AA

Motorist'~ ~~~~~
BRITAIN

Scale 1:250,000
or 3.95 miles to 1 inch

44th edition June 2022 © AA Media Limited 2022
Revised version of the atlas formerly known as *Complete Atlas of Britain*. Original edition printed 1979.

All cartography in this atlas edited, designed and produced by the Mapping Services Department of AA Media Limited (A05816).

This atlas contains Ordnance Survey data © Crown copyright and database right 2022 and Royal Mail data © Royal Mail copyright and database right 2022. Contains public sector information licensed under the Open Government Licence v3.0. Ireland mapping contains data available from openstreetmap.org © under the Open Database License found at opendatacommons.org

Published by AA Media Limited, whose registered office is Grove House, Lutyens Close, Basingstoke, Hampshire RG24 8AG, UK. Registered number 06112600.

ISBN: 978 0 7495 8298 2

A CIP catalogue record for this book is available from The British Library.

Acknowledgements: AA Media Limited would like to thank the following for information used in the creation of this atlas: Cadw, English Heritage, Forestry Commission, Historic Scotland, National Trust and National Trust for Scotland, RSPB, The Wildlife Trust, Scottish Natural Heritage, Natural England, The Countryside Council for Wales. Award winning beaches from 'Blue Flag' and 'Keep Scotland Beautiful' (summer 2021 data): for latest information visit *www.blueflag.org* and *www.keepscotlandbeautiful.org*. Transport for London (Central London Map), Nexus (Newcastle district map). Ireland mapping: Republic of Ireland census 2016 © Central Statistics Office and Northern Ireland census 2016 © NISRA (population data); Irish Public Sector Data (CC BY 4.0) (Gaeltacht); Logainm.ie (placenames); Roads Service and Transport Infrastructure Ireland.
Printed by 1010 Printing International Ltd, China

Contents

Map pages	inside front cover
Route planner	*II–VII*
Motorways	*VIII–XIV*
Restricted junctions	*VIII–XI*
M25 London Orbital motorway	*XII*
M6 Toll motorway	*XIII*
Smart motorways	*XIV*
Road map symbols	**1**
Road maps	**2–115**
Britain 1:250,000 scale	2–111
Some islands are shown at slightly smaller scales	
Ireland 1:1,000,000 scale	112–115
District maps	**116–127**
Birmingham	116–117
Glasgow	118–119
London	120–123
Manchester	124–125
Tyne & Wear	126–127
Street map symbols	**128**
Town plans	**129–141**
Central London street map and index	**142–157**
Index to place names	**158–194**
County, administrative area map	158
Place name index	159–194

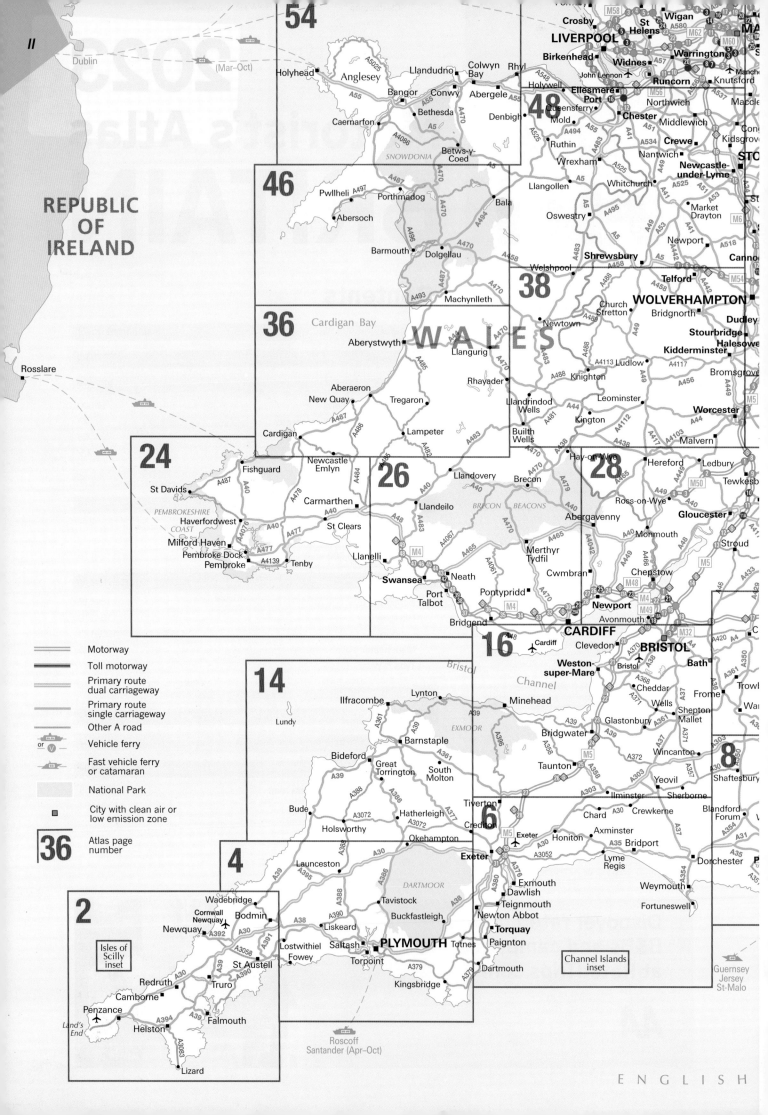

Motorway

Toll motorway

Primary route dual carriageway

Primary route single carriageway

Other A road

or V **Vehicle ferry**

Fast vehicle ferry or catamaran

National Park

City with clean air or low emission zone

36 **Atlas page number**

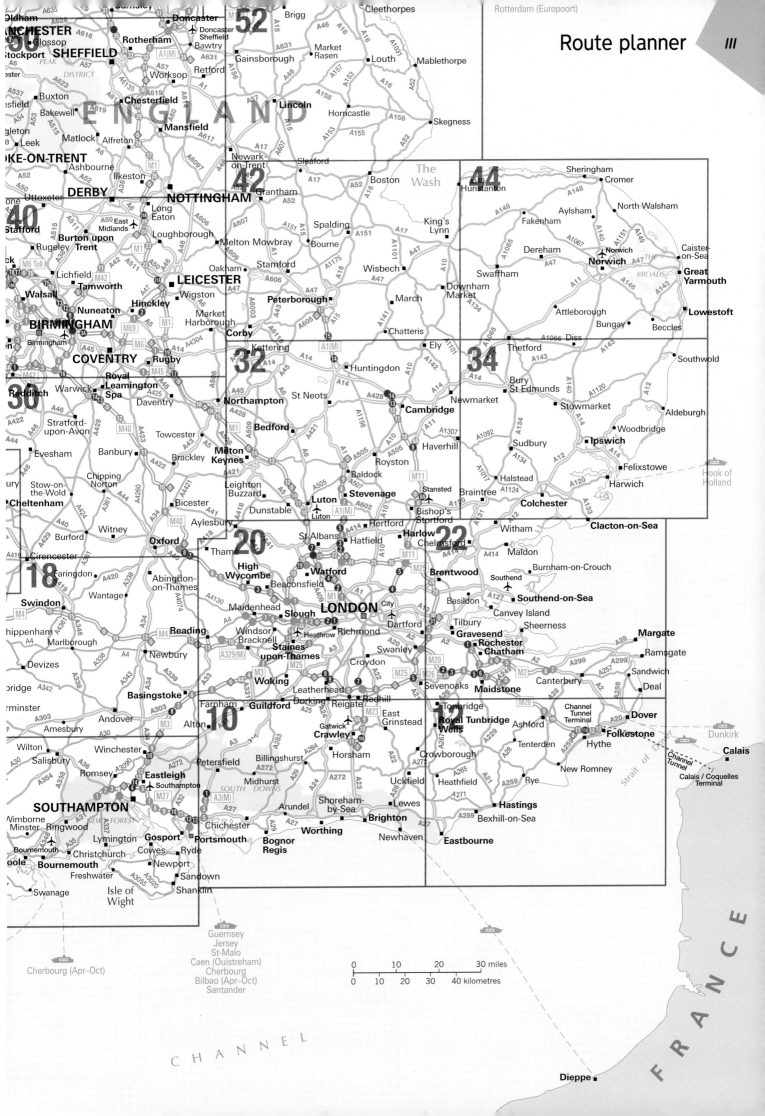

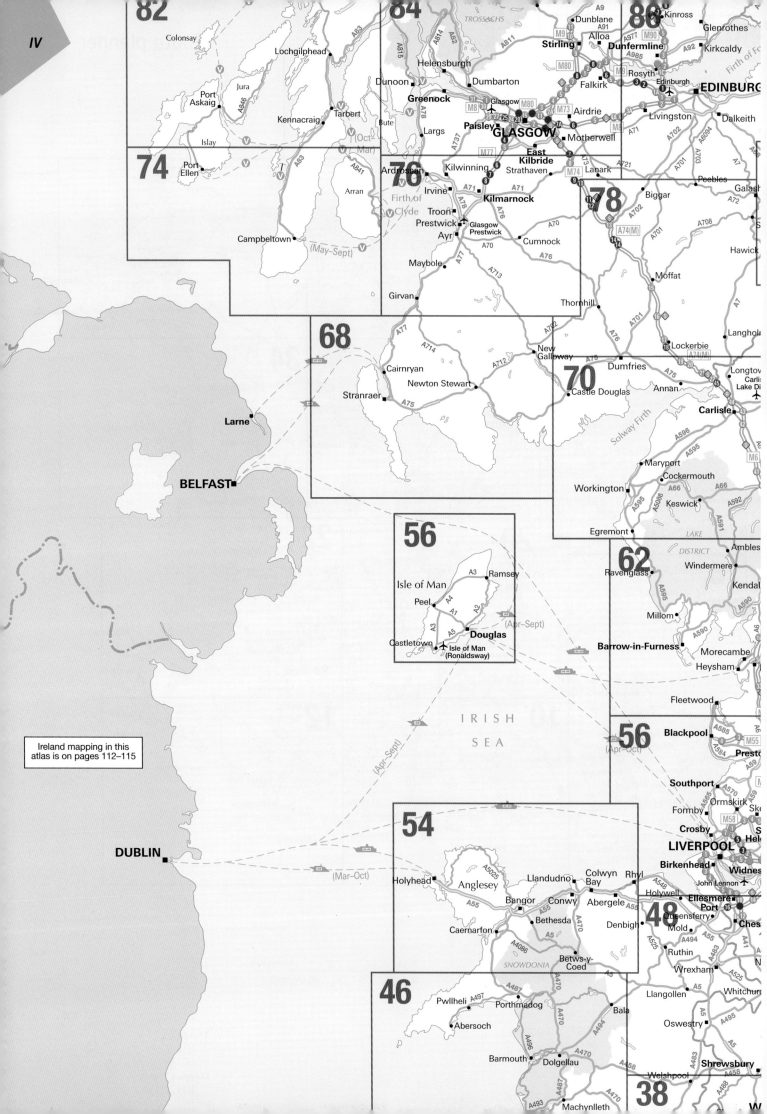

IV

82

84

86

Colonsay

Lochgilphead

Helensburgh

TROSSACHS

A9

Dunblane
A91

Kinross

Glenrothes

Port
Askaig

Jura

Dunoon

Dumbarton

Stirling

Alloa

Dunfermline

A92

Kirkcaldy

Kennacraig

Tarbert

Greenock

Bute

Glasgow

M8

Paisley

GLASGOW

Largs

Falkirk

Rosyth

Edinburgh

Airdrie

EDINBURGH

Livingston

Dalkeith

Islay

Motherwell

**East
Kilbride**

M77

Lanark

Port
Ellen

74

Arran

Campbeltown

(Oct
–Mar)

(May–Sept)

76

Ardrossan

Kilwinning

Irvine

Firth of
Clyde

Troon
Prestwick

Ayr

Kilmarnock

Strathaven

Glasgow
Prestwick

Cumnock

78

Peebles

Galash

Biggar

Hawick

Maybole

68

Girvan

Cairnryan

Newton Stewart

Stranraer

New
Galloway

Thornhill

Moffat

Lockerbie

Langhol

70

Dumfries

Castle Douglas

Annan

Longtov
Carli
Lake Di

BELFAST

Larne

Solway Firth

Carlisle

Maryport

Cockermouth

Workington

Keswick

56

Isle of Man

Peel

Ramsey

Douglas

Castletown

Isle of Man
(Ronaldsway)

(Apr–Sept)

Egremont

LAKE
DISTRICT

Ambles

Ravenglass

Windermere

Kendal

Millom

62

Barrow-in-Furness

Morecambe

Heysham

Fleetwood

I R I S H

S E A

(Apr–Oct)

56

Blackpool

Prest

Southport

Formby

Ormskirk

Ske

DUBLIN

Crosby

Hel

LIVERPOOL

Birkenhead

Widnes

John Lennon

Ellesmere
Port

Chest

(Mar–Oct)

54

Holyhead

Anglesey

Llandudno

Colwyn
Bay

Rhyl

Holywell

Queensferry

Bangor

Conwy

Abergele

Denbigh

Mold

48

Bethesda

Caernarfon

Ruthin

Wrexham

SNOWDONIA

Betws-y-
Coed

46

Pwllheli

Porthmadog

Bala

Llangollen

Oswestry

Abersoch

Barmouth

Dolgellau

Shrewsbury

Welshpool

38

Machynlleth

Ireland mapping in this
atlas is on pages 112–115

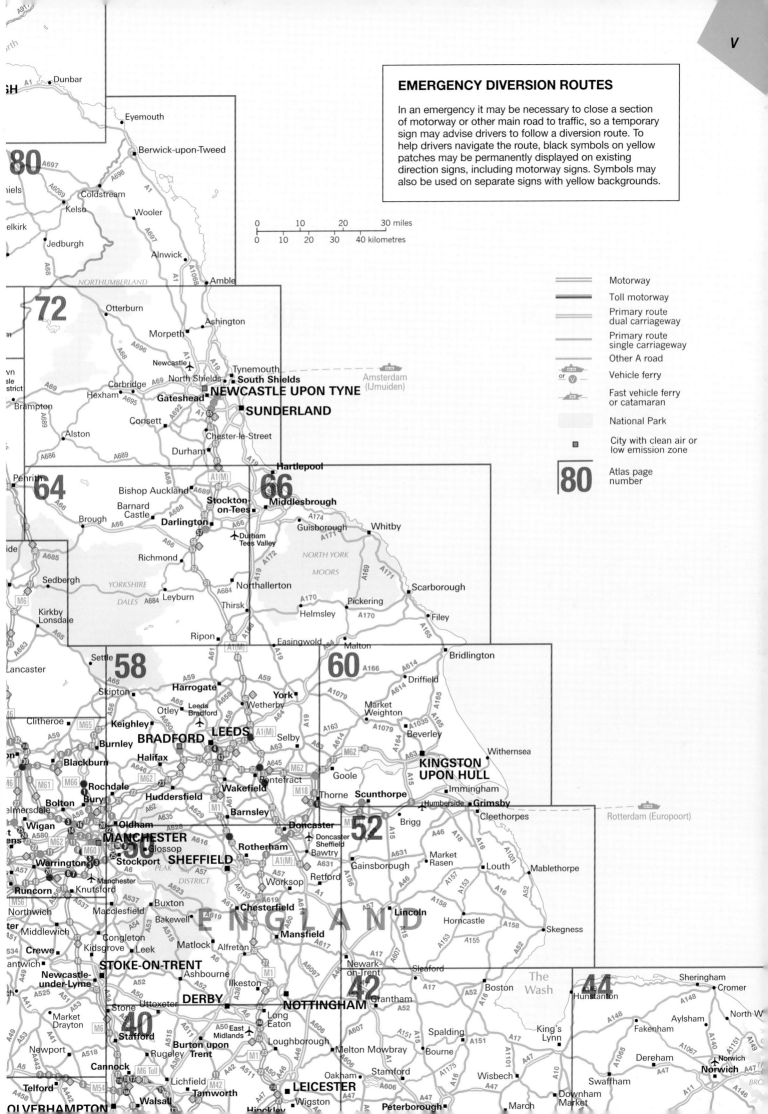

EMERGENCY DIVERSION ROUTES

In an emergency it may be necessary to close a section of motorway or other main road to traffic, so a temporary sign may advise drivers to follow a diversion route. To help drivers navigate the route, black symbols on yellow patches may be permanently displayed on existing direction signs, including motorway signs. Symbols may also be used on separate signs with yellow backgrounds.

0 10 20 30 miles		
0 10 20 30 40 kilometres		

Motorway
Toll motorway
Primary route dual carriageway
Primary route single carriageway
Other A road
or Vehicle ferry
Fast vehicle ferry or catamaran
National Park
City with clean air or low emission zone
80 Atlas page number

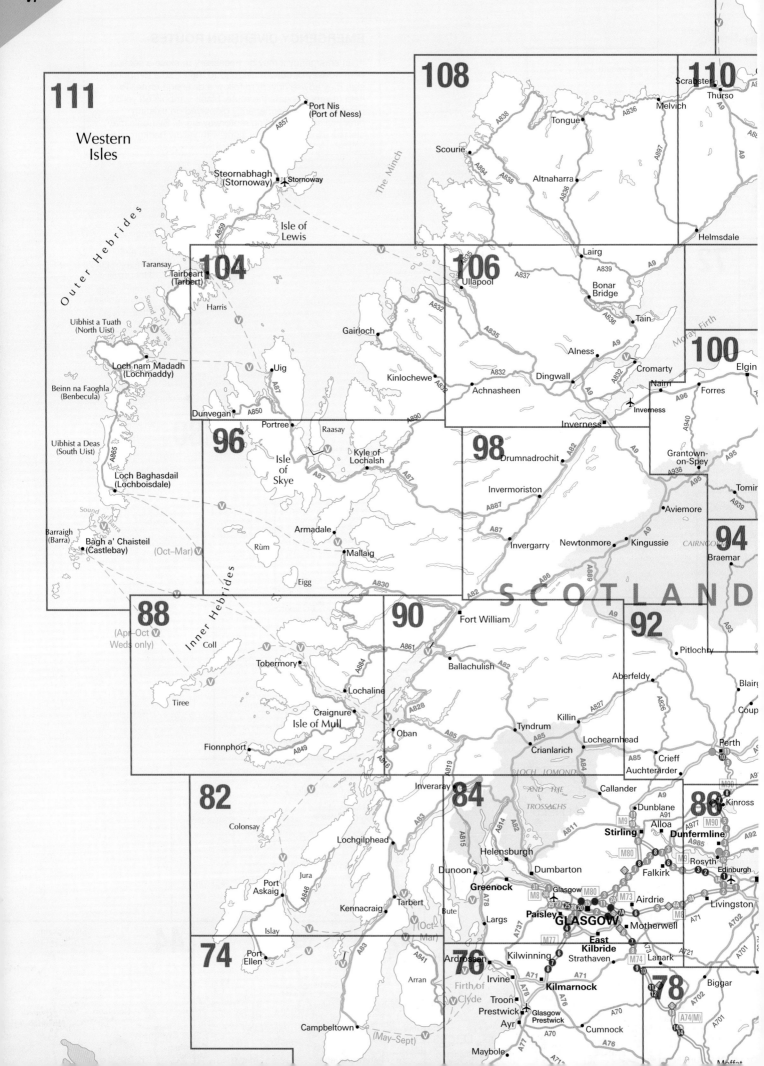

EMERGENCY DIVERSION ROUTES

111

Western Isles

Port Nis
(Port of Ness)

A857

Steornabhagh
(Stornoway) ✈ Stornoway

Isle of
Lewis

Outer Hebrides

Taransay

A859

Tairbeart
(Tarbert)

Harris

Uibhist a Tuath
(North Uist)

Beinn na Faoghla
(Benbecula)

Loch nam Madadh
(Lochmaddy)

Uibhist a Deas
(South Uist)

A865

Loch Baghasdail
(Lochboisdale)

Sound of Barra

Barraigh
(Barra)

Bàgh a' Chaisteil
(Castlebay)

(Oct–Mar) Ⓥ

88

(Apr–Oct) Ⓥ
Weds only)

Inner Hebrides

Coll

Tiree

Fionnphort

A849

82

Colonsay

Jura

Port
Askaig

A846

Islay

74

Port
Ellen

104

A865

Sound of Harris

Ⓥ

Uig

A850

Dunvegan

A87

Portree

96

Isle
of
Skye

A87

Armadale

Mallaig

Eigg

Rùm

A830

Tobermory

A884

Lochaline

Craignure

Isle of Mull

A828

Oban

A816

A819

Inveraray

84

A83

Lochgilphead

A816

Kennacraig

Tarbert

(Oct–Mar) Ⓥ

Bute

A841

Arran

Campbeltown

(May–Sept) Ⓥ

Ⓥ

Gairloch

Kinlochewe

A832

Achnasheen

106

A835

Ullapool

A832

A835

A832

A890

98

Drumnadrochit

A82

Invermoriston

A887

A87

Invergarry

90

A861

Fort William

A82

Ballachulish

A82

A85

Tyndrum

A85

Crianlarich

A84

LOCH LOMOND
AND THE
TROSSACHS

Callander

A84

Helensburgh

A814

A82

A811

Dunoon

Dumbarton

Greenock

A78

Paisley

Largs

A737

Ardrossan

A78

Kilwinning

A71

Irvine

76

A71

Troon

Prestwick

Glasgow
Prestwick

Ayr

A77

Maybole

A838

Tongue

A836

A838

A894

Scourie

A836

Altnaharra

Melvich

A836

108

A836

Scrabster

110

Thurso

A9

A887

A9

Helmsdale

A839

Lairg

Bonar
Bridge

A836

A9

Tain

A836

Alness

Dingwall

A832

A9

Cromarty

Inverness

✈ Inverness

Inverness

Nairn

A96

Forres

100

Elgin

A940

A938

A95

Grantown-
on-Spey

A95

Aviemore

A9

A889

A939

Tomin

Newtonmore

Kingussie

CAIRNGO

94

Braemar

A93

S C O T L A N D

92

Pitlochry

Aberfeldy

A827

A826

Blairg

Killin

Lochearnhead

Crianlarich

A85

Coup

Crieff

Auchterarder

Perth

10 9

A9

Dunblane

A91

Alloa

86

Kinross

A977

M90

M9

A9

Stirling

M9

M80

Falkirk

M9

Rosyth

Dunfermline

A985

M80

Airdrie

M73

Glasgow

M8

GLASGOW

Motherwell

East
Kilbride

M77

Strathaven

M74

Lanark

A721

Edinburgh

✈ Edinburgh

Livingston

A702

A71

M8

A71

Kilmarnock

A76

Cumnock

A76

Biggar

A74(M)

A702

A701

Moffat

Stromness

Stromness

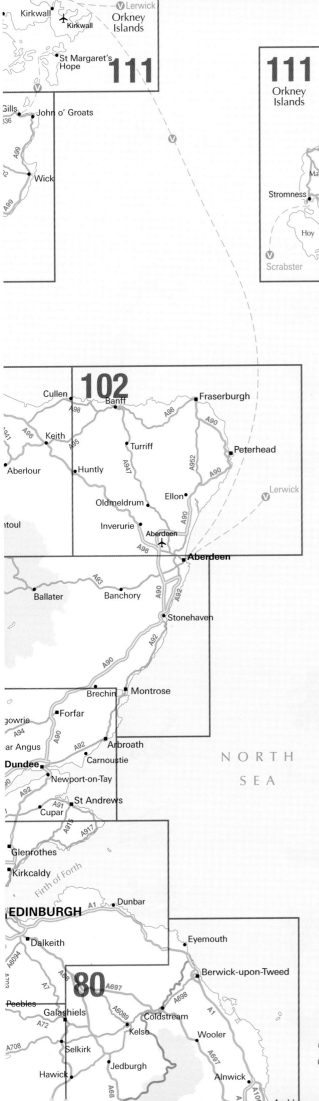

111
Orkney Islands

111
Shetland Islands

111

FERRY OPERATORS

Hebrides and west coast Scotland
calmac.co.uk
skyeferry.co.uk
western-ferries.co.uk

Orkney and Shetland
northlinkferries.co.uk
pentlandferries.co.uk
orkneyferries.co.uk
shetland.gov.uk/ferries

Isle of Man
steam-packet.com

Ireland
irishferries.com
poferries.com
stenaline.co.uk

North Sea (Scandinavia and Benelux)
dfdsseaways.co.uk
poferries.com

Isle of Wight
wightlink.co.uk
redfunnel.co.uk

Channel Islands
condorferries.co.uk

France and Belgium
brittany-ferries.co.uk
condorferries.co.uk
eurotunnel.com
dfdsseaways.co.uk
poferries.com

Northern Spain
brittany-ferries.co.uk

Motorway

Toll motorway

Primary route
dual carriageway

Primary route
single carriageway

Other A road

or Vehicle ferry

Fast vehicle ferry
or catamaran

National Park

City with clean air or
low emission zone

92 Atlas page
number

0   10   20   30 miles
0 10 20 30 40 kilometres

Restricted junctions

Motorway and primary route junctions which have access or exit restrictions are shown on the map pages thus:

M1 London - Leeds

Northbound
Access only from A1 (northbound)

Southbound
Exit only to A1 (southbound)

Northbound
Access only from A41 (northbound)

Southbound
Exit only to A41 (southbound)

Northbound
Access only from M25 (no link from A405)

Southbound
Exit only to M25 (no link from A405)

Northbound
Access only from A414

Southbound
Exit only to A414

Northbound
Exit only to M45

Southbound
Access only from M45

Northbound
Exit only to M6 (northbound)

Southbound
Exit only to A14 (southbound)

Northbound
Exit only, no access

Southbound
Access only, no exit

Northbound
No exit, access only

Southbound
Access only from A50 (eastbound)

Northbound
Exit only, no access

Southbound
Access only, no exit

Northbound
Exit only to M621

Southbound
Access only from M621

Northbound
Exit only to A1(M) (northbound)

Southbound
Access only from A1(M) (southbound)

M2 Rochester - Faversham

Westbound
No exit to A2 (eastbound)

Eastbound
No access from A2 (westbound)

M3 Sunbury - Southampton

Northeastbound
Access only from A303, no exit

Southwestbound
Exit only to A303, no access

Northbound
Exit only, no access

Southbound
Access only, no exit

Northeastbound
Access from M27 only, no exit

Southwestbound
No access to M27 (westbound)

M4 London - South Wales

For junctions 1 & 2 see London district map on pages 120–123

Westbound
Exit only to M48

Eastbound
Access only from M48

Westbound
Access only from M48

Eastbound
Exit only to M48

Westbound
Exit only, no access

Eastbound
Access only, no exit

Westbound
Exit only, no access

Eastbound
Access only, no exit

Westbound
Exit only to A48(M)

Eastbound
Access only from A48(M)

Westbound
Exit only, no access

Eastbound
No restriction

Westbound
Access only, no exit

Eastbound
No access or exit

M5 Birmingham - Exeter

Northeastbound
Access only, no exit

Southwestbound
Exit only, no access

Northeastbound
Access only from A417 (westbound)

Southwestbound
Exit only to A417 (eastbound)

Northeastbound
Exit only to M49

Southwestbound
Access only from M49

Northeastbound
No access, exit only

Southwestbound
No exit, access only

M6 Toll Motorway

See M6 Toll motorway map on page *XIII*

M6 Rugby - Carlisle

Northbound
Exit only to M6 Toll

Southbound
Access only from M6 Toll

Northbound
Exit only to M42 (southbound) and A446

Southbound
Exit only to A446

Northbound
Access only from M42 (southbound)

Southbound
Exit only to M42

Northbound
Exit only, no access

Southbound
Access only, no exit

Northbound
Exit only to M54

Southbound
Access only from M54

Northbound
Access only from M6 Toll

Southbound
Exit only to M6 Toll

Westbound map notes

Top right:
Westbound
Exit only to A483

Eastbound
Access only from A483

M8 Edinburgh - Bishopton

For junctions 7A to 29A see Glasgow district map on pages 118–119

Westbound
Exit only, no access

Eastbound
Access only, no exit

Westbound
Access only, no exit

Eastbound
Exit only, no access

Westbound
Access only, no exit

Eastbound
Exit only, no access

M9 Edinburgh - Dunblane

Northwestbound
Access only, no exit

Southeastbound
Exit only, no access

Northbound
No restriction

Southbound
Access only from M56 (eastbound)

Northbound
Exit only to M56 (westbound)

Southbound
Access only from M56 (eastbound)

Northbound
Access only, no exit

Southbound
Exit only, no access

Northbound
Exit only, no access

Southbound
Access only, no exit

Northbound
Access only from M61

Southbound
Exit only to M61

Northbound
Exit only, no access

Southbound
Access only, no exit

Northbound
Exit only, no access

Southbound
Access only, no exit

Northwestbound
Exit only, no access

Southeastbound
Access only, no exit

Northwestbound
Access only, no exit

Southeastbound
Exit only to A905

Northwestbound
Exit only to M876
(southwestbound)

Southeastbound
Access only from M876
(northeastbound)

M11 London - Cambridge

Northbound
Access only from A406
(eastbound)

Southbound
Exit only to A406

Northbound
Exit only, no access

Southbound
Access only, no exit

Northbound
Exit only, no access

Southbound
No direct access,
use jct 8

Northbound
Exit only to A11

Southbound
Access only from A11

Northbound
Exit only, no access

Southbound
Access only, no exit

Northbound
Exit only, no access

Southbound
Access only, no exit

M20 Swanley - Folkestone

Northwestbound
Staggered junction; follow
signs - access only

Southeastbound
Staggered junction; follow
signs - exit only

Northwestbound
Exit only to M26
(westbound)

Southeastbound
Access only from M26
(eastbound)

Northwestbound
Access only from A20

Southeastbound
For access follow signs -
exit only to A20

Northwestbound
No restriction

Southeastbound
For exit follow signs

Northwestbound
Access only, no exit

Southeastbound
Exit only, no access

M23 Hooley - Crawley

Northbound
Exit only to A23
(northbound)

Southbound
Access only from A23
(southbound)

Northbound
Access only, no exit

Southbound
Exit only, no access

M25 London Orbital Motorway

See M25 London Orbital motorway map on
page *XII*

M26 Sevenoaks - Wrotham

Westbound
Exit only to clockwise
M25 (westbound)

Eastbound
Access only from
anticlockwise M25
(eastbound)

Westbound
Access only from M20
(northwestbound)

Eastbound
Exit only to M20
(southeastbound)

M27 Cadnam - Portsmouth

Westbound
Staggered junction; follow
signs - access only from
M3 (southbound). Exit
only to M3 (northbound)

Eastbound
Staggered junction; follow
signs - access only from
M3 (southbound). Exit
only to M3 (northbound)

Westbound
Exit only, no access

Eastbound
Access only, no exit

Westbound
Staggered junction; follow
signs - exit only to M275
(southbound)

Eastbound
Staggered junction; follow
signs - access only from
M275 (northbound)

M40 London - Birmingham

Northwestbound
Exit only, no access

Southeastbound
Access only, no exit

Northwestbound
Exit only, no access

Southeastbound
Access only, no exit

Northwestbound
Exit only to M40/A40

Southeastbound
Access only from
M40/A40

Northwestbound
Exit only, no access

Southeastbound
Access only, no exit

Northwestbound
Access only, no exit

Southeastbound
Exit only, no access

Northwestbound
Access only, no exit

Southeastbound
Exit only, no access

M42 Bromsgrove - Measham

See Birmingham district map on pages
116–117

M45 Coventry - M1

Westbound
Access only from A45
(northbound)

Eastbound
Exit only, no access

Westbound
Access only from M1
(northbound)

Eastbound
Exit only to M1
(southbound)

M48 Chepstow

Westbound
Access only from M4
(westbound)

Eastbound
Exit only to M4
(eastbound)

Westbound
No exit to M4 (eastbound)

Eastbound
No access from M4
(westbound)

M53 Mersey Tunnel - Chester

Northbound
Access only from M56
(westbound). Exit only to
M56 (eastbound)

Southbound
Access only from M56
(westbound). Exit only to
M56 (eastbound)

M54 Telford - Birmingham

Westbound
Access only from M6
(northbound)

Eastbound
Exit only to M6
(southbound)

M56 Chester - Manchester

For junctions 1,2,3,4 & 7 see Manchester
district map on pages 124–125

Westbound
Access only, no exit

Eastbound
No access or exit

Westbound
No exit to M6
(southbound)

Eastbound
No access from M6
(northbound)

Westbound
Exit only to M53

Eastbound
Access only from M53

Westbound
No access or exit

Eastbound
No restriction

M57 Liverpool Outer Ring Road

Northwestbound
Access only, no exit

Southeastbound
Exit only, no access

Northwestbound
Access only from A580
(westbound)

Southeastbound
Exit only, no access

M60 Manchester Orbital

See Manchester district map on pages
124–125

M61 Manchester - Preston

Northwestbound
No access or exit

Southeastbound
Exit only, no access

Northwestbound
Exit only to M6
(northbound)

Southeastbound
Access only from M6
(southbound)

M62 Liverpool - Kingston upon Hull

Westbound
Access only, no exit

Eastbound
Exit only, no access

Westbound
No access to A1(M)
(southbound)

Eastbound
No restriction

M65 Preston - Colne

Northeastbound
Exit only, no access

Southwestbound
Access only, no exit

Northeastbound
Access only, no exit

Southwestbound
Exit only, no access

M66 Bury

Northbound
Exit only to A56
(northbound)

Southbound
Access only from A56
(southbound)

Northbound
Exit only, no access

Southbound
Access only, no exit

M67 Hyde Bypass

Westbound
Access only, no exit

Eastbound
Exit only, no access

Westbound
Exit only, no access

Eastbound
Access only, no exit

M69 Coventry - Leicester

Northbound
Access only, no exit

Southbound
Exit only, no access

M73 East of Glasgow

Northbound
No exit to A74 and A721

Southbound
No exit to A74 and A721

Northbound
No access from or exit to
A89. No access from M8
(eastbound)

Southbound
No access from or exit to
A89. No exit to M8
(westbound)

M74 and A74(M) Glasgow - Gretna

Northbound
Exit only, no access

Southbound
Access only, no exit

Northbound
Access only, no exit

Southbound
Exit only, no access

Northbound
No access from A74 and
A721

Southbound
Access only, no exit to
A74 and A721

Northbound
Access only, no exit

Southbound
Exit only, no access

Northbound
No access or exit

Southbound
Exit only, no access

Northbound
No restriction

Southbound
Access only, no exit

Northbound
Access only, no exit

Southbound
Exit only, no access

Northbound
Exit only, no access

Southbound
Access only, no exit

Northbound
Exit only, no access

Southbound
Access only, no exit

M77 Glasgow - Kilmarnock

Northbound
No exit to M8
(westbound)

Southbound
No access from M8
(eastbound)

Northbound
Access only, no exit

Southbound
Exit only, no access

Northbound
Access only, no exit

Southbound
Exit only, no access

Northbound
Access only, no exit

Southbound
No restriction

Northbound
Exit only, no access

Southbound
Exit only, no access

M80 Glasgow - Stirling

For junctions 1 & 4 see Glasgow district map
on pages 118–119

Northbound
Exit only, no access

Southbound
Access only, no exit

Northbound
Access only, no exit

Southbound
Exit only, no access

Northbound
Exit only to M876
(northeastbound)

Southbound
Access only from M876
(southwestbound)

M90 Edinburgh - Perth

Northbound
No exit, access only

Southbound
Exit only to A90
(eastbound)

Northbound
Exit only to A92
(eastbound)

Southbound
Access only from A92
(westbound)

Northbound
Access only, no exit

Southbound
Exit only, no access

Northbound
Exit only, no access

Southbound
Access only, no exit

Northbound
No access from A912
No exit to A912
(southbound)

Southbound
No access from A912
(northbound).
No exit to A912

M180 Doncaster - Grimsby

Westbound
Access only, no exit

Eastbound
Exit only, no access

M606 Bradford Spur

Northbound
Exit only, no access

Southbound
No restriction

M621 Leeds - M1

Clockwise
Access only, no exit

Anticlockwise
Exit only, no access

Clockwise
No exit or access

Anticlockwise
No restriction

Clockwise
Access only, no exit

Anticlockwise
Exit only, no access

Clockwise
Exit only, no access

Anticlockwise
Access only, no exit

Clockwise
Exit only to M1
(southbound)

Anticlockwise
Access only from M1
(northbound)

M876 Bonnybridge - Kincardine Bridge

Northeastbound
Access only from M80
(northbound)

Southwestbound
Exit only to M80
(southbound)

Northeastbound
Exit only to M9
(eastbound)

Southwestbound
Access only from M9
(westbound)

A1(M) South Mimms - Baldock

Northbound
Exit only, no access

Southbound
Access only, no exit

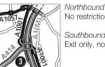

Northbound
No restriction

Southbound
Exit only, no access

Northbound
Access only, no exit

Southbound
No access or exit

A1(M) Pontefract - Bedale

Northbound
No access to M62 (eastbound)

Southbound
No restriction

Northbound
Access only from M1 (northbound)

Southbound
Exit only to M1 (southbound)

A1(M) Scotch Corner - Newcastle upon Tyne

Northbound
Exit only to A66(M) (eastbound)

Southbound
Access only from A66(M) (westbound)

Northbound
No access. Exit only to A194(M) & A1 (northbound)

Southbound
No exit. Access only from A194(M) & A1 (southbound)

A3(M) Horndean - Havant

Northbound
Access only from A3

Southbound
Exit only to A3

Northbound
Exit only, no access

Southbound
Access only, no exit

A38(M) Birmingham Victoria Road (Park Circus)

Northbound
No exit

Southbound
No access

A48(M) Cardiff Spur

Westbound
Access only from M4 (westbound)

Eastbound
Exit only to M4 (eastbound)

Westbound
Exit only to A48 (westbound)

Eastbound
Access only from A48 (eastbound)

A57(M) Manchester Brook Street (A34)

Westbound
No exit

Eastbound
No access

A58(M) Leeds Park Lane and Westgate

Northbound
No restriction

Southbound
No access

A64(M) Leeds Clay Pit Lane (A58)

Westbound
No exit (to Clay Pit Lane)

Eastbound
No access (from Clay Pit Lane)

A66(M) Darlington Spur

Westbound
Exit only to A1(M) (southbound)

Eastbound
Access only from A1(M) (northbound)

A74(M) Gretna - Abington

Northbound
Exit only, no access

Southbound
Access only, no exit

A194(M) Newcastle upon Tyne

Northbound
Access only from A1(M) (northbound)

Southbound
Exit only to A1(M) (southbound)

A12 M25 - Ipswich

Northeastbound
Access only, no exit

Southwestbound
No restriction

Northeastbound
Exit only, no access

Southwestbound
Access only, no exit

Northeastbound
Exit only, no access

Southwestbound
Access only, no exit

Northeastbound
Access only, no exit

Southwestbound
Exit only, no access

Northeastbound
No restriction

Southwestbound
Access only, no exit

Northeastbound
Exit only, no access

Southwestbound
Access only, no exit

Northeastbound
Access only, no exit

Southwestbound
Exit only, no access

Northeastbound
Exit only, no access

Southwestbound
Access only, no exit

Northeastbound
Exit only (for Stratford St Mary and Dedham)

Southwestbound
Access only

A14 M1 - Felixstowe

Westbound
Exit only to M6 & M1 (northbound)

Eastbound
Access only from M6 & M1 (southbound)

Westbound
Exit only, no access

Eastbound
Access only, no exit

Westbound
Access only, no exit

Eastbound
Exit only, no access

Westbound
Exit only, no access

Eastbound
Access only from A1 (southbound)

Westbound
Access only, no exit

Eastbound
Exit only, no access

Westbound
No restriction

Eastbound
Access only, no exit

Westbound
Access only, no exit

Eastbound
Exit only, no access

Westbound
Exit only to A11 Access only from A1303

Eastbound
Access only from A11

Westbound
Access only from A11

Eastbound
Exit only to A11

Westbound
Exit only, no access

Eastbound
Access only, no exit

Westbound
Access only, no exit

Eastbound
Exit only, no access

A55 Holyhead - Chester

Westbound
Exit only, no access

Eastbound
Access only, no exit

Westbound
Access only, no exit

Eastbound
Exit only, no access

Westbound
Exit only, no access

Eastbound
No access or exit.

Westbound
No restriction

Eastbound
No access or exit

Westbound
Exit only, no access

Eastbound
No access or exit

Westbound
Exit only, no access

Eastbound
Access only, no exit

Westbound
Exit only to A5104

Eastbound
Access only from A5104

Refer also to atlas pages 20–21

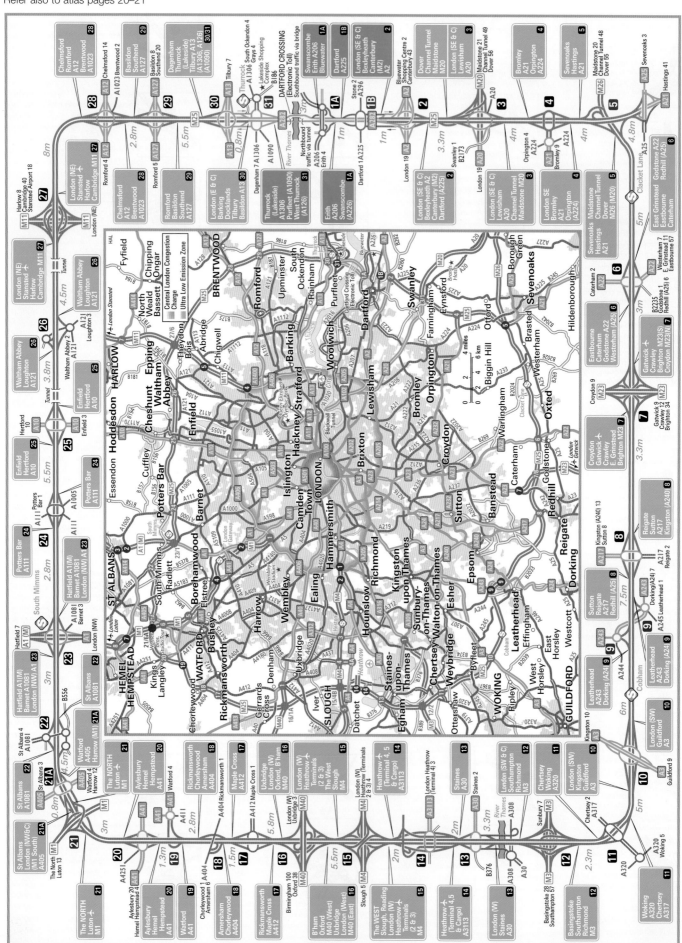

Refer also to atlas page 40

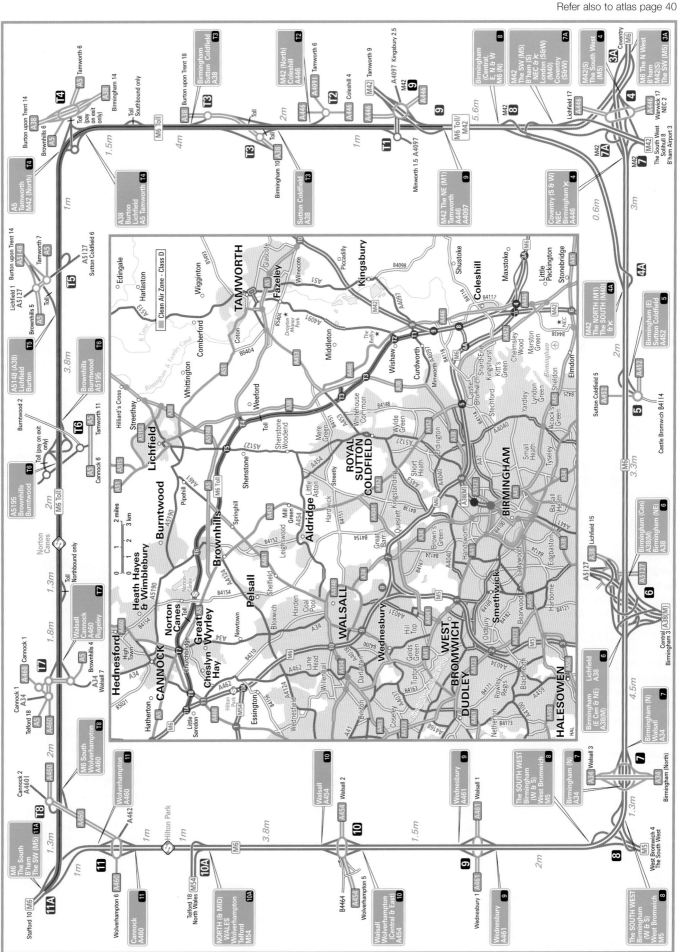

Smart motorways

Since Britain's first motorway (the Preston Bypass) opened in 1958, motorways have changed significantly. A vast increase in car journeys over the last 62 years has meant that motorways quickly filled to capacity. To combat this, the recent development of **smart motorways** uses technology to monitor and actively manage traffic flow and congestion.

How they work

Smart motorways utilise various active traffic management methods, monitored through a regional traffic control centre:

- Traffic flow is monitored using CCTV
- Speed limits are changed to smooth traffic flow and reduce stop-start driving
- Capacity of the motorway can be increased by either temporarily or permanently opening the hard shoulder to traffic
- Warning signs and messages alert drivers to hazards and traffic jams ahead
- Lanes can be closed in the case of an accident or emergency by displaying a red X sign

- Emergency refuge areas are located regularly along the motorway where there is no hard shoulder available

The map shows the main motorway network with the three different types of smart motorway in operation. Since January 2022, plans for the opening of further schemes have been put on hold to allow a review of safety data and the improvement of existing schemes.

Controlled motorway
Variable speed limits without hard shoulder (the hard shoulder is used in emergencies only)

Hard shoulder running
Variable speed limits with part-time hard shoulder (the hard shoulder is open to traffic at busy times when signs permit)

All lane running
Variable speed limits with hard shoulder as permanent running lane (there is no hard shoulder); this is standard for all new smart motorway schemes since 2013

Standard motorway

Quick tips

- Never drive in a lane closed by a red X
- Keep to the speed limit shown on the gantries
- A solid white line indicates the hard shoulder – do not drive in it unless directed or in the case of an emergency
- A broken white line indicates a normal running lane
- Exit the smart motorway where possible if your vehicle is in difficulty. In an emergency, move onto the hard shoulder where there is one, or the nearest emergency refuge area
- Put on your hazard lights if you break down

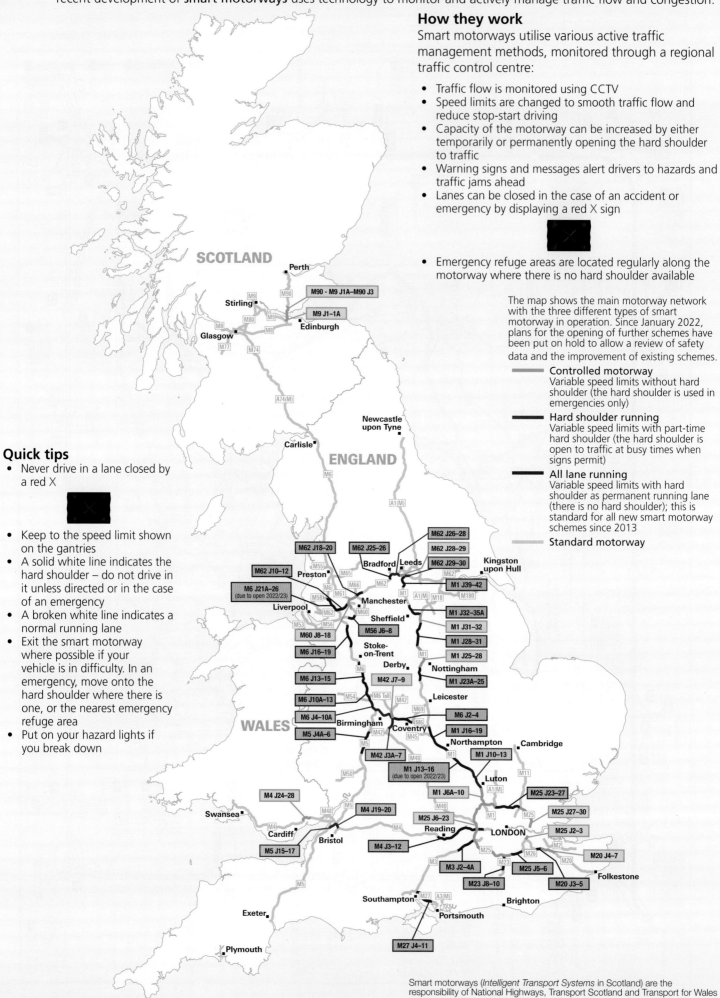

Smart motorways (*Intelligent Transport Systems* in Scotland) are the responsibility of National Highways, Transport Scotland and Transport for Wales

Motoring information

Symbol	Description
M4	Motorway with number
Toll	Toll motorway with toll station
6	Motorway junction with and without number
5	Restricted motorway junctions
Fleet / Todhills	Motorway service area, rest area
	Motorway and junction under construction
A3	Primary route single/dual carriageway
	Primary route junction with and without number
3	Restricted primary route junctions

Symbol	Description
S	Primary route service area
BATH	Primary route destination
A1123	Other A road single/dual carriageway
B2070	B road single/dual carriageway
	Minor road more than 4 metres wide, less than 4 metres wide
	Roundabout
	Interchange/junction
	Narrow primary/other A/B road with passing places (Scotland)
	Road under construction, road tunnel

Symbol	Description
	City with clean air zone, low emission zone (visit www.gov.uk/guidance/driving-in-a-clean-air-zone)
Toll	Road toll, steep gradient (arrows point downhill)
5	Distance in miles between symbols
or V V	Vehicle ferry (all year, seasonal)
	Fast vehicle ferry or catamaran
or P P	Passenger ferry (all year, seasonal)
	Railway line, in tunnel
X	Railway station, tram stop, level crossing
	Preserved or tourist railway

Symbol	Description
	Airport (major/minor), heliport
F	International freight terminal
H	24-hour Accident & Emergency hospital
C	Crematorium
P+R	Park and Ride (at least 6 days per week)
	City, town, village or other built-up area
628 / 637 Lecht Summit	Height in metres, mountain pass
	Snow gates (on main routes)
	National boundary, county or administrative boundary

Touring information To avoid disappointment, check opening times before visiting

Symbol	Description
	Scenic route
i	Tourist Information Centre
i	Tourist Information Centre (seasonal)
V	Visitor or heritage centre
	Picnic site
	Caravan site (AA inspected)
A	Camping site (AA inspected)
	Caravan & camping site (AA inspected)
	Abbey, cathedral or priory
	Ruined abbey, cathedral or priory
	Castle
	Historic house or building
	Museum or art gallery
	Industrial interest
	Aqueduct or viaduct
	Vineyard, brewery or distillery

Symbol	Description
	Garden
	Arboretum
	Country park
	Showground
	Theme park
	Farm or animal centre
	Zoological or wildlife collection
	Bird collection
	Aquarium
	RSPB site
	National Nature Reserve (England, Scotland, Wales)
	Local nature reserve
	Wildlife Trust reserve
	Forest drive
	National trail
	Viewpoint

Symbol	Description
	Waterfall
	Hill-fort
	Roman antiquity
	Prehistoric monument
1066	Battle site with year
	Preserved or tourist railway
	Cave or cavern
	Windmill, monument or memorial
	Beach (award winning)
	Lighthouse
	Golf course
	Football stadium
	County cricket ground
	Rugby Union national stadium
	International athletics stadium
	Horse racing, show jumping

Symbol	Description
	Motor-racing circuit
	Air show venue
	Ski slope (natural, artificial)
	National Trust site
	National Trust for Scotland site
	English Heritage site
	Historic Scotland site
	Cadw (Welsh heritage) site
★	Other place of interest
	Boxed symbols indicate attractions within urban area
	World Heritage Site (UNESCO)
	National Park and National Scenic Area (Scotland)
	Forest Park
	Sandy beach
	Heritage coast
	Major shopping centre

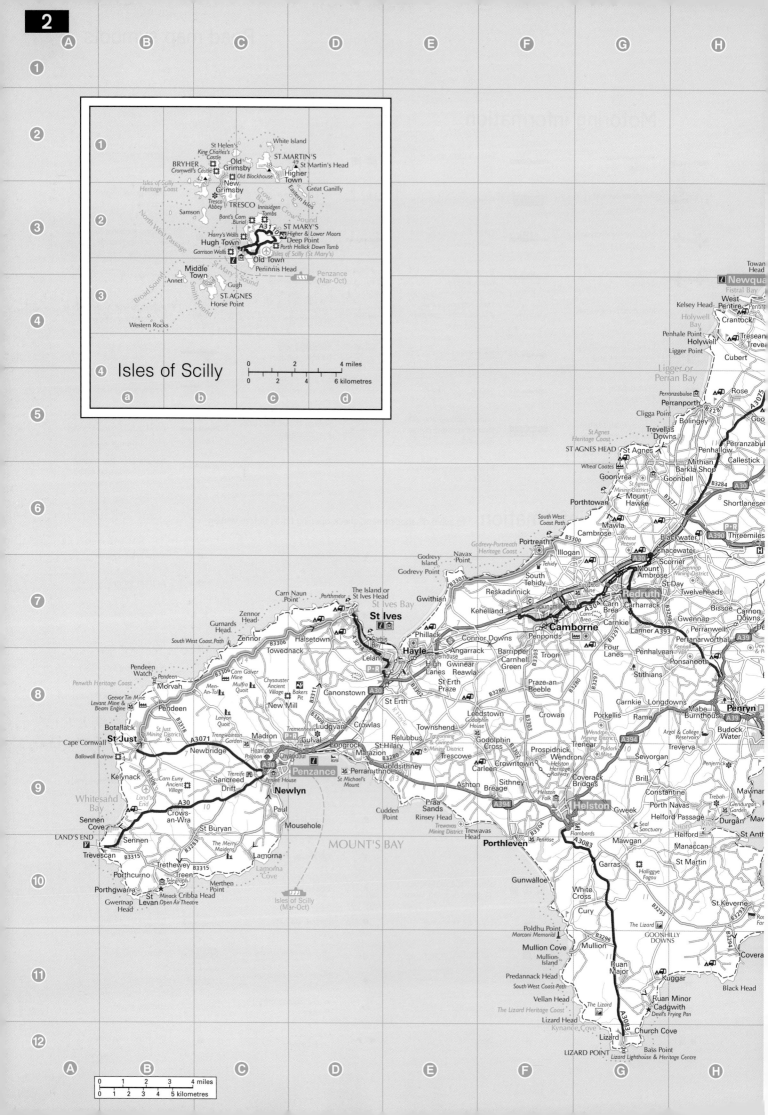

Isles of Scilly

⓵
St Helen's
King Charles's Castle
White Island
St.MARTIN'S
St Martin's Head
BRYHER
Cromwell's Castle
Old Grimsby
Old Blockhouse
Higher Town
New Grimsby
Great Ganilly
Tresco Abbey
TRESCO
Innisidgen Tombs
Samson
Bant's Carn Burial
Crow Bar
Eastern Isles
Crow Sound
ST MARY'S
⓶
Isles of Scilly Heritage Coast
Harry's Walls
Higher & Lower Moors
Hugh Town
Deep Point
Porth Hellick Down Tomb
Garrison Walls
Old Town
Isles of Scilly (St Mary's)
North West Passage
Penninis Head
Penzance (Mar-Oct)
Middle Town
St Mary's Sound
Broad Sound
Annet
Gugh
⓷
ST.AGNES
Smith Sound
Horse Point
Western Rocks

0   2   4 miles
0   2   6 kilometres

ⓐ   **ⓑ**   **ⓒ**   **ⓓ**

Towan Head
Newquay
Fistral Bay
West Pentire
Kelsey Head
Pentire
Holywell Bay
Crantock
Penhale Point
Holywell
Ligger Point
Tresean
Treve
Cubert
Ligger or Perran Bay
Perranzabuloe
Rose
Goo
Perranporth
Cligga Point
Bolingey
Trevellas Downs
Perranzabul
St Agnes Heritage Coast
ST AGNES HEAD
St Agnes
Penhallow
Callestick
Wheal Coates
Mithian
Barkla Shop
Goonvrea
Goonbell
Mount Hawke
Porthtowan
South West Coast Path
Mawla
Blackwater
Chacewater
Portreath
Wheal Peevor
Threemiles
Godrevy-Portreath Heritage Coast
Illogan
Scorrier
Mount Ambrose
Gwennap Mining District
St Day
Twelveheads
Godrevy Island
Navax Point
Redruth
Godrevy Point
South Tehidy
Tehidy
Reskadinnick
Carn Brea
Carharrack
Bissoe
Carnon Downs
Gwithian
Kehelland
Camborne
Carnkie
Lanner
Perranwell
Phillack
Connor Downs
Penponds
Four Lanes
Penhalvean
St Ives Bay
Angarrack
Barripper
Troon
Stithians
The Island or St Ives Head
Carn Naun Point
Porthmeor
Hayle
Copperhouse
Carnhell Green
Reawla
Praze-an-Beeble
Carnkie
Longdowns
Mabe
Penryn
Zennor Head
St Ives
High Gwinear Lanes
St Erth Praze
Crowan
Carnkie
Longdowns
Budock Water
Gurnards Head
Halsetown
Carbis Bay
Porkellis
Towednack
Lelant
Leedstown
Godolphin House
Wendron Mining District
Argal & College Reservoirs
Treverva
South West Coast Path
Zennor
Crowlas
St Erth
Townshend
Godolphin Cross
Prospidnick
Trenear
Penjerrick
Pendeen Watch
Morvah
Carn Galver Mine
Men-An-Tol
Mulfra Quoit
Chysauster Ancient Village
Bakers Pit
Canonstown
Relubbus
Crowntown
Wendron
Helston Folk
Coverack Bridges
Penwith Heritage Coast
Lanyon Quoit
New Mill
Ludgvan
St Hilary
Trescowe
Wendron Heritage Railway
Brill
Geevor Tin Mine
Levant Mine & Beam Engine
Pendeen
Trengwainton Garden
Madron
Tremenheere
Ashton
Sithney
Breage
Carleen
Helston
Constantine
Trebah Garden
Botallack
St Just Mining District
Heamoor
Polgoon
Gulval
Longrock
Marazion
Goldsithney
Helston
Gweek
Porth Navas
Mawnar
Cape Cornwall
St Just
A3071
Newbridge
Chyandour
Penzance
Perranuthnoe
St Michael's Mount
Helford Passage
Helford
St Anth
Ballowall Barrow
Trengwainton Garden
Penlee House
Praa Sands
Trewavas Head
Trewavas Mining District
Seal Sanctuary
Durgan
Kelynack
Carn Euny Ancient Village
Sancreed
Trereife
Newlyn
Cudden Point
Rinsey Head
Helston
Garras
St Martin
Manaccan
Whitesand Bay
Drift
Paul
Flambards
Mawgan
St Keverne
Sennen Cove
Crows-an-Wra
Mousehole
Helston
Halliggye Fogou
LAND'S END
Sennen
St Buryan
The Merry Maidens
MOUNT'S BAY
Porthleven
Mawgan
Trevescan
B3315
Trethewey
Treen
Lamorna
White Cross
Cury
Coverack
Porthcurno
Cribba Head
Merthen Point
Lamorna Cove
Poldhu Point
Marconi Memorial
Goonhilly Downs
Porthgwarra
Minack Open Air Theatre
St Levan
Isles of Scilly (Mar-Oct)
Mullion Cove
Mullion
Ruan Major
Kuggar
Gwennap Head
Gwennap
Mullion Island
Predannack Head
Ruan Minor
Cadgwith
Devil's Frying Pan
Black Head
Covera
Vellan Head
South West Coast Path
The Lizard
Lizard Head
Kynance Cove
The Lizard Heritage Coast
Lizard
Church Cove
Bass Point
LIZARD POINT
Lizard Lighthouse & Heritage Centre

0   1   2   3   4 miles
0 1 2 3 4 5 kilometres

A   B   C   D   E   F   G   H

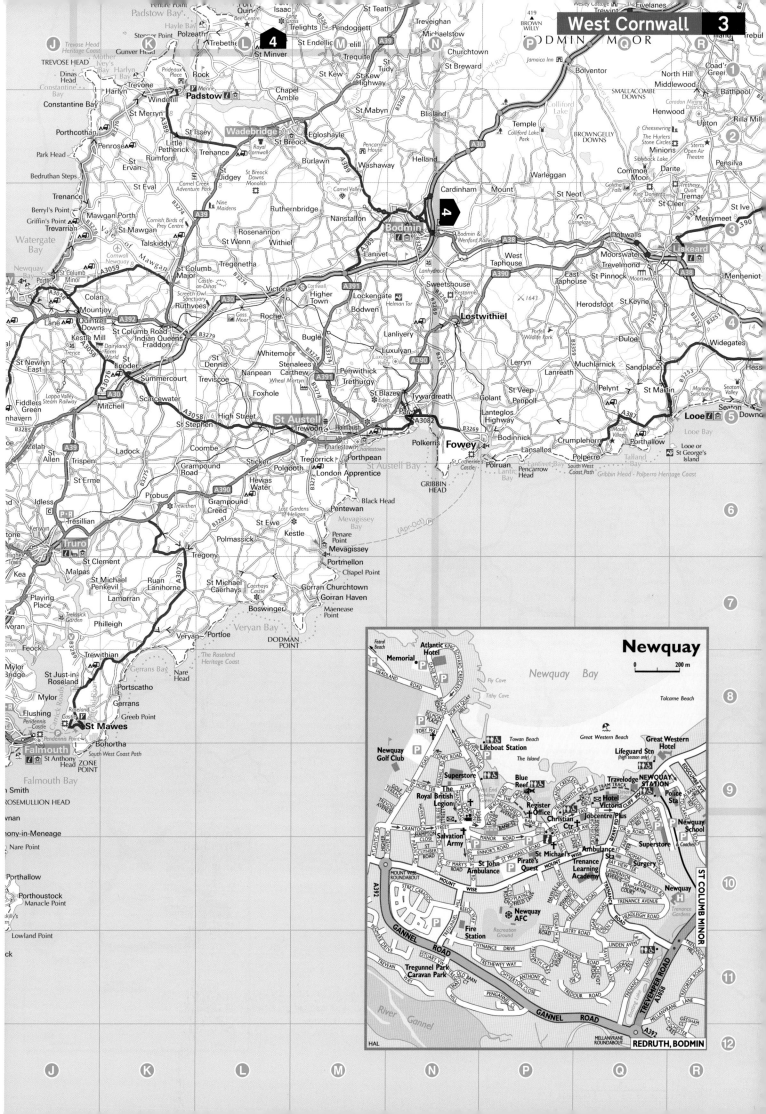

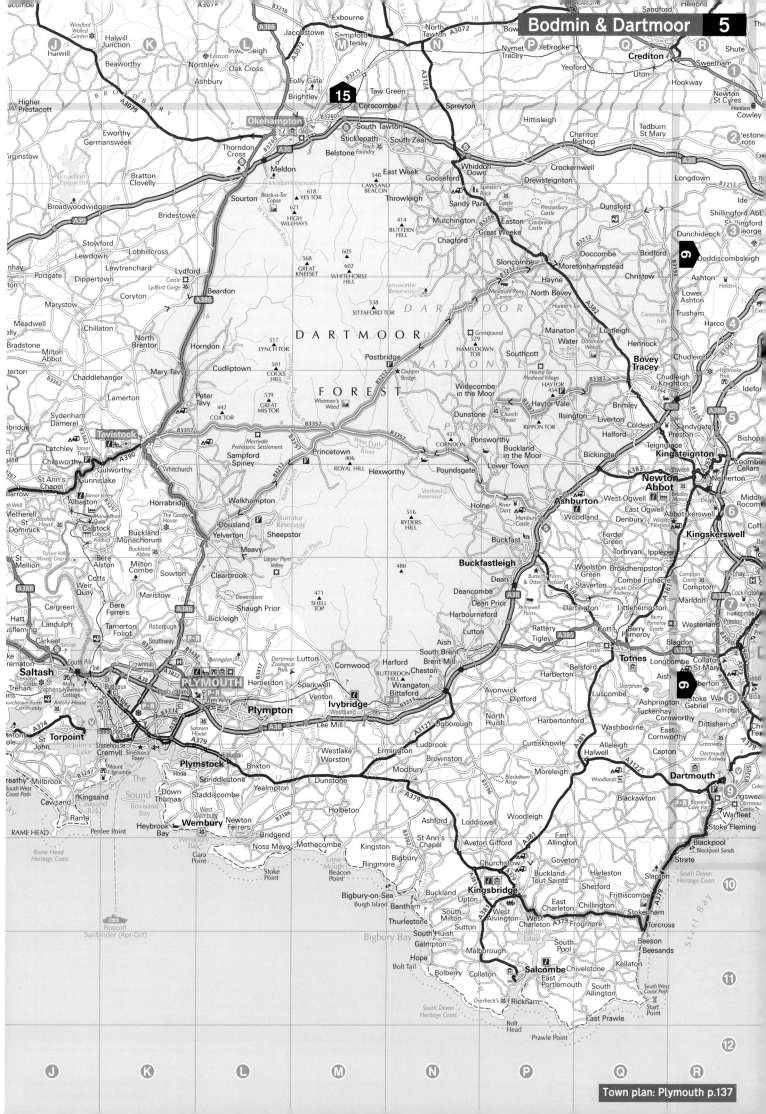

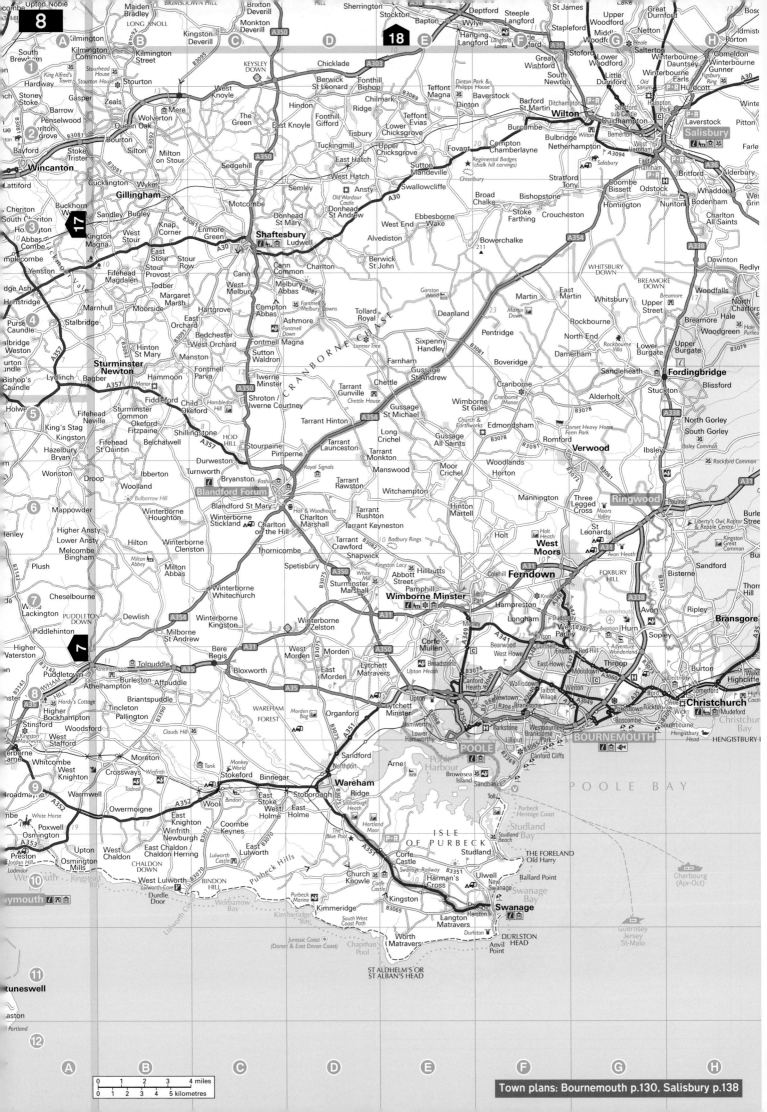

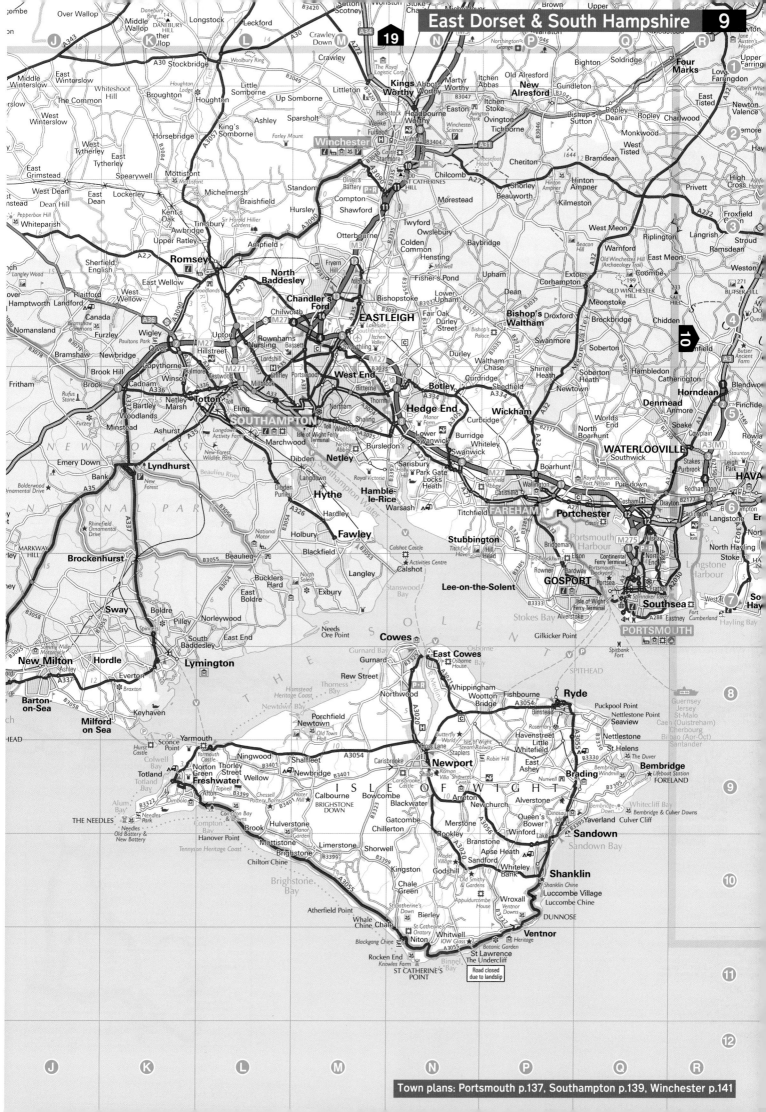

Town plan: Brighton p.131

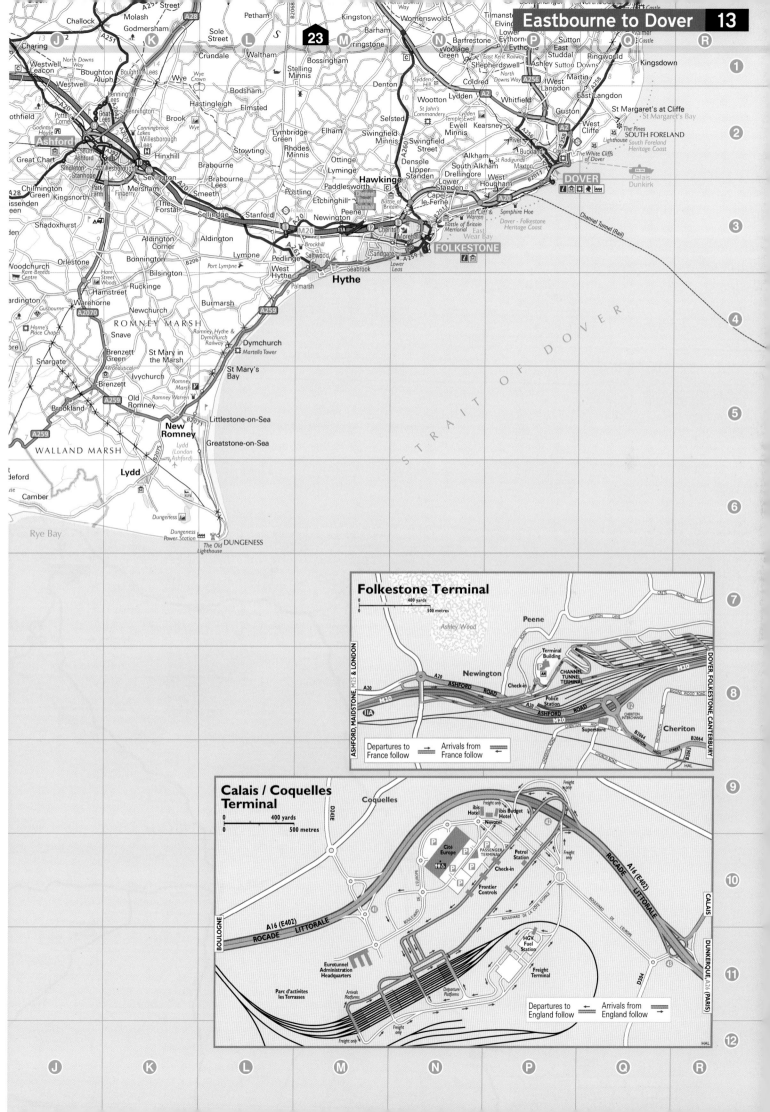

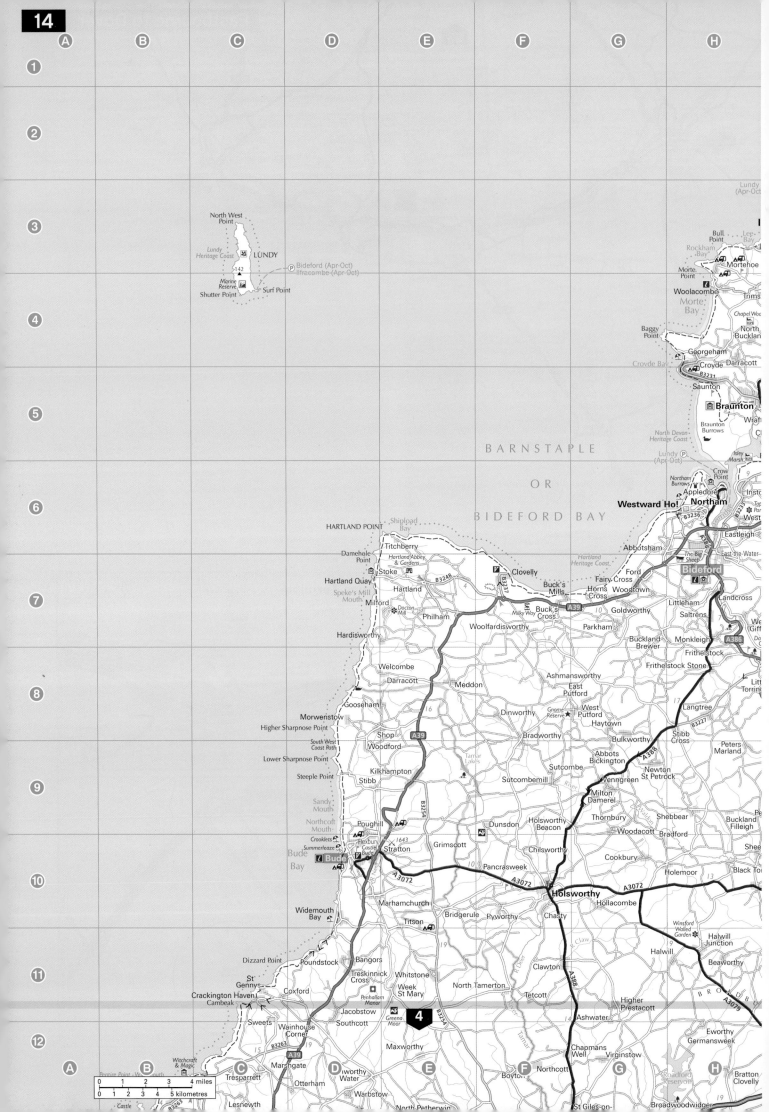

14

A   B   C   D   E   F   G   H

1 2 3 4 5 6 7 8 9 10 11 12

North West Point
Lundy Heritage Coast
LUNDY
▲142
Marine Reserve
Shutter Point
Surf Point
Bideford (Apr–Oct)
Ilfracombe (Apr–Oct)

Bull Point
Lee Bay
Rockham Bay
Mortehoe
Morte Point
Woolacombe
Trims
Morte Bay
Chapel Wood
Baggy Point
North Buckland
Georgeham
Croyde Darracott
Crovde Bay
B3231
Saunton

Braunton
Braunton Burrows
Wraf
Cl

North Devon Heritage Coast

BARNSTAPLE
OR
BIDEFORD BAY

Lundy (Apr–Oct)
Northam Burrows
Crow Point
Appledore
Westward Ho!
Northam
Inst
Tat Par
West

Shipload Bay
HARTLAND POINT
Titchberry
Damehole Point
Hartland Abbey & Gardens
Stoke
Hartland Quay
Speke's Mill Mouth
Hartland
Milford
Docton Mill
Philham
Hardisworthy

Clovelly
Buck's Mills
Milky Way
Buck's Cross
Woolfardisworthy

Hartland Heritage Coast

Abbotsham
The Big Sheep
Bideford
East-the-Water
Eastleigh
Ford
Fairy Cross
Horns Cross
Woodtown
A39
Goldworthy
Parkham
Buckland Brewer
Littleham
Saltrens
Landcross
We Giff
Monkleigh
A386
Frithelstock
Frithelstock Stone
Litt Torrin

Welcombe
Darracott
Gooseham
Morwenstow
Higher Sharpnose Point
South West Coast Path
Lower Sharpnose Point
Steeple Point
Sandy Mouth
Northcott Mouth
Crooklets
Summerleaze
Bude Bay
Bude
Widemouth Bay

Meddon
Shop
Woodford
A39
Kilkhampton
Stibb
Poughill
Flexbury
Castle Bude
Stratton
A3072

Ashmansworthy
East Putford
Dinworthy
Gnome Reserve
West Putford
Haytown
Bradworthy
Tamar Lakes
Sutcombe
Sutcombemill
Dunsdon
Holsworthy Beacon
Chilsworthy
Pancrasweek
A3072

Bulkworthy
Abbots Bickington
A388
Venngreen
Milton Damerel
Thornbury
Shebbear
Woodacott
Bradford
Cookbury
Holsworthy
Hollacombe
A3072
Holemoor

Langtree
B3227
Stibb Cross
Peters Marland
Newton St Petrock
Buckland Filleigh
Shee
Pe
Black To

Marhamchurch
Titson
Bridgerule
Pyworthy
Chasty
Winsford Walled Garden
Halwill Junction
Halwill
Beaworthy

Dizzard Point
Poundstock
Bangors
Treskinnick Cross
Whitstone
Week St Mary
North Tamerton
Tetcott
Higher Prestacott
BROAD

St Gennys
Crackington Haven
Cambeak
Coxford
Penhallam Manor
Jacobstow
Southcott
Greena Moor
4
B3254
Ashwater
Eworthy
Germansweek

Sweets
Wainhouse Corner
Maxworthy
Chapmans Well
Virginstow
Bratton Clovelly

Witchcraft & Magic
B3263
A39
Marshgate
Iworthy Water
Boyton
Northcott
Roadford Reservoir

Pentire Point – We mouth
Tresparrett
Otterham
Warbstow
St Giles-on-
Broadwoodwidger

Castle
B3263
Lesnewth
North Petherwin

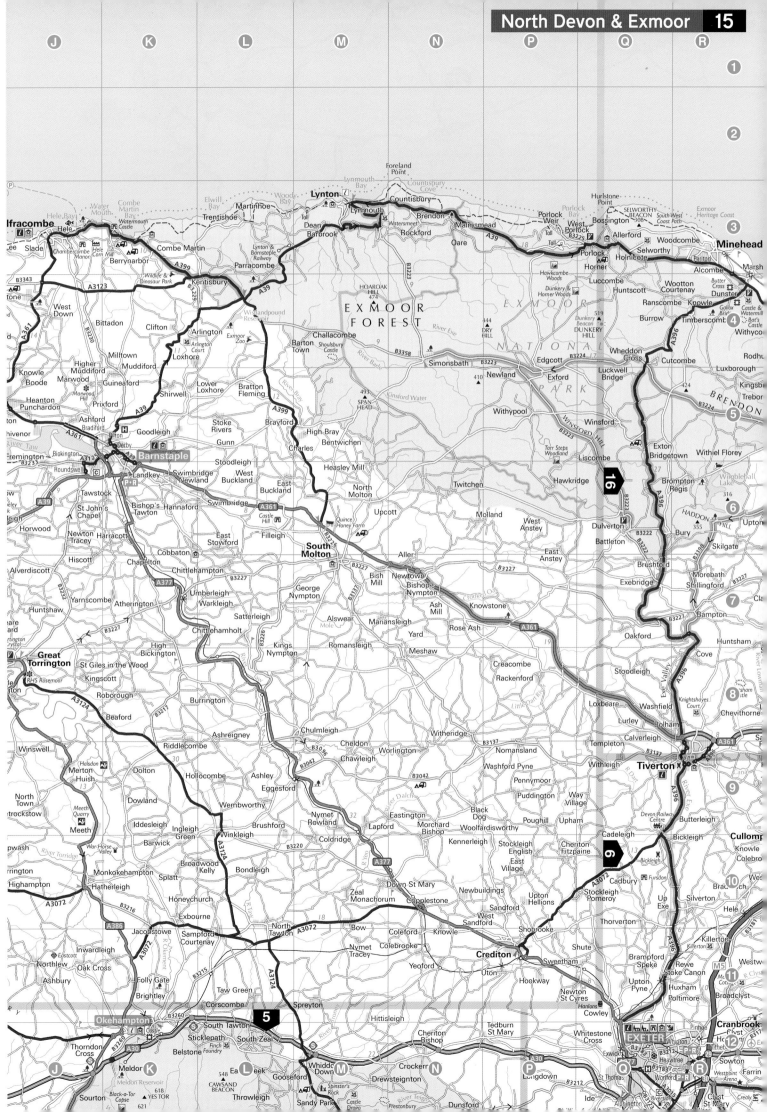

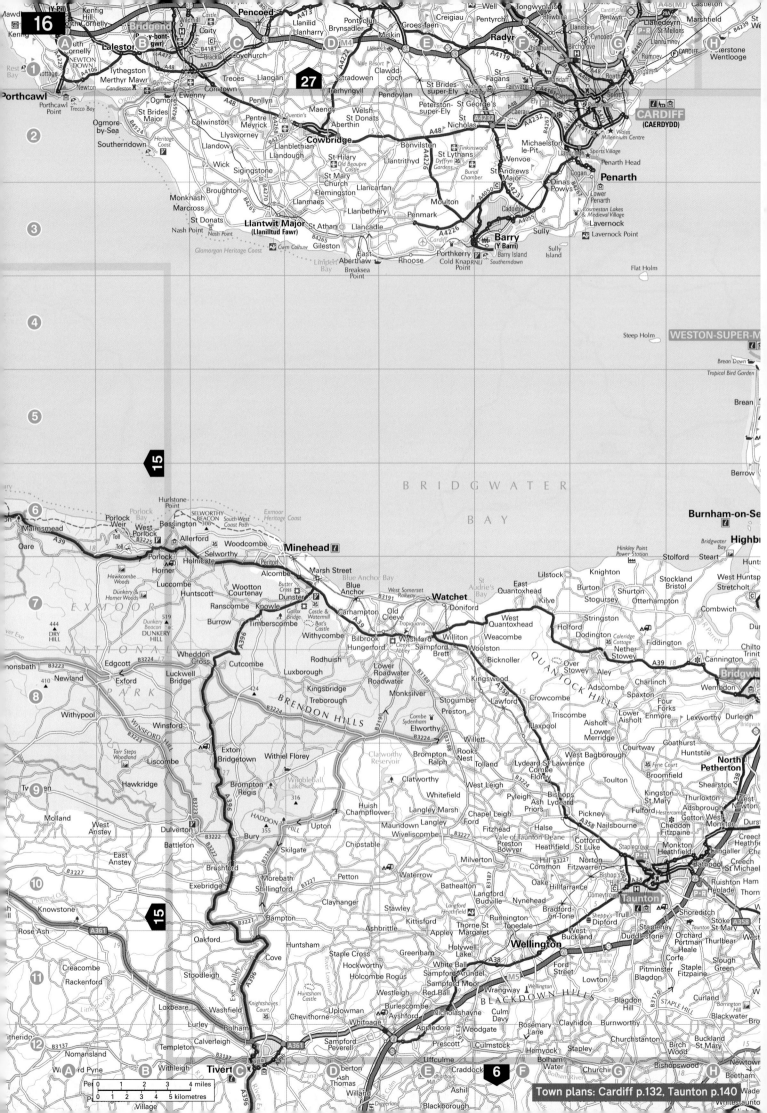

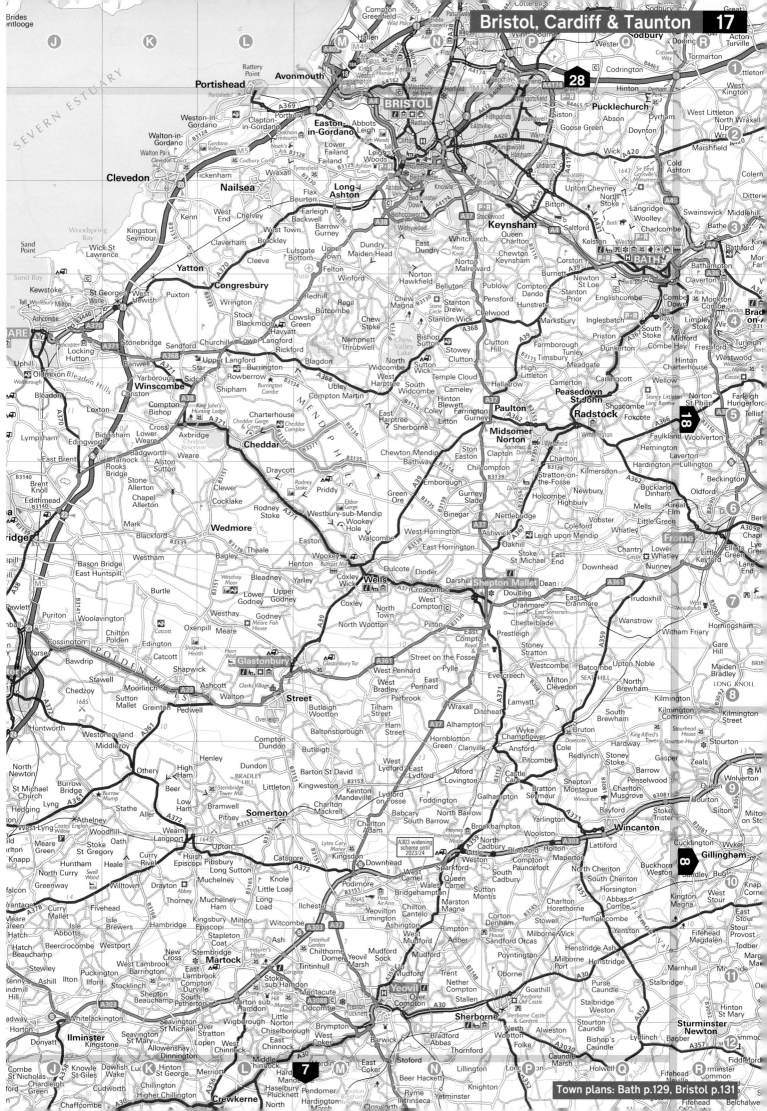

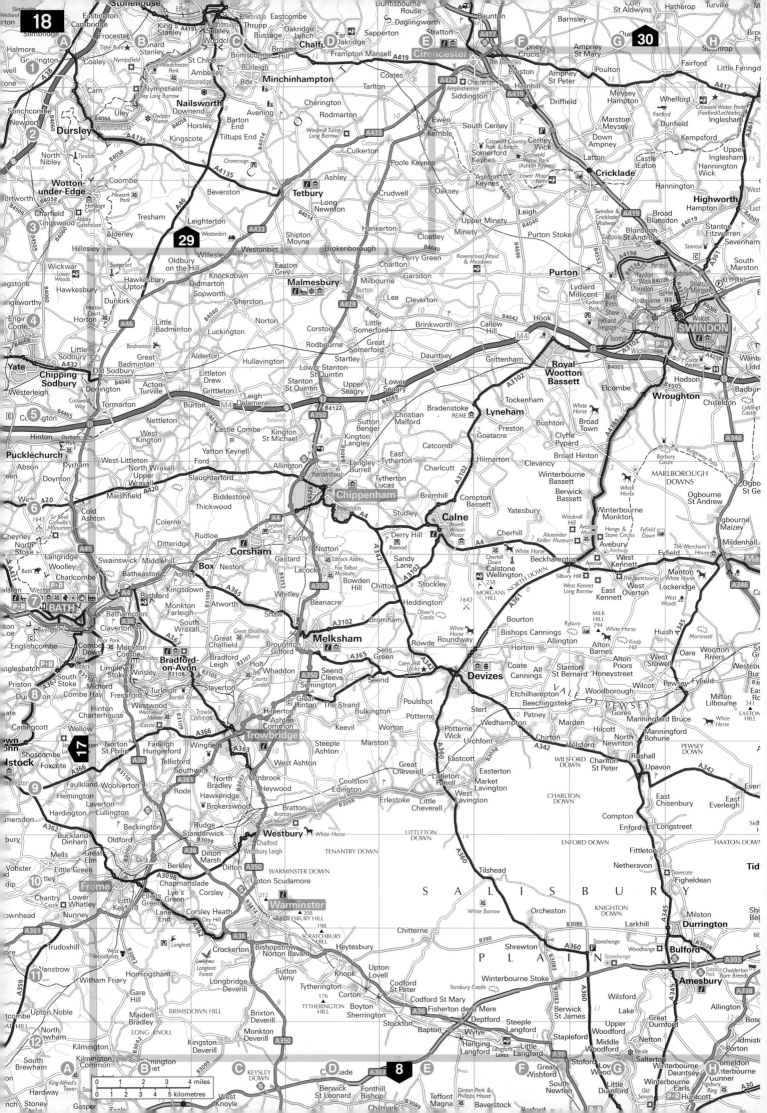

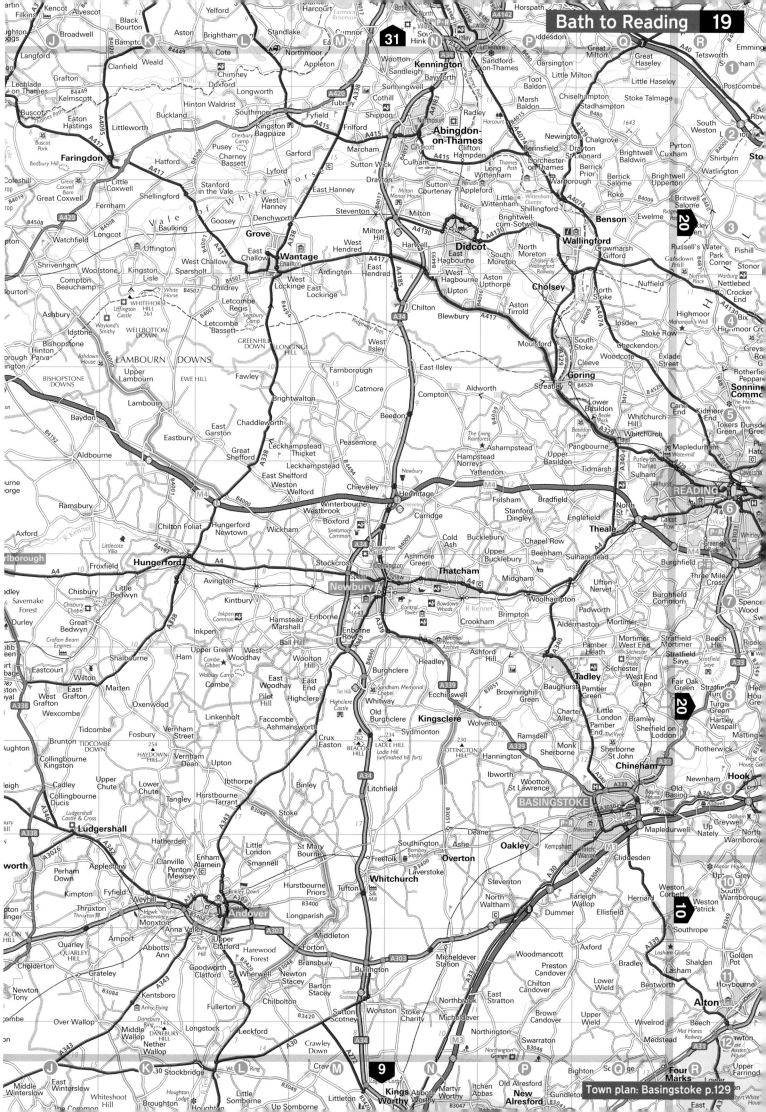

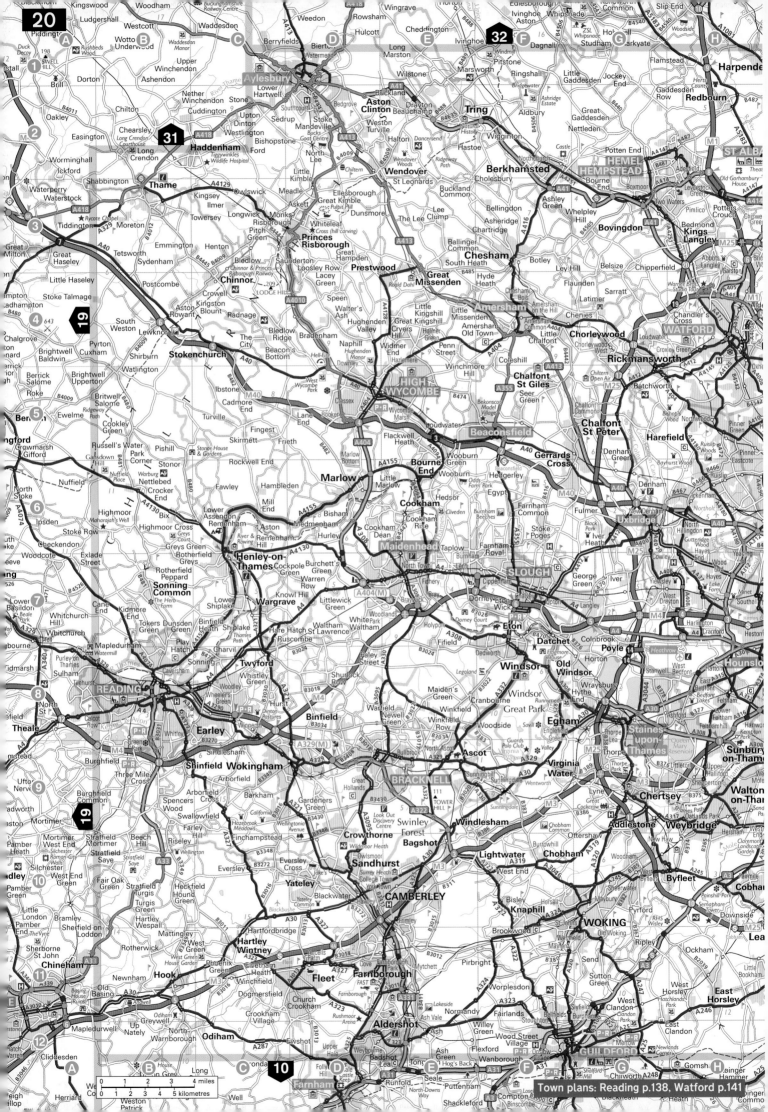

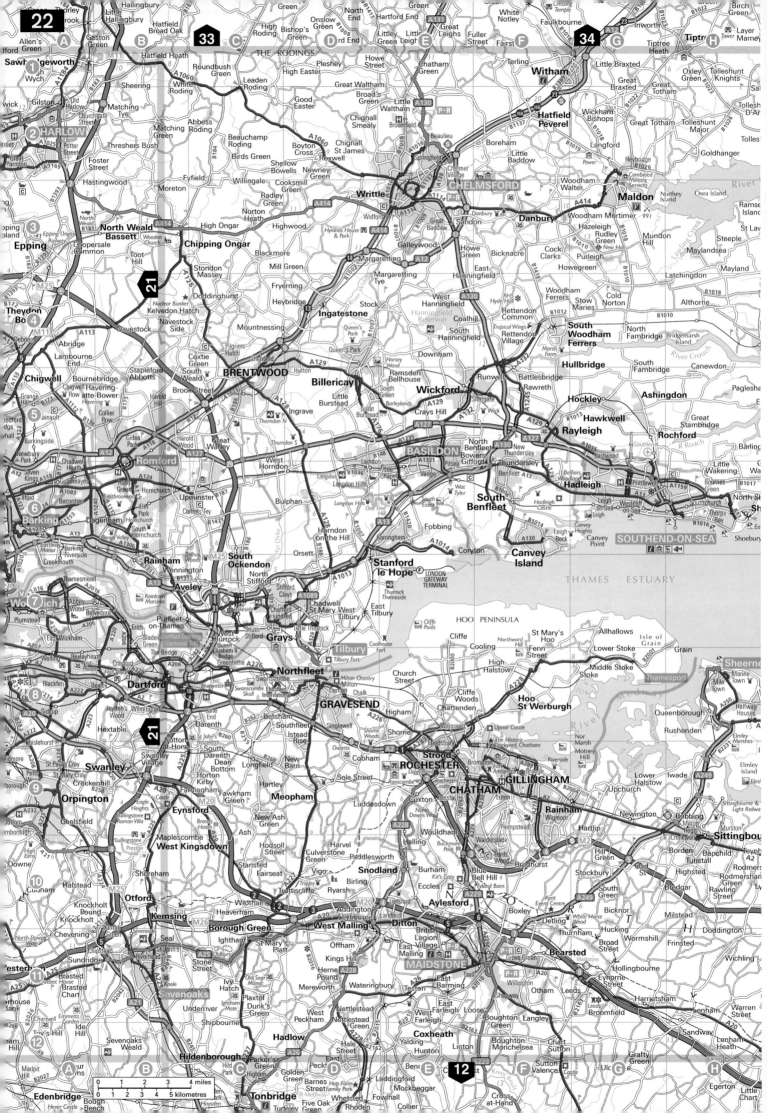

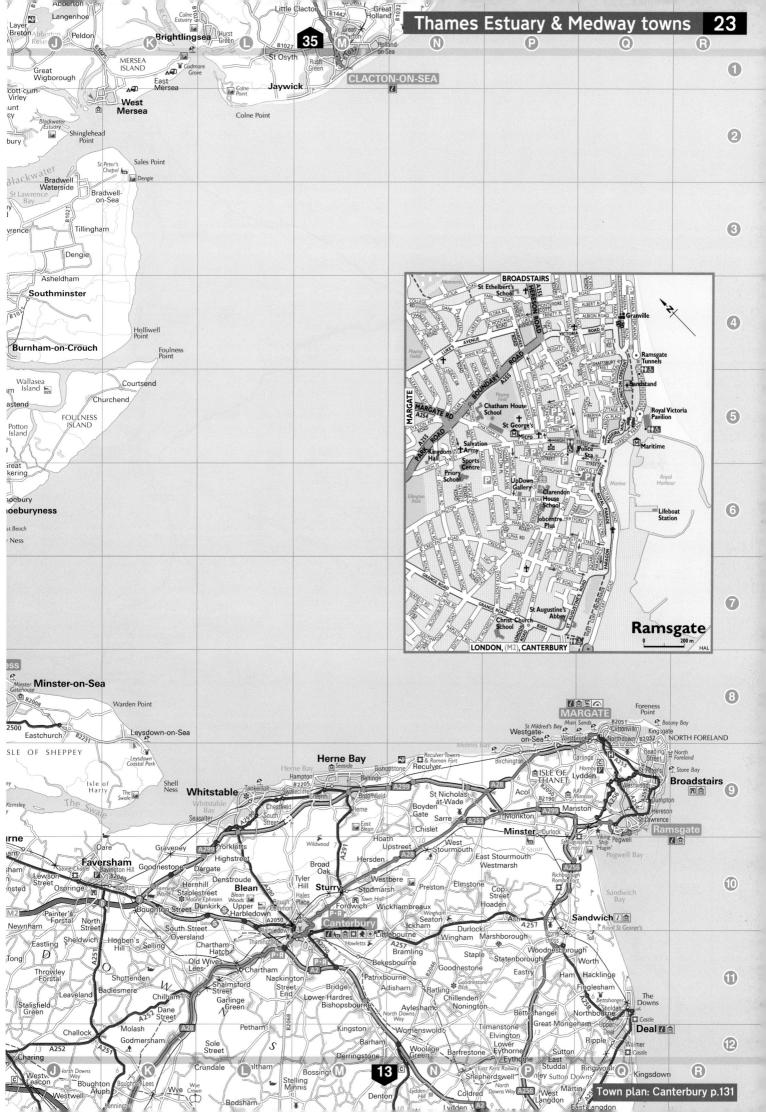

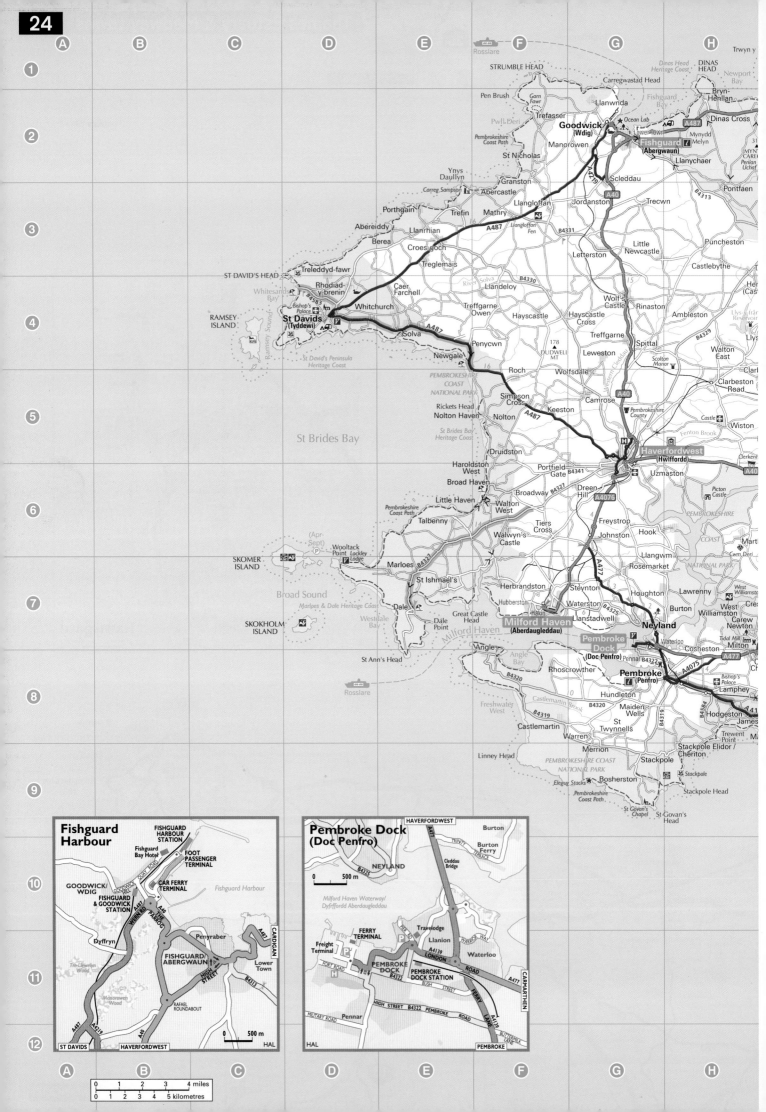

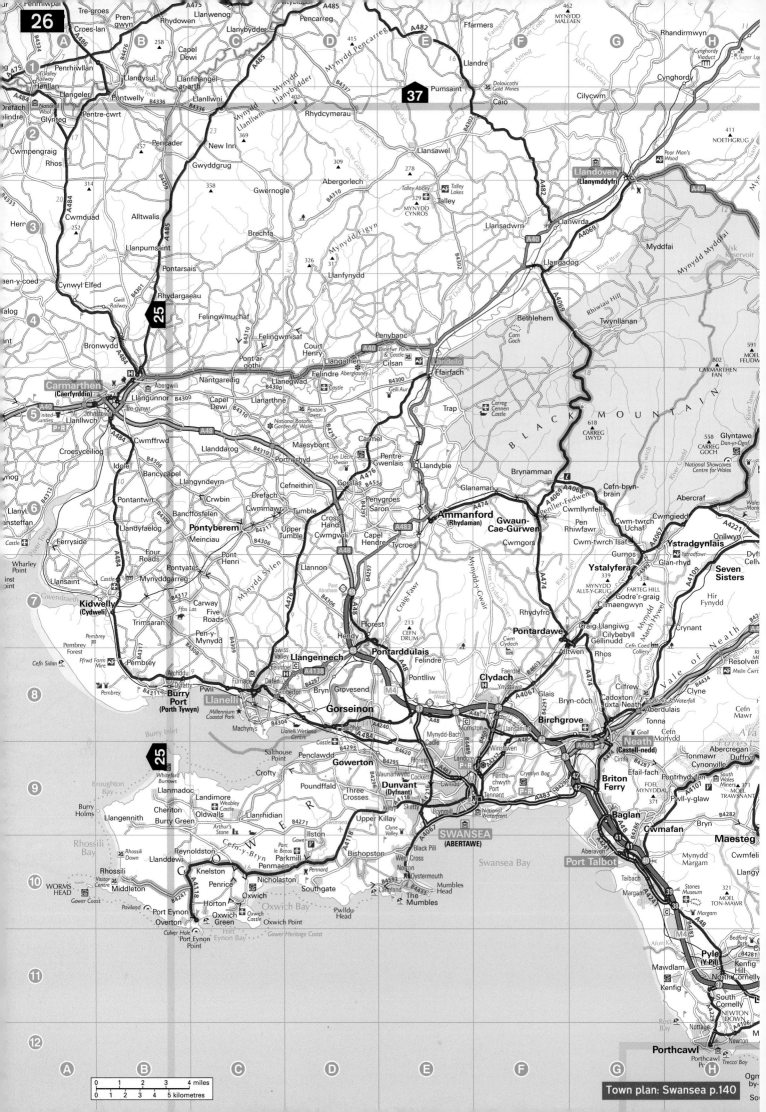

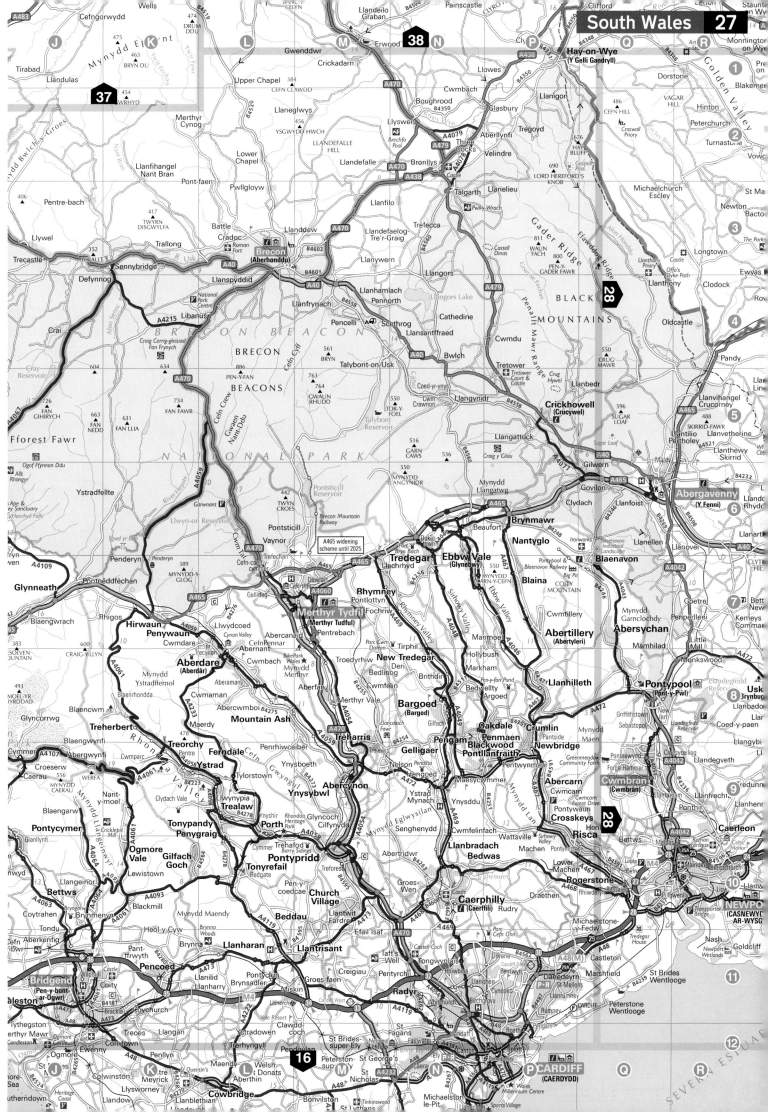

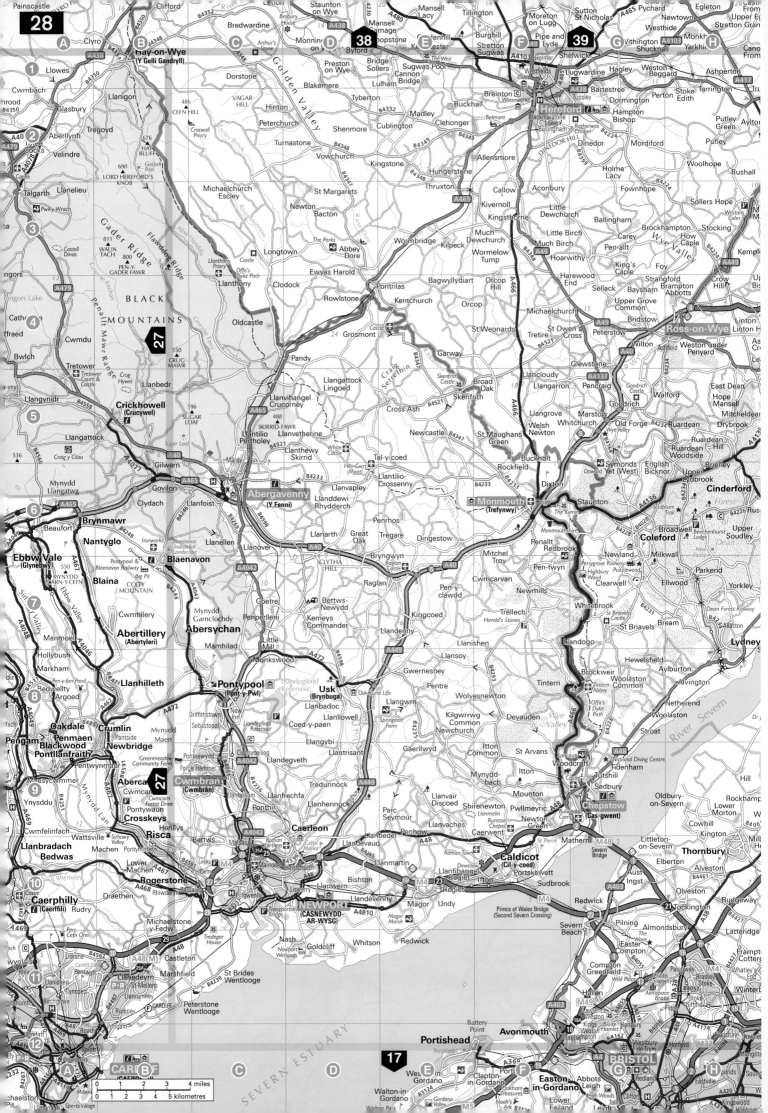

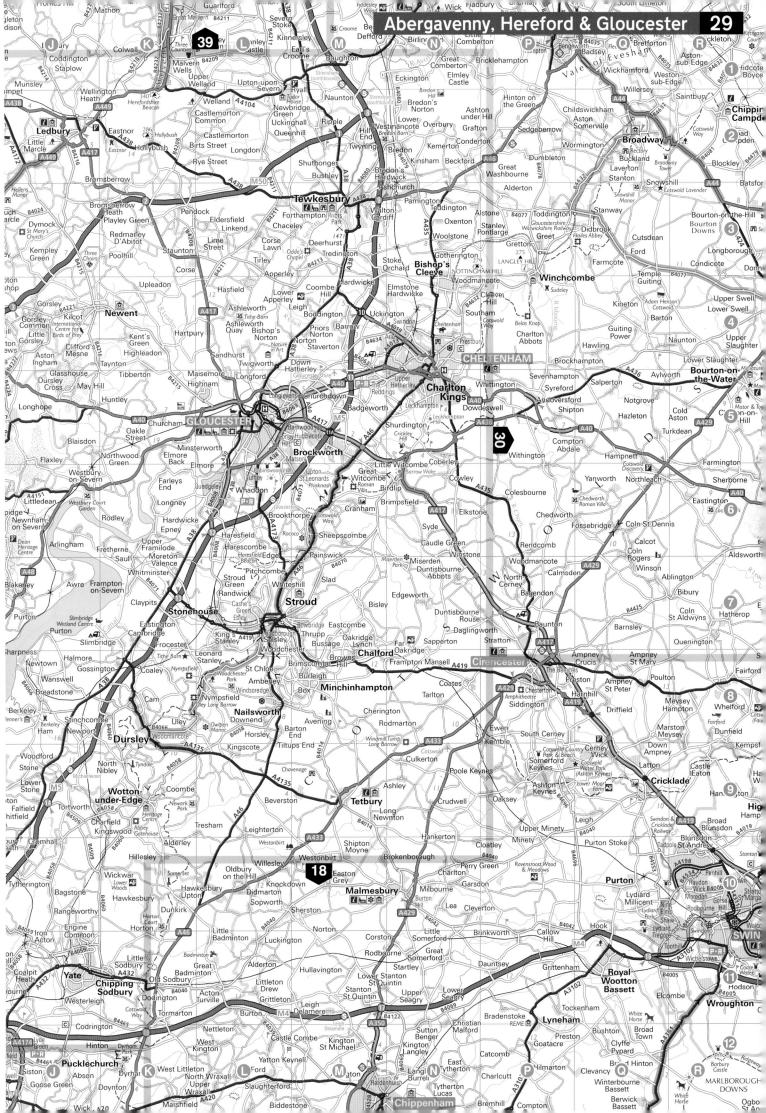

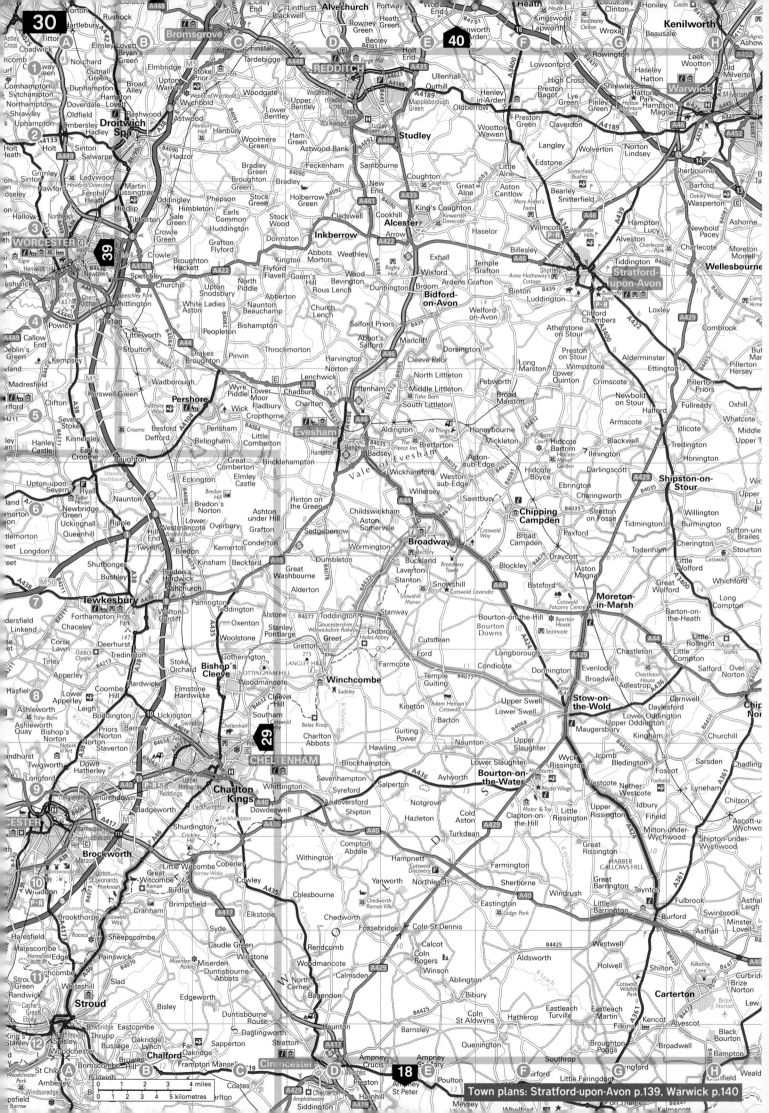

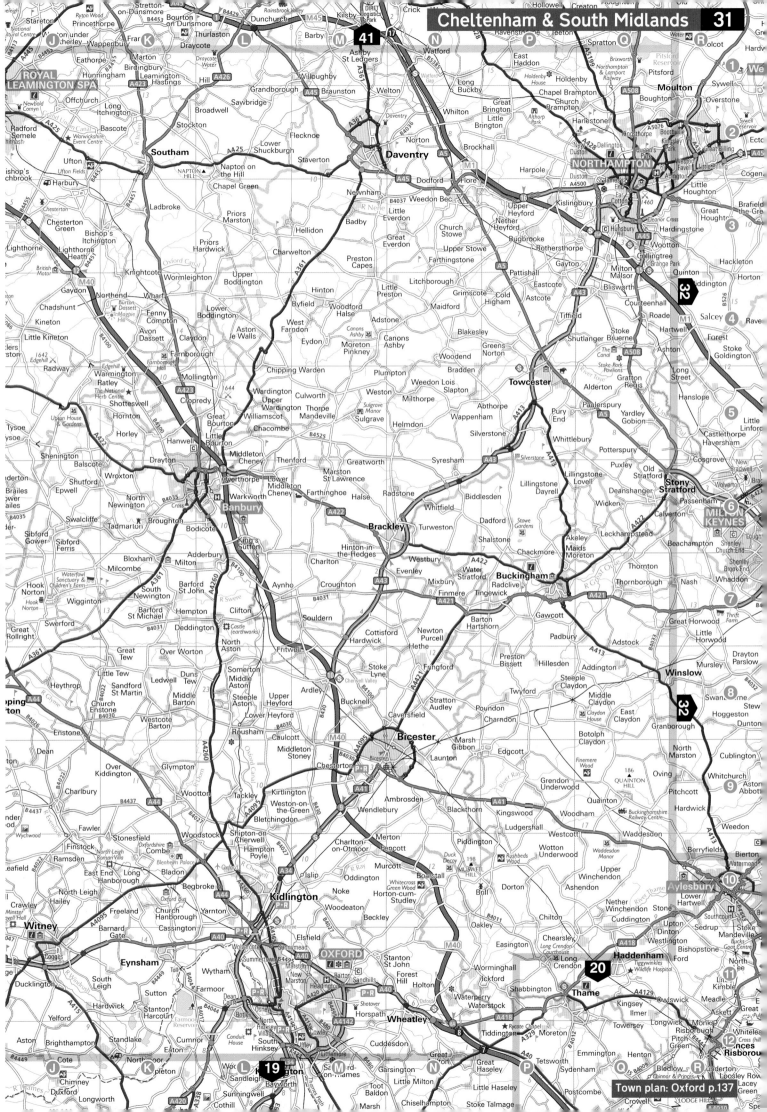

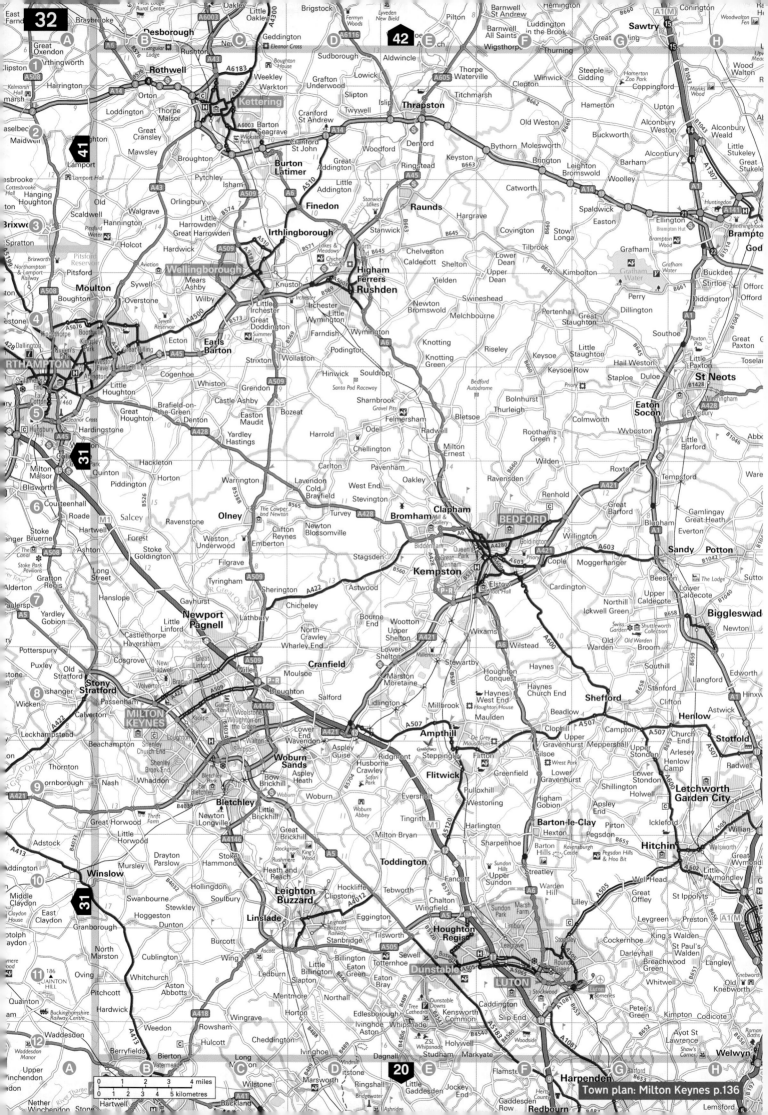

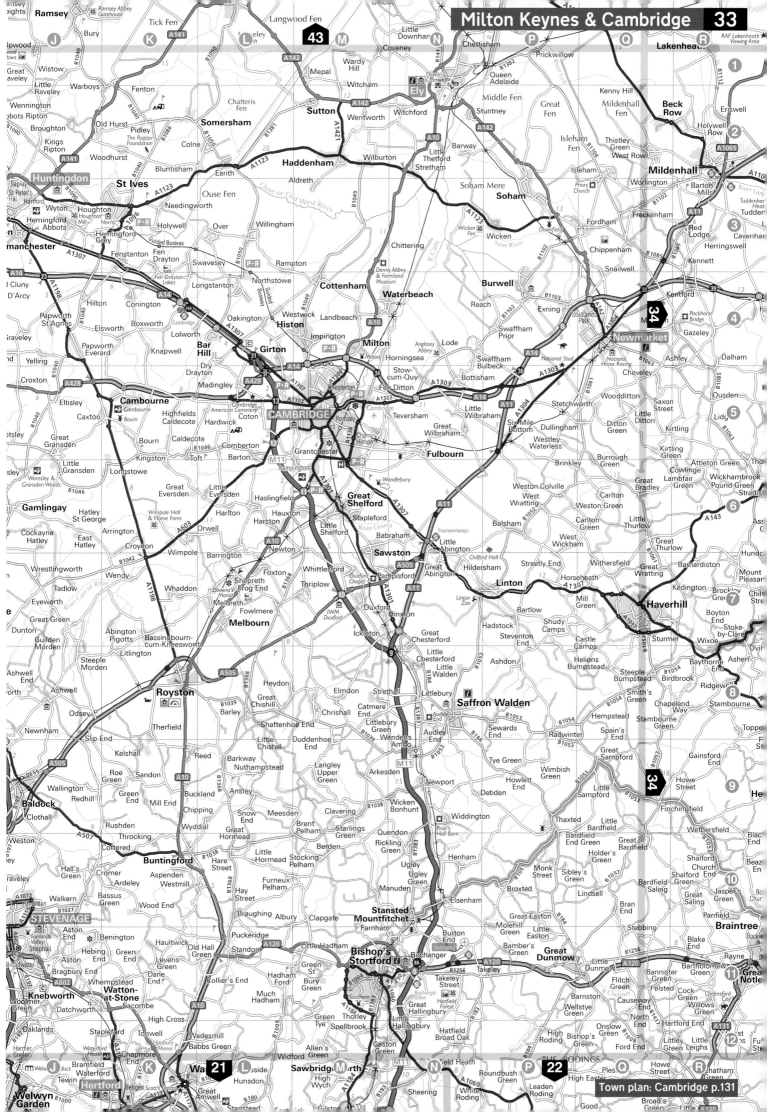

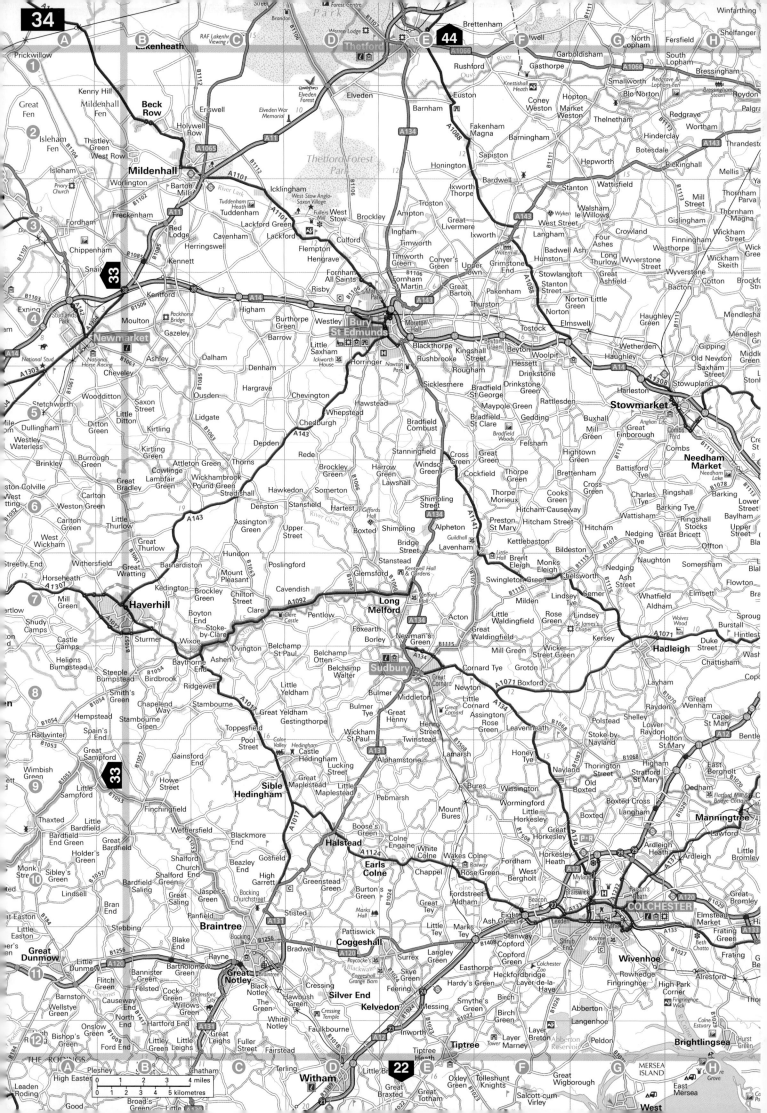

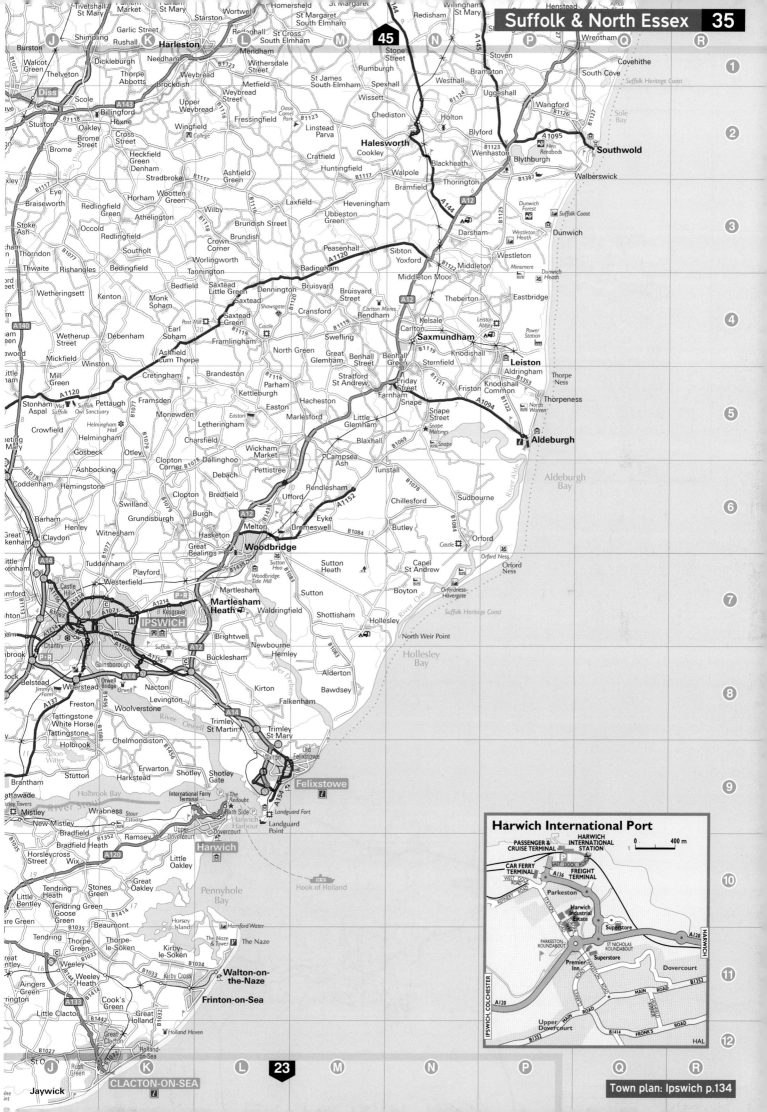

Suffolk Heritage Coast

45

P · R

Harwich International Port

PASSENGER & CRUISE TERMINAL
HARWICH INTERNATIONAL STATION
CAR FERRY TERMINAL
FREIGHT TERMINAL
EAST DOCK ROAD
WEST DOCK ROAD
A136
Parkeston
Harwich Industrial Estate
Superstore
PARKESTON ROUNDABOUT
ST NICHOLAS ROUNDABOUT
Superstore
Premier Inn
IPSWICH, COLCHESTER A120
HARWICH A120
Dovercourt
MAIN ROAD
B1352
FRONK'S ROAD
Upper Dovercourt
B1414
HAL
0   400 m

Town plan: Ipswich p.134

23

Aberystwyth

0   200 m

Cardigan Bay

Bandstand
Aberystwyth North Beach
St Paul Methodist
St David's URC
Surgery
The Morlan Centre
Capel y Morfa
Ceredigion
Royal Pier
Bethel
CAB
Coastguard Station
University (Old College)
Clock Tower
Market Hall
Salvation Army
Holy Trinity
ABERYSTWYTH STATION
Monument
Aberystwyth Castle (ruins)
St Michael's
Castle
Eglwys y Santes Fair
Superstores
Ystwyth Retail Park
Rheidol
Vale of Rheidol Steam Railway Station
Trefechan Bridge
Slipway
Justice Centre
River Rheidol
Afon Rheidol
Park Avenue (Aberystwyth Town FC)
Fire Station
Police Station
TA Centre
Lifeboat Station
Ro-fawr
Marina
Aqua Terra

MACHYNLLETH, LLANGURIG

CARDIGAN

C A R D I G A N

B A Y

Ceredigion Heritage Coast

Aberarth
Aberaeron
New Quay (Ceinewydd)
Marine
Llanina
Gilfachrheda
Llwyncelyn
Llanarth
A482
A487
Maen-y-groes
Cwmtydu
Cross Inn
Oakford
Nanternis
Caerwedros
Dihewyd
Mydroilyn
Temple B
Ynys-Lochtyn
Llwyndafydd
Llangrannog
Pontgarreg
Plwmp
Pentregat
Talgarreg
Cwrtnewydd
Gorsgoch
Pendinas Lochtyn
Penbryn
Brynhoffnant
Pontsian
Llanwnne
Ceredigion Heritage Coast
Tresaith
Sarnau
Tan-y-groes
Glynarthen
Rhydlewis
Ffostrasol
Drefach
Cardigan Island
Mwnt Beach
Aberporth
Bettws Ifan
Penrhiwpal
Llanwenog
Cardigan Island Coastal Farm
Blaenannerch
Hawen
Tre-groes
Rhydowen
Llanybydder
Y Ferwig
Penparc
Tremain
Blaenporth
Troedyraur
Prengwyn
Croes-lan
Llanfihangel-ar-arth
Poppit Sands
Beulah
Maesllyn
Capel Dewi
Pembrokeshire Coast Path
St Dogmaels
Abbey & Coach House
Cardigan (Aberteifi)
Ponthirwaun
Brongest
St Dogmaels Maylgrove Heritage Coast
Ceibwr Bay
Welsh Wildlife Centre
Llechryd
Llandygwydd
Cwm-cou
Penrhiwllan
Llandysul
Llanfihangel-ar-arth
Moylegrove
Pen-y-bryn
Teifi Marshes
TIVY SIDE
Llandyfriog
Llangeler
Llanllwni
Trwyn y bwa
Cilgerran
National Coracle Centre
Teifi Valley Railway
Henllan
Pontwelly
Bryn-Henllan
Abercych
Adpar
Newport
Pen-rhiw
Newcastle Emlyn (Castell Newydd Emlyn)
Drefach
Pentre-cwrt
Dinas Cross
Nevern
Felindre Farchog
Rhoshill
Genarth
National Wool Museum
Mynydd Llanllwni
Pontfaen
Pengelli Forest
Newchapel
Boncath
Drefach
Felindre
Glynteg
Pencader
MYNYDD CAREGOG
Penlan Uchaf
Brynberian
Crosswell
Blaenffos
Capel Iwan
Cwmhiraeth
New Inn
Eglwyswrw
Bwlch-y-groes
Cwmpengraig
Pontfaen
Carreg Coetan
Pentre Ifan
Hermon
Tegryn
Rhos
Gwyddgrug
PEMBROKESHIRE COAST
MYNYDD PRESELI NATIONAL PARK
Gwernol

0   1   2   3   4 miles
0 1 2 3 4 5 kilometres

HAL

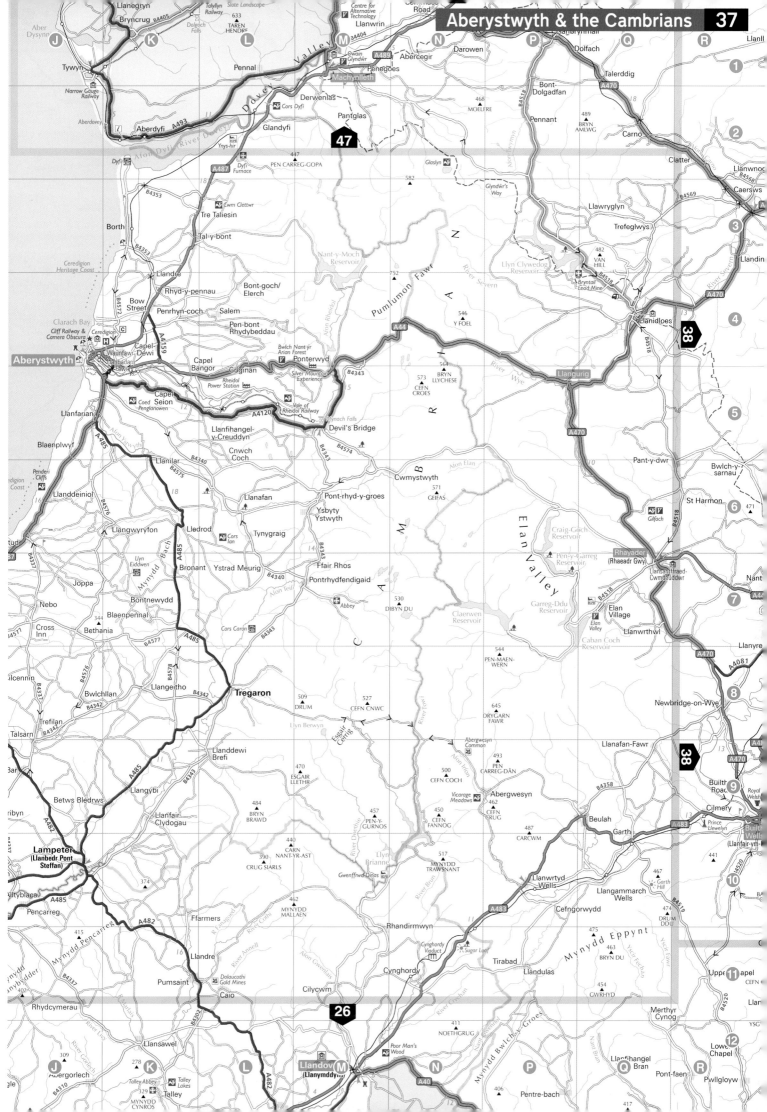

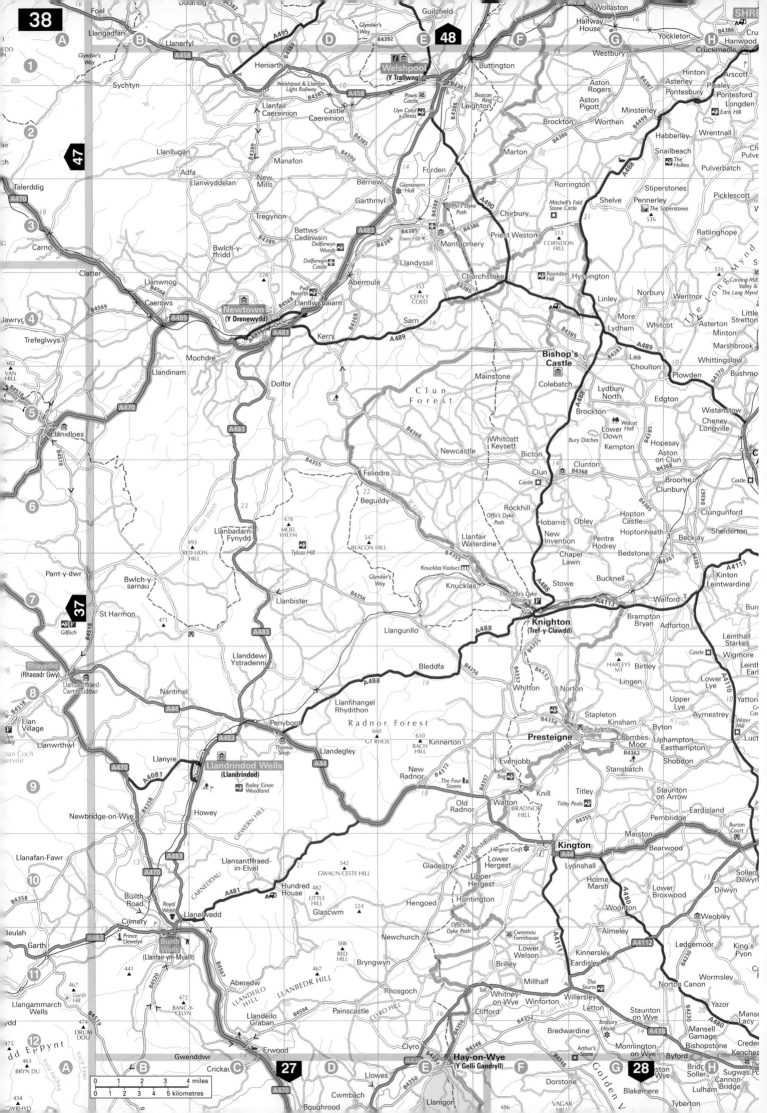

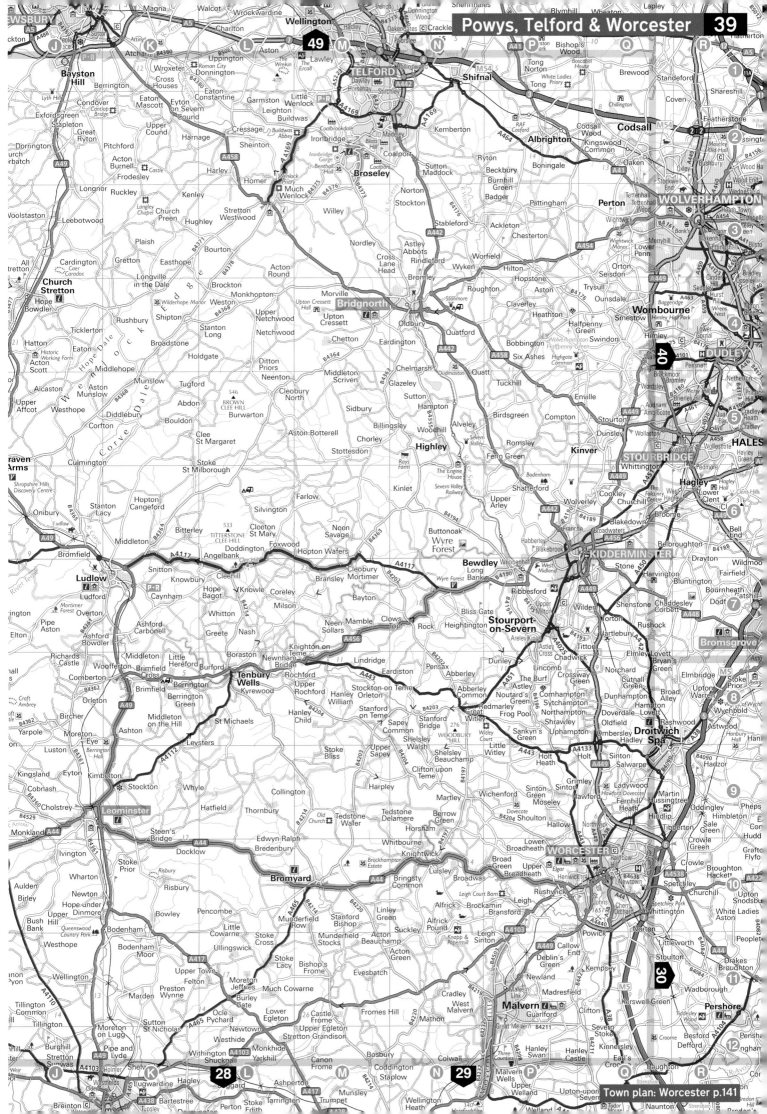

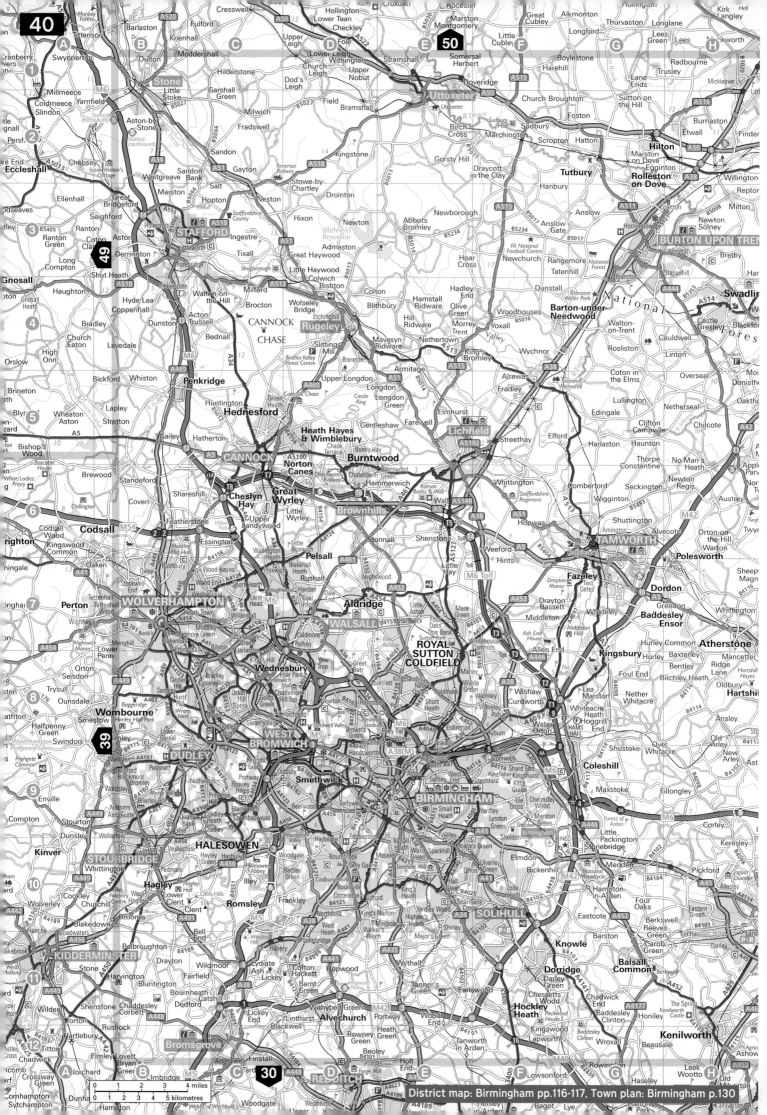

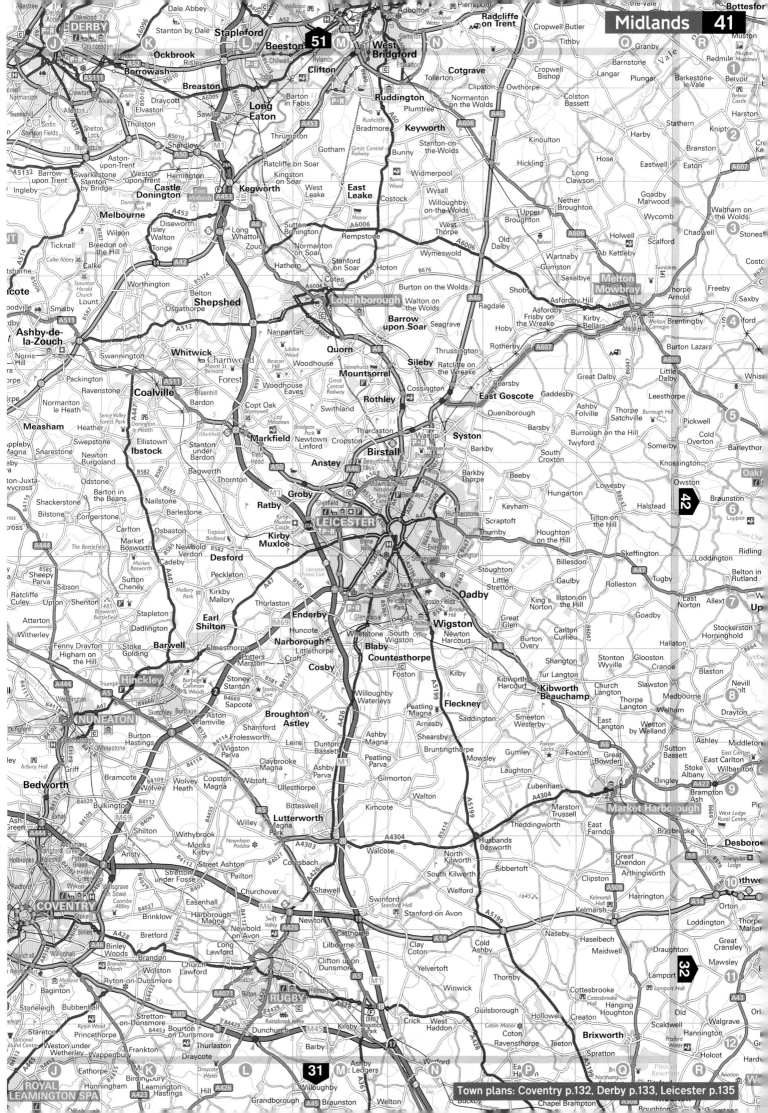

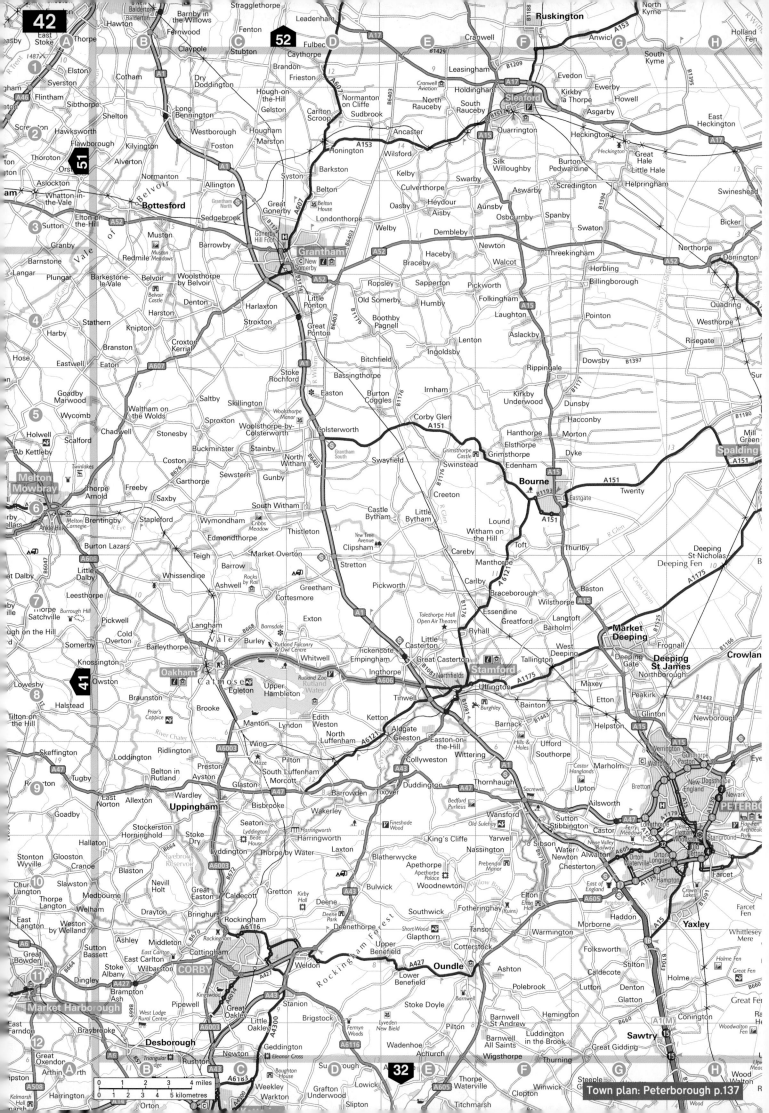

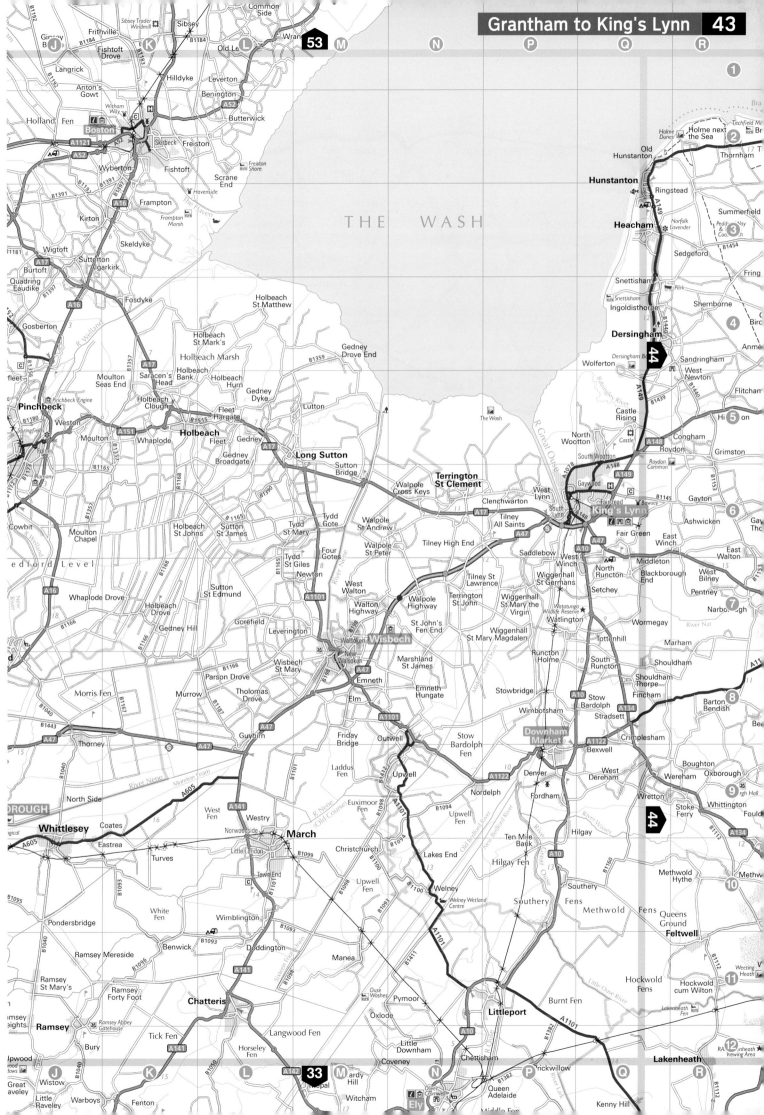

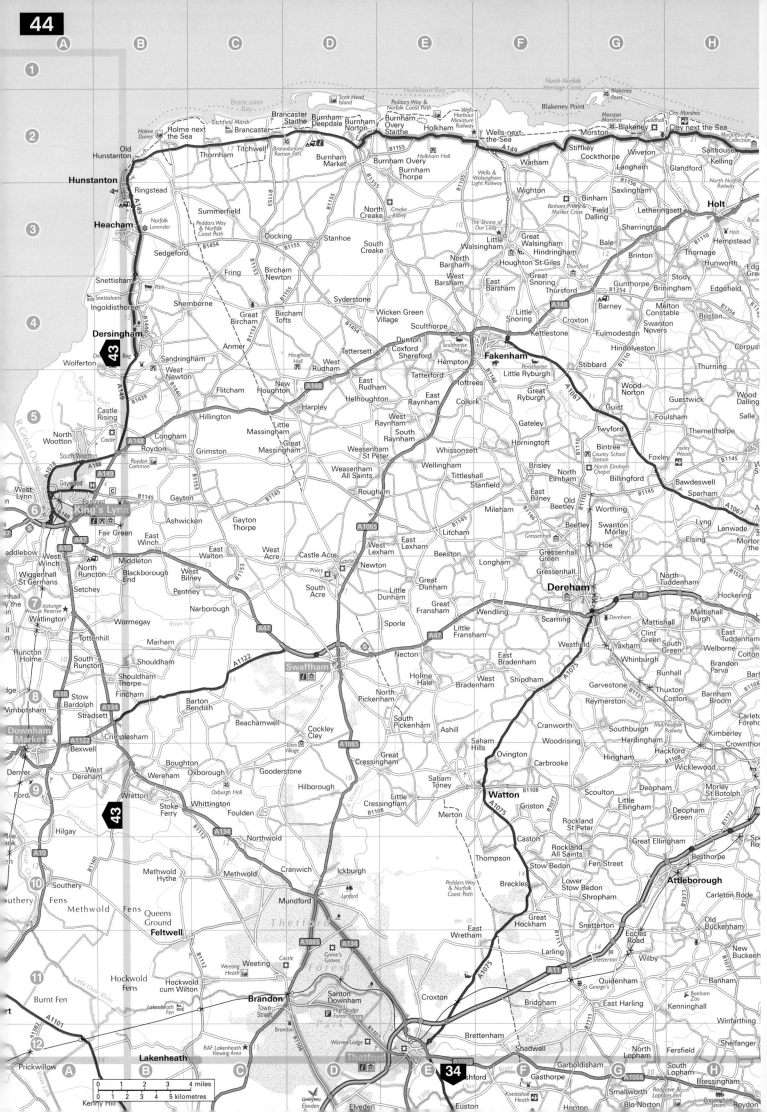

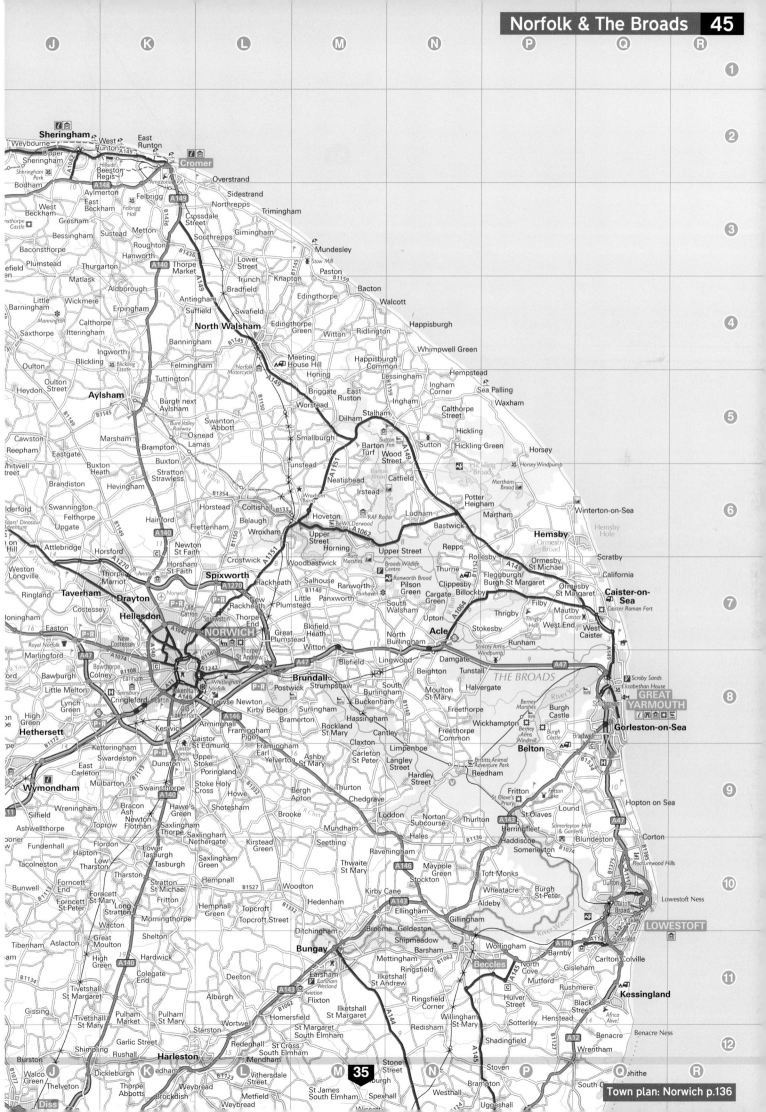

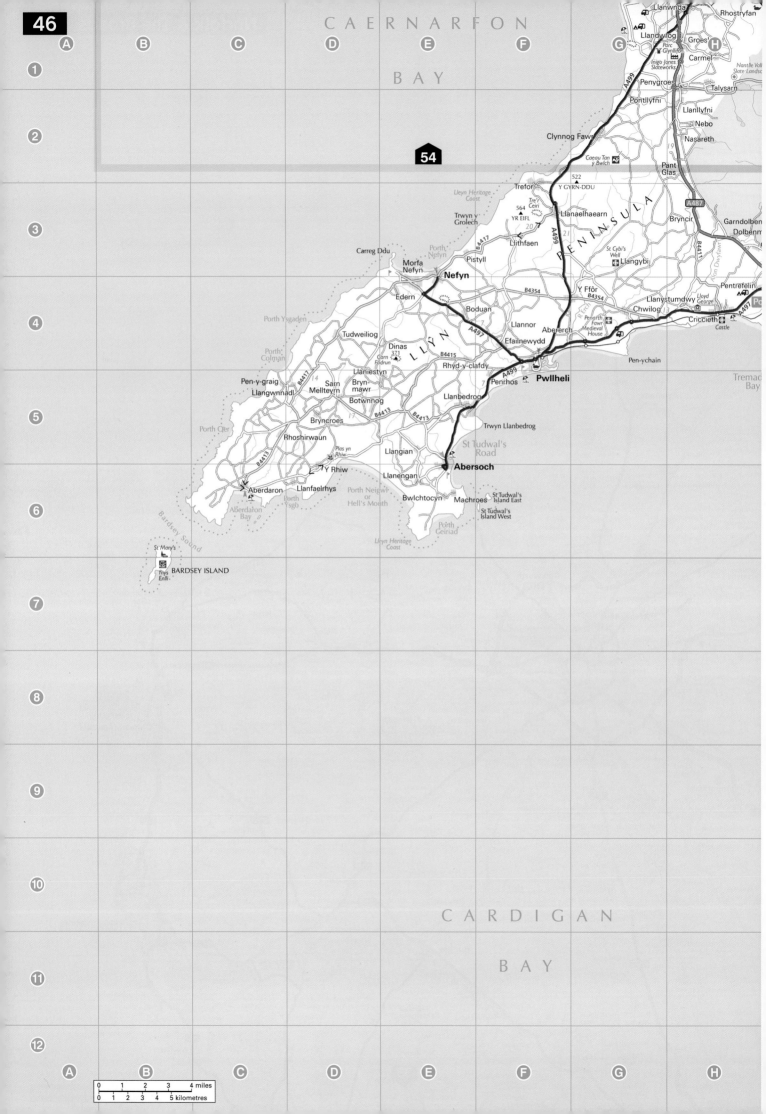

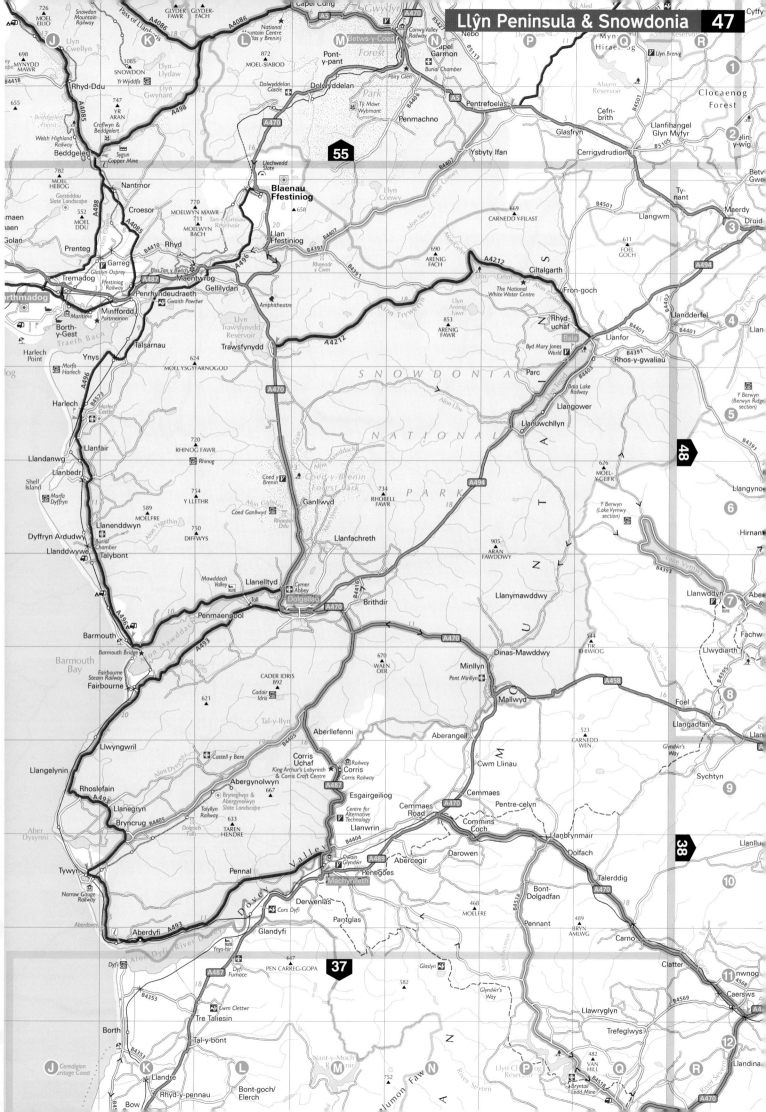

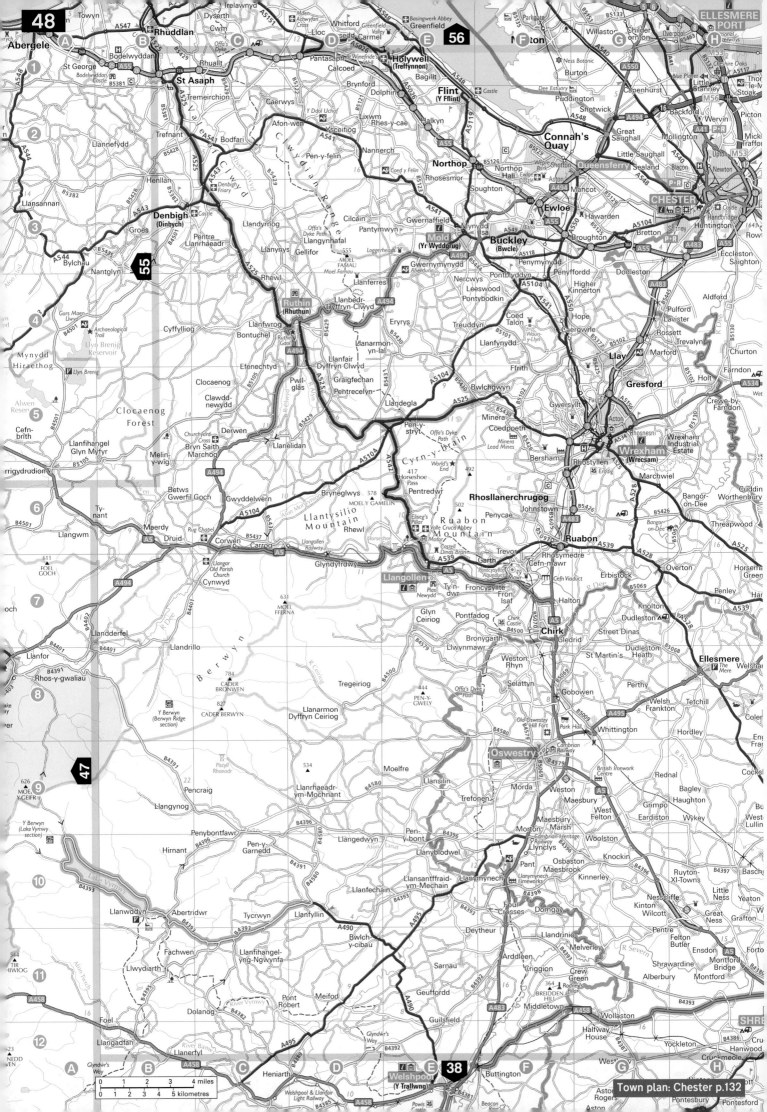

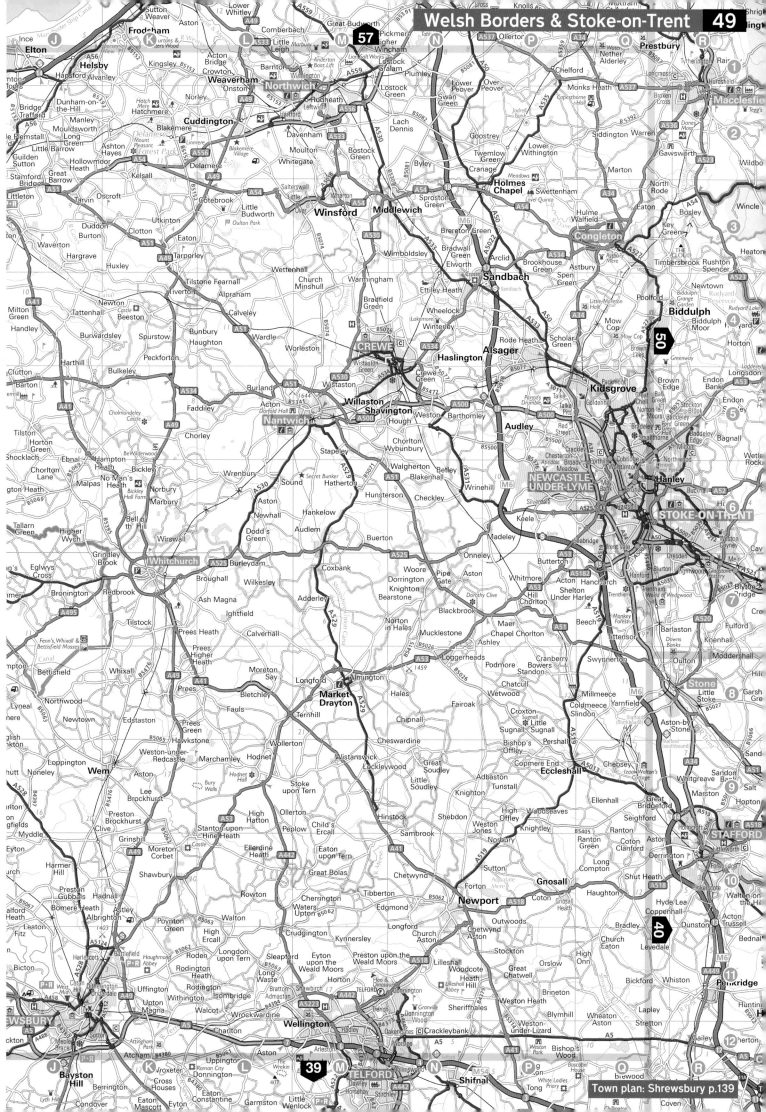

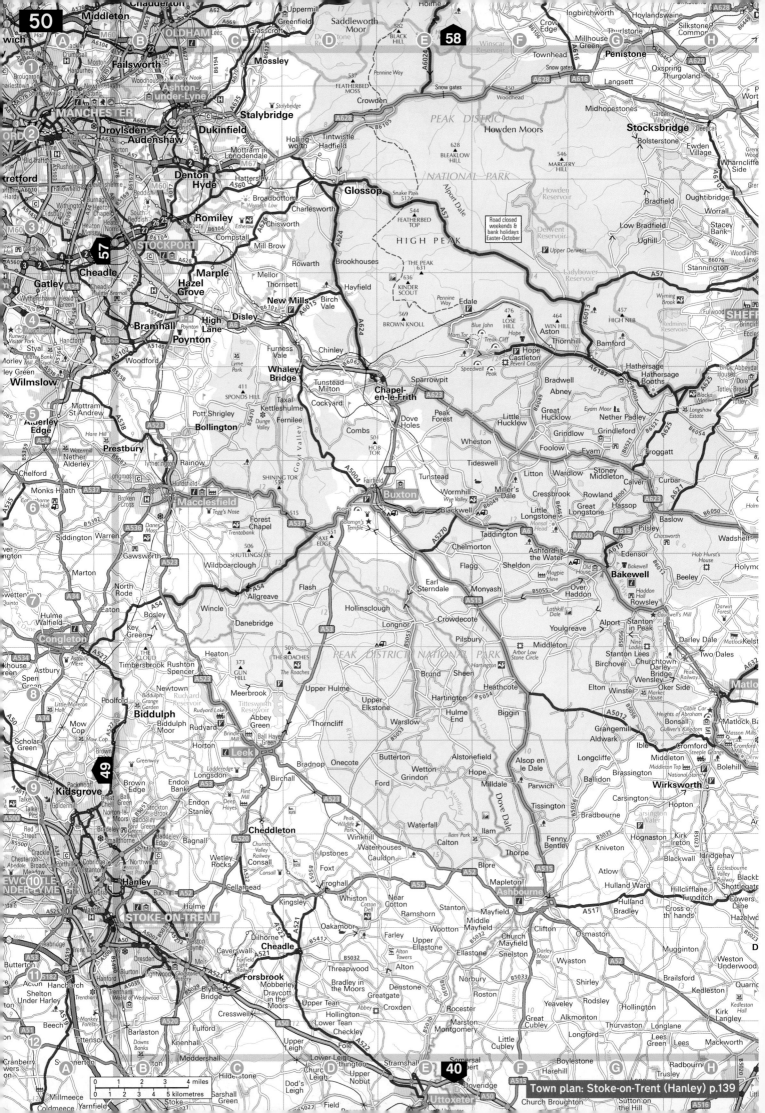

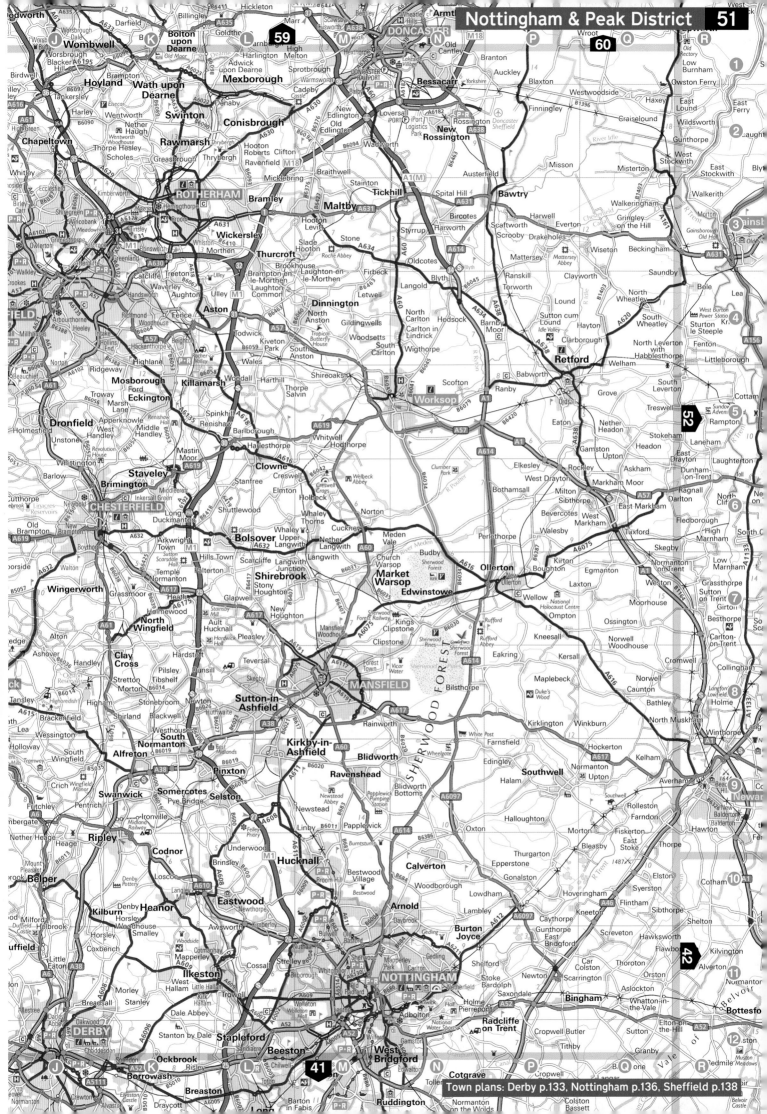

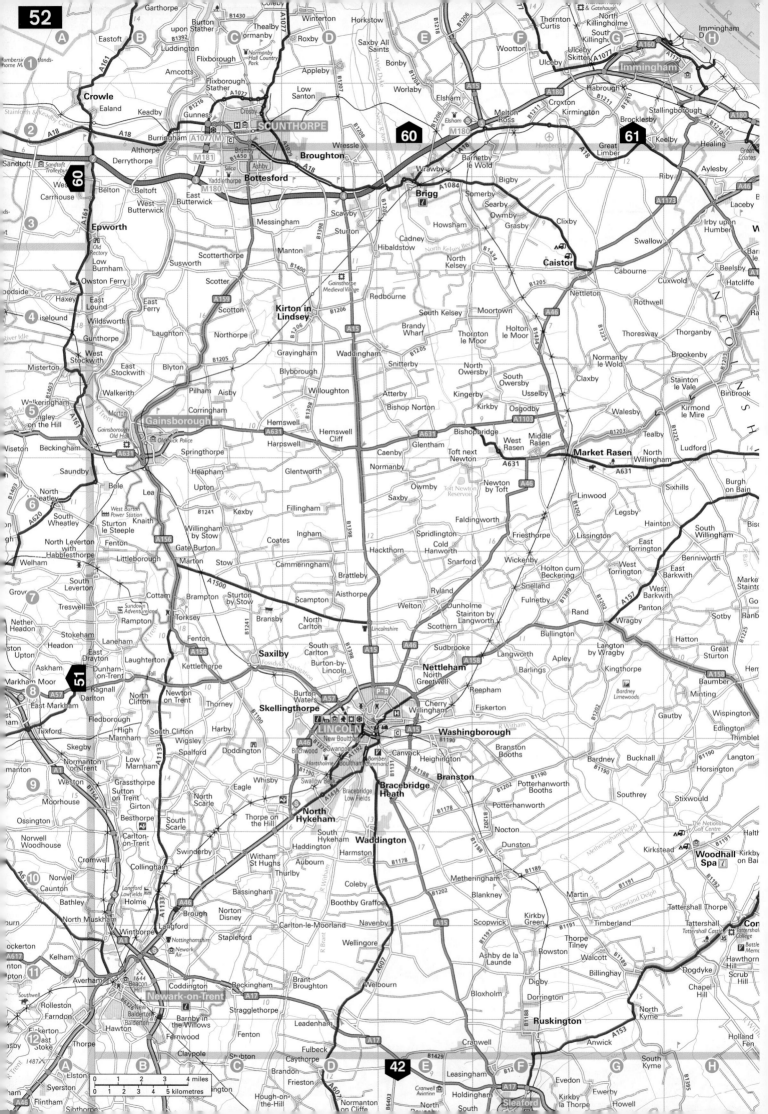

A map of the Lincoln & The Wolds area including Grimsby, Cleethorpes, Humberston, New Waltham, Louth, Mablethorpe, Sutton on Sea, Chapel St Leonards, Ingoldmells, Skegness, Horncastle, and Spilsby.

Grid references J–R (columns) and 1–12 (rows).

GRIMSBY
Cleethorpes
Humberston
New Waltham
Holton le Clay
Waithe
Tetney
North Cotes
Marshchapel
Grainthorpe
North Somercotes
Saltfleet
Saltfleetby St Clement
Saltfleetby All Saints
Saltfleetby St Peter
Theddlethorpe St Helen
Theddlethorpe All Saints
Mablethorpe
Trusthorpe
Sutton on Sea
Sandilands
Markby
Huttoft
Bilsby
Thurlby
Anderby
Mumby
Chapel St Leonards
Ingoldmells
Chapel Point
Addlethorpe
Habertoft
Sloothby
Willoughby
Hogsthorpe
Cumberworth
Farlesthorpe
Alford
Rigsby
Well
Ulceby
Sutterby
Skendleby
Welton le Marsh
Candlesby
Orby
Scremby
Burgh le Marsh
Skegness

Louth
Legbourne
North Reston
Little Cawthorpe
South Reston
Withern
Gayton le Marsh
Maltby le Marsh
Beesby
Saleby
Little Carlton
Great Carlton
Manby
Grimoldby
North Cockerington
South Cockerington
Alvingham
Yarburgh
Covenham St Mary
Covenham St Bartholomew
Conisholme
Fulstow
North Thoresby
North Ormsby
Utterby
Fotherby
Ludborough
Wold Newton
Kelstern
South Elkington
Welton le Wold
Hallington
Raithby
Withcall
Donington on Bain
Tathwell
Haugham
Muckton
Authorpe
Belleau
Aby
Swaby
South Thoresby
White Pit
Burwell
Walmsgate
Ormsby
South Ormsby
Brinkhill
Salmonby
Tetford
Harrington
Somersby
Bag Enderby
Langton
Aswardby
Sausthorpe
Partney
Ashby by Partney
Monksthorpe
Great Steeping
Bratoft
Irby in the Marsh
Croft

Horncastle
High Toynton
Greetham
Mareham on the Hill
Hameringham
Hagworthingham
Snipe Dales
Mavis Enderby
Raithby
Hundleby
Spilsby
Halton Holegate
Gunby Hall
Roughton
Moorby
Old Bolingbroke
Bolingbroke Castle
Miningsby
Toynton All Saints
Northcote
Firsby
Thorpe St Peter
Wainfleet St Mary
Wainfleet All Saints
Wood Enderby
East Kirkby
Revesby
Lincolnshire Aviation
East Keal
Keal Cotes
Little Steeping
Fendike Corner
Mareham le Fen
Tumby
Stickford
New Bolingbroke
New Leake
Eastville Lincolnshire
Friskney
Tumby Woodside
Stickney
East Fen
Leake Common Side
New York
West Fen
Northlands
Gipsey Bridge
Frithville
Sibsey
Sibsey Trader Windmill
Fishtoft Drove
Wrangle
Old Leake
Hilldyke
Leverton
Benington

Spurn Head
Kilnsea
Spurn Point
Spurn Heritage Coast
Rotterdam (Europoort)
Zeebrugge
Donna Nook
Tetney Marshes
Covenham Reservoir
Lincolnshire Wolds Railway
Saltfleetby – Theddlethorpe Dunes
Seal Sanctuary & Wildlife Centre
The Jungle Zoo
Cleethorpes Coast Light Railway
On Your Marques Model Car
Fantasy Island
Lincolnshire Coast Light Railway
Natureland Seal Sanctuary
Village Church Farm
Claythorpe Watermill
Cadwell Park
Lincolnshire Aviation
Battle of Britain Memorial Flight
Gibraltar Point
Wainfleet Haven

A16, A46, A18, A180, A1031, A157, A153, A158, A1104, A1028, A52, A155, A1111, B1219, B1200, B1201, B1373, B1196, B1449, B1195, B1183, B1184, B1192

61
43

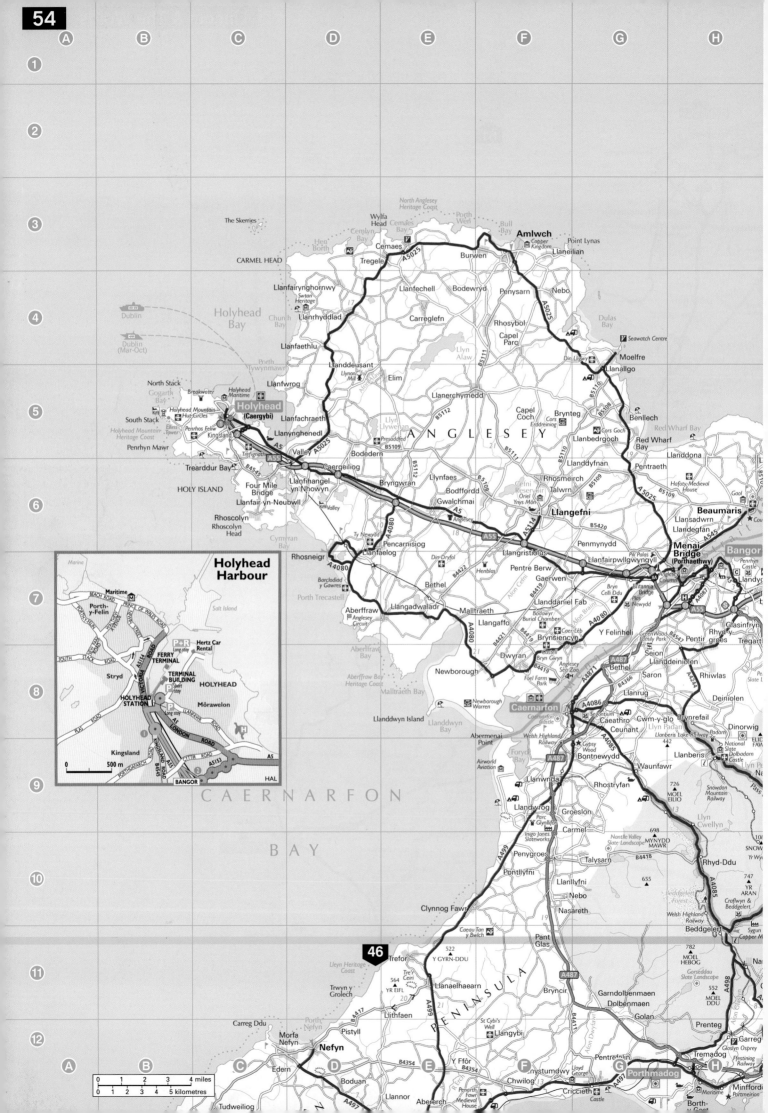

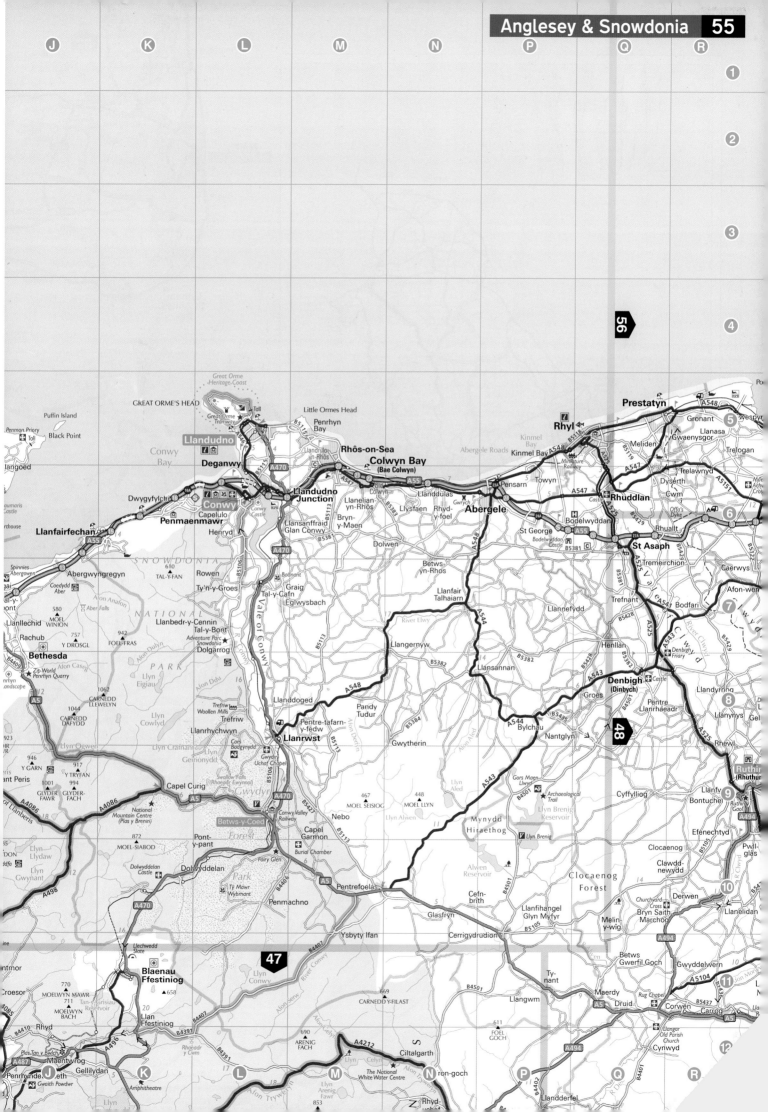

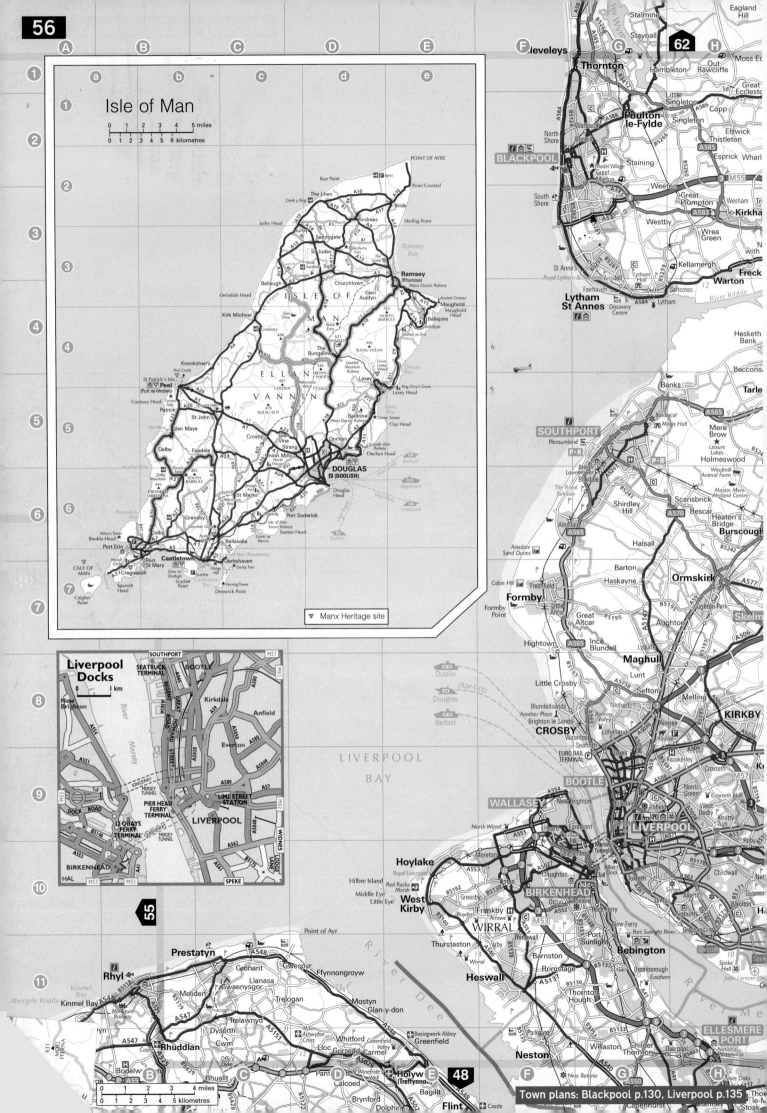

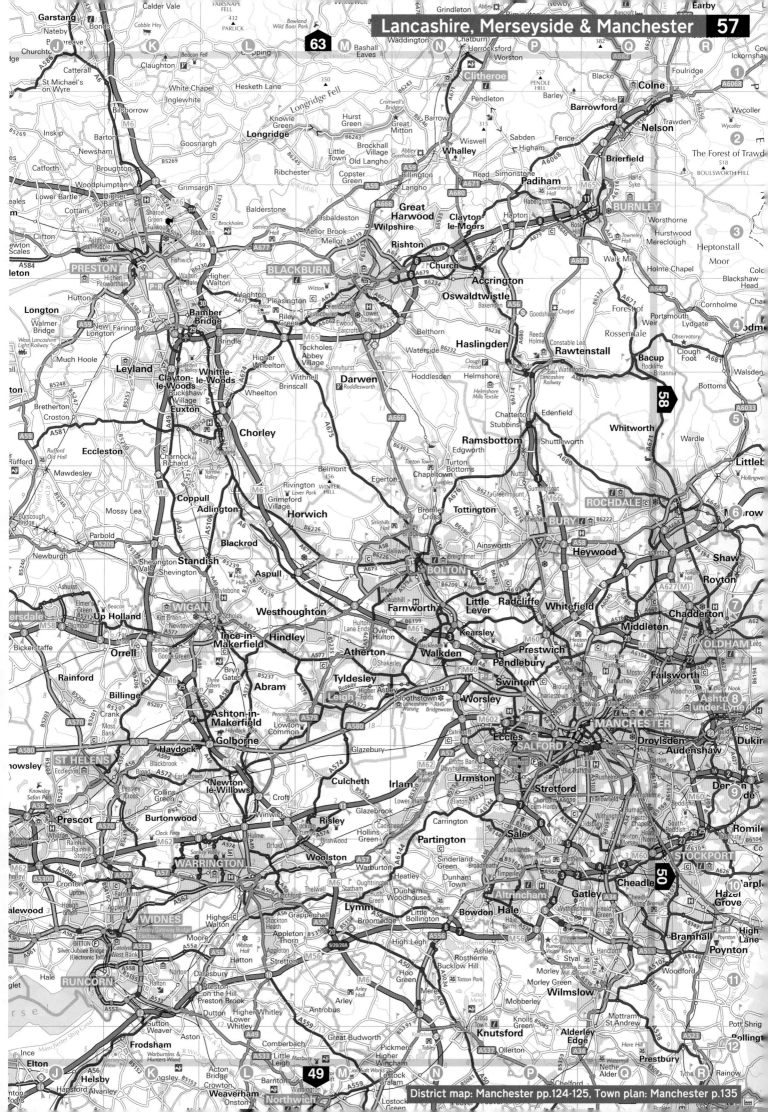

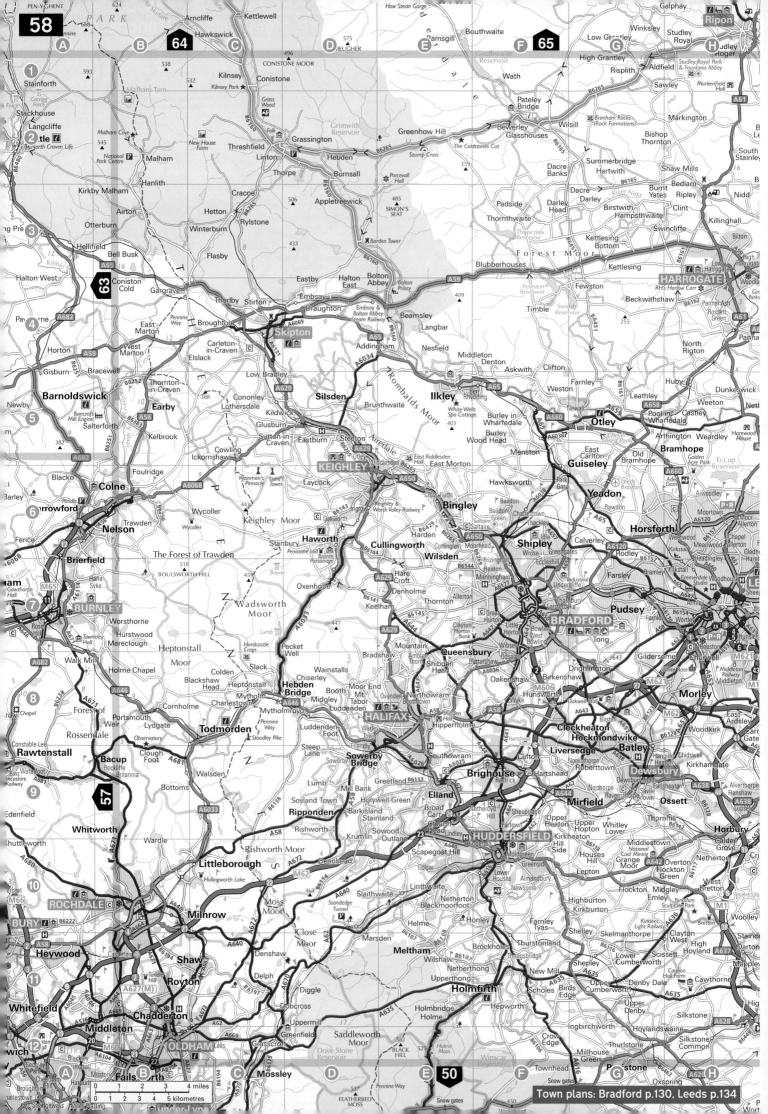

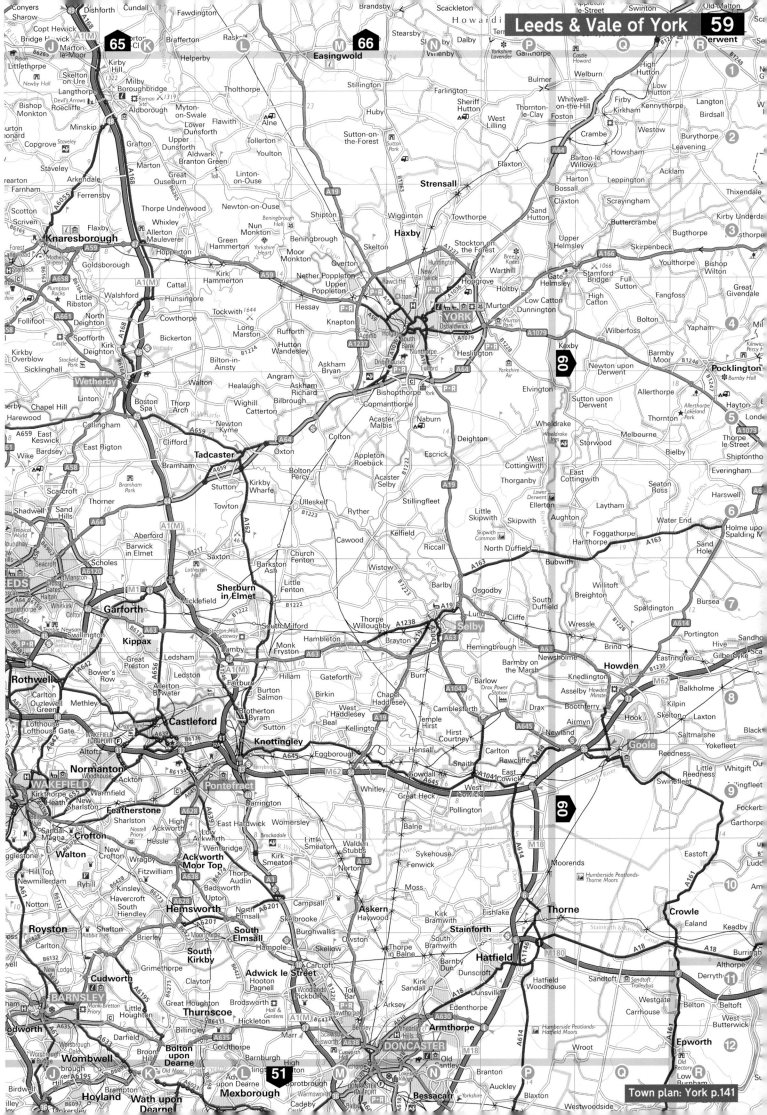

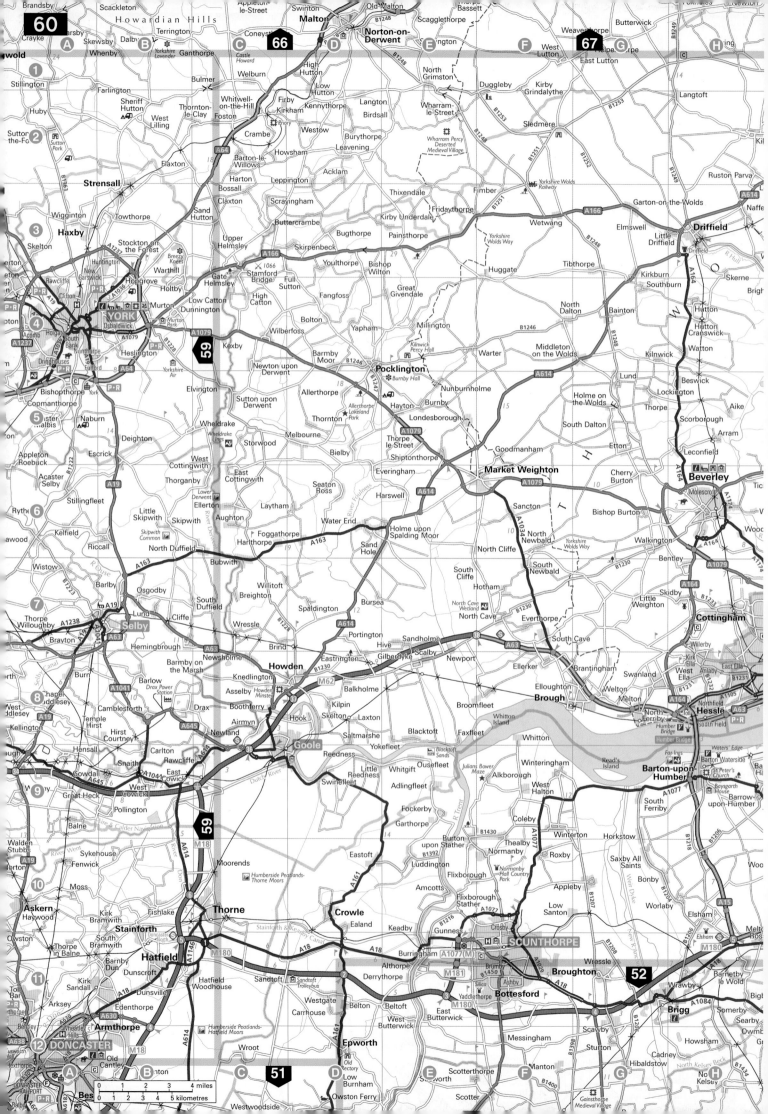

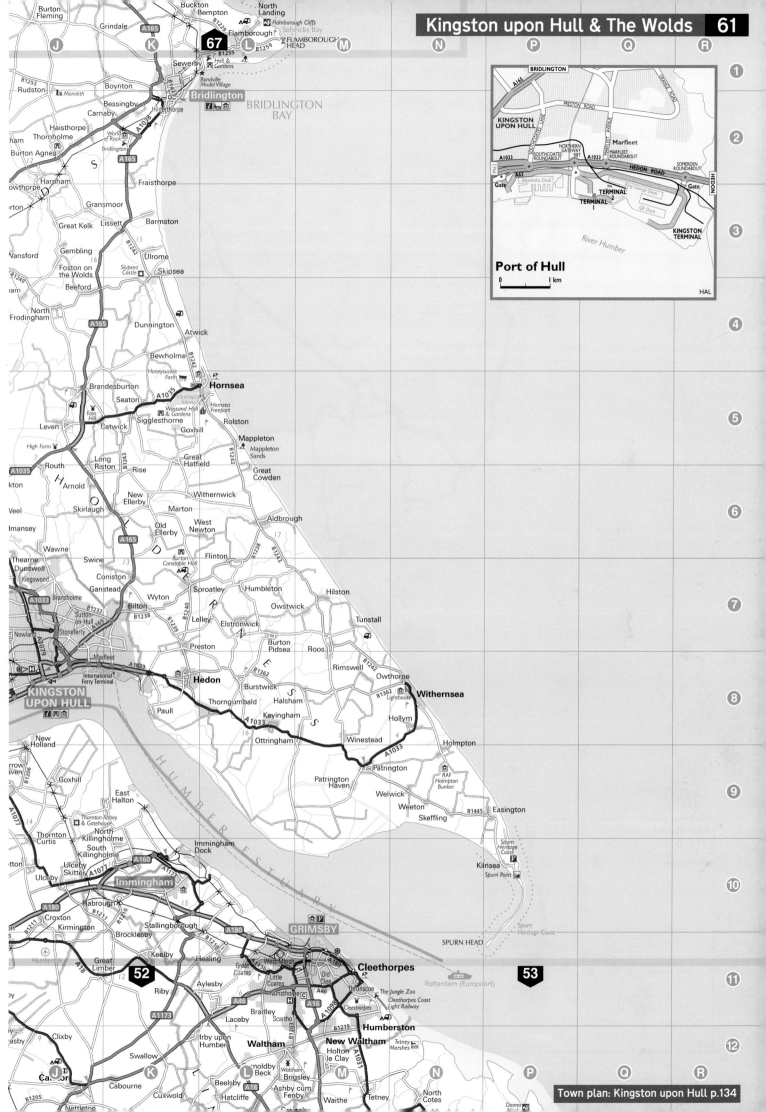

J **K** **67** **L** **M** **N** **P** **Q** **R**

1

2

3

4

5

6

7

8

9

10

11

12

BRIDLINGTON

PRESTON ROAD

KINGSTON UPON HULL

Marfleet

NORTHERN GATEWAY RBT

SOUTHCOATES ROUNDABOUT

MARFLEET ROUNDABOUT

HEDON ROAD

SOMERDEN ROUNDABOUT

HEDON

Gate

Alexandra Dock

TERMINAL 1

TERMINAL 2

Long George Dock

Q.E. Dock

Gate

KINGSTON TERMINAL

River Humber

Port of Hull

0   1 km

HAL

Burton Fleming

Buckton

Bempton

North Landing

Grindale

Flamborough Cliffs

Selwicks Bay

FLAMBOROUGH HEAD

Flamborough

Sewerby

Hall & Gardens

Bondville Model Village

Bridlington

BRIDLINGTON BAY

Rudston

Boynton

Bessingby

Carnaby

Hilderthorpe

World of Rock Bridlington

Haisthorpe

Thornholme

Burton Agnes

Harpham

Fraisthorpe

Gransmoor

Barmston

Great Kelk

Lissett

Wansford

Gembling

Foston on the Wolds

Skipsea Castle

Ulrome

Skipsea

Beeford

North Frodingham

Dunnington

Atwick

Bewholme

Honeysuckle Farm

Hornsea

Hornsea Mere

Hornsea Freeport

Brandesburton

Seaton

Wassand Hall & Gardens

Rolston

Foss Hill

Sigglesthorne

Goxhill

Mappleton

Mappleton Sands

Leven

Catwick

High Farm

Routh

Long Riston

Rise

Great Hatfield

Great Cowden

Arnold

New Ellerby

Withernwick

Skirlaugh

Marton

West Newton

Aldbrough

Veel

Old Ellerby

Imansey

Wawne

Swine

Coniston

Flinton

Humbleton

Hilston

Thearne Dunswell

Burton Constable Hall

Sproatley

Owstwick

Tunstall

Kingswood

Bransholme

Ganstead

Bilton

Wyton

Lelley

Elstronwick

Sutton-on-Hull

Stoneferry

Newland

KINGSTON UPON HULL

International Ferry Terminal

Marfleet

Preston

Burton Pidsea

Roos

Rimswell

Owthorne

Lighthouse

Withernsea

Hedon

Burstwick

Halsham

Hollym

Paull

Thorngumbald

Keyingham

Winestead

Holmpton

Ottringham

Patrington

RAF Holmpton Bunker

Patrington Haven

Welwick

Weeton

Holmpton

New Holland

Goxhill

East Halton

Skeffling

Easington

Thornton Abbey & Gatehouse

North Killingholme

South Killingholme

Thornton Curtis

Ulceby

Ulceby Skitter

Immingham Dock

Spurn Heritage Coast

Kilnsea

Spurn Point

Immingham

Habrough

Croxton

Kirmington

Brocklesby

Stallingborough

Healing

Humberside

Keelby

Great Limber

Riby

Aylesby

GRIMSBY

West Marsh

Great Coates

Little Coates

Nunsthorpe

Old Clee

Cleethorpes

Thrunscoe

The Jungle Zoo

Cleethorpes Coast Light Railway

SPURN HEAD

Rotterdam (Europoort)

Clixby

Swallow

Bradley

Laceby

Scartho

Irby upon Humber

Waltham

New Waltham

Holton le Clay

Humberston

Tetney Marshes

Cabourne

Cuxwold

Beelsby

Brigsley

Ashby cum Fenby

Waithe

North Cotes

Nettleton

Knoldby Beck

Tetney

52 **53**

HUMBER ESTUARY

Town plan: Kingston upon Hull p.134

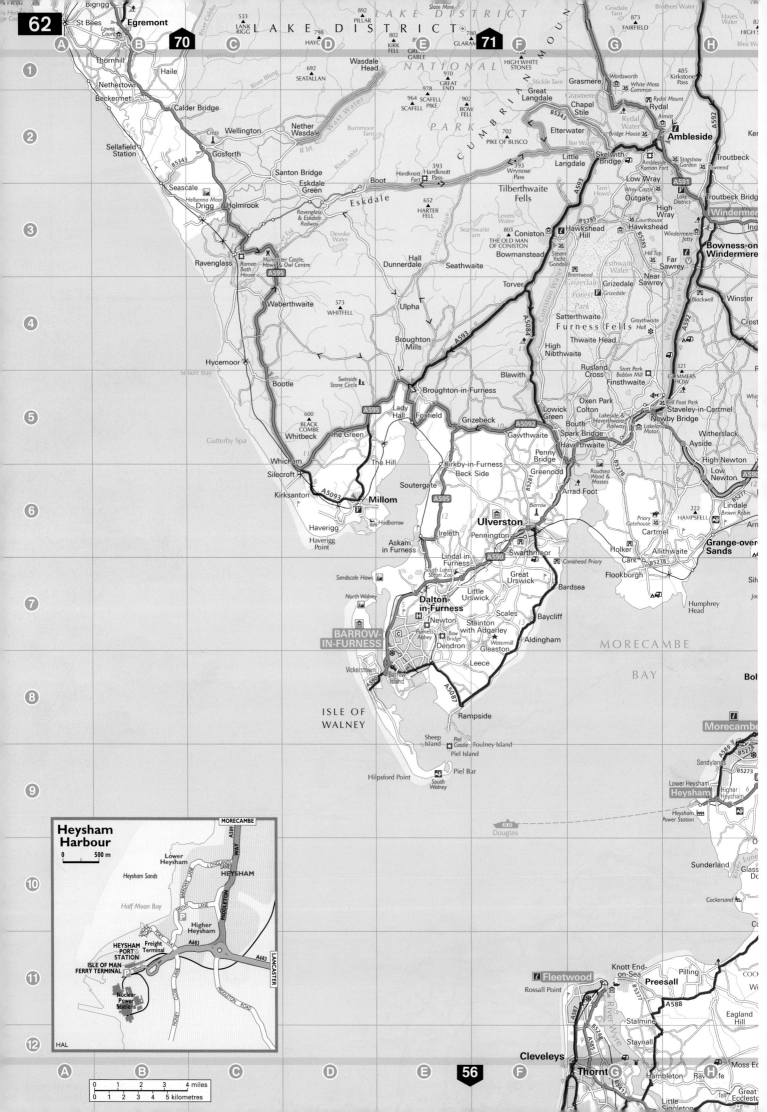

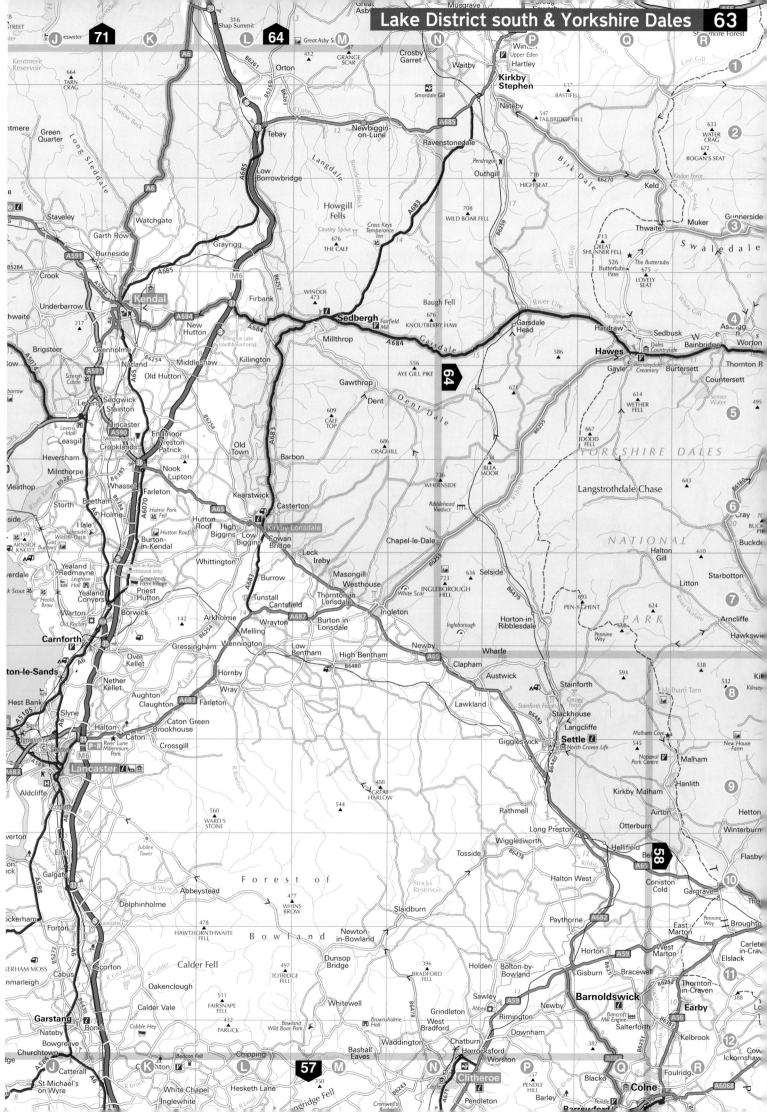

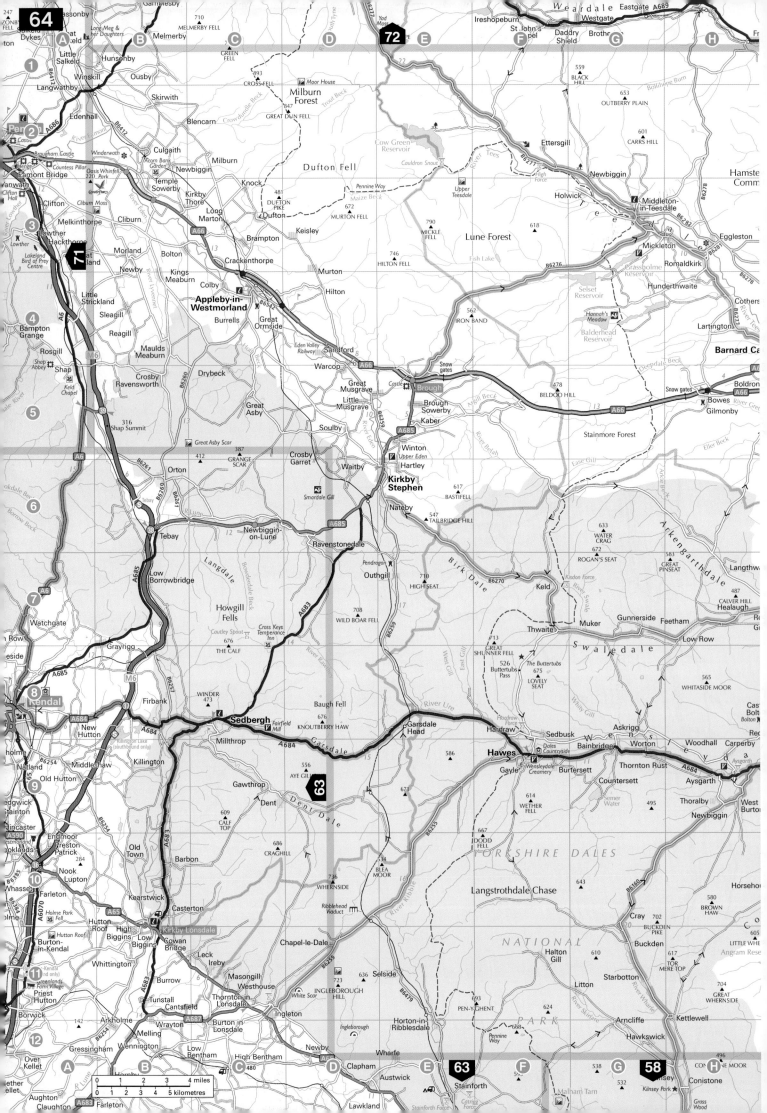

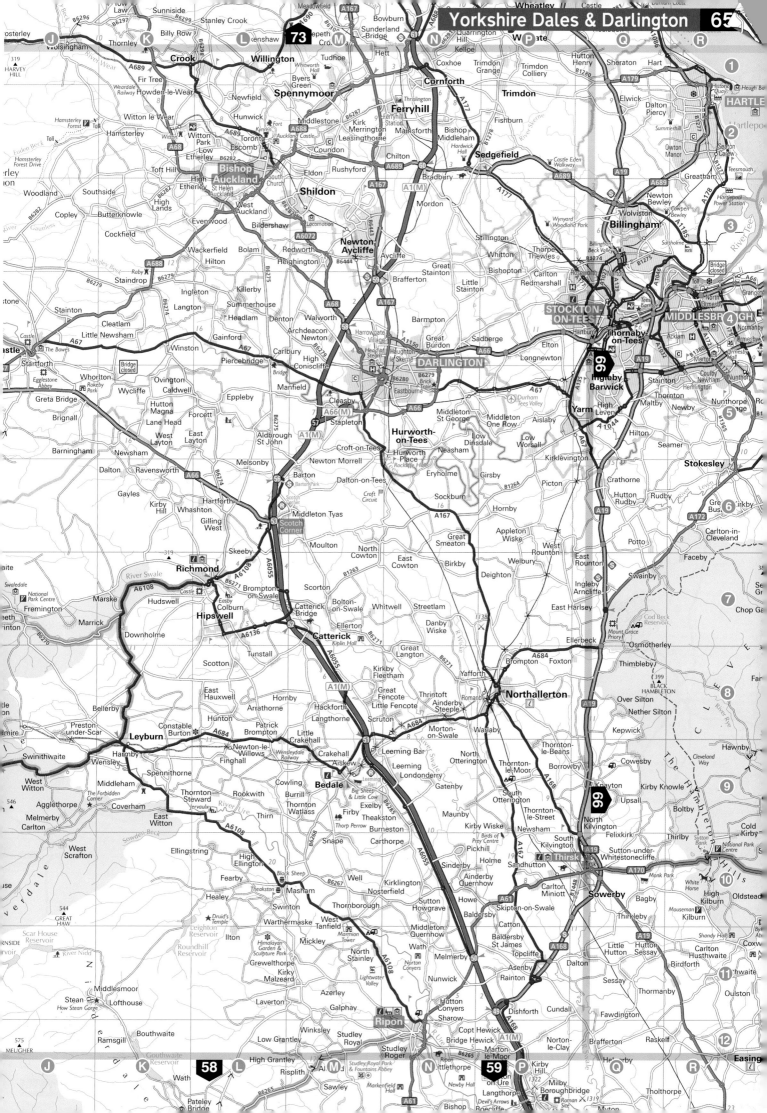

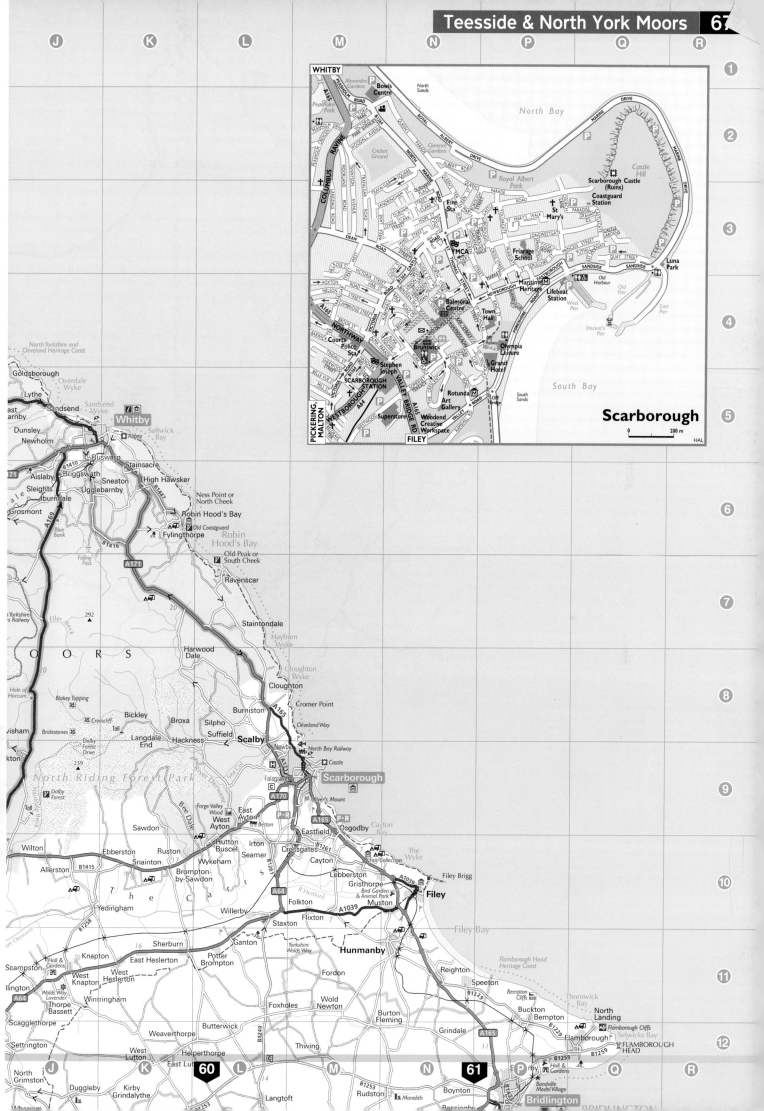

WHITBY

Alexandra Gardens
Bowls Centre
Peasholm Park
PEASHOLM ROAD
North Sands
VICTORIA PARK
COLUMBUS RAVINE
WOODALL AVENUE
QUEENS PARADE
North Bay
Cricket Ground
NORTH MARINE ROAD
ROYAL ALBERT DRIVE
MARINE DRIVE
Clarence Gardens
ALBERT ROAD
Castle Hill
Royal Albert Park
QUEEN STREET
Scarborough Castle (Ruins)
Coastguard Station
St Mary's
MARINE DRIVE
DEAN ROAD
Fire Sta
YMCA
St SEPULCHRE
LONGWESTGATE
PARADE
Princess Street
Paradise
CASTLE GARDENS
Luna Park
SANDSIDE
Old Harbour
Maritime Heritage
Lifeboat Station
West Pier
Vincent's Pier
East Pier
A165 NORTHWAY
Courts
Police Sta
Balmoral Centre
Town Hall
Brunswick
Olympia Leisure
Grand Hotel
South Bay
Stephen Joseph
SCARBOROUGH STATION
A64
WESTBOROUGH
VALLEY BRIDGE RD
A165
Cliff Bridge
Rotunda Art Gallery
South Sands
Superstore
Woodend Creative Workspace

PICKERING, MALTON

FILEY

Scarborough

0   200 m

HAL

North Yorkshire and Cleveland Heritage Coast
Goldsborough
Overdale Wyke
Lythe
Sandsend
Sandsend Wyke
barnby
Whitby
Saltwick Bay
Dunsley
Newholm
Abbey
B1410
Ruswarp
Stainsacre
71
Aislaby
Briggswath
Sneaton
High Hawsker
Sleights
Ugglebarnby
B1447
Ness Point or North Cheek
urndale
Grosmont
Blue Bank
B1416
Robin Hood's Bay
Old Coastguard
Falling Foss
A171
Fylingthorpe
Robin Hood's Bay
Old Peak or South Cheek
Ravenscar
292
20
Staintondale
Hayburn Wyke
Eller Beck
Cloughton Wyke
Harwood Dale
Cloughton
Cromer Point
MOORS
Blakey Topping
Burniston
A165
Cleveland Way
Hole of Horcum
Bickley
Broxa
Silpho
Crosscliff
Toll
Suffield
Bridestones
Langdale End
Hackness
Scalby
North Bay Railway
visham
239
Dalby Forest Drive
Newby
Castle
North Riding Forest Park
Dalby Forest
Falsgrave
Scarborough
ton
Toll
Staindale Beck
Sea Cut
River Derwent
Oliver's Mount
Bee Dale
Forge Valley Wood
East Ayton
P·R
Cayton Bay
A170
West Ayton
Betton
Eastfield
Osgodby
P·R
The Wyke
Sawdon
Hutton Buscel
Irton
Crossgates
A165
Wilton
Ebberston
Ruston
Cayton
Hair Collection
Allerston
B1415
Snainton
Wykeham
B1261
Lebberston
Filey Brigg
Brompton-by-Sawdon
Gristhorpe
A1039
Yedingham
Willerby
A64
R Hertford
Bird Garden & Animal Park
Filey
B1258
Folkton
Muston
Flixton
A1039
Staxton
Filey Bay
Scampston
Hall & Gardens
Sherburn
Ganton
Yorkshire Wolds Way
West Knapton
Knapton
East Heslerton
Potter Brompton
Hunmanby
16
llington
West Heslerton
Fordon
A64
Wold Newton
Reighton
Flamborough Head Heritage Coast
Wintringham
Foxholes
Burton Fleming
Speeton
Thorpe Bassett
Butterwick
Thwing
Grindale
Bempton Cliffs
Thornwick Bay
Scagglethorpe
Weaverthorpe
B1249
Buckton
North Landing
Settrington
West Lutton
Helperthorpe
Bempton
Flamborough Cliffs
B1229
Selwicks Bay
North Grimston
East Lu
C
Wold Newton
A165
Flamborough
FLAMBOROUGH HEAD
Duggleby
Kirby Grindalythe
Langtoft
B1253
Rudston
Monolith
Boynton
Bessingby
Bandville Model Village
Bridlington
Wherron
B1255
B1259
B1253
BRIDLINGTON

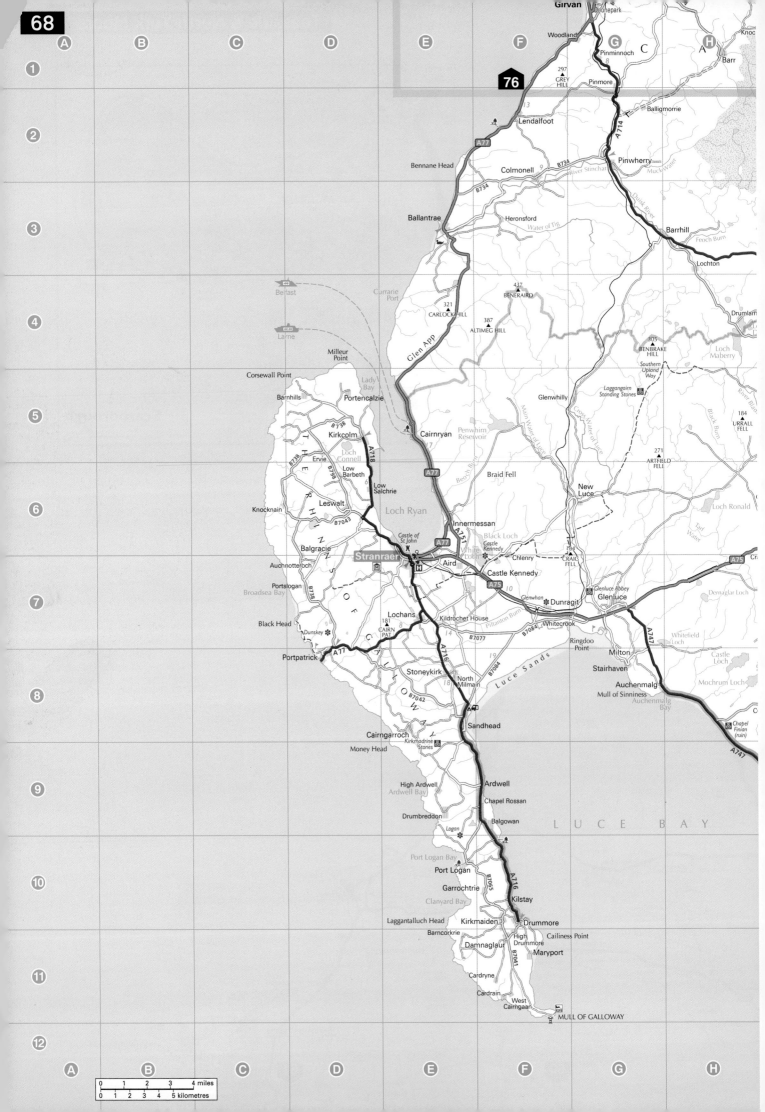

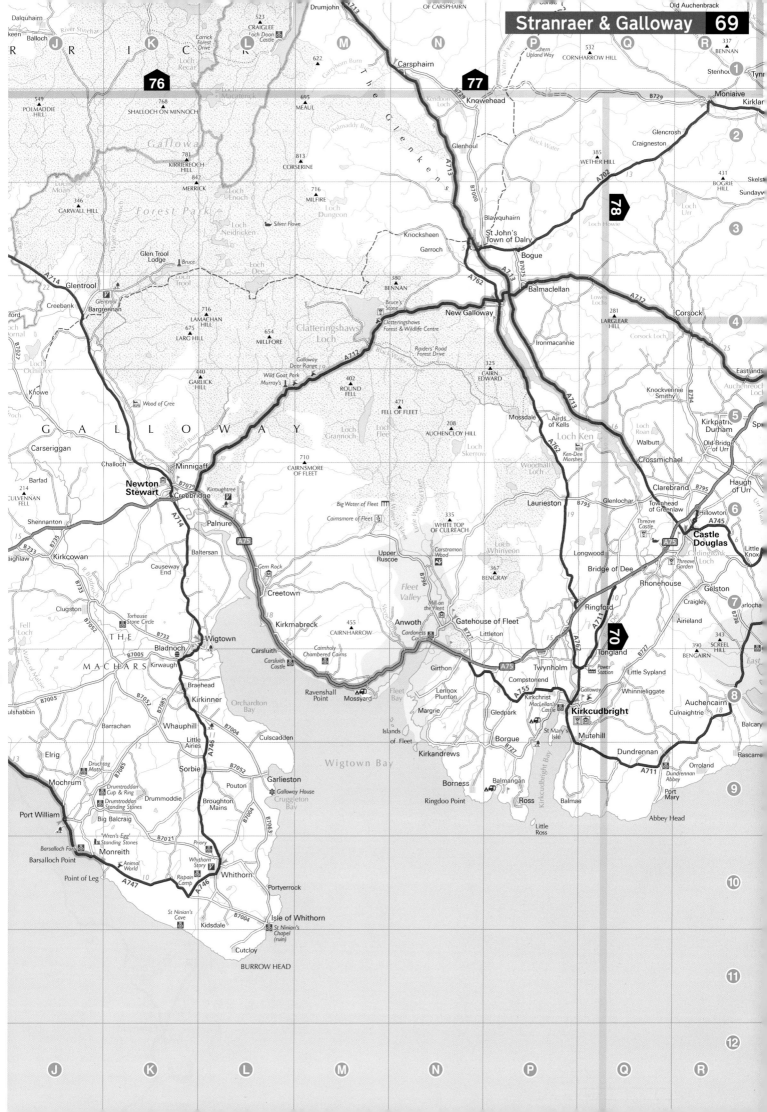

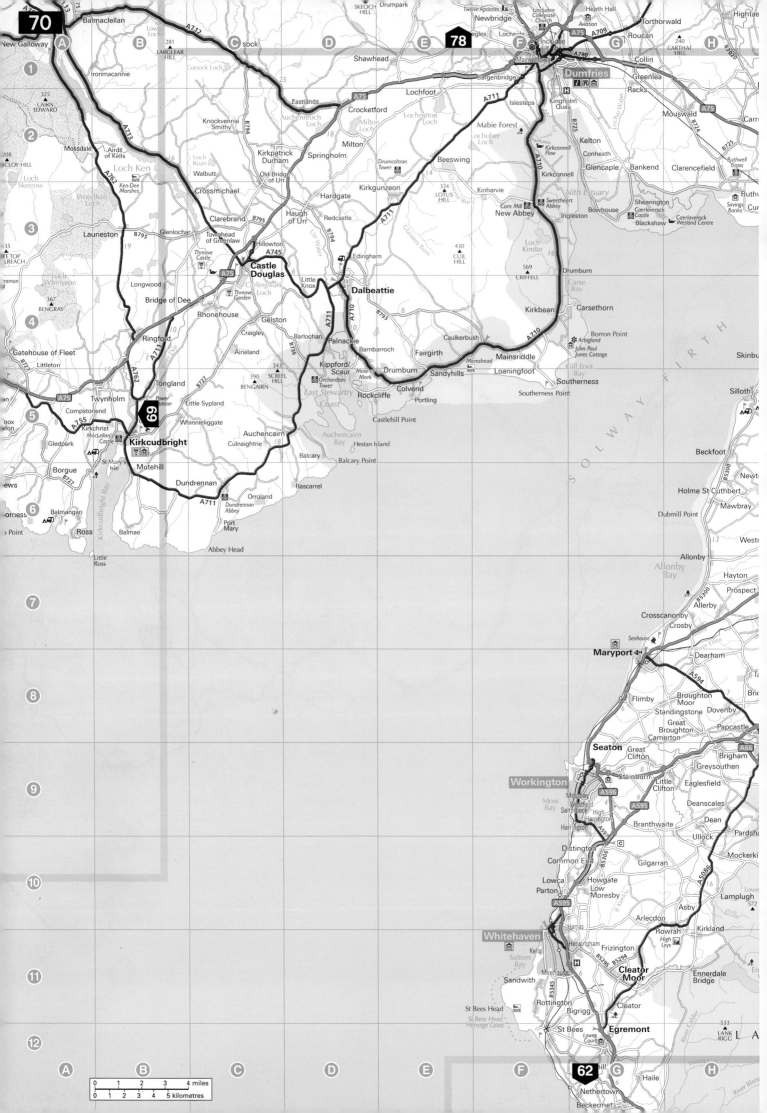

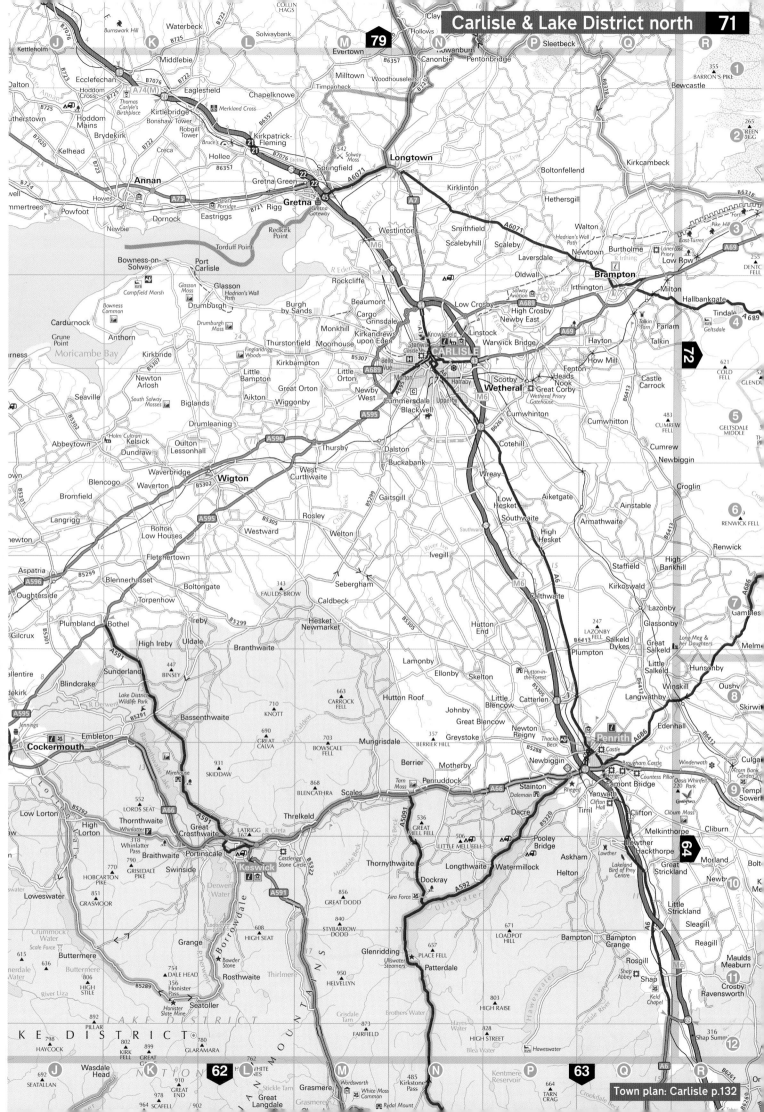

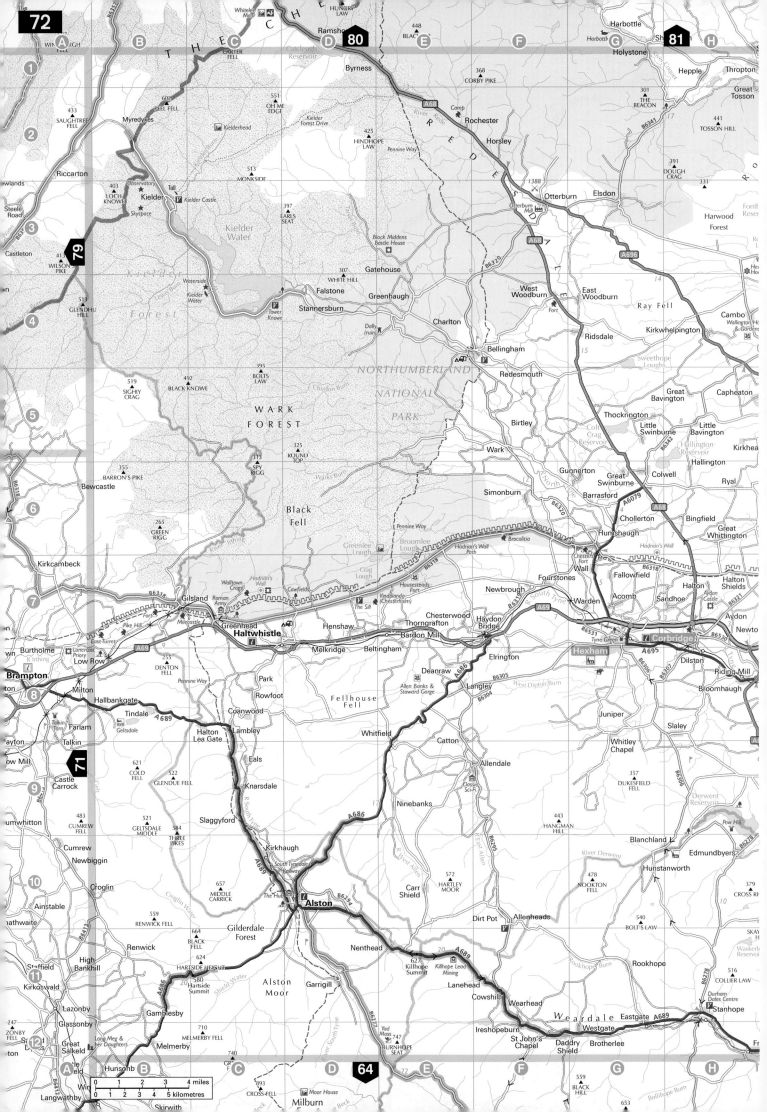

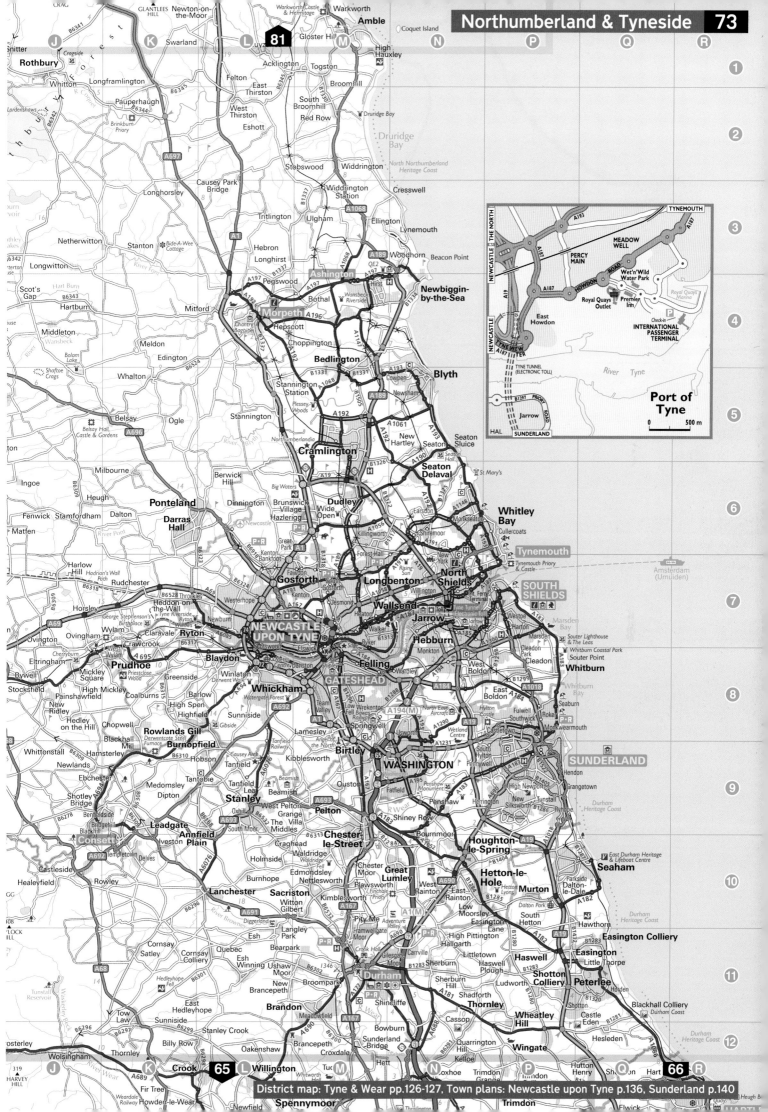

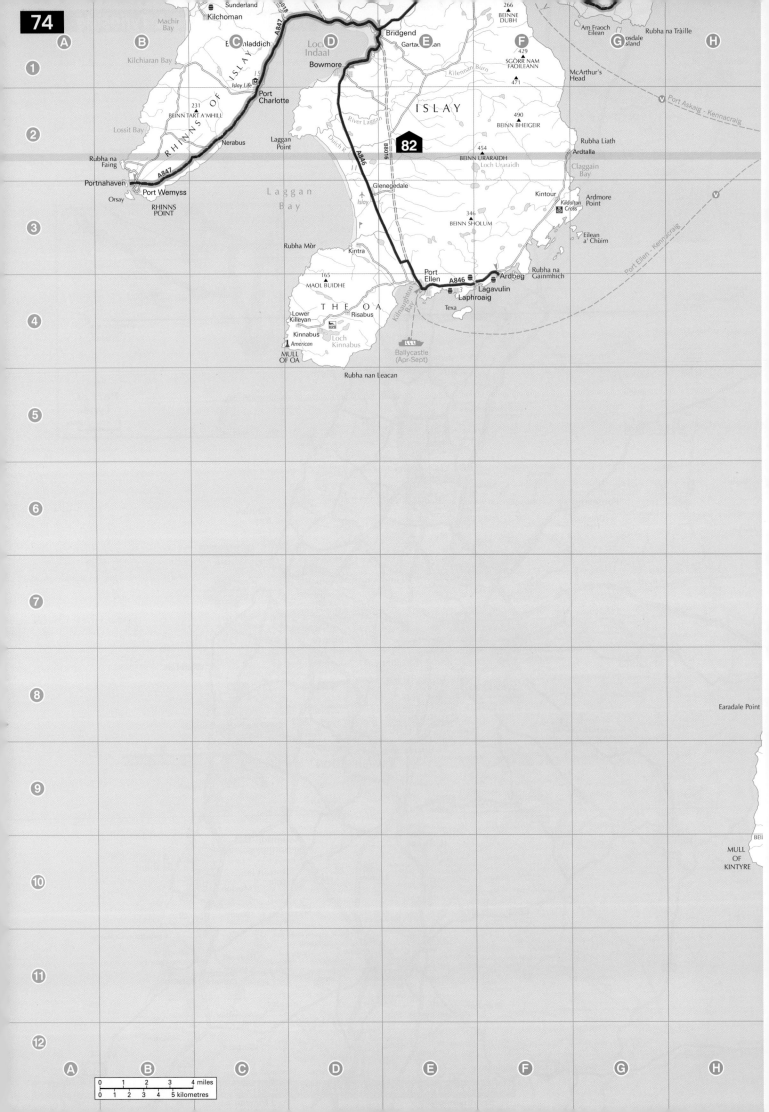

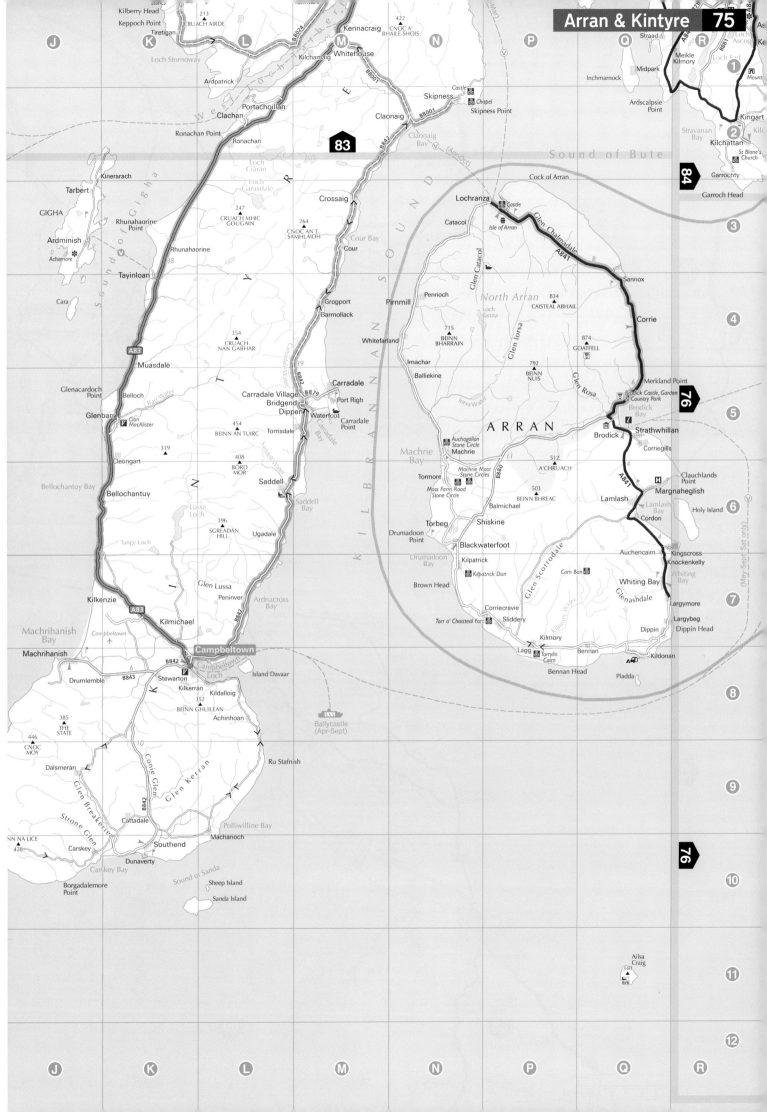

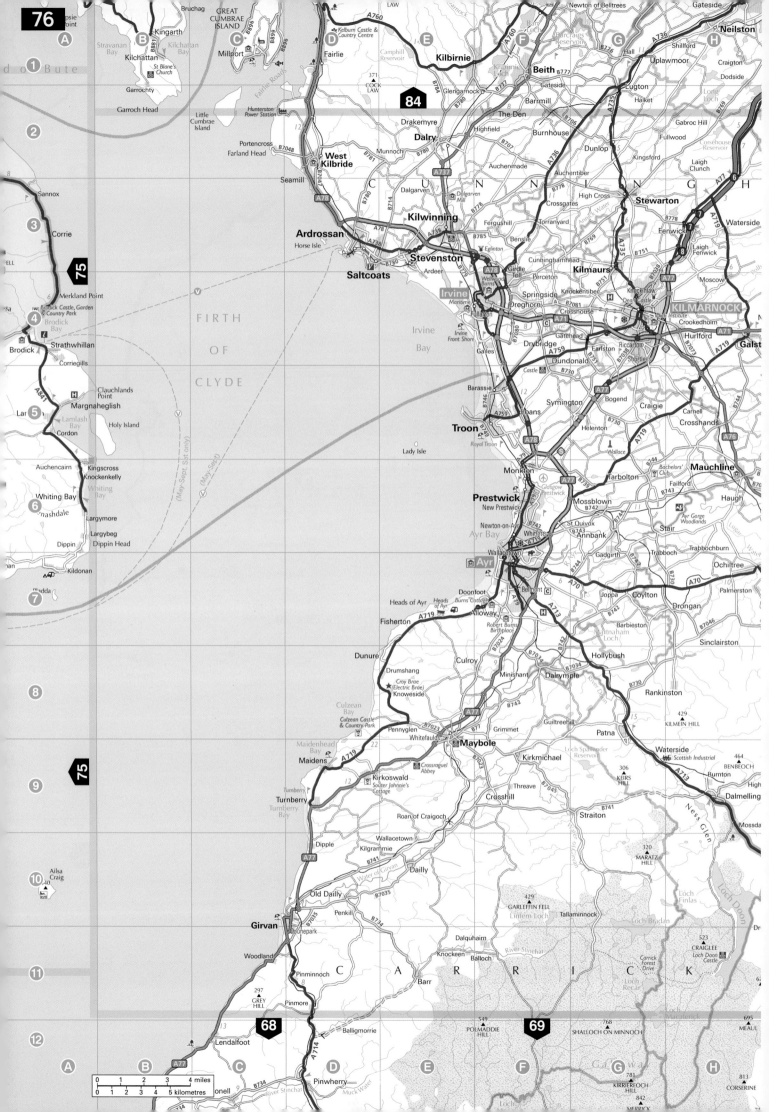

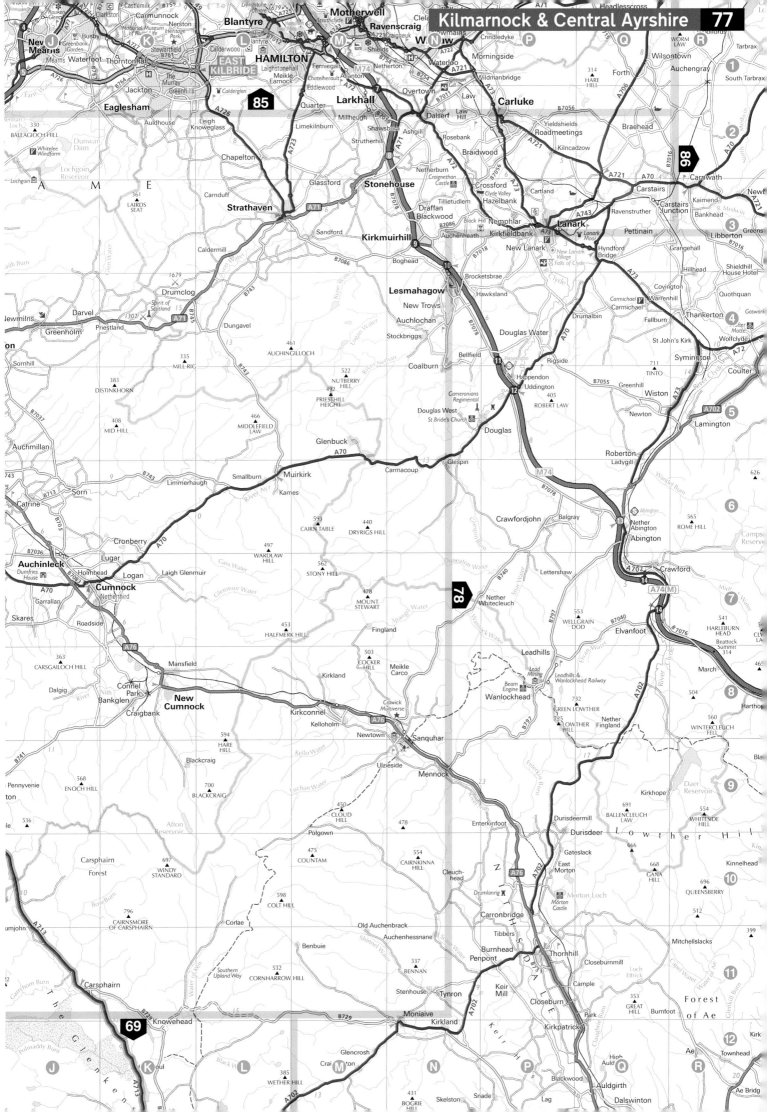

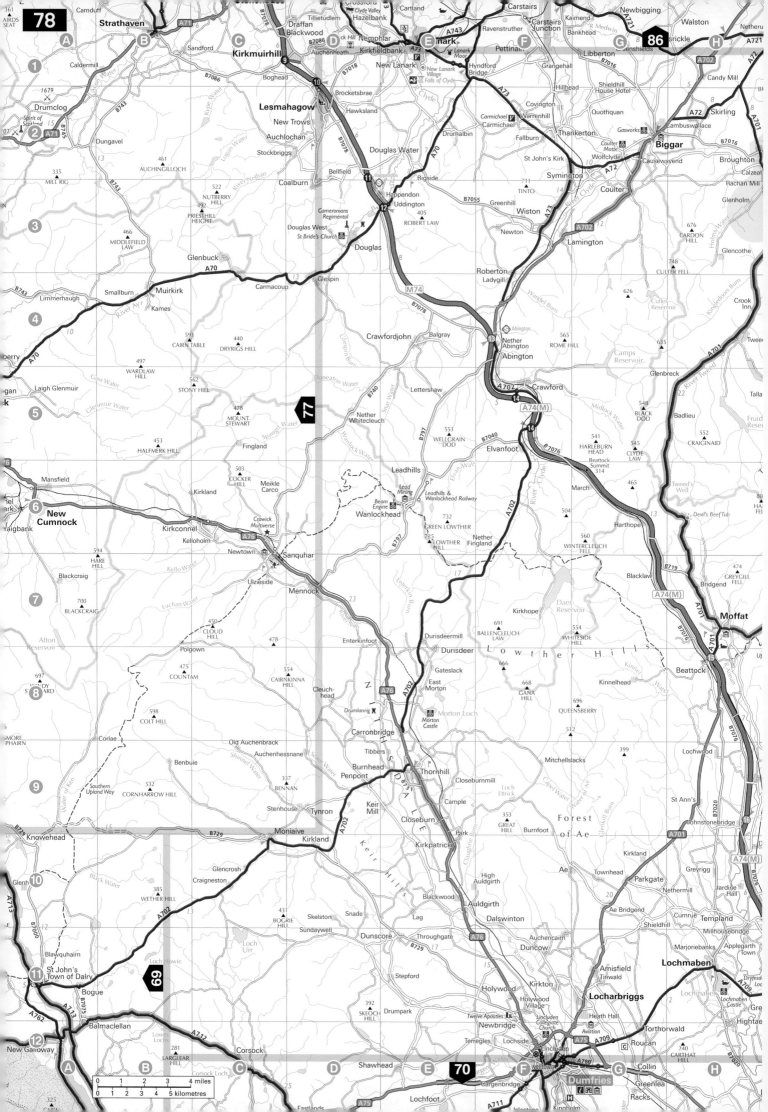

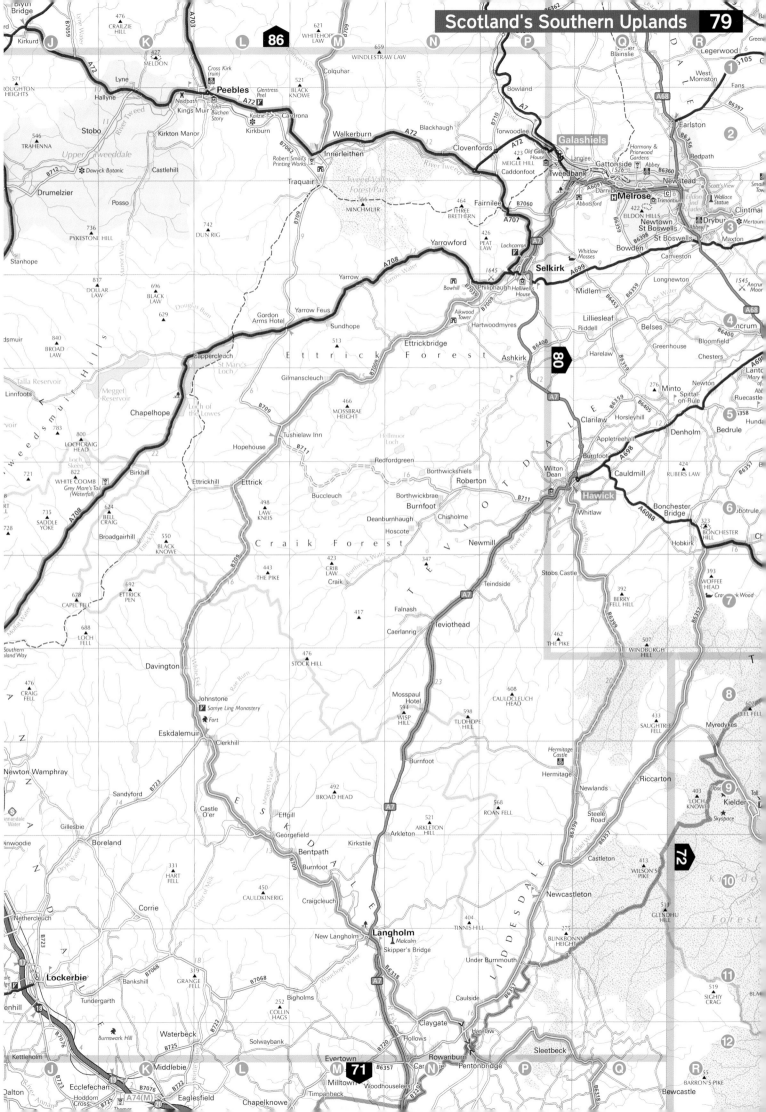

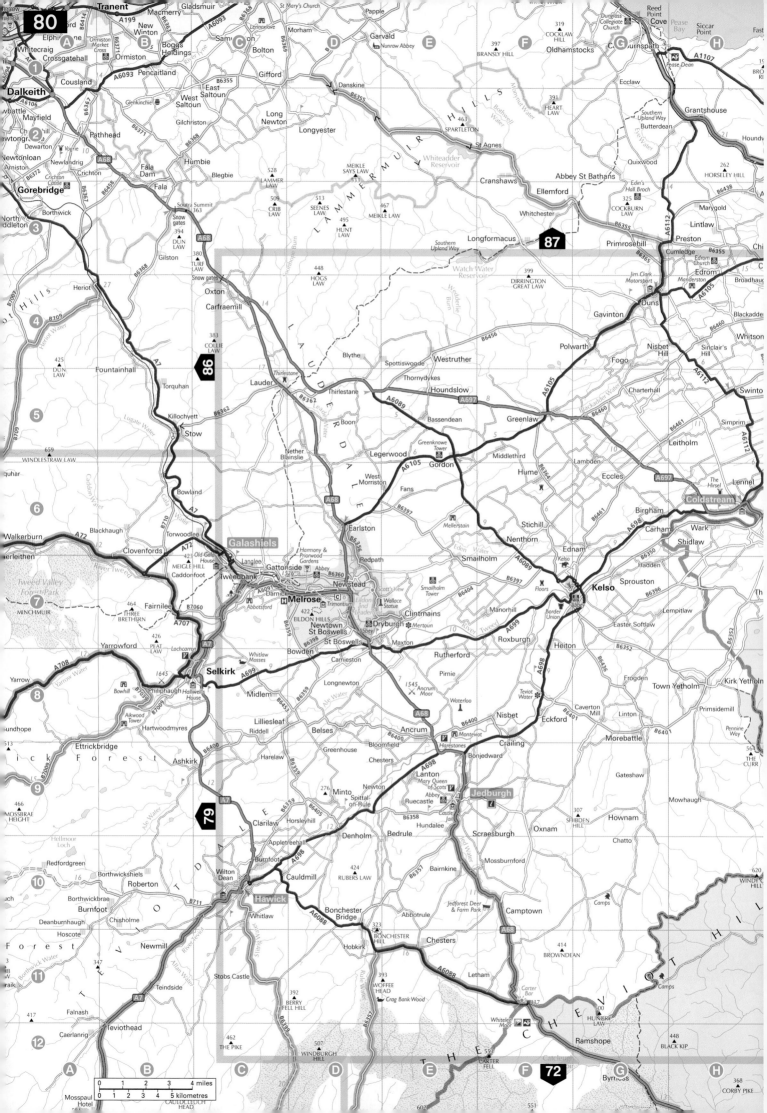

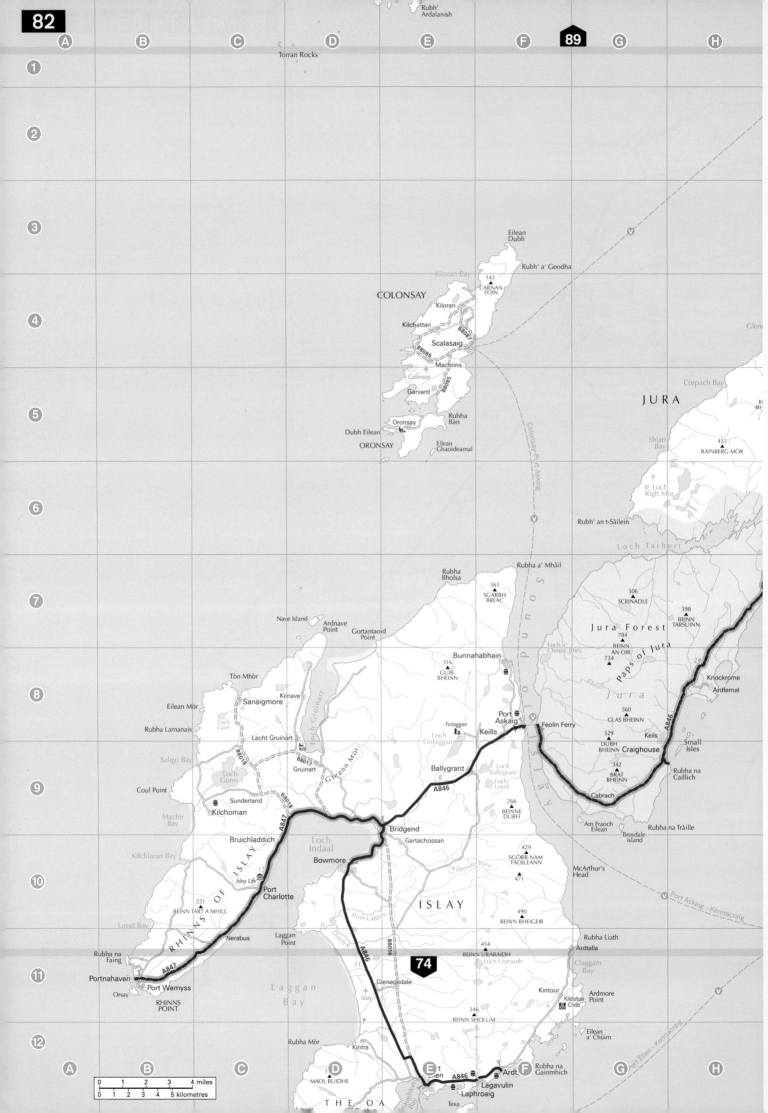

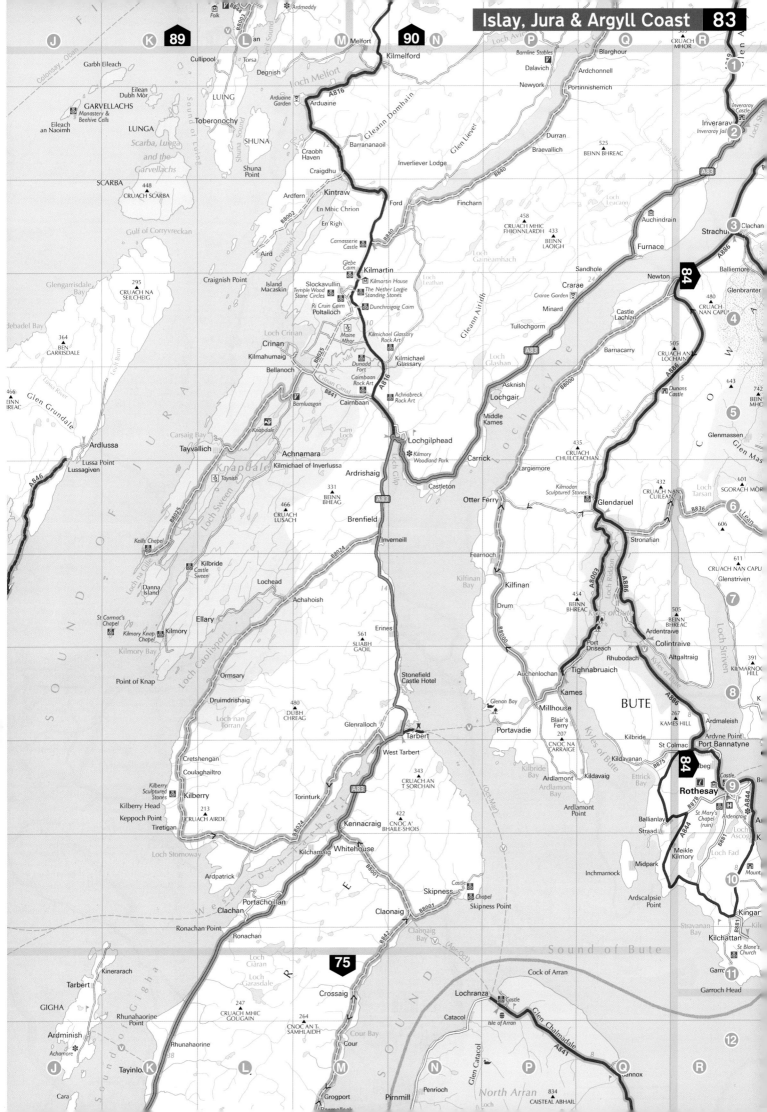

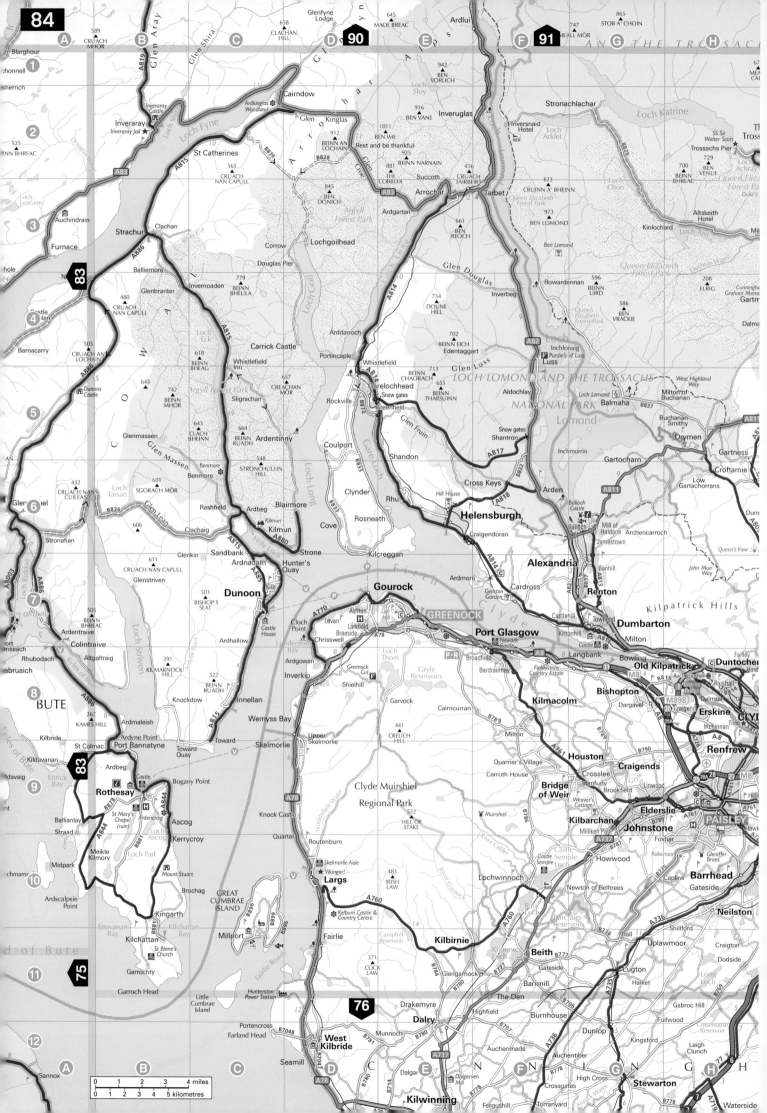

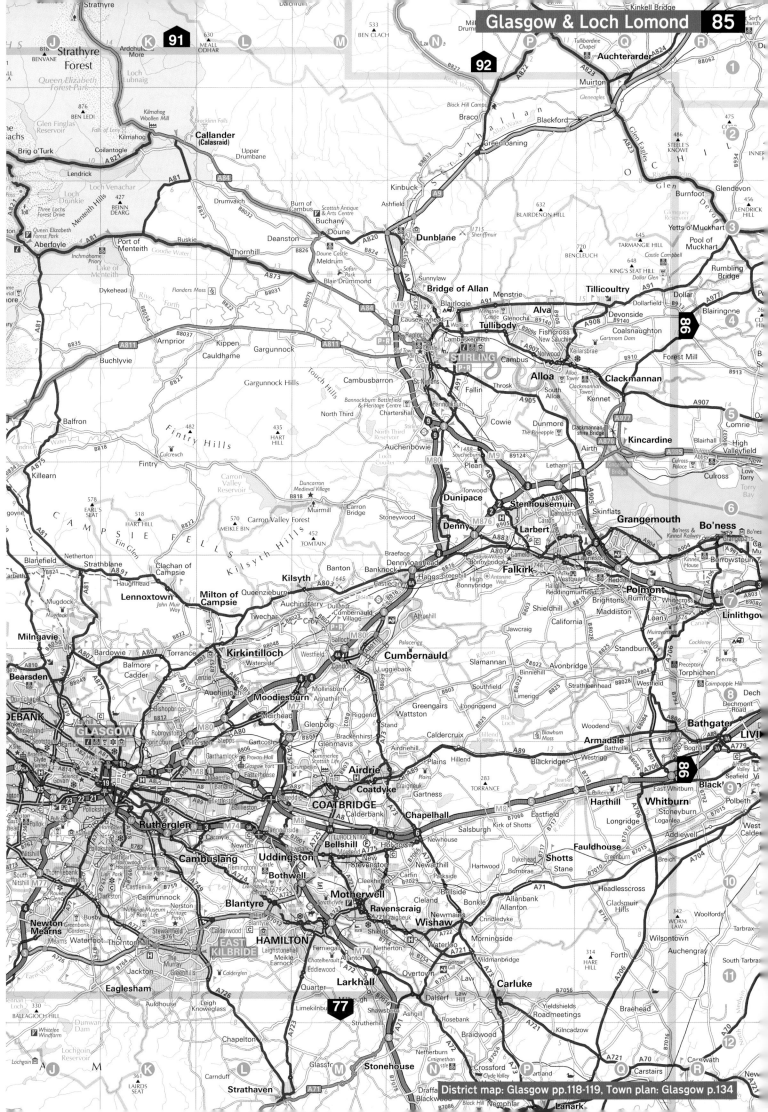

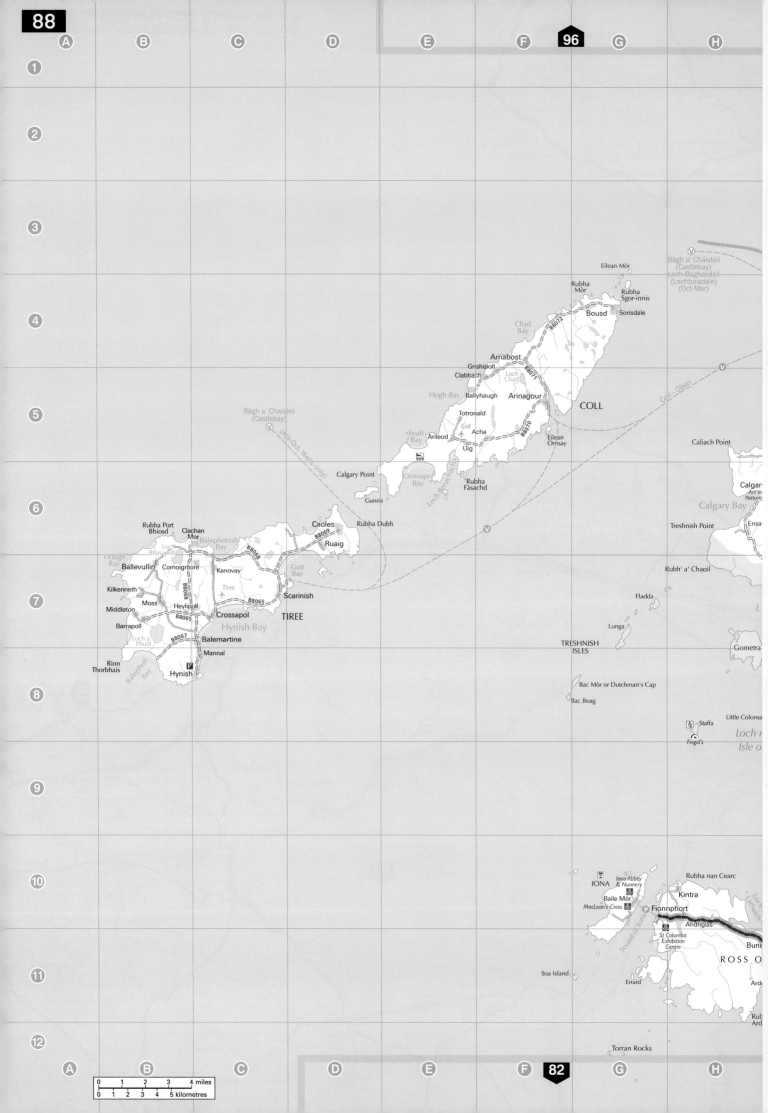

1

2

3

Eilean Mòr

Bàgh a' Chàisteil
(Castlebay)
Loch-Baghasdail
(Lochboisdale)
(Oct-Mar)

Rubha
Mòr

Rubha
Sgor-innis

4

Cliad
Bay

B8072

Bousd

Sorisdale

Arnabost

Grishipoll
Clabhach

Hogh Bay

Loch
Cliad

B8071

Ballyhaugh

Arinagour

COLL

Coll - Oban

Caliach Point

5

Bàgh a' Chàisteil
(Castlebay)

(Apr-Oct. Weds only)

Feall
Bay

Arileod

Totronald

Coll

Acha

Uig

Eilean
Ornsay

B8070

Calgar

Calgary Bay

6

Calgary Point

Crossapol
Bay

Loch Breachacha

Rubha
Fàsachd

Gunna

Rubha Dubh

Caoles

B8069

Ruaig

Treshnish Point

Ensa

Rubh' a' Chaoil

Rubha Port
Bhiosd

Clachan
Mòr

Balephetrish
Bay

B8068

Loch
Bhasapoll

Hough
Bay

Ballevullin

Cornoigmore

Kenovay

Tiree

Gott
Bay

Fladda

Lunga

7

Kilkenneth

B8066

Moss

Heylipoll

Scarinish

B8065

TIREE

**TRESHNISH
ISLES**

Gometra

Middleton

Crossapol

Barrapoll

B8065

Hynish Bay

Loch a'
Phuill

B8067

Balemartine

Mannal

8

Rinn
Thorbhais

Balephuil
Bay

Hynish

Bac Mòr or Dutchman's Cap

Bac Beag

Staffa

Little Colonsa

Fingal's

Loch r
Isle o

9

10

IONA

Iona Abbey
& Nunnery

Rubha nan Cearc

Baile Mòr

MacLean's Cross

Kintra

Fionnphort

Loch
Lathaich

Ardnglas

St Columba
Exhibition
Centre

Bune

11

ROSS O

Soa Island

Erraid

Ardo

Rub
Ard

12

Torran Rocks

0   1   2   3   4 miles
0 1 2 3 4 5 kilometres

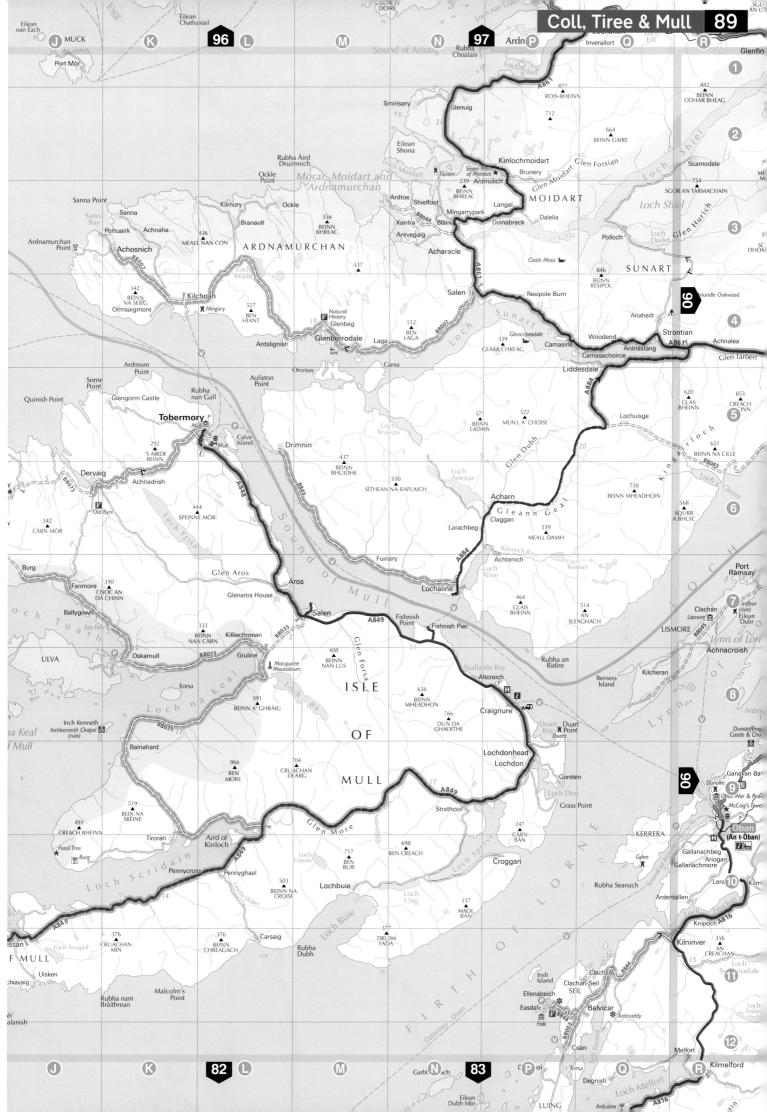

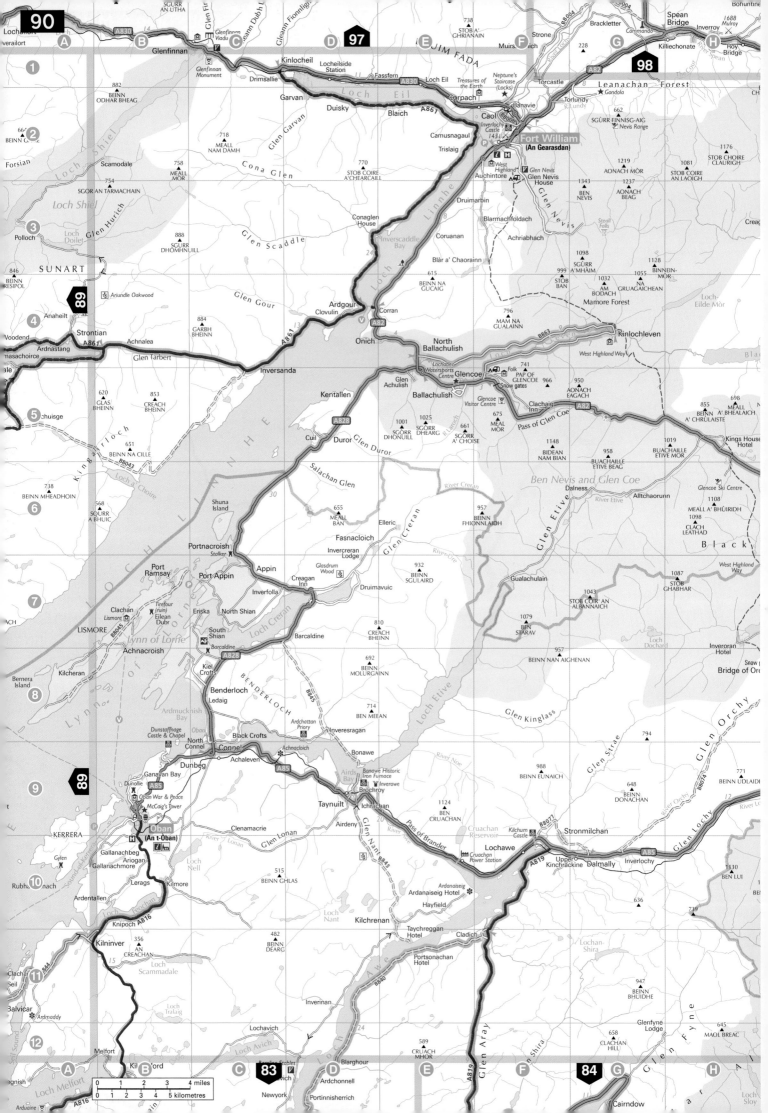

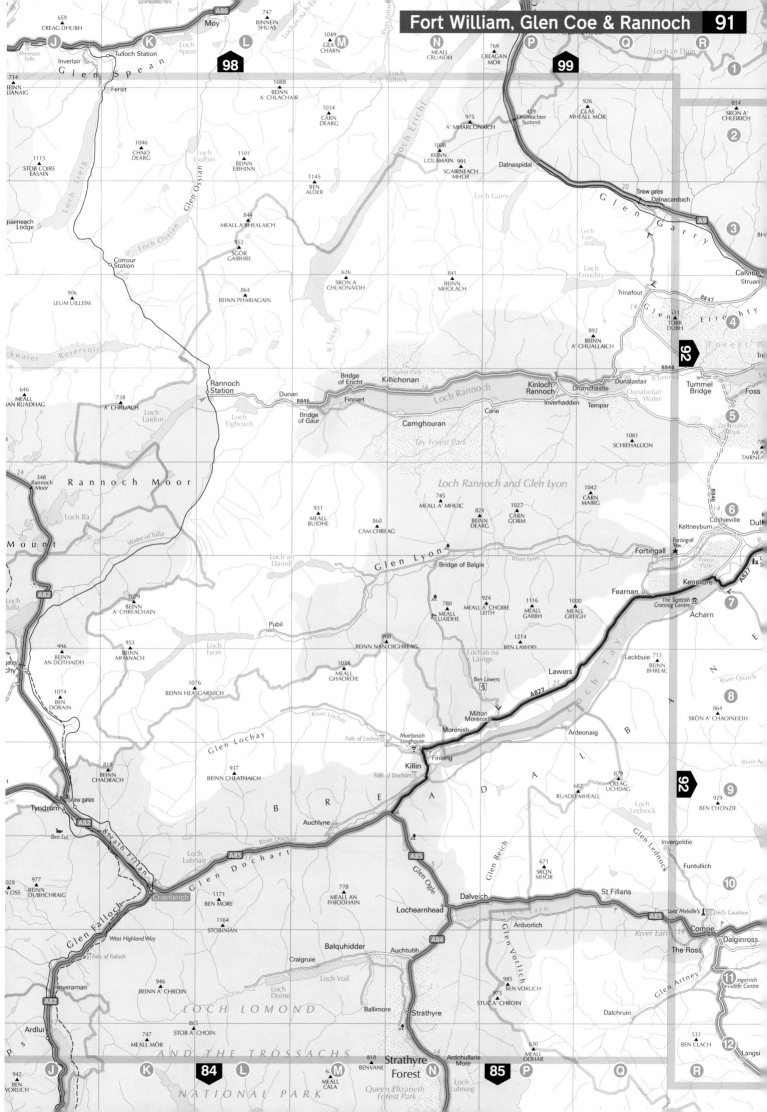

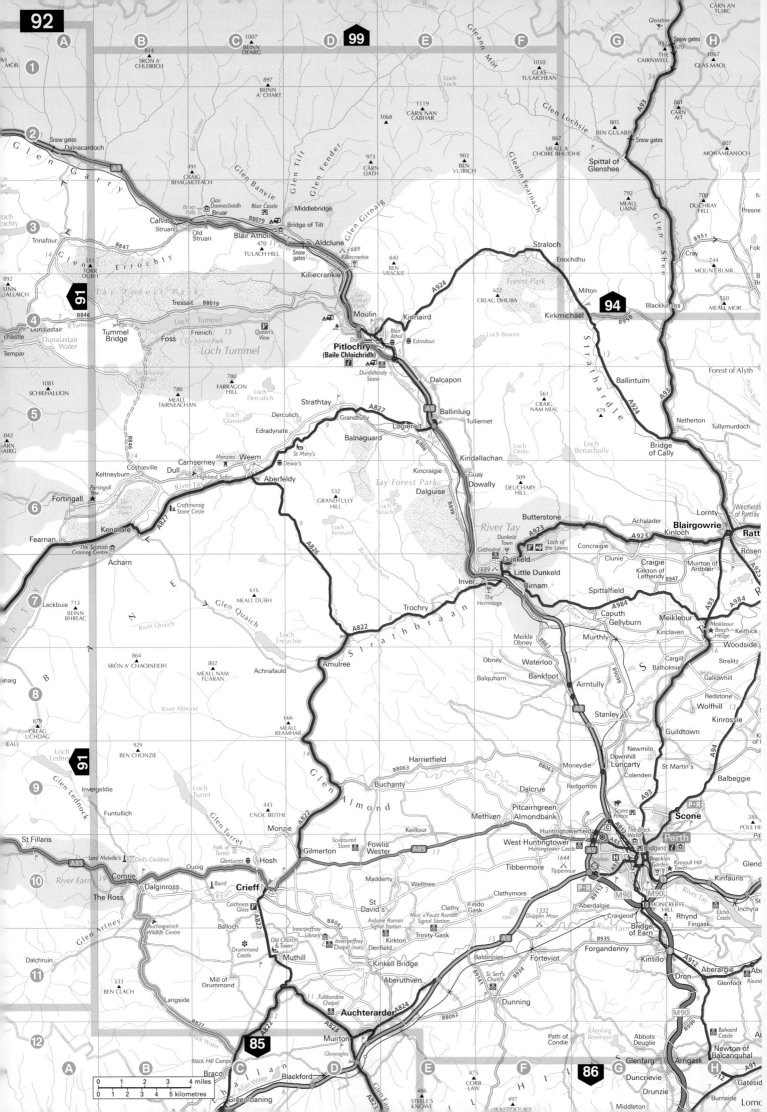

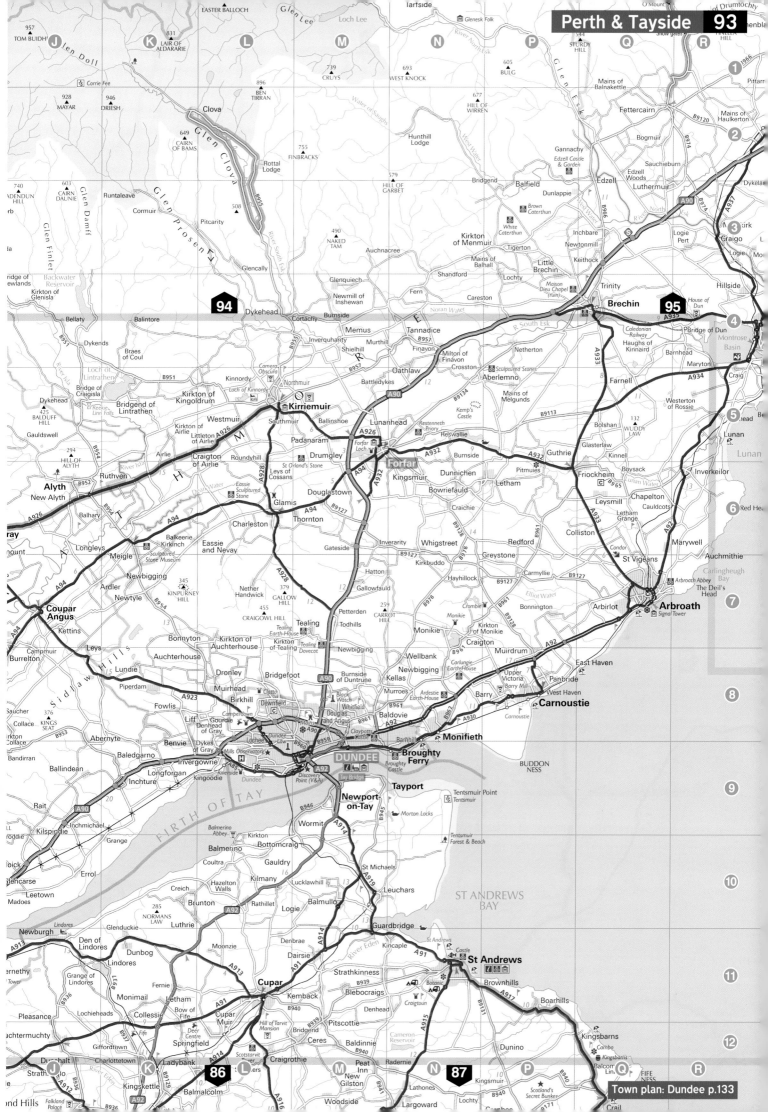

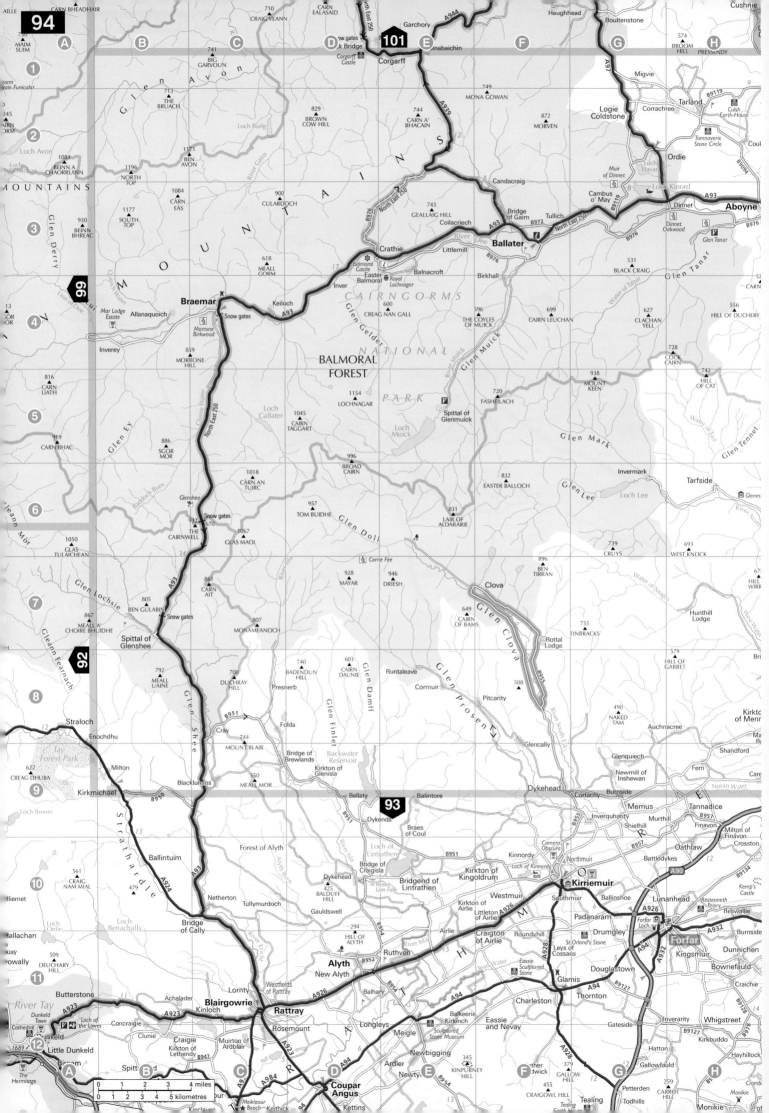

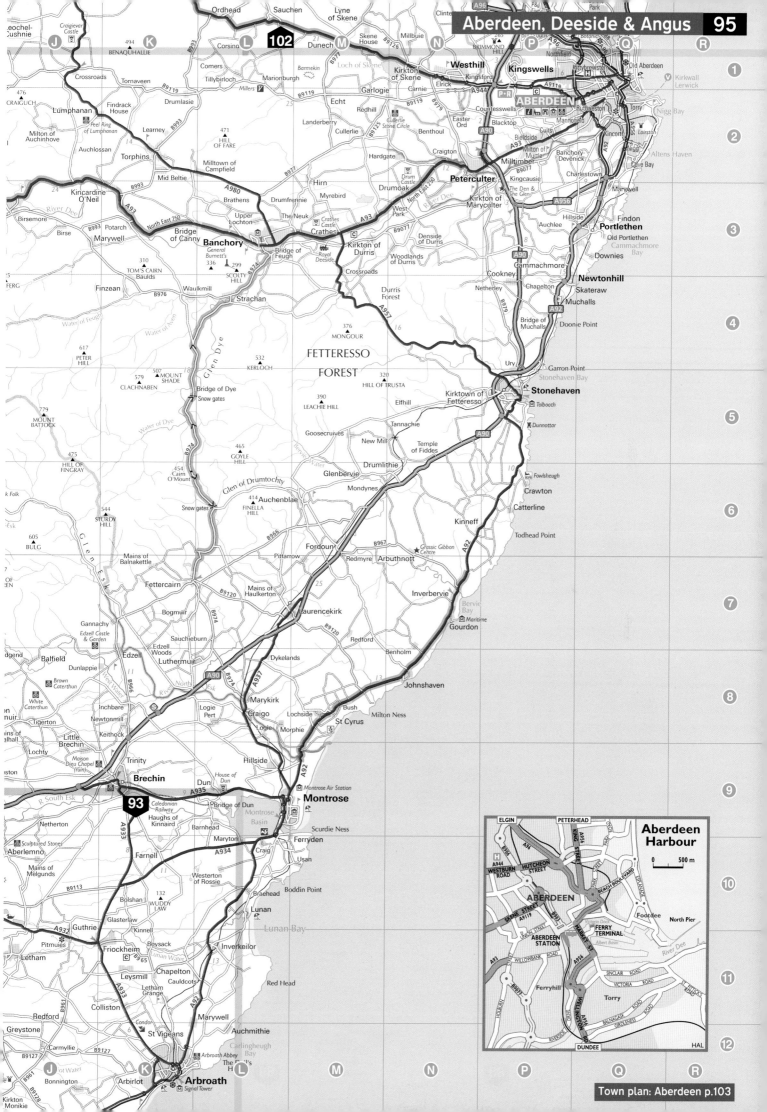

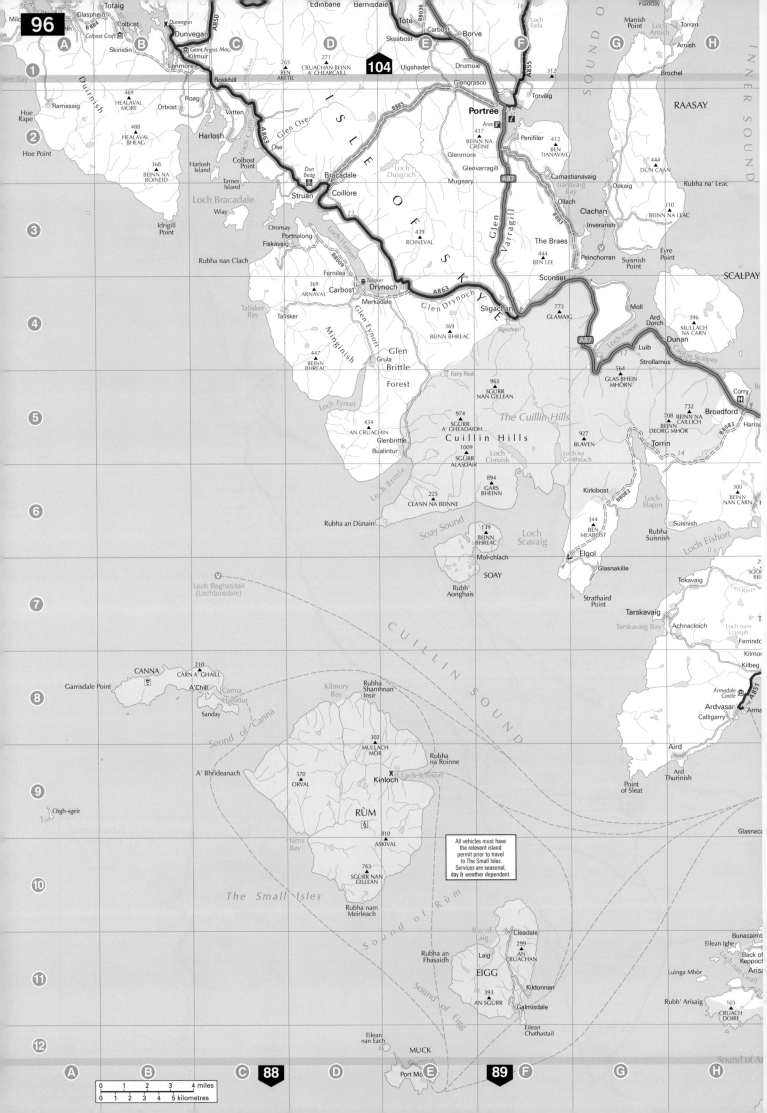

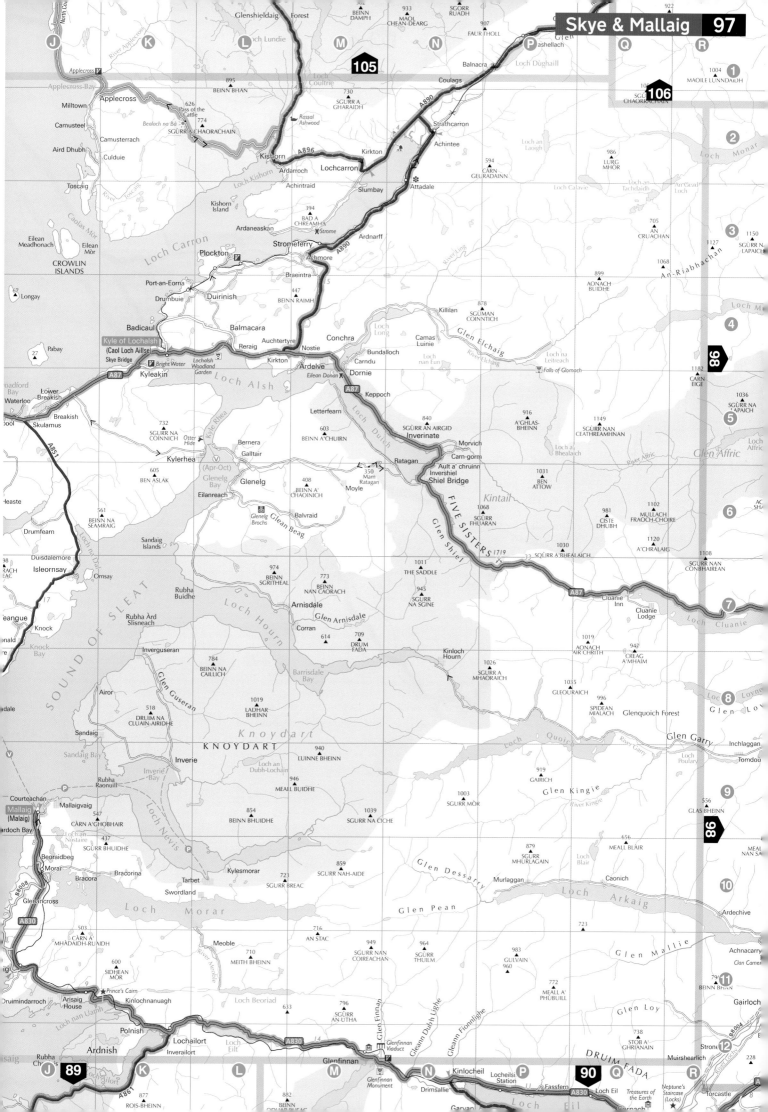

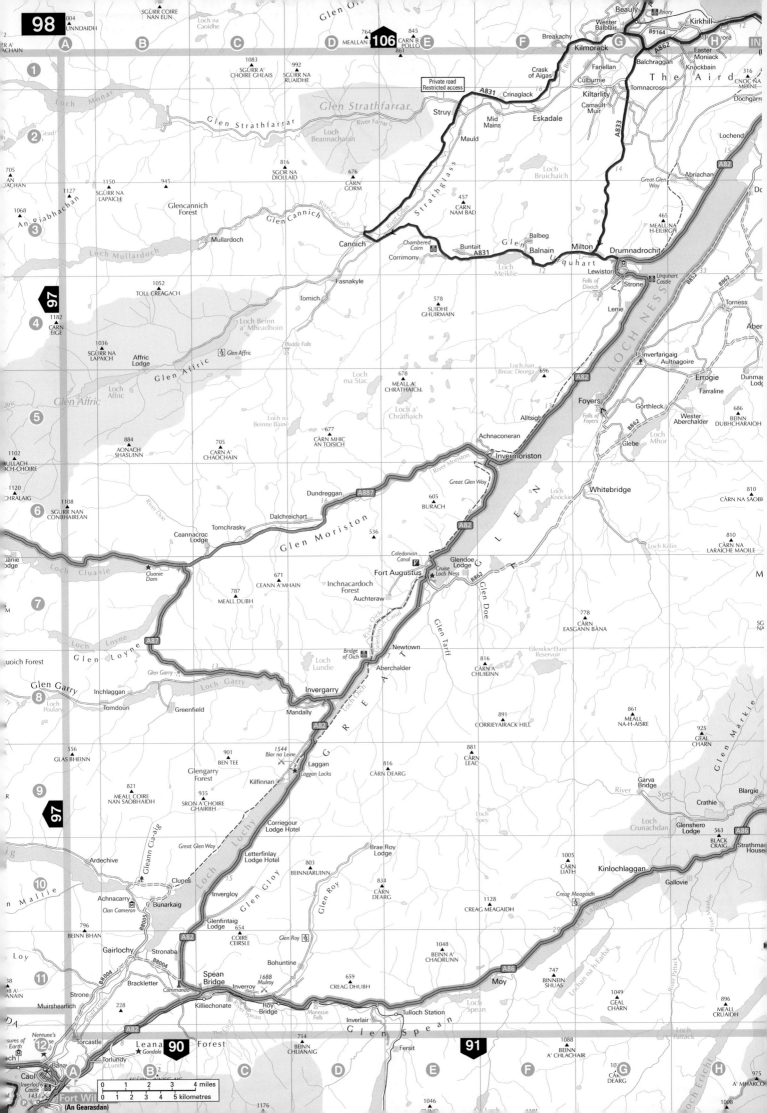

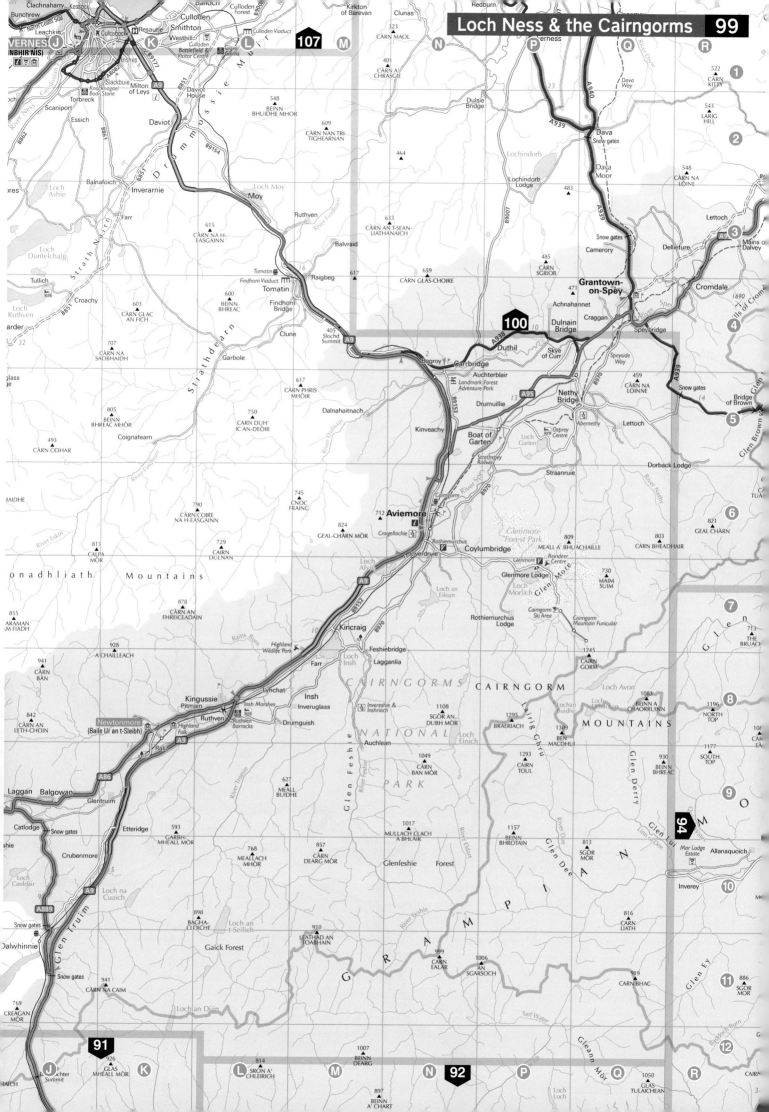

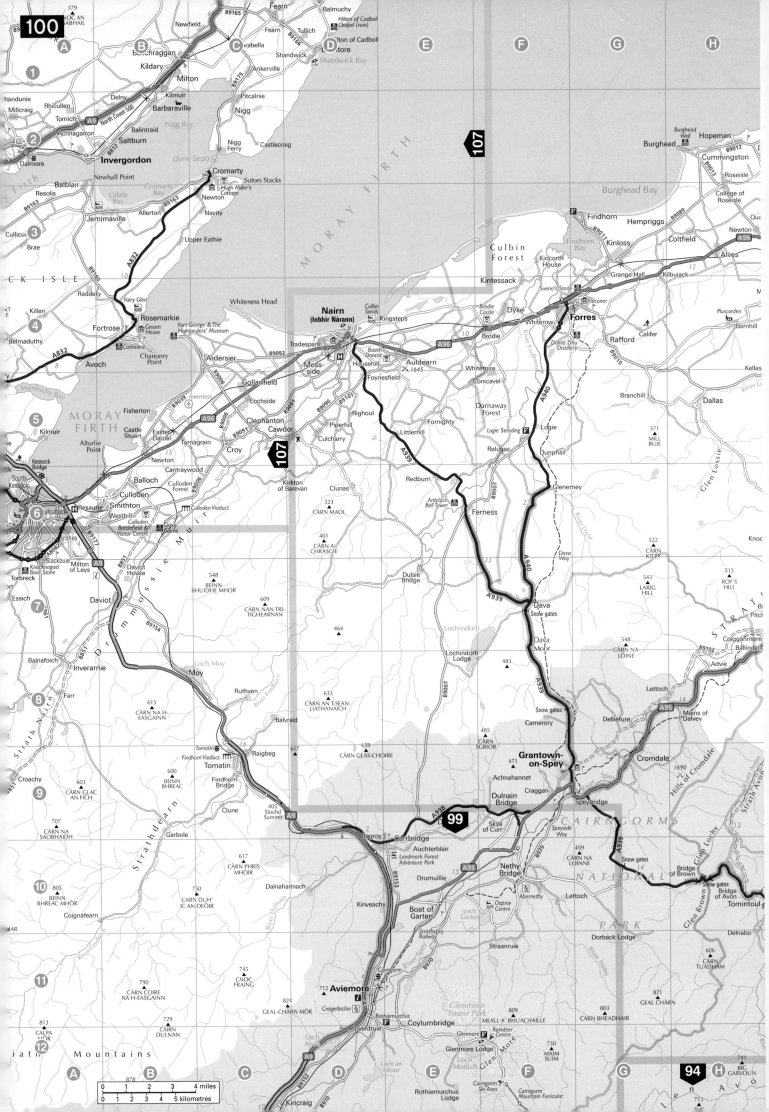

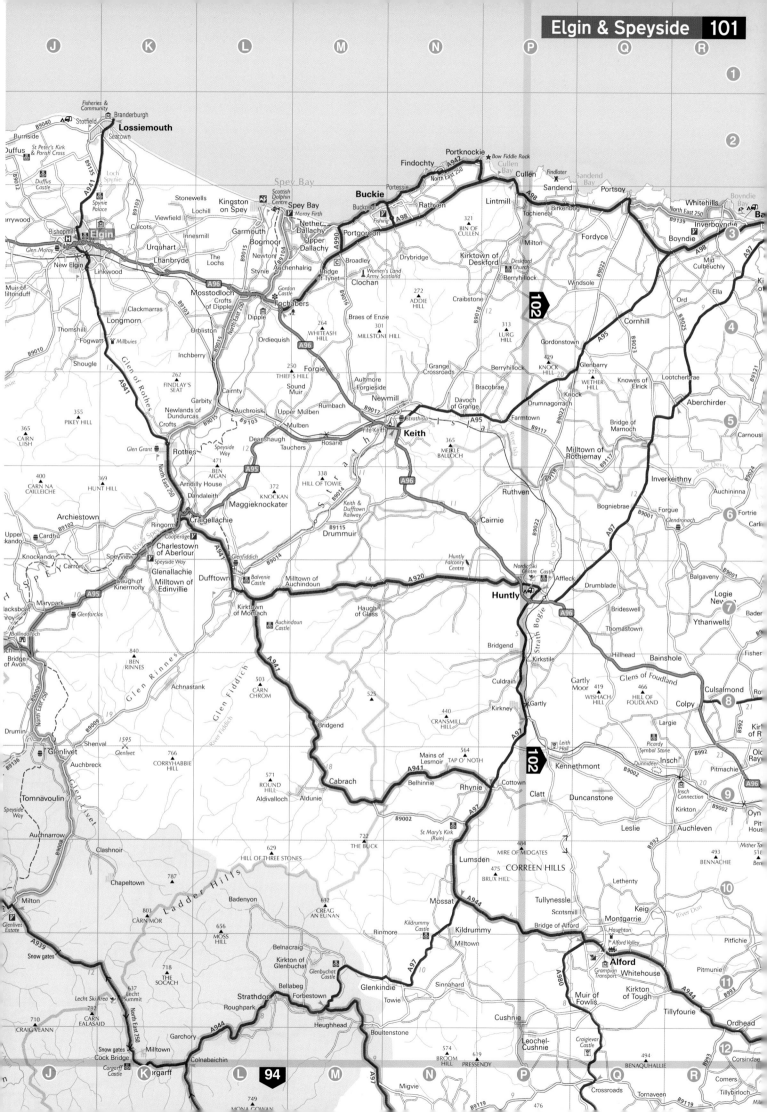

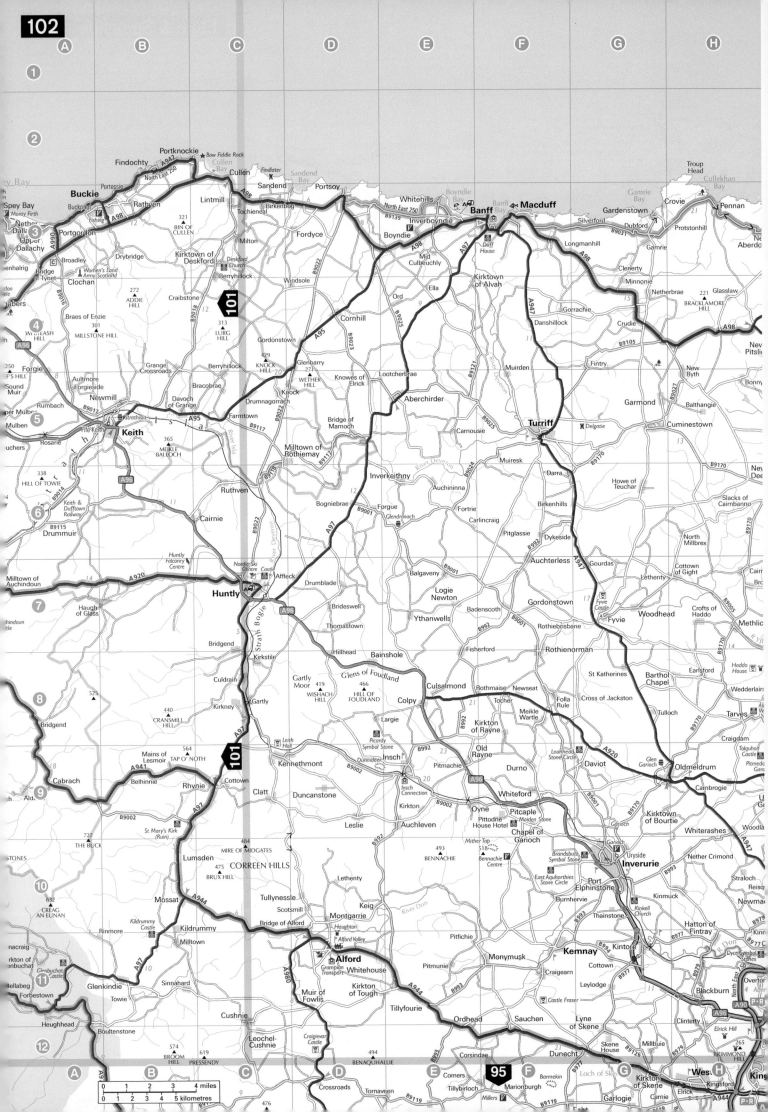

Port plan: Aberdeen p.95

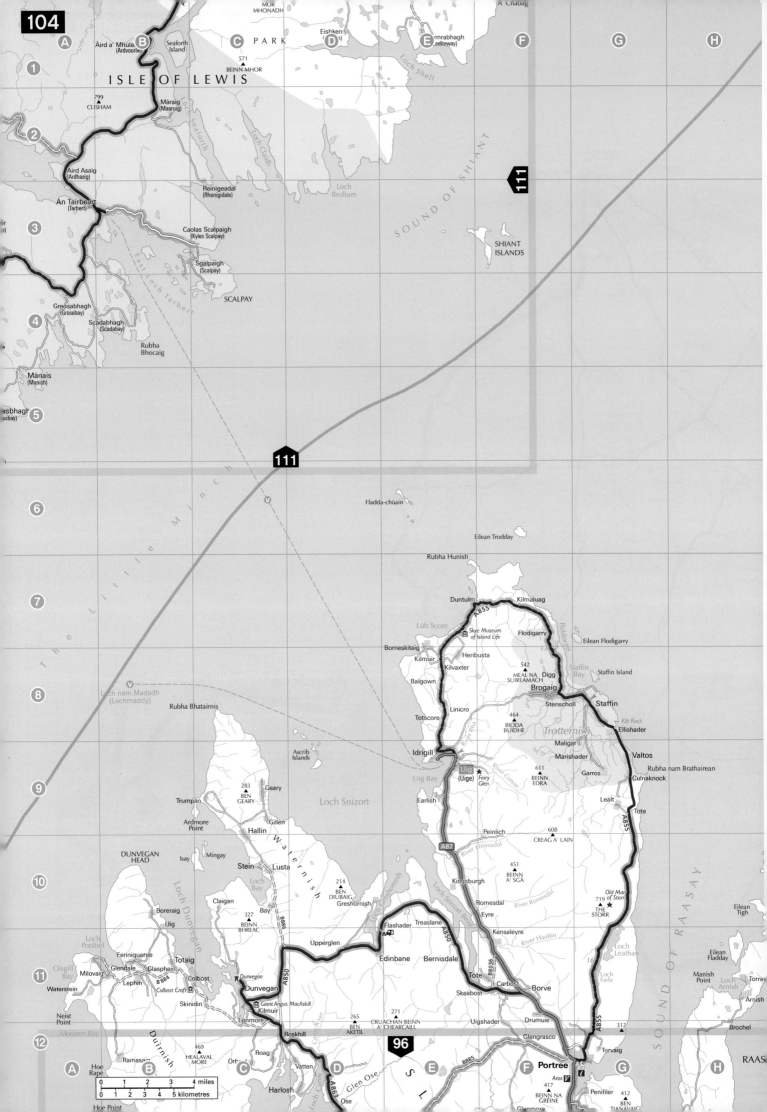

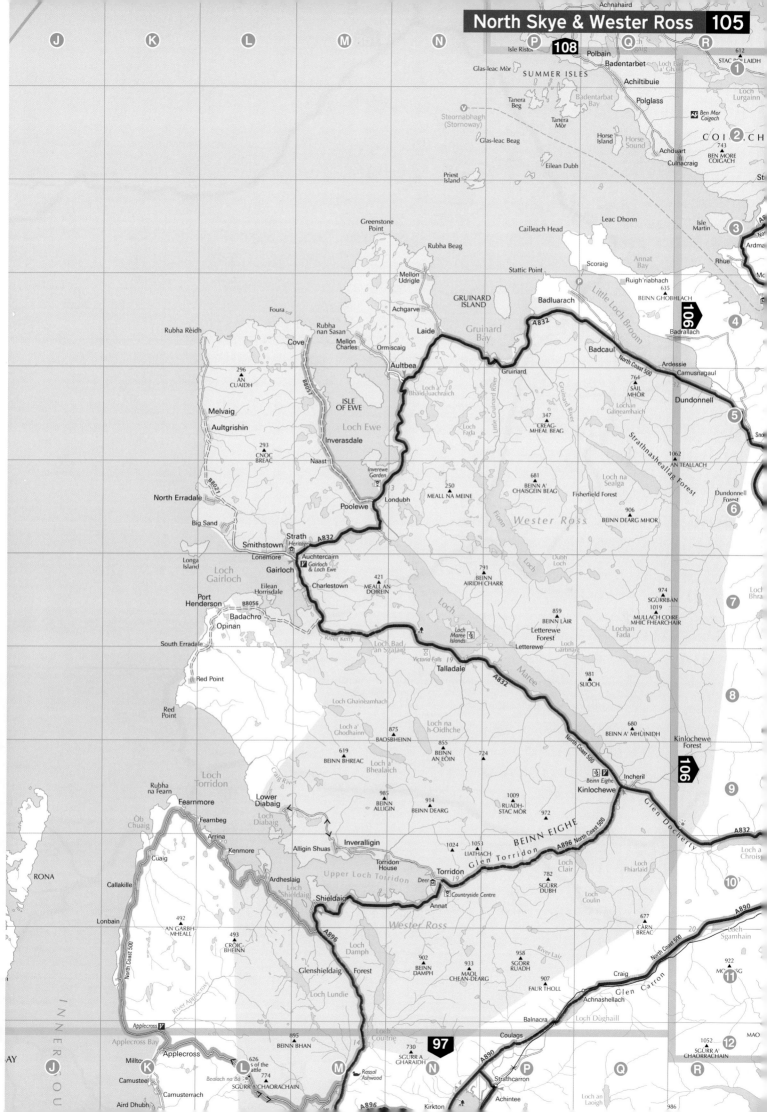

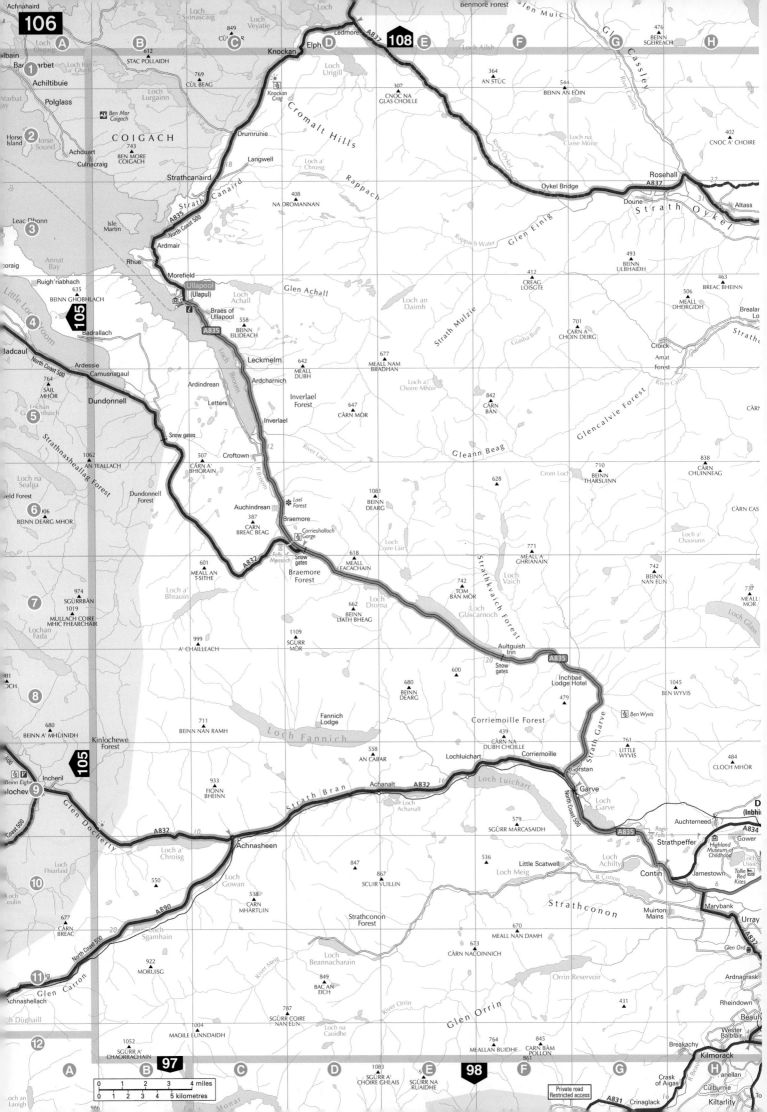

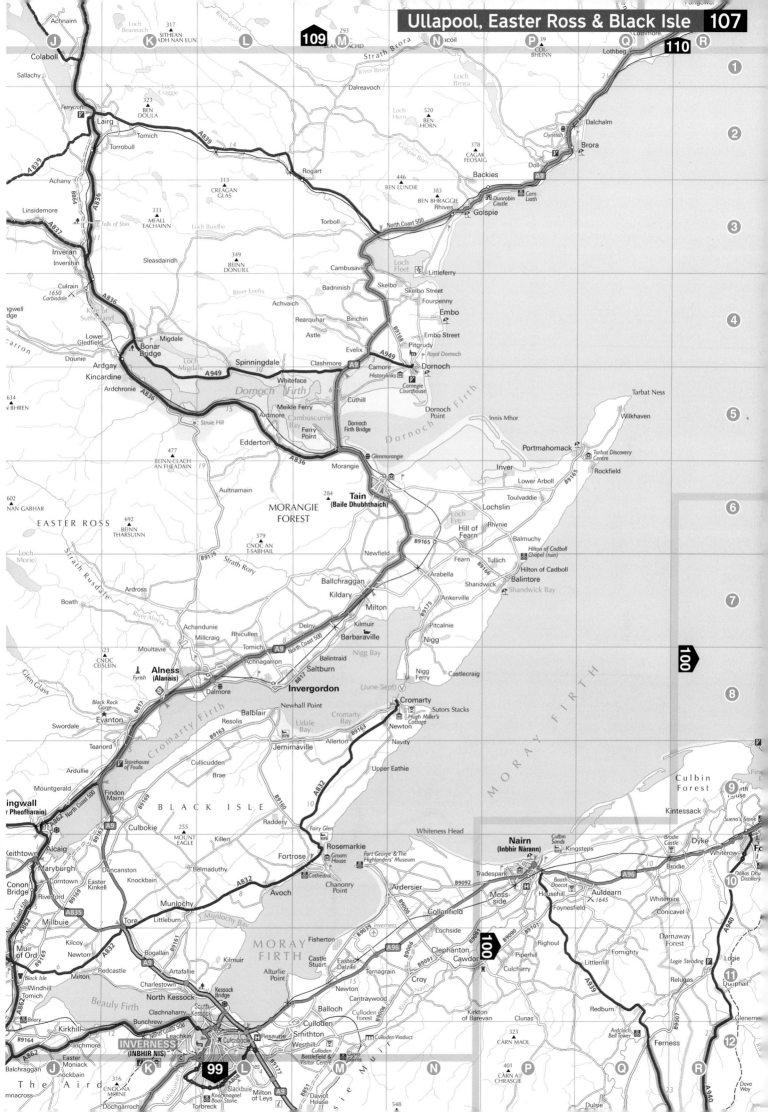

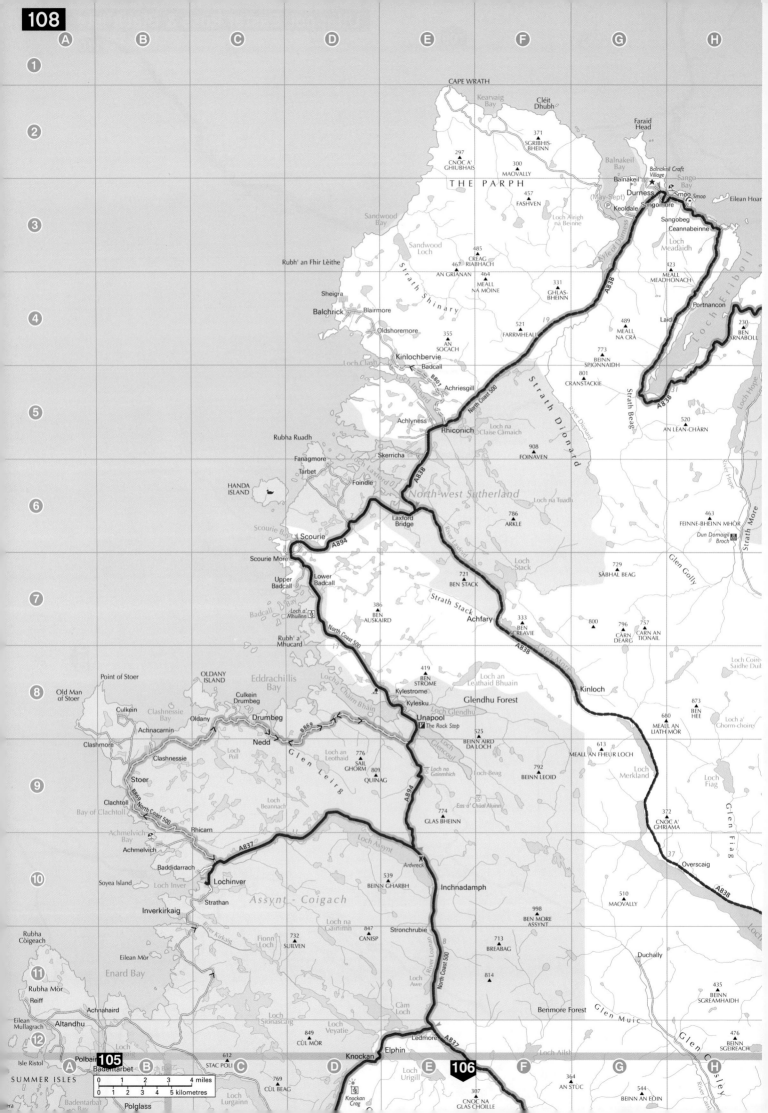

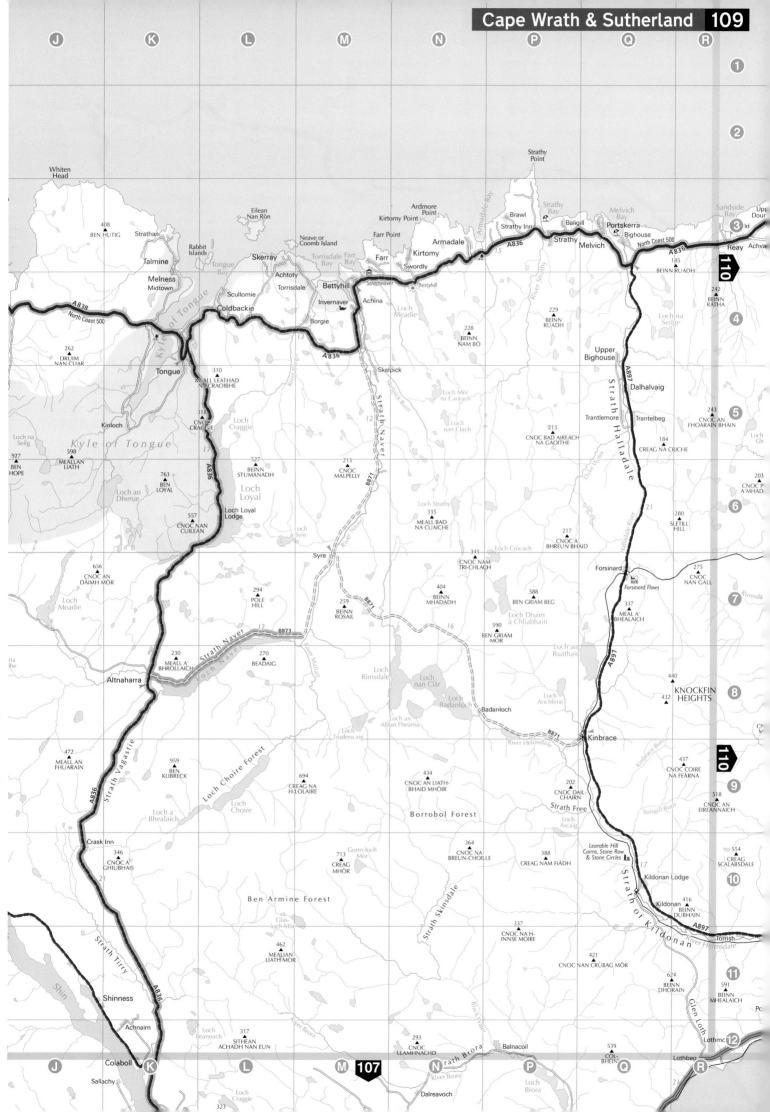

J   K   L   M   N   P   Q   R

1
2
3
4
5
6
7
8
9
10
11
12

110
110

Whiten Head
408 BEN HUTIG
Strathan
Talmine
Melness
Midtown
Rabbit Islands
Eilean Nan Ròn
Skerray
Achtoty
Torrisdale
Scullomie
Coldbackie
Tongue Bay
Neave or Coomb Island
Torrisdale Bay
Farr Bay
Farr Point
Farr
Swordly
Achina
Bettyhill
Invernaver
Borgie
Strathnaver
Bettyhill
Strathy Point
Ardmore Point
Kirtomy Point
Kirtomy
Armadale
Brawl
Strathy Inn
Strathy Bay
Baligill
Melvich
Strathy
Melvich Bay
Portskerra
Bighouse
Sandside Bay
Upp Dou
Reay
Achva
Id
North Coast 500
A836
15
Armadale-Bay
Strathy
185 BEINN RUADH
242 BEINN RATHA
Loch na Seilge
A838
North Coast 500
Kyle of Tongue
Coldbackie
Tongue
262 DRUIM NAN CLIAR
A836
13
Loch Meadie
228 BEINN NAM BÒ
229 BEINN RUADH
Upper Bighouse
Strath Halladale
Dalhalvaig
A897
Trantlemore
Trantelbeg
243 CNOC AN FHOARAIN BHÀIN
184 CREAG NA CRICHE
Skelpick
Skelpick Burn
310 MEALL LEATHAD NA CRAOIBHE
318 CNOC CRAGGIE
Loch Craggie
17
Kinloch
Loch na Seilg
Kyle of Tongue
927 BEN HOPE
598 MEALLAN LIATH
Loch an Dherue
763 BEN LOYAL
A836
527 BEINN STUMANADH
Loch Loyal
213 CNOC MALPELLY
B871
Strath Naver
12
Loch Mòr na Caoirach
Loch nan Clach
213 CNOC BAD AIREACH NA GAOITHE
Loch Strathy
335 MEALL BAD NA CUAICHE
217 CNOC A' BHREUN BHAID
203 CNOC A'MHAD...
280 SLETILL HILL
21
557 CNOC NAN CUILEAN
Loch Loyal Lodge
Loch Syre
Loch Crocach
345 CNOC NAM TRI-CHLACH
Dyke Water
Forsinard
Forsinard Flows
275 CNOC NAN GALL
Rumsda
656 CNOC AN DÀIMH MÒR
Loch Meadie
Syre
River Naver
294 POLE HILL
259 BEINN ROSAIL
B871
16
404 BEINN MHADADH
588 BEN GRIAM BEG
Lòch Druim à Chliabhain
337 MEALL A' BHEALAICH
A897
7
230 MEALL A' BHROLLAICH
Strath Naver
12
B873
Loch Naver
270 BEADAIG
River Mallart
Loch Rimsdale
Loch nan Clàr
590 BEN GRIAM MÒR
Loch an Ruathair
440
432
KNOCKFIN HEIGHTS
8
Altnaharra
472 MEALL AN FHUARAIN
Strath Vagastie
959 BEN KLIBRECK
Loch Choire Forest
Loch Truderscaig
Loch Badanloch
Loch an Allan Fhearna
Badanloch
River Helmsdale
B871
Kinbrace
437 CNOC COIRE NA FEÀRNA
9
518 CNOC AN EIREANNAICH
Crask Inn
346 CNOC A' GHIUBHAIS
21
694 CREAG NA H-IOLAIRE
Loch a' Bhealaich
Loch Choire
713 CREAG MHÒR
Gorm-loch Mòr
434 CNOC AN LIATH-BHAID MHÒIR
Borrobol Forest
Loch Ascaig
202 CNOC DAIL-CHAIRN
Strath Free
554 CREAG SCALABSDALE
10
A836
Ben Armine Forest
364 CNOC NA BREUN-CHOILLE
Strath Skinsdale
388 CREAG NAM FIADH
Learable Hill Cairns, Stone Row & Stone Circles
17
Strath of Kildonan
Kildonan Lodge
Kildonan
416 BEINN DUBHAIN
A897
River Helmsdale
Torrish
Strath Tirry
462 MEALIAN LIATH MÒR
Glas-loch Mòr
337 CNOC NA H-INNSE MOIRE
421 CNOC NAN CRÙBAG MÒR
624 BEINN DHORAIN
591 BEINN MHEALAICH
Glen Loth
Lothmo
11
Shinness
Achnairn
A836
Shin
317 SITHEAN ACHADH NAN EUN
Loch Beannach
293 CNOC LEAMHNACHD
Strath Brora
Balnacoil
539 COL-BHEINN
River Helmsdale
Lothbeg
12
Colaboll
Sallachy
Loch Craggie
323
J   K   L   M   N   P   Q   R

107

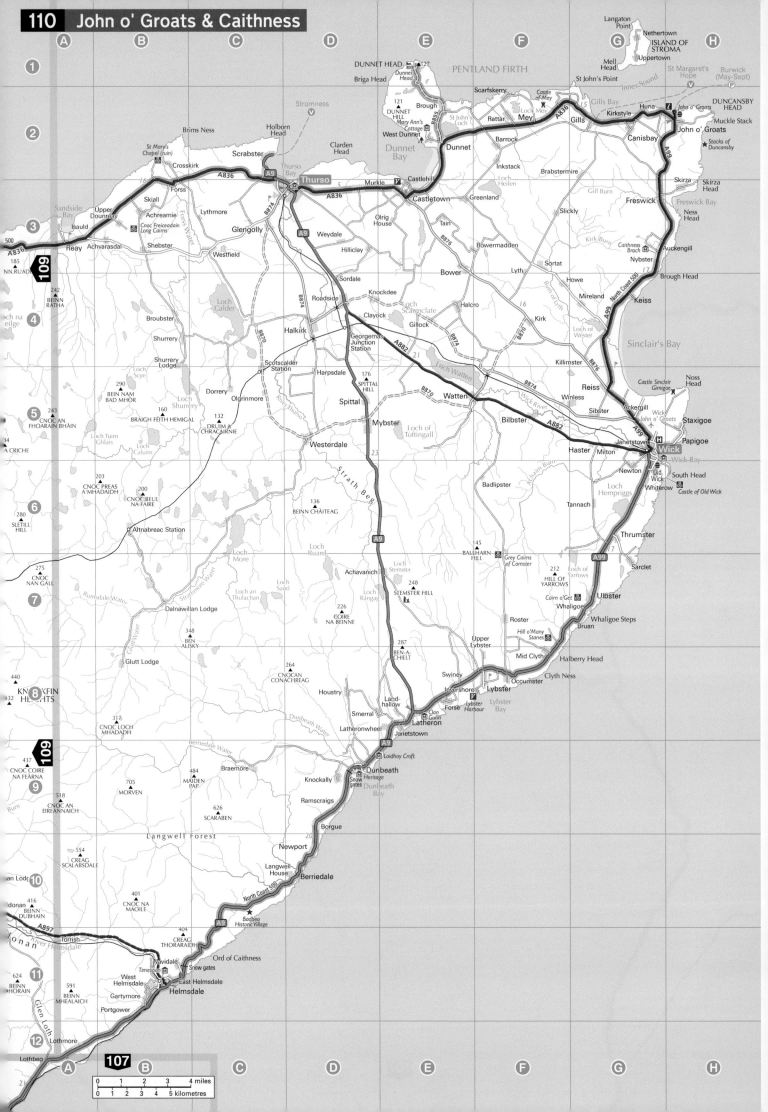

A B C D E F G H

1
2
3
4
5
6
7
8
9
10
11
12

109
109

PENTLAND FIRTH

ISLAND OF STROMA

Langaton Point
Netherton
Uppertown
Mell Head
St Margaret's Hope
Burwick (May-Sept)

DUNNET HEAD
Briga Head
Dunnet Head
127
Scarfskerry
Castle of Mey
St John's Point
St John's Loch
DUNNET HILL
Mary Ann's Cottage
West Dunnet
Brough
Rattar
Mey
A836
Gills
Kirkstyle
Huna
Gills Bay
Inner Sound
DUNCANSBY HEAD
John o' Groats
Muckle Stack

121
Stromness
Brims Ness
Holborn Head
Scrabster
St Mary's Chapel (ruin)
Crosskirk
Skiall
Forss
A836
A9
Thurso Bay
Thurso
Murkle
Castlehill
Castletown
Dunnet
Dunnet Bay
Barrock
Inkstack
Brabstermire
Canisbay
Stacks of Duncansby
Skirza
Skirza Head
Freswick
Freswick Bay
Ness Head

Sandside Bay
Isauld
Upper Dounreay
Achreamie
Cnoc Freiceadain Long Cairns
Lythmore
Shebster
Westfield
Glengolly
A9
Weydale
Hilliclay
Olrig House
Greenland
Loch Heilen
Bowermadden
Slickly
Gill Burn
Caithness Broch
Auckengill
Nybster
Brough Head
Keiss
North Coast 500

500
A836
Reay
Achvarasdal
185
NN.RUADH
242
BEINN RATHA
Broubster
Shurrery
Shurrery Lodge
290
BEIN NAM BAD MHÒR
Loch Calder
B870
B874
Roadside
Knockdee
Clayock
Loch Scarmclate
Halcro
Tain
Bower
Sortat
Lyth
Howe
Mireland
Sinclair's Bay
Noss Head

loch na eilge
203
CNOC PREAS A'MHADAIDH
160
BRÀIGH FÉITH HEMIGAL
Loch Scye
132
DRUIM A' CHRACAIRNIE
Dorrery
Olgrinmore
River Thurso
Halkirk
Scotscalder Station
Harpsdale
Spittal
176
SPITTAL HILL
Georgemas Junction Station
A882
21
Gillock
Kirk
Killimster
B876
Reiss
Ackergill
Wick John o' Groats
Castle Sinclair Girnigoe

CRICHE
243
CNOC AN FHOARAIN BHÀIN
200
CNOC BEUL NA FAIRE
Loch Caluim
Loch Tuim Ghlais
Westerdale
23
Mybster
Loch of Toftingall
Watten
Loch Watten
B870
Bilbster
A882
Winless
Sibster
Staxigoe
Papigoe

280
SLETILL HILL
Altnabreac Station
136
BEINN CHÀITEAG
Loch More
Loch Ruard
Loch Sand
Achavanich
Loch Stemster
248
STEMSTER HILL
Loch Rangag
145
BALLHARN HILL
Grey Cairns of Camster
212
HILL OF YARROWS
Loch of Yarrows
Cairn o'Get
Ulbster
Whaligoe
Whaligoe Steps
Bruan
Haster
Milton
Janetstown
Wick
Wick Bay
Newton
Old Wick
Whiterow
South Head
Castle of Old Wick
Loch Hempriggs
Tannach
Badlipster
Thrumster
Sarclet

275
CNOC NAN GALL
Rumsdale Water
Strathmore Water
Dalnawillan Lodge
Loch an Thulachan
348
BEN ALISKY
226
COIRE NA BEINNE
Houstry
287
BEN-A-CHIELT
Upper Lybster
Roster
Hill o'Many Stanes
Mid Clyth
Halberry Head
Clyth Ness
Occumster
Lybster
Lybster Harbour
Lybster Bay
Swiney
Invershore
Forse

440
KNOCKFIN HEIGHTS
132
264
CNOCAN CONACHREAG
Glutt Lodge
Glutt Water
317
CNOC LOCH MHADADH
Landhallow
Smerral
Latheronwheel
Latheron
Janetstown
Clan Gunn
A9

109
437
CNOC COIRE NA FEARNA
518
CNOC AN EIREANNAICH
Dunbeath Water
Berriedale Water
484
MAIDEN PAP
Braemore
705
MORVEN
Knockally
Ramscraigs
Dunbeath
Laidhay Croft
Snow gates
Dunbeath Heritage
Dunbeath Bay

Burn
Langwell Forest
626
SCARABEN
Borgue
Newport
20
Langwell House
Berriedale
North Coast 500

an Lodg
554
CREAG SCALABSDALE
401
CNOC NA MAOILE
404
CREAG THORARAIDH
Ord of Caithness
Snow gates
A9
Badbea Historic Village

donan
416
BEINN DUBHAIN
A897
Torrish
River Helmsdale
Navidale
Timespan
East Helmsdale

624
BEINN HORAIN
591
BEINN MHEALAICH
West Helmsdale
Helmsdale
Gartymore
Portgower

Glen Loth
Lothmore
Lothbeg

0 1 2 3 4 miles
0 1 2 3 4 5 kilometres

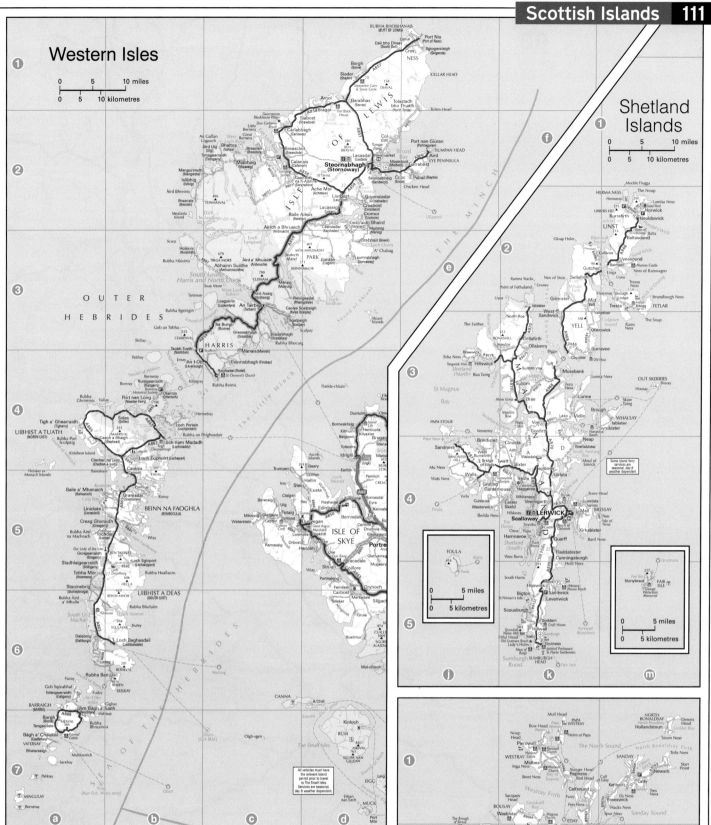

FERRY SERVICES

Western Isles

There are numerous and varied sailings from the west coast of Scotland and between Scottish islands, most of which are operated by Caledonian MacBrayne.

Shetland Islands

The main service is from Aberdeen on the mainland to the island port of Lerwick. A service from Kirkwall (Orkney) to Lerwick is also available. Shetland Islands Council operates an inter-island car ferry service.

Orkney Islands

The main service is from Scrabster on the Caithness coast to the island port of Stromness and there is a further service from Gills (Caithness) to St Margaret's Hope on South Ronaldsay. A service from Aberdeen to Kirkwall provides a link to Shetland at Lerwick. Inter-island car ferry services are also operated by Orkney Ferries.

Note

Some island services are day dependant and advance reservations are recommended. Before setting off on your journey, confirm and book sailings by contacting the ferry operator listed on page VII of this atlas.

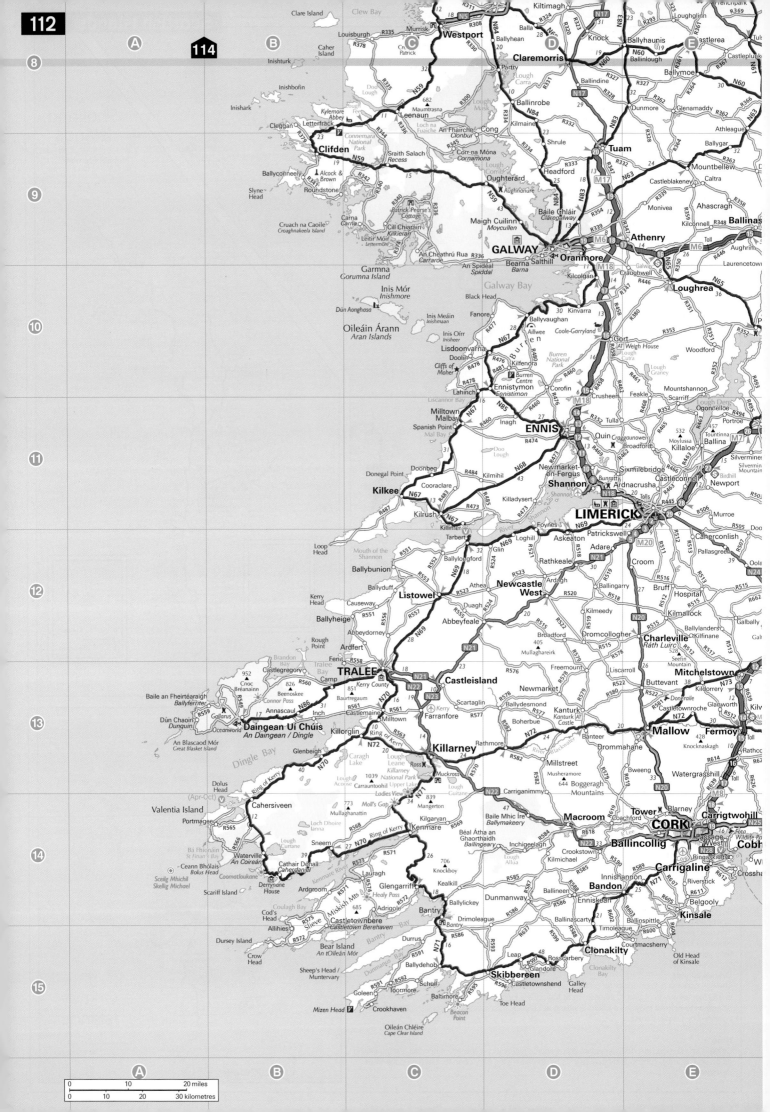

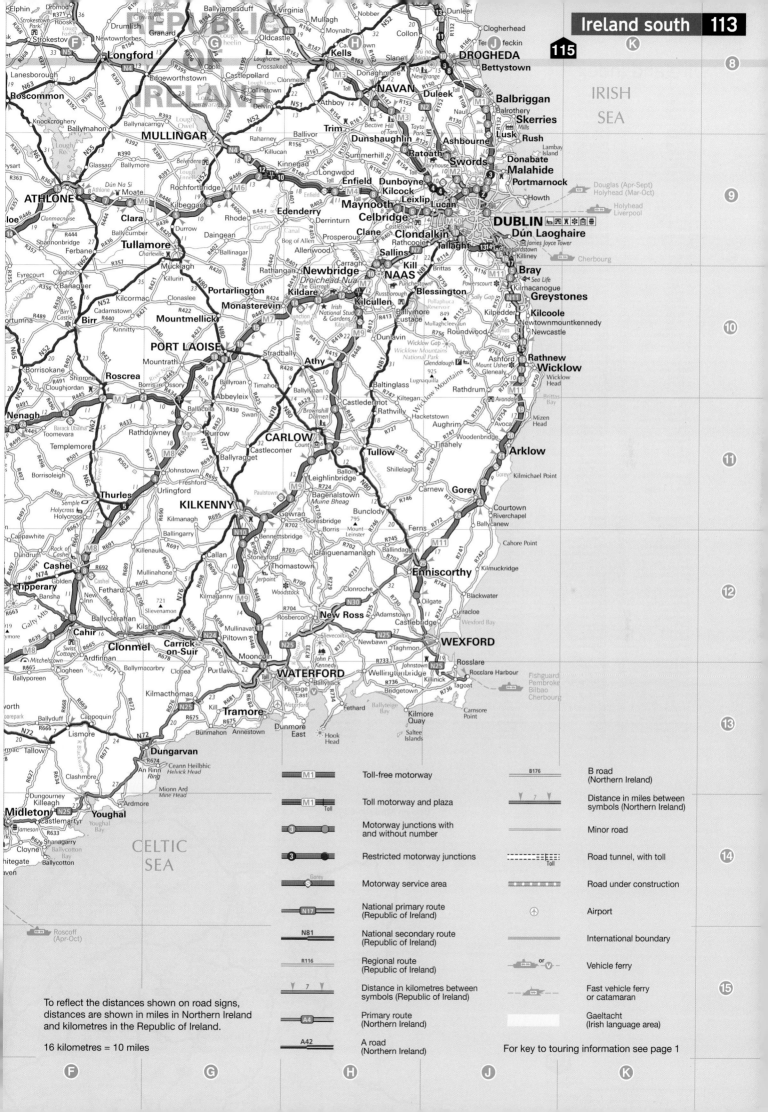

Ireland index

Abbeydorney....C12
Abbeyfeale....D12
Abbeyleix....G11
Adamstown....H12
Adare....D12
Adrigole....C14
Aghalee....J5
Ahascragh....E9
Ahoghill....J4
Allenwood....H9
Allihies....B15
An Bun Beag....E4
An Charraig....E5
An Cheathrú Rua....C9
An Clochán Liath....E4
An Coireán....B14
An Daingean....B13
An Fál Carrach....F3
An Fhairche....C9
Annahilt....J6
Annalong....J7
Annascaul....B13
Annestown....G13
An Rinn....G13
An Spidéal....D9
Antrim....J5
Ardagh....D12
Ardara....E5
Ardee....H8
Ardfert....C12
Ardfinnan....F12
Ardglass....K6
Ardgroom....B14
Ardmore....F14
Ardnacrusha....E11
Arklow....J11
Armagh....H6
Armoy....J3
Arvagh....G7
Ashbourne....J9
Ashford....J10
Askeaton....D12
Athea....D12
Athenry....E9
Athleague....E8
Athlone....F9
Athy....H10
Augher....G6
Aughnacloy....H6
Aughrim....E9
Aughrim....J11
Avoca....J11

Bagenalstown....H11
Baile an Fheirtéaraigh....B13
Baile Chláir....D9
Baile Mhic Íre....D14
Baile na Finne....F4
Bailieborough....H7
Balbriggan....J8
Balla....D8
Ballacolla....G11
Ballaghaderreen....E7
Ballina....D7
Ballina....E11
Ballinafad....F7
Ballinagar....G9
Ballinamallard....G6
Ballinamore....F7
Ballinascarty....D14
Ballinasloe....E9
Ballincollig....E14
Ballindaggan....H12
Ballindine....D8
Ballineen....D14
Ballingarry....D12
Ballingarry....G12
Ballingeary....D14
Ballinlough....E8
Ballinrobe....D8
Ballinspittle....E14
Ballintra....F5
Ballivor....H9
Ballon....H11
Ballybay....H7
Ballybofey....F5
Ballybunion....C12
Ballycanew....J11
Ballycarry....K5

Ballycastle....J3
Ballycastle....C6
Ballyclare....J5
Ballyclerahan....F12
Ballyconneely....B9
Ballyconnell....G7
Ballycotton....F14
Ballycumber....F9
Ballydehob....C15
Ballydesmond....D13
Ballyduff....C12
Ballyduff....F13
Ballyfarnon....E7
Ballyferriter....B13
Ballygally....J4
Ballygar....E9
Ballygawley....H6
Ballygawley....E6
Ballygowan....K5
Ballyhack....H13
Ballyhaise....G7
Ballyhalbert....K5
Ballyhaunis....E8
Ballyhean....D8
Ballyheige....C12
Ballyjamesduff....G8
Ballylanders....E12
Ballylickey....C14
Ballyliffin....G3
Ballylongford....C12
Ballylynan....H10
Ballymacarbry....F13
Ballymahon....F8
Ballymakeery....D14
Ballymena....J4
Ballymoe....E8
Ballymoney....H4
Ballymore....F9
Ballymore Eustace....H10
Ballymote....E7
Ballynacarrigy....G8
Ballynahinch....J6
Ballynure....J5
Ballyporeen....F13
Ballyragget....G11
Ballyroan....G10
Ballyshannon....F5
Ballysadare....E6
Ballyvaughan....D10
Ballywalter....K5
Balrothery....J8
Baltimore....C15
Baltinglass....H10
Banagher....F10
Banbridge....J6
Bandon....E14
Bangor....K5
Bangor Erris....C7
Bansha....F12
Banteer....D13
Bantry....C14
Barna....D9
Béal an Mhuirthead....B6
Béal Átha an Ghaorthaidh....D14
Bearna....D9
Belcoo....F6
Belfast....J5
Belgooly....E14
Bellaghy....H4
Belleek....F6
Belmullet....B6
Belturbet....G7
Benburb....H6
Bennettsbridge....G12
Beragh....G5
Bessbrook....J6
Bettystown....J8
Birr....F10
Blacklion....F6
Blackwater....J12
Blarney....E14
Blessington....H10
Boherbue....D13
Borris....H12
Borris-in-Ossory....F10
Borrisokane....F10
Borrisoleigh....F11
Boyle....E7
Bray....J10
Bridgetown....H13

Brittas....J9
Broadford....E11
Broadford....D12
Brookeborough....G6
Broughshane....J4
Bruff....E12
Bunbeg....E4
Bunclody....H11
Buncrana....G3
Bundoran....E6
Bunmahon....G13
Bunnyconnellan....D7
Bushmills....H3
Buttevant....E13
Bweeng....E13

Cadamstown....F10
Caherconlish....E12
Caherdaniel....B14
Cahersiveen....B14
Cahir....F12
Caledon....H6
Callan....G12
Caltra....E9
Camp....B13
Carndonagh....G3
Cappawhite....F12
Cappoquin....F13
Carlanstown....H8
Carlingford....J7
Carlow....H11
Carna....C9
Carnew....J11
Carnlough....J4
Carragh....H9
Carraig Airt....F3
Carraroe....C9
Carrick....E5
Carrickfergus....K5
Carrickmacross....H7
Carrickmore....G5
Carrick-on-Shannon....F7
Carrick-on-Suir....G12
Carrigaline....E14
Carrigallen....F7
Carriganimmy....D13
Carrigart....F3
Carrigtwohill....E14
Carryduff....J5
Cashel....F12
Castlebar....D8
Castlebellingham....J7
Castleblakeney....E9
Castleblayney....H7
Castlebridge....J12
Castlecomer....G11
Castleconnell....E11
Castlederg....G5
Castledermot....H11
Castlegregory....B13
Castleisland....C13
Castlemaine....C13
Castlemartyr....F14
Castleplunket....E8
Castlepollard....G8
Castlerea....E8
Castlerock....H3
Castletownbere....B15
Castletownroche....E13
Castletownshend....D15
Castlewellan....J6
Cathair Dónall....B14
Causeway....C12
Cavan....G7
Celbridge....H9
Charlestown....D7
Charleville....E12
Cill Charthaigh....E5
Cill Chiaráin....C9
Clady....G5
Clane....H9
Clara....G9
Claregalway....D9
Claremorris....D8
Clashmore....F13
Claudy....G4
Cleggan....B8
Clifden....B9
Cliffoney....E6
Cloghan....F10
Clogheen....F13

Clogher....G6
Clogherhead....J8
Clogh Mills....J4
Clonakilty....D15
Clonaslee....G10
Clonbur....C9
Clondalkin....J9
Clonea....G13
Clones....G7
Clonmany....G3
Clonmel....F12
Clonmellon....H8
Clonroche....H12
Clough....K6
Cloughjordan....F10
Cloyne....F14
Coachford....D14
Coagh....H5
Coalisland....H5
Cobh....E14
Coleraine....H3
Collinstown....G8
Collon....H8
Collooney....E7
Comber....K5
Cong....D9
Convoy....F4
Cookstown....H5
Coole....G8
Cooraclare....C11
Cootehill....G7
Cork....E14
Cornamona....C9
Corofin....D10
Corr na Móna....C9
Courtmacsherry....E15
Courtown....J11
Craigavon....J6
Craughwell....E10
Creeslough....F4
Croithlí....E4
Crolly....E4
Crookhaven....C15
Crookstown....D14
Croom....E12
Crossakeel....H8
Crosshaven....E14
Crossmaglen....H7
Crossmolina....D7
Crumlin....J5
Crusheen....D10
Culdaff....G3
Cullybackey....J4
Culmore....G4
Curracloe....J12
Curry....E7
Cushendall....J4
Cushendun....J3

Daingean....G9
Daingean Uí Chúis....B13
Delvin....G8
Derrinturn....H9
Derry....G4
Derrygonnelly....F6
Derrylin....G6
Dervock....H3
Dingle....B13
Doagh....J5
Donabate....J9
Donaghadee....K5
Donaghmore....H5
Donaghmore....H8
Donegal....F5
Donemana....G4
Doolin....C10
Doon....E12
Doonbeg....C11
Downings....F3
Downpatrick....K6
Dowra....F6
Draperstown....H5
Drimoleague....D14
Drogheda....J8
Droichead Nua....H10
Dromahair....E6
Dromara....J6
Dromcolloher....D12
Dromiskin....J7
Dromod....F8
Dromore....J6

Dromore....G5
Dromore West....D6
Drumaness....K6
Drumfries....G3
Drumkeeran....F7
Drumlish....F8
Drumquin....G5
Drumshanbo....F7
Drumsna....F8
Duagh....C12
Dublin....J9
Duleek....J8
Dunboyne....J9
Dún Chaoin....A13
Dundalk....J7
Dundonald....K5
Dundrum....F12
Dunfanaghy....F3
Dungannon....H5
Dungarvan....G13
Dungiven....H4
Dunglow....E4
Dungourney....E5
Dunkineely....E5
Dún Laoghaire....J9
Dunlavin....H10
Dunleer....J8
Dunloy....J4
Dunmanway....D14
Dunmore....E8
Dunmore East....H13
Dunquin....A13
Dunshaughlin....H9
Durrow....G11
Durrow....G9
Durrus....C15
Dysart....E9

Easky....D6
Edenderry....H9
Edgeworthstown....G8
Eglinton....G4
Elphin....F8
Emyvale....H4
Enfield....H9
Ennis....D11
Enniscorthy....H12
Enniscrone....D6
Enniskean....D14
Enniskillen....F6
Ennistymon....D10
Eyrecourt....F10

Fahan....G4
Falcarragh....F3
Fanore....D10
Farranfore....C13
Feakle....E11
Fenagh....F7
Fenit....B13
Ferbane....F9
Fermoy....E13
Ferns....J12
Fethard....F12
Fethard....H13
Fintona....G6
Fintown....F4
Fivemiletown....G6
Foxford....D7
Foynes....D12
Freemount....D13
Frenchpark....E8
Freshford....G11

Galbally....E12
Galway....D9
Garrison....F6
Garvagh....H4
Gilford....J6
Glandore....D15
Glanworth....E13
Glaslough....H6
Glassan....F9
Gleann Cholm Cille....E5
Glenamaddy....E8
Glenarm....J4
Glenavy....J5
Glenbeigh....B13
Glencolumbkille....E5
Glenealy....J10
Glengarriff....C14
Glenties....E5

Glin....D12
Golden....F12
Goleen....C15
Goresbridge....H11
Gorey....J11
Gort....D10
Gorteen....E7
Gortin....G5
Gowran....H11
Graiguenamanagh....H12
Granard....G8
Grange....E6
Greencastle....H3
Greencastle....G5
Greenore....J7
Greyabbey....K5
Greystones....J10
Gulladuff....H4

Hacketstown....H11
Headford....D9
Hillsborough....J6
Hilltown....J6
Holycross....F11
Holywood....K5
Hospital....E12
Howth....J9

Inagh....D11
Inch....B13
Inchigeelagh....D14
Inishcrone....D6
Innishannon....E14
Irvinestown....F6

Johnstown....G11

Kanturk....D13
Keadue....F7
Keady....H6
Kealkill....C14
Keel....B7
Kells....J4
Kells....H8
Kenmare....C14
Kesh....F5
Kilbeggan....G9
Kilcar....E5
Kilcock....H9
Kilcolgan....D10
Kilconnell....E9
Kilcoole....J10
Kilcormac....F10
Kilcullen....H10
Kildare....H10
Kildorrery....E13
Kilfenora....D10
Kilfinane....E12
Kilgarvan....C14
Kilkee....C11
Kilkeel....J7
Kilkenny....G11
Kilkieran....C9
Kill....H9
Kill....G13
Killadysert....D11
Killala....D6
Killaloe....E11
Killarney....C13
Killashandra....G7
Kileagh....F14
Killenaule....F12
Killimer....C11
Killiney....J9
Killinick....J13
Killorglin....C13
Killough....K6
Killucan....G9
Killurin....G10
Killybegs....E5
Killyleagh....K6
Kilmacanogue....J10
Kilmacrenan....F4
Kilmacthomas....G13
Kilmaganny....G12
Kilmaine....D8
Kilmallock....E12
Kilmanagh....G11
Kilmeedy....D12
Kilmichael....D14
Kilmihil....C11
Kilmore Quay....H13

Kilmuckridge....J12
Kilpedder....J10
Kilrea....H4
Kilrush....C11
Kilsheelan....G12
Kiltegan....H11
Kiltimagh....D8
Kilworth....E13
Kingscourt....H7
Kinlough....E6
Kinnegad....G9
Kinnitty....F10
Kinsale....E14
Kinvarra....D10
Kircubbin....K5
Knock....D8
Knockcroghery....F8

Lahinch....C10
Lanesborough....F8
Laragh....J10
Larne....K4
Lauragh....C14
Laurencetown....F10
Leap....D15
Leenaun....C8
Leighlinbridge....H11
Leitrim....F7
Leixlip....H9
Letterfrack....B8
Letterkenny....F4

Lifford....G4
Limavady....H4
Limerick....E11
Lisbellaw....G6
Liscarroll....D13
Lisdoonvarna....D10
Lismore....F13
Lisnaskea....G6
Listowel....C12
Loghill....D12
Londonderry....G4
Longford....F8
Longwood....H9
Loughbrickland....J6
Loughglinn....E8
Loughrea....E10
Louisburgh....C8
Lucan....J9
Lurgan....J6
Lusk....J9

Macroom....D14
Maghera....H4
Magherafelt....H5
Maguiresbridge....G6
Maigh Cuilinn....D9
Malahide....J9
Málainn Mhóir....E5
Malin....G3
Malin More....E5

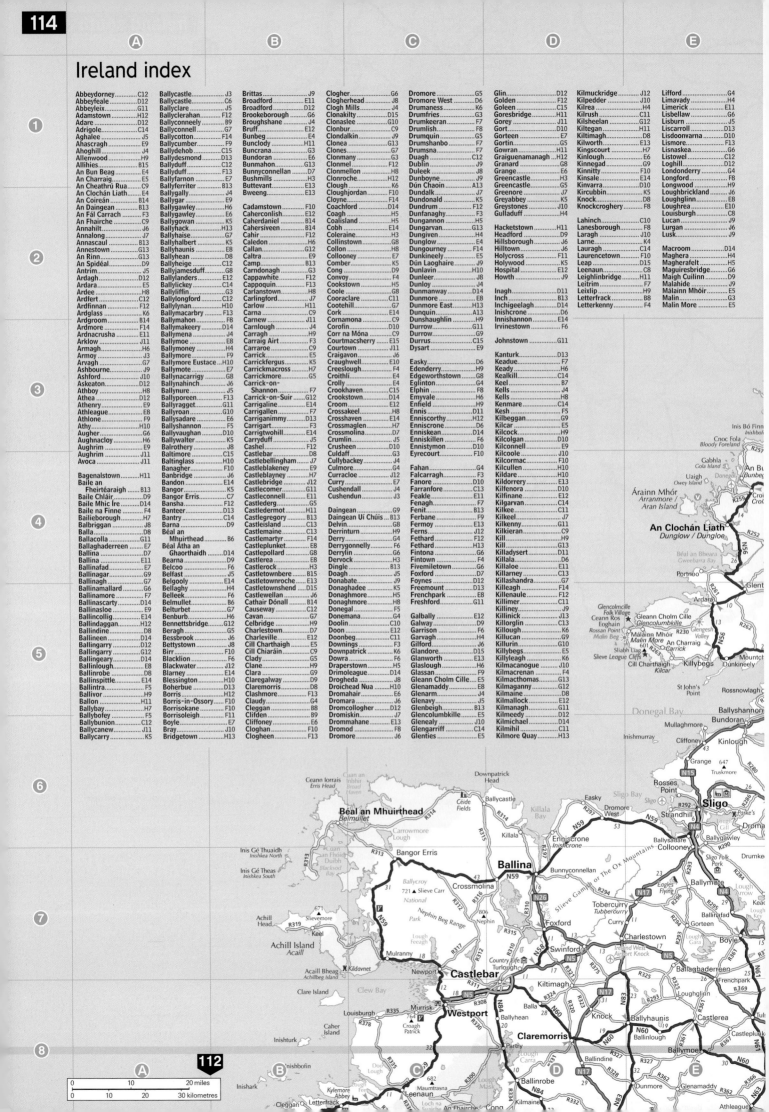

Mallow............E13	Mullagh...........H8	Newtown	Portballintrae......H3	Rathmullan......G4
Manorhamilton......F6	Mullaghmore......E6	Cunningham......G4	Portglenone......H4	Rathnew..........J10
Markethill.........H6	Mullinahone......G12	Newtownforbes......F8	Port Laoise......G10	Rathvilly.........H11
Martinstown........J4	Mullinavat........G12	Newtownhamilton......H6	Portlaw..........G13	Ratoath...........J9
Maynooth..........H9	Mullingar.........G9	Newtownmount-	Portmagee........B14	Recess............C9
Mayobridge........J6	Mulranny..........C7	kennedy..........J10	Portmarnock......J9	Rhode.............G9
Midleton..........F14	Murrisk...........C8	Newtownstewart......G5	Portnablagh......F3	Ring.............G13
Milford...........F4	Murroe............E11	Nobber............H8	Portnoo...........E4	Ringaskiddy......E14
Millstreet........D13			Portroe..........E11	Riverchapel......J11
Milltown..........C13	Naas.............H10	Ogonnelloe.......E11	Portrush..........H3	Riverstick.......E14
Milltown Malbay......C11	Na Dúnaibh........F3	Oilgate.........H12	Portstewart......H3	Rochfortbridge......G9
Mitchelstown......E13	Naul..............J8	Oldcastle........G8	Portumna.........E10	Rockcorry.........H7
Moate.............F9	Navan.............H8	Omagh............G5	Poyntzpass........J6	Roosky............F8
Mohill............F7	Nenagh...........E11	Omeath............J7	Prosperous........H9	Rosbercon.......H12
Monaghan..........H6	Newbawn.........H12	Oola.............E12		Roscommon.........F8
Monasterevin......G10	Newbliss..........G7	Oranmore.........D9	Quin.............D11	Roscrea..........F10
Moneymore.........H5	Newbridge........H10	Oughterard.......D9		Rosscarbery......D15
Monivea...........E9	Newcastle.........J6		Raharney.........G9	Rosses Point......E6
Mooncoin.........G13	Newcastle........J10	Pallasgreen......E12	Ramelton..........F4	Rosslare.........J13
Mountbellew.......E9	Newcastle West......D12	Partry...........D8	Randalstown.......J5	Rosslare Harbour......J13
Mountcharles......F5	New Inn..........F12	Passage East......H13	Raphoe............G4	Rosslea...........G6
Mountmellick......G10	Newmarket........D13	Passage West......E14	Rasharkin.........H4	Rossnowlagh.......E5
Mountrath........G10	Newmarket-on-	Patrickswell......E12	Rathangan.......H10	Rostrevor.........J7
Mountshannon......E10	Fergus..........D11	Pettigo...........F5	Rathcoole.........J9	Roundstone.......B9
Moville...........G3	Newport...........C7	Piltown.........G12	Rathcormac......E13	Roundwood........J10
Moy...............H6	Newport..........E11	Plumbridge........G5	Rathdowney......G11	Rush..............J9
Moycullen.........D9	New Ross.........H12	Pomeroy..........H5	Rathdrum.........J10	
Moynalty..........H8	Newry.............J6	Portadown.........H6	Rathfriland.......J6	Saintfield........K6
Mucklagh..........G9	Newtownabbey......J5	Portaferry........K6	Rathkeale.......D12	St Johnston......G4
Muff..............G4	Newtownards.......K5	Portarlington......G10	Ráth Luirc......E12	Sallins...........H9
Muine Bheag......H11	Newtownbutler......G7	Portavogie........K6	Rathmore.........D13	Salthill..........D9

Rathnew..........J10	Scarriff.........E11	Strokestown.......F8	Tubbercurry......E7	
Rathvilly.........H11	Scartaglin.......C13	Summerhill........H9	Tulla............D11	
Ratoath..........J9	Schull...........C15	Swan.............G11	Tullamore.........G9	
Recess...........C9	Seskinore.........G5	Swanlinbar........F6	Tullow...........H11	
Rhode............G9	Shanagarry.......F14	Swinford..........D7	Tulsk............E8	
Ring............G13	Shannon..........D11	Swords............J9	Turlough..........D7	
Ringaskiddy......E14	Shannonbridge......F9			
Riverchapel......J11	Shercock..........H7	Taghmon.........H12	Urlingford.......G11	
Riverstick.......E14	Shillelagh.......H11	Tagoat..........J13		
Rochfortbridge......G9	Shinrone.........F10	Tallaght..........J9	Virginia..........G8	
Rockcorry.........H7	Shrule...........D9	Tallow...........F13		
Roosky...........F8	Silvermines......E11	Tandragee.........J6	Warrenpoint.......J7	
Rosbercon.......H12	Sion Mills........G5	Tarbert.........C12	Waterford........G13	
Roscommon.........F8	Sixmilebridge......D11	Templemore.......F11	Watergrasshill......E13	
Roscrea..........F10	Skerries..........J8	Termonfeckin......J8	Waterville.......B14	
Rosscarbery......D15	Slane............H8	Thomastown.......G12	Wellingtonbridge......H13	
Rosses Point......E6	Sligo............E6	Thurles..........F11	Westport.........C8	
Rosslare.........J13	Smithborough......G6	Timahoe.........G10	Wexford..........J12	
Rosslare Harbour......J13	Sneem...........B14	Timoleague.......D15	Whitegate........E14	
Rosslea...........G6	Spanish Point......C11	Tinahely.........J11	Whitehead.........K5	
Rossnowlagh.......E5	Spiddal..........D9	Tipperary........F12	Wicklow..........J10	
Rostrevor.........J7	Sraith Salach......C9	Tobercurry........E7	Woodenbridge......J11	
Roundstone.......B9	Stewartstown......H5	Tobermore.........H4	Woodford.........E10	
Roundwood........J10	Stoneyford.......G12	Toome............H5		
Rush..............J9	Strabane.........G4	Toomevara........F11	Youghal..........F14	
	Stradbally.......G10	Toormore.........C15		
Saintfield........K6	Stradone..........G7	Tower............E14		
St Johnston......G4	Strandhill........E6	Tralee...........C13		
Sallins...........H9	Strangford........K6	Tramore..........G13		
Salthill..........D9	Stranorlar........F5	Trim.............H8		
	Tuam.............D9			

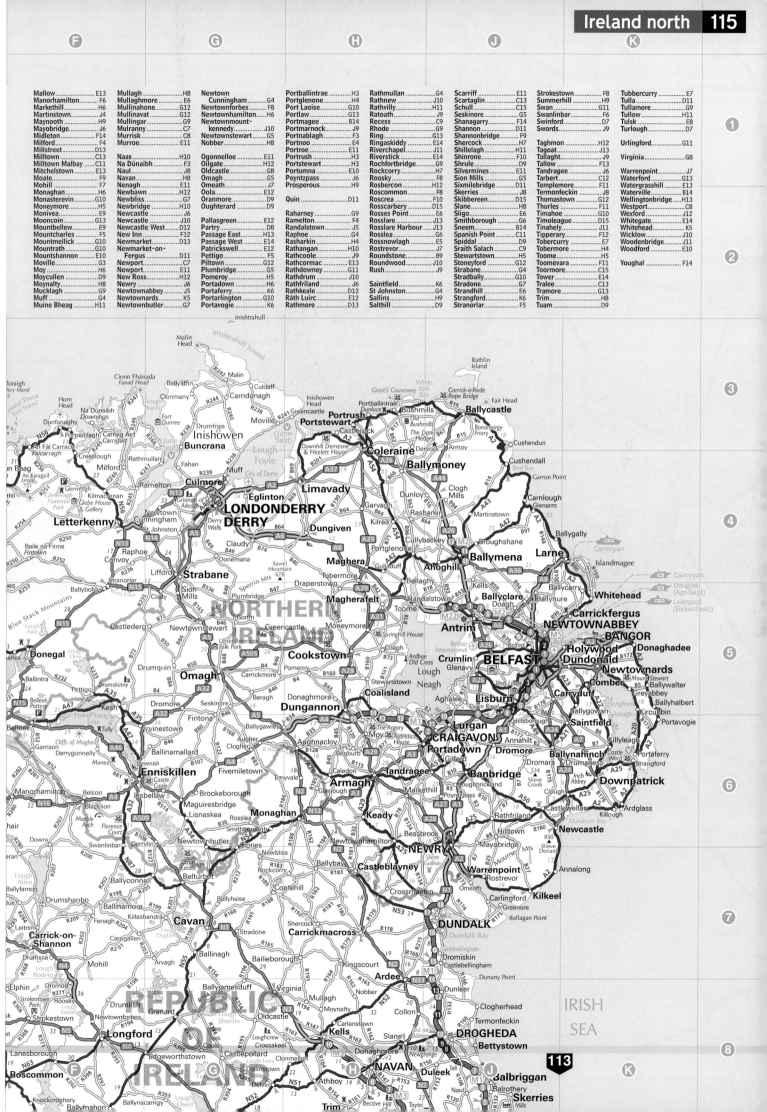

Town plan : Glasgow p.134

St Mary's Island

Whitley Bay C
Links Art Gallery
Whitley Bay
WHITLEY BAY
East Holywell
Holywell
Bates Cottages
Earsdon
Shiremoor
SHIREMOOR
Monkseaton
WEST MONKSEATON
West Monkseaton
MONKSEATON
Murton
NORTHUMBERLAND PARK
West Allotment
New York
North Tyneside General H
Cullercoats
CULLERCOATS
Marden Park Nature Reserve
Marden
Farringdon Rd
Blue Reef
Longsands South
Benton Square
Preston
Tynemouth
West Chirton
NORTH SHIELDS
TYNEMOUTH
King Edwards Bay
Tynemouth Priory & Castle
Billy Mill
Tynemouth C
Stephenson Railway
Willington Square
SILVERLINK ROUNDABOUT
North Tyneside Steam Railway
HOWDON INTERCHANGE
Waterville Road
MEADOW WELL
Meadow Well
NORTH SHIELDS
Arbeia Roman Fort & Museum
The Lawe
Sandhaven
Holy Cross
Willington
Howdon
Percy Main
SOUTH SHIELDS
South Shields
WALLSEND
Willington Quay
East Howdon
Point Pleasant
HADRIAN ROAD
Royal Quays
International Passenger Terminal
Mill Dam
CHICHESTER
Westoe
Cauldwell
Harton
Marsden Rock
Segedunum Roman Fort & Baths
River Tyne
Tyne Tunnel (Electronic Toll)
Tyne Dock
Chichester
JARROW
Jarrow Hall
St Paul's Monastery
East Jarrow
TYNE DOCK
Harton Nook
Marsden
Marsden Bay
Hebburn-Jarrow Colliery
BEDE
Simonside
SIMONSIDE
West Harton
South Tyneside General H
Cleadon Park
Souter Lighthouse & The Leas
Whitburn
Hebburn New Town
HEBBURN
Monkton
Primrose
Primrose
Brockley Whins
BROCKLEY WHINS
South Shields C
Whiteleas
Biddick Hall
Whitburn Coastal Park
Riverside Park
LINDISFARNE ROUNDABOUT
Hedworth
FELLGATE
Cleadon
Whitburn
Fellgate
Boldon Colliery
NEW ROAD
Wardley
West Boldon
East Boldon
EAST BOLDON
South Bents
A184 NEWCASTLE ROAD
TESTOS ROUNDABOUT
Greyhound Stadium
Whitburn Bay
Folingsby
Seaburn
Boldon
Witherwack
Carley Hill
Seaburn
Roker
Downhill
Marley Pots
High Southwick
George Washington
North East Aircraft
Roker
Usworth
Hylton Castle
Castletown
Northern Spire Bridge
Low Southwick
Southwick
Monkwearmouth
STADIUM OF LIGHT
Sunderland Harbour
Concord
Sulgrave
Hylton Plantation
Deptford
Queen Alexandra Bridge
Stadium of Light (Sunderland AFC)
National Glass Centre
Albany
Hertburn
River Wear
Pallion
Ayre's Quay
ST PETER'S
Washington Old Hall
Barmston
South Hylton
SOUTH HYLTON
Pallion
Millfield
MILLFIELD
Bishopwearmouth
SUNDERLAND
Washington Village
Washington Wetland Centre
Ford
Sunderland Royal H
PARK LANE
Hendon
Teal Farm
Pennywell
Sunderland C
SUNDERLAND
UNIVERSITY
Columbia
Biddick
Wearside
High Barnes
Barnes Park
Ashbrooke
Sunderland Eye Infirmary H
Fatfield
Humbledon
Hillview
Grangetown
Mount Pleasant
Hastings Hill
Grindon
Springwell
Plains Farm
Penshaw Monument
Thorney Close
Silksworth Sports Complex & Ski Centre
Penshaw
Herrington Country Park
Middle Herrington
New Silksworth
East Herrington
Silksworth
Shiney Row
New Herrington
Hylton Colliery

NORTH SEA

Amsterdam (IJmuiden)

Street map symbols

Town, port and airport plans

② Motorway and junction	→ One-way, gated/ closed road	━● Railway station	Toilet, with facilities for the less able
④ Primary road single/ dual carriageway and numbered junction	Restricted access road	·········· Preserved or tourist railway	**P** **P** Car park, with electric charging point
37 A road single/ dual carriageway and numbered junction	Pedestrian area	○ Light rapid transit system station	**P+R** Park and Ride (at least 6 days per week)
B road single/ dual carriageway	- - - - Footpath	━┼━ Level crossing	Bus/coach station
Local road single/ dual carriageway	─ ─ ─ Road under construction	●━●━● Tramway	**H** **H** Hospital, 24-hour Accident & Emergency hospital
Other road single/ dual carriageway, minor road	|: : : : :| Road tunnel	✈ Ⓗ Airport, heliport	Beach (award winning)
Building of interest	🗼 Lighthouse	Ⓡ Railair terminal	City wall
Ruined building	✕ Castle	Theatre or performing arts centre	Escarpment
🅘 Tourist Information Centre	✳ Castle mound	Cinema	Cliff lift
🆅 Visitor or heritage centre	• Monument, memorial, statue	✝ Abbey, chapel, church	River/canal, lake
◉ World Heritage Site (UNESCO)	✉ Post Office	✡ Synagogue	Lock, weir
Ⓜ Museum	📖 Public library	☾ Mosque	☼ Viewpoint
♯ English Heritage site	Shopping centre	⚑ Golf course	Park/sports ground
Historic Scotland site	Shopmobility	Racecourse	Cemetery
Cadw (Welsh heritage) site	⚽ Football stadium	Nature reserve	Woodland
National Trust site	🏉 Rugby stadium	Aquarium	Built-up area
National Trust Scotland site	🏏 County cricket ground	Showground	Beach

Central London street map (see pages 142–151)

⊖ London Underground station	⊖ London Overground station
⊖ Docklands Light Railway (DLR) station	Central London Congestion Charge boundary

Royal Parks

Green Park — Park open 5am–midnight. Constitution Hill and The Mall closed to traffic Sundays and public holidays 8am–dusk.

Hyde Park — Park open 5am–midnight. Park roads closed to traffic midnight–5am.

Kensington Gardens — Park open 6am–dusk.

Regent's Park — Park open 5am–dusk. Park roads closed to traffic midnight–7am, except for residents.

St James's Park — Park open 5am–midnight. The Mall closed to traffic Sundays and public holidays 8am–dusk.

Victoria Tower Gardens — Park open dawn–dusk.

Traffic regulations in the City of London include security checkpoints and restrict the number of entry and exit points.

Note: Oxford Street is closed to through-traffic (except buses & taxis) 7am–7pm Monday–Saturday.

Bishopsgate Streetspace Scheme: Temporary traffic restrictions are in operation between Shoreditch and London Bridge, 7am–7pm Monday–Friday. Follow local road signs for changes to permitted routes.

Central London Congestion Charge Zone (CCZ)

You need to pay a £15 daily charge for driving a vehicle on public roads in this central London area. Payment permits entry, travel within and exit from the CCZ by the vehicle as often as required on that day.

The daily charge applies 07:00–18:00 Mon–Fri, 12:00–18:00 Sat–Sun and bank holidays. There is no charge between Christmas Day and New Year's Day bank holiday (inclusive).

For up to date information on the CCZ, exemptions, discounts or ways to pay, visit **tfl.gov.uk/modes/driving/congestion-charge**

Ultra Low Emission Zone (ULEZ)

Most vehicles in Central London, including cars and vans, need to meet minimum exhaust emission standards or drivers must pay a daily charge to drive within the zone. It covers central London and includes the area up to, but not including, the North Circular Road (A406) and South Circular Road (A205). The ULEZ operates 24 hours a day, every day of the year, except Christmas Day (25 December). The charge is £12.50 for motorcycles, cars and vans and is in addition to the Congestion Charge.

For further information visit **tfl.gov.uk/ULEZ**

In addition the Low Emission Zone (LEZ) operates across Greater London, 24 hours every day of the year and is aimed at the most heavy-polluting vehicles. It does not apply to cars or motorcycles. For details visit **tfl.gov.uk/LEZ**

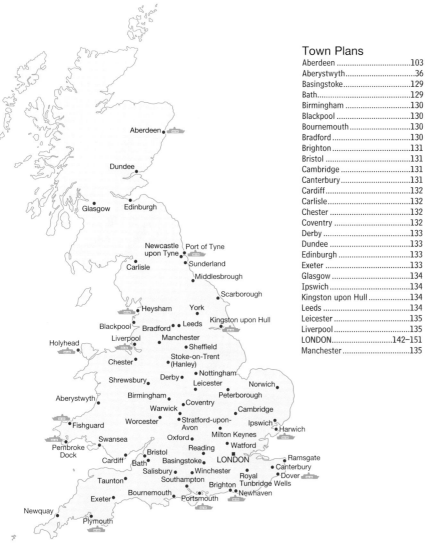

Town Plans

Central London

Basingstoke | Bath

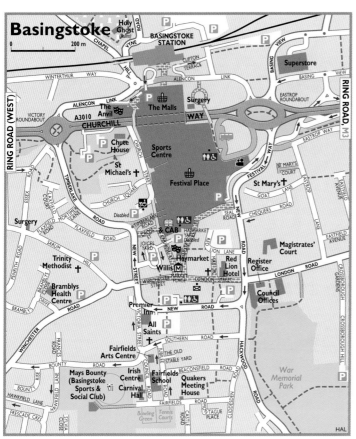

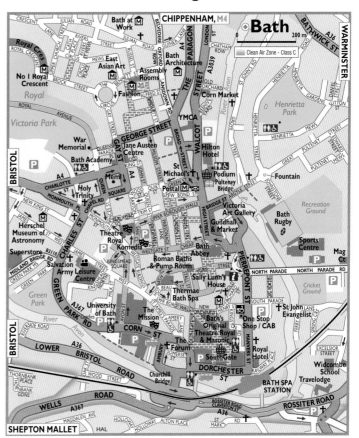

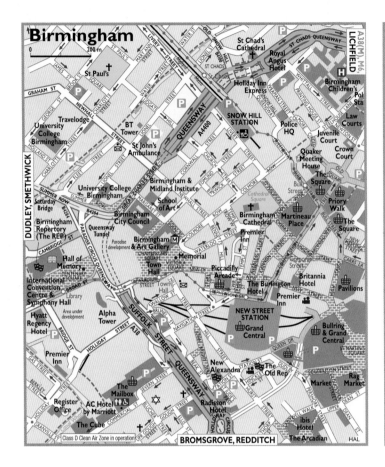

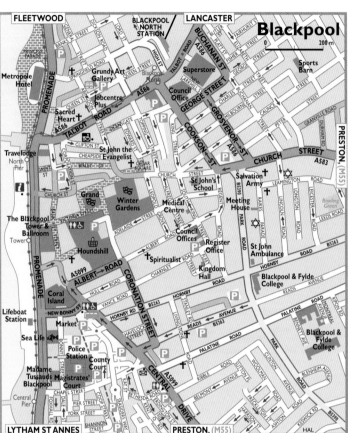

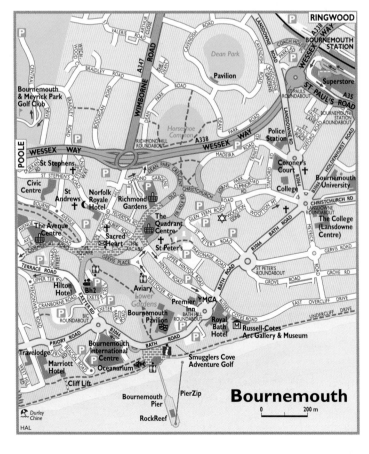

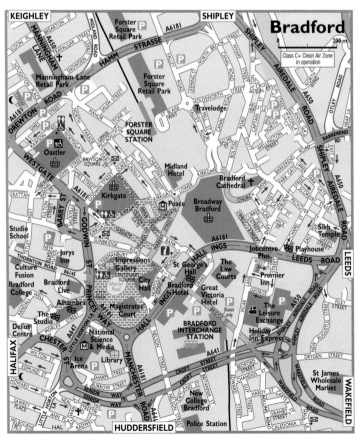

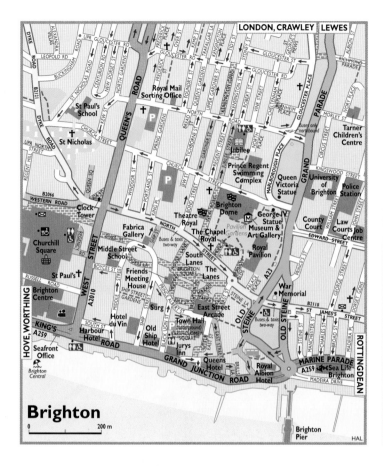

Brighton

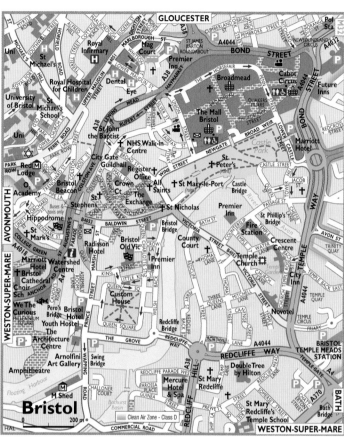

Bristol

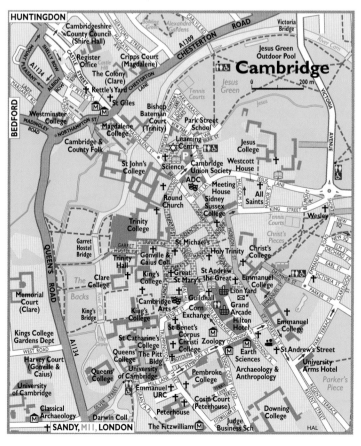

Cambridge

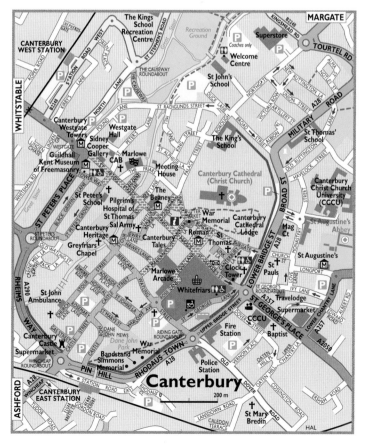

Canterbury

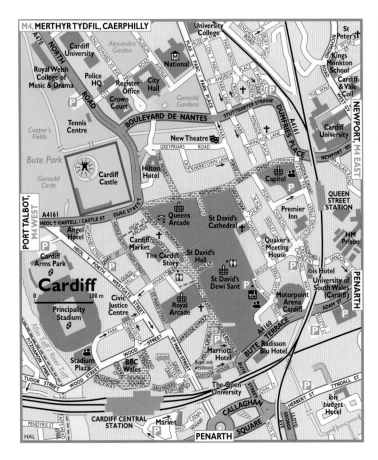

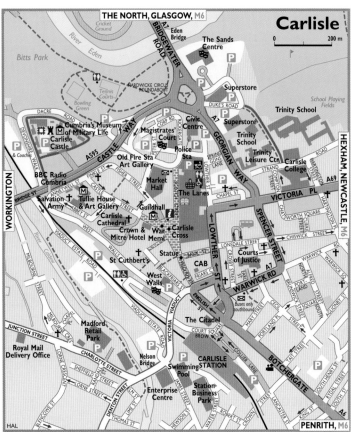

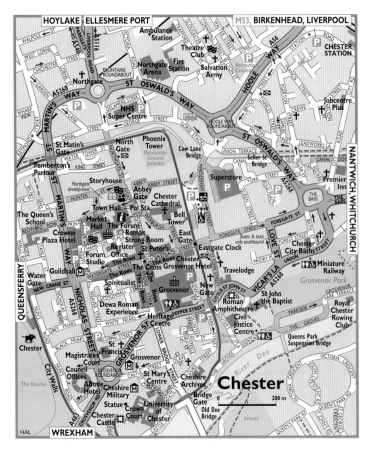

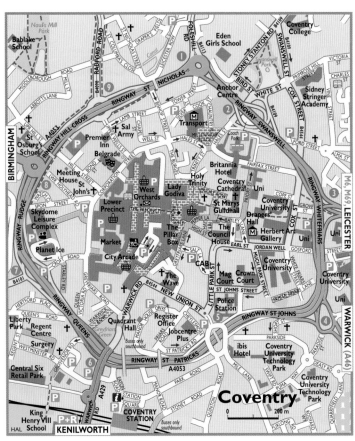

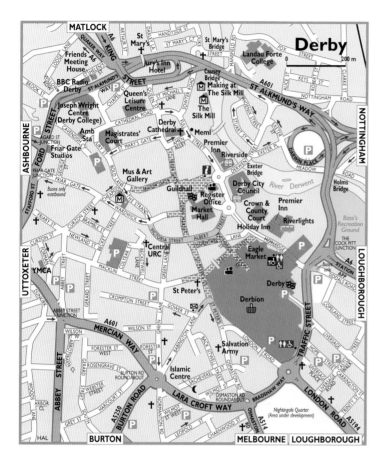

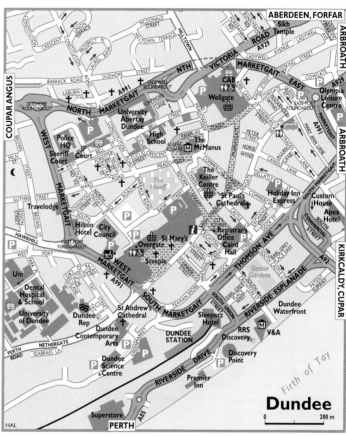

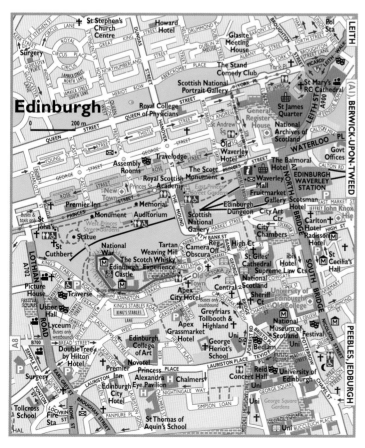

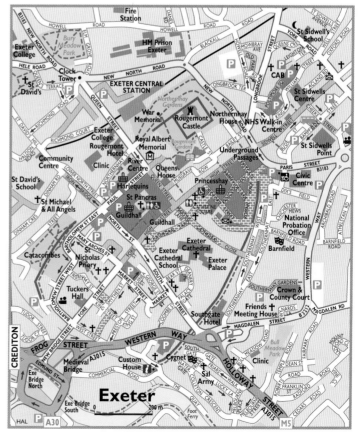

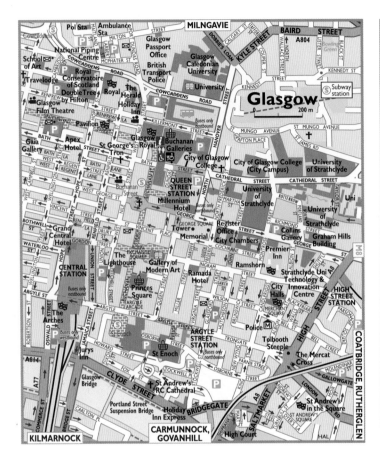

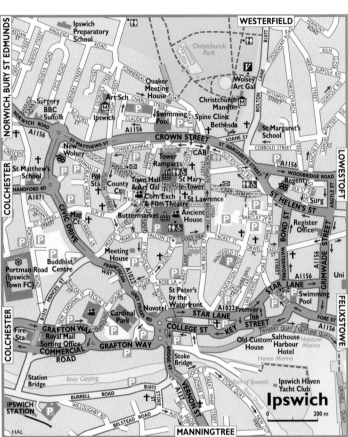

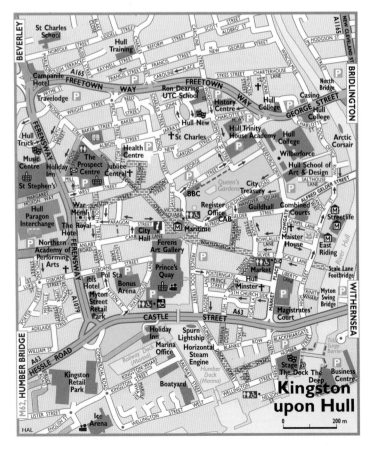

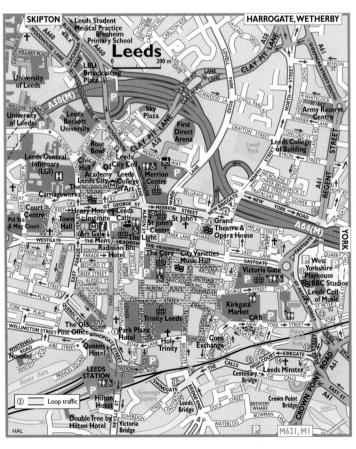

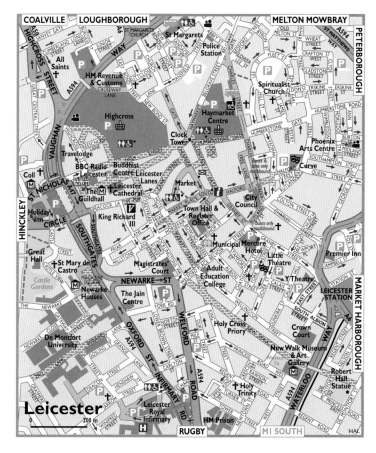

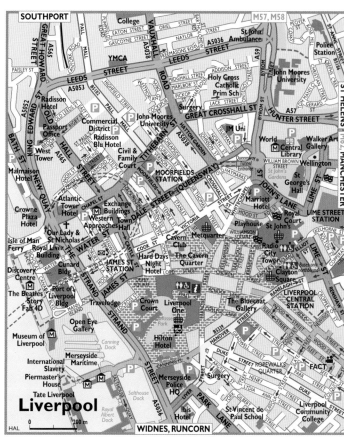

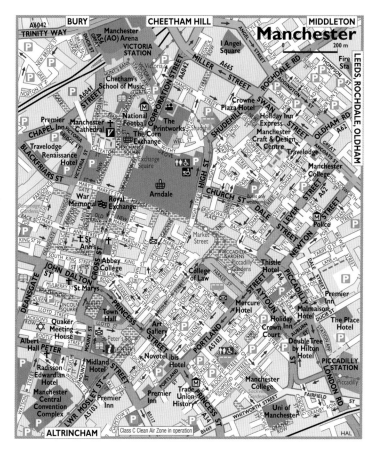

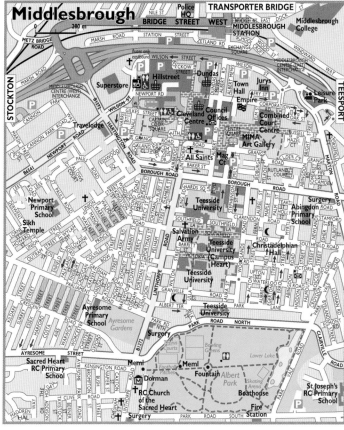

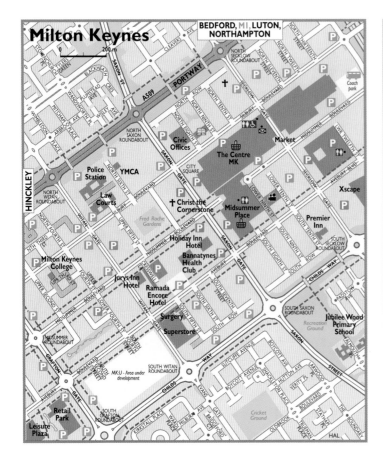

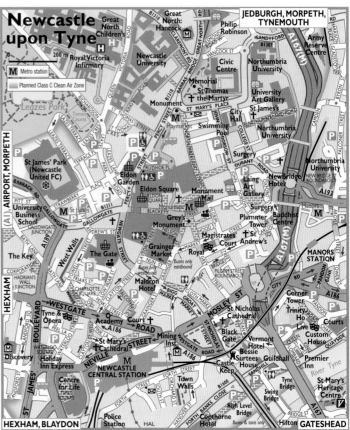

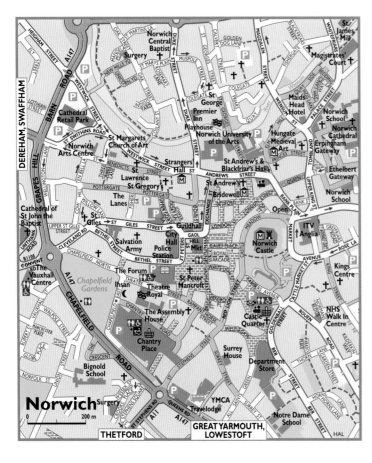

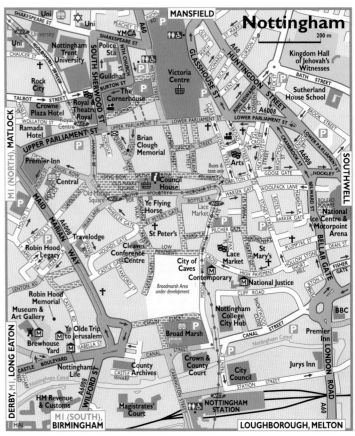

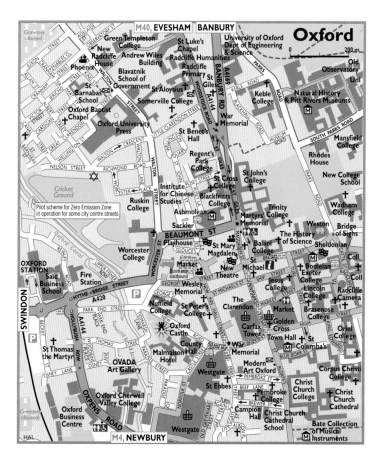

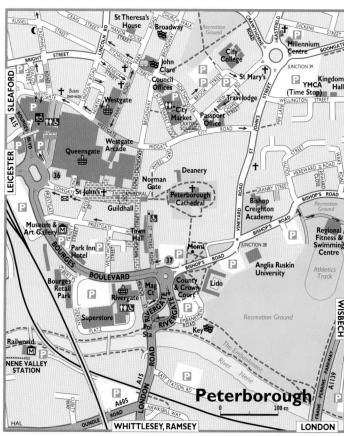

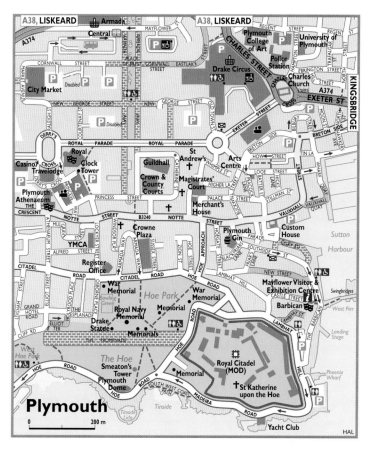

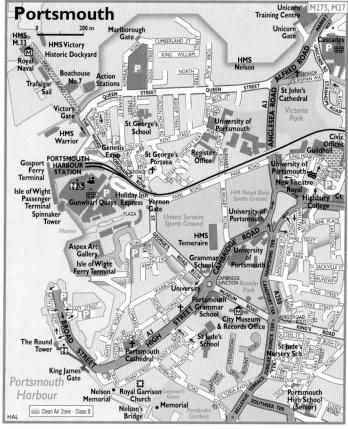

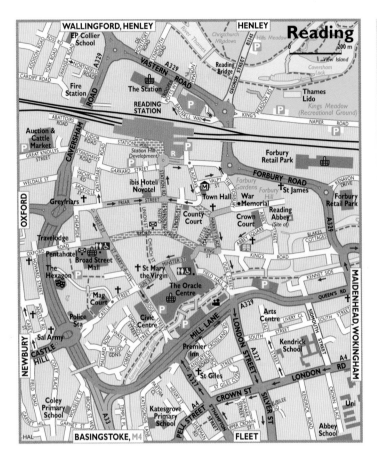

Reading

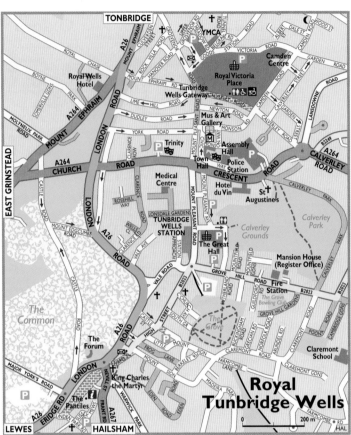

Royal Tunbridge Wells

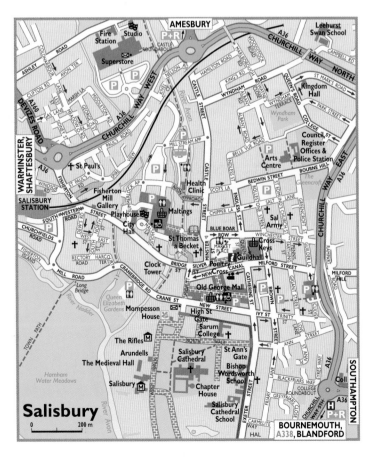

Salisbury

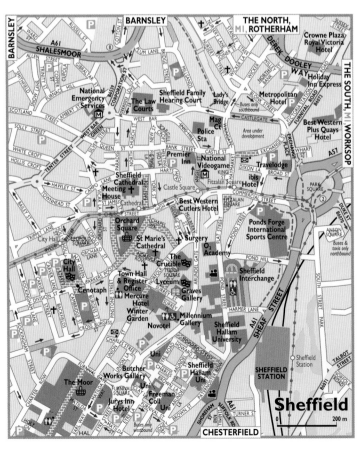

Sheffield

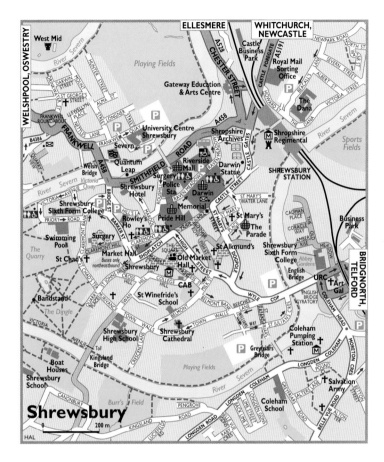

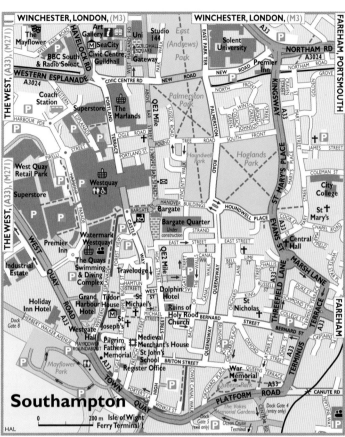

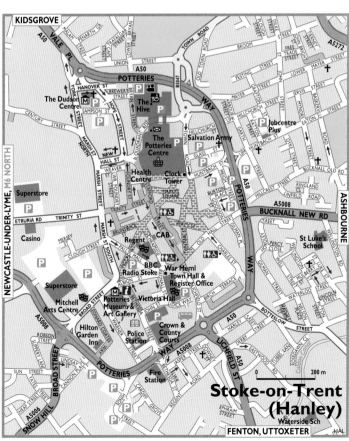

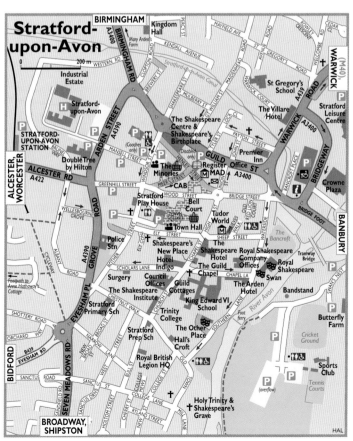

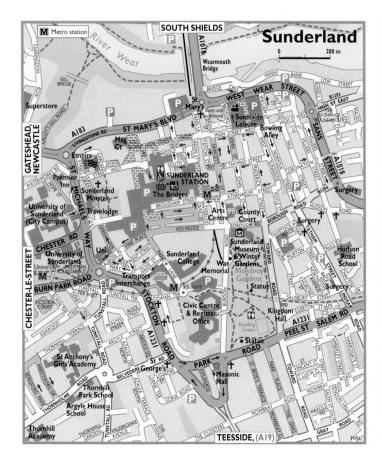

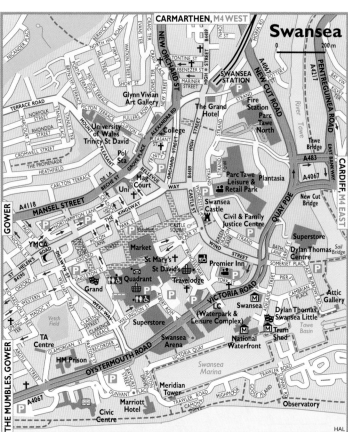

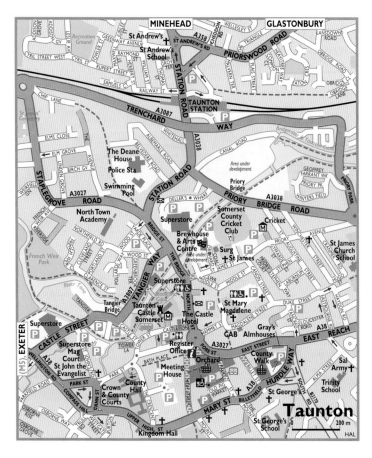

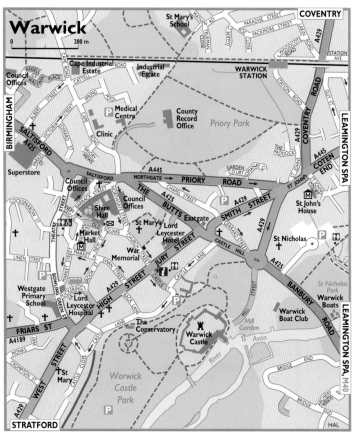

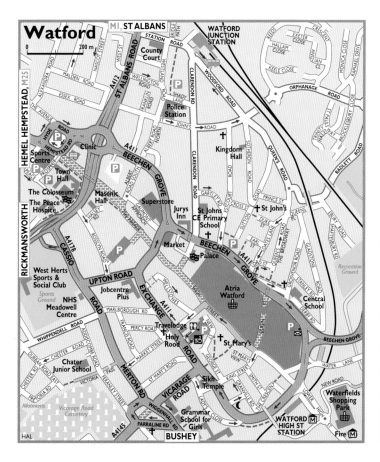

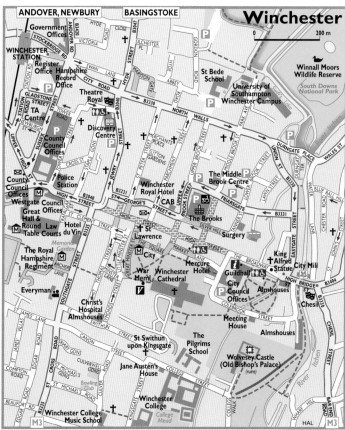

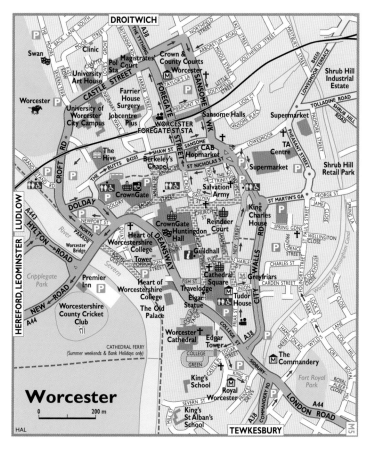

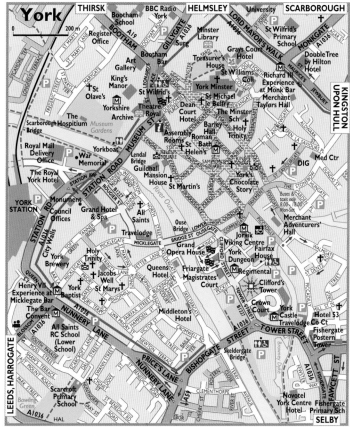

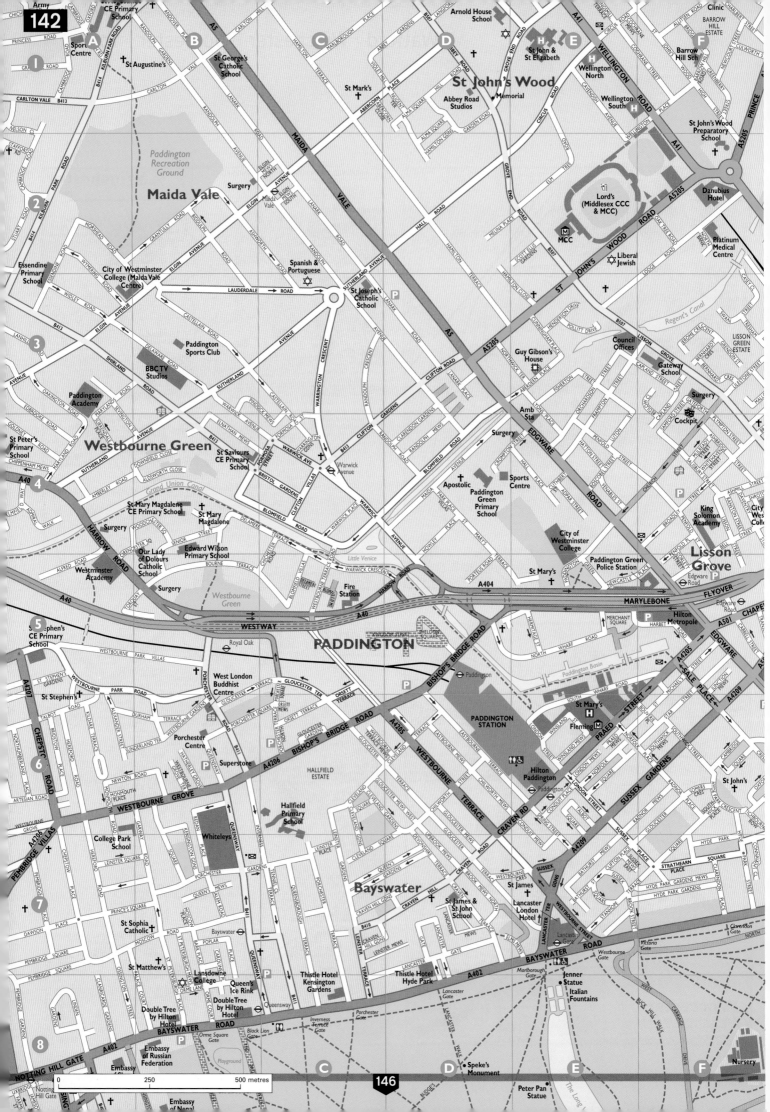

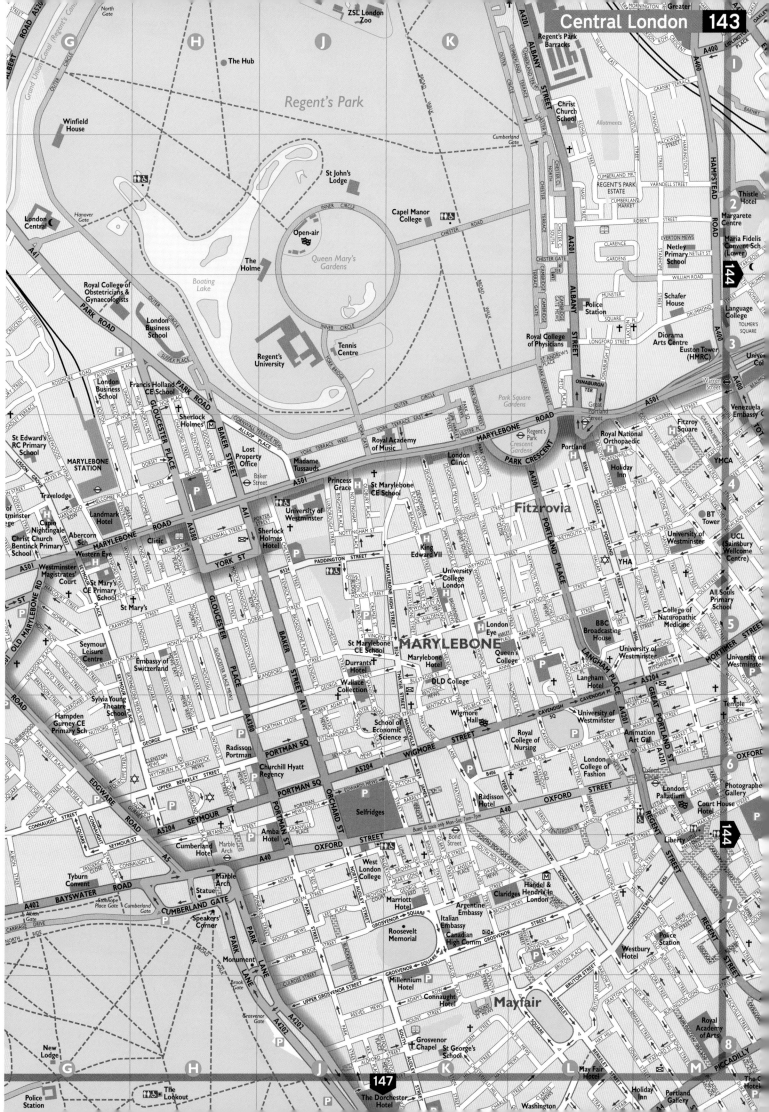

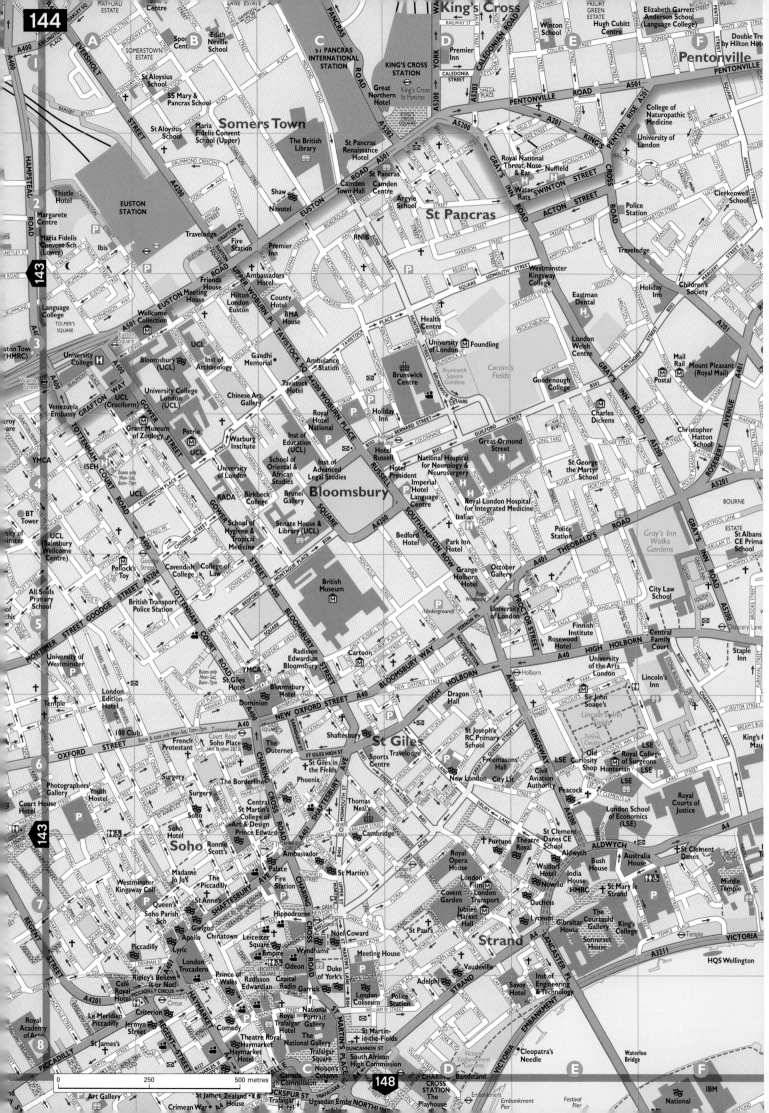

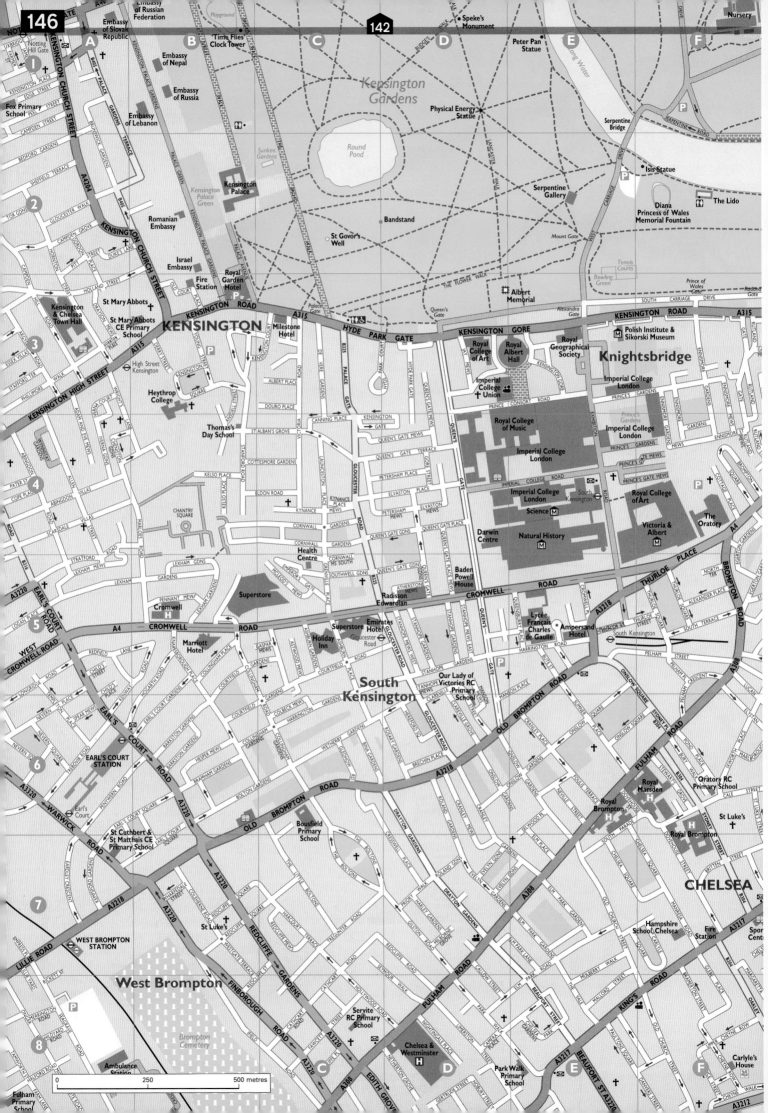

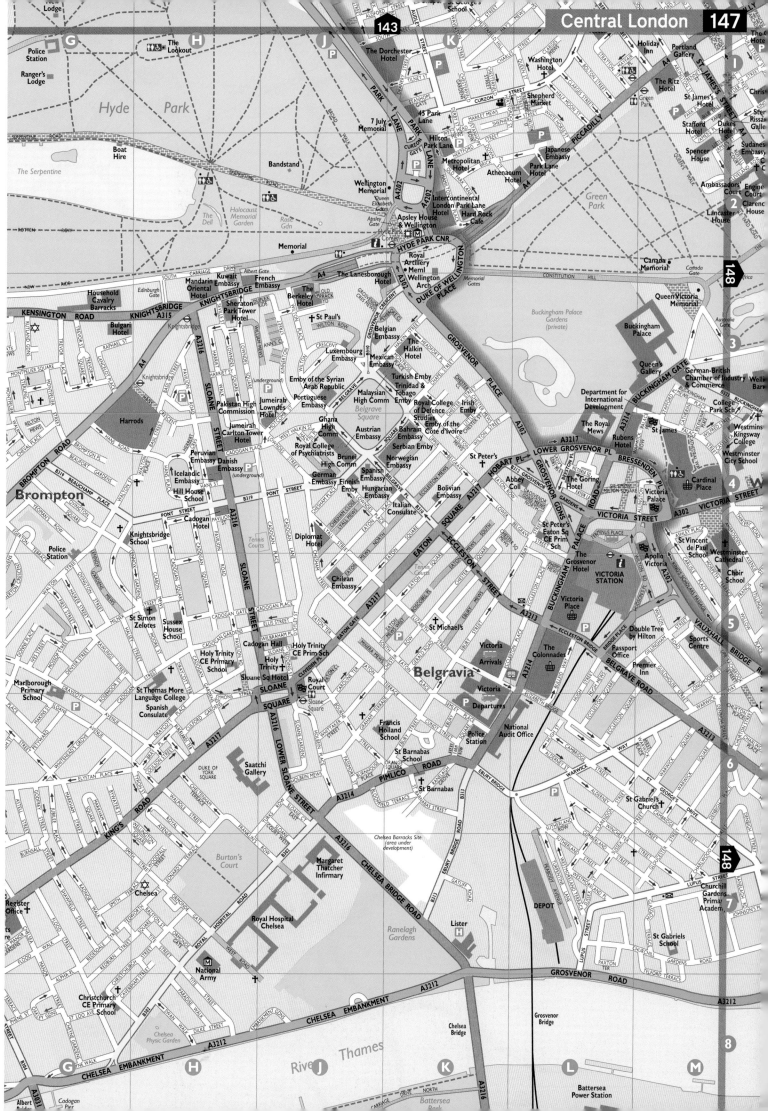

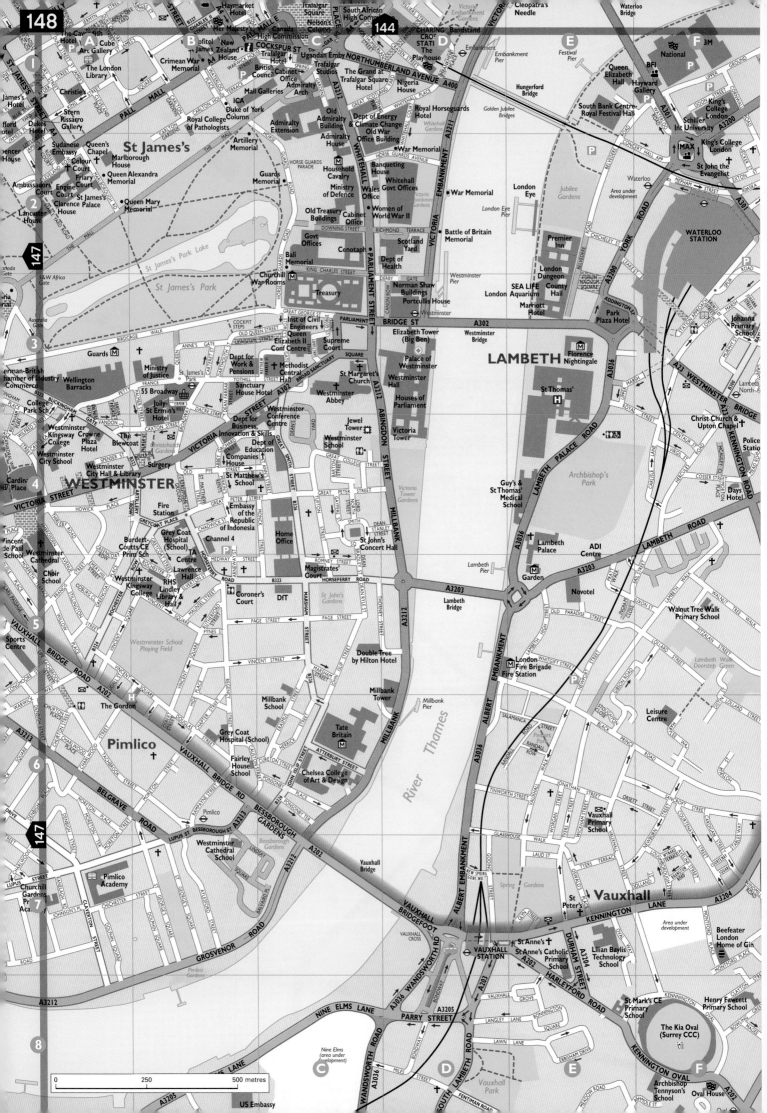

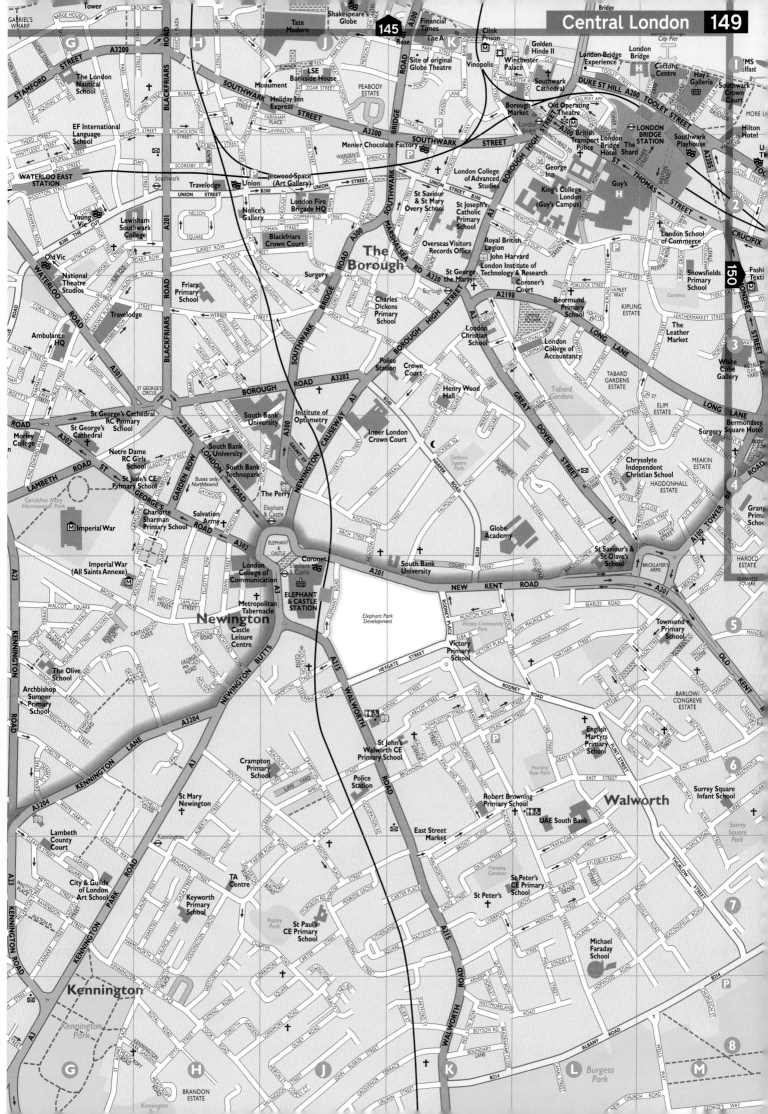

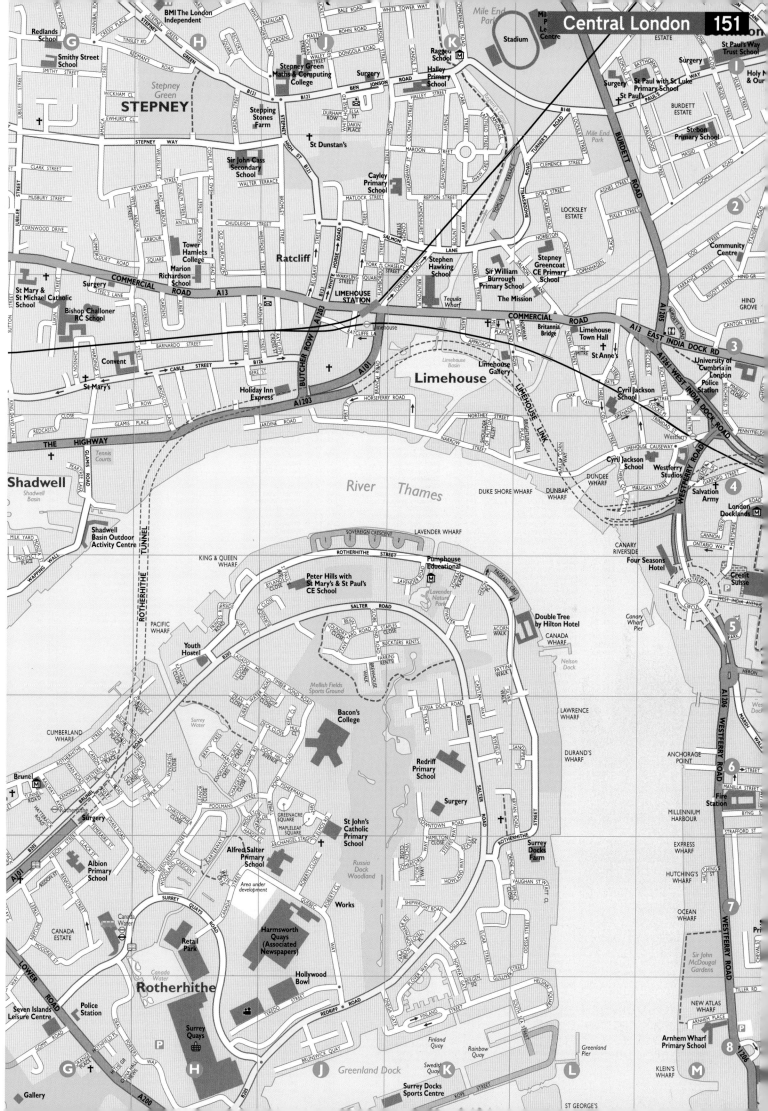

This index lists street and station names, and top places of tourist interest shown in red. Names are listed in alphabetical order and written in full, but may be abbreviated on the map. Each entry is followed by its Postcode District and then the page number and grid reference to the square in which the name is found. Names are asterisked (*) in the index where there is insufficient space to show them on the map.

A

Abbey Gardens NW8......................142 C1
Abbey Orchard Street SW1P......148 B4
Abbey Road NW8.........................142 C1
Abbey Street SE1..........................150 B7
Abchurch Lane EC4N...................145 L7
Abercorn Close NW8....................142 C1
Abercorn Place NW8.....................142 C1
Aberdeen Place NW8....................142 E3
Aberdour Street SE1......................149 M5
Abingdon Road W8.......................146 A4
Abingdon Street SW1P................148 C3
Abingdon Villas W8......................146 A4
Ackroyd Drive E3...........................151 L1
Acorn Walk SE16..........................151 K5
Acton Street WC1X.......................144 E2
Adam and Eve Mews W8..............146 A3
Adam's Row W1K...........................143 K8
Adam Street WC2N.......................144 D8
Addington Street SE1....................148 E3
Addle Hill EC4V.............................145 H7
Adelina Grove E1..........................150 F1
Adeline Place WC1B.....................144 B5
Adler Street E1...............................150 D2
Admiral Place SE16.......................151 K5
Admiral Walk W9..........................142 A4
Adpar Street W2............................142 E4
Agar Street WC2N.........................144 D8
Agdon Street EC1V.......................145 H3
Agnes Street E14...........................151 L2
Ainsty Street SE16........................151 G6
Air Street W1B...............................144 A8
Alaska Street SE1..........................148 F2
Albany Road SE5...........................149 L8
Albany Street NW1........................143 L1
Albemarle Street W1S..................143 L8
Albermarle Way EC1V..................145 H4
Alberta Street SE17.......................149 H6
Albert Bridge SW3........................147 G8
Albert Embankment SE1..............148 D7
Albert Gardens E1.........................151 H3
Albert Gate SW1X.........................147 H2
Albert Place W8.............................146 C3
Albion Gate W2.............................143 G7
Albion Place EC1M.......................145 H4
Albion Street SE16........................151 G7
Albion Street W2............................143 G7
Aldenham Street NW1..................144 A1
Aldermanbury EC2V.....................145 K6
Alderney Mews SE1......................149 K4
Alderney Street SW1V..................147 L6
Aldersgate Street EC1A...............145 J4
Aldford Street W1K.......................143 J8
Aldgate EC3N...............................150 B3
Aldgate ⊖ EC3N...........................150 B3
Aldgate East ⊖ E1........................150 C2
Aldgate High Street EC3N...........150 B3
Aldgate Square EC3N...................150 B3
Aldsworth Close W9.....................142 B4
Aldwych WC2E..............................144 E7
Alexander Place SW7...................146 F5
Alexander Street W2.....................142 A6
Alexandra Gate SW7.....................146 E3
Alfred Mews WC1E.......................144 B4
Alfred Place WC1E........................144 B4
Alfred Road W2..............................142 A5
Alice Street SE1.............................149 M4
Alie Street E1..................................150 C3
Allen Street W8..............................146 A4
Allhallows Lane EC4R..................145 L8
Allington Street SW1E..................147 M4
Allitsen Road NW8........................142 F1
Allsop Place NW1..........................143 H4
Alma Square NW8.........................142 D1
Alpha Place SW3...........................147 G8
Alsace Road SE17.........................149 M7
Alscot Road * SE1.........................150 C8
Alvey Street SE17..........................149 M6
Ambergate Street SE17................149 H7
Amberley Road W9.......................142 A4
Ambrosden Avenue SW1P...........148 A4
Amelia Street SE17........................149 J6
America Square EC3N...................150 B3
America Street SE1........................149 J2
Ampton Street WC1X....................144 E2
Amwell Street EC1R......................144 F2
Anchorage Point E14.....................151 M6
Andover Place NW6......................142 B1
Angel ⊖ N1....................................145 G1
Angela Hooper Place * SW1E.....148 A4
Angel Junction N1.........................145 G1
Angel Lane EC4R..........................145 L8
Angel Street EC1A........................145 J6
Ann Moss Way SE16......................150 F8
Ann's Close SW1X.........................147 J3
Ansdell Street W8..........................146 B4
Antill Terrace E1............................151 H2
Antizan Street E1...........................150 B2
Apple Tree Yard SW1Y.................144 A8
Appold Street EC2A......................145 M4
Apsley Gate W1J...........................147 J2
Apsley House & Wellington
    Museum W1J.............................147 K2
Aquinas Street SE1.......................149 G1
Arbour Square E1..........................151 H2
Archangel Street SE16.................151 J7
Archer Street W1B.........................144 B7
Arch Street SE1.............................149 J4
Arden Estate N1.............................145 M1
Argyle Square WC1H....................144 D2
Argyle Street WC1H......................144 D2
Argyll Road W8..............................146 A3
Argyll Street W1F...........................143 M6
Arlington Street SW1A..................147 M1
Arlington Way EC1R.....................145 G2
Arne Street WC2H........................144 D6
Arneway Street SW1P...................148 B5
Arnhem Place E14........................151 M8
Arnold Estate SE1.........................150 C7
Arnside Street SE17......................149 K8
Artesian Road W11.......................142 A6
Arthur Street EC4V.......................145 L7
Artichoke Hill E1W........................150 E4
Artillery Lane E1............................150 A1
Artillery Row SW1P......................148 B4
Arundel Street WC2R....................144 F7

Ashbridge Street NW8.................142 F4
Ashburn Gardens SW7.................146 C5
Ashburn Place SW7......................146 C5
Ashby Street EC1V.......................145 H2
Asher Way E1W.............................150 D4
Ashfield Street E1..........................150 E2
Ashford Street N1..........................145 M2
Ashley Place SW1P.......................147 M4
Ashmill Street NW1......................142 F4
Ashmole Street SW8.....................148 F8
Ashworth Road W9.......................142 B2
Assam Street E1.............................150 C2
Assembly Passage * E1................151 G1
Astell Street SW3...........................147 G6
Aston Street E14............................151 K1
Astwood Mews SW7......................146 C5
Atherstone Mews SW7.................146 D5
Atterbury Street SW1P.................148 C6
Attneave Street WC1X..................144 F3
Augustus Street NW1....................143 L1
Aulton Place SE11.........................149 G7
Austin Friars EC2N........................145 L6
Australia Gate SW1A.....................147 M3
Austral Street SE11.......................149 H5
Aveline Street SE11.......................148 F7
Ave Maria Lane EC1A...................145 H6
Avenue Dock Hill SE16................151 J6
Avery Farm Row SW1W...............147 K6
Avery Row W1K.............................143 L7
Aybrook Street W1U......................143 J5
Aylesbury Road SE17...................149 L7
Aylesbury Street EC1R.................145 H4
Aylesford Street SW1V..................148 B7
Aylward Street E1..........................151 G2
Ayres Street SE1............................149 K2

B

Babmaes Street SW1Y..................144 B8
Bache's Street N1...........................145 L2
Back Church Lane E1....................150 D3
Back Hill EC1R..............................145 G4
Bacon Grove SE1..........................150 B8
Bainbridge Street WC1A..............144 C6
Bakers Mews W1U........................143 J6
Baker's Row EC1R........................145 G4
Baker Street NW1.........................143 H4
Baker Street W1U..........................143 J5
Baker Street ⊖ W1U.....................143 H4
Balcombe Street NW1..................143 G3
Balderton Street W1K...................143 J7
Baldwin's Gardens EC1N.............144 F5
Baldwin Street EC1V....................145 L2
Bale Road E1..................................151 J1
Balfe Street N1...............................144 D1
Balfour Mews W1K........................143 K8
Balfour Place W1K.........................143 J8
Balfour Street SE17.......................149 K5
Baltic Street East EC1Y................145 J3
Baltic Street West EC1Y...............145 J4
Balvaird Place SW1V....................148 C7
Bank ⊖ EC2R...............................145 L6
Bank End SE1................................149 K1
Bankside SE1.................................145 J8
Banner Street EC1Y......................145 K3
Banyard Road SE16......................150 B8
Barbican ⊖ EC1A.........................145 J4
Barbican Estate EC2Y..................145 J5
Barge House Street SE1...............149 G1
Bark Place W2...............................142 B7
Barkston Gardens SW5................146 B6
Barley Corn Way E14....................151 L4
Barlow/Congreve Estate SE17....149 M5
Barlow Place W1J.........................143 L7
Barlow Street SE17.......................149 L5
Barnardo Street E1.......................151 H3
Barnby Street NW1.......................144 A1
Barnes Street E14.........................151 J2
Barnham Street SE1......................150 A6
Baron's Place SE1.........................149 G3
Baron Street N1.............................145 G1
Barrett Street W1U........................143 K6
Barrow Hill Estate NW8...............142 F1
Barrow Hill Road NW8.................142 F1
Barter Street WC1A......................144 D5
Bartholomew Close EC1A............145 J5
Bartholomew Lane EC2R.............145 L6
Bartholomew Street SE1...............149 L5
Bartlett Court EC4A......................145 G6
Barton Street SW1P......................148 C4
Basil Street SW3............................147 H4
Basin Approach E14......................151 J3
Basinghall Avenue EC2V.............145 K5
Basinghall Street EC2V................145 K5
Bastwick Street EC1V...................145 J3
Bateman's Buildings W1D...........144 B6
Bateman Street W1D.....................144 B6
Bath Street EC1V..........................145 K2
Bath Terrace SE1..........................149 J4
Bathurst Mews W2........................142 E7
Bathurst Street W2........................142 E7
Battle Bridge Lane SE1................149 M1
Batty Street E1...............................150 D2
Bayley Street WC1B......................144 B5
Baylis Road SE1.............................148 F3
Bayswater ⊖ W2...........................142 B7
Bayswater Road W2......................142 B8
Baythorne Street E3......................151 L1
Beaconsfield Road SE17..............149 M7
Beak Street W1F............................144 A7
Bear Gardens SE1.........................145 J8
Bear Lane SE1...............................149 H1
Beauchamp Place SW3................147 G4
Beaufort Gardens SW3.................147 G4
Beaufort Street SW3......................146 E8
Beaumont Place W1T....................144 A3
Beaumont Street W1G..................143 K4
Beccles Street E14........................151 M3
Beckett Street SE1........................149 L3
Beckway Street SE17....................149 M6
Bedale Street SE1.........................149 L1
Bedford Avenue WC1B.................144 C5
Bedfordbury WC2N.......................144 C7
Bedford Gardens W8....................146 A2
Bedford Place WC1N...................144 D4

Bedford Row WC1R......................144 E4
Bedford Square WC1B.................144 B5
Bedford Street WC2E....................144 D7
Bedford Way WC1H.....................144 C3
Bedlow Close NW8......................142 F3
Beech Street EC2Y........................145 J4
Beeston Place SW1W...................147 L4
Belgrave Mews North * SW1X.....147 J3
Belgrave Mews South * SW1X.....147 K4
Belgrave Place SW1X...................147 J4
Belgrave Road SW1V....................147 L5
Belgrave Road SW1V....................148 A6
Belgrave Square SW1X................147 J3
Belgrave Street E1.........................151 J2
Belgrove Street WC1H.................144 D2
Bell Lane E1...................................150 B1
Bell Street NW1.............................142 F4
Bell Yard WC2A.............................144 F6
Belvedere Road SE1.....................148 E2
Benjamin Street EC1M.................145 H4
Ben Jonson Road E1.....................151 J1
Bennett Street SW1A....................147 M1
Ben Smith Way SE16....................150 D7
Benson Quay E1W........................151 F4
Bentinck Mews W1U....................143 K6
Bentinck Street W1U.....................143 K6
Bere Street E1W............................151 H3
Bergen Square SE16.....................151 K8
Berkeley Mews W1H.....................143 H6
Berkeley Square W1J....................143 L8
Berkeley Street W1J......................143 L8
Bermondsey ⊕ ⊖ SE16...............150 E7
Bermondsey Spa SE16.................150 C8
Bermondsey Square SE1..............150 A8
Bermondsey Street SE1................150 A6
Bermondsey Wall East SE16........150 E7
Bermondsey Wall Estate SE16....150 D7
Bermondsey Wall West SE16......150 C6
Bernard Street WC1N...................144 D4
Berners Mews W1T.......................144 A5
Berners Place W1F........................144 A6
Berners Street W1T.......................144 A5
Bernhardt Crescent NW8.............142 F3
Berryfield Road SE17....................149 J6
Berry Street EC1V.........................145 H3
Berwick Street W1F.......................144 A6
Bessborough Gardens SW1V.......148 C6
Bessborough Street SW1V...........148 B6
Betterton Street WC2H.................144 D6
Bevenden Street N1......................145 L2
Bevin Close SE16.........................151 J5
Bevington Street SE16.................150 D7
Bevin Way WC1X..........................144 F1
Bevis Marks EC3A........................150 A2
Bewley Street E1...........................150 F3
Bickenhall Street W1U.................143 H4
Bidborough Street WC1H.............144 C2
Biddulph Road W9.......................142 B2
Big Ben (Elizabeth Tower) SW1A...148 D3
Bigland Street E1..........................150 E3
Billiter Square EC3M....................150 A3
Billiter Street EC3M......................150 A3
Bina Gardens SW5.......................146 C6
Bingham Place W1U.....................143 J4
Binney Street W1K........................143 K7
Birchfield Street E14.....................151 M3
Birchin Lane EC3V.......................145 L7
Birdcage Walk SW1H...................148 A3
Birde Lane EC4Y...........................145 H6
Bird Street W1C............................143 K6
Birkenhead Street N1...................144 D1
Bishop's Bridge Road W2............142 C6
Bishopsgate EC2M.......................150 A2
Bishops Square E1........................150 B1
Bishop's Terrace SE11.................149 G5
Bittern Street SE1..........................149 J3
Blackall Street EC2A....................145 M3
Blackburne's Mews W1K.............143 J7
Blackfriars ⊕ ⊖ EC4V................145 H7
Blackfriars Bridge SE1.................145 H8
Blackfriars Road SE1....................149 H3
Blackhorse Court SE1...................149 L4
Black Lion Gate W2.....................142 B8
Black Prince Road SE11..............148 E6
Blackwood Street SE17................149 K6
Blandford Street W1U...................143 H5
Blenheim Street W1S....................143 L7
Bletchley Street N1.......................145 K1
Blomfield Mews W2......................142 C5
Blomfield Road W2......................142 C5
Blomfield Street EC2M.................145 M5
Blomfield Villas W2.......................142 C5
Bloomfield Terrace SW1W...........147 J6
Bloomsbury Square WC1A..........144 D5
Bloomsbury Street WC1B.............144 C5
Bloomsbury Way WC1A...............144 C5
Blount Street E14..........................151 K2
Blue Ball Yard SW1A....................147 M1
Bohn Road E1...............................151 J1
Bolsover Street W1W....................143 L4
Bolton Gardens SW5....................146 B6
Bolton Street W1J.........................147 L1
Bond Street ⊖ W1C......................143 K6
Bondway SW8...............................148 D8
Bonhill Street EC2A......................145 L4
Bonnington Square SW8..............148 B8
Boot Street N1...............................145 M2
Borough ⊖ SE1.............................149 K3
Borough High Street SE1.............149 K3
Borough Road SE1.......................149 H3
Boscobel Place SW1W.................147 K5
Boscobel Street NW8...................142 E4
Boss Street SE1.............................150 B6
Boston Place NW1........................143 G3
Botolph Lane EC3R......................145 M7
Boundary Lane SE17....................149 K8
Boundary Row SE1.......................149 G2
Bourdon Street W1K.....................143 L7
Bourlet Close W1W.......................143 M5
Bourne Estate EC1N.....................144 F4
Bourne Street SW1W....................147 J6
Bourne Terrace W2.......................142 B5
Bouverie Place W2........................142 F6
Bouverie Street EC4Y...................145 G6
Bowland Yard * SW1X..................147 J3
Bow Lane EC4M...........................145 K6

Bowling Green Lane EC1R..........145 G3
Bowling Green Place SE1............149 L2
Bowling Green Street SE11..........148 F8
Bowling Green Walk N1...............145 M2
Bowsell Street WC1N....................144 D4
Bow Street WC2E..........................144 D7
Boyd Street E1...............................150 D3
Boyfield Street SE1.......................149 H3
Boyle Street W1S..........................143 M7
Boyson Road SE17.......................149 K8
Brackley Street EC1Y...................145 J4
Bradenham Close SE17................149 K8
Brad Street SE1.............................149 G2
Braganza Street SE17...................149 H7
Braham Street E1..........................150 C3
Bramerton Street SW3..................146 F7
Bramham Gardens SW5...............146 B6
Branch Road E14..........................151 J3
Brandon Estate SE17....................149 H8
Brandon Street SE17....................149 K6
Brangton Road SE11....................148 F7
Bray Crescent SE16......................151 H6
Bray Place SW3.............................147 H6
Bread Street EC4M.......................145 K7
Bream's Buildings EC4A..............144 F6
Brechin Place SW7.......................146 D6
Breezer's Hill E1W........................150 D4
Brendon Street W1H.....................143 G5
Bressenden Place SW1W.............147 L4
Brettell Street SE17.......................149 L7
Brewers Green SW1H..................148 A3
Brewer Street W1F........................144 A7
Brewhouse Lane E1W..................151 F6
Brick Court WC2R........................144 F7
Brick Lane E1................................150 C1
Brick Street W1J...........................147 K2
Bridewell Place EC4V..................145 H7
Bridgeman Street NW8................142 F1
Bridge Place SW1V.......................147 L5
Bridgeport Place E1W..................150 D4
Bridge Street SW1A......................148 D3
Bridgewater Street EC2Y.............145 J4
Bridgeway Street NW1.................144 A1
Bridle Lane W1F...........................144 A7
Bridstow Place W2........................142 A6
Bridlingsea Place E14..................151 L4
Brill Place NW1.............................144 C1
Briset Street EC1M.......................145 H4
Bristol Gardens W9......................142 B4
Britannia Street WC1X.................144 E2
Britannia Walk N1.........................145 L2
Britannia Way SW1X....................145 L2
Britten Street SW3.........................146 F7
Britton Street EC1M......................145 H4
Broadbent Street W1K..................143 L7
Broadgate Circle EC2M...............145 M5
Broadley Street NW8....................142 F4
Broadley Terrace NW1.................142 F4
Broadstone Place W1U.................143 J5
Broad Walk NW1..........................143 K1
Broad Walk W2.............................143 H7
Broadwall SE1...............................149 G1
Broadway SW1H...........................148 B4
Broadwick Street W1F..................144 A7
Brockham Street SE1....................149 K4
Brodlove Lane E1W......................151 H3
Bromley Street E1..........................151 J2
Brompton Place SW3....................147 G4
Brompton Road SW3....................147 G4
Brompton Road SW3....................146 F5
Brompton Square SW3.................146 F4
Bronti Close SE17.........................149 K7
Brook Drive SE11..........................149 G5
Brooke Street EC1N.....................144 F5
Brook Gate W2..............................143 H8
Brook Mews North W2.................142 D7
Brook's Mews W1K.......................143 K7
Brook Street W1K..........................143 K7
Brook Street W2............................142 E7
Brown Heart Gardens W1K.........143 K7
Browning Mews W1G...................143 K5
Browning Street SE17...................149 K6
Brownlow Mews WC1N................144 E4
Brownlow Street WC1V................144 E5
Brown Street W1H.........................143 G6
Brunel Road SE16........................151 G6
Brune Street E1.............................150 B1
Brunswick Close SE1....................150 A6
Brunswick Gardens W8................146 A1
Brunswick Place N1......................145 L2
Brunswick Quay SE16..................151 J8
Brunswick Square WC1N.............144 D3
Brunswick Street WC1N...............144 D3
Brunton Place E14.........................151 K3
Brushfield Street E1......................150 B1
Bruton Lane W1J..........................143 L8
Bruton Place W1J..........................143 L7
Bruton Street W1J.........................143 L8
Bryan Road SE16.........................151 K6
Bryanstone Mews West W1H.......143 G5
Bryanston Mews East W1H..........143 H5
Bryanston Place W1H...................143 G5
Bryanston Square W1H................143 H5
Bryanston Street W1C...................143 H7
Buck Hill Walk W2........................142 E8
Buckingham Gate SW1E..............147 L3
Buckingham Mews SW1E.............147 M3
Buckingham Palace SW1A...........147 L3
Buckingham Palace Road SW1W...147 L5
Buckingham Street WC2N...........144 M4
Buckland Street N1.......................145 L1
Buckle Street E1............................150 C2
Bucknall Street WC2H..................144 C6
Buckters Rents SE16....................151 J5
Budge's Walk W2..........................146 D2
Bulleid Way SW1V........................147 L5
Bulstrode Street W1U...................143 K5
Bunhill Row EC1Y.........................145 L3
Burdett Estate E14........................151 M1
Burdett Road E14..........................151 L2
Burdett Street SE1.........................148 F3
Burgess Street E14.......................151 M1
Burge Street SE1...........................149 L4
Burlington Arcade W1J.................143 M8
Burlington Gardens W1S..............143 M8
Burnhouse Place SW1V...............147 J6
Burnsall Street SW3......................147 G7

Burnside Close SE16...................151 J5
Burrell Street SE1..........................149 H1
Burslem Street E1.........................150 D3
Burton Grove SE17.......................149 L7
Burton Street WC1H.....................144 C3
Burwood Place W2.......................143 G6
Bury Close SE16...........................151 H5
Bury Court EC3A..........................150 A2
Bury Place WC1A.........................144 D5
Bury Street EC3A..........................150 A2
Bury Street SW1Y.........................148 A1
Bury Walk SW3.............................146 F6
Bushell Street E1W.......................150 D5
Bush Lane EC4V...........................145 L7
Butcher Row E1............................151 J3
Bute Street SW7............................146 E5
Butler Place SW1H.......................148 B4
Butler's Wharf SE1........................150 C6
Buttesland Street N1....................145 L2
Byefield Close SE16.....................151 K6
Bylands Close SE16.....................151 J5
Byng Place WC1E........................144 B4
Byng Street E14............................151 M6
Byward Street EC3R.....................150 A4
Bywater Place SE16......................151 K5
Bywater Street SW3......................147 G6

C

Cabbell Street NW1.....................142 F5
Cable Street E1..............................150 F3
Cadiz Street SE17.........................149 K7
Cadogan Gardens SW3................147 H5
Cadogan Gate SW1X...................147 H5
Cadogan Lane SW1X...................147 J4
Cadogan Place SW1X..................147 J4
Cadogan Square SW1X...............147 H5
Cadogan Street SW3....................147 G6
Caledonian Road N1....................144 D1
Caledonia Street N1.....................144 D1
Cale Street SW3............................146 F6
Callow Street SW3........................146 D7
Calshot Street N1..........................144 E1
Calthorpe Street WC1X................144 E3
Cambridge Circus WC2H............144 C7
Cambridge Gardens NW6...........142 A1
Cambridge Gate NW1.................143 L3
Cambridge Road NW6.................142 A1
Cambridge Road NW6.................142 A2
Cambridge Square W2.................142 F6
Cambridge Terrace NW1.............147 L6
Cambridge Terrace NW1.............143 L2
Cambridge Terrace Mews NW1...143 L3
Camdenhurst Street E14..............151 K2
Camera Place SW10.....................146 D8
Camomile Street EC3A.................150 A2
Campden Grove W8.....................146 A2
Campden Hill Road W8................146 A2
Campden Street W8......................146 A1
Camperdown Street E1.................150 C3
Canada Estate SE16.....................151 G7
Canada Gate SW1A......................147 M3
Canada Street SE16.....................151 H7
Canada Water ⊖ ⊕ SE16............151 G7
Canada Wharf SE16.....................151 L5
Canal Street SE5...........................149 L8
Canary Riverside E14...................151 L4
Candle Street E1............................151 K1
Canning Place W8........................146 C4
Cannon Drive E14.........................151 M4
Cannon Street EC4N....................145 K7
Cannon Street ⇄ ⊖ EC4R............145 K7
Cannon Street Road E1................150 E3
Canon Beck Road SE16...............151 G6
Canon Row SW1A........................148 D3
Canton Street E14.........................151 M3
Capeners Close * SW1X..............147 J3
Capland Street NW8....................142 E3
Capper Street WC1E....................144 A4
Capstan Way SE16.......................151 K5
Carbis Road E14...........................151 L2
Carburton Street W1W.................143 L4
Cardigan Street SE11...................148 F6
Cardington Street NW1................144 A2
Carey Street WC2A.......................144 F6
Carlisle Avenue EC3N..................150 B3
Carlisle Lane SE1..........................148 E4
Carlisle Place SW1P.....................147 M5
Carlisle Street W1D.......................144 B6
Carlos Place W1K.........................143 K7
Carlton Gardens SW1Y................148 B2
Carlton Hill NW6..........................142 B1
Carlton House Terrace SW1Y......148 B1
Carlton Street W1J........................147 L1
Carlton Vale NW6.........................142 A1
Carlton Vale NW6.........................142 B1
Carlyle Square SW3......................146 F7
Carmelite Street EC4Y.................145 G7
Carnaby Street W1F......................143 M7
Caroline Place W2........................142 B7
Caroline Street E1.........................151 H3
Caroline Terrace SW1W...............147 J5
Carpenter Street W1K..................143 K7
Carrington Street W1J..................147 L1
Carr Street E14..............................151 K1
Carteret Street SW1H...................148 B3
Carter Lane EC4V.........................145 H7
Carter Place SE17.........................149 K7
Carter Street SE17........................149 J7
Carthusian Street EC1M...............145 J4
Carting Lane WC2R......................144 D8
Cartwright Gardens WC1H..........144 C2
Cartwright Street E1......................150 C4
Casey Close NW8.........................142 F3
Casson Street E1...........................150 C1
Castellain Road W9......................142 B3
Castlebrook Close SE11...............149 G5
Castle Lane SW1E........................147 M4
Catesby Street SE17.....................149 L6
Cathay Street SE16........................150 F7
Cathcart Road SW10....................146 C8
Cathedral Walk SW1E..................147 M4
Catherine Place SW1E.................147 M4
Catherine Street WC2E................144 D7
Cato Street W1H............................143 G5
Causton Street SW1P....................148 C6

Street	Page	Grid
Cavell Street E1	150	F1
Cavendish Avenue NW8	142	E1
Cavendish Place W1G	143	L6
Cavendish Square W1G	143	L6
Cavendish Street N1	145	L1
Caversham Street SW3	147	G8
Caxton Street SW1H	148	B4
Cayton Street EC1V	145	K2
Centaur Street SE1	148	F4
Central Street EC1V	145	J2
Chadwell Street EC1R	145	G1
Chadwick Street SW1P	148	B4
Chagford Street NW1	143	H4
Chalton Street NW1	144	B1
Chambers Street SE16	150	D7
Chamber Street E1	150	C3
Chambers Wharf SE16	150	D6
Chancel Street SE1	149	H1
Chancery Lane WC2A	144	F5
Chancery Lane ⊖ WC1V	144	F5
Chandos Place WC2N	144	C8
Chandos Street W1G	143	L5
Chantry Square W8	146	B4
Chapel Market * N1	144	F1
Chapel Street NW1	142	F5
Chapel Street SW1X	147	K3
Chaplin Close SE1	149	G3
Chapman Street E1	150	E3
Chapter Road SE17	149	H7
Chapter Street SW1P	148	B6
Chargrove Close SE16	151	H6
Charing Cross ⇌ ⊖ WC2N	148	D1
Charing Cross Road WC2H	144	B6
Charing Cross Road WC2N	144	C7
Charlbert Street NW8	142	F1
Charles II Street SW1Y	144	B8
Charles Square N1	145	M2
Charles Street W1J	147	K1
Charleston Street SE17	149	K6
Charlotte Road EC2A	145	M3
Charlotte Place SW1V	148	A6
Charlotte Street W1T	144	A4
Charlwood Place SW1V	148	A6
Charlwood Street SW1V	147	M7
Charlwood Street SW1V	148	A6
Charrington Street NW1	144	B1
Charterhouse Square EC1M	145	H4
Charterhouse Street EC1M	145	G5
Chart Street N1	145	L2
Chaseley Street E14	151	J2
Chatham Street SE17	149	L5
Cheapside EC2V	145	K6
Chelsea Bridge SW1W	147	K8
Chelsea Bridge Road SW1W	147	J7
Chelsea Embankment SW3	147	G8
Chelsea Manor Gardens SW3	146	F7
Chelsea Manor Street SW3	147	G7
Chelsea Park Gardens SW3	146	E8
Chelsea Physic Garden SW3	147	H8
Chelsea Square SW3	146	E7
Cheltenham Terrace SW3	147	H6
Chenies Mews WC1E	144	B4
Chenies Street WC1E	144	B4
Cheniston Gardens W8	146	A4
Chepstow Place W2	142	A7
Chepstow Road W2	142	A6
Chequer Street EC1Y	145	K3
Cherbury Street N1	145	L1
Cherry Garden Street SE16	150	E7
Chesham Close SW1X	147	J4
Chesham Place SW1X	147	J4
Chesham Street SW1X	147	J4
Chester Close SW1X	147	K3
Chester Close North NW1	143	L2
Chester Close South NW1	143	L2
Chesterfield Gardens W1J	147	K1
Chesterfield Hill W1J	143	K8
Chesterfield Street W1J	147	K1
Chester Gate NW1	143	L2
Chester Mews SW1X	147	K3
Chester Place NW1	143	L1
Chester Road NW1	143	K2
Chester Row SW1W	147	K5
Chester Square SW1W	147	K5
Chester Square Mews SW1W	147	K4
Chester Street SW1X	147	K4
Chester Terrace NW1	143	L2
Chester Way SE11	149	G6
Cheval Place SW7	147	G4
Cheval Street E14	151	M7
Cheyne Gardens SW3	147	G8
Cheyne Row SW3	146	F8
Cheyne Walk SW3	146	F8
Chicheley Street SE1	148	E2
Chichester Road NW6	142	A1
Chichester Road W2	142	C5
Chichester Street SW1V	148	A7
Chicksand Street E1	150	C1
Chigwell Hill E1W	150	E4
Child's Place SW5	146	A5
Child's Street SW5	146	A5
Chiltern Street W1U	143	J4
Chilton Mews W2	142	D6
Chilworth Street W2	142	D6
China Hall Mews SE16	151	G8
Chinatown W1D	144	B7
Chippenham Mews W9	142	A4
Chiswell Street EC1Y	145	K4
Chitty Street W1T	144	A4
Christchurch Street SW3	147	G8
Christian Street E1	150	D3
Christina Street EC2A	145	M3
Christopher Close SE16	151	H6
Christopher Street EC2A	145	L4
Chudleigh Street E1	151	H2
Chumleigh Street SE5	149	M8
Churchill Gardens Road SW1V	147	L7
Churchill War Rooms SW1A	148	C3
Church Street NW8	142	F4
Church Way NW1	144	B2
Churchyard Row SE1	149	H5
Churton Place SW1V	148	A6
Churton Street SW1V	148	A6
Circus Road NW8	142	E1
Cirencester Square W2	142	A5
City Garden Row N1	145	J1
City Road EC1V	145	J1
City Road EC1Y	145	L3
City Thameslink ⇌ EC4M	145	H6
Clabon Mews SW1X	147	H5
Clack Street SE16	151	G7
Clanricarde Gardens W2	142	A8
Claremont Square N1	144	F1
Clarence Gardens NW1	143	L2
Clarence Mews SE16	151	G6
Clarendon Gardens W9	142	D4
Clarendon Gate W2	142	F7
Clarendon Place W2	142	F7
Clarendon Street SW1V	147	L6
Clareville Grove SW7	146	D6
Clareville Street SW7	146	D6
Clarges Mews W1J	147	L1
Clarges Street W1J	147	L1
Clark Street E1	150	F2
Clarkson Row NW1	143	M1
Claverton Street SW1V	148	A7
Clave Street E1W	150	F5
Clay Street W1U	143	H5
Clayton Street SE11	148	F8
Cleaver Square SE11	149	G7
Cleaver Street SE11	149	G7
Clegg Street E1	150	F5
Clemence Street E14	151	L2
Clements Lane EC4N	145	L7
Clement's Road SE16	150	E8
Clenston Mews W1H	143	H6
Clere Street EC2A	145	L3
Clerkenwell Close EC1R	145	G3
Clerkenwell Green EC1R	145	G4
Clerkenwell Road EC1M	145	G4
Cleveland Gardens W2	142	C6
Cleveland Mews W1T	143	M4
Cleveland Place SW1Y	148	A1
Cleveland Row SW1A	148	A2
Cleveland Square W2	142	C6
Cleveland Street W1T	143	M4
Cleveland Terrace W2	142	D6
Clifford Street W1S	143	M7
Clifton Gardens W9	142	C4
Clifton Place SE16	151	G6
Clifton Place W2	142	E7
Clifton Road W9	142	D3
Clifton Street EC2A	145	M3
Clifton Villas W9	142	C4
Clink Street SE1	149	K1
Clipper Close SE16	151	H6
Clipstone Mews W1W	143	M4
Clipstone Street W1W	143	L4
Cliveden Place SW1W	147	J5
Cloak Lane EC4R	145	K7
Cloth Fair EC1A	145	J5
Cloth Street EC1A	145	J5
Cluny Place SE1	150	A8
Cobb Street E1	150	B2
Cobourg Street NW1	144	A2
Coburg Close SW1P	148	A5
Cochrane Mews NW8	142	E1
Cochrane Street NW8	142	E1
Cock Lane EC1A	145	H5
Cockspur Street SW1Y	148	C1
Codling Close * E1W	150	D5
Coin Street SE1	149	G1
Coke Street E1	150	D2
Colbeck Mews SW7	146	C6
Colebrook Row N1	145	H1
Coleherne Road SW10	146	B7
Coleman Street EC2R	145	L6
Cole Street SE1	149	K3
Coley Street WC1X	144	F3
College Hill EC4R	145	K7
College Street EC4R	145	K7
Collett Road SE16	150	D8
Collier Street N1	144	E1
Collingham Gardens SW5	146	B6
Collingham Place SW5	146	B5
Collingham Road SW5	146	B5
Colnbrook Street SE1	149	H4
Colombo Street SE1	149	H1
Colonnade WC1N	144	D4
Coltman Street E14	151	K2
Commercial Road E1	150	D2
Commercial Road E14	151	K3
Commercial Street E1	150	B1
Compton Street EC1V	145	H3
Concert Hall Approach SE1	148	E2
Conder Street E14	151	K2
Conduit Mews W2	142	E6
Conduit Place W2	142	E6
Conduit Street W1S	143	L7
Congreve Street SE17	149	M5
Connaught Close W2	142	F7
Connaught Place W2	143	G7
Connaught Square W2	143	G6
Connaught Street W2	143	G6
Cons Street SE1	149	G2
Constitution Hill SW1A	147	L3
Content Street SE17	149	K5
Conway Street W1T	143	M4
Cookham Crescent SE16	151	H6
Cook's Road SE17	149	H8
Coombs Street N1	145	J1
Cooper's Lane Estate NW1	144	B1
Cooper's Row EC3N	150	B3
Copenhagen Place E14	151	L2
Cope Place W8	146	A4
Copley Court SE17	149	J8
Copley Street E1	151	H2
Copperfield Road E3	151	K1
Copperfield Street SE1	149	J2
Copthall Avenue EC2R	145	L6
Coptic Street WC1A	144	C5
Coral Street SE1	149	G3
Coram Street WC1H	144	C3
Cork Square E1W	150	E5
Cork Street W1S	143	M8
Corlett Street NW1	142	F5
Cornhill EC3V	145	L6
Cornwall Gardens SW7	146	C4
Cornwall Mews South SW7	146	C5
Cornwall Road SE1	148	F1
Cornwall Road SE1	149	G2
Cornwall Street E1	150	E3
Cornwall Terrace Mews NW1	143	H4
Cornwood Drive E1	151	G2
Coronet Street N1	145	M2
Corporation Row EC1R	145	G3
Corsham Street N1	145	L2
Cosser Street SE1	148	F4
Cosway Street NW1	143	G4
Cottage Place SW3	146	F4
Cottesmore Gardens W8	146	B4
Cottons Lane SE1	149	M1
Coulson Street SW3	147	H6
Counter Street SE1	149	M1
County Street SE1	149	K5
Courtenay Square SE11	148	F7
Courtenay Street SE11	148	F6
Courtfield Gardens SW5	146	B5
Courtfield Mews * SW5	146	C5
Courtfield Road SW7	146	C5
Court Street E1	150	E1
Cousin Lane EC4R	145	K8
Covent Garden ⊖ WC2E	144	D7
Covent Garden WC2E	144	D7
Coventry Street W1D	144	B8
Cowcross Street EC1M	145	H4
Cowper Street EC2A	145	L3
Crail Row SE17	149	L5
Cramer Street W1U	143	J5
Crampton Street SE17	149	J6
Cranbourn Street WC2H	144	C7
Cranleigh Street NW1	144	A1
Cranley Gardens SW7	146	D6
Cranley Mews SW7	146	D6
Cranley Place SW7	146	E6
Cranston Estate N1	145	L1
Cranwood Street EC1V	145	L2
Craven Hill W2	142	D7
Craven Hill Gardens W2	142	C7
Craven Road W2	142	D7
Craven Street WC2N	148	D1
Craven Terrace W2	142	D7
Crawford Passage EC1R	145	G3
Crawford Place W1H	143	G5
Crawford Street W1H	143	G5
Creechurch Lane EC3A	150	A3
Creed Lane EC4V	145	H7
Cresswell Place SW10	146	D6
Cressy Row SE1	151	G1
Crestfield Street WC1H	144	D2
Crimscott Street SE1	150	A8
Crispin Street E1	150	B1
Cromer Street WC1H	144	D2
Crompton Street W2	142	D4
Cromwell Mews * SW7	146	E5
Cromwell Place SW7	146	E5
Cromwell Road SW5	146	B5
Cromwell Road SW7	146	E5
Crondall Court N1	145	M1
Crondall Street N1	145	L1
Cropley Street N1	145	K1
Crosby Row SE1	149	L3
Cross Lane EC3R	150	A4
Crosswall EC3N	150	B3
Crowder Street E1	150	E3
Crucifix Lane SE1	150	A6
Cruikshank Street WC1X	144	F1
Crutched Friars EC3N	150	A3
Cuba Street E14	151	M6
Cubitt Street WC1X	144	E2
Culford Gardens SW3	147	H6
Culling Road SE16	150	F7
Cullum Street EC3M	145	M7
Culross Street W1K	143	J8
Culworth Street NW8	142	F1
Cumberland Gardens WC1X	144	F2
Cumberland Gate W2	143	H7
Cumberland Market NW1	143	L2
Cumberland Street SW1V	147	L6
Cumberland Terrace NW1	143	K1
Cumberland Terrace Mews NW1	143	L1
Cumberland Wharf SE16	151	G6
Cumming Street N1	144	E1
Cundy Street SW1W	147	K6
Cunningham Place NW8	142	E3
Cureton Street SW1P	148	C6
Curlew Street SE1	150	B6
Cursitor Street EC4A	144	F6
Curtain Road EC2A	145	M3
Curtain Road EC2A	145	M4
Curzon Gate W2	147	K2
Curzon Street W1J	147	K1
Cuthbert Street W2	142	E4
Cutler Street EC3A	150	A2
Cynthia Street N1	144	F1
Cypress Place W1T	144	A4
Cyrus Street EC1V	145	H3

D

Street	Page	Grid
Dacre Street SW1H	148	B3
Dakin Place E1	151	J1
Dallington Street EC1V	145	H3
Damien Street E1	150	F2
Dane Street WC1R	144	E5
Dansey Place W1D	144	B7
Dante Road SE11	149	H5
Danvers Street SW3	146	F8
D'Arblay Street W1F	144	A6
Dartford Street SE17	149	K8
Dartmouth Street SW1H	148	B3
Darwin Street SE17	149	L5
Date Street SE17	149	K7
Davenant Street E1	150	D1
Daventry Street NW1	142	F4
Davidge Street SE1	149	H3
Davies Mews W1K	143	K7
Davies Street W1K	143	K7
Dawes Street SE17	149	L6
Dawson Place W2	142	A7
Deal Porters Way SE16	151	G8
Deal Street E1	150	D1
Dean Bradley Street SW1P	148	C5
Dean Close SE16	151	H6
Deancross Street E1	150	F3
Deanery Street W1K	147	K1
Dean Farrar Street SW1H	148	B3
Dean Ryle Street SW1P	148	C5
Dean's Buildings SE17	149	L6
Dean Stanley Street SW1P	148	C4
Dean Street W1D	144	B6
Dean's Yard SW1P	148	C4
Decima Street SE1	149	M4
Deck Close SE16	151	J6
Defoe Close SE16	151	K7
Delamere Street W2	142	C5
Delamere Terrace W2	142	C4
De Laune Street SE17	149	H7
Delaware Road W9	142	B3
Dellow Street E1	150	F3
Delverton Road SE17	149	H7
Denbigh Place SW1V	147	M6
Denbigh Street SW1V	148	A6
Denman Street W1D	144	A7
Denmark Street WC2H	144	C6
Denny Close SE11	149	G6
Denny Street SE11	149	G6
Denyer Street SW3	147	G5
Derby Gate SW1A	148	D3
Derby Street W1J	147	K1
Dering Street W1S	143	L6
Derry Street W8	146	B3
De Vere Gardens W8	146	C3
Deverell Street SE1	149	L4
Devonport Street E1	151	G3
Devonshire Close W1G	143	K4
Devonshire Mews South W1G	143	K4
Devonshire Mews West W1G	143	K4
Devonshire Place W1G	143	K4
Devonshire Place Mews W1G	143	K4
Devonshire Row EC2M	150	A2
Devonshire Square EC2M	150	A2
Devonshire Street W1G	143	K4
Devonshire Terrace W2	142	D7
De Walden Street W1G	143	K5
Dickens Estate SE16	150	D7
Dickens Square SE1	149	K4
Dilke Street SW3	147	H8
Dingley Place EC1V	145	K2
Dingley Road EC1V	145	J2
Disney Place SE1	149	K2
Distaff Lane EC4V	145	J7
Distin Street SE11	148	F6
Dockhead SE1	150	C7
Dockley Road SE16	150	D8
Dock Street E1	150	D4
Doddington Grove SE17	149	H7
Doddington Place SE17	149	H8
Dodson Street SE1	149	G3
Dod Street E14	151	M2
Dolben Street SE1	149	H2
Dolland Street SE11	148	E7
Dolphin Square SW1V	148	A7
Dolphin Square SW1V	148	B7
Dombey Street WC1N	144	E4
Dominion Drive SE16	151	H7
Dominion Street EC2A	145	L5
Donegal Street N1	144	F1
Dongola Road E1	151	J1
Donne Place SW3	147	G5
Doon Street SE1	148	F1
Dora Street E14	151	L2
Doric Way NW1	144	B2
Dorset Rise EC4Y	145	G7
Dorset Square NW1	143	H4
Dorset Street W1U	143	H5
Doughty Mews WC1N	144	E3
Doughty Street WC1N	144	E3
Douglas Street SW1P	148	B6
Douro Place W8	146	C3
Douthwaite Square * E1W	150	D5
Dovehouse Street SW3	146	E6
Dover Street W1J	147	L1
Dover Street W1S	143	L8
Dowgate Hill EC4R	145	K7
Downfield Close W9	142	B4
Downing Street SW1A	148	C2
Downtown Road SE16	151	K6
D'Oyley Street SW1X	147	J5
Draco Street SE17	149	J8
Drake Close SE16	151	H6
Draycott Avenue SW3	147	G5
Draycott Place SW3	147	H6
Draycott Terrace SW3	147	H5
Drayson Mews W8	146	A3
Drayton Gardens SW10	146	D6
Druid Street SE1	150	A6
Druid Street SE1	150	B6
Drummond Crescent NW1	144	B2
Drummond Gate * SW1V	148	B6
Drummond Road SE16	150	E8
Drummond Street NW1	144	A3
Drury Lane WC2B	144	D6
Dryden Court SE11	149	G5
Dryden Street WC2B	144	D6
Duchess Mews W1G	143	L5
Duchess Street W1B	143	L5
Duchy Street SE1	149	G1
Duckett Street E1	151	J1
Duck Lane W1F	144	B6
Dufferin Street EC1Y	145	K4
Duke of Wellington Place SW1W	147	K3
Duke of York Square SW3	147	H6
Duke of York Street SW1Y	148	A1
Duke Shore Wharf E14	151	K4
Duke's Lane W8	146	A2
Duke's Place EC3A	150	B2
Duke's Road WC1H	144	C2
Duke Street W1K	143	K7
Duke Street W1U	143	J6
Duke Street Hill SE1	149	L1
Duke Street St James's SW1Y	148	A1
Dunbar Wharf E14	151	L4
Duncannon Street WC2N	144	C8
Duncan Terrace N1	145	H1
Dundee Street E1W	150	E5
Dundee Wharf E14	151	L4
Dunelm Street E1	151	H2
Dunlop Place SE16	150	C8
Dunraven Street W1K	143	H7
Dunster Court EC3R	150	A3
Duplex Ride SW1X	147	H3
Durand's Wharf SE16	151	L6
Durham Row E1	151	J1
Durham Street SE11	148	E7
Durham Terrace W2	142	A6
Dyott Street WC1A	144	C6
Dysart Street EC2A	145	M4

E

Street	Page	Grid
Eagle Court EC1M	145	H4
Eagle Street WC1R	144	E5
Eamont Street * NW8	143	G1
Eardley Crescent SW5	146	A7
Earlham Street WC2H	144	C7
Earl's Court ⇌ ⊖ SW5	146	A6
Earl's Court Gardens SW5	146	B6
Earl's Court Road SW5	146	A6
Earl's Court Square SW5	146	A6
Earlstoke Street EC1V	145	H2
Earnshaw Street WC2H	144	C6
East Arbour Street E1	151	H2
Eastbourne Mews W2	142	D6
Eastbourne Terrace W2	142	D6
Eastcastle Street W1W	144	A6
Eastcheap EC3M	145	M7
Eastfield Street E14	151	K1
East India Dock Road E14	151	M3
East Lane SE16	150	D6
Easton Street WC1X	144	F3
East Poultry Avenue EC1A	145	H5
East Road N1	145	L2
East Smithfield E1W	150	C4
East Street SE17	149	L6
East Tenter Street E1	150	C3
Eaton Close SW1W	147	J5
Eaton Gate SW1W	147	J5
Eaton Lane SW1W	147	L4
Eaton Mews North SW1W	147	J5
Eaton Mews South SW1W	147	K5
Eaton Mews West SW1W	147	K5
Eaton Place SW1X	147	J4
Eaton Row SW1W	147	K4
Eaton Square SW1W	147	K5
Eaton Terrace SW1W	147	J5
Ebbisham Drive SW8	148	E8
Ebury Bridge SW1W	147	K6
Ebury Bridge Road SW1W	147	K7
Ebury Mews SW1W	147	K5
Ebury Square SW1W	147	K6
Ebury Street SW1W	147	K5
Eccleston Bridge SW1W	147	L5
Eccleston Mews SW1X	147	K4
Eccleston Place SW1W	147	L5
Eccleston Square SW1V	147	L6
Eccleston Street SW1X	147	K4
Edbrooke Road W9	142	A3
Edge Street W8	146	A1
Edgware Road W2	142	F5
Edgware Road ⊖ NW1	142	F5
Edinburgh Gate SW1X	147	H3
Edith Grove SW10	146	C8
Edwards Mews W1	143	J6
Egerton Crescent SW3	146	F5
Egerton Gardens SW3	146	F5
Egerton Terrace SW3	147	G4
Eglington Court SE17	149	J7
Elba Place SE17	149	K5
Eldon Road W8	146	B4
Eldon Street EC2M	145	L5
Eleanor Close SE16	151	H6
Elephant & Castle SE1	149	J4
Elephant & Castle ⇌ ⊖ SE1	149	J5
Elephant Lane SE16	150	F6
Elephant Road SE17	149	J5
Elf Row E1W	151	G3
Elgar Street SE16	151	K7
Elgin Avenue W9	142	B2
Elgin Mews North W9	142	C2
Elgin Mews South W9	142	C2
Elia Mews N1	145	H1
Elia Street N1	145	H1
Elim Estate SE1	149	M3
Elim Street SE1	149	M3
Elizabeth Bridge SW1V	147	L6
Elizabeth Street SW1W	147	K5
Ellen Street E1	150	D3
Elliott's Row SE11	149	H5
Ellis Street SW1X	147	J5
Elmfield Way W9	142	A4
Elm Park Gardens SW10	146	E7
Elm Park Lane SW3	146	E7
Elm Park Road SW3	146	E8
Elm Place SW7	146	E7
Elms Mews W2	142	D7
Elm Street WC1X	144	F4
Elm Tree Road NW8	142	E2
Elnathan Mews W9	142	B4
Elsa Street E1	151	J1
Elsted Street SE17	149	L6
Elvaston Mews SW7	146	D4
Elvaston Place SW7	146	D4
Elverton Street SW1P	148	B5
Ely Place EC1N	145	G5
Elystan Place SW3	147	G6
Elystan Street SW3	146	F6
Embankment ⊖ WC2N	148	D1
Embankment Gardens SW3	147	H8
Embankment Place WC2N	148	D1
Emba Street SE16	150	D7
Emerald Street WC1N	144	E4
Emerson Street SE1	149	J1
Emery Hill Street SW1P	148	A5
Emery Street SE1	149	G3
Emperor's Gate SW7	146	C5
Empire Square SE1	149	L3
Empress State SW6	146	A7
Endell Street WC2H	144	C6
Endsleigh Gardens WC1H	144	B3
Endsleigh Place WC1H	144	B3
Endsleigh Street WC1H	144	B3
Enford Street W1H	143	G5
English Grounds SE1	149	M1
Enid Street SE16	150	C8
Ennismore Gardens SW7	146	F3
Ennismore Gardens Mews SW7	146	F3
Ennismore Mews SW7	146	F3
Ennismore Street SW7	146	F4
Ensign Street E1	150	D4
Epworth Street EC2A	145	L3
Erasmus Street SW1P	148	C6
Errol Street EC1Y	145	K4
Essendine Road W9	142	A3
Essex Street WC2R	144	F7
Essex Villas W8	146	A3
Europa Place EC1V	145	J2
Euston ⇌ ⊖ NW1	144	B2
Euston Road NW1	144	B3
Euston Square NW1	144	A3
Euston Square ⊖ NW1	144	A3
Euston Street NW1	144	A3
Evelyn Gardens SW7	146	D7
Evelyn Walk N1	145	L1
Eversholt Street NW1	144	A1
Everton Mews NW1	143	M2
Ewer Street SE1	149	J2
Ewhurst Close E1	151	G1
Exchange Square EC2A	145	M4
Exeter Street WC2E	144	D7
Exhibition Road SW7	146	E3
Exmouth Market EC1R	145	G3
Exon Street SE17	149	M6
Exton Street SE1	148	F2
Eyre Street Hill EC1R	144	F4

F

Street	Page	Grid
Fairclough Street E1	150	D3
Fair Street SE1	150	B6
Falmouth Road SE1	149	K4
Fann Street EC1M	145	J4
Fanshaw Street N1	145	M1
Farmer Street W8	146	A1
Farm Lane SW6	146	A8
Farm Street W1K	143	K8
Farnham Place SE1	149	J1
Farrance Street E14	151	M3
Farringdon ⇌ ⊖ EC1M	145	G4
Farringdon Lane EC1R	145	G4
Farringdon Road EC1R	144	F3

Farringdon Street EC1M 145 H5
Farrins Rents SE16 151 J5
Farrow Place E14 151 K7
Farthing Fields * E1W 150 F5
Fashion Street E1 150 B1
Faunce Street SE17 149 H7
Fawcett Street SW10 146 C8
Featherstone Street EC1Y 145 L3
Fenchurch Avenue EC3M 150 A3
Fenchurch Buildings EC3M 150 A3
Fenchurch Place EC3M 150 A3
Fenchurch Street EC3M 150 A3
Fenchurch Street ⇌ EC3M 150 A3
Fendall Street SE1 150 B8
Fenning Street SE1 149 M2
Fentiman Road SW8 148 D8
Fernsbury Street WC1X 144 F2
Fetter Lane EC4A 145 G6
Fieldgate Street E1 150 D2
Fielding Street SE17 149 J7
Field Street WC1X 144 E1
Finborough Road SW10 146 B8
Finch Lane EC3V 145 L6
Finland Street SE16 151 K8
Finsbury Circus EC2M 145 L5
Finsbury Estate EC1R 145 G3
Finsbury Market EC2A 145 M4
Finsbury Square EC2A 145 L4
Finsbury Street EC2Y 145 L4
First Street SW3 147 G5
Fishermans Drive SE16 151 J6
Fisher Street WC1R 144 D5
Fisherton Street NW8 142 E3
Fish Street Hill EC3R 145 L7
Fitzalan Street SE11 148 F5
Fitzhardinge Street W1H 143 J6
Fitzroy Square W1T 143 M4
Fitzroy Street W1T 143 M4
Flamborough Street E14 151 J3
Flank Street E1 150 C4
Flaxman Terrace WC1H 144 C3
Fleet Street EC4A 145 G6
Fleming Road SE17 149 H8
Fletcher Street E1 150 D3
Flint Street SE17 149 L6
Flitcroft Street WC2H 144 C6
Flockton Street SE16 150 D7
Flood Street SW3 147 G7
Flood Walk SW3 147 G7
Floral Street WC2E 144 D7
Foley Street W1W 143 M5
Forbes Street E1 150 D3
Fordham Street E1 150 D2
Ford Square E1 150 F2
Fore Street EC2Y 145 K5
Formosa Street W9 142 C4
Forset Street W1H 143 G6
Forsyth Gardens SE17 149 H8
Fort Street E1 150 B1
Fortune Street EC1Y 145 K4
Forum Magnum Square SE1 148 E3
Foster Lane EC2V 145 J6
Foulis Terrace SW7 146 E6
Foundry Close SE16 151 J5
Fournier Street E1 150 B1
Fowey Close E1W 150 E5
Frampton Street NW8 142 E4
Francis Street SW1P 148 A5
Franklin's Row SW3 147 H6
Frazier Street SE1 149 G3
Frean Street SE16 150 C8
Frederick Close W2 143 G7
Frederick Street WC1X 144 E2
Frederic Mews * SW1X 147 J3
Freemantle Street SE17 149 M6
Friday Street EC4V 145 J7
Friend Street EC1V 145 H2
Frith Street W1D 144 B6
Fulbourne Street E1 150 E1
Fulford Street SE16 150 F7
Fulham Road SW10 146 D8
Fulham Road SW3 146 F6
Furnival Street EC4A 144 F5
Fynes Street SW1P 148 B5

G
Gabriel's Wharf SE1 149 G1
Gainsford Street SE1 150 B6
Galleon Close SE16 151 G6
Galsworthy Avenue E14 151 K2
Galway Street EC1V 145 K2
Gambia Street SE1 149 H2
Garden Road NW8 142 D1
Garden Row SE1 149 H4
Garden Street E1 151 H1
Garden Terrace * SW1V 148 B6
Garden Walk EC2A 145 M3
Gard Street EC1V 145 J2
Garford Street E14 151 M4
Garnault Place EC1R 145 G3
Garnet Street E1W 150 F4
Garrett Street EC1Y 145 K3
Garrick Street WC2E 144 C7
Garterway SE16 151 H7
Garway Road W2 142 B6
Gaspar Mews SW7 146 C5
Gataker Street * SE16 150 E8
Gate Mews SW7 146 F3
Gateforth Street NW8 142 F3
Gate Mews NW1 143 L3
Gatesborough Street * EC2A 145 M3
Gate Street WC2A 144 E5
Gatliff Road SW1W 147 K7
Gaunt Street SE1 149 J4
Gayfere Street SW1P 148 C4
Gaywood Street SE1 149 H4
Gaza Street SE17 149 H7
Gedling Place SE1 150 C7
Gee Street EC1V 145 J3
George Mathers Road SE11 149 H5
George Row SE16 150 C7
George Street W1H 143 H6
George Yard W1K 143 K7
Geraldine Street SE1 149 H4
Gerald Road SW1W 147 K5
Gerrard Street W1D 144 B7
Gerridge Street SE1 149 G3
Gertrude Street SW10 146 D8
Gibson Road SE11 148 E5
Gilbert Place WC1A 144 C5
Gilbert Road SE11 149 G5
Gilbert Street W1K 143 K7
Gildea Street W1W 143 L5

Gillingham Street SW1V 147 M5
Gill Street E14 151 L3
Gilston Road SW10 146 D7
Giltspur Street EC1A 145 H5
Gladstone Street SE1 149 H4
Glamis Place E1W 151 G4
Glamis Road E1W 151 G4
Glasgow Terrace SW1V 147 M7
Glasshill Street SE1 149 J3
Glasshouse Street W1B 144 A8
Glasshouse Walk SE11 148 D7
Glasshouse Yard EC1 145 J4
Glebe Place SW3 146 F7
Gledhow Road SW5 146 C6
Glentworth Street NW1 143 H4
Globe Pond Road SE16 151 J5
Globe Street SE1 149 K3
Gloucester Court * EC3R 150 A4
Gloucester Gardens W2 142 C6
Gloucester Mews W2 142 D6
Gloucester Mews West W2 142 C6
Gloucester Place NW1 143 H4
Gloucester Place W1U 143 H5
Gloucester Place Mews W1U 143 H5
Gloucester Road SW7 146 C4
Gloucester Road SW7 146 D6
Gloucester Road ⊖ SW7 146 C5
Gloucester Square W2 142 F6
Gloucester Street SW1V 147 M7
Gloucester Terrace W2 142 B5
Gloucester Terrace W2 142 D6
Gloucester Walk W8 146 A2
Gloucester Way EC1R 145 G2
Glyn Street SE11 148 E7
Godfrey Street SW3 147 G6
Goding Street SE11 148 D7
Godliman Street EC4V 145 J7
Godwin Close * N1 145 K1
Golden Hinde II SE1 149 L1
Golden Jubilee Bridge WC2N 148 D1
Golden Lane EC1Y 145 J4
Golden Square W1F 144 A7
Golding Street E1 150 E3
Goldney Road W9 142 A4
Goldsmith Street EC2V 145 K6
Gomm Road SE16 151 G8
Goodge Place W1T 144 A5
Goodge Street W1T 144 A5
Goodge Street ⊖ W1T 144 B5
Goodwin Close SE16 150 C8
Gordon Place W8 146 A2
Gordon Square WC1H 144 B3
Gordon Street WC1H 144 B3
Gore Street SW7 146 D4
Goring Street * EC3A 150 A2
Gosfield Street W1W 143 L5
Goslett Yard WC2H 144 B6
Goswell Road EC1V 145 H1
Gough Street WC1X 144 F3
Goulston Street E1 150 B2
Gower Mews WC1E 144 B5
Gower Place NW1 144 A3
Gower Street WC1E 144 B3
Gower's Walk E1 150 D2
Gracechurch Street EC3V 145 M7
Grafton Mews W1T 143 M4
Grafton Place NW1 144 B2
Grafton Street W1S 143 L8
Grafton Way W1T 144 A4
Graham Street N1 145 J1
Graham Terrace SW1W 147 J6
Granby Terrace NW1 143 M1
Grand Avenue EC1A 145 H5
Grange Road SE1 150 B8
Grange Walk SE1 150 B8
Grange Yard SE1 150 B8
Grantully Road W9 142 B2
Granville Place W1H 143 J6
Granville Road NW6 142 A1
Granville Square WC1X 144 F2
Grape Street WC2H 144 C6
Gravel Lane E1 150 B2
Gray's Inn Road WC1X 144 D2
Gray's Inn Square WC1R 144 F5
Gray Street SE1 149 G3
Great Castle Street W1G 143 L6
Great Central Street NW1 143 G4
Great Chapel Street W1D 144 B6
Great College Street SW1P 148 C4
Great Cumberland Place W1H 143 H6
Great Dover Street SE1 149 K3
Great Eastern Street EC2A 145 M3
Great George Street SW1P 148 C3
Great Guildford Street SE1 149 J1
Great James Street WC1N 144 E4
Great Marlborough Street W1F 143 M7
Great Maze Pond SE1 149 L2
Great Newport Street WC2H 144 C7
Greatorex Street E1 150 D1
Great Ormond Street WC1N 144 D4
Great Percy Street WC1X 144 F2
Great Peter Street SW1P 148 B4
Great Portland Street W1W 143 L4
Great Portland Street ⊖ W1W 143 L4
Great Pulteney Street W1F 144 A7
Great Queen Street WC2B 144 D6
Great Russell Street WC1B 144 C5
Great St Helen's EC3A 145 M6
Great Scotland Yard SW1A 148 C1
Great Smith Street SW1P 148 C4
Great Suffolk Street SE1 149 H2
Great Sutton Street EC1V 145 H4
Great Swan Alley EC2R 145 L6
Great Titchfield Street W1W 143 M4
Great Tower Street EC3M 145 M7
Great Tower Street EC3R 150 A4
Great Winchester Street EC2N 145 L6
Great Windmill Street W1D 144 B7
Greek Street W1D 144 B6
Greenacre Square SE16 151 J6
Green Bank E1W 150 E5
Greenberry Street NW8 142 F1
Greencoat Place SW1P 148 A5
Green Coat Row SW1P 148 A4
Greenfield Road E1 150 D2
Greenham Close SE1 148 F3
Green Park ⊖ W1J 147 M1
Green Street W1K 143 J7
Greenwell Street W1W 143 L4
Greet Street SE1 149 G2
Grenade Street E14 151 L4
Grendon Street NW8 142 F3
Grenville Place SW7 146 C5
Gresham Street EC2V 145 J6
Gresse Street W1T 144 B5

Greville Street EC1N 145 G5
Greycoat Place SW1P 148 B4
Greycoat Street SW1P 148 B4
Grigg's Place SE1 150 A8
Grosvenor Bridge SW8 147 L8
Grosvenor Crescent SW1X 147 J3
Grosvenor Crescent Mews SW1X 147 J3
Grosvenor Gardens SW1W 147 L4
Grosvenor Gardens Mews East SW1W 147 L4
Grosvenor Gardens Mews North SW1W 147 L4
Grosvenor Gardens Mews South * SW1W 147 L4
Grosvenor Gate W2 143 H8
Grosvenor Hill W1K 143 L7
Grosvenor Place SW1X 147 K3
Grosvenor Road SW1V 147 L8
Grosvenor Square W1K 143 J7
Grosvenor Street W1K 143 K7
Grosvenor Terrace SE5 149 J8
Grove End Road NW8 142 D2
Guildhouse Street SW1V 147 M5
Guilford Street WC1N 144 D4
Guinness Square SE1 149 M5
Gulliver Street SE16 151 K8
Gunpowder Square EC4A 145 G6
Gun Street E1 150 B1
Gunthorpe Street E1 150 C2
Gutter Lane EC2V 145 J6
Guy Street SE1 149 L3

H
Haberdasher Street N1 145 L2
Haddonhall Estate SE1 149 M4
Hainton Close E1 150 F3
Halcrow Street * E1 150 F2
Half Moon Street W1J 147 L1
Halford Road SW6 146 A8
Halkin Place SW1X 147 J4
Halkin Street SW1X 147 K3
Hallam Street W1W 143 L5
Halley Street E14 151 K1
Hallfield Estate W2 142 C6
Hall Place W2 142 E4
Hall Road NW8 142 D2
Hall Street EC1V 145 H2
Halpin Place SE17 149 M6
Halsey Street SW3 147 G5
Hamilton Close NW8 142 D2
Hamilton Close SE16 151 K7
Hamilton Gardens NW8 142 D2
Hamilton Place W1J 147 K2
Hamilton Terrace NW8 142 C1
Hamlet Way SE1 149 L3
Hammett Street EC3N 150 B4
Hampden Close NW1 144 B1
Hampden Gurney Street W2 143 H6
Hampstead Road NW1 143 M2
Hampton Street SE17 149 J6
Hanbury Street E1 150 C1
Hand Court WC1V 144 E5
Handel Street WC1N 144 D3
Hankey Place SE1 149 L3
Hannibal Road E1 151 G1
Hanover Square W1S 143 L6
Hanover Street W1S 143 L7
Hans Crescent SW3 147 H3
Hanson Street W1W 143 M4
Hans Place SW1X 147 H4
Hans Road SW3 147 G4
Hans Street SW1X 147 H4
Hanway Place W1T 144 B6
Hanway Street W1T 144 B6
Harbet Road W2 142 F5
Harcourt Street W1H 143 G5
Harcourt Terrace SW10 146 C7
Hardinge Street E1 151 G3
Hardwick Street EC1R 145 G2
Hardwidge Street SE1 149 M2
Hardy Close SE16 151 H6
Harewood Place W1G 143 L6
Harewood Row NW1 143 G4
Harewoood Avenue NW1 143 G4
Harford Street E1 151 J1
Harleyford Street SE11 148 E8
Harley Gardens SW10 146 D7
Harley Place W1G 143 K5
Harley Street W1G 143 K4
Harmsworth Street SE17 149 G7
Harold Estate SE1 150 A8
Harper Road SE1 149 K4
Harpour Street WC1N 144 E4
Harriet Street SW1X 147 H3
Harriet Walk SW1X 147 H3
Harrington Gardens SW7 146 C6
Harrington Road SW7 146 E5
Harrington Square NW1 143 M1
Harrington Street NW1 143 M2
Harrison Street WC1H 144 D2
Harrods SW1X 147 G4
Harrowby Street W1H 143 G6
Harrow Place E1 150 B2
Harrow Road W2 142 A4
Hart Street EC3R 150 A3
Hasker Street SW3 147 G5
Hastings Street WC1H 144 C2
Hatfields SE1 149 G1
Hatherley Grove W2 142 B6
Hatteraick Road SE16 151 G6
Hatton Garden EC1N 145 G4
Hatton Street NW8 142 E4
Hatton Wall EC1N 145 G4
Havering Street E1 151 H3
Haverstock Street N1 145 J1
Hawke Place * SE16 151 H6
Haydon Street EC3N 150 B3
Hayes Place NW1 143 G4
Hay Hill W1J 143 L8
Hayles Street SE11 149 H5
Haymarket SW1Y 144 B8
Hayne Street EC1A 145 J4
Hay's Lane SE1 149 M1
Hay's Mews W1J 143 L8
Haywood Place EC1R 145 J4
Headfort Place SW1X 147 K3
Head Street E1 151 H2
Hearnshaw Street E14 151 K2
Hearn Street EC2A 145 M4
Heathcote Street WC1N 144 E3
Heddon Street W1B 143 M7
Heddon Street W1S 144 A7
Hedger Street SE11 149 H5

Heiron Street SE17 149 J8
Hellings Street E1W 150 D5
Helmet Row EC1V 145 K3
Helsinki Square SE16 151 L8
Henderson Drive NW8 142 E3
Heneage Lane EC3A 150 A3
Heneage Street E1 150 C1
Henrietta Place W1G 143 L6
Henrietta Street WC2E 144 D7
Henriques Street E1 150 D2
Henshaw Street SE17 149 L5
Herbal Hill EC1R 145 G4
Herbert Crescent SW1X 147 H4
Herbrand Street WC1H 144 C3
Hercules Road SE1 148 F4
Hereford Road W2 142 A6
Hereford Square SW7 146 D6
Hermitage Street W2 142 E5
Hermitage Wall E1W 150 D5
Hermit Street EC1V 145 H2
Heron Place SE16 151 K5
Heron Quays E14 151 M5
Herrick Street SW1P 148 C6
Hertford Street W1J 147 K2
Hertsmere Road E14 151 M4
Hesper Mews SW5 146 B6
Hessel Street E1 150 E3
Hewett Street EC2A 145 M3
Heygate Street SE17 149 J5
Hide Place SW1P 148 B6
High Holborn WC1V 144 E5
High Street Kensington ⊖ W8 146 A3
Hildyard Road SW6 146 A8
Hilliards Court E1W 150 F5
Hillingdon Street SE17 149 J8
Hill Road NW8 142 D1
Hills Place W1F 143 M6
Hill Street W1J 143 K8
Hinde Street W1U 143 K6
Hind Grove E14 151 M3
Hindgrove Area E14 151 M3
HMS Belfast SE1 150 A5
Hobart Place SW1W 147 K4
Hobury Street SW10 146 D8
Hogarth Road SW5 146 B6
Holbein Mews SW1W 147 J6
Holbein Place SW1W 147 J6
Holborn EC1N 145 G5
Holborn ⊖ WC2B 144 E5
Holborn Circus EC1N 145 G5
Holborn Viaduct EC1A 145 G5
Holford Street WC1X 144 F2
Holland Street SE1 149 H1
Holland Street W8 146 A3
Hollen Street W1F 144 A6
Holles Street W1C 143 L6
Hollywood Road SW10 146 C8
Holyoak Road SE11 149 H5
Holyrood Street SE1 149 M2
Holywell Row EC2A 145 M4
Homefield Street * N1 145 M1
Homer Row W1H 143 G5
Homer Street W1H 143 G5
Hooper Street E1 150 D3
Hopetown Street E1 150 C1
Hopkins Street W1F 144 A7
Hopton Street SE1 149 H1
Hopwood Road SE17 149 L8
Hornton Place W8 146 A3
Hornton Street W8 146 A2
Horse & Dolphin Yard W1D 144 B7
Horseferry Road E14 151 J3
Horseferry Road SW1P 148 B4
Horse Guards Avenue SW1A 148 C2
Horse Guards Parade SW1A 148 C2
Horse Guards Road SW1A 148 C2
Horselydown Lane SE1 150 B6
Horsley Street SE17 149 K8
Hosier Lane EC1A 145 H5
Hothfield Place SE16 151 G8
Hotspur Street SE11 148 F6
Houghton Street WC2A 144 E6
Houndsditch EC3A 150 A2
Houses of Parliament SW1A 148 D3
Howick Place SW1E 148 A4
Howland Street W1T 144 A4
Howland Way SE16 151 K7
Howley Place W2 142 D5
Hoxton Square N1 145 M2
Hoxton Street N1 145 M1
Hudson's Place SW1V 147 M5
Hugh Mews SW1V 147 L6
Hugh Street SW1V 147 L6
Hull Close SE16 151 J6
Hull Street EC1V 145 J2
Hungerford Bridge SE1 148 E1
Hunter Close SE1 149 M4
Hunter Street WC1N 144 D3
Huntley Street WC1E 144 A4
Huntsman Street SE17 149 M6
Huntsworth Mews NW1 143 H3
Hurley Crescent SE16 151 H6
Hutching's Street E14 151 M7
Hutton Street EC4Y 145 G7
Hyde Park W2 147 G1
Hyde Park Corner W1J 147 K2
Hyde Park Corner ⊖ W1J 147 K2
Hyde Park Crescent W2 146 D3
Hyde Park Crescent W2 142 F6
Hyde Park Gardens Mews W2 142 F7
Hyde Park Gardens W2 142 F7
Hyde Park Gate SW7 146 C3
Hyde Park Gate SW7 146 D3
Hyde Park Square W2 142 F7
Hyde Park Street W2 142 F7

I
Idol Lane EC3R 145 M7
Ifield Road SW10 146 B8
Iliffe Street SE17 149 J6
Iliffe Yard SE17 149 J6
Imperial College Road SW7 146 D4
Imperial War Museum SE1 149 G4
India Street EC3N 150 B3
Ingestre Place W1F 144 A7
Inglebert Street EC1R 145 G2
Ingram Close SE11 148 E5
Inner Circle NW1 143 J2
Inverness Terrace W2 142 B6
Inverness Terrace Gate W2 142 C8

Invicta Plaza SE1 149 H1
Inville Road SE17 149 L7
Ironmonger Lane EC2V 145 K6
Ironmonger Row EC1V 145 K2
Irving Street WC2N 144 C8
Isambard Place SE16 151 G6
Island Row E14 151 K3
Iverna Court W8 146 A4
Iverna Gardens W8 146 A4
Ives Street SW3 147 G5
Ivor Place NW1 143 G4
Ixworth Place SW3 146 F6

J
Jacob Street SE1 150 C6
Jamaica Gate SE16 150 E8
Jamaica Road SE1 150 C7
Jamaica Road SE16 150 E7
Jamaica Street E1 151 G2
Jamaica Wharf SE1 150 C6
James Street W1U 143 K6
James Street WC2E 144 D7
Jameson Street W8 146 A1
Jamuna Close E14 151 K1
Janeway Street SE16 150 D7
Jardine Road E1W 151 J4
Java Wharf SE1 150 C6
Jay Mews SW7 146 D3
Jermyn Street SW1Y 144 A8
Jerome Crescent NW8 142 F3
Jewery Street EC3N 150 B3
Joan Street SE1 149 G2
Jockey's Fields WC1R 144 E4
Johanna Street SE1 148 F3
John Adam Street WC2N 144 D8
John Carpenter Street EC4Y 145 G7
John Fisher Street E1 150 C4
John Islip Street SW1P 148 C5
John Prince's Street W1G 143 L6
John Roll Way SE16 150 D7
John Ruskin Street SE5 149 J8
John's Mews WC1N 144 E4
Johnson's Place SW1V 148 A7
Johnson Street E1 151 G3
John Street WC1N 144 E4
Joiner Street SE1 149 L1
Jonathan Street SE11 148 E6
Jubilee Place SW3 147 G6
Jubilee Street E1 151 G2
Jubilee Walk W8 146 B1
Judd Street WC1H 144 C2
Junction Mews W2 142 F5
Juxon Street SE11 148 E5

K
Katherine Close SE16 151 H5
Kean Street WC2B 144 E6
Keel Close SE16 151 J6
Keeley Street WC2B 144 E6
Keeton's Road SE16 150 E7
Kell Street SE1 149 H3
Kelso Place W8 146 B4
Kemble Street WC2B 144 E6
Kempsford Gardens SW5 146 A7
Kempsford Road SE11 149 G6
Kendall Place W1U 143 J5
Kendal Street W2 143 G6
Kennet Street E1W 150 D5
Kenning Street SE16 151 G6
Kennings Way SE11 149 G7
Kennington ⊖ SE11 149 H7
Kennington Lane SE11 148 E7
Kennington Oval SE11 148 E8
Kennington Park Gardens SE11 149 G8
Kennington Park Place SE11 149 G7
Kennington Park Road SE11 149 G7
Kennington Road SE1 148 F4
Kennington Road SE11 149 G5
Kennington Oval SE11 148 F8
Kenrick Place W1U 143 J5
Kensington Church Street W8 146 A1
Kensington Court W8 146 B3
Kensington Gardens W2 146 C1
Kensington Gardens Square W2 142 B6
Kensington Gate W8 146 C4
Kensington Gore SW7 146 E3
Kensington High Street W8 146 A4
Kensington Palace W8 146 B2
Kensington Palace Gardens W8 146 B1
Kensington Palace Gardens W8 146 B2
Kensington Place W8 146 A1
Kensington Road SW7 147 G3
Kensington Road W8 146 B3
Kensington Square W8 146 B3
Kenton Street WC1H 144 C3
Kenway Road SW5 146 A6
Keystone Close N1 144 D1
Keyworth Street SE1 149 H4
Kia Oval (Surrey County Cricket Ground) SE11 148 F8
Kilburn Park Road NW6 142 A2
Kildare Terrace W2 142 A6
Killick Street N1 144 E1
Kinburn Street SE16 151 H6
Kinder Street E1 150 E2
King & Queen Wharf SE16 151 H5
King and Queen Street SE17 149 K6
King Charles Street SW1A 148 C3
King David Lane E1 151 G3
Kingdom Street W2 142 C5
King Edward Street EC1A 145 J6
King Edward Walk SE1 149 G4
King James Street SE1 149 H3
Kingly Street W1F 143 M7
King's Arms Yard EC2R 145 L6
King's Bench Street SE1 149 H2
Kingscote Street EC4V 145 H7
King's Cross ⇌ N1C 144 D1
King's Cross Road WC1X 144 E2
King's Cross Square N1C 144 D1
King's Cross St Pancras ⊖ N1C 144 D1
Kingsgate Walk * SW1E 148 A4
King's Head Yard SE1 149 L1
King's Mews WC1N 144 F4
Kingsmill Terrace NW8 142 E1
King Square EC1V 145 J2
King's Scholars Passage SW1P 147 M5
King's Stairs Close SE16 150 F6
King Street WC2E 144 D7

King Street SW1Y ...148 A1
King Street EC2V ...145 K6
Kingsway WC2B ...144 E6
King William Street EC4N ...145 L7
Kinnerton Place North * SW1X ...147 J3
Kinnerton Place South * SW1X ...147 J3
Kinnerton Street SW1X ...147 J3
Kinnerton Yard * SW1X ...147 J3
Kipling Estate SE1 ...149 L3
Kipling Street SE1 ...149 L3
Kirby Estate SE16 ...150 D7
Kirby Grove SE1 ...149 M3
Kirby Street EC1N ...145 G4
Knaresborough Place SW5 ...146 B5
Knightrider Street EC4V ...145 H7
Knightsbridge SW1X ...147 H3
Knightsbridge SW3 ...147 H3
Knox Street W1H ...143 H4
Kynance Mews SW7 ...146 C4
Kynance Place SW7 ...146 C4

L

Lackington Street EC2A ...145 L4
Lafone Street SE1 ...150 B6
Lagado Mews SE16 ...151 H5
Lambeth Bridge SE1 ...148 D5
Lambeth High Street SE1 ...148 E5
Lambeth Hill EC4V ...145 J7
Lambeth North ⊖ SE1 ...148 F3
Lambeth Palace Road SE1 ...148 E4
Lambeth Road SE1 ...148 F4
Lambeth Walk SE11 ...148 F5
Lamb's Conduit Street WC1N ...144 E4
Lamb's Passage EC1Y ...145 K4
Lamb Street E1 ...150 B1
Lamb Way SE1 ...150 A7
Lamlash Street SE11 ...149 H6
Lanark Place W9 ...142 D3
Lanark Road W9 ...142 B1
Lancaster Gate W2 ...142 D7
Lancaster Gate W2 ...142 D8
Lancaster Gate ⊖ W2 ...142 E7
Lancaster Mews W2 ...142 D7
Lancaster Place WC2E ...144 E7
Lancaster Street SE1 ...149 H3
Lancaster Terrace W2 ...142 E7
Lancaster Walk W2 ...142 D8
Lancelot Place SW7 ...147 G3
Lancing Street NW1 ...144 B2
Lanesborough Place * SW1X ...147 J3
Langdale Street E1 ...150 E3
Langford Place NW8 ...142 D1
Langham Place W1B ...143 L5
Langham Street W1W ...143 L5
Langham Street W1W ...143 M5
Langley Lane SW8 ...148 D8
Langley Street WC2H ...144 C7
Langton Close WC1X ...144 E3
Lanhill Road W9 ...142 A3
Lansdowne Place SE1 ...149 L4
Lant Street SE1 ...149 J3
Larcom Street SE17 ...149 K6
Lauderdale Road W9 ...142 B3
Laud Street SE11 ...148 E7
Launcelot Street SE1 ...148 F3
Launceston Place W8 ...146 C4
Laurence Pountney Lane EC4V ...145 L7
Lavender Road SE16 ...151 K5
Lavender Wharf SE16 ...151 K4
Lavington Street SE1 ...149 J1
Lawn Lane SW8 ...148 D8
Lawrence Street SW3 ...146 F8
Lawrence Wharf SE16 ...151 L4
Law Street SE1 ...149 L4
Laxton Place NW1 ...143 L3
Laystall Street EC1R ...144 F4
Leadenhall Street EC3A ...150 A3
Leadenhall Street EC3V ...145 M6
Leake Street SE1 ...148 E2
Leather Lane EC1N ...145 G4
Leathermarket Street SE1 ...149 M3
Leeke Street WC1X ...144 E2
Lees Place W1K ...143 J7
Leicester Square ⊖ WC2H ...144 C7
Leicester Square WC2H ...144 C7
Leicester Street WC2H ...144 B7
Leigh Street WC1H ...144 C3
Leinster Gardens W2 ...142 C6
Leinster Mews W2 ...142 C7
Leinster Place W2 ...142 C7
Leinster Square W2 ...142 A7
Leinster Terrace W2 ...142 C7
Leman Street E1 ...150 C3
Lennox Gardens SW1X ...147 G4
Lennox Gardens Mews SW1X ...147 G5
Leonard Street EC2A ...145 L3
Leopold Estate E3 ...151 M1
Leopold Street E3 ...151 L1
Leroy Street SE1 ...149 M5
Lever Street EC1V ...145 J2
Lewisham Street SW1H ...148 B3
Lexham Gardens W8 ...146 A5
Lexham Mews W8 ...146 A5
Lexington Street W1F ...144 A7
Leyden Street E1 ...150 B2
Leydon Close SE16 ...151 H5
Library Street SE1 ...149 H3
Lidlington Place NW1 ...144 A1
Lilestone Street NW8 ...142 F3
Lilley Close E1W ...150 D5
Lillie Road SW6 ...146 A7
Lillie Yard SW6 ...146 A7
Limeburner Lane EC4M ...145 H6
Lime Close E1W ...150 D5
Limehouse Causeway E14 ...151 L4
Limehouse Link E14 ...151 L3
Limehouse ≥ ⊖ E14 ...151 J3
Limerston Street SW10 ...146 D8
Lime Street EC3M ...145 M7
Lincoln's Inn Fields WC2A ...144 E6
Linden Gardens W2 ...142 A8
Lindley Street E1 ...150 F1
Lindsay Square SW1V ...148 B7
Lindsey Street EC1A ...145 H4
Linhope Street NW1 ...143 G3
Linsey Street SE16 ...150 D8
Lisle Street WC2H ...144 B7
Lisson Green Estate NW8 ...142 F3
Lisson Grove NW1 ...143 G4
Lisson Grove NW8 ...142 F3
Lisson Street NW1 ...142 F4
Litchfield Street WC2H ...144 C7
Little Argyll Street W1F ...143 M6

Little Britain EC1A ...145 J5
Little Chester Street SW1X ...147 K4
Little George Street SW1P ...148 C3
Little Marlborough Street W1F ...144 A7
Little New Street EC4A ...145 G6
Little Portland Street W1G ...143 L6
Little Russell Street WC1A ...144 C5
Little St James's Street SW1A ...147 M2
Little Sanctuary SW1A ...148 C3
Little Somerset Street E1 ...150 B3
Little Titchfield Street W1W ...143 M5
Liverpool Grove SE17 ...149 K7
Liverpool Street EC2M ...145 M5
Liverpool Street ≥ ⊖ EC2M ...145 M5
Lizard Street EC1V ...145 K3
Llewellyn Street SE16 ...150 D7
Logan Place W8 ...146 A5
Lolesworth Close E1 ...150 B1
Lollard Street SE11 ...148 F5
Lollard Street SE11 ...148 F6
Loman Street SE1 ...149 J2
Lomas Street E1 ...150 D1
Lombard Lane EC4Y ...145 G6
Lombard Street EC3V ...145 L7
London Bridge EC4R ...145 L8
London Bridge ≥ ⊖ NW1 ...149 L1
London Bridge Street SE1 ...149 L1
London Dungeon SE1 ...148 E2
London Eye SE1 ...148 E2
London Mews W2 ...142 E6
London Road SE1 ...149 H4
London Street EC3R ...150 A3
London Street W2 ...142 E6
London Transport
  Museum WC2E ...144 D7
London Wall EC2M ...145 K5
London Zoo ZSL NW1 ...143 J1
Long Acre WC2E ...144 D7
Longford Street NW1 ...143 L3
Long Lane EC1A ...145 J5
Long Lane SE1 ...149 L3
Longmoore Street SW1V ...147 M5
Longridge Road SW5 ...146 A5
Longville Road SE11 ...149 H5
Long Walk SE1 ...150 A8
Long Yard WC1N ...144 E4
Lord North Street SW1P ...148 C4
Lord's Cricket Ground NW8 ...142 E2
Lorenzo Street WC1X ...144 E1
Lorrimore Road SE17 ...149 J8
Lorrimore Square SE17 ...149 H8
Lothbury EC2R ...145 L6
Loughborough Street SE11 ...148 F7
Lovat Lane EC3R ...145 M7
Love Lane EC2V ...145 K6
Lovell Place SE16 ...151 K7
Lowell Street E14 ...151 L1
Lower Belgrave Street SW1W ...147 K4
Lower Grosvenor Place SW1W ...147 L4
Lower James Street W1F ...144 A7
Lower John Street W1F ...144 A7
Lower Marsh SE1 ...148 F3
Lower Road SE16 ...151 G7
Lower Sloane Street SW1W ...147 J6
Lower Thames Street EC3R ...150 A4
Lower Thames Street EC3R ...145 M8
Lowndes Close * SW1X ...147 J4
Lowndes Place SW1X ...147 J4
Lowndes Square SW1X ...147 H3
Lowndes Street SW1X ...147 J4
Lucan Place SW3 ...146 F5
Lucey Road SE16 ...150 C8
Ludgate Circus EC4M ...145 H6
Ludgate Hill EC4M ...145 H6
Luke Street EC2A ...145 M3
Lukin Street E1 ...151 G3
Lumley Street W1K ...143 K7
Lupus Street SW1V ...147 L7
Lupus Street SW1V ...148 B7
Luton Street NW8 ...142 F4
Luxborough Street W1U ...143 J4
Lyall Mews SW1X ...147 J4
Lyall Street SW1X ...147 J4
Lyons Place NW8 ...142 E3
Lytham Street SE17 ...149 K7

M

Macclesfield Road EC1V ...145 J2
Macclesfield Street * W1D ...144 B7
Mace Close E1W ...150 E5
Macklin Street WC2B ...144 D6
Mackworth Street NW1 ...143 M2
Macleod Street SE17 ...149 K7
Madame Tussauds NW1 ...143 J4
Maddox Street W1S ...143 M7
Magdalen Street SE1 ...149 M2
Magee Street SE11 ...148 F8
Maguire Street SE1 ...150 C6
Maida Avenue W9 ...142 D4
Maida Vale W9 ...142 C2
Maida Vale ⊖ W9 ...142 C2
Maiden Lane SE1 ...149 L1
Maiden Lane WC2E ...144 D7
Major Road SE16 ...150 D7
Makins Street SW3 ...147 G6
Malet Street WC1E ...144 B4
Mallord Street SW3 ...146 E8
Mallory Street NW8 ...142 F3
Mallow Street EC1Y ...145 L3
Malta Street EC1V ...145 H3
Maltby Street SE1 ...150 B7
Manchester Square W1U ...143 J6
Manchester Street W1U ...143 J5
Manciple Street SE1 ...149 L3
Mandeville Place W1U ...143 K6
Manette Street W1D ...144 B6
Manilla Street E14 ...151 M6
Manningford Close EC1V ...145 H2
Manor Place SE17 ...149 J7
Manresa Road SW3 ...146 F7
Mansell Street E1 ...150 C3
Mansfield Mews W1G ...143 L5
Mansfield Street W1G ...143 L5

Mansion House ⊖ EC4V ...145 K7
Manson Mews SW7 ...146 D5
Manson Place SW7 ...146 D6
Mapleleaf Square SE16 ...151 J6
Maples Place E1 ...150 F1
Maple Street W1T ...143 M4
Marble Arch ⊖ W1C ...143 H7
Marchmont Street WC1H ...144 C3
Margaret Street W1G ...143 L6
Margaretta Terrace SW3 ...146 F7
Margery Street WC1X ...144 F3
Marigold Street SE16 ...150 E7
Marine Street SE16 ...150 C7
Market Mews W1J ...147 K1
Market Place W1W ...143 M6
Markham Square SW3 ...147 G6
Markham Street SW3 ...147 G6
Mark Lane EC3R ...150 A4
Marlborough Gate W2 ...142 E7
Marlborough Place NW8 ...142 C1
Marlborough Road SW1A ...148 A2
Marlborough Street SW3 ...146 F6
Marloes Road W8 ...146 B4
Marlow Way SE16 ...151 H6
Maroon Street E14 ...151 K2
Marshall Street W1F ...144 A7
Marshalsea Road SE1 ...149 K2
Marsham Street SW1P ...148 C5
Marsh Wall E14 ...151 M5
Martha's Buildings EC1V ...145 K3
Martha Street E1 ...150 F3
Martin Lane EC4V ...145 L7
Maryland Road W9 ...142 A4
Marylands Road W9 ...142 A4
Marylebone ≥ ⊖ NW1 ...143 G4
Marylebone Flyover W2 ...142 E5
Marylebone High Street W1U ...143 K5
Marylebone Lane W1U ...143 K6
Marylebone Road NW1 ...143 G4
Marylebone Street W1G ...143 K5
Marylee Way SE11 ...148 F6
Masjid Lane E14 ...151 M2
Mason Street SE17 ...149 M5
Massinger Street SE17 ...149 M6
Masters Street E1 ...151 J1
Matlock Street E14 ...151 J2
Matthew Parker Street SW1H ...148 C3
Maunsel Street SW1P ...148 B5
Mayfair Place W1J ...147 L1
Mayflower Street SE16 ...150 F7
Mayford Estate NW1 ...144 A1
Maynards Quay E1W ...150 F4
May's Court WC2N ...144 C8
McAuley Close SE1 ...148 F4
McLeod's Mews SW7 ...146 C5
Meadcroft Road SE11 ...149 G8
Meadcroft Road SE11 ...149 H8
Meadow Road SW8 ...148 E8
Meadow Row SE1 ...149 J5
Mead Row SE1 ...148 F4
Meakin Estate SE1 ...149 M4
Mecklenburgh Square WC1N ...144 E3
Medway Street SW1P ...148 B5
Meeting House Alley E1W ...150 E5
Melcombe Place NW1 ...143 G4
Melcombe Street W1U ...143 H4
Melina Place NW8 ...142 D2
Melior Street SE1 ...149 M2
Melton Street NW1 ...144 A2
Memorial Gates SW1W ...147 K3
Mepham Street SE1 ...148 F2
Mercer Street WC2H ...144 C7
Merchant Square W2 ...142 E5
Merlin Street EC1R ...144 F2
Mermaid Court SE1 ...149 K2
Merrick Square SE1 ...149 K4
Merrington Road SW6 ...146 A8
Merrow Street SE17 ...149 L7
Methley Street SE11 ...149 G7
Meymott Street SE1 ...149 G2
Micawber Street N1 ...145 K1
Micklethwaite Road SW6 ...146 A8
Middlesex Street E1 ...150 A1
Middlesex Street E1 ...150 B2
Middle Street EC1A ...145 J5
Middle Temple WC2R ...144 F7
Middle Temple Lane EC4Y ...144 F7
Middleton Drive SE16 ...151 H6
Midland Road NW1 ...144 C1
Midship Close SE16 ...151 H6
Milborne Grove SW10 ...146 D7
Milcote Street SE1 ...149 H3
Miles Street SW8 ...148 D8
Milford Lane WC2R ...144 F7
Milk Street EC2V ...145 K6
Milk Yard E1W ...151 G4
Millbank SW1P ...148 D4
Millennium Bridge SE1 ...145 J8
Millennium Harbour E14 ...151 M6
Milligan Street E14 ...151 L4
Millman Mews WC1N ...144 E4
Millman Street WC1N ...144 E4
Mill Place E14 ...151 K3
Millstream Road SE1 ...150 B7
Mill Street SE1 ...150 C6
Mill Street W1S ...143 L7
Milner Street SW3 ...147 G5
Milton Street EC2Y ...145 K4
Milverton Street SE11 ...149 G7
Mincing Lane EC3M ...150 A4
Minera Mews SW1W ...147 J5
Minories EC3N ...150 B3
Mitchell Street EC1V ...145 J3
Mitre Road SE1 ...149 G2
Mitre Street EC3A ...150 A3
Molyneux Street W1H ...143 G5
Monck Street SW1P ...148 C4
Monkton Street SE11 ...149 G5
Monkwell Square EC2Y ...145 K5
Monmouth Place W2 ...142 A6
Monmouth Road W2 ...142 A6
Monmouth Street WC2H ...144 C6
Montague Close SE1 ...149 L1
Montague Place WC1B ...144 C5
Montague Street WC1B ...144 C5
Montagu Mansions W1U ...143 H5
Montagu Mews North W1H ...143 H5
Montagu Mews West W1H ...143 H5
Montagu Place W1H ...143 H5
Montagu Row W1U ...143 H5
Montagu Square W1H ...143 H6
Montford Place SE11 ...148 F7
Monthorpe Road E1 ...150 C1
Montpelier Square SW7 ...147 G3
Montpelier Street SW7 ...147 G3

Montpelier Walk SW7 ...146 G3
Montrose Place SW1X ...147 K3
Monument ⊖ EC4R ...145 L7
Monument Street EC3R ...145 L7
Monument Street EC3R ...145 M7
Monza Street E1W ...151 G4
Moodkee Street SE16 ...151 G7
Moore Street SW3 ...147 H5
Moorfields EC2Y ...145 L5
Moorgate EC2R ...145 L6
Moorgate ⊖ EC2Y ...145 L5
Moor Lane EC2Y ...145 K5
Moor Street W1D ...144 C7
Mora Street EC1V ...145 K2
Morecambe Street SE17 ...149 K6
Moreland Street EC1V ...145 H2
Moreton Place SW1V ...148 A6
Moreton Street SW1V ...148 B6
Moreton Terrace SW1V ...148 A6
Morgan's Lane SE1 ...149 M2
Morgan's Lane SE1 ...150 A5
Morley Street SE1 ...149 G3
Mornington Crescent NW1 ...143 M1
Mornington Place NW1 ...143 L1
Mornington Terrace NW1 ...143 L1
Morocco Street SE1 ...150 A7
Morpeth Terrace SW1P ...147 M5
Morris Street E1 ...150 F3
Morshead Road W9 ...142 A2
Mortimer Market WC1E ...144 A4
Mortimer Street W1T ...144 A5
Mortimer Street W1W ...143 M5
Morton Place SE1 ...148 F4
Morwell Street WC1B ...144 B5
Moscow Place W2 ...142 B7
Moscow Road W2 ...142 B7
Mossop Street SW3 ...147 G5
Motcomb Street SW1X ...147 J4
Mount Gate W2 ...146 E2
Mount Mills EC1V ...145 J3
Mount Pleasant WC1X ...144 F4
Mount Row W1K ...143 K8
Mount Street W1K ...143 K8
Mount Street Mews W1K ...143 K8
Mount Terrace E1 ...150 E1
Moxon Street W1U ...143 J5
Mulberry Street E1 ...150 D2
Mulberry Walk SW3 ...146 E8
Mulready Street NW8 ...142 F4
Mundy Street N1 ...145 M2
Munster Square NW1 ...143 L3
Munton Road SE17 ...149 K5
Murphy Street SE1 ...148 F3
Murray Grove N1 ...145 K1
Musbury Street E1 ...151 G2
Muscovy Street EC3N ...150 A4
Museum of London EC2Y ...145 J5
Museum Street WC1A ...144 C5
Myddelton Passage EC1R ...145 G2
Myddelton Square EC1R ...145 G1
Myddelton Street EC1R ...145 G3
Myrdle Street E1 ...150 D2

N

Naoroji Street WC1X ...144 F2
Napier Grove N1 ...145 K1
Narrow Street E14 ...151 K4
Nash Street NW1 ...143 L2
Nassau Street W1W ...143 M5
Nathaniel Close * E1 ...150 C2
National Portrait
  Gallery WC2N ...144 C8
Natural History Museum SW7 ...146 E4
Neal Street WC2H ...144 C6
Neathouse Place * SW1V ...147 M5
Neckinger SE1 ...150 C8
Needleman Street SE16 ...151 H7
Nelson Close NW6 ...142 A1
Nelson Place N1 ...145 H1
Nelson's Column WC2N ...144 C8
Nelson Square SE1 ...149 H2
Nelson Street E1 ...150 E2
Nelson Terrace N1 ...145 H1
Neptune Street SE16 ...151 G7
Nesham Street E1W ...150 D4
Netherby Grove SW10 ...146 D8
Netley Street NW1 ...143 M2
Nevern Place SW5 ...146 A6
Nevern Road SW5 ...146 A6
Nevern Square SW5 ...146 A6
Neville Street SW7 ...146 E6
Newark Street E1 ...150 E2
New Atlas Wharf E14 ...151 M8
New Bond Street W1S ...143 L7
New Bond Street W1S ...143 L8
New Bridge Street EC4V ...145 H6
New Broad Street EC2M ...145 M5
New Burlington Street W1S ...143 M7
Newburn Street SE11 ...148 F7
Newbury Street EC1A ...145 J5
Newcastle Place W2 ...142 E5
New Cavendish Street W1G ...143 L5
New Change EC4M ...145 J6
New Church Road SE5 ...149 L8
Newcomen Street SE1 ...149 K2
New Compton Street WC2H ...144 C6
Newcourt Street NW8 ...142 F1
Newell Street E14 ...151 L3
New Fetter Lane EC4A ...145 G6
Newgate Street EC1A ...145 H6
New Globe Walk SE1 ...145 J8
New Goulston Street E1 ...150 B2
Newham's Row SE1 ...150 A7
Newington Butts SE1 ...149 H5
Newington Causeway SE1 ...149 K4
New Kent Road SE1 ...149 K5
Newlands Quay E1W ...150 F4
Newman Street W1T ...144 A5
New North Place EC2A ...145 M3
New North Road N1 ...145 L1
New North Street WC1N ...144 D4
New Oxford Street WC1A ...144 C6
Newport Street SE11 ...148 E5
New Quebec Street W1H ...143 H6
New Ride SW7 ...146 E3
New Road E1 ...150 E2
New Row WC2N ...144 C7
New Spring Gardens Walk SE1 ...148 D7
New Square WC2A ...144 F6
New Street EC2M ...150 A2
New Street Square EC4A ...145 G6
Newton Road W2 ...142 A6
Newton Street WC2B ...144 D5

New Union Street EC2Y ...145 K5
Nicholas Lane EC3V ...145 L7
Nicholson Street SE1 ...149 H1
Nightingale Place SW10 ...146 D8
Nile Street N1 ...145 K2
Nine Elms Lane SW8 ...148 C8
Noble Street EC2V ...145 J6
Noel Road * N1 ...145 J1
Noel Street W1F ...144 A6
Norbiton Road E14 ...151 L2
Norfolk Crescent W2 ...143 G6
Norfolk Place W2 ...142 E6
Norfolk Square W2 ...142 E6
Norman Street EC1V ...145 J3
Norris Street SW1Y ...144 B8
Northampton Road EC1R ...145 G3
Northampton Square EC1V ...145 H2
North Audley Street W1K ...143 J7
North Bank NW8 ...142 F2
Northburgh Street EC1V ...145 H3
North Carriage Drive W2 ...142 F7
Northdown Street N1 ...144 D1
Northey Street E14 ...151 K4
North Gower Street NW1 ...144 A2
Northington Street WC1N ...144 E4
North Mews WC1N ...144 E4
North Ride W2 ...143 G7
North Row W1K ...143 J7
North Terrace SW3 ...146 F5
Northumberland Alley EC3N ...150 B3
Northumberland
  Avenue WC2N ...148 C1
Northumberland Place W2 ...142 A6
Northumberland Street WC2N ...148 C1
North Wharf Road W2 ...142 E5
Northwick Terrace NW8 ...142 D3
Norway Gate SE16 ...151 K7
Norway Place E14 ...151 L3
Norwich Street EC4A ...144 F5
Nottingham Place W1U ...143 J4
Nottingham Street W1U ...143 J4
Notting Hill Gate W11 ...142 A8
Notting Hill Gate ⊖ W11 ...146 A1
Nugent Terrace NW8 ...142 D1
Nutford Place W1H ...143 G6

O

Oakden Street SE11 ...149 G5
Oakington Road W9 ...142 A3
Oak Lane E14 ...151 L3
Oakley Close EC1V ...145 H1
Oakley Gardens SW3 ...147 G8
Oakley Square NW1 ...144 A1
Oakley Street SW3 ...146 F8
Oak Tree Road NW8 ...142 F2
Oat Lane EC2V ...145 J5
Occupation Road SE17 ...149 J6
Ocean Square E1 ...151 J1
Ocean Street E1 ...151 J1
Odessa Street SE16 ...151 L7
Ogle Street W1W ...143 M5
Old Bailey EC4M ...145 H6
Old Barrack Yard SW1X ...147 J3
Old Bond Street W1S ...143 M8
Old Broad Street EC2N ...145 M6
Old Brompton Road SW5 ...146 B6
Old Brompton Road SW7 ...146 D6
Old Burlington Street W1S ...143 M7
Oldbury Place W1U ...143 J4
Old Castle Street E1 ...150 B2
Old Cavendish Street W1G ...143 L6
Old Church Road E1 ...151 H2
Old Church Street SW3 ...146 E7
Old Compton Street W1D ...144 B7
Old Court Place W8 ...146 B3
Old Gloucester Street WC1N ...144 D4
Old Jamaica Road SE16 ...150 C7
Old Jewry EC2R ...145 K6
Old Kent Road SE1 ...149 M5
Old Marylebone Road NW1 ...143 G5
Old Montague Street E1 ...150 C1
Old North Street WC1X ...144 E5
Old Paradise Street SE11 ...148 E5
Old Park Lane W1J ...147 K2
Old Pye Street SW1P ...148 B4
Old Queen Street SW1H ...148 B3
Old Square WC2A ...144 F6
Old Street EC1V ...145 K3
Old Street ≥ ⊖ EC1V ...145 L3
Old Street Junction EC1Y ...145 L3
Oliver's Yard EC1Y ...145 L3
Olney Road SE17 ...149 J8
O'Meara Street SE1 ...149 K2
Omega Place N1 ...144 D1
Onega Gate SE16 ...151 K8
Ongar Road SW6 ...146 A8
Onslow Gardens SW7 ...146 D6
Onslow Square SW7 ...146 E5
Onslow Square SW7 ...146 E6
Ontario Street SE1 ...149 J4
Ontario Way E14 ...151 M4
Opal Street SE11 ...149 H6
Orange Place SE16 ...151 G8
Orange Square SW1W ...147 K6
Orange Street WC2H ...144 B8
Orange Street E1W ...150 D5
Orb Street SE17 ...149 L6
Orchardson Street NW8 ...142 E4
Orchard Street W1H ...143 J6
Orde Hall Street WC1N ...144 E4
Orient Street SE11 ...149 H5
Orme Court W2 ...142 B8
Orme Lane W2 ...142 B8
Orme Square Gate W2 ...142 B8
Ormond Close WC1N ...144 D4
Ormonde Gate SW3 ...147 H7
Ormond Yard SW1Y ...144 A8
Orsett Mews W2 ...142 C6
Orsett Street SE11 ...148 E6
Orsett Terrace W2 ...142 C5
Orton Street E1W ...150 D5
Osbert Street SW1V ...148 B6
Osborn Street E1 ...150 C2
Oslo Square SE16 ...151 K7
Osnaburgh Street NW1 ...143 L3
Osnaburgh Terrace NW1 ...143 L3
Ossington Buildings W1U ...143 J5
Ossington Street W2 ...142 A7
Ossulston Street NW1 ...144 B1
Oswin Street SE11 ...149 H5
Othello Close SE11 ...149 H6
Otto Street SE17 ...149 H8
Outer Circle NW1 ...143 H3

Outer Circle NW1 ... 143 K1
Oval ⊖ SE11 ... 148 F8
Oval Way SE11 ... 148 E7
Ovington Square SW3 ... 147 G4
Ovington Street SW3 ... 147 G5
Owen Street EC1V ... 145 G1
Oxendon Street SW1Y ... 144 B8
Oxford Circus ⊖ W1B ... 143 M6
Oxford Road NW6 ... 142 A1
Oxford Square W2 ... 142 F6
Oxford Street W1C ... 143 L6
Oxford Street WC1A ... 144 A6

P

Pace Place E1 ... 150 E3
Pacific Wharf SE16 ... 151 H5
Paddington ≷⊖ W2 ... 142 D6
Paddington Green W2 ... 142 E5
Paddington Street W1U ... 143 J5
Pageant Crescent SE16 ... 151 K5
Page Street SW1P ... 148 B5
Paget Street EC1V ... 145 H2
Pakenham Street WC1X ... 144 E3
Palace Avenue W8 ... 146 B2
Palace Court W2 ... 142 A7
Palace Gardens Terrace W8 ... 146 A1
Palace Gate W8 ... 146 C3
Palace Green W8 ... 146 B2
Palace of Westminster SW1A ... 148 D3
Palace Place SW1E ... 147 M4
Palace Street SW1E ... 147 M4
Pall Mall SW1Y ... 148 A1
Pall Mall East SW1Y ... 148 B1
Palmer Street SW1H ... 148 B3
Pancras Lane EC4N ... 145 K6
Pancras Road N1C ... 144 C1
Panton Street SW1Y ... 144 B8
Paradise Street SE16 ... 150 E7
Paradise Walk SW3 ... 147 H8
Pardoner Street SE1 ... 149 L4
Pardon Street EC1V ... 145 H3
Parfett Street E1 ... 150 D2
Paris Garden SE1 ... 149 G1
Park Crescent W1B ... 143 K4
Park Crescent Mews
  West W1G ... 143 K4
Parker's Row SE1 ... 150 C7
Parker Street WC2B ... 144 D6
Park Lane W1K ... 143 H7
Park Lane W1 ... 147 J1
Park Place SW1A ... 147 M1
Park Place Villas W2 ... 142 D4
Park Road NW1 ... 143 H3
Park Square East NW1 ... 143 L3
Park Square Mews NW1 ... 143 K3
Park Square West NW1 ... 143 K3
Park Street SE1 ... 149 K1
Park Street W1K ... 143 J7
Park Village East NW1 ... 143 L1
Park Walk SW10 ... 146 D8
Park West Place W2 ... 143 G6
Parliament Street SW1A ... 148 C2
Parry Street SW8 ... 148 D8
Passmore Street SW1W ... 147 J6
Paternoster Square EC4 ... 145 J6
Pater Street W8 ... 146 A4
Pattina Walk SE16 ... 151 K5
Paul Street EC2A ... 145 M3
Paultons Square SW3 ... 146 E8
Paveley Street NW1 ... 143 G3
Pavilion Road SW1X ... 147 H3
Pavilion Street SW1X ... 147 H4
Paxton Terrace SW1V ... 147 L7
Peabody Avenue SW1V ... 147 L7
Peabody Estate SE1 ... 149 J1
Peacock Street SE17 ... 149 J6
Pearl Street E1W ... 150 F5
Pearman Street SE1 ... 149 G3
Pear Tree Court EC1R ... 145 G3
Peartree Lane E1W ... 151 G4
Pear Tree Street EC1V ... 145 J3
Peel Street W8 ... 146 A1
Peerless Street EC1V ... 145 K2
Pelham Crescent SW7 ... 146 F6
Pelham Place SW7 ... 146 F5
Pelham Street SW7 ... 146 F5
Pelier Street SE17 ... 149 K8
Pemberton Row EC4A ... 145 G6
Pembridge Gardens W2 ... 142 A8
Pembridge Place W2 ... 142 A7
Pembridge Square W2 ... 142 A7
Pembridge Villas W11 ... 142 A7
Pembroke Close SW1X ... 147 J3
Penang Street E1W ... 150 F5
Penfold Place NW1 ... 142 F5
Penfold Street NW8 ... 142 E4
Pennant Mews W8 ... 146 B5
Pennington Street E1W ... 150 D4
Pennyfields E14 ... 151 M4
Penrose Grove SE17 ... 149 J7
Penrose Street SE17 ... 149 J7
Penton Place SE17 ... 149 H6
Penton Rise WC1X ... 144 E2
Penton Street N1 ... 144 F1
Pentonville Road N1 ... 144 E1
Penywern Road SW5 ... 146 A6
Pepper Street SE1 ... 149 J2
Pepys Street EC3N ... 150 A4
Percival Street EC1V ... 145 H3
Percy Circus WC1X ... 144 F2
Percy Street W1T ... 144 B5
Perkin's Rents SW1P ... 148 B4
Perryn Road SE16 ... 150 E7
Petersham Mews SW7 ... 146 D4
Petersham Place SW7 ... 146 C4
Peter Street W1F ... 144 B7
Peto Place NW1 ... 143 L3
Petticoat Lane E1 ... 150 B2
Petty France SW1H ... 148 A3
Petyward SW3 ... 147 G6
Phelp Street SE17 ... 149 L7
Phene Street SW3 ... 147 G8
Phillimore Walk W8 ... 146 A3
Philpot Lane EC3M ... 145 M7
Philpot Street E1 ... 150 E2
Phipp's Mews SW1W ... 147 L5
Phipp Street EC2A ... 145 M3
Phoenix Place WC1X ... 144 F3
Phoenix Road NW1 ... 144 B1
Phoenix Street WC2H ... 144 C6
Piccadilly W1J ... 147 L2
Piccadilly Arcade SW1Y ... 147 M1

Piccadilly Circus W1B ... 144 A8
Piccadilly Circus ⊖ W1J ... 144 B8
Pickard Street EC1V ... 145 J2
Picton Place W1U ... 143 K6
Pier Head E1W ... 150 E6
Pigott Street E14 ... 151 M3
Pilgrimage Street SE1 ... 149 L3
Pimlico SW1V ... 148 B6
Pimlico Road SW1W ... 147 J6
Pinchin Street E1 ... 150 D3
Pindar Street EC2A ... 145 M4
Pindock Mews W9 ... 142 B3
Pine Street EC1R ... 144 F3
Pitfield Street N1 ... 145 M1
Pitsea Street E1 ... 151 H3
Pitt's Head Mews W1J ... 147 K2
Pitt Street W8 ... 146 A2
Pixley Street E14 ... 151 L2
Platina Street * EC2A ... 145 L3
Plover Way SE16 ... 151 K8
Plumbers Row E1 ... 150 D2
Plumtree Court EC4A ... 145 G5
Plympton Street NW8 ... 142 F4
Pocock Street SE1 ... 149 H2
Poland Street W1F ... 144 A6
Pollen Street W1S ... 143 L7
Pollitt Drive NW8 ... 142 E3
Polperro Mews SE11 ... 149 G5
Polygon Road NW1 ... 144 B1
Pond Place SW3 ... 146 F6
Ponler Street E1 ... 150 E3
Ponsonby Place SW1P ... 148 C6
Ponsonby Terrace SW1P ... 148 C6
Ponton Road * SW1V ... 148 B8
Pont Street SW1X ... 147 H4
Poolmans Street SE16 ... 151 H6
Pope Street SE1 ... 150 B7
Poplar Place W2 ... 142 B7
Poppin's Court EC4A ... 145 H6
Porchester Gardens W2 ... 142 B7
Porchester Gate W2 ... 142 C8
Porchester Place W2 ... 143 G6
Porchester Road W2 ... 142 B5
Porchester Square W2 ... 142 B6
Porchester Terrace W2 ... 142 C7
Porchester Terrace
  North W2 ... 142 C6
Porlock Street SE1 ... 149 L3
Porter Street NW1 ... 143 H4
Porteus Road W2 ... 142 D5
Portland Place W1B ... 143 L4
Portland Place W1B ... 143 L5
Portland Square E1W ... 150 E5
Portland Street SE17 ... 149 L7
Portman Close W1H ... 143 J6
Portman Mews South W1H ... 143 J6
Portman Square W1H ... 143 J6
Portman Street W1H ... 143 J6
Portpool Lane EC1N ... 144 F4
Portsea Place W2 ... 143 G6
Portsmouth Street WC2A ... 144 E6
Portsoken Street E1 ... 150 B3
Portugal Street WC2A ... 144 E6
Potier Street SE1 ... 149 L4
Potters Fields SE1 ... 150 B6
Pottery Street SE16 ... 150 F7
Poultry EC2V ... 145 K6
Powis Place WC1N ... 144 D4
Praed Mews W2 ... 142 E6
Praed Street W2 ... 142 E6
Pratt Walk SE1 ... 148 E5
Premier Place E14 ... 151 M4
Prescot Street E1 ... 150 C3
Preston Close SE1 ... 149 M5
Price's Street SE1 ... 149 H1
Prideaux Place WC1X ... 144 F2
Primrose Street EC2A ... 150 A1
Prince Albert Road NW8 ... 142 F1
Prince Consort Road SW7 ... 146 D3
Princelet Street E1 ... 150 C1
Prince of Wales Gate SW7 ... 146 F3
Princes Arcade SW1Y ... 144 A8
Prince's Gardens SW7 ... 146 E3
Prince's Gate Mews SW7 ... 146 E4
Princes Riverside
  Road SE16 ... 151 H5
Prince's Square W2 ... 142 A7
Princess Road NW6 ... 142 A1
Princess Street SE1 ... 149 H4
Princes Street W1B ... 143 L6
Prince's Street EC2R ... 145 L6
Princeton Street WC1R ... 144 E5
Prioress Street SE1 ... 149 L4
Priory Green Estate N1 ... 144 E1
Priory Walk SW10 ... 146 D7
Proctor Street WC1V ... 144 E5
Prospect Place E1W ... 151 G5
Prospect Street SE16 ... 150 E7
Provident Court W1K ... 143 J7
Provost Street N1 ... 145 L1
Prusom Street E1W ... 150 F5
Pudding Lane EC3R ... 145 M7
Pumphouse Mews E1 ... 150 D3
Purbrook Street SE1 ... 150 A7
Purcell Street N1 ... 145 M1
Purchese Street NW1 ... 144 B1

Q

Quebec Way SE16 ... 151 J7
Queen Anne's Gate SW1H ... 148 B3
Queen Anne Street W1G ... 143 K5
Queen Elizabeth Street SE1 ... 150 B6
Queen Mother Gate W2 ... 147 J2
Queensborough Terrace W2 ... 142 C7
Queensburry Place SW7 ... 146 E5
Queen's Gardens W2 ... 142 C7
Queen's Gate SW7 ... 146 D3
Queen's Gate SW7 ... 146 D4
Queen's Gate Gardens SW7 ... 146 D5
Queen's Gate Mews SW7 ... 146 D4
Queen's Gate Place SW7 ... 146 D4
Queen's Gate
  Place Mews SW7 ... 146 D4
Queen's Gate Terrace SW7 ... 146 C4
Queen's Mews W2 ... 142 B7
Queen Square WC1N ... 144 D4
Queen's Row SE17 ... 149 K7
Queen Street EC4N ... 145 K7
Queen Street W1J ... 147 L1
Queen Street Place EC4R ... 145 K7
Queen's Walk SE1 ... 150 A5
Queen's Walk SW1A ... 147 M2
Queensway W2 ... 142 B6

Queensway ⊖ W2 ... 142 B8
Queen Victoria Street EC4V ... 145 J7
Quick Street N1 ... 145 H1

R

Raby Street E14 ... 151 K2
Radcliffe Road SE1 ... 150 B8
Radcot Street SE11 ... 149 G2
Radnor Mews W2 ... 142 E6
Radnor Place W2 ... 142 F6
Radnor Street EC1V ... 145 K3
Radnor Walk SW3 ... 147 G7
Railway Approach SE1 ... 149 L1
Railway Avenue SE16 ... 151 G6
Railway Street N1 ... 144 D1
Raine Street E1W ... 150 F5
Ralston Street SW3 ... 147 H7
Ramillies Place W1F ... 143 M6
Ramillies Street W1F ... 143 M6
Rampart Street E1 ... 150 E2
Rampayne Street SW1V ... 148 B6
Randall Road SE11 ... 148 D6
Randall Row SE11 ... 148 E6
Randolph Avenue W9 ... 142 B1
Randolph Crescent W9 ... 142 C3
Randolph Gardens NW6 ... 142 B1
Randolph Mews W9 ... 142 D4
Randolph Road W9 ... 142 C4
Ranelagh Grove SW1W ... 147 K6
Ranelagh Road SW1V ... 148 A7
Rangoon Street * EC3N ... 150 B3
Ranston Street NW8 ... 142 F4
Raphael Street SW7 ... 147 G3
Ratcliffe Cross Street E1W ... 151 J3
Ratcliffe Lane E14 ... 151 J3
Rathbone Place W1T ... 144 B5
Rathbone Street W1T ... 144 A5
Raven Row E1 ... 150 F1
Ravensdon Street SE11 ... 149 G7
Ravey Street EC2A ... 145 M3
Rawlings Street SW3 ... 147 G5
Rawstorne Street EC1V ... 145 H2
Ray Street EC1R ... 145 G4
Reardon Place E1W ... 150 E5
Reardon Street E1W ... 150 E5
Rectory Square E1 ... 151 H1
Redan Place W2 ... 142 B6
Redburn Street SW3 ... 147 G7
Redcastle Close E1W ... 151 G4
Redcliffe Gardens SW10 ... 146 B7
Redcliffe Mews SW10 ... 146 C7
Redcliffe Place SW10 ... 146 C8
Redcliffe Road SW10 ... 146 D7
Redcliffe Square SW10 ... 146 B7
Redcliffe Street SW10 ... 146 B8
Redcross Way SE1 ... 149 K2
Redesdale Street SW3 ... 147 G7
Redfield Lane SW5 ... 146 A5
Redhill Street NW1 ... 143 L1
Red Lion Row SE5 ... 149 K8
Red Lion Square WC1R ... 144 E5
Red Lion Street WC2B ... 144 E5
Redman's Road E1 ... 151 G1
Redmead Lane E1W ... 150 D5
Reedworth Street SE11 ... 149 G6
Reeves Mews W1K ... 143 J8
Regal Close E1 ... 150 D1
Regan Way N1 ... 145 M1
Regency Street SW1P ... 148 B5
Regent Place W1B ... 144 A7
Regent's Park ⊖ W1B ... 143 L4
Regent's Park NW1 ... 143 J1
Regent's Park Estate NW1 ... 143 L2
Regent Square WC1H ... 144 D2
Regent Street SW1Y ... 144 B8
Regent Street W1S ... 143 M7
Relton Mews SW7 ... 147 G4
Remington Street N1 ... 145 H1
Remnant Street WC2A ... 144 E6
Renforth Street SE16 ... 151 G7
Renfrew Road SE11 ... 149 H5
Rennie Street SE1 ... 149 H1
Rephidim Street SE1 ... 149 M4
Repton Street E14 ... 151 K2
Reveley Square SE16 ... 151 K7
Rex Place W1K ... 143 J8
Rhodeswell Road E14 ... 151 L2
Rich Street E14 ... 151 M3
Rickett Street SW6 ... 146 A8
Ridgemount Street WC1E ... 144 B4
Ridgemount Gardens WC1E ... 144 B4
Riding House Street W1W ... 143 M5
Riley Road SE1 ... 150 B7
Ripley's Believe It or Not! W1J ... 144 B8
Risborough Street SE1 ... 149 J2
Risdon Street SE16 ... 151 G7
Rissinghill Street N1 ... 144 F1
River Street EC1R ... 144 F2
Rivington Street EC2A ... 145 M3
Robert Adam Street W1U ... 143 J6
Roberts Close SE16 ... 151 J7
Robert Street NW1 ... 143 L2
Rochester Row SW1P ... 148 A5
Rochester Street SW1P ... 148 B5
Rockingham Street SE1 ... 149 J4
Rocliffe Street N1 ... 145 H1
Roding Mews E1W ... 150 D5
Rodmarton Street W1U ... 143 H5
Rodney Place SE17 ... 149 K5
Rodney Road SE17 ... 149 K5
Rodney Street N1 ... 144 E1
Roger Street WC1N ... 144 E4
Roland Gardens SW7 ... 146 D6
Roland Way SE17 ... 149 L7
Romford Street E1 ... 150 E2
Romilly Street W1D ... 144 B7
Romney Street SW1P ... 148 C5
Rood Lane EC3M ... 145 M7
Ropemaker Road SE16 ... 151 K7
Ropemaker Street EC2Y ... 145 L4
Roper Lane SE1 ... 150 B7
Rope Street SE16 ... 151 K8
Rope Walk Gardens E1 ... 150 E2
Rosary Gardens SW7 ... 146 D6
Roscoe Street EC1Y ... 145 K3
Rose Alley SE1 ... 145 K8
Rosebery Avenue EC1R ... 144 F3
Rosemoor Street SW3 ... 147 G6
Rose Street WC2E ... 144 C7
Rossmore Road NW1 ... 143 G3
Rotary Street SE1 ... 149 H3
Rotherhithe ⊖ SE16 ... 151 G6

Rotherhithe Street SE16 ... 151 G6
Rotherhithe Street SE16 ... 151 J4
Rotherhithe Tunnel SE16 ... 151 H5
Rothsay Street SE1 ... 149 M4
Rotten Row W2 ... 146 F2
Rouel Road SE16 ... 150 C8
Roupell Street SE1 ... 149 G2
Royal Albert Hall SW7 ... 146 E3
Royal Avenue SW3 ... 147 H6
Royal Hospital Road SW3 ... 147 H7
Royal Mint Street E1 ... 150 C4
Royal Oak ⊖ W2 ... 142 B5
Royal Oak Yard SE1 ... 150 A7
Royal Opera House WC2E ... 144 D7
Royal Road SE17 ... 149 H8
Royal Street SE1 ... 148 E3
Rudolph Road NW6 ... 142 A1
Rugby Street WC1N ... 144 E4
Rum Close E1W ... 150 F4
Rupack Street SE16 ... 151 G7
Rupert Street W1D ... 144 B7
Rushworth Street SE1 ... 149 H2
Russell Court SW1A ... 148 A2
Russell Square WC1B ... 144 C4
Russell Square ⊖ WC1B ... 144 D4
Russell Street WC2B ... 144 D7
Russia Dock Road SE16 ... 151 K6
Rutherford Street SW1P ... 148 B5
Rutland Gardens SW7 ... 147 G3
Rutland Gate SW7 ... 146 F3
Rutland Mews SW7 ... 146 F4
Rutland Street SW7 ... 147 G4
Ryder Street SW1Y ... 148 A1

S

Sackville Street W1S ... 144 A8
Saffron Hill EC1N ... 145 G4
Saffron Street EC1N ... 145 G4
Sail Street SE11 ... 148 F5
St Agnes Place SE11 ... 149 G8
St Alban's Grove W8 ... 146 B4
St Alban's Street SW1Y ... 144 B8
St Alphage Garden EC2Y ... 145 K5
St Andrews Hill EC4V ... 145 H7
St Andrew's Place NW1 ... 143 L3
St Andrew Street EC4A ... 145 G5
St Anne's Court W1F ... 144 B6
St Ann's Court SW1P ... 148 C4
St Anselm's Place W1K ... 143 K7
St Barnabas Street SW1W ... 147 K6
St Botolph Street EC3N ... 150 B2
St Bride Street EC4A ... 145 G6
St Chad's Street WC1H ... 144 D2
St Clare Street EC3N ... 150 B3
St Clements Lane WC2A ... 144 E6
St Cross Street EC1N ... 145 G4
St Dunstan's Hill EC3R ... 145 M8
St Dunstan's Lane EC3R ... 145 M7
St Elmos Road SE16 ... 151 J7
St Ermin's Hill SW1H ... 148 B3
St George's Circus SE1 ... 149 H3
St George's Drive SW1V ... 147 M6
St George's Estate E1 ... 150 D3
St George's Lane * EC3R ... 145 M7
St George's Road SE1 ... 149 G4
St George's Square SW1V ... 148 B7
St Giles High Street WC2H ... 144 C6
St Helen's Place EC3A ... 145 M6
St James Market * SW1Y ... 144 B8
St James's Park ⊖ SW1H ... 148 B3
St James's Park SW1A ... 148 B3
St James's Place SW1A ... 147 M2
St James's Road SE16 ... 150 D8
St James's Square SW1Y ... 148 A1
St James's Street SW1A ... 147 M1
St James Walk EC1R ... 145 G3
St John's Lane EC1M ... 145 H4
St John's Place EC1M ... 145 H4
St John's Square EC1V ... 145 H4
St John Street EC1V ... 145 H2
St John's Wood High Street NW8 ... 142 F1
St John's Wood Road NW8 ... 142 E3
St Katharine's Way E1W ... 150 C5
St Leonard's Terrace SW3 ... 147 H7
St Loo Avenue SW3 ... 147 G8
St Luke's Close EC1V ... 145 K3
St Luke's Street SW3 ... 146 F6
St Manningtree E1 ... 150 C2
St Mark Street E1 ... 150 C3
St Martin's Lane WC2N ... 144 C7
St Martin's le Grand EC1A ... 145 J6
St Martin's Street WC2N ... 144 C8
St Mary at Hill EC3R ... 145 M8
St Mary Axe EC3A ... 150 A3
St Marychurch Street SE16 ... 150 F7
St Mary's Gardens SE11 ... 149 G5
St Mary's Terrace W2 ... 142 D4
St Mary's Walk SE11 ... 149 G5
St Matthew Street SW1P ... 148 B4
St Michael's Street W2 ... 142 F6
St Olav's Square SE16 ... 150 F7
St Oswald's Place SE11 ... 148 E7
St Oswulf Street * SW1P ... 148 C5
St Pancras International ≷ N1C ... 144 C1
St Paul's ⊖ EC1A ... 145 J6
St Paul's Avenue SE16 ... 151 J5
St Paul's Cathedral EC4M ... 145 J6
St Paul's Churchyard EC4M ... 145 J6
St Paul's Way E1 ... 151 L1
St Petersburgh Mews W2 ... 142 B7
St Petersburgh Place W2 ... 142 B7
St Saviours Wharf SE1 ... 150 C6
St Stephen's Gardens W2 ... 142 A5
St Swithin's Lane EC4N ... 145 L7
St Thomas Street SE1 ... 149 L2
St Vincent Street W1U ... 143 J5
Salamanca Street SE1 ... 148 D6
Sale Place W2 ... 142 F5
Salisbury Court EC4Y ... 145 G6
Salisbury Place W1H ... 143 H4
Salisbury Street NW8 ... 142 F4
Salmon Lane E14 ... 151 J2
Salter Road SE16 ... 151 J5
Salter Street E14 ... 151 M4
Samford Street NW8 ... 142 F4
Sampson Street E1W ... 150 D5
Sancroft Street SE11 ... 148 F6
Sandland Street WC1R ... 144 E5
Sandpiper Close SE16 ... 151 L6
Sandwich Street WC1H ... 144 C2
Sandy's Row E1 ... 150 B1

Sans Walk EC1R ... 145 G3
Sardinia Street WC2A ... 144 E6
Savage Gardens EC3N ... 150 B3
Savile Row W1S ... 143 M7
Savoy Hill WC2R ... 144 E8
Savoy Place WC2R ... 144 D8
Savoy Street WC2E ... 144 E7
Sawyer Street SE1 ... 149 J2
Scala Street W1T ... 144 A5
Scandrett Street E1W ... 150 E5
Scarborough Street E1 ... 150 C3
Scarsdale Villas W8 ... 146 A4
Schooner Close * SE16 ... 151 H6
Science Museum SW7 ... 146 E4
Scoresby Street SE1 ... 149 H2
Scotch House Junction SW1X ... 147 H3
Scotland Street SW1A ... 148 C1
Scott Ellis Gardens NW8 ... 142 E2
Scott Lidgett Crescent SE16 ... 150 D7
Scrutton Street EC2A ... 145 M3
Seaford Street WC1H ... 144 D2
Seagrave Road SW6 ... 146 A8
Sea Life London Aquarium SE1 ... 148 E3
Searles Road SE1 ... 149 L5
Sebastian Street EC1V ... 145 H2
Secker Street SE1 ... 148 F2
Sedan Way SE17 ... 149 M6
Sedding Street SW1X ... 147 J5
Seddon Street WC1X ... 144 E3
Seething Lane EC3N ... 150 A4
Sekforde Street EC1R ... 145 H3
Selfridges W1A ... 143 J6
Selsey Street E14 ... 151 M1
Selwood Place SW7 ... 146 E6
Semley Place SW1W ... 147 K6
Senior Street W2 ... 142 B4
Senrab Street E1 ... 151 H2
Serle Street WC2A ... 144 F6
Serpentine Bridge W2 ... 146 E1
Serpentine Road W2 ... 146 F2
Seth Street SE16 ... 151 G7
Settles Street E1 ... 150 D2
Seven Dials WC2H ... 144 C6
Seville Street SW1X ... 147 H3
Sevington Street W9 ... 142 A3
Seward Street EC1V ... 145 J3
Seymour Mews W1H ... 143 J6
Seymour Place W1H ... 143 G5
Seymour Street W1H ... 143 H6
Seymour Street W2 ... 143 G7
Seymour Walk SW10 ... 146 C7
Shad Thames SE1 ... 150 B6
Shad Thames SE1 ... 150 C6
Shadwell ⊖ E1 ... 151 G3
Shadwell Gardens E1 ... 150 F3
Shaftesbury Avenue W1D ... 144 B7
Shaftesbury Avenue WC2H ... 144 C6
Shaftesbury Street N1 ... 145 K1
Shakespeare's Globe SE1 ... 145 J8
Shand Street SE1 ... 150 A6
Sharsted Street SE17 ... 149 H7
Shaw Crescent E14 ... 151 K2
Shawfield Street SW3 ... 147 G7
Sheffield Terrace W8 ... 146 A2
Sheldon Square W2 ... 142 D5
Shelmerdine Close E3 ... 151 M1
Shelton Street WC2H ... 144 D6
Shepherdess Walk N1 ... 145 K1
Shepherd Street W1J ... 147 K1
Sheraton Street W1F ... 144 B6
Sherborne Lane EC4N ... 145 L7
Sherwood Street W1D ... 144 A7
Ship and Mermaid Row SE1 ... 149 M2
Shipwright Road SE16 ... 151 K7
Shirland Road W9 ... 142 A3
Shoe Lane EC4A ... 145 G5
Shorter Street EC3N ... 150 B4
Shorts Gardens WC2H ... 144 C6
Short Street SE1 ... 149 G2
Shoulder of Mutton Alley E14 ... 151 K4
Shouldham Street W1H ... 143 G5
Shroton Street NW1 ... 142 F4
Siddons Lane W1H ... 143 H4
Sidmouth Street WC1N ... 144 D3
Sidney Square E1 ... 150 F2
Sidney Street E1 ... 150 F1
Silex Street SE1 ... 149 H3
Silk Street EC2Y ... 145 K4
Silver Walk SE16 ... 151 K5
Silvester Street SE1 ... 149 K3
Singer Street EC2A ... 145 L3
Sir John Soane's Museum WC2A ... 144 E5
Sir Simon Milton Square SW1V ... 147 L4
Skinner Place * SW1W ... 147 J6
Skinners Lane EC4V ... 145 K7
Skinner Street EC1R ... 145 G3
Slippers Place SE16 ... 150 F8
Sloane Avenue SW3 ... 147 G6
Sloane Court East SW3 ... 147 J6
Sloane Court West SW3 ... 147 J6
Sloane Gardens SW1W ... 147 J6
Sloane Square SW1W ... 147 J6
Sloane Square ⊖ SW1W ... 147 J6
Sloane Street SW1X ... 147 H3
Sloane Terrace SW1X ... 147 J5
Smeaton Street E1W ... 150 E5
Smithfield Street EC1A ... 145 H5
Smith Square SW1P ... 148 C4
Smith Street SW3 ... 147 G7
Smith Terrace SW3 ... 147 G7
Smithy Street E1 ... 151 G1
Snowden Street EC2A ... 145 M4
Snow Hill EC1A ... 145 H5
Snowsfields SE1 ... 149 L2
Soho Square W1D ... 144 B6
Soho Street W1D ... 144 B6
Somerford Way SE16 ... 151 K7
Somers Crescent W2 ... 142 F6
Somerset House WC2R ... 144 E7
Somerstown Estate NW1 ... 144 A1
Sondes Street SE17 ... 149 L7
South & West Africa Gate SW1A ... 148 A3
Southall Place SE1 ... 149 L3
Southampton Buildings WC2A ... 144 F5
Southampton Place WC1A ... 144 D5
Southampton Row WC1B ... 144 D4
Southampton Street WC2E ... 144 D7
South Audley Street W1K ... 143 K8
South Carriage Drive SW1X ... 147 H3
South Carriage Drive SW7 ... 146 F3
South Eaton Place SW1W ... 147 J5
Southern Street N1 ... 144 E1
South Kensington SW7 ... 146 E4
South Kensington ⊖ SW7 ... 146 E5
South Lambeth Road SW8 ... 148 D8
South Molton Lane W1K ... 143 K7

South Molton Street W1K 143 K7
South Parade SW3 .... 146 E7
South Place EC2M 145 L5
South Sea Street SE16 .... 151 L8
South Square WC1R 144 F5
South Street W1K 147 J1
South Tenter Street E1 .... 150 C3
South Terrace SW7 .... 146 F5
Southwark ≥ SE1 .... 149 H2
Southwark Bridge SE1 .... 145 K8
Southwark Bridge Road SE1 .... 149 J3
Southwark Park Road SE16 .... 150 E8
Southwark Street SE1 .... 149 H1
Southwell Gardens SW7 .... 146 C5
South Wharf Road W2 .... 142 E6
Southwick Mews W2 .... 142 F6
Southwick Place W2 .... 142 F6
Southwick Street W2 .... 142 F6
Sovereign Close E1W 150 F4
Sovereign Crescent SE16 .... 151 J4
Spanish Place W1U 143 J5
Spa Road SE16 .... 150 C8
Spear Mews SW5 .... 146 A6
Spelman Street E1 .... 150 C1
Spence Close SE16 .... 151 K7
Spencer Street EC1V 145 H2
Spenser Street SW1E 148 A4
Spert Street E14 .... 151 J4
Spital Square E1 .... 150 A1
Spring Gardens SW1A 148 C1
Spring Street W2 .... 142 E6
Spurgeon Street SE1 .... 149 L4
Spur Road SE1 .... 148 F3
Stables Way SE11 .... 148 F7
Stable Yard Road SW1A 148 A2
Stacey Street WC2H 144 C6
Stafford Place SW1E 147 M3
Stafford Road NW6 .... 142 A2
Stafford Street W1S 143 M8
Stafford Terrace W8 .... 146 A3
Stainer Street SE1 .... 149 L2
Staining Lane EC2V 145 K6
Stainsby Road E14 .... 151 M2
Stalham Street SE16 .... 150 F8
Stamford Street SE1 .... 149 G1
Stanford Place SE1 .... 149 M6
Stanford Road W8 .... 146 B4
Stanford Street * SW1V 148 B6
Stanhope Close * SE16 .... 151 H6
Stanhope Gardens SW7 .... 146 D5
Stanhope Gate W1K 147 K1
Stanhope Mews SW7 .... 146 D5
Stanhope Mews East SW7 .... 146 D5
Stanhope Mews West SW7 .... 146 D5
Stanhope Place W2 .... 143 G7
Stanhope Place Gate W2 .... 143 G7
Stanhope Row W1J 147 K1
Stanhope Street NW1 .... 143 M1
Stanhope Terrace W2 .... 142 E7
Stannary Street SE11 .... 149 G7
Staples Close SE16 .... 151 J5
Staple Street SE1 .... 149 L3
Starcross Street NW1 .... 144 A2
Star Road W14 .... 142 F6
Station Approach SE1 .... 148 F3
Stave Yard Road SE16 .... 151 J5
Stead Street SE17 .... 149 K6
Steedman Street SE17 .... 149 J5
Steel's Lane E1 .... 151 G3
Steeres Way SE16 .... 151 K7
Stephenson Way NW1 .... 144 A3
Stephen Street W1T 144 B5
Stepney Green E1 .... 151 H1
Stepney High Street E1 .... 151 J1
Stepney Way E1 .... 150 E1
Sterling Street SW7 .... 147 G3
Stevedore Street E1W 150 E5
Stevens Street SE1 .... 150 A7
Steward Street * E1 .... 150 B1
Stewart's Grove SW3 .... 146 F6
Stew Lane EC4V 145 J7
Stillington Street SW1P 148 A5
Stockholm Way E1W 150 D5
Stocks Place E14 .... 151 M3
Stone Buildings WC2A 144 F5
Stoney Lane E1 .... 150 B2
Stoney Street SE1 .... 149 K1
Stopford Road SE17 .... 149 J7
Store Street WC1E 144 B5
Storey's Gate SW1H 148 C3
Storks Road SE16 .... 150 D8
Stoughton Close SE11 .... 148 E6
Stourcliffe Street W1H 143 G6
Strafford Street E14 .... 151 M6
Strand WC2R 144 D8
Stratford Place W1C 143 K6
Stratford Road W8 .... 146 A5
Strathearn Place W2 .... 142 F7
Stratton Street W1J 147 L1
Strutton Ground SW1P 148 B4
Strype Street E1 .... 150 B2
Stuart Road NW6 .... 142 A2
Stukeley Street WC2B 144 D6
Sturgeon Road SE17 .... 149 J7
Sturge Street SE1 .... 149 J3
Sturt Street N1 .... 145 K1
Stutfield Street E1 .... 150 D3
Sudley Street N1 .... 145 H1
Sudrey Street SE1 .... 149 J3
Suffolk Lane EC4V 145 L7
Suffolk Street SW1Y 144 B8
Sugar Lane SE16 .... 150 D7
Sugar Quay Walk EC3R 150 A4
Sullivan Road SE11 .... 149 G5
Summercourt Road E1 .... 151 G2
Summers Street EC1R 144 F4
Sumner Place SW7 .... 146 E6
Sumner Street SE1 .... 149 J1
Sunderland Terrace W2 .... 142 A6
Sun Passage SE16 .... 150 D8
Sun Street EC2M 145 M4
Sun Street Passage EC2M 145 M5
Surrendale Place W9 .... 142 A4
Surrey Quays Road SE16 .... 151 H7
Surrey Row SE1 .... 149 H2
Surrey Square SE17 .... 149 M6
Surrey Street WC2E 144 E7
Surrey Water Road SE16 .... 151 H6
Sussex Gardens W2 .... 142 E6
Sussex Mews East W2 .... 142 E7
Sussex Place NW1 .... 143 H3
Sussex Place W2 .... 142 E6
Sussex Square W2 .... 142 E7
Sussex Street SW1V 147 L7
Sutherland Avenue W9 .... 142 A4

Sutherland Row SW1V 147 L6
Sutherland Square SE17 .... 149 J7
Sutherland Street SW1V 147 L7
Sutton Row W1D 144 B6
Sutton Street E1 .... 151 G3
Suttons Way EC1Y 145 K4
Swain Street NW8 .... 142 F3
Swallow Place W1B 143 L6
Swallow Street W1B 144 A8
Swan Lane EC4R 145 L8
Swan Mead SE1 .... 149 M4
Swan Road SE16 .... 151 G6
Swan Street SE1 .... 149 K3
Swan Walk SW3 .... 147 H8
Swedenborg Gardens E1 .... 150 E4
Sweeney Crescent SE1 .... 150 C7
Swinton Street WC1X 144 E2
Sydney Place SW7 .... 146 F6
Sydney Street SW3 .... 146 F6
Symons Street SW3 .... 147 H6

T

Tabard Gardens Estate SE1 .... 149 L3
Tabard Street SE1 .... 149 L3
Tabernacle Street EC2A 145 L3
Tachbrook Street SW1V 148 A6
Talbot Road W2 .... 142 A6
Talbot Square W2 .... 142 E6
Talbot Yard SE1 .... 149 L2
Tallis Street EC4Y 145 G7
Tamworth Street SW6 .... 146 A8
Tanner Street SE1 .... 150 A7
Taplow Street N1 .... 145 K1
Tarling Street E1 .... 150 F3
Tarver Road SE17 .... 149 H7
Tate Britain SW1P 148 C6
Tate Modern SE1 .... 145 J8
Tatum Street SE17 .... 149 M6
Taunton Street N1 .... 143 G3
Tavistock Place WC1H 144 C3
Tavistock Square WC1H 144 C3
Tavistock Street WC2E 144 D7
Taviton Street WC1H 144 B3
Teak Close SE16 .... 151 K6
Tedworth Square SW3 .... 147 G7
Telford Terrace SW1V 147 M7
Temeraire Street SE16 .... 151 G6
Temple ⊖ WC2R 144 F7
Temple Avenue EC4Y 145 G7
Temple Lane EC4Y 145 G7
Temple Place WC2R 144 F7
Templeton Place SW5 .... 146 A5
Tench Street E1W 150 E5
Tenniel Close W2 .... 142 C7
Tennis Street SE1 .... 149 L2
Tenterden Street W1S 143 L6
Tenterground E1 .... 150 B1
Teredo Street SE16 .... 151 J8
Terminus Place SW1V 147 L4
Thame Road SE16 .... 151 H6
Thanet Street WC1H 144 C2
Thavies Inn EC4A 145 G6
Thayer Street W1U 143 K5
The Arches WC2N 144 D8
The Boltons SW10 .... 146 C7
The British Library NW1 .... 144 C2
The British Museum WC1B 144 C5
The Broad Walk NW1 .... 142 B8
The Broad Walk W8 .... 146 C2
The Cut SE1 .... 149 G2
Theed Street SE1 .... 149 G2
The Flower Walk W2 .... 146 D3
The Grange SE1 .... 150 B8
The Highway E1W 150 E4
The Little Boltons SW10 .... 146 C7
The Mall SW1A 148 B2
The Mitre E14 .... 151 L3
The Monument EC3R 145 L7
The National Gallery WC2N 144 C8
Theobald's Road WC1X 144 E4
Theobald Street SE1 .... 149 L5
The Oval (Surrey County
  Cricket Ground) SE11 .... 148 F8
The Shard SE1 .... 149 L2
The Vale SW3 .... 146 E8
Thirleby Road SW1P 148 A4
Thomas More Street E1W 150 D4
Thomas Road E14 .... 151 M2
Thoresby Street N1 .... 145 K1
Thorney Street SW1P 148 C5
Thornton Place W1H 143 H4
Thrale Street SE1 .... 149 K1
Thrawl Street E1 .... 150 C1
Threadneedle Street EC2R 145 L6
Three Colt Street E14 .... 151 L3
Three Oak Lane SE1 .... 150 B6
Throgmorton Avenue EC2N 145 L6
Throgmorton Street EC2N 145 L6
Thurland Road SE16 .... 150 D8
Thurloe Place SW7 .... 146 F5
Thurloe Square SW7 .... 146 F5
Thurloe Street SW7 .... 146 E5
Thurlow Street SE17 .... 149 M7
Tichbourne Row W2 .... 142 F6
Tiller Road E14 .... 151 M8
Tillman Street E1 .... 150 E3
Tilney Street W1J 147 K1
Timber Pond Road SE16 .... 151 J6
Tinsley Road E1 .... 151 G1
Tinworth Street SE11 .... 148 D6
Tisdall Place SE17 .... 149 L6
Tite Street SW3 .... 147 H8
Tiverton Street SE1 .... 149 J4
Token House Yard EC2R 145 L6
Tolmer's Square NW1 .... 144 A3
Tolmin's Terrace E14 .... 151 K2
Tonbridge Street WC1H 144 D2
Tooley Street SE1 .... 149 L1
Tooley Street SE1 .... 150 B6
Tor Gardens W8 .... 146 A2
Torquay Street W2 .... 142 A5
Torrens Street EC1V 145 G1
Torrington Place E1W 150 D5
Torrington Place WC1E 144 B4
Torrington Square WC1E 144 B4
Tothill Street SW1H 148 B3
Tottenham Court Road ⊖ W1T 144 B6
Tottenham Court Road ⊖ W1D 144 B6
Tottenham Street W1T 144 A5
Toulmin Street SE1 .... 149 J3
Tower Bridge EC3N 150 B5
Tower Bridge Approach EC3N 150 B5
Tower Bridge Road SE1 .... 150 A7

Tower Bridge Wharf E1W 150 C5
Tower Gateway ⊖ EC3N 150 B4
Tower Hill EC3N 150 B4
Tower Hill ⊖ EC3N 150 B4
Tower of London EC3N 150 B4
Tower Place EC3R 150 A4
Tower Street WC2H 144 C7
Townsend Street SE17 .... 149 M5
Toynbee Street E1 .... 150 B1
Trafalgar Gardens E1 .... 151 H1
Trafalgar Square WC2N 144 C8
Trafalgar Street SE17 .... 149 L7
Transept Street NW1 .... 142 F5
Trebeck Street W1J 147 L1
Trebovir Road SW5 .... 146 A6
Tregunter Road SW10 .... 146 C7
Trenton Road SE16 .... 150 E8
Tresham Crescent NW8 .... 142 F3
Trevor Place SW7 .... 147 G3
Trevor Square SW7 .... 147 G3
Trevor Street SW7 .... 147 G3
Trinidad Street E14 .... 151 M4
Trinity Church Square SE1 .... 149 K3
Trinity Square EC3N 150 B4
Trinity Street SE1 .... 149 K3
Trump Street EC2V 145 K6
Tudor Street EC4Y 145 G7
Tufton Street SW1P 148 C4
Tunnel Road SE16 .... 151 G6
Turks Row SW3 .... 147 J6
Turner's Road E3 .... 151 L2
Turner Street E1 .... 150 E2
Turnmill Street EC1N 145 G4
Turpentine Lane SW1V 147 L7
Turquand Street SE17 .... 149 K6
Tyers Gate SE1 .... 149 M3
Tyers Street SE11 .... 148 E7
Tyers Terrace SE11 .... 148 E7
Tyron Street SW3 .... 147 H6
Tysoe Street EC1R 145 G3

U

Udall Street SW1P 148 A5
Ufford Street SE1 .... 149 G2
Ulster Place NW1 .... 143 K4
Umberston Street E1 .... 150 E2
Undershaft EC3A 150 A2
Underwood Road N1 .... 145 K2
Underwood Street N1 .... 145 K1
Union Street SE1 .... 149 H2
University Street WC1E 144 A4
Upbrook Mews W2 .... 142 D6
Upper Belgrave Street SW1X 147 K4
Upper Berkeley Street W1H 143 H6
Upper Brook Street W1K 143 J7
Upper Cheyne Row SW3 .... 146 F8
Upper Grosvenor Street W1K 143 J8
Upper Ground SE1 .... 148 F1
Upper Harley Street NW1 .... 143 K3
Upper James Street W1F 144 A7
Upper John Street W1F 144 A7
Upper Marsh SE1 .... 148 E3
Upper Montagu Street W1H 143 H5
Upper St Martin's WC2H 144 C7
Upper Tachbrook Street SW1V 148 A5
Upper Thames Street EC4V 145 J7
Upper Wimpole Street W1G 143 K4
Upper Woburn Place WC1H 144 B2
Urlwin Street SE5 .... 149 J8
Uxbridge Street W8 .... 146 A1

V

Valentine Place SE1 .... 149 G3
Vandon Passage SW1H 148 A3
Vandon Street SW1H 148 A4
Varden Street E1 .... 150 E2
Varndell Street NW1 .... 143 M2
Vauban Street SE16 .... 150 C8
Vaughan Street SE16 .... 151 L7
Vaughan Way E1W 150 D5
Vauxhall ≥ ⊖ SW8 .... 148 D7
Vauxhall Bridge SW1V 148 C7
Vauxhall Bridgefoot SE1 .... 148 D7
Vauxhall Bridge Road SW1V 147 M5
Vauxhall Cross SE1 .... 148 D7
Vauxhall Grove SW8 .... 148 D8
Vauxhall Street SE11 .... 148 E6
Vauxhall Walk SE11 .... 148 E6
Venables Street W2 .... 142 E4
Vere Street W1G 143 K6
Vernon Place WC1A 144 D5
Vernon Rise WC1X 144 E2
Verulam Street WC1X 144 F4
Vestry Street N1 .... 145 L2
Victoria ≥ ⊖ SW1V 147 L5
Victoria & Albert Museum SW7 .... 146 F4
Victoria Embankment SW1A 148 D2
Victoria Embankment WC2R 144 F7
Victoria Gate W2 .... 142 F7
Victoria Road W8 .... 146 C4
Victoria Square SW1W 147 L4
Victoria Street SW1E 147 L4
Victory Place SE17 .... 149 K5
Victory Way SE16 .... 151 K7
Vigo Street W1S 143 M8
Villa Street SE17 .... 149 L7
Villiers Street WC2N 144 D8
Vincent Close SE16 .... 151 K7
Vincent Square SW1P 148 B5
Vincent Street SW1P 148 B5
Vincent Terrace N1 .... 145 H1
Vine Court E1 .... 150 D1
Vinegar Street E1W 150 E5
Vine Hill EC1R 144 F4
Vine Lane SE1 .... 150 A6
Vine Street EC3N 150 B3
Violet Hill NW8 .... 142 C1
Virgil Street SE1 .... 148 E4
Virginia Street E1W 150 D4
Viscount Street EC2Y 145 J4

W

Wadding Street SE17 .... 149 K6
Wakefield Street WC1H 144 D3
Wakeling Street E14 .... 151 J3
Wakley Street EC1V 145 H2

Walbrook EC4N 145 L7
Walcorde Avenue SE17 .... 149 K6
Walcot Square SE11 .... 149 G5
Walden Street E1 .... 150 E2
Waley Street E1 .... 151 J1
Wallwood Street E14 .... 151 M1
Walnut Tree Walk SE11 .... 148 F5
Walpole Street SW3 .... 147 H6
Walter Terrace E1 .... 151 H2
Walton Place SW3 .... 147 H4
Walton Street SW3 .... 147 G4
Walworth Place SE17 .... 149 K7
Walworth Road SE17 .... 149 J5
Wandsworth Road SW8 .... 148 C8
Wansey Street SE17 .... 149 J6
Wapping ⊖ E1W 150 F5
Wapping High Street E1W 150 E6
Wapping Lane E1 .... 150 F4
Wapping Wall E1W 151 G5
Warden's Grove SE1 .... 149 J2
Wardour Street W1F 144 B6
Warner Street EC1R 144 F4
Warren Street W1T 143 M4
Warren Street ⊖ W1T 143 M3
Warrington Crescent W9 .... 142 C3
Warrington Gardens W9 .... 142 C4
Warwick Avenue ⊖ W9 .... 142 C4
Warwick Avenue W9 .... 142 B3
Warwick Crescent W2 .... 142 C5
Warwick House Street SW1Y 148 B1
Warwick Lane EC4M 145 H6
Warwick Place W9 .... 142 C4
Warwick Road SW5 .... 146 A6
Warwick Row SW1E 147 L4
Warwick Square SW1V 147 M6
Warwick Street W1B 144 A7
Warwick Way SW1V 147 L6
Waterhouse Square EC1N 145 G5
Waterloo ≥ ⊖ SE1 .... 148 F2
Waterloo Bridge SE1 .... 148 E1
Waterloo Bridge WC2R 144 E8
Waterloo East ≥ SE1 .... 149 G2
Waterloo Place SW1Y 148 B1
Waterloo Road SE1 .... 148 F1
Waterloo Road SE1 .... 149 G2
Waterman Way E1W 150 E5
Waterside Close SE16 .... 150 D7
Watling Street EC4N 145 K7
Watney Street E1 .... 150 F3
Watts Street E1W 150 E5
Waveney Close E1W 150 D5
Waverton Street W1J 143 K8
Weavers Lane SE1 .... 150 A6
Webber Row SE1 .... 149 G3
Webber Street SE1 .... 149 H3
Webb Street SE1 .... 150 A8
Webster Road SE16 .... 150 D8
Weighhouse Street W1K 143 K7
Welbeck Street W1G 143 K5
Welbeck Way W1G 143 K6
Welland Mews E1W 150 E5
Wellclose Square E1 .... 150 D4
Wellesley Street E1 .... 151 H2
Wellesley Terrace N1 .... 145 K2
Wellington Arch W1J 147 K2
Wellington Square SW3 .... 147 H6
Wellington Place NW8 .... 142 E2
Wellington Road NW8 .... 142 E1
Wellington Street WC2E 144 D7
Wells Mews W1T 144 A5
Wells Street W1T 144 A5
Wells Way SE5 .... 149 M8
Wenlock Road N1 .... 145 K1
Wenlock Street N1 .... 145 K1
Wentworth Street E1 .... 150 B2
Werrington Street NW1 .... 144 A1
Wesley Street W1G 143 K5
West Arbour Street E1 .... 151 G2
Westbourne Crescent W2 .... 142 D7
Westbourne Gardens W2 .... 142 B6
Westbourne Gate W2 .... 142 E7
Westbourne Grove W2 .... 142 A6
Westbourne Grove Terrace W2 .... 142 B6
Westbourne Park Road W2 .... 142 A5
Westbourne Park Villas W2 .... 142 A5
Westbourne Street W2 .... 142 E7
Westbourne Terrace W2 .... 142 D6
Westbourne Terrace Mews W2 .... 142 C6
Westbourne Terrace Road W2 .... 142 C5
West Brompton ≥ ⊖ SW5 .... 146 A7
West Carriage Drive W2 .... 146 E2
Westcott Road SE17 .... 149 H8
West Cromwell Road SW5 .... 146 A5
Western Place SE16 .... 151 G6
Westferry ⊖ E14 .... 151 M4
Westferry Circus E14 .... 151 M5
Westferry Road E14 .... 151 M5
West Gardens E1W 150 F4
Westgate Terrace SW10 .... 146 B7
West Halkin Street SW1X 147 J4
West Harding Street EC4A 145 G6
West India Avenue E14 .... 151 M5
West India Dock Road E14 .... 151 M3
Westland Place N1 .... 145 K2
West Lane SE16 .... 150 E7
Westminster ⊖ SW1A 148 D3
Westminster Abbey SW1A 148 C3
Westminster Bridge SE1 .... 148 D3
Westminster Bridge Road SE1 .... 148 F3
Westmoreland Place SW1V 147 L7
Westmoreland Road SE17 .... 149 K8
Westmoreland Street W1G 143 K5
Westmoreland Terrace
  SW1V 147 L7
Weston Rise WC1X 144 E1
Weston Street SE1 .... 149 M2
Weston Street SE1 .... 149 M3
Westport Street E1 .... 151 H2
West Poultry Avenue EC1A 145 H5
West Road SW3 .... 147 H7
West Smithfield EC1A 145 H5
West Square SE11 .... 149 H4
West Street WC2H 144 C7
West Tenter Street E1 .... 150 C3
West Warwick Place SW1V 147 M6
Westway W2 .... 142 B5
Wetherby Gardens SW5 .... 146 C6
Weyhill Road E1 .... 150 D2
Weymouth Mews W1G 143 L5
Weymouth Street W1G 143 K5
Wharfdale Road * N1 .... 144 D1
Wharfedale Street SW10 .... 146 B7
Wharf Road N1 .... 145 J1
Wharton Street WC1X 144 F2
Wheatley Street W1G 143 K5
Whetstone Park WC2A 144 E6

Whidborne Street WC1H 144 D2
Whiskin Street EC1R 145 G2
Whitcomb Street WC2H 144 B8
Whitechapel ≥ ⊖ E1 .... 150 E1
Whitechapel Estate E1 .... 150 C4
Whitechapel High Street E1 .... 150 C2
Whitechapel Road E1 .... 150 D1
Whitecross Street EC1Y 145 K3
Whitefriars Street EC4Y 145 G6
Whitehall SW1A 148 C2
Whitehall Court SW1A 148 D2
Whitehall Place SW1A 148 D1
White Hart Street SE11 .... 149 G6
White Hart Yard SE1 .... 149 L2
Whitehaven Street NW8 .... 142 F4
Whitehead's Grove SW3 .... 147 G6
White Horse Lane E1 .... 151 H1
White Horse Road E1 .... 151 J1
White Horse Road E1 .... 151 J3
White Horse Street W1J 147 L1
White Kennett Street E1 .... 150 B2
White Lion Hill EC4V 145 H7
White Lion Street N1 .... 144 F1
White's Grounds SE1 .... 150 A7
White's Row E1 .... 150 B1
White Tower Way E1 .... 151 J1
Whitfield Place W1T 144 A4
Whitfield Street W1T 144 A4
Whitgift Street SE11 .... 148 E5
Whittaker Street SW1W 147 J6
Whittlesey Street SE1 .... 149 G2
Wicker Street E1 .... 150 E3
Wickham Close E1 .... 151 G1
Wickham Street SE11 .... 148 E7
Wicklow Street WC1X 144 E2
Widegate Street E1 .... 150 A1
Widley Road W9 .... 142 A3
Wigmore Place W1G 143 K5
Wigmore Street W1U 143 K6
Wigton Place SE11 .... 149 G7
Wilbraham Place SW1X 147 J5
Wilcox Place * SW1E 148 A4
Wild Court WC2B 144 E6
Wild's Rents SE1 .... 149 M4
Wild Street WC2B 144 D6
Wilfred Street SW1E 147 M4
Wilkes Street E1 .... 150 B1
William IV Street WC2N 144 C8
William Mews SW1X 147 H3
William Road NW1 .... 143 M3
Willow Place SW1P 148 A5
Willow Street EC2A 145 M3
Wilmington Square WC1X 144 F3
Wilmington Street WC1X 144 F2
Wilson Grove SE16 .... 150 E7
Wilson Street EC2A 145 L4
Wilton Crescent SW1X 147 J3
Wilton Mews SW1X 147 K4
Wilton Place SW1X 147 J3
Wilton Road SW1V 147 M5
Wilton Row SW1X 147 J3
Wilton Street SW1X 147 K4
Wimpole Mews W1G 143 K5
Wimpole Street W1G 143 K5
Winchester Street SW1V 147 L6
Winchester Walk SE1 .... 149 K1
Wincott Street SE11 .... 149 G5
Windmill Road SE11 .... 148 F7
Windmill Street W1T 144 B5
Windrose Close SE16 .... 151 H6
Windsor Terrace N1 .... 145 K1
Wine Close E1W 150 F5
Winnett Street W1D 144 B7
Winsland Mews W2 .... 142 E6
Winsland Street W2 .... 142 E6
Winsley Street W1W 144 A6
Winthrop Street E1 .... 150 E1
Woburn Place WC1H 144 C3
Woburn Square WC1H 144 C4
Wodeham Gardens E1 .... 150 E1
Wolfe Crescent SE16 .... 151 H7
Wolseley Street SE1 .... 150 C6
Woodbridge Street EC1R 145 G3
Woodchester Square W9 .... 142 A4
Woodfall Street SW3 .... 147 H7
Woodland Crescent SE16 .... 151 H7
Woodseer Street E1 .... 150 C1
Woods Mews W1K 143 J7
Woods Place SE1 .... 150 A8
Woodstock Street W1C 143 K6
Wood Street EC2V 145 K6
Woolaston Close SE1 .... 149 J5
Wooler Street SE17 .... 149 L7
Wootton Street SE1 .... 149 G2
Worgan Street SE11 .... 148 E6
Worgan Street * SE16 .... 151 H8
Wormwood Street EC2M 145 M5
Worship Street EC2A 145 M4
Wren Street WC1X 144 E3
Wright's Lane W8 .... 146 A3
Wyatt Close SE16 .... 151 L7
Wyclif Street EC1V 145 H2
Wymering Road W9 .... 142 A2
Wynard Terrace SE11 .... 148 F7
Wyndham Place W1H 143 H5
Wyndham Street W1H 143 G4
Wynnstay Gardens W8 .... 146 A4
Wynyatt Street EC1V 145 H2
Wythburn Place W1H 143 H6

Y

Yalding Road * SE16 .... 150 C8
Yardley Street WC1X 144 F2
Yeoman's Row SW3 .... 147 G4
York Boulevard WC2N 144 D8
York Bridge NW1 .... 143 J3
York Gate NW1 .... 143 J4
York Road SE1 .... 148 E2
Yorkshire Road E14 .... 151 K3
York Square E14 .... 151 J2
York Street W1H 143 G5
York Street W1U 143 H5
York Terrace East NW1 .... 143 J4
York Terrace West NW1 .... 143 J4
York Way N1 .... 144 D1
Young Street W8 .... 146 B3

Z

Zoar Street SE1 .... 149 J1
ZSL London Zoo NW1 .... 143 J1

This index lists places appearing in the main map section of the atlas in alphabetical order. The reference following each name gives the atlas page number and grid reference of the square in which the place appears. The map shows counties, unitary authorities and administrative areas, together with a list of the abbreviated name forms used in the index. The top 100 places of tourist interest are indexed in **red**, World Heritage sites in **green**, motorway service areas in **blue**, airports in blue *italic* and National Parks in green *italic*.

Scotland

Abers	Aberdeenshire
Ag & B	Argyll and Bute
Angus	Angus
Border	Scottish Borders
C Aber	City of Aberdeen
C Dund	City of Dundee
C Edin	City of Edinburgh
C Glas	City of Glasgow
Clacks	Clackmannanshire (1)
D & G	Dumfries & Galloway
E Ayrs	East Ayrshire
E Duns	East Dunbartonshire (2)
E Loth	East Lothian
E Rens	East Renfrewshire (3)
Falk	Falkirk
Fife	Fife
Highld	Highland
Inver	Inverclyde (4)
Mdloth	Midlothian (5)
Moray	Moray
N Ayrs	North Ayrshire
N Lans	North Lanarkshire (6)
Ork	Orkney Islands
P & K	Perth & Kinross
Rens	Renfrewshire (7)
S Ayrs	South Ayrshire
S Lans	South Lanarkshire
Shet	Shetland Islands
Stirlg	Stirling
W Duns	West Dunbartonshire (8)
W Isls	Western Isles (Na h-Eileanan an Iar)
W Loth	West Lothian

Wales

Blae G	Blaenau Gwent (9)
Brdgnd	Bridgend (10)
Caerph	Caerphilly (11)
Cardif	Cardiff
Carmth	Carmarthenshire
Cerdgn	Ceredigion
Conwy	Conwy
Denbgs	Denbighshire
Flints	Flintshire
Gwynd	Gwynedd
IoA	Isle of Anglesey
Mons	Monmouthshire
Myr Td	Merthyr Tydfil (12)
Neath	Neath Port Talbot (13)
Newpt	Newport (14)
Pembks	Pembrokeshire
Powys	Powys
Rhondd	Rhondda Cynon Taf (15)
Swans	Swansea
Torfn	Torfaen (16)
V Glam	Vale of Glamorgan (17)
Wrexhm	Wrexham

Channel Islands & Isle of Man

Guern	Guernsey
Jersey	Jersey
IoM	Isle of Man

England

BaNES	Bath & N E Somerset (18)
Barns	Barnsley (19)
BCP	Bournemouth, Christchurch and Poole (20)
Bed	Bedford
Birm	Birmingham
Bl w D	Blackburn with Darwen (21)
Bolton	Bolton (22)
Bpool	Blackpool
Br & H	Brighton & Hove (23)
Br For	Bracknell Forest (24)
Bristl	City of Bristol
Bucks	Buckinghamshire
Bury	Bury (25)
C Beds	Central Bedfordshire
C Brad	City of Bradford
C Derb	City of Derby
C KuH	City of Kingston upon Hull
C Leic	City of Leicester
C Nott	City of Nottingham

C Pete	City of Peterborough
C Plym	City of Plymouth
C Port	City of Portsmouth
C Sotn	City of Southampton
C Stke	City of Stoke-on-Trent
C York	City of York
Calder	Calderdale (26)
Cambs	Cambridgeshire
Ches E	Cheshire East
Ches W	Cheshire West and Chester
Cnwll	Cornwall
Covtry	Coventry
Cumb	Cumbria
Darltn	Darlington (27)
Derbys	Derbyshire
Devon	Devon
Donc	Doncaster (28)
Dorset	Dorset
Dudley	Dudley (29)
Dur	Durham
E R Yk	East Riding of Yorkshire
E Susx	East Sussex
Essex	Essex
Gatesd	Gateshead (30)
Gloucs	Gloucestershire
Gt Lon	Greater London
Halton	Halton (31)
Hants	Hampshire
Hartpl	Hartlepool (32)
Herefs	Herefordshire
Herts	Hertfordshire
IoS	Isles of Scilly
IoW	Isle of Wight
Kent	Kent
Kirk	Kirklees (33)
Knows	Knowsley (34)
Lancs	Lancashire
Leeds	Leeds
Leics	Leicestershire
Lincs	Lincolnshire
Lpool	Liverpool
Luton	Luton

M Keyn	Milton Keynes
Manch	Manchester
Medway	Medway
Middsb	Middlesbrough
N Linc	North Lincolnshire
N Som	North Somerset
N Tyne	North Tyneside (35)
N u Ty	Newcastle upon Tyne
N York	North Yorkshire
NE Lin	North East Lincolnshire
Nhants	Northamptonshire
Norfk	Norfolk
Notts	Nottinghamshire
Nthumb	Northumberland
Oldham	Oldham (36)
Oxon	Oxfordshire
R & Cl	Redcar & Cleveland
Readg	Reading
Rochdl	Rochdale (37)
Rothm	Rotherham (38)
Rutlnd	Rutland
S Glos	South Gloucestershire (39)
S on T	Stockton-on-Tees (40)
S Tyne	South Tyneside (41)
Salfd	Salford (42)
Sandw	Sandwell (43)
Sefton	Sefton (44)
Sheff	Sheffield
Shrops	Shropshire
Slough	Slough (45)
Solhll	Solihull (46)
Somset	Somerset
St Hel	St Helens (47)
Staffs	Staffordshire
Sthend	Southend-on-Sea
Stockp	Stockport (48)
Suffk	Suffolk
Sundld	Sunderland
Surrey	Surrey
Swindn	Swindon
Tamesd	Tameside (49)
Thurr	Thurrock (50)
Torbay	Torbay
Traffd	Trafford (51)
W & M	Windsor & Maidenhead (52)
W Berk	West Berkshire
W Susx	West Sussex
Wakefd	Wakefield (53)
Warrtn	Warrington (54)
Warwks	Warwickshire
Wigan	Wigan (55)
Wilts	Wiltshire
Wirral	Wirral (56)
Wokham	Wokingham (57)
Wolves	Wolverhampton (58)
Worcs	Worcestershire
Wrekin	Telford & Wrekin (59)
Wsall	Walsall (60)

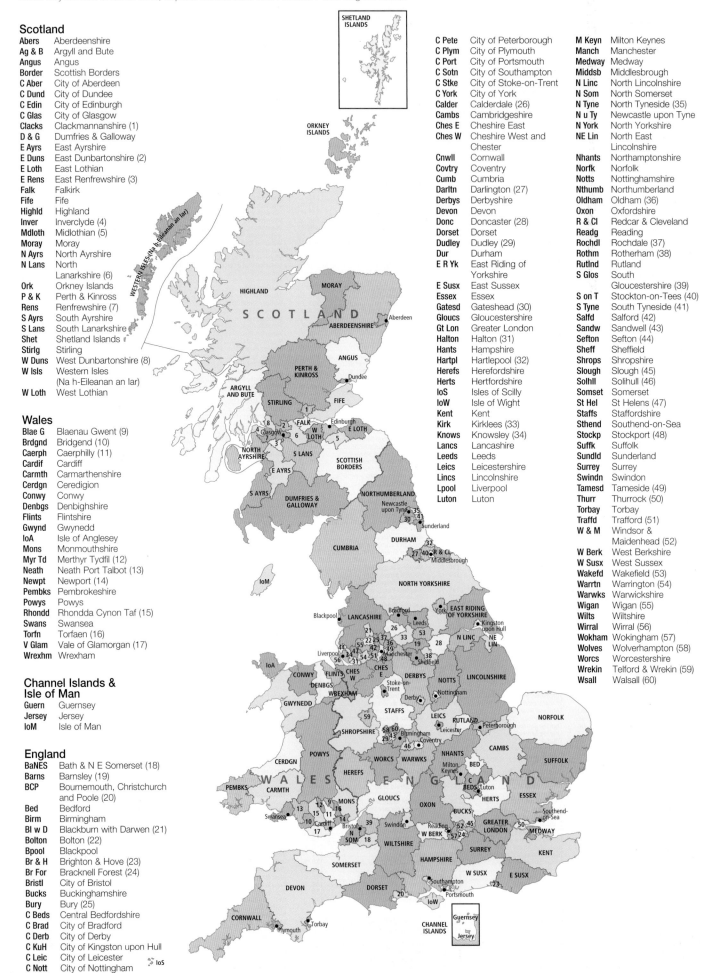

Abbas Combe – Ardnamurchan 159

A

Abbas Combe Somset 17 Q10
Abberley Worcs 39 N8
Abberley Common Worcs 39 N8
Abberton Essex 34 G11
Abberton Worcs 30 C4
Abbess Roding Essex 22 C2
Abbeydale Sheff 50 H4
Abbey Dore Herefs 28 D3
Abbey Green Staffs 50 C8
Abbey St Bathans Border 87 P9
Abbeystead Lancs 63 K10
Abbeytown Cumb 71 J5
Abbey Village Lancs 57 M4
Abbey Wood Gt Lon 21 P7
Abbotrule Border 80 E10
Abbots Bickington Devon 14 G9
Abbots Bromley Staffs 40 E3
Abbotsbury Dorset 7 N6
Abbots Deuglie P & K 92 G12
Abbotsham Devon 14 H6
Abbotskerswell Devon 6 B8
Abbots Langley Herts 20 H3
Abbots Leigh N Som 17 M2
Abbotsley Cambs 32 H5
Abbots Morton Worcs 30 D3
Abbots Ripton Cambs 32 H2
Abbot's Salford Warwks 30 E4
Abbots Worthy Hants 9 N2
Abbotts Ann Hants 19 K11
Abbott Street Dorset 8 E7
Abdon Shrops 39 L5
Aberaeron Cerdgn 36 G7
Aberaman Rhondd 27 L8
Aberangell Gwynd 47 N8
Aberarder Highld 99 J4
Aberargie P & K 92 H11
Aberarth Cerdgn 36 H7
Aberavon Neath 26 G10
Abercanaid Myr Td 27 M7
Abercarn Caerph 27 P9
Abercastle Pembks 24 F3
Abercegir Powys 47 N10
Aberchalder Highld 98 D8
Aberchirder Abers 102 E5
Abercorn W Loth 86 C6
Abercraf Powys 26 H6
Abercregan Neath 26 H9
Abercwmboi Rhondd 27 L8
Abercych Pembks 36 D11
Abercynon Rhondd 27 M9
Aberdalgie P & K 92 G10
Aberdare Rhondd 27 L8
Aberdaron Gwynd 46 C6
Aberdeen C Aber 95 Q1
Aberdeen Airport C Aber 103 J11
Aberdour Fife 86 E5
Aberdulais Neath 26 G8
Aberdyfi Gwynd 47 K11
Aberedw Powys 38 C11
Abereiddy Pembks 24 E3
Abererch Gwynd 46 G4
Aberfan Myr Td 27 M8
Aberfeldy P & K 92 C6
Aberffraw IoA 54 E7
Aberford Leeds 59 K6
Aberfoyle Stirlg 85 J3
Abergavenny Mons 28 C6
Abergele Conwy 55 P6
Abergorlech Carmth 26 D3
Abergwesyn Powys 37 P9
Abergwili Carmth 25 Q5
Abergwynfi Neath 27 J9
Abergwyngregyn Gwynd 55 J7
Abergynolwyn Gwynd 47 L9
Aberkenfig Brdgnd 27 J11
Aberlady E Loth 87 J6
Aberlemno Angus 93 N5
Aberllefenni Gwynd 47 M8
Aberllynfi Powys 27 N2
Aberlour, Charlestown of Moray 101 K6
Abermule Powys 38 D4
Abernant Carmth 25 N4
Abernant Rhondd 27 L7
Abernethy P & K 92 H11
Abernyte P & K 93 J8
Aberporth Cerdgn 36 D9
Abersoch Gwynd 46 E6
Abersychan Torfn 28 B7
Aberthin V Glam 16 D2
Abertillery Blae G 27 P7
Abertridwr Caerph 27 N10
Abertridwr Powys 48 B10
Aberuthven P & K 92 E11
Aberystwyth Cerdgn 37 J4
Abingdon-on-Thames Oxon 19 N2
Abinger Common Surrey 10 H2
Abinger Hammer Surrey 10 H1
Abington Nhants 32 A5
Abington S Lans 78 F4
Abington Pigotts Cambs 33 K7
Abington Services S Lans 78 F4
Abingworth W Susx 10 H6
Ab Kettleby Leics 41 Q3
Ablington Gloucs 30 E11
Abney Derbys 50 G5
Aboyne Abers 95 J3
Abhainn Suidhe W Isls 111 c3
Abram Wigan 57 L8
Abriachan Highld 98 H2
Abridge Essex 21 P4
Abronhill N Lans 85 N7
Abson S Glos 17 Q2
Abthorpe Nhants 31 N5
Aby Lincs 53 L7
Acaster Malbis C York 59 N5
Acaster Selby N York 59 M6
Accrington Lancs 57 N3
Acha Ag & B 88 F5
Achahoish Ag & B 83 L7
Achalader P & K 92 G6
Achaleven Ag & B 90 C9
Acha Mor W Isls 111 d2
Achanalt Highld 106 D9
Achandunie Highld 107 K7
Achany Highld 107 J3
Acharacle Highld 89 N3
Acharn Highld 89 P6
Acharn P & K 92 B6
Achavanich Highld 110 E7
Achduart Highld 105 Q2
Achfary Highld 108 F7
Achgarve Highld 105 N4
A'Chill Highld 96 C8
Achiltibuie Highld 105 Q1
Achina Highld 109 M4
Achinhoan Ag & B 75 L8
Achintee Highld 97 N2
Achintraid Highld 97 L2
Achlyness Highld 108 E5
Achmelvich Highld 108 B10
Achmore Highld 97 M3
Achmore W Isls 111 d2
Achnacarnin Highld 108 B8
Achnacarry Highld 98 B10
Achnacloich Highld 96 H7
Achnaconeran Highld 98 F5
Achnacroish Ag & B 90 B7
Achnadrish Ag & B 89 K6
Achnafauld P & K 92 D8
Achnagarron Highld 107 L8
Achnaha Highld 89 K3
Achnahaird Highld 108 A11
Achnahannet Highld 100 F9
Achnairn Highld 109 K12
Achnalea Highld 90 B4
Achnamara Ag & B 83 L5
Achnasheen Highld 106 C10
Achnashellach Highld 105 Q11
Achnastank Moray 101 K8
Achosnich Highld 89 K3
Achranich Highld 89 P6
Achreamie Highld 110 B3
Achriabhach Highld 90 F3
Achriesgill Highld 108 E5
Achtoty Highld 109 M3
Achurch Nhants 42 E12
Achvaich Highld 107 L4
Achvarasdal Highld 110 B3
Ackergill Highld 110 G5
Acklam Middsb 66 C4
Acklam N York 60 D2
Ackleton Shrops 39 P3
Acklington Nthumb 73 M1
Ackton Wakefd 59 K9
Ackworth Moor Top Wakefd 59 K10
Acle Norfk 45 N7
Acock's Green Birm 40 E10
Acol Kent 23 P9
Acomb C York 59 M4
Acomb Nthumb 72 G7
Aconbury Herefs 28 F3
Acton Ches E 49 L5
Acton Gt Lon 21 K7
Acton Staffs 49 P7
Acton Suffk 34 E7
Acton Wrexhm 48 G5
Acton Beauchamp Herefs 39 M11
Acton Bridge Ches W 49 L1
Acton Burnell Shrops 39 K2
Acton Green Herefs 39 M11
Acton Round Shrops 39 L3
Acton Scott Shrops 39 J4
Acton Trussell Staffs 40 C4
Acton Turville S Glos 18 B5
Adbaston Staffs 49 N9
Adber Dorset 17 N11
Adbolton Notts 51 N12
Adderbury Oxon 31 L7
Adderley Shrops 49 M7
Addiewell W Loth 86 B9
Addingham C Brad 58 E4
Addington Bucks 31 Q8
Addington Gt Lon 21 M9
Addington Kent 22 D10
Addiscombe Gt Lon 21 M9
Addlestone Surrey 20 G9
Addlethorpe Lincs 53 N9
Adeyfield Herts 20 H2
Adfa Powys 38 C2
Adforton Herefs 38 H7
Adisham Kent 23 N11
Adlestrop Gloucs 30 G8
Adlingfleet E R Yk 60 E9
Adlington Lancs 57 L6
Admaston Staffs 40 D3
Admaston Wrekin 49 L11
Adpar Cerdgn 36 E11
Adsborough Somset 16 H9
Adscombe Somset 16 G8
Adstock Bucks 31 Q7
Adstone Nhants 31 N4
Adversane W Susx 10 H5
Advie Highld 100 H8
Adwick le Street Donc 59 M11
Adwick upon Dearne Donc 51 L1
Ae D & G 78 G10
Ae Bridgend D & G 78 G10
Afan Forest Park Neath 26 H8
Affleck Abers 102 D7
Affpuddle Dorset 8 B8
Affric Lodge Highld 98 B5
Afon-wen Flints 48 D2
Afton IoW 9 L9
Agglethorpe N York 65 J9
Aigburth Lpool 56 H10
Aike E R Yk 60 H5
Aiketgate Cumb 71 P6
Aikton Cumb 71 L5
Ailsworth C Pete 42 G9
Ainderby Quernhow N York 65 N10
Ainderby Steeple N York 65 N8
Aingers Green Essex 35 J11
Ainsdale Sefton 56 F6
Ainstable Cumb 71 Q6
Ainsworth Bury 57 N6
Ainthorpe N York 66 G6
Aintree Sefton 56 H8
Ainville W Loth 86 D9
Aird Ag & B 83 L3
Aird D & G 68 E7
Aird Highld 96 H9
Aird W Isls 111 e2
Àird a' Mhulaidh W Isls 111 c3
Aird Asaig W Isls 111 c3
Aird Dhubh Highld 97 J2
Airdeny Ag & B 90 D9
Airdrie N Lans 85 M9
Airdriehill N Lans 85 N9
Airds of Kells D & G 69 P5
Àird Uig W Isls 111 c2
Airidh a bhruaich W Isls 111 c3
Airieland D & G 70 C4
Airlie Angus 93 K5
Airmyn E R Yk 60 C8
Airntully P & K 92 G8
Airor Highld 97 J8
Airth Falk 85 Q5
Airton N York 58 B3
Aisby Lincs 42 E3
Aisby Lincs 52 C5
Aish Devon 5 N7
Aish Devon 6 A10
Aisholt Somset 16 G8
Aiskew N York 65 M9
Aislaby N York 66 H9
Aislaby N York 67 J6
Aislaby S on T 65 P5
Aisthorpe Lincs 52 D7
Aith Shet 111 k4
Akeld Nthumb 81 K8
Akeley Bucks 31 P6
Albaston Cnwll 5 J6
Alberbury Shrops 48 G11
Albourne W Susx 11 K6
Albrighton Shrops 39 P2
Albrighton Shrops 49 J10
Alburgh Norfk 45 L11
Albury Herts 33 M10
Albury Surrey 10 G1
Albury Heath Surrey 10 G2
Alcaig Highld 107 J10
Alcaston Shrops 39 J5
Alcester Warwks 30 E3
Alciston E Susx 11 P8
Alcombe Somset 16 C7
Alconbury Cambs 32 H2
Alconbury Weald Cambs 32 H2
Alconbury Weston Cambs 32 H2
Aldborough N York 59 K2
Aldborough Norfk 45 K4
Aldbourne Wilts 19 J5
Aldbrough E R Yk 61 L6
Aldbrough St John N York 65 L5
Aldbury Herts 20 F2
Aldcliffe Lancs 63 J9
Aldclune P & K 92 D3
Aldeburgh Suffk 35 P5
Aldeby Norfk 45 P10
Aldenham Herts 21 J4
Alderbury Wilts 8 H2
Alderford Norfk 45 J6
Alderholt Dorset 8 G5
Alderley Gloucs 29 K10
Alderley Edge Ches E 57 Q12
Aldermans Green Covtry 41 J10
Aldermaston W Berk 19 P7
Alderminster Warwks 30 G4
Aldershot Hants 20 D12
Alderton Gloucs 30 D7
Alderton Nhants 31 Q5
Alderton Suffk 35 M8
Alderton Wilts 18 C4
Aldfield N York 58 H1
Aldford Ches W 48 H4
Aldgate Rutlnd 42 E8
Aldham Essex 34 F10
Aldham Suffk 34 H7
Aldingbourne W Susx 10 E8
Aldingham Cumb 62 F7
Aldington Kent 13 K3
Aldington Worcs 30 E5
Aldington Corner Kent 13 K3
Aldivalloch Moray 101 M9
Aldochlay Ag & B 84 F5
Aldreth Cambs 33 M3
Aldridge Wsall 40 D7
Aldringham Suffk 35 P5
Aldsworth Gloucs 30 F11
Aldunie Moray 101 M9
Aldwark Derbys 50 G8
Aldwark N York 59 L2
Aldwick W Susx 10 E9
Aldwincle Nhants 32 E1
Aldworth W Berk 19 P5
Alexandria W Duns 84 G7
Aley Somset 16 G8
Alfington Devon 6 F4
Alfold Surrey 10 G4
Alfold Crossways Surrey 10 G3
Alford Abers 102 D11
Alford Lincs 53 M8
Alford Somset 17 N9
Alfreton Derbys 51 K9
Alfrick Worcs 39 N10
Alfrick Pound Worcs 39 N10
Alfriston E Susx 11 P9
Algarkirk Lincs 43 J3
Alhampton Somset 17 P8
Alkborough N Linc 60 F9
Alkham Kent 13 N2
Alkmonton Derbys 50 F12
Allaleigh Devon 5 Q9
Allanaquoich Abers 94 B4
Allanbank N Lans 85 P10
Allanton Border 81 J4
Allanton N Lans 85 P10
Allanton S Lans 85 M11
Allaston Gloucs 28 H7
Allbrook Hants 9 M4
All Cannings Wilts 18 F8
Allendale Nthumb 72 F9
Allen End Warwks 40 F7
Allenheads Nthumb 72 F10
Allen's Green Herts 33 M12
Allensmore Herefs 28 F2
Allenton C Derb 41 J2
Aller Devon 15 N7
Aller Somset 17 K9
Allerby Cumb 70 H7
Allercombe Devon 6 E4
Allerford Somset 16 B6
Allerston N York 67 J10
Allerthorpe E R Yk 60 D5
Allerton C Brad 58 E7
Allerton Highld 107 M8
Allerton Lpool 56 H10
Allerton Bywater Leeds 59 K8
Allerton Mauleverer N York 59 K3
Allesley Covtry 40 H10
Allestree C Derb 51 J11
Allexton Leics 42 B9
Allgreave Ches E 50 C7
Allhallows Medway 22 G7
Alligin Shuas Highld 105 M10
Allington Dorset 7 L4
Allington Lincs 42 C3
Allington Wilts 18 D5
Allington Wilts 18 F8
Allington Wilts 18 H11
Allithwaite Cumb 62 H6
Alloa Clacks 85 P4
Allonby Cumb 70 H7
Alloway S Ayrs 76 F7
Allowenshay Somset 17 K12
All Stretton Shrops 39 J3
Alltchaorunn Highld 90 G6
Alltsigh Highld 98 F5
Alltwalis Carmth 25 Q3
Alltwen Neath 26 G7
Alltyblaca Cerdgn 36 H10
Almeley Herefs 38 G11
Almington Staffs 49 N8
Almondbank P & K 92 F9
Almondbury Kirk 58 F10
Almondsbury S Glos 28 H11
Alne N York 59 L2
Alness Highld 107 L8
Alnham Nthumb 81 L11
Alnmouth Nthumb 81 P11
Alnwick Nthumb 81 P10
Alperton Gt Lon 21 J6
Alphamstone Essex 34 E9
Alpheton Suffk 34 E6
Alphington Devon 6 C5
Alport Derbys 50 G7
Alpraham Ches E 49 L4
Alresford Essex 34 H11
Alrewas Staffs 40 F5
Alsager Ches E 49 P4
Alsop en le Dale Derbys 50 F9
Alston Cumb 72 D10
Alston Devon 7 J3
Alstone Gloucs 29 N3
Alstonefield Staffs 50 F9
Alston Sutton Somset 17 K6
Alswear Devon 15 M7
Altandhu Highld 108 A12
Altarnun Cnwll 4 F4
Altass Highld 106 H3
Altcreich Ag & B 89 N8
Altgaltraig Ag & B 83 Q8
Althorne Essex 22 H4
Althorpe N Linc 60 E11
Altnabreac Station Highld 110 B6
Altnaharra Highld 109 K8
Altofts Wakefd 59 J9
Alton Derbys 51 J7
Alton Hants 10 B3
Alton Staffs 50 E11
Alton Barnes Wilts 18 G8
Alton Pancras Dorset 7 Q3
Alton Priors Wilts 18 G8
Alton Towers Staffs 50 E11
Altrincham Traffd 57 P10
Altskeith Hotel Stirlg 84 H3
Alva Clacks 85 P4
Alvanley Ches W 49 J1
Alvaston C Derb 41 K2
Alvechurch Worcs 40 D11
Alvecote Warwks 40 G6
Alvediston Wilts 8 E3
Alveley Shrops 39 N5
Alverdiscott Devon 15 J7
Alverstoke Hants 9 P7
Alverstone IoW 9 P9
Alverthorpe Wakefd 58 H9
Alverton Notts 42 B2
Alves Moray 100 H3
Alvescot Oxon 30 H12
Alveston S Glos 28 H10
Alveston Warwks 30 G3
Alvingham Lincs 53 K5
Alvington Gloucs 28 H8
Alwalton C Pete 42 G10
Alweston Dorset 17 P12
Alwinton Nthumb 81 J11
Alwoodley Leeds 58 H6
Alyth P & K 93 J6
Am Bàgh a Tuath W Isls 111 a7
Ambergate Derbys 51 J9
Amberley Gloucs 29 L8
Amberley W Susx 10 G7
Amble Nthumb 81 Q12
Amblecote Dudley 40 B9
Ambler Thorn C Brad 58 E8
Ambleside Cumb 62 G2
Ambleston Pembks 24 H4
Ambrosden Oxon 31 N9
Amcotts N Linc 60 E10
Amersham Bucks 20 F4
Amersham Common Bucks 20 F4
Amersham Old Town Bucks 20 F4
Amersham on the Hill Bucks 20 F4
Amesbury Wilts 18 H11
Amhuinnsuidhe W Isls 111 c3
Amington Staffs 40 G6
Amisfield D & G 78 G11
Amlwch IoA 54 F3
Ammanford Carmth 26 E6
Amotherby N York 66 G11
Ampfield Hants 9 L3
Ampleforth N York 66 E10
Ampney Crucis Gloucs 30 E12
Ampney St Mary Gloucs 18 G1
Ampney St Peter Gloucs 18 F1
Amport Hants 19 K11
Ampthill C Beds 32 E8
Ampton Suffk 34 E3
Amroth Pembks 25 K7
Amulree P & K 92 D8
Amwell Herts 21 J2
Anaheilt Highld 89 Q4
Ancaster Lincs 42 E2
Ancells Farm Hants 20 D11
Ancroft Nthumb 81 L5
Ancrum Border 80 E8
Ancton W Susx 10 F9
Anderby Lincs 53 N8
Andover Hants 19 L10
Andoversford Gloucs 30 D9
Andreas IoM 56 d2
Anerley Gt Lon 21 M9
Anfield Lpool 56 G9
Angarrack Cnwll 2 E7
Angelbank Shrops 39 L7
Angle Pembks 24 F8
Anglesey IoA 54 F5
Anglesey Abbey Cambs 33 N4
Angmering W Susx 10 H8
Angram N York 59 M5
Ankerville Highld 107 N7
Ankle Hill Leics 41 Q4
Anlaby E R Yk 60 H8
Anmer Norfk 44 C4
Anmore Hants 9 Q5
Annan D & G 71 K3
Annandale Water Services D & G 78 H9
Annat Highld 105 N10
Annathill N Lans 85 M8
Anna Valley Hants 19 L11
Annbank S Ayrs 76 G6
Anne Hathaway's Cottage Warwks 30 F3
Annfield Plain Dur 73 L9
Anniesland C Glas 85 J8
Ansdell Lancs 56 G3
Ansford Somset 17 P9
Ansley Warwks 40 H8
Anslow Staffs 40 G3
Anslow Gate Staffs 40 G3
Anstey Herts 33 L9
Anstey Leics 41 M6
Anstruther Fife 87 L2
Ansty W Susx 11 L5
Ansty Warwks 41 K10
Ansty Wilts 8 E3
An Tairbeart W Isls 111 c3
Anthorn Cumb 71 K4
Antingham Norfk 45 L4
An t-Ob W Isls 111 c4
Antonine Wall 85 P7
Anton's Gowt Lincs 43 J1
Antony Cnwll 5 J8
Antrobus Ches W 57 M11
Anwick Lincs 52 G12
Anwoth D & G 69 N7
Aperfield Gt Lon 21 N10
Apethorpe Nhants 42 E10
Apley Lincs 52 G8
Apperknowle Derbys 51 J5
Apperley Gloucs 29 M3
Appin Ag & B 90 C7
Appleby N Linc 60 G10
Appleby-in-Westmorland Cumb 64 C4
Appleby Magna Leics 40 H5
Appleby Parva Leics 40 H6
Applecross Highld 97 J2
Appledore Devon 14 H6
Appledore Devon 16 E12
Appledore Kent 13 J4
Appleford Oxon 19 N3
Applegarth Town D & G 78 H11
Appleshaw Hants 19 K10
Appleton Halton 57 K10
Appleton Oxon 19 M1
Appleton Warrtn 57 L11
Appleton-le-Moors N York 66 G9
Appleton-le-Street N York 66 G11
Appleton Roebuck N York 59 M6
Appleton Thorn Warrtn 57 M11
Appleton Wiske N York 65 P6
Appletreehall Border 80 C10
Appletreewick N York 58 D3
Appley Somset 16 E10
Apse Heath IoW 9 P10
Apsley End C Beds 32 G9
Apuldram W Susx 10 D9
Arabella Highld 107 N7
Arbirlot Angus 93 Q7
Arborfield Wokham 20 C9
Arborfield Cross Wokham 20 C9
Arbourthorne Sheff 51 J4
Arbroath Angus 93 Q7
Arbuthnott Abers 95 N6
Archddu Carmth 25 Q8
Archdeacon Newton Darltn 65 M4
Archencarroch W Duns 84 G6
Archiestown Moray 101 J6
Arclid Ches E 49 P3
Ardallie Abers 103 L7
Ardanaiseig Hotel Ag & B 90 E10
Ardaneaskan Highld 97 L3
Ardarroch Highld 97 L2
Ardbeg Ag & B 74 F4
Ardbeg Ag & B 84 B9
Ardbeg Ag & B 84 C6
Ardcharnich Highld 106 C5
Ardchiavaig Ag & B 89 J11
Ardchonnell Ag & B 83 P1
Ardchronie Highld 107 K5
Ardchullarie More Stirlg 91 N12
Arddarroch Ag & B 84 D4
Arddleen Powys 48 F11
Ard Dorch Highld 96 G4
Ardechive Highld 98 A10
Ardeer N Ayrs 76 E4
Ardeley Herts 33 K10
Ardelve Highld 97 M4
Arden Ag & B 84 F6
Ardens Grafton Warwks 30 E4
Ardentallen Ag & B 90 B10
Ardentinny Ag & B 84 D5
Ardentraive Ag & B 83 Q7
Ardeonaig Stirlg 91 P8
Ardersier Highld 107 N10
Ardessie Highld 105 Q5
Ardfern Ag & B 83 M3
Ardfernal Ag & B 82 H8
Ardgartan Ag & B 84 E3
Ardgay Highld 107 K4
Ardgour Highld 90 D4
Ardgowan Inver 84 D8
Ardhallow Ag & B 84 C7
Ardhasig W Isls 111 c3
Ardheslaig Highld 105 L10
Ardindrean Highld 106 C5
Ardingly W Susx 11 M4
Ardington Oxon 19 M3
Ardlamont Ag & B 83 P9
Ardleigh Essex 34 H10
Ardleigh Heath Essex 34 H10
Ardler P & K 93 J7
Ardley Oxon 31 M8
Ardlui Ag & B 91 J12
Ardlussa Ag & B 83 J5
Ardmair Highld 106 B3
Ardmaleish Ag & B 84 B8
Ardminish Ag & B 75 J3
Ardmolich Highld 89 P2
Ardmore Ag & B 84 F7
Ardmore Highld 107 L5
Ardnadam Ag & B 84 C7
Ardnagrask Highld 106 H11
Ardnamurchan Highld 89 L3

Ardnarff Highld 97 M3
Ardnastang Highld 89 Q4
Ardpatrick Ag & B 83 L10
Ardrishaig Ag & B 83 M6
Ardross Highld 107 K7
Ardrossan N Ayrs 76 D3
Ardslignish Highld 89 L4
Ardtalla Ag & B 82 G11
Ardtoe Highld 89 M3
Arduaine Ag & B 83 M2
Ardullie Highld 107 J9
Ardvasar Highld 96 H8
Ardvorlich P & K 91 P10
Ardvourlie W Isls 111 c3
Ardwell D & G 68 F9
Ardwick Manch 57 Q9
Areley Kings Worcs 39 P7
Arevegaig Highld 89 N3
Arford Hants 10 D3
Argoed Caerph 27 N8
Argyll Forest Park Ag & B 84 D3
Aribruach W Isls 111 c3
Aridhglas Ag & B 88 H10
Arileod Ag & B 88 E5
Arinagour Ag & B 88 F5
Ariogan Ag & B 90 B10
Arisaig Highld 97 J11
Arisaig House Highld 97 J11
Arkendale N York 59 K2
Arkesden Essex 33 M9
Arkholme Lancs 63 L7
Arkleton D & G 79 N10
Arkley Gt Lon 21 K4
Arksey Donc 59 M11
Arkwright Town Derbys 51 K6
Arle Gloucs 29 N4
Arlecdon Cumb 70 G10
Arlesey C Beds 32 H9
Arleston Wrekin 49 M12
Arley Ches E 57 M11
Arlingham Gloucs 29 J6
Arlington Devon 15 K4
Arlington E Susx 12 B8
Armadale Highld 96 H8
Armadale Highld 109 N3
Armadale W Loth 85 Q8
Armathwaite Cumb 71 Q6
Arminghall Norfk 45 L8
Armitage Staffs 40 E4
Armley Leeds 58 H7
Armscote Warwks 30 G6
Armthorpe Donc 59 N12
Arnabost Ag & B 88 F4
Arncliffe N York 64 G12
Arncroach Fife 87 K2
Arndilly House Moray 101 K6
Arne Dorset 8 E9
Arnesby Leics 41 N8
Arngask P & K 92 H12
Arnisdale Highld 97 L7
Arnish Highld 104 H11
Arniston Mdloth 86 G9
Arnol W Isls 111 d1
Arnold E R Yk 61 J6
Arnold Notts 51 N10
Arnprior Stirlg 85 K4
Arnside Cumb 63 J6
Aros Ag & B 89 L7
Arrad Foot Cumb 62 F6
Arram E R Yk 60 H5
Arran N Ayrs 75 P5
Arrathorne N York 65 L8
Arreton IoW 9 N9
Arrina Highld 105 L10
Arrington Cambs 33 K6
Arrochar Ag & B 84 E3
Arrow Warwks 30 E3
Arscott Shrops 38 H1
Artafallie Highld 107 K11
Arthington Leeds 58 H5
Arthingworth Nhants 41 Q10
Arthrath Abers 103 K7
Artrochie Abers 103 L8
Arundel W Susx 10 G8
Asby Cumb 70 H10
Ascog Ag & B 84 B9
Ascot W & M 20 E9
Ascott-under-Wychwood
    Oxon 30 H9
Asenby N York 65 P11
Asfordby Leics 41 P4
Asfordby Hill Leics 41 Q4
Asgarby Lincs 42 G2
Ash Kent 22 C9
Ash Kent 23 P10
Ash Somset 17 L11
Ash Surrey 20 E12
Ashampstead W Berk 19 P5
Ashbocking Suffk 35 K6
Ashbourne Derbys 50 F10
Ashbrittle Somset 16 E11
Ashburton Devon 5 P6
Ashbury Devon 15 J11
Ashbury Oxon 19 J4
Ashby N Linc 52 C2
Ashby by Partney Lincs 53 L9
Ashby cum Fenby NE Lin 53 J4
Ashby de la Launde Lincs 52 F11
Ashby Folville Leics 41 P5
Ashby Magna Leics 41 M9
Ashby Parva Leics 41 M9
Ashby Puerorum Lincs 53 K8
Ashby St Ledgers Nhants 31 M1
Ashby St Mary Norfk 45 N9
Ashchurch Gloucs 29 N3
Ashcombe N Som 17 J4
Ashcott Somset 17 L8
Ashdon Essex 33 P8
Ashdown Forest E Susx 11 P4
Ashe Hants 19 N10
Asheldham Essex 23 J3
Ashen Essex 34 C8
Ashendon Bucks 31 P10
Asheridge Bucks 20 F3
Ashfield Herefs 28 H4
Ashfield Stirlg 85 N3
Ashfield cum Thorpe Suffk 35 K4
Ashfield Green Suffk 35 L3
Ashford Devon 5 N9
Ashford Devon 15 J5
Ashford Kent 13 J2
Ashford Surrey 20 H8

Ashford Bowdler Shrops 39 K7
Ashford Carbonell Shrops 39 K7
Ashford Hill Hants 19 P8
Ashford in the Water Derbys 50 G6
Ashgill S Lans 77 N2
Ash Green Surrey 20 E12
Ash Green Warwks 41 J9
Ashill Devon 6 E1
Ashill Norfk 44 E8
Ashill Somset 17 J11
Ashingdon Essex 22 G5
Ashington Nthumb 73 M4
Ashington Somset 17 N11
Ashington W Susx 11 J7
Ashkirk Border 79 P4
Ashleworth Gloucs 29 L4
Ashleworth Quay Gloucs 29 L4
Ashley Cambs 34 B5
Ashley Ches E 57 P11
Ashley Devon 15 L9
Ashley Gloucs 29 N9
Ashley Hants 9 J3
Ashley Hants 9 L2
Ashley Kent 13 P1
Ashley Nhants 42 B11
Ashley Staffs 49 N7
Ashley Wilts 18 B7
Ashley Green Bucks 20 F3
Ash Magna Shrops 49 K7
Ashmansworth Hants 19 M8
Ashmansworthy Devon 14 F9
Ash Mill Devon 15 N7
Ashmore Dorset 8 D4
Ashmore Green W Berk 19 N6
Ashorne Warwks 30 H3
Ashover Derbys 51 J8
Ashow Warwks 40 H12
Ashperton Herefs 28 H1
Ashprington Devon 5 Q8
Ash Priors Somset 16 F9
Ashreigney Devon 15 L9
Ash Street Suffk 34 G7
Ashtead Surrey 21 J10
Ash Thomas Devon 6 D1
Ashton Cnwll 2 F9
Ashton Devon 6 B6
Ashton Herefs 39 K8
Ashton Inver 84 D7
Ashton Nhants 31 Q4
Ashton Nhants 42 F11
Ashton Common Wilts 18 D8
Ashton Hayes Ches W 49 J2
Ashton-in-Makerfield Wigan 57 L3
Ashton Keynes Wilts 18 F2
Ashton-on-Ribble Lancs 57 K3
Ashton under Hill Worcs 30 C6
Ashton-under-Lyne Tamesd 50 C2
Ashton Vale Bristl 17 N3
Ashurst Hants 9 K5
Ashurst Kent 11 P3
Ashurst Lancs 57 J7
Ashurst W Susx 11 J6
Ashurst Wood W Susx 11 N3
Ash Vale Surrey 20 E12
Ashwater Devon 5 J2
Ashwell Herts 33 J8
Ashwell Rutlnd 42 C7
Ashwell End Herts 33 J8
Ashwellthorpe Norfk 45 J9
Ashwick Somset 17 P6
Ashwicken Norfk 44 B6
Askam in Furness Cumb 62 E6
Askern Donc 59 M10
Askerswell Dorset 7 M4
Askett Bucks 20 D3
Askham Cumb 71 Q10
Askham Notts 51 Q6
Askham Bryan C York 59 M5
Askham Richard C York 59 M5
Asknish Ag & B 83 P5
Askrigg N York 64 G8
Askwith N York 58 F5
Aslackby Lincs 42 F4
Aslacton Norfk 45 J11
Aslockton Notts 51 Q11
Aspatria Cumb 71 J7
Aspenden Herts 33 K10
Aspley Guise C Beds 32 D9
Aspley Heath C Beds 32 D9
Aspull Wigan 57 L7
Asselby E R Yk 60 C8
Assington Suffk 34 F8
Assington Green Suffk 34 C6
Astbury Ches E 49 Q3
Astcote Nhants 31 P4
Asterby Lincs 53 J7
Asterley Shrops 38 G1
Asterton Shrops 38 H4
Asthall Oxon 30 H10
Asthall Leigh Oxon 30 H10
Astle Highld 107 M4
Astley Shrops 49 K10
Astley Warwks 40 H9
Astley Wigan 57 M8
Astley Worcs 39 P8
Astley Abbotts Shrops 39 N3
Astley Bridge Bolton 57 N6
Astley Cross Worcs 39 P8
Aston Birm 40 E9
Aston Ches E 49 L6
Aston Ches W 57 K12
Aston Derbys 50 F4
Aston Flints 48 F3
Aston Herts 33 J11
Aston Oxon 31 J12
Aston Rothm 51 L4
Aston Shrops 39 P4
Aston Staffs 40 B3
Aston Staffs 49 N7
Aston Wokham 20 C6
Aston Abbotts Bucks 32 C11
Aston Botterell Shrops 39 L5
Aston-by-Stone Staffs 40 B2
Aston Cantlow Warwks 30 F3
Aston Clinton Bucks 20 E2
Aston Crews Herefs 29 J4
Aston End Herts 33 J11
Aston Fields Worcs 40 C12
Aston Flamville Leics 41 L8
Aston Ingham Herefs 29 J4
Aston le Walls Nhants 31 L4
Aston Magna Gloucs 30 G7

Aston Munslow Shrops 39 K5
Aston on Clun Shrops 38 H6
Aston Pigott Shrops 38 G2
Aston Rogers Shrops 38 G2
Aston Rowant Oxon 20 B4
Aston Somerville Worcs 30 D6
Aston-sub-Edge Gloucs 30 F6
Aston Tirrold Oxon 19 P4
Aston-upon-Trent Derbys 41 K2
Aston Upthorpe Oxon 19 P4
Astwick C Beds 32 H8
Astwood M Keyn 32 D7
Astwood Worcs 30 C2
Astwood Bank Worcs 30 D2
Aswarby Lincs 42 F3
Aswardby Lincs 53 L9
Atcham Shrops 39 K1
Athelhampton Dorset 8 B8
Athelington Suffk 35 K3
Athelney Somset 17 J9
Athelstaneford E Loth 87 K6
Atherington Devon 15 K7
Atherstone Warwks 40 H7
Atherstone on Stour Warwks 30 G4
Atherton Wigan 57 M8
Atlow Derbys 50 G10
Attadale Highld 97 N3
Atterby Lincs 52 E5
Attercliffe Sheff 51 J3
Atterton Leics 41 J7
Attingham Park Shrops 49 K12
Attleborough Norfk 44 H10
Attleborough Warwks 41 J8
Attlebridge Norfk 45 J6
Attleton Green Suffk 34 C6
Atwick E R Yk 61 K4
Atworth Wilts 18 C7
Auburn Lincs 52 D10
Auchbreck Moray 101 J9
Auchedly Abers 103 J8
Auchenblae Abers 95 M6
Auchenbowie Stirlg 85 N5
Auchencairn D & G 70 D5
Auchencairn D & G 78 F11
Auchencairn N Ayrs 75 Q6
Auchencrow Border 87 Q9
Auchendinny Mdloth 86 F9
Auchengray S Lans 86 B10
Auchenhalrig Moray 101 M3
Auchenheath S Lans 77 N3
Auchenhessnane D & G 77 N11
Auchenlochan Ag & B 83 P8
Auchenmade N Ayrs 76 F2
Auchentiber N Ayrs 76 F2
Auchindrain Ag & B 83 Q3
Auchindrean Highld 106 C6
Auchininna Abers 102 F6
Auchinleck E Ayrs 77 J7
Auchinloch N Lans 85 L8
Auchinstarry N Lans 85 M7
Auchintore Highld 90 F2
Auchiries Abers 103 M7
Auchlean Highld 99 M9
Auchlee Abers 95 P3
Auchleven Abers 102 E9
Auchlochan S Lans 77 N4
Auchlossan Abers 95 J2
Auchlyne Stirlg 91 M9
Auchmillan E Ayrs 77 J5
Auchmithie Angus 93 R6
Auchmuirbridge Fife 86 E3
Auchnacree Angus 94 H8
Auchnagatt Abers 103 J7
Auchnarrow Moray 101 J9
Auchnotteroch D & G 68 D7
Auchroisk Moray 101 L5
Auchterarder P & K 92 E12
Auchteraw Highld 98 E7
Auchterblair Highld 99 N5
Auchtercairn Highld 105 M7
Auchterderran Fife 86 E3
Auchterhouse Angus 93 L8
Auchterless Abers 102 F7
Auchtermuchty Fife 93 J12
Auchterneed Highld 106 H9
Auchtertool Fife 86 E4
Auchtertyre Highld 97 L4
Auchtubh Stirlg 91 N11
Auckengill Highld 110 G3
Auckley Donc 51 P1
Audenshaw Tamesd 50 B2
Audlem Ches E 49 M6
Audley Staffs 49 P5
Audley End Essex 33 N8
Audley End House &
    Gardens Essex 33 N8
Audnam Dudley 40 B9
Aughton E R Yk 60 C6
Aughton Lancs 56 H7
Aughton Lancs 63 K8
Aughton Rothm 51 L4
Aughton Wilts 19 J9
Aughton Park Lancs 56 H7
Auldearn Highld 100 E4
Aulden Herefs 39 J10
Auldgirth D & G 78 E10
Auldhouse S Lans 77 K2
Ault a' chruinn Highld 97 N5
Aultbea Highld 105 N5
Aultgrishin Highld 105 L6
Aultguish Inn Highld 106 F8
Ault Hucknall Derbys 51 L7
Aultmore Moray 101 M5
Aultnagoire Highld 98 H4
Aultnamain Highld 107 L6
Aunsby Lincs 42 F3
Aust S Glos 28 G10
Austerfield Donc 51 P2
Austrey Warwks 40 H6
Austwick N York 63 N8
Authorpe Lincs 53 L7
Avebury Wilts 18 G6
Aveley Thurr 22 C7
Avening Gloucs 29 M8
Averham Notts 51 Q9
Aveton Gifford Devon 5 N10
Aviemore Highld 99 N6
Avington W Berk 19 L7
Avoch Highld 107 L10
Avon Hants 8 G7
Avonbridge Falk 85 Q8
Avon Dassett Warwks 31 K4

Avonmouth Bristl 28 F12
Avonwick Devon 5 N8
Awbridge Hants 9 K3
Awliscombe Devon 6 F3
Awre Gloucs 29 J7
Awsworth Notts 51 L11
Axbridge Somset 17 L5
Axford Hants 19 Q11
Axford Wilts 19 J6
Axminster Devon 6 H3
Axmouth Devon 6 H5
Aycliffe Dur 65 M3
Aydon Nthumb 72 H7
Aylburton Gloucs 28 H8
Aylesbeare Devon 6 D4
Aylesbury Bucks 20 D1
Aylesby NE Lin 52 H3
Aylesford Kent 22 E10
Aylesham Kent 23 N11
Aylestone C Leic 41 M7
Aylestone Park C Leic 41 N7
Aylmerton Norfk 45 K3
Aylsham Norfk 45 K5
Aylton Herefs 28 H2
Aylworth Gloucs 30 E9
Aymestrey Herefs 38 H8
Aynho Nhants 31 L7
Ayot St Lawrence Herts 32 H12
Ayr S Ayrs 76 F7
Aysgarth N York 64 H9
Ayshford Devon 16 E11
Ayside Cumb 62 H5
Ayston Rutlnd 42 C9
Ayton Border 81 J3
Azerley N York 65 M11

B

Babbacombe Torbay 6 C9
Babbs Green Herts 33 L12
Babcary Somset 17 N9
Babraham Cambs 33 N6
Babworth Notts 51 P5
Backaland Ork 111 h1
Backfolds Abers 103 L5
Backford Ches W 48 H2
Backies Highld 107 N3
Back of Keppoch Highld 97 J11
Backwell N Som 17 L3
Baconsthorpe Norfk 45 J3
Bacton Herefs 28 D3
Bacton Norfk 45 M4
Bacton Suffk 34 H4
Bacup Lancs 57 Q4
Badachro Highld 105 L7
Badanloch Highld 109 N8
Badbury Swindn 18 H5
Badby Nhants 31 M3
Badcall Highld 108 E5
Badcaul Highld 105 Q4
Baddeley Edge C Stke 50 B9
Baddeley Green C Stke 50 B9
Baddesley Clinton Warwks 40 G11
Baddesley Ensor Warwks 40 H7
Baddidarrach Highld 108 C10
Baddinsgill Border 86 D10
Badenscoth Abers 102 F7
Badentarbet Highld 105 Q1
Badenyon Abers 101 L10
Badger Shrops 39 N3
Badgeworth Gloucs 29 M5
Badgworth Somset 17 K5
Badicaul Highld 97 K4
Badingham Suffk 35 M3
Badlesmere Kent 23 J11
Badlieu Border 78 H5
Badlipster Highld 110 F6
Badluarach Highld 105 P4
Badninish Highld 107 M4
Badrallach Highld 105 Q4
Badsey Worcs 30 E5
Badshot Lea Surrey 10 E1
Badsworth Wakefd 59 L10
Badwell Ash Suffk 34 G3
Bagber Dorset 17 Q12
Bagby N York 66 C10
Bag Enderby Lincs 53 K8
Bagendon Gloucs 30 D11
Bàgh a' Chaisteil W Isls 111 a7
Bagillt Flints 48 E1
Baginton Warwks 41 J11
Baglan Neath 26 G9
Bagley Shrops 48 H9
Bagley Somset 17 L7
Bagnall Staffs 50 B10
Bagshot Surrey 20 E10
Bagshot Wilts 19 K6
Bagstone S Glos 29 J10
Bagworth Leics 41 K6
Bagwyllydiart Herefs 28 E4
Baildon C Brad 58 F6
Baildon Green C Brad 58 F6
Baile Ailein W Isls 111 d2
Baile a' Mhanaich W Isls 111 b5
Baile Mòr Ag & B 88 G10
Bailieston C Glas 85 L9
Bainbridge N York 64 G9
Bainshole Abers 102 D8
Bainton C Pete 42 F8
Bainton E R Yk 60 G4
Baintown Fife 86 G2
Bairnkine Border 80 E10
Bakewell Derbys 50 G7
Bala Gwynd 47 Q4
Balallan W Isls 111 d2
Balbeg Highld 98 F3
Balbeggie P & K 92 H9
Balblair Highld 107 L8
Balby Donc 51 M1
Balcary D & G 70 D5
Balchraggan Highld 98 G1
Balchrick Highld 108 D4
Balcombe W Susx 11 L4
Balcomie Links Fife 87 M1
Baldersby N York 65 N10
Baldersby St James N York 65 P11
Balderstone Lancs 57 L3
Balderton Notts 52 B12
Baldinnie Fife 93 M12
Baldinnies P & K 92 F11
Baldock Herts 33 J9
Baldock Services Herts 32 H9
Baldovie C Dund 93 M8

Baldrine IoM 56 d5
Baldslow E Susx 12 F7
Bale Norfk 44 G3
Baledgarno P & K 93 K9
Balemartine Ag & B 88 C7
Balerno C Edin 86 D8
Balfarg Fife 86 F2
Balfield Angus 95 J8
Balfour Ork 111 h2
Balfron Stirlg 85 J5
Balgaveny Abers 102 E7
Balgonar Fife 86 B4
Balgowan D & G 68 F9
Balgowan Highld 99 J9
Balgown Highld 104 E8
Balgracie D & G 68 D7
Balgray S Lans 78 G8
Balham Gt Lon 21 L8
Balhary P & K 93 J6
Balholmie P & K 92 H7
Baligill Highld 109 P3
Balintore Angus 93 K4
Balintore Highld 107 P7
Balintraid Highld 107 M8
Balivanich W Isls 111 b5
Balkeerie Angus 93 K6
Balkholme E R Yk 60 D8
Ballachulish Highld 90 E5
Ballajora IoM 56 e4
Ballantrae S Ayrs 68 E3
Ballasalla IoM 56 b6
Ballater Abers 94 F3
Ballaugh IoM 56 c3
Ballchraggan Highld 107 M7
Ballencrieff E Loth 87 J6
Ballevullin Ag & B 88 B7
Ball Green C Stke 50 B9
Ball Haye Green Staffs 50 C9
Ball Hill Hants 19 M8
Ballianlay Ag & B 83 Q9
Ballidon Derbys 50 G9
Balliekine N Ayrs 75 N5
Balliemore Ag & B 84 B3
Balligmorrie S Ayrs 68 E5
Ballimore Stirlg 91 M11
Ballindalloch Moray 101 J7
Ballindean P & K 93 J9
Ballinger Common Bucks 20 E3
Ballingham Herefs 28 G3
Ballingry Fife 86 E3
Ballinluig P & K 92 E5
Ballinshoe Angus 93 M5
Ballintuim P & K 92 H4
Balloch Highld 107 M11
Balloch N Lans 85 M7
Balloch P & K 92 C10
Balloch S Ayrs 76 F11
Balloch W Duns 84 G6
Balls Cross W Susx 10 F5
Balls Green E Susx 11 P3
Ballygown Ag & B 89 J7
Ballygrant Ag & B 82 E9
Ballyhaugh Ag & B 88 E5
Balmacara Highld 97 L4
Balmaclellan D & G 69 P4
Balmae D & G 69 P9
Balmaha Stirlg 84 G5
Balmalcolm Fife 86 G1
Balmangan D & G 69 P9
Balmedie Abers 103 K10
Balmerino Fife 93 L9
Balmichael N Ayrs 75 P6
Balmore E Duns 85 K8
Balmuchy Highld 107 P6
Balmule Fife 86 E5
Balmullo Fife 93 M10
Balnacoil Highld 109 P12
Balnacra Highld 105 P12
Balnacroft Abers 94 E2
Balnafoich Highld 99 K2
Balnaguard P & K 92 E5
Balnahard Ag & B 89 K9
Balnain Highld 98 F3
Balnakeil Highld 108 G3
Balne N York 59 N9
Balquharn P & K 92 F8
Balquhidder Stirlg 91 M11
Balsall Common Solhll 40 G11
Balsall Heath Birm 40 E10
Balscote Oxon 31 K6
Balsham Cambs 33 P6
Baltasound Shet 111 m2
Baltersan D & G 69 K6
Balthangie Abers 102 H5
Baltonsborough Somset 17 M8
Balvicar Ag & B 89 Q11
Balvraid Highld 97 M6
Balvraid Highld 99 M3
Bamber Bridge Lancs 57 K4
Bamber's Green Essex 33 P11
Bamburgh Nthumb 81 N7
Bamburgh Castle Nthumb 81 N7
Bamford Derbys 50 G4
Bampton Cumb 71 Q10
Bampton Devon 16 C10
Bampton Oxon 30 H12
Bampton Grange Cumb 71 Q11
Banavie Highld 90 F2
Banbury Oxon 31 L5
Bancffosfelen Carmth 26 C6
Banchory Abers 95 L3
Banchory-Devenick Abers 95 P2
Bancycapel Carmth 25 P6
Bancyfelin Carmth 25 N5
Bandirran P & K 93 J9
Banff Abers 102 F3
Bangor Gwynd 54 H7
Bangor-on-Dee Wrexhm 48 H6
Bangors Cnwll 14 D11
Banham Norfk 44 H10
Bank Hants 9 K6
Bankend D & G 70 G2
Bankfoot P & K 92 F8
Bankglen E Ayrs 77 K8
Bankhead C Aber 103 J12
Bankhead S Lans 86 B12
Banknock Falk 85 N7
Banks Lancs 56 H5
Bankshill D & G 79 K11
Banningham Norfk 45 K4
Bannister Green Essex 34 B11
Bannockburn Stirlg 85 N5
Banstead Surrey 21 K10
Bantham Devon 5 N10

Place	County	Page	Grid
Banton	N Lans	85	M7
Banwell	N Som	17	K4
Bapchild	Kent	22	H10
Bapton	Wilts	18	E12
Barabhas	W Isls	111	d1
Barassie	S Ayrs	76	F5
Barbaraville	Highld	107	M7
Barbieston	S Ayrs	76	G7
Barbon	Cumb	63	L6
Barbrook	Devon	15	M3
Barby	Nhants	41	M12
Barcaldine	Ag & B	90	D7
Barcombe	E Susx	11	N7
Barcombe Cross	E Susx	11	N6
Barden Park	Kent	12	C2
Bardfield End Green	Essex	33	Q9
Bardfield Saling	Essex	34	B10
Bardney	Lincs	52	G9
Bardon	Leics	41	K5
Bardon Mill	Nthumb	72	E7
Bardowie	E Duns	85	K8
Bardrainney	Inver	84	F8
Bardsea	Cumb	62	F7
Bardsey	Leeds	59	J5
Bardsey Island	Gwynd	46	B7
Bardwell	Suffk	34	F3
Bare	Lancs	63	J8
Barfad	D & G	69	J6
Barford	Norfk	45	J8
Barford	Warwks	30	H2
Barford St John	Oxon	31	K7
Barford St Martin	Wilts	8	F2
Barford St Michael	Oxon	31	K7
Barfrestone	Kent	23	N12
Bargeddie	N Lans	85	L9
Bargood	Cerdgn	27	N8
Bargrennan	D & G	69	J4
Barham	Cambs	32	G2
Barham	Kent	23	N12
Barham	Suffk	35	J6
Bar Hill	Cambs	33	L4
Barholm	Lincs	42	F7
Barkby	Leics	41	N5
Barkby Thorpe	Leics	41	N5
Barkestone-le-Vale	Leics	41	R1
Barkham	Wokham	20	C9
Barking	Gt Lon	21	N6
Barking	Suffk	34	H4
Barking Riverside	Gt Lon	21	P6
Barkingside	Gt Lon	21	N5
Barking Tye	Suffk	34	H6
Barkisland	Calder	58	D9
Barkla Shop	Cnwll	2	H5
Barkston	Lincs	42	D2
Barkston Ash	N York	59	L7
Barkway	Herts	33	L9
Barlanark	C Glas	85	L9
Barlaston	Staffs	50	B12
Barlavington	W Susx	10	F6
Barlborough	Derbys	51	L5
Barlby	N York	59	N7
Barlestone	Leics	41	K6
Barley	Herts	33	L8
Barley	Lancs	57	P1
Barleythorpe	Rutlnd	42	C8
Barling	Essex	22	H5
Barlings	Lincs	52	F8
Barlochan	D & G	70	D4
Barlow	Derbys	51	J6
Barlow	Gatesd	73	K8
Barlow	N York	59	N8
Barmby Moor	E R Yk	60	D4
Barmby on the Marsh	E R Yk	59	P8
Barmollack	Ag & B	75	M4
Barmouth	Gwynd	47	K7
Barmpton	Darltn	65	N4
Barmston	E R Yk	61	K3
Barnacarry	Ag & B	83	Q4
Barnack	C Pete	42	F8
Barnard Castle	Dur	65	J4
Barnard Gate	Oxon	31	K11
Barnardiston	Suffk	34	B7
Barnbarroch	D & G	70	D4
Barnburgh	Donc	59	L12
Barnby	Suffk	45	P11
Barnby Dun	Donc	59	N11
Barnby in the Willows	Notts	52	C11
Barnby Moor	Notts	51	P4
Barncorkrie	D & G	68	E11
Barnes	Gt Lon	21	K7
Barnes Street	Kent	12	D1
Barnet	Gt Lon	21	K4
Barnetby le Wold	N Linc	52	F2
Barney	Norfk	44	G4
Barnham	Suffk	34	E2
Barnham	W Susx	10	F8
Barnham Broom	Norfk	44	H8
Barnhead	Angus	93	R4
Barnhill	C Dund	93	N8
Barnhill	Moray	100	H4
Barnhills	D & G	68	D5
Barningham	Dur	65	J5
Barningham	Suffk	34	F2
Barnoldby le Beck	NE Lin	53	H3
Barnoldswick	Lancs	63	Q11
Barns Green	W Susx	10	H5
Barnsley	Barns	59	J11
Barnsley	Gloucs	30	E12
Barnstaple	Devon	15	K5
Barnston	Essex	33	Q11
Barnston	Wirral	56	F11
Barnstone	Notts	41	Q1
Barnt Green	Worcs	40	D11
Barnton	C Edin	86	E7
Barnton	Ches W	49	L1
Barnwell All Saints	Nhants	42	F12
Barnwell St Andrew	Nhants	42	F12
Barnwood	Gloucs	29	M5
Barr	S Ayrs	76	E11
Barra Airport	W Isls	111	a6
Barrachan	D & G	69	J8
Barraigh	W Isls	111	a7
Barrananaoil	Ag & B	83	M2
Barrapoll	Ag & B	88	B7
Barrasford	Nthumb	72	G6
Barrhead	E Rens	84	H10
Barrhill	S Ayrs	68	H3
Barrington	Cambs	33	L6
Barrington	Somset	17	K11
Barripper	Cnwll	2	F7
Barmill	N Ayrs	84	F11
Barrock	Highld	110	F2
Barrow	Gloucs	29	M4
Barrow	Lancs	57	N2
Barrow	Rutlnd	42	C7
Barrow	Somset	17	Q9
Barrow	Suffk	34	C4
Barrowby	Lincs	42	C3
Barrowden	Rutlnd	42	D9
Barrowford	Lancs	57	Q2
Barrow Gurney	N Som	17	M3
Barrow Haven	N Linc	60	H9
Barrow-in-Furness	Cumb	62	E8
Barrow Island	Cumb	62	E8
Barrow-upon-Humber	N Linc	60	H9
Barrow upon Soar	Leics	41	M4
Barrow upon Trent	Derbys	41	J2
Barry	Angus	93	P8
Barry	V Glam	16	F3
Barry Island	V Glam	16	F3
Barsby	Leics	41	P5
Barsham	Suffk	45	N11
Barston	Solhll	40	G10
Bartestree	Herefs	28	G1
Barthol Chapel	Abers	102	H8
Bartholomew Green	Essex	34	C11
Barthomley	Ches E	49	N5
Bartley	Hants	9	K5
Bartley Green	Birm	40	D10
Bartlow	Cambs	33	P7
Barton	Cambs	33	L5
Barton	Ches W	49	J5
Barton	Gloucs	30	E8
Barton	Lancs	56	G7
Barton	Lancs	57	K2
Barton	N York	65	M6
Barton	Oxon	31	M11
Barton	Torbay	6	C8
Barton Bendish	Norfk	44	B8
Barton End	Gloucs	29	L8
Barton Hartshorn	Bucks	31	N7
Barton in Fabis	Notts	41	M2
Barton in the Beans	Leics	41	K6
Barton-le-Clay	C Beds	32	F9
Barton-le-Street	N York	66	G11
Barton-le-Willows	N York	60	C2
Barton Mills	Suffk	34	C3
Barton-on-Sea	Hants	9	J8
Barton-on-the-Heath	Warwks	30	G7
Barton Park Services	N York	65	L6
Barton St David	Somset	17	M9
Barton Seagrave	Nhants	32	C2
Barton Stacey	Hants	19	M11
Barton Town	Devon	15	L4
Barton Turf	Norfk	45	M5
Barton-under-Needwood	Staffs	40	F4
Barton-upon-Humber	N Linc	60	H9
Barton Waterside	N Linc	60	H9
Barvas	W Isls	111	d1
Barway	Cambs	33	N2
Barwell	Leics	41	K8
Barwick	Devon	15	K10
Barwick	Herts	17	M12
Barwick in Elmet	Leeds	59	K6
Baschurch	Shrops	48	H10
Bascote	Warwks	31	K2
Bashall Eaves	Lancs	63	M12
Basildon	Essex	22	E5
Basingstoke	Hants	19	Q9
Baslow	Derbys	50	G6
Bason Bridge	Somset	17	J7
Bassaleg	Newpt	28	C10
Bassendean	Border	80	E5
Bassenthwaite	Cumb	71	K8
Bassett	C Sotn	9	M4
Bassingbourn-cum-Kneesworth	Cambs	33	K7
Bassingham	Lincs	52	C10
Bassingthorpe	Lincs	42	D5
Bassus Green	Herts	33	K10
Baston	Lincs	42	G7
Bastwick	Norfk	45	N6
Batchworth	Herts	20	G5
Batcombe	Dorset	7	N3
Batcombe	Somset	17	Q8
Batford	Herts	21	J1
Bath	BaNES	17	Q3
Bathampton	BaNES	18	B7
Bathealton	Somset	16	E10
Batheaston	BaNES	18	B7
Bathford	BaNES	18	B7
Bathgate	W Loth	86	B8
Bathley	Notts	51	Q8
Bathpool	Cnwll	4	G5
Bathpool	Somset	16	H10
Bath Side	Essex	35	L9
Bathville	W Loth	85	Q9
Bathway	Somset	17	N6
Batley	Kirk	58	H9
Batsford	Gloucs	30	F7
Battersby	N York	66	E6
Battersea	Gt Lon	21	L7
Battisford Tye	Suffk	34	G6
Battle	E Susx	12	E7
Battle	Powys	27	L3
Battledykes	Angus	93	M5
Battlefield	Shrops	49	K11
Battlesbridge	Essex	22	F5
Battleton	Somset	16	C10
Baughton	Worcs	29	M1
Baughurst	Hants	19	P8
Baulds	Abers	95	K4
Baulking	Oxon	19	K3
Baumber	Lincs	52	H8
Baunton	Gloucs	30	D12
Baverstock	Wilts	8	F2
Bawburgh	Norfk	45	J8
Bawdeswell	Norfk	44	H6
Bawdrip	Somset	17	J8
Bawdsey	Suffk	35	M8
Bawtry	Donc	51	P3
Baxenden	Lancs	57	P4
Baxterley	Warwks	40	H7
Bay	Highld	104	C10
Baybridge	Hants	9	N3
Baycliff	Cumb	62	F7
Baydon	Wilts	19	K5
Bayford	Herts	21	L2
Bayford	Somset	17	Q9
Bayhead	W Isls	111	a4
Baylham	Suffk	34	H6
Baysham	Herefs	28	G4
Bayston Hill	Shrops	49	J1
Baythorne End	Essex	34	C8
Bayton	Worcs	39	M7
Bayworth	Oxon	31	N1
Beachampton	Bucks	31	Q6
Beachamwell	Norfk	44	C8
Beachy Head	E Susx	12	C10
Beacon	Devon	6	G2
Beacon End	Essex	34	F10
Beacon Hill	Notts	52	B11
Beacon Hill	Surrey	10	E3
Beacon's Bottom	Bucks	20	C4
Beaconsfield	Bucks	20	F5
Beaconsfield Services	Bucks	20	F6
Beadlam	N York	66	F9
Beadlow	C Beds	32	F8
Beadnell	Nthumb	81	P8
Beaford	Devon	15	K8
Beal	N York	59	M8
Beal	Nthumb	81	M6
Bealsmill	Cnwll	4	H5
Beaminster	Dorset	7	L3
Beamish	Dur	73	M9
Beamish - The Living Museum of the North	Dur	73	L9
Beamsley	N York	58	E4
Beanacre	Wilts	18	D7
Beanley	Nthumb	81	M9
Beardon	Devon	5	L4
Beare Green	Surrey	11	J2
Bearley	Warwks	30	F3
Bearpark	Dur	73	M11
Bearsden	E Duns	85	J8
Bearsted	Kent	22	F11
Bearstone	Shrops	49	N7
Bearwood	BCP	8	F7
Bearwood	Birm	40	D9
Bearwood	Herefs	38	H10
Beattock	D & G	78	H8
Beauchamp Roding	Essex	22	C2
Beauchief	Sheff	51	J5
Beaufort	Blae G	27	N6
Beaulieu	Essex	22	E2
Beaulieu	Hants	9	L7
Beauly	Highld	107	J11
Beaumaris	IoA	54	H6
Beaumaris Castle	IoA	54	H6
Beaumont	Cumb	71	M4
Beaumont	Essex	35	J10
Beaumont	Jersey	7	b2
Beaumont Leys	C Leic	41	M6
Beausale	Warwks	40	G12
Beauworth	Hants	9	P3
Beaworthy	Devon	14	H11
Beazley End	Essex	34	C10
Bebington	Wirral	56	G11
Beccles	Suffk	45	N11
Becconsall	Lancs	57	J4
Beckbury	Shrops	39	N2
Beckenham	Gt Lon	21	M9
Beckermet	Cumb	62	B2
Beckfoot	Cumb	70	H5
Beckford	Worcs	29	N2
Beckhampton	Wilts	18	G7
Beckingham	Lincs	52	C11
Beckingham	Notts	51	R3
Beckington	Somset	18	B9
Beckjay	Shrops	38	H6
Beckley	E Susx	12	G5
Beckley	Oxon	31	M10
Beck Row	Suffk	34	B2
Beck Side	Cumb	62	E6
Beckton	Gt Lon	21	N7
Beckwithshaw	N York	58	H4
Becontree	Gt Lon	21	P6
Bedale	N York	65	M9
Bedchester	Dorset	8	C4
Beddau	Rhondd	27	M10
Beddgelert	Gwynd	54	H11
Beddingham	E Susx	11	N8
Beddington	Gt Lon	21	L9
Beddington Corner	Gt Lon	21	L9
Bedfield	Suffk	35	K4
Bedford	Bed	32	F6
Bedgrove	Bucks	20	D2
Bedhampton	Hants	10	B8
Bedingfield	Suffk	35	K3
Bedlam	N York	58	H2
Bedlington	Nthumb	73	M5
Bedlinog	Myr Td	27	M8
Bedminster	Bristl	17	N2
Bedminster Down	Bristl	17	N3
Bedmond	Herts	20	H3
Bednall	Staffs	40	C4
Bedrule	Border	80	E10
Bedstone	Shrops	38	G6
Bedwas	Caerph	27	N10
Bedwellty	Caerph	27	N8
Bedworth	Warwks	41	J9
Beeby	Leics	41	P6
Beech	Hants	10	B3
Beech	Staffs	49	Q7
Beech Hill	W Berk	20	B9
Beechingstoke	Wilts	18	G8
Beedon	W Berk	19	N5
Beeford	E R Yk	61	J4
Beeley	Derbys	50	H7
Beelsby	NE Lin	52	H3
Beenham	W Berk	19	P7
Beer	Devon	6	G5
Beer	Somset	17	K9
Beercrocombe	Somset	17	J11
Beer Hackett	Dorset	7	N1
Beesands	Devon	5	Q11
Beesby	Lincs	53	M7
Beeson	Devon	5	Q11
Beeston	C Beds	32	G7
Beeston	Ches W	49	K4
Beeston	Leeds	58	H7
Beeston	Norfk	44	E7
Beeston	Notts	51	M12
Beeston Regis	Norfk	45	J2
Beeswing	D & G	70	E2
Beetham	Cumb	63	J6
Beetham	Somset	16	H1
Beetley	Norfk	44	F6
Begbroke	Oxon	31	L10
Begelly	Pembks	25	K7
Beguildy	Powys	38	E6
Beighton	Norfk	45	N8
Beighton	Sheff	51	K4
Beinn Na Faoghla	W Isls	111	b5
Beith	N Ayrs	84	F11
Bekesbourne	Kent	23	M11
Belaugh	Norfk	45	L6
Belbroughton	Worcs	40	B11
Belchalwell	Dorset	8	B5
Belchamp Otten	Essex	34	D8
Belchamp St Paul	Essex	34	D8
Belchamp Walter	Essex	34	D8
Belchford	Lincs	53	J8
Belford	Nthumb	81	M7
Belgrave	C Leic	41	N6
Belhaven	E Loth	87	M6
Belhelvie	Abers	103	K10
Belhinnie	Abers	101	N9
Bellabeg	Abers	101	L11
Bellanoch	Ag & B	83	M5
Bellaty	Angus	93	J4
Bell Busk	N York	58	B3
Belleau	Lincs	53	L7
Bell End	Worcs	40	C11
Bellerby	N York	65	K8
Belle Vue	Cumb	71	M4
Belle Vue	Wakefd	59	J9
Bellfield	S Lans	78	D2
Bellfields	Surrey	20	F11
Bellingdon	Bucks	20	F3
Bellingham	Nthumb	72	F4
Belloch	Ag & B	75	K5
Bellochantuy	Ag & B	75	K6
Bell o' th' Hill	Ches W	49	K6
Bellshill	N Lans	85	M10
Bellshill	Nthumb	81	N10
Bellsquarry	W Loth	86	C8
Bells Yew Green	E Susx	12	C3
Belluton	BaNES	17	N4
Belmaduthy	Highld	107	K10
Belmont	Bl w D	57	M6
Belmont	Gt Lon	21	K10
Belmont	S Ayrs	76	F7
Belmont	Shet	111	m2
Belnacraig	Abers	101	M11
Belper	Derbys	51	J10
Belsay	Nthumb	73	K5
Belses	Border	80	D8
Belsford	Devon	5	P8
Belsize	Herts	20	G4
Belstead	Suffk	35	J8
Belstone	Devon	5	M2
Belthorn	Bl w D	57	N4
Beltinge	Kent	23	M9
Beltingham	Nthumb	72	E7
Beltoft	N Linc	52	B3
Belton	Leics	41	K4
Belton	Lincs	42	D3
Belton	Lincs	52	B3
Belton	Norfk	45	P9
Belton House	Lincs	42	D3
Belton in Rutland	Rutlnd	42	B9
Belvedere	Gt Lon	21	P7
Belvoir	Leics	42	B4
Bembridge	IoW	9	Q9
Bemerton	Wilts	8	G2
Bempton	E R Yk	67	P12
Benacre	Suffk	45	Q12
Benbecula	W Isls	111	b5
Benbecula Airport	W Isls	111	b5
Benbuie	D & G	77	M11
Benderloch	Ag & B	90	C8
Benenden	Kent	12	F4
Benfieldside	Dur	73	J9
Benfleet	Essex	22	F6
Bengeo	Herts	21	L1
Bengeworth	Worcs	30	D5
Benhall Green	Suffk	35	N5
Benhall Street	Suffk	35	N5
Benholm	Abers	95	N7
Beningbrough	N York	59	M3
Benington	Herts	33	J11
Benington	Lincs	43	L2
Benllech	IoA	54	G5
Benmore	Ag & B	84	C6
Bennan	N Ayrs	75	Q7
Ben Nevis	Highld	90	G3
Benniworth	Lincs	52	H7
Benover	Kent	12	E1
Ben Rhydding	C Brad	58	F5
Benslie	N Ayrs	76	F3
Benson	Oxon	19	Q3
Benthoul	C Aber	95	N2
Bentley	Donc	59	M11
Bentley	E R Yk	60	H7
Bentley	Hants	10	C2
Bentley	Suffk	35	J8
Bentley	Warwks	40	H8
Bentpath	D & G	79	M10
Bentwichen	Devon	15	M6
Bentworth	Hants	19	Q11
Benvie	Angus	93	K8
Benville	Dorset	7	M3
Benwick	Cambs	43	K11
Beoley	Worcs	40	E12
Beoraidbeg	Highld	97	J10
Bepton	W Susx	10	D6
Berden	Essex	33	M10
Berea	Pembks	24	E3
Bere Alston	Devon	5	K7
Bere Ferrers	Devon	5	K7
Bere Regis	Dorset	8	C8
Bergh Apton	Norfk	45	M9
Berinsfield	Oxon	19	P2
Berkeley	Gloucs	29	J8
Berkhamsted	Herts	20	F2
Berkley	Somset	18	B10
Berkswell	Solhll	40	G10
Bermondsey	Gt Lon	21	M7
Bernera	Highld	97	L3
Bernisdale	Highld	104	E11
Berrick Prior	Oxon	19	Q2
Berrick Salome	Oxon	19	Q3
Berriedale	Highld	110	D10
Berrier	Cumb	71	N9
Berriew	Powys	38	E2
Berrington	Shrops	39	K2
Berrington	Worcs	39	L8
Berrington Green	Worcs	39	L8
Berrow	Somset	16	H6
Berrow	Worcs	39	N9
Berryfields	Bucks	20	C1
Berryhillock	Moray	101	P3
Berryhillock	Moray	101	P5
Berrynarbor	Devon	15	K3
Berry Pomeroy	Devon	5	Q8
Bersham	Wrexhm	48	F5
Berwick	E Susx	11	P8
Berwick Bassett	Wilts	18	G6
Berwick Hill	Nthumb	73	L5
Berwick St James	Wilts	18	F11
Berwick St John	Wilts	8	D3
Berwick St Leonard	Wilts	8	D2
Berwick-upon-Tweed	Nthumb	81	L4
Bescar	Lancs	56	H6
Besford	Worcs	30	B5
Bessacarr	Donc	51	N1
Bessingby	E R Yk	61	K2
Bessingham	Norfk	45	J3
Besthorpe	Norfk	44	H10
Besthorpe	Notts	52	B9
Bestwood Village	Notts	51	M10
Beswick	E R Yk	60	H5
Betchworth	Surrey	21	K12
Bethania	Cerdgn	37	J7
Bethel	Gwynd	54	G8
Bethel	IoA	54	E7
Bethersden	Kent	12	H3
Bethesda	Gwynd	55	J8
Bethesda	Pembks	25	J5
Bethlehem	Carmth	26	F4
Bethnal Green	Gt Lon	21	M6
Betley	Staffs	49	N6
Betsham	Kent	22	C8
Betteshanger	Kent	23	P11
Bettiscombe	Dorset	7	K3
Bettisfield	Wrexhm	49	J8
Bettws	Brdgnd	27	J10
Bettws	Newpt	28	C10
Bettws Cedewain	Powys	38	D3
Bettws Ifan	Cerdgn	36	E10
Bettws-Newydd	Mons	28	D7
Bettyhill	Highld	109	M4
Betws Bledrws	Cerdgn	37	K9
Betws Gwerfil Goch	Denbgs	48	B6
Betws-y-Coed	Conwy	55	L9
Betws-yn-Rhos	Conwy	55	N6
Beulah	Cerdgn	36	E10
Beulah	Powys	37	Q9
Bevercotes	Notts	51	P6
Beverley	E R Yk	60	H6
Beverston	Gloucs	29	M9
Bewcastle	Cumb	71	Q1
Bewdley	Worcs	39	P7
Bewerley	N York	58	F2
Bewholme	E R Yk	61	K4
Bexhill-on-Sea	E Susx	12	E8
Bexley	Gt Lon	21	P8
Bexleyheath	Gt Lon	21	P8
Bexwell	Norfk	43	Q9
Beyton	Suffk	34	F4
Beyton Green	Suffk	34	F4
Bhaltos	W Isls	111	c2
Bhatarsaigh	W Isls	111	a7
Bibury	Gloucs	30	E11
Bicester	Oxon	31	N9
Bickenhill	Solhll	40	F10
Bicker	Lincs	42	H3
Bickerstaffe	Lancs	57	J7
Bickerton	N York	59	K4
Bickford	Staffs	40	B5
Bickington	Devon	5	Q6
Bickington	Devon	15	J6
Bickleigh	Devon	5	L7
Bickleigh	Devon	6	C2
Bickley	Ches W	49	K6
Bickley	Gt Lon	21	N9
Bickley	N York	67	K8
Bicknacre	Essex	22	F3
Bicknoller	Somset	16	G10
Bicknor	Kent	22	G10
Bicton	Shrops	38	F5
Bicton	Shrops	49	J11
Bidborough	Kent	12	C2
Biddenden	Kent	12	G3
Biddenham	Bed	32	E6
Biddestone	Wilts	18	C6
Biddisham	Somset	17	K5
Biddlesden	Bucks	31	N6
Biddulph	Staffs	50	B8
Biddulph Moor	Staffs	50	B8
Bideford	Devon	14	H6
Bidford-on-Avon	Warwks	30	E4
Bielby	E R Yk	60	D5
Bieldside	C Aber	95	P2
Bierley	IoW	9	N10
Bierton	Bucks	32	B12
Big Balcraig	D & G	69	K9
Bigbury	Devon	5	N10
Bigbury-on-Sea	Devon	5	N10
Bigby	Lincs	52	F3
Biggar	S Lans	78	G2
Biggin	Derbys	50	F8
Biggin	N York	59	M5
Biggin Hill	Gt Lon	21	N10
Biggleswade	C Beds	32	H7
Bigholms	D & G	79	M11
Bighouse	Highld	109	Q3
Bighton	Hants	9	Q1
Biglands	Cumb	71	L5
Bignor	W Susx	10	F7
Bigrigg	Cumb	70	G11
Big Sand	Highld	105	L6
Bigton	Shet	111	k5
Bilborough	C Nott	51	M11
Bilbrook	Somset	16	D7
Bilbrough	N York	59	M5
Bilbster	Highld	110	F5
Bildershaw	Dur	65	L3
Bildeston	Suffk	34	F7
Billericay	Essex	22	D5
Billesdon	Leics	41	Q7
Billesley	Warwks	30	F3
Billingborough	Lincs	42	G4
Billinge	St Hel	57	K8
Billingford	Norfk	44	H5
Billingford	Norfk	45	K4
Billingham	S on T	66	C3
Billinghay	Lincs	52	G11
Billingley	Barns	59	K12
Billingshurst	W Susx	10	H5
Billingsley	Shrops	39	N5
Billington	C Beds	32	D11
Billington	Lancs	57	N2
Billockby	Norfk	45	N7
Billy Row	Dur	73	L12
Bilsborrow	Lancs	57	K2
Bilsby	Lincs	53	M8
Bilsham	W Susx	10	F9
Bilsington	Kent	13	K3
Bilsthorpe	Notts	51	N8
Bilston	Mdloth	86	F8
Bilston	Wolves	40	C8

Place	County	Page	Grid
Bilstone	Leics	41	J6
Bilton	E R Yk	61	K7
Bilton	N York	58	H3
Bilton	Warwks	41	L11
Bilton-in-Ainsty	N York	59	L4
Binbrook	Lincs	52	H5
Bincombe	Dorset	7	P6
Binegar	Somset	17	N6
Binfield	Br For	20	D8
Binfield Heath	Oxon	20	C7
Bingfield	Nthumb	72	H6
Bingham	Notts	51	P11
Bingley	C Brad	58	E6
Binham	Norfk	44	G3
Binley	Covtry	41	J10
Binley	Hants	19	M9
Binley Woods	Warwks	41	K11
Binnegar	Dorset	8	C9
Binniehill	Falk	85	P8
Binscombe	Surrey	10	F2
Binstead	IoW	9	P8
Binsted	Hants	10	C2
Binsted	W Susx	10	F8
Binton	Warwks	30	F4
Bintree	Norfk	44	G5
Birch	Essex	34	F11
Birchall	Staffs	50	C9
Bircham Newton	Norfk	44	C4
Bircham Tofts	Norfk	44	C4
Birchanger	Essex	33	N11
Birchanger Green Services Essex		33	N11
Birch Cross	Staffs	40	E2
Bircher	Herefs	39	J8
Birchfield	Birm	40	E8
Birch Green	Essex	34	F11
Birchgrove	Cardif	27	N11
Birchgrove	Swans	26	F8
Birchgrove	W Susx	11	N4
Birchington	Kent	23	P9
Birchley Heath	Warwks	40	H8
Birchover	Derbys	50	G8
Birch Services	Rochdl	57	Q7
Birch Vale	Derbys	50	D4
Birchwood	Lincs	52	D9
Birch Wood	Somset	16	H12
Birchwood	Warrtn	57	M9
Bircotes	Notts	51	N3
Birdbrook	Essex	34	B8
Birdforth	N York	66	C11
Birdham	W Susx	10	D9
Birdingbury	Warwks	31	K1
Birdlip	Gloucs	29	N6
Birdsall	N York	60	E2
Birds Edge	Kirk	58	G11
Birds Green	Essex	22	C2
Birdsgreen	Shrops	39	P5
Birdsmoorgate	Dorset	7	K3
Birdwell	Barns	51	J1
Birgham	Border	80	G6
Birichin	Highld	107	M4
Birkby	N York	65	N7
Birkdale	Sefton	56	G6
Birkenbog	Abers	102	C3
Birkenhead	Wirral	56	G10
Birkenhead (Queensway) Tunnel Lpool		56	G10
Birkenhills	Abers	102	F6
Birkenshaw	Kirk	58	G8
Birkhall	Abers	94	F4
Birkhill	Angus	93	L8
Birkhill	D & G	79	K6
Birkin	N York	59	M8
Birley	Herefs	39	J10
Birley Carr	Sheff	51	J3
Birling	Kent	22	D10
Birlingham	Worcs	30	C5
Birmingham	Birm	40	E9
Birmingham Airport	Solhll	40	F10
Birnam	P & K	92	F7
Birness	Abers	103	K8
Birse	Abers	95	J3
Birsemore	Abers	95	J3
Birstall	Kirk	58	G8
Birstall	Leics	41	N5
Birstwith	N York	58	G3
Birtley	Gatesd	73	M9
Birtley	Herefs	38	G8
Birtley	Nthumb	72	F5
Birts Street	Worcs	29	K2
Bisbrooke	Rutlnd	42	C9
Biscathorpe	Lincs	52	H6
Bisham	W & M	20	D6
Bishampton	Worcs	30	C4
Bish Mill	Devon	15	M7
Bishop Auckland	Dur	65	L2
Bishopbridge	Lincs	52	E5
Bishopbriggs	E Duns	85	K8
Bishop Burton	E R Yk	60	G7
Bishop Middleham	Dur	65	N2
Bishopmill	Moray	101	J3
Bishop Monkton	N York	59	J2
Bishop Norton	Lincs	52	E5
Bishopsbourne	Kent	23	M11
Bishops Cannings	Wilts	18	F7
Bishop's Castle	Shrops	38	G4
Bishop's Caundle	Dorset	17	Q12
Bishop's Cleeve	Gloucs	29	N4
Bishop's Frome	Herefs	39	M11
Bishop's Green	Essex	33	Q12
Bishop's Hull	Somset	16	G10
Bishops Itchington	Warwks	31	K3
Bishops Lydeard	Somset	16	G10
Bishop's Norton	Gloucs	29	L4
Bishop's Nympton	Devon	15	N7
Bishop's Offley	Staffs	49	P9
Bishop's Stortford	Herts	33	M11
Bishop's Sutton	Hants	9	Q2
Bishop's Tachbrook	Warwks	30	H2
Bishop's Tawton	Devon	15	K6
Bishopsteignton	Devon	6	B7
Bishopstoke	Hants	9	M4
Bishopston	Swans	26	D10
Bishopstone	Bucks	20	C2
Bishopstone	E Susx	11	P9
Bishopstone	Herefs	38	H12
Bishopstone	Kent	23	N9
Bishopstone	Swindn	19	J4
Bishopstone	Wilts	8	F3
Bishopstrow	Wilts	18	D11
Bishop Sutton	BaNES	17	N4
Bishop's Waltham	Hants	9	P4
Bishopswood	Somset	16	H1
Bishop's Wood	Staffs	49	Q12
Bishopsworth	Bristl	17	N3
Bishop Thornton	N York	58	H2
Bishopthorpe	C York	59	N5
Bishopton	Darltn	65	P4
Bishopton	Rens	84	G8
Bishop Wilton	E R Yk	60	D3
Bishton	Newpt	28	D10
Bishton	Staffs	40	D4
Bisley	Gloucs	29	M7
Bisley	Surrey	20	F10
Bissoe	Cnwll	2	H7
Bisterne	Hants	8	G7
Bitchfield	Lincs	42	E4
Bittadon	Devon	15	J4
Bittaford	Devon	5	N8
Bitterley	Shrops	39	M6
Bitterne	C Sotn	9	M5
Bitteswell	Leics	41	M9
Bitton	S Glos	17	P3
Bix	Oxon	20	B6
Bixter	Shet	111	k4
Blaby	Leics	41	M7
Blackadder	Border	80	H4
Blackawton	Devon	5	Q9
Blackborough	Devon	6	E2
Blackborough End	Norfk	43	Q7
Black Bourton	Oxon	30	H12
Blackboys	E Susx	11	Q6
Blackbrook	Derbys	51	J10
Blackbrook	St Hel	57	K9
Blackbrook	Staffs	49	N7
Blackburn	Abers	102	H11
Blackburn	Bl w D	57	M4
Blackburn	W Loth	86	B8
Blackburn with Darwen Services Bl w D		57	M4
Blackcraig	E Ayrs	77	K9
Black Crofts	Ag & B	90	C8
Blackdog	Abers	103	K11
Black Dog	Devon	15	N9
Blackdown	Dorset	7	K3
Blacker Hill	Barns	51	J1
Blackfen	Gt Lon	21	P8
Blackfield	Hants	9	M7
Blackford	P & K	85	P2
Blackford	Somset	17	K6
Blackford	Somset	17	P10
Blackfordby	Leics	41	J4
Blackhall	C Edin	86	E7
Blackhall Colliery	Dur	73	Q11
Blackhall Mill	Gatesd	73	K9
Blackhaugh	Border	79	N2
Blackheath	Gt Lon	21	M7
Blackheath	Sandw	40	C9
Blackheath	Suffk	35	N3
Blackheath	Surrey	10	G2
Blackhill	Abers	103	M4
Blackhill	Abers	103	M6
Blackhill	Dur	73	J9
Blackhill of Clackriach	Abers	103	J6
Blacklaw	D & G	78	G7
Blackley	Manch	57	Q8
Blacklunans	P & K	94	C9
Blackmarstone	Herefs	28	F2
Blackmill	Brdgnd	27	K10
Blackmoor	Hants	10	C4
Blackmoor	N Som	17	L4
Blackmoorfoot	Kirk	58	E10
Blackmore	Essex	22	C3
Blackmore End	Essex	34	C9
Black Mountains		27	Q4
Blackness	Falk	86	C6
Blacknest	Hants	10	C2
Black Notley	Essex	34	C11
Blacko	Lancs	57	Q1
Black Pill	Swans	26	E10
Blackpool	Bpool	56	F2
Blackpool	Devon	6	B12
Blackpool Zoo	Bpool	56	G2
Blackridge	W Loth	85	P9
Blackrod	Bolton	57	L6
Blacksboat	Moray	101	J7
Blackshaw	D & G	70	G3
Blackshaw Head	Calder	58	C8
Blackstone	W Susx	11	K6
Black Street	Suffk	45	Q11
Blackthorn	Oxon	31	N9
Blackthorpe	Suffk	34	E4
Blacktoft	E R Yk	60	E8
Blacktop	C Aber	95	P2
Black Torrington	Devon	14	H10
Blackwall	Derbys	50	G10
Blackwall Tunnel	Gt Lon	21	M7
Blackwater	Cnwll	2	H6
Blackwater	Hants	20	D10
Blackwater	IoW	9	N9
Blackwater	Somset	16	H11
Blackwaterfoot	N Ayrs	75	N6
Blackwell	Cumb	71	N5
Blackwell	Derbys	50	E6
Blackwell	Derbys	51	K8
Blackwell	Warwks	30	G5
Blackwell	Worcs	40	C11
Blackwood	Caerph	27	N8
Blackwood	D & G	78	E10
Blackwood	S Lans	77	N3
Blacon	Ches W	48	H2
Bladnoch	D & G	69	K8
Bladon	Oxon	31	K10
Blaenannerch	Cerdgn	36	D10
Blaenau Ffestiniog	Gwynd	47	L3
Blaenau Ffestiniog	Gwynd	47	L3
Blaenavon Industrial Landscape Torfn		27	P7
Blaencwm	Rhondd	27	K8
Blaenffos	Pembks	25	L2
Blaengarw	Brdgnd	27	J7
Blaengwrach	Neath	27	J7
Blaengwynfi	Neath	27	J9
Blaenpennal	Cerdgn	37	K7
Blaenplwyf	Cerdgn	37	J5
Blaenporth	Cerdgn	36	D10
Blaenrhondda	Rhondd	27	K8
Blaenwaun	Carmth	25	L4
Blaen-y-coed	Carmth	25	N4
Blagdon	N Som	17	M4
Blagdon	Somset	16	G11
Blagdon	Torbay	6	B9
Blagdon Hill	Somset	16	G11
Blaich	Highld	90	G2
Blaina	Blae G	27	P7
Blair Atholl	P & K	92	C3
Blair Drummond	Stirlg	85	M3
Blairgowrie	P & K	92	H6
Blairhall	Fife	86	B5
Blairingone	P & K	86	B3
Blairlogie	Stirlg	85	N4
Blairmore	Ag & B	84	D6
Blairmore	Highld	108	D4
Blair's Ferry	Ag & B	83	P8
Blaisdon	Gloucs	29	J5
Blakebrook	Worcs	39	P6
Blakedown	Worcs	39	Q6
Blake End	Essex	34	B11
Blakemere	Ches W	49	K2
Blakemere	Herefs	28	D1
Blakenall Heath	Wsall	40	D7
Blakeney	Gloucs	29	J7
Blakeney	Norfk	44	G2
Blakenhall	Ches E	49	N6
Blakenhall	Wolves	40	B7
Blakesley	Nhants	31	N4
Blanchland	Nthumb	72	H10
Blandford Forum	Dorset	8	C6
Blandford St Mary	Dorset	8	C6
Blanefield	Stirlg	85	J7
Blankney	Lincs	52	F10
Blantyre	S Lans	85	L10
Blàr a' Chaorainn	Highld	90	F3
Blarghour	Ag & B	83	Q1
Blargie	Highld	98	H9
Blarmachfoldach	Highld	90	F3
Blaston	Leics	42	B10
Blatherwycke	Nhants	42	D10
Blawith	Cumb	62	F5
Blawquhairn	D & G	69	N3
Blaxhall	Suffk	35	M5
Blaxton	Donc	51	P2
Blaydon	Gatesd	73	L8
Bleadney	Somset	17	L7
Bleadon	N Som	17	J5
Blean	Kent	23	L10
Bleasby	Notts	51	Q10
Bleasdale	Lancs	63	P11
Blebocraigs	Fife	93	M11
Bleddfa	Powys	38	E8
Bledington	Gloucs	30	G9
Bledlow	Bucks	20	C3
Bledlow Ridge	Bucks	20	C4
Blegbie	E Loth	87	J9
Blencarn	Cumb	64	B2
Blencogo	Cumb	71	K6
Blendworth	Hants	10	B7
Blenheim Palace	Oxon	31	K10
Blennerhasset	Cumb	71	J7
Bletchingdon	Oxon	31	L9
Bletchingley	Surrey	21	M12
Bletchley	M Keyn	32	C9
Bletchley	Shrops	49	L8
Bletchley Park Museum M Keyn		32	C9
Bletherston	Pembks	25	J5
Bletsoe	Bed	32	E5
Blewbury	Oxon	19	N4
Blickling	Norfk	45	K4
Blidworth	Notts	51	N9
Blidworth Bottoms	Notts	51	N9
Blindcrake	Cumb	71	J8
Blindley Heath	Surrey	11	M2
Blisland	Cnwll	4	D5
Blissford	Hants	8	H5
Bliss Gate	Worcs	39	N7
Blisworth	Nhants	31	Q4
Blithbury	Staffs	40	E4
Blockley	Gloucs	30	F7
Blofield	Norfk	45	M8
Blofield Heath	Norfk	45	M7
Blo Norton	Norfk	34	G2
Bloomfield	Border	80	D8
Blore	Staffs	50	F10
Bloxham	Oxon	31	K7
Bloxholm	Lincs	52	F11
Bloxwich	Wsall	40	C7
Bloxworth	Dorset	8	C8
Blubberhouses	N York	58	F3
Blue Anchor	Somset	16	D7
Blue Bell Hill	Kent	22	E10
Blue John Cavern	Derbys	50	F4
Blundellsands	Sefton	56	F8
Blundeston	Suffk	45	Q10
Blunham	C Beds	32	G6
Blunsdon St Andrew	Swindn	18	G3
Bluntington	Worcs	40	B11
Bluntisham	Cambs	33	K2
Blurton	C Stke	50	B11
Blyborough	Lincs	52	D5
Blyford	Suffk	35	N2
Blymhill	Staffs	49	P11
Blyth	Notts	51	N4
Blyth	Nthumb	73	N5
Blyth Bridge	Border	86	D12
Blythburgh	Suffk	35	P2
Blythe	Border	80	D4
Blythe Bridge	Staffs	50	C11
Blyth Services	Notts	51	N3
Blyton	Lincs	52	C5
Boarhills	Fife	93	P11
Boarhunt	Hants	9	P6
Boarstall	Bucks	31	N10
Boath	Highld	107	J7
Boat of Garten	Highld	99	P5
Bobbing	Kent	22	H9
Bobbington	Staffs	39	P4
Bocking	Essex	34	C10
Bocking Churchstreet	Essex	34	C10
Boddam	Abers	103	M6
Boddam	Shet	111	k5
Boddington	Gloucs	29	M4
Bodedern	IoA	54	D5
Bodelwyddan	Denbgs	55	Q6
Bodenham	Herefs	39	K11
Bodenham	Wilts	8	H3
Bodenham Moor	Herefs	39	K11
Bodewryd	IoA	54	E4
Bodfari	Denbgs	48	C2
Bodffordd	IoA	54	F6
Bodham	Norfk	45	J3
Bodiam	E Susx	12	F5
Bodicote	Oxon	31	L6
Bodinnick	Cnwll	4	E9
Bodle Street Green	E Susx	12	C7
Bodmin	Cnwll	3	N3
Bodmin Moor	Cnwll	4	F5
Bodsham	Kent	13	L2
Boduan	Gwynd	46	E4
Bodwen	Cnwll	3	M4
Bogallan	Highld	107	K11
Bogbrae	Abers	103	L8
Bogend	S Ayrs	76	G5
Boggs Holdings	E Loth	87	J7
Boghall	Mdloth	86	F8
Boghall	W Loth	86	B8
Boghead	S Lans	77	N3
Bogmoor	Moray	101	L3
Bogmuir	Abers	95	K7
Bogniebrae	Abers	102	D6
Bognor Regis	W Susx	10	E9
Bogroy	Highld	99	N4
Bogue	D & G	69	P3
Bohortha	Cnwll	3	J8
Bohuntine	Highld	98	D11
Bolam	Dur	65	L3
Bolberry	Devon	5	N11
Boldmere	Birm	40	E8
Boldre	Hants	9	K7
Boldron	Dur	65	J5
Bole	Notts	52	B6
Bolehill	Derbys	50	H9
Bolham	Devon	16	C12
Bolham Water	Devon	6	F1
Bolingey	Cnwll	2	H5
Bollington	Ches E	50	C5
Bolney	W Susx	11	L5
Bolnhurst	Bed	32	F5
Bolnore	W Susx	11	M5
Bolshan	Angus	93	Q5
Bolsover	Derbys	51	L6
Bolsterstone	Sheff	50	H2
Boltby	N York	66	C9
Bolton	Bolton	57	N7
Bolton	Cumb	64	B3
Bolton	E Loth	87	K8
Bolton	E R Yk	60	D4
Bolton	Nthumb	81	M10
Bolton Abbey	N York	58	E4
Bolton-by-Bowland	Lancs	63	P11
Boltonfellend	Cumb	71	P2
Boltongate	Cumb	71	K7
Bolton-le-Sands	Lancs	63	J8
Bolton Low Houses	Cumb	71	K6
Bolton-on-Swale	N York	65	M7
Bolton Percy	N York	59	M6
Bolton upon Dearne	Barns	51	L1
Bolventor	Cnwll	4	E5
Bomere Heath	Shrops	49	J10
Bonar Bridge	Highld	107	K4
Bonawe	Ag & B	90	D9
Bonby	N Linc	60	G10
Boncath	Pembks	25	L2
Bonchester Bridge	Border	80	D10
Bondleigh	Devon	15	L10
Bonds	Lancs	63	J12
Bo'ness	Falk	86	B6
Boney Hay	Staffs	40	D5
Bonhill	W Duns	84	G7
Boningale	Shrops	39	P2
Bonjedward	Border	80	E9
Bonkle	N Lans	85	P10
Bonnington	Angus	93	M7
Bonnington	Kent	13	K3
Bonnybank	Fife	86	G2
Bonnybridge	Falk	85	N7
Bonnykelly	Abers	102	H5
Bonnyrigg	Mdloth	86	G8
Bonnyton	Angus	93	L7
Bonsall	Derbys	50	H8
Bonshaw Tower	D & G	71	K2
Bont-Dolgadfan	Powys	47	P10
Bont-goch	Cerdgn	37	L4
Bontnewydd	Cerdgn	37	K7
Bontnewydd	Gwynd	54	G9
Bontuchel	Denbgs	48	C4
Bonvilston	V Glam	16	E2
Boode	Devon	15	J4
Booker	Bucks	20	D5
Boon	Border	80	D5
Boosbeck	R & Cl	66	F4
Boose's Green	Essex	34	E9
Boot	Cumb	62	D3
Boothby Graffoe	Lincs	52	E10
Boothby Pagnell	Lincs	42	D4
Boothferry	E R Yk	60	C8
Boothstown	Salfd	57	N8
Boothtown	Calder	58	E8
Boothville	Nhants	32	B4
Bootle	Cumb	62	C5
Bootle	Sefton	56	G9
Boraston	Shrops	39	L8
Bordeaux	Guern	6	c1
Borden	Kent	22	G10
Bordon	Hants	10	C3
Boreham	Essex	22	F2
Boreham Street	E Susx	12	D7
Borehamwood	Herts	21	J4
Boreland	D & G	79	J10
Boreraig	Highld	104	B10
Borgh	W Isls	111	a7
Borgh	W Isls	111	d1
Borgie	Highld	109	M4
Borgue	D & G	69	P9
Borgue	Highld	110	D9
Borley	Essex	34	E7
Borneskitaig	Highld	104	E7
Borness	D & G	69	N9
Boroughbridge	N York	59	K2
Borough Green	Kent	22	C11
Borrowash	Derbys	41	K1
Borrowby	N York	65	Q9
Borrowdale	Cumb	71	L11
Borrowstoun	Falk	86	B6
Borstal	Medway	22	E9
Borth	Cerdgn	37	K3
Borthwick	Mdloth	86	H9
Borthwickbrae	Border	79	N6
Borthwickshiels	Border	79	N6
Borth-y-Gest	Gwynd	47	J4
Borve	Highld	104	F11
Borve	W Isls	111	a7
Borve	W Isls	111	c3
Borve	W Isls	111	d1
Borwick	Lancs	63	K7
Bosbury	Herefs	39	M12
Boscastle	Cnwll	4	D3
Boscombe	BCP	8	G8
Boscombe	Wilts	18	H11
Bosham	W Susx	10	D9
Bosherston	Pembks	24	G9
Bosley	Ches E	50	B7
Bossall	N York	60	D2
Bossiney	Cnwll	4	D3
Bossingham	Kent	13	M1
Bossington	Somset	16	B6
Bostock Green	Ches W	49	M2
Boston	Lincs	43	K2
Boston Spa	Leeds	59	K5
Boswinger	Cnwll	3	L7
Botallack	Cnwll	2	B8
Botany Bay	Gt Lon	21	L4
Botesdale	Suffk	34	H2
Bothal	Nthumb	73	M4
Bothamsall	Notts	51	P6
Bothel	Cumb	71	J7
Bothenhampton	Dorset	7	L5
Bothwell	S Lans	85	L10
Bothwell Services (southbound) S Lans		85	M10
Botley	Bucks	20	F3
Botley	Hants	9	N5
Botley	Oxon	31	L11
Botolph Claydon	Bucks	31	Q8
Botolphs	W Susx	11	J8
Bottesford	Leics	42	B3
Bottesford	N Linc	52	C3
Bottisham	Cambs	33	N5
Bottomcraig	Fife	93	L10
Bottoms	Calder	58	B9
Botusfleming	Cnwll	5	J7
Botwnnog	Gwynd	46	D5
Bough Beech	Kent	11	P1
Boughrood	Powys	27	N2
Boughton	Nhants	31	Q2
Boughton	Norfk	44	B9
Boughton	Notts	51	P7
Boughton Aluph	Kent	13	K1
Boughton Green	Kent	22	F12
Boughton Lees	Kent	13	K1
Boughton Monchelsea	Kent	22	F12
Boughton Street	Kent	23	K10
Bouldon	Shrops	39	K5
Boulmer	Nthumb	81	Q10
Boultenstone	Abers	101	M12
Boultham	Lincs	52	D9
Bourn	Cambs	33	K5
Bournbrook	Birm	40	D10
Bourne	Lincs	42	F6
Bournebridge	Essex	21	P5
Bourne End	Bucks	20	E6
Bourne End	C Beds	32	D7
Bourne End	Herts	20	G3
Bournemouth	BCP	8	G8
Bournemouth Airport	BCP	8	G8
Bournes Green	Shend	22	H6
Bournheath	Worcs	40	C11
Bournmoor	Dur	73	N9
Bournville	Birm	40	D10
Bourton	Dorset	8	B2
Bourton	Oxon	19	J4
Bourton	Shrops	39	L3
Bourton	Wilts	18	F7
Bourton on Dunsmore Warwks		41	K12
Bourton-on-the-Hill	Gloucs	30	F7
Bourton-on-the-Water Gloucs		30	F9
Bousd	Ag & B	88	G4
Bouth	Cumb	62	G5
Bouthwaite	N York	65	K12
Boveridge	Dorset	8	F4
Bovey Tracey	Devon	5	Q5
Bovingdon	Herts	20	G3
Bow	Devon	15	M10
Bow	Gt Lon	21	M6
Bow	Ork	111	h3
Bow Brickhill	M Keyn	32	C9
Bowbridge	Gloucs	29	M7
Bowburn	Dur	73	N12
Bowcombe	IoW	9	M9
Bowd	Devon	6	F5
Bowden	Border	80	D7
Bowden Hill	Wilts	18	D7
Bowdon	Traffd	57	N10
Bower	Highld	110	F3
Bowerchalke	Wilts	8	F3
Bowermadden	Highld	110	F3
Bowers	Staffs	49	P8
Bowers Gifford	Essex	22	E6
Bowershall	Fife	86	C4
Bower's Row	Leeds	59	K8
Bowes	Dur	64	H5
Bowgreave	Lancs	63	J12
Bowhouse	D & G	70	G3
Bowland	Border	79	P2
Bowley	Herefs	39	K10
Bowlhead Green	Surrey	10	E3
Bowling	C Brad	58	F7
Bowling	W Duns	84	G8
Bowmanstead	Cumb	62	F3
Bowmore	Ag & B	82	D10
Bowness-on-Solway	Cumb	71	K3
Bowness-on-Windermere Cumb		62	H3
Bow of Fife	Fife	93	K12
Bowriefauld	Angus	93	N6
Bowsden	Nthumb	81	L6
Bow Street	Cerdgn	37	K4
Bowthorpe	Norfk	45	K8
Box	Gloucs	29	M8
Box	Wilts	18	C7
Boxford	Suffk	34	F8
Boxford	W Berk	19	M6
Boxgrove	W Susx	10	E8
Boxley	Kent	22	F10
Boxmoor	Herts	20	G3
Boxted	Essex	34	G9
Boxted	Suffk	34	D6
Boxted Cross	Essex	34	G9
Boxworth	Cambs	33	K4
Boyden Gate	Kent	23	N9
Boylestone	Derbys	40	F1
Boyndie	Abers	102	E3
Boyndlie	Abers	103	J3
Boynton	E R Yk	61	K1
Boysack	Angus	93	Q6
Boythorpe	Derbys	51	J6
Boyton	Cnwll	4	H2
Boyton	Suffk	35	N7
Boyton	Wilts	18	D11
Boyton Cross	Essex	22	D2
Boyton End	Suffk	34	C7
Bozeat	Nhants	32	C5
Brabourne	Kent	13	L2
Brabourne Lees	Kent	13	L3
Brabstermire	Highld	110	G2
Bracadale	Highld	96	D2

Name	Page	Grid
Braceborough Lincs	42	F7
Bracebridge Heath Lincs	52	E9
Bracebridge Low Fields Lincs	52	D9
Braceby Lincs	42	E3
Bracewell Lancs	63	Q11
Brackenfield Derbys	51	J8
Brackenhirst N Lans	85	M8
Brackla Brdgnd	27	K11
Bracklesham W Susx	10	D10
Brackletter Highld	98	B11
Brackley Nhants	31	N6
Bracknell Br For	20	E9
Braco P & K	85	N2
Bracobrae Moray	101	P5
Bracon Ash Norfk	45	K9
Bracora Highld	97	K10
Bracorina Highld	97	K10
Bradbourne Derbys	50	G9
Bradbury Dur	65	N2
Bradden Nhants	31	N5
Bradeley C Stke	49	Q5
Bradenham Bucks	20	D4
Bradenstoke Wilts	18	E5
Bradfield Devon	6	E2
Bradfield Essex	35	J9
Bradfield Norfk	45	L4
Bradfield Sheff	50	H3
Bradfield W Berk	19	P6
Bradfield Combust Suffk	34	E5
Bradfield Green Ches E	49	M4
Bradfield Heath Essex	35	J10
Bradfield St Clare Suffk	34	E5
Bradfield St George Suffk	34	E5
Bradford C Brad	58	F7
Bradford Devon	14	G10
Bradford Abbas Dorset	17	N12
Bradford Leigh Wilts	18	C8
Bradford-on-Avon Wilts	18	C8
Bradford-on-Tone Somset	16	G10
Bradford Peverell Dorset	7	P4
Bradiford Devon	15	K5
Brading IoW	9	Q9
Bradley Derbys	50	G10
Bradley Hants	19	Q11
Bradley NE Lin	53	J3
Bradley Staffs	49	Q11
Bradley Wolves	40	C8
Bradley Worcs	30	C2
Bradley Green Worcs	30	C2
Bradley in the Moors Staffs	50	D11
Bradley Stoke S Glos	28	H11
Bradmore Notts	41	N2
Bradninch Devon	6	D3
Bradnop Staffs	50	D9
Bradpole Dorset	7	L4
Bradshaw Calder	58	E8
Bradstone Devon	4	H4
Bradwall Green Ches E	49	N3
Bradwell Derbys	50	F5
Bradwell Essex	34	D11
Bradwell M Keyn	32	B8
Bradwell Norfk	45	Q8
Bradwell-on-Sea Essex	23	J3
Bradwell Waterside Essex	23	J2
Bradworthy Devon	14	F8
Brae Highld	107	L9
Brae Shet	111	k3
Braeface Falk	85	N7
Braehead Angus	95	L10
Braehead D & G	69	K8
Braehead S Lans	77	Q2
Braeintra Highld	97	M3
Braemar Abers	94	C4
Braemore Highld	106	C6
Braemore Highld	110	C9
Brae Roy Lodge Highld	98	D10
Braeside Inver	84	D7
Braes of Coul Angus	93	K4
Braes of Enzie Moray	101	M4
Braes of Ullapool Highld	106	C4
Braeswick Ork	111	i1
Braevallich Ag & B	83	P2
Braewick Shet	111	j3
Brafferton Darltn	65	N4
Brafferton N York	66	B12
Brafield-on-the-Green Nhants	32	B5
Bragar W Isls	111	d1
Bragbury End Herts	33	J11
Braidwood S Lans	77	P2
Brailsford Derbys	50	G11
Braintree Essex	34	C11
Braiseworth Suffk	35	J3
Braishfield Hants	9	L3
Braiswick Essex	34	G10
Braithwaite Cumb	71	K10
Braithwaite Donc	51	M2
Braithwell Donc	51	L2
Bramber W Susx	11	J7
Bramcote Warwks	41	K9
Bramdean Hants	9	Q2
Bramerton Norfk	45	L8
Bramfield Herts	21	L1
Bramfield Suffk	35	N3
Bramford Suffk	35	J7
Bramhall Stockp	50	B4
Bramham Leeds	59	K5
Bramhope Leeds	58	G5
Bramley Hants	19	Q8
Bramley Leeds	58	G7
Bramley Rothm	51	L3
Bramley Surrey	10	G2
Bramling Kent	23	N11
Brampford Speke Devon	6	C3
Brampton Cambs	32	H3
Brampton Cumb	64	C3
Brampton Cumb	71	Q4
Brampton Lincs	52	B7
Brampton Norfk	45	K5
Brampton Rothm	51	K1
Brampton Suffk	35	P1
Brampton Abbotts Herefs	28	H3
Brampton Ash Nhants	42	B11
Brampton Bryan Herefs	38	G7
Brampton-en-le-Morthen Rothm	51	L4
Bramshall Staffs	40	D2
Bramshaw Hants	9	J4
Bramshott Hants	10	D4
Bramwell Somset	17	L9
Branault Highld	89	L3
Brancaster Norfk	44	C2
Brancaster Staithe Norfk	44	D2
Brancepeth Dur	73	L12
Branchill Moray	100	G5

Name	Page	Grid
Branderburgh Moray	101	K2
Brandesburton E R Yk	61	J5
Brandeston Suffk	35	L5
Brandiston Norfk	45	J6
Brandon Dur	73	M11
Brandon Lincs	42	C1
Brandon Suffk	44	D11
Brandon Warwks	41	K11
Brandon Parva Norfk	44	H8
Brandsby N York	66	E11
Brandy Wharf Lincs	52	E4
Bran End Essex	33	Q10
Branksome BCP	8	F8
Branksome Park BCP	8	F8
Bransbury Hants	19	M11
Bransby Lincs	52	C7
Branscombe Devon	6	G5
Bransford Worcs	39	P10
Bransgore Hants	8	H7
Bransholme C KuH	61	J7
Bransley Shrops	39	M7
Branston Leics	42	B4
Branston Lincs	52	E9
Branston Staffs	40	G4
Branston Booths Lincs	52	F9
Branstone IoW	9	P10
Brant Broughton Lincs	52	D11
Brantham Suffk	35	J9
Branthwaite Cumb	70	H9
Branthwaite Cumb	71	L7
Brantingham E R Yk	60	G8
Branton Donc	51	N1
Branton Nthumb	81	L10
Branton Green N York	59	K2
Branxton Nthumb	81	J6
Brassington Derbys	50	G9
Brasted Kent	21	P11
Brasted Chart Kent	21	P11
Brathens Abers	95	L3
Bratoft Lincs	53	M9
Brattleby Lincs	52	D7
Bratton Wilts	18	D9
Bratton Wrekin	49	L11
Bratton Clovelly Devon	5	K2
Bratton Fleming Devon	15	L5
Bratton Seymour Somset	17	P9
Braughing Herts	33	L10
Braunston Nhants	31	M2
Braunston Rutlnd	42	B8
Braunton Devon	14	H5
Brawby N York	66	G11
Brawl Highld	109	P3
Bray W & M	20	E7
Braybrooke Nhants	41	Q9
Brayford Devon	15	M5
Bray Shop Cnwll	4	H5
Brayton N York	59	N7
Braywick W & M	20	E7
Breachwood Green Herts	32	G11
Breaclete W Isls	111	c2
Breaclete W Isls	111	c2
Breadsall Derbys	51	J11
Breadstone Gloucs	29	J8
Breage Cnwll	2	F9
Breakachy Highld	106	H12
Breakish Highld	97	J5
Brealangwell Lodge Highld	106	H4
Bream Gloucs	28	H7
Breamore Hants	8	H4
Brean Somset	16	H5
Breanais W Isls	111	b2
Brearton N York	58	H3
Breascleit W Isls	111	c2
Breasclete W Isls	111	c2
Breaston Derbys	41	L2
Brechfa Carmth	26	C3
Brechin Angus	95	K9
Breckles Norfk	44	F10
Brecon Powys	27	L3
Brecon Beacons National Park	27	L4
Bredbury Stockp	50	B3
Brede E Susx	12	G6
Bredenbury Herefs	39	L10
Bredfield Suffk	35	L6
Bredgar Kent	22	G10
Bredhurst Kent	22	F10
Bredon Worcs	29	N2
Bredon's Hardwick Worcs	29	M2
Bredon's Norton Worcs	29	N2
Bredwardine Herefs	38	G12
Breich W Loth	85	Q10
Breightmet Bolton	57	N7
Breighton E R Yk	60	C7
Breinton Herefs	28	F2
Bremhill Wilts	18	E6
Brenchley Kent	12	D2
Brendon Devon	15	N3
Brenfield Ag & B	83	M6
Brenish W Isls	111	b2
Brent Cross Gt Lon	21	K6
Brent Eleigh Suffk	34	F7
Brentford Gt Lon	21	J7
Brentingby Leics	42	B6
Brent Knoll Somset	17	J6
Brent Mill Devon	5	N8
Brent Pelham Herts	33	M10
Brentwood Essex	22	C5
Brenzett Kent	13	J5
Brenzett Green Kent	13	J4
Brereton Staffs	40	D4
Brereton Green Ches E	49	P3
Bressay Shet	111	k4
Bressingham Norfk	34	H1
Bretby Derbys	40	H3
Bretford Warwks	41	K11
Bretforton Worcs	30	E5
Bretherton Lancs	57	J5
Brettabister Shet	111	k4
Brettenham Norfk	44	F12
Brettenham Suffk	34	F6
Bretton C Pete	42	G9
Bretton Flints	48	G3
Brewood Staffs	40	B6
Briantspuddle Dorset	8	B8
Brickendon Herts	21	L2
Bricket Wood Herts	21	H3
Brick Houses Sheff	50	H5
Brickhampton Worcs	29	N1
Bride IoM	56	e2
Bridekirk Cumb	71	J8
Bridestowe Devon	5	L3
Brideswell Abers	102	D7

Name	Page	Grid
Bridford Devon	5	Q3
Bridge Kent	23	M11
Bridgefoot Angus	93	L8
Bridgehampton Somset	17	N10
Bridge Hewick N York	65	N12
Bridgehill Dur	73	K9
Bridgemary Hants	9	P6
Bridgend Abers	101	P7
Bridgend Ag & B	75	J4
Bridgend Ag & B	82	E9
Bridgend Angus	95	J8
Bridgend Brdgnd	27	J11
Bridgend Cerdgn	36	C10
Bridgend D & G	78	H7
Bridgend Devon	5	J9
Bridgend Fife	93	L12
Bridgend Moray	101	M8
Bridgend P & K	92	G10
Bridgend W Loth	86	C7
Bridgend of Lintrathen Angus	93	J4
Bridge of Alford Abers	102	D10
Bridge of Allan Stirlg	85	N4
Bridge of Avon Moray	100	H10
Bridge of Avon Moray	101	J7
Bridge of Balgie P & K	91	N7
Bridge of Brewlands Angus	94	C9
Bridge of Brown Highld	100	H10
Bridge of Cally P & K	92	H5
Bridge of Canny Abers	95	K3
Bridge of Craigisla Angus	93	J5
Bridge of Dee D & G	70	C4
Bridge of Don C Aber	103	K12
Bridge of Dun Angus	93	R4
Bridge of Dye Abers	94	K5
Bridge of Earn P & K	92	G11
Bridge of Ericht P & K	91	M5
Bridge of Feugh Abers	95	L3
Bridge of Gairn Abers	94	F3
Bridge of Gaur P & K	91	M5
Bridge of Marnoch Abers	102	D5
Bridge of Muchalls Abers	95	P4
Bridge of Orchy Ag & B	91	J8
Bridge of Tilt P & K	92	D3
Bridge of Tynet Moray	101	M3
Bridge of Walls Shet	111	j4
Bridge of Weir Rens	84	G9
Bridgerule Devon	14	E10
Bridge Sollers Herefs	28	E1
Bridge Street Suffk	34	E6
Bridgetown Somset	16	C9
Bridge Trafford Ches W	49	J2
Bridgnorth Shrops	39	N4
Bridgwater Somset	16	H8
Bridgwater Services Somset	17	J8
Bridlington E R Yk	61	K2
Bridport Dorset	7	L4
Bridstow Herefs	28	G4
Brierfield Lancs	57	Q2
Brierley Barns	59	K11
Brierley Gloucs	28	H6
Brierley Hill Dudley	40	B9
Brigg N Linc	52	E3
Briggate Norfk	45	M5
Briggswath N York	67	J6
Brigham Cumb	70	H9
Brigham E R Yk	61	J4
Brighouse Calder	58	F9
Brighstone IoW	9	M10
Brighthampton Oxon	31	K12
Brightley Devon	5	L1
Brightling E Susx	12	D6
Brightlingsea Essex	34	H12
Brighton Br & H	11	L8
Brighton City Airport W Susx	11	K8
Brighton le Sands Sefton	56	F8
Brightons Falk	85	Q7
Brightwalton W Berk	19	M5
Brightwell Suffk	35	L7
Brightwell Baldwin Oxon	19	Q2
Brightwell-cum-Sotwell Oxon	19	P3
Brightwell Upperton Oxon	19	Q2
Brignall Dur	65	J5
Brig o'Turk Stirlg	85	J2
Brigsley NE Lin	53	J3
Brigsteer Cumb	63	J4
Brigstock Nhants	42	D11
Brill Bucks	31	P10
Brill Cnwll	2	G9
Brilley Herefs	38	F11
Brimfield Herefs	39	K8
Brimfield Cross Herefs	39	K8
Brimington Derbys	51	K6
Brimley Devon	5	Q5
Brimpsfield Gloucs	29	N6
Brimpton W Berk	19	P7
Brimscombe Gloucs	29	M8
Brimstage Wirral	56	F11
Brincliffe Sheff	51	J4
Brind E R Yk	60	C7
Brindister Shet	111	j4
Brindle Lancs	57	L4
Brineton Staffs	49	P11
Bringhurst Leics	42	B10
Bringsty Common Herefs	39	M10
Brington Cambs	32	F2
Brinian Ork	111	h2
Briningham Norfk	44	G4
Brinkhill Lincs	53	L8
Brinkley Cambs	33	Q6
Brinklow Warwks	41	K10
Brinkworth Wilts	18	E4
Brinscall Lancs	57	L5
Brinsley Notts	51	L10
Brinsworth Rothm	51	K3
Brinton Norfk	44	G3
Brisley Norfk	44	F6
Brislington Bristl	17	N3
Brissenden Green Kent	12	H3
Bristol Bristl	17	N2
Bristol Airport N Som	17	M3
Briston Norfk	44	H4
Britannia Lancs	58	B9
Britford Wilts	8	H2
Brithdir Caerph	27	N8
Brithdir Gwynd	47	M7
British Legion Village Kent	22	E11
Briton Ferry Neath	26	G9
Britwell Salome Oxon	19	R3
Brixham Torbay	6	C10
Brixton Devon	5	L9
Brixton Gt Lon	21	L8
Brixton Deverill Wilts	18	C11

Name	Page	Grid
Brixworth Nhants	41	Q12
Brize Norton Oxon	30	H11
Brize Norton Airport Oxon	30	H11
Broad Alley Worcs	30	B1
Broad Blunsdon Swindn	18	G3
Broadbottom Tamesd	50	C3
Broadbridge W Susx	10	D8
Broadbridge Heath W Susx	11	J4
Broad Campden Gloucs	30	F6
Broad Carr Calder	58	E9
Broad Chalke Wilts	8	F3
Broadclyst Devon	6	D4
Broadfield Inver	84	F8
Broadford Highld	96	H5
Broadford Bridge W Susx	10	H5
Broadgairhill Border	79	K6
Broad Green Worcs	39	P10
Broadhaugh Border	81	J4
Broad Haven Pembks	24	F6
Broadheath Traffd	57	N10
Broadhembury Devon	6	E2
Broadhempston Devon	5	Q7
Broad Hinton Wilts	18	G5
Broadland Row E Susx	12	G6
Broadley Moray	101	M3
Broad Marston Worcs	30	F5
Broadmayne Dorset	7	Q5
Broadmoor Pembks	25	J7
Broadoak Dorset	7	L4
Broad Oak E Susx	12	C5
Broad Oak E Susx	12	G6
Broad Oak Herefs	28	F5
Broad Oak Kent	23	M10
Broad Oak St Hel	57	K9
Broadsands Torbay	6	B10
Broad's Green Essex	22	E2
Broadstairs Kent	23	Q9
Broadstone BCP	8	E8
Broadstone Shrops	39	K4
Broad Street E Susx	12	G6
Broad Street Kent	22	G11
Broad Town Wilts	18	G5
Broadwas Worcs	39	N10
Broadwater Herts	33	J11
Broadwater W Susx	11	J8
Broadwaters Worcs	39	Q6
Broadway Pembks	24	F6
Broadway Somset	17	J11
Broadway Worcs	30	E6
Broadwell Gloucs	28	G6
Broadwell Gloucs	30	G8
Broadwell Oxon	30	G12
Broadwell Warwks	31	L2
Broadwindsor Dorset	7	L3
Broadwood Kelly Devon	15	K10
Broadwoodwidger Devon	5	J3
Brochel Highld	104	H12
Brochroy Ag & B	90	D9
Brockamin Worcs	39	P10
Brockbridge Hants	9	Q4
Brockdish Norfk	35	K2
Brockenhurst Hants	9	K7
Brocketsbrae S Lans	78	D2
Brockford Street Suffk	35	J4
Brockhall Nhants	31	N2
Brockhall Village Lancs	57	N2
Brockham Surrey	21	K12
Brockhampton Gloucs	30	D9
Brockhampton Hants	10	B8
Brockhampton Herefs	28	H3
Brockholes Kirk	58	F11
Brocklesby Lincs	61	K11
Brockley N Som	17	L3
Brockley Suffk	34	D3
Brockley Green Suffk	34	C7
Brockley Green Suffk	34	D6
Brockmoor Dudley	40	B9
Brockton Shrops	38	G2
Brockton Shrops	39	K4
Brockton Shrops	39	L4
Brockweir Gloucs	28	G8
Brockworth Gloucs	29	M5
Brocton Staffs	40	C4
Brodick N Ayrs	75	Q5
Brodie Moray	100	F4
Brodsworth Donc	59	L11
Brogaig Highld	104	F8
Brokenborough Wilts	18	D3
Broken Cross Ches E	50	B6
Brokerswood Wilts	18	C9
Bromborough Wirral	56	G11
Brome Suffk	35	J2
Brome Street Suffk	35	J2
Bromeswell Suffk	35	M6
Bromfield Cumb	71	J6
Bromfield Shrops	39	J6
Bromham Bed	32	E6
Bromham Wilts	18	E7
Bromley Dudley	40	B9
Bromley Gt Lon	21	N9
Bromley Shrops	39	N3
Bromley Cross Bolton	57	N6
Brompton Medway	22	F9
Brompton N York	65	P8
Brompton-by-Sawdon N York	67	K10
Brompton-on-Swale N York	65	L7
Brompton Ralph Somset	16	E9
Brompton Regis Somset	16	C9
Bromsberrow Gloucs	29	J2
Bromsberrow Heath Gloucs	29	K3
Bromsgrove Worcs	40	C12
Bromyard Herefs	39	M10
Bronant Cerdgn	37	K7
Brongest Cerdgn	36	E10
Bronington Wrexhm	49	J7
Bronllys Powys	27	N3
Bronwydd Carmth	25	P4
Brongarth Shrops	48	F7
Brook IoW	9	J5
Brook Kent	13	K2
Brook Surrey	10	E3
Brooke Norfk	45	L9
Brooke Rutlnd	42	C8
Brookenby Lincs	52	H4
Brookhampton Somset	17	P9
Brook Hill Hants	9	J4
Brookhouse Lancs	63	K8
Brookhouse Rothm	51	L4
Brookhouse Green Ches E	49	P4
Brookhouses Derbys	50	D3
Brookland Kent	13	J5

Name	Page	Grid
Brooklands Traffd	57	P10
Brookmans Park Herts	21	K3
Brook Street Essex	22	C5
Brook Street Kent	12	H4
Brookthorpe Gloucs	29	L6
Brookwood Surrey	20	F11
Broom C Beds	32	G8
Broom Rothm	51	K3
Broom Warwks	30	E4
Broome Norfk	45	M10
Broome Shrops	38	H6
Broome Worcs	40	B10
Broomedge Warttn	57	N10
Broomfield Essex	22	E2
Broomfield Kent	22	G11
Broomfield Kent	23	M9
Broomfield Somset	16	G9
Broomfleet E R Yk	60	F8
Broomhaugh Nthumb	72	H8
Broom Hill Barns	59	K12
Broom Hill Notts	51	M10
Broomhill Nthumb	73	M1
Broompark Dur	73	M11
Brora Highld	107	P2
Broseley Shrops	39	M2
Brotherlee Dur	72	G12
Brotherton N York	59	L8
Brotton R & Cl	66	F4
Broubster Highld	110	B4
Brough Cumb	64	E5
Brough E R Yk	60	F8
Brough Highld	110	E2
Brough Notts	52	B10
Brough Shet	111	m3
Broughall Shrops	49	K7
Brough Lodge Shet	111	m2
Brough Sowerby Cumb	64	E5
Broughton Border	78	H2
Broughton Cambs	33	J2
Broughton Flints	48	G3
Broughton Hants	9	K2
Broughton Lancs	57	K2
Broughton M Keyn	32	C8
Broughton N Linc	52	D2
Broughton N York	58	C4
Broughton N York	66	H11
Broughton Nhants	32	B2
Broughton Oxon	31	K6
Broughton Salfd	57	P8
Broughton V Glam	16	C3
Broughton Astley Leics	41	M8
Broughton Gifford Wilts	18	C7
Broughton Green Worcs	30	C2
Broughton Hackett Worcs	30	B3
Broughton-in-Furness Cumb	62	E5
Broughton Mains D & G	69	L9
Broughton Mills Cumb	62	E4
Broughton Moor Cumb	70	H8
Broughton Poggs Oxon	30	G12
Broughty Ferry C Dund	93	N9
Brown Candover Hants	19	P11
Brown Edge Staffs	50	B9
Brownhill Abers	102	H7
Brownhills Fife	93	P11
Brownhills Wsall	40	D6
Browninghill Green Hants	19	P8
Brown Lees Staffs	49	Q4
Brownsea Island Dorset	8	F9
Brown's Green Birm	40	D8
Browns Hill Gloucs	29	M8
Brownston Devon	5	N9
Broxa N York	67	K8
Broxbourne Herts	21	M3
Broxburn E Loth	87	N6
Broxburn W Loth	86	C7
Broxted Essex	33	P10
Bruan Highld	110	G7
Bruar P & K	92	C3
Bruchag Ag & B	84	B10
Bruichladdich Ag & B	82	C10
Bruisyard Suffk	35	M4
Bruisyard Street Suffk	35	M4
Brumby N Linc	52	C2
Brund Staffs	50	E8
Brundall Norfk	45	M8
Brundish Suffk	35	L3
Brundish Street Suffk	35	L3
Brunery Highld	89	P2
Brunswick Village N u Ty	73	M6
Bruntcliffe C Brad	58	D5
Bruntingthorpe Leics	41	N9
Brunton Fife	93	K10
Brunton Wilts	19	J9
Brushford Devon	15	L9
Brushford Somset	16	C10
Bruton Somset	17	P8
Bryan's Green Worcs	30	B1
Bryanston Dorset	8	C6
Brydekirk D & G	71	K2
Bryher IoS	2	b2
Brympton Somset	17	M11
Bryn Carmth	26	D8
Bryn Neath	26	H9
Bryn Wigan	57	K8
Brynamman Carmth	26	F6
Brynberian Pembks	25	J2
Bryncir Gwynd	46	H3
Bryn-côch Neath	26	G8
Bryncroes Gwynd	46	D5
Bryncrug Gwynd	47	K9
Bryneglwys Denbgs	48	D6
Bryneglwys & Abergynolwyn Slate Landscape Gwynd	47	L9
Brynford Flints	48	D1
Bryn Gates Wigan	57	L8
Bryngwran IoA	54	D6
Bryngwyn Mons	28	D7
Bryngwyn Powys	38	E11
Bryn-Henllan Pembks	24	H2
Brynhoffnant Cerdgn	36	F9
Brynmawr Blae G	27	P6
Bryn-mawr Gwynd	46	D5
Brynmenyn Brdgnd	27	J10
Brynmill Swans	26	E9
Brynna Rhondd	27	L11
Brynrefail Gwynd	54	H8
Brynrefail IoA	54	G5
Bryn Saith Marchog Denbgs	48	C5
Brynsadler Rhondd	27	L11
Brynsiencyn IoA	54	F7
Brynteg IoA	54	G5
Bryn-y-Maen Conwy	55	M6
Bualintur Highld	96	E5
Bubbenhall Warwks	41	J11
Bubwith E R Yk	60	C7

Buccleuch Border 79 M6
Buchanan Smithy Stirlg 84 H5
Buchanhaven Abers 103 M6
Buchanty P & K 92 D9
Buchany Stirlg 85 M3
Buchlyvie Stirlg 85 J4
Buckabank Cumb 71 M6
Buckden Cambs 32 H4
Buckden N York 64 G11
Buckenham Norfk 45 M8
Buckerell Devon 6 F3
Buckfast Devon 5 P6
Buckfastleigh Devon 5 P7
Buckhaven Fife 86 G3
Buckholt Mons 28 F5
Buckhorn Weston Dorset 17 R10
Buckhurst Hill Essex 21 N5
Buckie Moray 101 M3
Buckingham Bucks 31 P7
Buckland Bucks 20 E2
Buckland Devon 5 N10
Buckland Gloucs 30 E7
Buckland Herts 33 K9
Buckland Kent 13 P2
Buckland Oxon 19 K2
Buckland Surrey 21 K12
Buckland Brewer Devon 14 G7
Buckland Common Bucks 20 E3
Buckland Dinham Somset 17 R6
Buckland Filleigh Devon 14 H9
Buckland in the Moor Devon 5 P5
Buckland Monachorum Devon 5 K8
Buckland Newton Dorset 7 P2
Buckland Ripers Dorset 7 P6
Buckland St Mary Somset 16 H12
Buckland-Tout-Saints Devon 5 P10
Bucklebury W Berk 19 P6
Bucklers Hard Hants 9 L7
Bucklesham Suffk 35 L8
Buckley Flints 48 F3
Bucklow Hill Ches E 57 N11
Buckminster Leics 42 C5
Bucknall C Stke 50 B10
Bucknall Lincs 52 G9
Bucknell Oxon 31 M8
Bucknell Shrops 38 G7
Buckpool Moray 101 M3
Bucksburn C Aber 103 J12
Buck's Cross Devon 14 F7
Bucks Green W Susx 10 H4
Buckshaw Village Lancs 57 K5
Bucks Horn Oak Hants 10 D2
Buck's Mills Devon 14 F7
Buckton E R Yk 67 P11
Buckton Nthumb 81 M6
Buckworth Cambs 32 G2
Budby Notts 51 N6
Bude Cnwll 14 D10
Budge's Shop Cnwll 4 H8
Budleigh Salterton Devon 6 E6
Budock Water Cnwll 2 H9
Buerton Ches E 49 M6
Bugbrooke Nhants 31 P3
Bugle Cnwll 3 M4
Bugley Dorset 8 B3
Bugthorpe E R Yk 60 D3
Buildwas Shrops 39 L2
Builth Road Powys 38 B10
Builth Wells Powys 38 B11
Bulbridge Wilts 8 G2
Bulford Wilts 18 H11
Bulkeley Ches E 49 K5
Bulkington Warwks 41 K9
Bulkington Wilts 18 D8
Bulkworthy Devon 14 G8
Bullbrook Br For 20 E9
Bullington Hants 19 M11
Bullington Lincs 52 F7
Bulmer Essex 34 D8
Bulmer N York 60 C1
Bulmer Tye Essex 34 D8
Bulphan Thurr 22 D6
Bulwark Abers 103 J6
Bulwell C Nott 51 M11
Bulwick Nhants 42 D10
Bumble's Green Essex 21 N3
Bunacaimb Highld 97 J11
Bunarkaig Highld 98 B10
Bunbury Ches E 49 K4
Bunchrew Highld 107 K12
Bundalloch Highld 97 M4
Bunessan Ag & B 89 J11
Bungay Suffk 45 M11
Bunnahabhain Ag & B 82 F8
Bunny Notts 41 N2
Buntait Highld 98 E3
Buntingford Herts 33 K10
Bunwell Norfk 45 J10
Burbage Leics 41 K8
Burbage Wilts 19 J8
Burchett's Green W & M 20 D7
Burcombe Wilts 8 F2
Burcott Bucks 32 C11
Bures Essex 34 E9
Burford Oxon 30 G10
Burford Shrops 39 L8
Burg Ag & B 89 J7
Burgess Hill W Susx 11 L6
Burgh Suffk 35 K6
Burgh by Sands Cumb 71 M4
Burgh Castle Norfk 45 P8
Burghclere Hants 19 M8
Burghead Moray 100 H2
Burghfield W Berk 19 Q7
Burghfield Common W Berk 19 Q7
Burgh Heath Surrey 21 K10
Burghill Herefs 39 J12
Burgh Island Devon 5 M10
Burgh le Marsh Lincs 53 N9
Burgh next Aylsham Norfk 45 K3
Burgh on Bain Lincs 52 H6
Burgh St Margaret Norfk 45 P7
Burgh St Peter Norfk 45 P10
Burghwallis Donc 59 M10
Burham Kent 22 E10
Buriton Hants 10 C6
Burland Ches E 49 L5
Burlawn Cnwll 3 M2
Burleigh Gloucs 29 M8
Burlescombe Devon 16 E11
Burleston Dorset 8 B8
Burley Hants 8 H6
Burley Rutlnd 42 C7

Burleydam Ches E 49 L7
Burley Gate Herefs 39 L11
Burley in Wharfedale C Brad 58 F5
Burley Street Hants 8 H6
Burley Wood Head C Brad 58 F5
Burlton Shrops 49 J9
Burmarsh Kent 13 L4
Burmington Warwks 30 H6
Burn N York 59 N8
Burnage Manch 57 Q9
Burnaston Derbys 40 H2
Burnbrae N Lans 85 P10
Burnby E R Yk 60 E5
Burneside Cumb 63 J3
Burneston N York 65 N9
Burnett BaNES 17 P3
Burnfoot Border 79 N6
Burnfoot Border 80 C10
Burnfoot D & G 78 F9
Burnfoot D & G 79 M10
Burnfoot D & G 79 N9
Burnfoot P & K 86 B2
Burnham Bucks 20 E7
Burnham Deepdale Norfk 44 D2
Burnham Market Norfk 44 D2
Burnham Norton Norfk 44 D2
Burnham-on-Crouch Essex 23 J4
Burnham-on-Sea Somset 17 J6
Burnham Overy Norfk 44 D2
Burnham Overy Staithe Norfk 44 D2
Burnham Thorpe Norfk 44 E2
Burnhead D & G 78 E9
Burnhervie Abers 102 F10
Burnhill Green Staffs 39 P3
Burnhope Dur 73 L10
Burnhouse N Ayrs 76 G2
Burniston N York 67 L8
Burnley Lancs 57 Q3
Burnmouth Border 81 K3
Burn of Cambus Stirlg 85 M3
Burnopfield Dur 73 L9
Burnsall N York 58 D2
Burnside Angus 93 M4
Burnside Angus 93 N5
Burnside Fife 86 D1
Burnside Moray 101 J2
Burnside W Loth 86 C7
Burnside of Duntrune Angus 93 M8
Burntisland Fife 86 F5
Burnton E Ayrs 76 H9
Burntwood Staffs 40 D5
Burntwood Green Staffs 40 E6
Burnt Yates N York 58 G2
Burnworthy Somset 16 G11
Burpham Surrey 20 G11
Burpham W Susx 10 G8
Burradon Nthumb 81 K11
Burrafirth Shet 111 m2
Burravoe Shet 111 k3
Burray Village Ork 111 h3
Burrells Cumb 64 C4
Burrelton P & K 92 H8
Burridge Devon 7 J2
Burridge Hants 9 N5
Burrill N York 65 M9
Burringham N Linc 60 B2
Burrington Devon 15 L8
Burrington Herefs 38 H7
Burrington N Som 17 L4
Burrough Green Cambs 33 Q6
Burrough on the Hill Leics 41 Q5
Burrow Lancs 63 L7
Burrow Somset 16 C7
Burrow Bridge Somset 17 J9
Burrowhill Surrey 20 F10
Burry Green Swans 26 B9
Burry Port Carmth 25 Q8
Burscough Lancs 56 H6
Burscough Bridge Lancs 57 J6
Bursea E R Yk 60 D7
Burshill E R Yk 60 H5
Bursledon Hants 9 N5
Burstall Suffk 34 H7
Burstock Dorset 7 K3
Burston Norfk 45 J12
Burstow Surrey 11 L2
Burstwick E R Yk 61 L8
Burtersett N York 64 F9
Burtholme Cumb 71 Q3
Burtle Somset 17 K7
Burtoft Lincs 43 J3
Burton BCP 8 H8
Burton Ches W 48 G5
Burton Ches W 49 K3
Burton Pembks 24 H7
Burton Somset 16 G7
Burton Wilts 18 B5
Burton Agnes E R Yk 61 J2
Burton Bradstock Dorset 7 L5
Burton-by-Lincoln Lincs 52 D8
Burton Coggles Lincs 42 E5
Burton End Essex 33 N11
Burton Fleming E R Yk 67 M12
Burton Hastings Warwks 41 K9
Burton Hill Wilts 18 D4
Burton-in-Kendal Cumb 63 K7
Burton-in-Kendal Services Cumb 63 K7
Burton in Lonsdale N York 63 M7
Burton Joyce Notts 51 N11
Burton Latimer Nhants 32 C2
Burton Lazars Leics 41 Q4
Burton Leonard N York 59 J2
Burton on the Wolds Leics 41 N4
Burton Overy Leics 41 P7
Burton Pedwardine Lincs 42 G2
Burton Pidsea E R Yk 61 L7
Burton Salmon N York 59 L8
Burton's Green Essex 34 D10
Burton upon Stather N Linc 60 E10
Burton upon Trent Staffs 40 H3
Burton Waters Lincs 52 D8
Burtonwood Warrtn 57 K9
Burtonwood Services Warrtn 57 K9
Burwardsley Ches W 49 K4
Burwarton Shrops 39 L5
Burwash E Susx 12 D5
Burwash Common E Susx 12 D5
Burwash Weald E Susx 12 D5
Burwell Cambs 33 P4
Burwell Lincs 53 K7
Burwen IoA 54 F3
Burwick Ork 111 h3
Bury Bury 57 P6

Bury Cambs 43 J12
Bury Somset 16 C10
Bury W Susx 10 G7
Bury Green Herts 33 M11
Bury St Edmunds Suffk 34 E4
Burythorpe N York 60 D2
Busby E Rens 85 K10
Buscot Oxon 19 J2
Bush Abers 95 M8
Bush Bank Herefs 39 J10
Bushbury Wolves 40 B7
Bushey Herts 21 J4
Bushey Heath Herts 21 J5
Bush Hill Park Gt Lon 21 M4
Bushley Worcs 29 M2
Bushmoor Shrops 38 H5
Bushton Wilts 18 F5
Bussage Gloucs 29 M7
Butcombe N Som 17 M4
Bute Ag & B 83 Q8
Butleigh Somset 17 M9
Butleigh Wootton Somset 17 M8
Butlers Marston Warwks 30 H4
Butley Suffk 35 N6
Buttercrambe N York 60 C3
Butterdean Border 87 P8
Butterknowle Dur 65 K3
Butterleigh Devon 6 D2
Buttermere Cumb 71 J11
Buttershaw C Brad 58 F8
Butterstone P & K 92 F6
Butterton Staffs 50 E7
Butterton Staffs 50 E9
Butterwick Lincs 43 L2
Butterwick N York 66 G11
Butterwick N York 67 L12
Buttington Powys 38 F1
Buttonoak Shrops 39 N6
Buttsash Hants 9 M6
Buxhall Suffk 34 G5
Buxted E Susx 11 P5
Buxton Derbys 50 D6
Buxton Norfk 45 K5
Buxton Heath Norfk 45 K6
Bwlch Powys 27 N4
Bwlchgwyn Wrexhm 48 F5
Bwlchllan Cerdgn 37 J8
Bwlchtocyn Gwynd 46 E6
Bwlch-y-cibau Powys 48 D11
Bwlch-y-ffridd Powys 38 C3
Bwlch-y-groes Pembks 25 M2
Bwlch-y-sarnau Powys 38 B7
Byers Green Dur 65 L2
Byfield Nhants 31 M4
Byfleet Surrey 20 G10
Byford Herefs 38 H12
Byker N u Ty 73 M7
Bylchau Conwy 55 P8
Byley Ches W 49 N2
Byram N York 59 L8
Byrness Nthumb 72 D1
Bystock Devon 6 D6
Bythorn Cambs 32 F2
Byton Herefs 38 G8
Bywell Nthumb 73 J8
Byworth W Susx 10 F6

C

Cabourne Lincs 52 G3
Cabrach Ag & B 82 G9
Cabrach Moray 101 M9
Cabus Lancs 63 J11
Cadbury Devon 6 C2
Cadbury World Birm 40 D10
Cadder E Duns 85 K8
Caddington C Beds 32 F11
Caddonfoot Border 79 P2
Cadeby Donc 51 L1
Cadeby Leics 41 K7
Cadeleigh Devon 6 C2
Cade Street E Susx 12 C6
Cadgwith Cnwll 2 G11
Cadham Fife 86 F2
Cadishead Salfd 57 N9
Cadle Swans 26 E9
Cadley Lancs 57 K3
Cadley Wilts 18 H7
Cadley Wilts 19 J9
Cadmore End Bucks 20 C5
Cadnam Hants 9 K5
Cadney N Linc 52 E3
Cadoxton V Glam 16 F3
Cadoxton Juxta-Neath Neath 26 G8
Caeathro Gwynd 54 G8
Caenby Lincs 52 E5
Caerau Brdgnd 27 J9
Caerau Cardif 16 F2
Caer Farchell Pembks 24 E4
Caergeiliog IoA 54 D6
Caergwrle Flints 48 F4
Caerlanrig Border 79 N7
Caerleon Newpt 28 D10
Caernarfon Gwynd 54 F8
Caernarfon Castle Gwynd 54 F8
Caerphilly Caerph 27 N10
Caersws Powys 38 B4
Caerwedros Cerdgn 36 F9
Caerwent Mons 28 F10
Caerwys Flints 48 D2
Caio Carmth 37 L11
Cairinis W Isls 111 b5
Cairnbaan Ag & B 83 M5
Cairnbulg Abers 103 L3
Cairncross Border 81 J2
Cairncurran Inver 84 F8
Cairndow Ag & B 84 C2
Cairneyhill Fife 86 C5
Cairngarroch D & G 68 E8
Cairngorms National Park 99 N8
Cairnie Abers 101 N6
Cairnorrie Abers 102 H7
Cairnryan D & G 68 E5
Cairnty Moray 101 L5
Caister-on-Sea Norfk 45 Q7
Caistor Lincs 52 G3
Caistor St Edmund Norfk 45 K8
Calanais W Isls 111 c2
Calbourne IoW 9 M9
Calceby Lincs 53 K7
Calcoed Flints 48 D1
Calcot Gloucs 30 E11
Calcot Row W Berk 19 R6
Calcots Moray 101 K3

Caldbeck Cumb 71 M7
Caldecote Cambs 33 K5
Caldecote Cambs 42 G11
Caldecott Nhants 32 E3
Caldecott Oxon 19 N2
Caldecott Rutlnd 42 C10
Calder Bridge Cumb 62 B2
Caldercruix N Lans 85 N9
Calder Grove Wakefd 58 H10
Caldermill S Lans 77 L3
Calder Vale Lancs 63 K11
Calderwood S Lans 85 L11
Caldey Island Pembks 25 K9
Caldicot Mons 28 F10
Caldmore Wsall 40 D7
Caldwell N York 65 L5
Calf of Man IoM 56 a7
Calfsound Ork 111 h1
Calgary Ag & B 89 J6
Califer Moray 100 G4
California Falk 85 Q7
California Norfk 45 Q7
Calke Derbys 41 J3
Calke Abbey Derbys 41 J3
Callakille Highld 105 K10
Callander Stirlg 85 K2
Callanish W Isls 111 c2
Callestick Cnwll 2 H6
Calligarry Highld 96 H8
Callington Cnwll 4 H6
Callow Herefs 28 F2
Callow End Worcs 39 Q11
Callow Hill Wilts 18 F4
Calmore Hants 9 K5
Calmsden Gloucs 30 D11
Calne Wilts 18 E6
Calshot Hants 9 N7
Calstock Cnwll 5 J6
Calstone Wellington Wilts 18 F7
Calthorpe Norfk 45 K4
Calthorpe Street Norfk 45 N5
Calthwaite Cumb 71 P7
Calton Staffs 50 E10
Calveley Ches E 49 L4
Calver Derbys 50 G6
Calverhall Shrops 49 L7
Calverleigh Devon 16 C12
Calverley Leeds 58 G6
Calverton M Keyn 32 B8
Calverton Notts 51 N10
Calvine P & K 92 B3
Calzeat Border 78 H2
Cam Gloucs 29 K8
Camasachoirce Highld 89 Q4
Camasine Highld 89 P4
Camas Luinie Highld 97 N4
Camastianavaig Highld 96 F2
Camault Muir Highld 98 G2
Camber E Susx 13 J6
Camberley Surrey 20 E10
Camberwell Gt Lon 21 L7
Camblesforth N York 59 N8
Cambo Nthumb 72 H4
Camborne Cnwll 2 F7
Camborne & Redruth Mining District Cnwll 2 F7
Cambourne Cambs 33 K5
Cambridge Cambs 33 M5
Cambridge Gloucs 29 K7
Cambridge Airport Cambs 33 M5
Cambrose Cnwll 2 G6
Cambus Clacks 85 P4
Cambusavie Highld 107 M3
Cambusbarron Stirlg 85 N5
Cambuskenneth Stirlg 85 N4
Cambuslang S Lans 85 L10
Cambus o' May Abers 94 G3
Cambuswallace S Lans 78 G2
Camden Town Gt Lon 21 L6
Cameley BaNES 17 N5
Camelford Cnwll 4 D4
Camelon Falk 85 P6
Camerory Highld 100 F8
Camerton BaNES 17 P5
Camerton Cumb 70 G8
Camghouran P & K 91 N5
Camieston Border 80 D8
Cammachmore Abers 95 P3
Cammeringham Lincs 52 D7
Camore Highld 107 N4
Campbeltown Ag & B 75 K8
Campbeltown Airport Ag & B 75 K7
Cample D & G 78 E9
Campmuir P & K 93 J7
Camps W Loth 86 C8
Campsall Donc 59 M10
Campsea Ash Suffk 35 M5
Campton C Beds 32 G8
Camptown Border 80 F10
Camrose Pembks 24 G5
Camserney P & K 92 C6
Camusnagaul Highld 90 E2
Camusnagaul Highld 105 Q5
Camusteel Highld 97 J2
Camusterrach Highld 97 J2
Canada Hants 9 K4
Candacraig Abers 94 F3
Candlesby Lincs 53 M9
Candy Mill Border 78 H1
Cane End Oxon 20 B7
Canewdon Essex 22 H5
Canford Cliffs BCP 8 F8
Canford Heath BCP 8 F8
Canisbay Highld 110 G2
Canley Covtry 40 H11
Cann Dorset 8 C3
Canna Highld 96 B8
Cann Common Dorset 8 C4
Cannich Highld 98 D3
Cannington Somset 16 H8
Canning Town Gt Lon 21 N7
Cannock Staffs 40 C5
Cannock Chase Staffs 40 C4
Cannon Bridge Herefs 28 E1
Canonbie D & G 71 N1
Canon Frome Herefs 39 M12
Canon Pyon Herefs 39 J11
Canons Ashby Nhants 31 N4
Canonstown Cnwll 2 E7
Canterbury Kent 23 M10
Canterbury Cathedral Kent 23 M10
Cantley Norfk 45 N8
Canton Cardif 16 F2

Cantraywood Highld 107 N11
Cantsfield Lancs 63 L7
Canvey Island Essex 22 F6
Canwick Lincs 52 D9
Canworthy Water Cnwll 4 F2
Caol Highld 90 F2
Caolas Scalpaigh W Isls 111 c3
Caoles Ag & B 88 D6
Caonich Highld 97 Q10
Capel Kent 12 D2
Capel Surrey 11 J2
Capel Bangor Cerdgn 37 K5
Capel Coch IoA 54 F5
Capel Curig Conwy 55 K9
Capel Dewi Carmth 26 C5
Capel Dewi Cerdgn 36 G11
Capel Dewi Cerdgn 37 K4
Capel Garmon Conwy 55 M9
Capel Hendre Carmth 26 E6
Capel Iwan Carmth 25 M2
Capel-le-Ferne Kent 13 N3
Capel Parc IoA 54 F4
Capel St Andrew Suffk 35 N7
Capel St Mary Suffk 34 H8
Capel Seion Cerdgn 37 K5
Capelulo Conwy 55 L6
Capenhurst Ches W 48 G2
Cape Wrath Highld 108 E1
Capheaton Nthumb 73 J5
Caplaw E Rens 84 G10
Cappercleuch Border 79 K4
Capton Devon 5 Q9
Caputh P & K 92 G7
Caradon Mining District Cnwll 4 G5
Carbeth Stirlg 85 J7
Carbis Bay Cnwll 2 D7
Carbost Highld 96 D4
Carbost Highld 104 F11
Carbrook Sheff 51 J3
Carbrooke Norfk 44 F9
Car Colston Notts 51 Q11
Carcroft Donc 59 M11
Cardenden Fife 86 E4
Cardhu Moray 101 J6
Cardiff Cardif 16 F2
Cardiff Airport V Glam 16 E3
Cardiff Gate Services Cardif 27 P11
Cardiff West Services Cardif 27 M11
Cardigan Cerdgn 36 C10
Cardington Bed 32 F7
Cardington Shrops 39 J3
Cardinham Cnwll 4 D6
Cardrain D & G 68 F11
Cardrona Border 79 L2
Cardross Ag & B 84 F7
Cardryne D & G 68 F11
Cardurnock Cumb 71 J4
Careby Lincs 42 E6
Careston Angus 95 J9
Carew Pembks 24 H7
Carew Cheriton Pembks 24 H8
Carew Newton Pembks 24 H7
Carey Herefs 28 G3
Carfin N Lans 85 N10
Carfraemill Border 80 C4
Cargate Green Norfk 45 N7
Cargenbridge D & G 70 F1
Cargill P & K 92 H8
Cargo Cumb 71 M4
Cargreen Cnwll 5 J7
Carham Nthumb 80 H6
Carhampton Somset 16 D7
Carharrack Cnwll 2 G7
Carie P & K 91 P5
Carinish W Isls 111 b5
Carisbrooke IoW 9 N9
Cark Cumb 62 G6
Carkeel Cnwll 5 J7
Càrlabhagh W Isls 111 c2
Carlbury Darltn 65 L4
Carlby Lincs 42 F7
Carleen Cnwll 2 F9
Carleton Forehoe Norfk 44 H8
Carleton-in-Craven N York 58 C4
Carleton Rode Norfk 44 H10
Carleton St Peter Norfk 45 M9
Carlincraig Abers 102 E6
Carlingcott BaNES 17 Q5
Carlisle Cumb 71 N4
Carlisle Lake District Airport Cumb 71 P4
Carlops Border 86 D10
Carloway W Isls 111 c2
Carlton Barns 59 J11
Carlton Bed 32 D6
Carlton Cambs 33 Q6
Carlton Leeds 59 J8
Carlton Leics 41 K6
Carlton N York 59 N9
Carlton N York 65 J9
Carlton N York 65 L9
Carlton Notts 51 N11
Carlton S on T 65 P3
Carlton Suffk 35 N4
Carlton Colville Suffk 45 Q11
Carlton Curlieu Leics 41 P7
Carlton Green Cambs 33 Q6
Carlton Husthwaite N York 66 C11
Carlton-in-Cleveland N York 66 C6
Carlton in Lindrick Notts 51 N4
Carlton-le-Moorland Lincs 52 C10
Carlton Miniott N York 65 P10
Carlton-on-Trent Notts 52 B10
Carlton Scroop Lincs 42 D2
Carluke S Lans 77 P2
Carmacoup S Lans 77 N6
Carmarthen Carmth 25 P5
Carmel Carmth 26 D5
Carmel Flints 56 D12
Carmel Gwynd 54 G9
Carmichael S Lans 78 F2
Carmunnock C Glas 85 K10
Carmyle C Glas 85 L9
Carmyllie Angus 93 P7
Carnaby E R Yk 61 K2
Carnbee Fife 87 K2
Carnbo P & K 86 C2
Carn Brea Cnwll 2 G7
Carnbrogie Abers 102 H9
Carndu Highld 97 M4
Carnduff S Lans 77 L3
Carnell E Ayrs 76 H5
Carnforth Lancs 63 J7

Carn-gorm – Cilfrew 165

Carn-gorm Highld 97 N5
Carnhell Green Cnwll 2 F8
Carnie Abers 95 N2
Carnkie Cnwll 2 G7
Carnkie Cnwll 2 G8
Carno Powys 47 Q11
Carnock Fife 86 C4
Carnon Downs Cnwll 3 J7
Carnousie Abers 102 E5
Carnoustie Angus 93 P8
Carnwath S Lans 86 B11
Carol Green Solhll 40 H11
Carperby N York 64 H9
Carradale Ag & B 75 M5
Carradale Village Ag & B 75 M5
Carrbridge Highld 99 N4
Carrefour Jersey 7 b1
Carreglefn IoA 54 E4
Carr Gate Wakefd 58 H8
Carrhouse N Linc 60 D11
Carrick Ag & B 83 N5
Carrick Castle Ag & B 84 D4
Carriden Falk 86 B6
Carrington Mdloth 86 G9
Carrington Traffd 57 N9
Carrog Denbgs 48 C6
Carron Falk 85 P6
Carron Moray 101 J7
Carronbridge D & G 78 E8
Carron Bridge Stirlg 85 M6
Carronshore Falk 85 P6
Carr Shield Nthumb 72 E10
Carrutherstown D & G 70 H2
Carruth House Inver 84 F9
Carrville Dur 73 N11
Carsaig Ag & B 89 L11
Carseriggan D & G 69 J5
Carsethorn D & G 70 G4
Carshalton Gt Lon 21 L9
Carsington Derbys 50 G9
Carskey Ag & B 75 J10
Carsluith D & G 69 L8
Carsphairn D & G 77 J11
Carstairs S Lans 77 Q3
Carstairs Junction S Lans 77 Q3
Carterton Oxon 30 H11
Carthew Cnwll 3 N5
Carthorpe N York 65 N10
Cartland S Lans 77 P3
Cartmel Cumb 62 H6
Carway Carmth 26 C7
Cashe's Green Gloucs 29 L7
Cassington Oxon 31 L11
Cassop Dur 73 N12
Castel Guern 6 b2
Casterton Cumb 63 L6
Castle Acre Norfk 44 D7
Castle Ashby Nhants 32 C5
Castlebay W Isls 111 a7
Castle Bolton N York 65 J8
Castle Bromwich Solhll 40 F9
Castle Bytham Lincs 42 E6
Castlebythe Pembks 24 H3
Castle Caereinion Powys 38 D2
Castle Camps Cambs 33 P8
Castle Carrock Cumb 71 Q5
Castlecary N Lans 85 N7
Castle Cary Somset 17 P9
Castle Combe Wilts 18 C5
Castlecraig Highld 107 N8
Castle Donington Leics 41 K3
Castle Douglas D & G 70 C3
Castle Eaton Swindn 18 G2
Castle Eden Dur 73 Q12
Castleford Wakefd 59 K8
Castle Frome Herefs 39 M11
Castle Gresley Derbys 40 H4
Castle Hedingham Essex 34 D9
Castlehill Border 79 K2
Castlehill Highld 110 E3
Castle Hill Suffk 35 J7
Castlehill W Duns 84 G7
Castle Howard N York 66 G12
Castle Kennedy D & G 68 F7
Castle Lachlan Ag & B 83 Q4
Castlemartin Pembks 24 F8
Castlemilk C Glas 85 K10
Castlemorton Worcs 29 L2
Castlemorton Common
Worcs 29 K2
Castle O'er D & G 79 L9
Castle Rising Norfk 43 Q5
Castleside Dur 73 J10
Castle Stuart Highld 107 M11
Castlethorpe M Keyn 32 B7
Castleton Ag & B 83 N6
Castleton Border 79 Q10
Castleton Derbys 50 F4
Castleton N York 66 F6
Castleton Newpt 27 Q11
Castleton Rochdl 58 B11
Castletown Highld 110 E3
Castletown IoM 56 b7
Castletown Sundld 73 P8
Castley N York 58 H5
Caston Norfk 44 F9
Castor C Pete 42 G9
Catacol N Ayrs 75 N3
Catcliffe Rothm 51 K3
Catcomb Wilts 18 E5
Catcott Somset 17 K8
Caterham Surrey 21 M11
Catfield Norfk 45 N6
Catford Gt Lon 21 M8
Catforth Lancs 57 J2
Cathcart C Glas 85 K10
Cathedine Powys 27 N4
Catherington Hants 10 B7
Catherston Leweston Dorset 7 K4
Catisfield Hants 9 P6
Catlodge Highld 99 J9
Catmere End Essex 33 M8
Catmore W Berk 19 M5
Caton Lancs 63 K8
Caton Green Lancs 63 K8
Catrine E Ayrs 77 J6
Catsfield E Susx 12 E7
Catsgore Somset 17 M10
Catshill Worcs 40 C11
Cattadale Ag & B 75 K9
Cattal N York 59 K4
Cattawade Suffk 34 H9
Catterall Lancs 57 J1
Catterick N York 65 M7
Catterick Bridge N York 65 M7
Catterlen Cumb 71 P8
Catterline Abers 95 P6
Catterton N York 59 L5
Catteshall Surrey 10 F2
Catthorpe Leics 41 M10
Cattistock Dorset 7 N3
Catton N York 65 P11
Catton Nthumb 72 E8
Catwick E R Yk 61 J5
Catworth Cambs 32 F3
Caudle Green Gloucs 29 N6
Caulcott Oxon 31 L8
Cauldcots Angus 93 Q6
Cauldhame Stirlg 85 L4
Cauldmill Border 80 C10
Cauldon Staffs 50 E10
Cauldwell Derbys 40 G4
Caulkerbush D & G 70 F4
Caulside D & G 79 P11
Caundle Marsh Dorset 17 P12
Caunton Notts 51 Q8
Causeway End D & G 69 K7
Causeway End Essex 34 B11
Causewayend S Lans 78 G2
Causewayhead Stirlg 85 N4
Causeyend Abers 103 K10
Causey Park Bridge Nthumb 73 L2
Cavendish Suffk 34 D7
Cavenham Suffk 34 C3
Caversfield Oxon 31 M8
Caversham Readg 20 B8
Caverswall Staffs 50 C11
Caverton Mill Border 80 G8
Cawdor Highld 100 D5
Cawood N York 59 M6
Cawsand Cnwll 5 J9
Cawston Norfk 45 J5
Cawthorne Barns 58 H11
Caxton Cambs 33 K5
Caynham Shrops 39 K7
Caythorpe Lincs 42 D1
Caythorpe Notts 51 P10
Cayton N York 67 M10
Ceannabeinne Highld 108 H3
Ceann a Bhaigh W Isls 111 a4
Ceannacroc Lodge Highld 98 C6
Cearsiadar W Isls 111 d2
Cefn Newpt 28 C10
Cefn-brîth Conwy 55 N10
Cefn-bryn-brain Carmth 26 G6
Cefn-coed-y-cymmer Myr Td 27 L7
Cefn Cribwr Brdgnd 27 J11
Cefneithin Carmth 26 D6
Cefngorwydd Powys 37 P10
Cefn-mawr Wrexhm 48 F7
Cefn-y-pant Carmth 25 L4
Cellardyke Fife 87 L2
Cellarhead Staffs 50 C10
Cemaes IoA 54 E3
Cemmaes Powys 47 N9
Cemmaes Road Powys 47 N9
Cenarth Cerdgn 36 E11
Ceres Fife 93 M12
Cerne Abbas Dorset 7 P3
Cerney Wick Gloucs 18 F2
Cerrigydrudion Conwy 55 P11
Ceunant Gwynd 54 G8
Chaceley Gloucs 29 M3
Chacewater Cnwll 2 H6
Chackmore Bucks 31 P7
Chacombe Nhants 31 L5
Chadbury Worcs 30 D5
Chadderton Oldham 58 B12
Chaddesden C Derb 51 J12
Chaddesley Corbett Worcs 40 B11
Chaddlehanger Devon 5 K5
Chaddleworth W Berk 19 M5
Chadlington Oxon 31 J9
Chadshunt Warwks 31 J4
Chadwell Leics 42 B5
Chadwell Heath Gt Lon 21 P6
Chadwell St Mary Thurr 22 D7
Chadwick Worcs 39 Q8
Chadwick End Solhll 40 G11
Chaffcombe Somset 7 J2
Chafford Hundred Thurr 22 C7
Chagford Devon 5 N3
Chailey E Susx 11 N6
Chainhurst Kent 12 E1
Chaldon Surrey 21 L11
Chaldon Herring Dorset 8 B10
Chale IoW 9 N11
Chale Green IoW 9 N11
Chalfont Common Bucks 20 G5
Chalfont St Giles Bucks 20 F5
Chalfont St Peter Bucks 20 G5
Chalford Gloucs 29 M8
Chalford Wilts 18 C10
Chalgrove Oxon 19 Q2
Chalk Kent 22 D8
Chalkwell Kent 22 H10
Challacombe Devon 15 M4
Challoch D & G 69 K5
Challock Kent 23 J12
Chalton C Beds 32 E10
Chalton Hants 10 B6
Chalvey Slough 20 F7
Chalvington E Susx 11 P8
Chandler's Cross Herts 20 H4
Chandler's Ford Hants 9 M4
Channel Tunnel Terminal Kent 13 M3
Chantry Somset 17 Q6
Chantry Suffk 35 J7
Chapel Fife 86 F4
Chapel Allerton Leeds 58 H6
Chapel Allerton Somset 17 K6
Chapel Amble Cnwll 3 M1
Chapel Brampton Nhants 31 Q2
Chapel Chorlton Staffs 49 P7
Chapelend Way Essex 34 B8
Chapel-en-le-Frith Derbys 50 D5
Chapel Green Warwks 31 L3
Chapel Haddlesey N York 59 M8
Chapelhall N Lans 85 N9
Chapel Hill Abers 103 L8
Chapel Hill Lincs 52 H11
Chapel Hill N York 59 J5
Chapelhope Border 79 K5
Chapelknowe D & G 71 M2
Chapel Lawn Shrops 38 G6
Chapel-le-Dale N York 64 D11
Chapel Leigh Somset 16 F9
Chapel of Garioch Abers 102 F9
Chapel Rossan D & G 68 F9
Chapel Row W Berk 19 P6
Chapel St Leonards Lincs 53 N8
Chapel Stile Cumb 62 G2
Chapelton Abers 95 P4
Chapelton Angus 93 Q6
Chapelton Devon 15 K6
Chapelton S Lans 77 L2
Chapeltown Bl w D 57 N6
Chapeltown Moray 101 K10
Chapeltown Sheff 51 J2
Chapmanslade Wilts 18 C10
Chapmans Well Devon 4 H2
Chapmore End Herts 33 K12
Chappel Essex 34 E10
Chard Somset 7 J2
Chard Junction Somset 7 J2
Chardleigh Green Somset 7 J1
Chardstock Devon 7 J2
Charfield S Glos 29 J9
Charing Kent 23 J12
Charingworth Gloucs 30 G6
Charlbury Oxon 31 J9
Charlcombe BaNES 17 Q3
Charlcutt Wilts 18 E5
Charlecote Warwks 30 H3
Charlemont Sandw 40 D8
Charles Devon 15 M5
Charleston Angus 93 L6
Charlestown C Aber 95 Q2
Charlestown C Brad 58 F6
Charlestown Calder 58 C8
Charlestown Cnwll 3 M5
Charlestown Cnwll 3 M5
Charlestown Fife 86 C5
Charlestown Highld 105 M7
Charlestown Highld 107 K11
Charlestown Salfd 57 P8
Charlestown of Aberlour
Moray 101 K6
Charles Tye Suffk 34 G6
Charlesworth Derbys 50 D3
Charlinch Somset 16 H8
Charlottetown Fife 93 K12
Charlton Gt Lon 21 N7
Charlton Nhants 31 M7
Charlton Nthumb 72 E4
Charlton Oxon 19 L3
Charlton Somset 16 H10
Charlton Somset 17 P6
Charlton W Susx 10 E7
Charlton Wilts 8 D3
Charlton Wilts 18 E3
Charlton Worcs 30 D5
Charlton Wrekin 49 L12
Charlton Abbots Gloucs 30 D8
Charlton Adam Somset 17 M9
Charlton All Saints Wilts 8 H3
Charlton Down Dorset 7 P4
Charlton Horethorne Somset 17 P10
Charlton Kings Gloucs 29 N5
Charlton Mackrell Somset 17 M9
Charlton Marshall Dorset 8 D6
Charlton Musgrove Somset 17 Q9
Charlton-on-Otmoor Oxon 31 M10
Charlton on the Hill Dorset 8 D6
Charlton St Peter Wilts 18 G9
Charlwood Hants 10 A4
Charlwood Surrey 11 K2
Charminster Dorset 7 P4
Charmouth Dorset 7 J4
Charndon Bucks 31 P8
Charney Bassett Oxon 19 L2
Charnock Richard Lancs 57 K6
Charnock Richard Services
Lancs 57 K6
Charsfield Suffk 35 L5
Charter Alley Hants 19 P8
Charterhall Border 80 G5
Charterhouse Somset 17 M5
Chartershall Stirlg 85 N5
Chartham Kent 23 L11
Chartham Hatch Kent 23 L11
Chartridge Bucks 20 E3
Chart Sutton Kent 22 F12
Charvil Wokham 20 C8
Charwelton Nhants 31 M3
Chase Terrace Staffs 40 D5
Chasetown Staffs 40 D6
Chastleton Oxon 30 G8
Chasty Devon 14 F10
Chatburn Lancs 63 P12
Chatcull Staffs 49 P8
Chatham Medway 22 F9
Chatham Green Essex 22 E1
Chathill Nthumb 81 P8
Chatsworth House Derbys 50 H6
Chattenden Medway 22 F8
Chatteris Cambs 43 L11
Chatterton Lancs 57 P5
Chattisham Suffk 34 H8
Chatto Border 80 G10
Chatton Nthumb 81 M8
Chawleigh Devon 15 M9
Chawton Hants 10 B3
Cheadle Staffs 50 D11
Cheadle Stockp 57 Q10
Cheadle Hulme Stockp 57 Q10
Cheam Gt Lon 21 K10
Chearsley Bucks 31 Q11
Chebsey Staffs 49 Q9
Checkendon Oxon 19 Q4
Checkley Ches E 49 N6
Checkley Staffs 50 D12
Chedburgh Suffk 34 D5
Cheddar Somset 17 L5
Cheddington Bucks 32 D12
Cheddleton Staffs 50 C9
Cheddon Fitzpaine Somset 16 H9
Chedgrave Norfk 45 M9
Chedington Dorset 7 L2
Chediston Suffk 35 M2
Chedworth Gloucs 30 D10
Chedzoy Somset 17 J8
Cheetham Hill Manch 57 Q8
Cheldon Devon 15 M9
Chelford Ches E 49 P1
Chellaston C Derb 41 J2
Chellington Bed 32 D5
Chelmarsh Shrops 39 N5
Chelmer Village Essex 22 E2
Chelmondiston Suffk 35 K8
Chelmorton Derbys 50 E6
Chelmsford Essex 22 E3
Chelmsley Wood Solhll 40 F9
Chelsea Gt Lon 21 L7
Chelsfield Gt Lon 21 P9
Chelsworth Suffk 34 G7
Cheltenham Gloucs 29 N4
Chelveston Nhants 32 E3
Chelvey N Som 17 L3
Chelwood BaNES 17 P4
Chelwood Gate E Susx 11 N4
Cheney Longville Shrops 38 H5
Chenies Bucks 20 G4
Chepstow Mons 28 G9
Cherhill Wilts 18 F6
Cherington Gloucs 29 M8
Cherington Warwks 30 H6
Cheriton Hants 9 P2
Cheriton Kent 13 M3
Cheriton Pembks 24 H8
Cheriton Swans 26 B9
Cheriton Bishop Devon 5 P2
Cheriton Fitzpaine Devon 15 P10
Cherrington Wrekin 49 M10
Cherry Burton E R Yk 60 G6
Cherry Hinton Cambs 33 M5
Cherry Orchard Worcs 39 Q10
Cherry Willingham Lincs 52 E8
Chertsey Surrey 20 G9
Cherwell Valley Services
Oxon 31 M8
Cheselbourne Dorset 8 B7
Chesham Bucks 20 F3
Chesham Bury 57 P6
Chesham Bois Bucks 20 F4
Cheshunt Herts 21 M3
Chesil Beach Dorset 7 N6
Cheslyn Hay Staffs 40 C6
Chessetts Wood Warwks 40 F11
Chessington Gt Lon 21 J10
Chessington World of
Adventures Gt Lon 21 J10
Chester Ches W 48 H3
Chesterblade Somset 17 P7
Chesterfield Derbys 51 J6
Chesterfield Staffs 40 E6
Chesterhill Mdloth 86 H8
Chester-le-Street Dur 73 M9
Chester Moor Dur 73 M10
Chesters Border 80 E11
Chesters Border 80 E9
Chester Services Ches W 49 J1
Chesterton Cambs 33 M5
Chesterton Cambs 42 G10
Chesterton Gloucs 18 E1
Chesterton Oxon 31 M9
Chesterton Shrops 39 P3
Chesterton Staffs 49 P5
Chesterton Green Warwks 31 J3
Chesterwood Nthumb 72 E7
Chester Zoo Ches W 48 H2
Chestfield Kent 23 L9
Cheston Devon 5 N8
Cheswardine Shrops 49 N9
Cheswick Nthumb 81 L5
Chetnole Dorset 7 N2
Chettisham Cambs 43 N12
Chettle Dorset 8 D5
Chetton Shrops 39 M4
Chetwynd Wrekin 49 N10
Chetwynd Aston Wrekin 49 N11
Cheveley Cambs 34 B5
Chevening Kent 21 P11
Chevington Suffk 34 D5
Cheviot Hills 80 G11
Chevithorne Devon 16 D11
Chew Magna BaNES 17 N4
Chew Stoke BaNES 17 M4
Chewton Keynsham BaNES 17 P3
Chewton Mendip Somset 17 N5
Chicheley M Keyn 32 C7
Chichester W Susx 10 D8
Chickerell Dorset 7 P6
Chicklade Wilts 8 D1
Chidden Hants 9 Q4
Chiddingfold Surrey 10 F3
Chiddingly E Susx 12 B7
Chiddingstone Kent 11 P2
Chiddingstone Causeway
Kent 11 Q1
Chideock Dorset 7 K4
Chidham W Susx 10 C8
Chidswell Kirk 58 H9
Chieveley W Berk 19 M6
Chieveley Services W Berk 19 N6
Chignall St James Essex 22 D2
Chignall Smealy Essex 22 D2
Chigwell Essex 21 N5
Chigwell Row Essex 21 P5
Chilbolton Hants 19 L11
Chilcomb Hants 9 N2
Chilcombe Dorset 7 M5
Chilcompton Somset 17 P6
Chilcote Leics 40 H5
Childer Thornton Ches W 56 G12
Child Okeford Dorset 8 C5
Childrey Oxon 19 L3
Child's Ercall Shrops 49 M9
Childswickham Worcs 30 E6
Childwall Lpool 56 H10
Chilfrome Dorset 7 N3
Chilgrove W Susx 10 D7
Chilham Kent 23 K11
Chillaton Devon 5 J4
Chillenden Kent 23 N11
Chillerton IoW 9 N10
Chillesford Suffk 35 N6
Chillington Devon 5 Q10
Chillington Somset 7 K1
Chilmark Wilts 8 E2
Chilmington Green Kent 13 J3
Chilson Oxon 30 H9
Chilsworthy Cnwll 5 J6
Chilsworthy Devon 14 F10
Chiltern Hills 20 C4
Chilthorne Domer Somset 17 M11
Chilton Bucks 31 P10
Chilton Dur 65 M2
Chilton Oxon 19 N4
Chilton Candover Hants 19 P11
Chilton Cantelo Somset 17 N10
Chilton Foliat Wilts 19 K6
Chilton Polden Somset 17 K7
Chilton Street Suffk 34 C7
Chilton Trinity Somset 16 H8
Chilwell Notts 41 L1
Chilworth Hants 9 L4
Chilworth Surrey 10 G1
Chimney Oxon 19 L1
Chineham Hants 19 Q9
Chingford Gt Lon 21 M5
Chinley Derbys 50 D4
Chinnor Oxon 20 C3
Chipnall Shrops 49 N8
Chippenham Cambs 33 Q3
Chippenham Wilts 18 D6
Chipperfield Herts 20 G3
Chipping Herts 33 K9
Chipping Lancs 63 L12
Chipping Campden Gloucs 30 F6
Chipping Norton Oxon 30 H8
Chipping Ongar Essex 22 B3
Chipping Sodbury S Glos 29 K11
Chipping Warden Nhants 31 L5
Chipstable Somset 16 E10
Chipstead Kent 21 P11
Chipstead Surrey 21 L11
Chirbury Shrops 38 F3
Chirk Wrexhm 48 F7
Chirnside Border 81 J3
Chirnsidebridge Border 80 H3
Chirton Wilts 18 F8
Chisbury Wilts 19 J7
Chiselborough Somset 17 L12
Chiseldon Swindn 18 H5
Chiselhampton Oxon 19 P2
Chiserley Calder 58 D8
Chisholme Border 79 N6
Chislehurst Gt Lon 21 N9
Chislet Kent 23 N9
Chiswell Green Herts 21 J3
Chiswick Gt Lon 21 K7
Chisworth Derbys 50 C3
Chithurst W Susx 10 D5
Chittering Cambs 33 M3
Chitterne Wilts 18 E11
Chittlehamholt Devon 15 L7
Chittlehampton Devon 15 L7
Chittoe Wilts 18 E7
Chivelstone Devon 5 Q11
Chivenor Devon 15 J5
Chlenry D & G 68 F6
Chobham Surrey 20 F10
Cholderton Wilts 19 J11
Cholesbury Bucks 20 E3
Chollerton Nthumb 72 G6
Cholsey Oxon 19 P4
Cholstrey Herefs 39 J9
Chop Gate N York 66 D7
Choppington Nthumb 73 M4
Chopwell Gatesd 73 K8
Chorley Ches E 49 K5
Chorley Lancs 57 L5
Chorley Shrops 39 M5
Chorleywood Herts 20 G4
Chorleywood West Herts 20 G4
Chorlton Ches E 49 N5
Chorlton-cum-Hardy Manch 57 P9
Chorlton Lane Ches W 49 J6
Choulton Shrops 38 H5
Chrishall Essex 33 M8
Chrisswell Inver 84 D7
Christchurch BCP 8 H8
Christchurch Cambs 43 M10
Christchurch Newpt 28 D10
Christian Malford Wilts 18 E5
Christon N Som 17 K5
Christon Bank Nthumb 81 P9
Christow Devon 5 Q4
Chudleigh Devon 6 B6
Chudleigh Knighton Devon 6 B7
Chulmleigh Devon 15 M8
Church Lancs 57 N3
Churcham Gloucs 29 K5
Church Aston Wrekin 49 N11
Church Brampton Nhants 31 Q2
Church Broughton Derbys 40 G2
Church Cove Cnwll 2 G12
Church Crookham Hants 20 D11
Churchdown Gloucs 29 M5
Church Eaton Staffs 49 Q11
Church End C Beds 32 H8
Churchend Essex 23 J5
Church End Essex 34 C10
Church End Gt Lon 21 K5
Church Enstone Oxon 31 J8
Church Fenton N York 59 L6
Churchfield Sandw 40 D8
Churchgate Street Essex 21 P2
Church Green Devon 6 G4
Church Hanborough Oxon 31 K10
Church Houses N York 66 F7
Churchill Devon 6 H3
Churchill N Som 17 L4
Churchill Oxon 30 H8
Churchill Worcs 30 B4
Churchill Worcs 39 Q6
Churchinford Somset 6 G1
Church Knowle Dorset 8 D10
Church Langton Leics 41 Q8
Church Lawford Warwks 41 L11
Church Leigh Staffs 40 D1
Church Lench Worcs 30 D4
Church Mayfield Staffs 50 F11
Church Minshull Ches E 49 M4
Church Norton W Susx 10 E10
Churchover Warwks 41 L10
Church Preen Shrops 39 K3
Church Pulverbatch Shrops 38 H2
Churchstanton Somset 16 G12
Churchstoke Powys 38 F4
Churchstow Devon 5 P10
Church Stowe Nhants 31 N3
Church Street Kent 22 E8
Church Stretton Shrops 39 J4
Churchtown Cnwll 4 D5
Churchtown Derbys 50 H8
Churchtown IoM 56 d3
Churchtown Lancs 63 J12
Church Village Rhondd 27 M10
Church Warsop Notts 51 M7
Churston Ferrers Torbay 6 B10
Churt Surrey 10 D3
Churton Ches W 48 H4
Churwell Leeds 58 H8
Chwilog Gwynd 46 G4
Chyandour Cnwll 2 D9
Cilcain Flints 48 D3
Cilcennin Cerdgn 36 H8
Cilfrew Neath 26 G8

Cilfynydd Rhondd......27 M9
Cilgerran Pembks......36 C11
Cilmaengwyn Neath......26 G7
Cilsan Carmth......26 E4
Ciltalgarth Gwynd......47 P4
Cilycwm Carmth......37 M11
Cimla Neath......26 G9
Cinderford Gloucs......28 H6
Cinder Hill Wolves......40 B8
Cippenham Slough......20 F7
Cirencester Gloucs......18 F1
City Gt Lon......21 M7
City Airport Gt Lon......21 N7
Clabhach Ag & B......88 F5
Clachaig Ag & B......84 B6
Clachaig Inn Highld......90 F5
Clachan Ag & B......83 L10
Clachan Ag & B......84 B3
Clachan Ag & B......89 Q11
Clachan Ag & B......90 B7
Clachan Highld......96 G3
Clachan-a-Luib W Isls......111 b4
Clachan Mor Ag & B......88 C6
Clachan na Luib W Isls......111 b4
Clachan of Campsie E Duns......85 K7
Clachan-Seil Ag & B......89 Q10
Clachnaharry Highld......107 K11
Clachtoll Highld......108 B9
Clacket Lane Services Surrey......21 N11
Clackmannan Clacks......85 Q5
Clackmannanshire Bridge
   Fife......85 Q5
Clackmarras Moray......101 K4
Clacton-on-Sea Essex......23 M1
Cladich Ag & B......90 F11
Cladswell Worcs......30 D3
Claggan Highld......89 P6
Claigan Highld......104 C10
Clanfield Hants......10 B6
Clanfield Oxon......19 K1
Clanville Hants......19 K10
Clanville Somset......17 P9
Claonaig Ag & B......83 N10
Clapgate Herts......33 M10
Clapham Bed......32 E6
Clapham Gt Lon......21 L8
Clapham N York......63 N8
Clapham W Susx......10 H8
Clapton Somset......7 K2
Clapton Somset......17 P5
Clapton-in-Gordano N Som......17 L2
Clapton-on-the-Hill Gloucs......30 F9
Claravale Gatesd......73 K7
Clarbeston Pembks......25 J5
Clarbeston Road Pembks......24 H5
Clarborough Notts......51 Q4
Clare Suffk......34 C7
Clarebrand D & G......70 C3
Clarencefield D & G......70 H2
Clarilaw Border......80 C9
Clarkston E Rens......85 J10
Clashmore Highld......107 M5
Clashmore Highld......108 B9
Clashnessie Highld......108 B9
Clashnoir Moray......101 J10
Clathy P & K......92 E10
Clathymore P & K......92 F10
Clatt Abers......102 C9
Clatter Powys......38 B4
Clatworthy Somset......16 E9
Claughton Lancs......57 K1
Claughton Lancs......63 K8
Claughton Wirral......56 F10
Claverdon Warwks......30 G2
Claverham N Som......17 L3
Clavering Essex......33 M9
Claverley Shrops......39 P4
Claverton BaNES......18 B7
Clawdd-coch V Glam......27 M12
Clawdd-newydd Denbgs......48 C5
Clawton Devon......14 F11
Claxby Lincs......52 G5
Claxton N York......59 P3
Claxton Norfk......45 M9
Claybrooke Magna Leics......41 L9
Clay Coton Nhants......41 N11
Clay Cross Derbys......51 K8
Claydon Oxon......31 L4
Claydon Suffk......35 J6
Claygate D & G......79 N11
Claygate Kent......12 E2
Claygate Surrey......21 J10
Clayhall Gt Lon......21 N5
Clayhanger Devon......16 D10
Clayhidon Devon......16 F11
Clayhill E Susx......12 G5
Clayock Highld......110 D4
Claypits Gloucs......29 K7
Claypole Lincs......42 C1
Clayton C Brad......58 E7
Clayton Donc......59 L11
Clayton W Susx......11 L7
Clayton-le-Moors Lancs......57 N3
Clayton-le-Woods Lancs......57 K4
Clayton West Kirk......58 H11
Clayworth Notts......51 Q4
Cleadale Highld......96 F11
Cleadon S Tyne......73 P8
Cleadon Park S Tyne......73 P7
Clearbrook Devon......5 L7
Clearwell Gloucs......28 G7
Cleasby N York......65 M5
Cleat Ork......111 h3
Cleatlam Dur......65 K4
Cleator Cumb......70 G11
Cleator Moor Cumb......70 G11
Cleckheaton Kirk......58 F8
Cleehill Shrops......39 L7
Clee St Margaret Shrops......39 K5
Cleethorpes NE Lin......53 K2
Cleeton St Mary Shrops......39 L6
Cleeve N Som......17 L3
Cleeve Oxon......19 Q5
Cleeve Hill Gloucs......29 N4
Cleeve Prior Worcs......30 E4
Cleghornie E Loth......87 L5
Clehonger Herefs......28 E2
Cleish P & K......86 C3
Cleland N Lans......85 N10
Clenamacrie Ag & B......90 C9
Clenchwarton Norfk......43 P6
Clenerty Abers......102 G3

Clent Worcs......40 B10
Cleobury Mortimer Shrops......39 M7
Cleobury North Shrops......39 L5
Cleongart Ag & B......75 K5
Clephanton Highld......107 N11
Clerkhill D & G......79 L8
Cleuch-head D & G......78 D8
Clevancy Wilts......18 F6
Clevedon N Som......17 K2
Cleveleys Lancs......62 G12
Cleverton Wilts......18 E4
Clewer Somset......17 L6
Cley next the Sea Norfk......44 H2
Cliburn Cumb......64 B3
Cliddesden Hants......19 Q10
Cliffe Medway......22 E7
Cliffe N York......59 P7
Cliff End E Susx......12 H7
Cliffe Woods Medway......22 E8
Clifford Herefs......38 E11
Clifford Leeds......59 K5
Clifford Chambers Warwks......30 G4
Clifford's Mesne Gloucs......29 J4
Clifton Bristl......17 M2
Clifton C Beds......32 G8
Clifton C Nott......41 M1
Clifton C York......59 N4
Clifton Calder......58 F9
Clifton Cumb......71 Q9
Clifton Derbys......50 F11
Clifton Donc......51 M2
Clifton Lancs......57 J3
Clifton N York......58 F5
Clifton Oxon......31 L7
Clifton Worcs......39 Q11
Clifton Campville Staffs......40 G5
Clifton Hampden Oxon......19 P2
Clifton Reynes M Keyn......32 C6
Clifton upon Dunsmore
   Warwks......41 M11
Clifton upon Teme Worcs......39 N9
Cliftonville Kent......23 Q8
Climping W Susx......10 F9
Clink Somset......18 B10
Clint N York......58 H3
Clinterty C Aber......102 H11
Clint Green Norfk......44 G7
Clintmains Border......80 E7
Clippesby Norfk......45 N7
Clipsham Rutlnd......42 D6
Clipston Nhants......41 Q10
Clipston Notts......41 N1
Clipstone C Beds......32 D10
Clipstone Notts......51 N8
Clitheroe Lancs......57 N1
Clive Shrops......49 K9
Cliveden Bucks......20 E6
Clixby Lincs......52 F3
Cloatley Wilts......29 N10
Clocaenog Denbgs......48 C5
Clochan Moray......101 M3
Clodock Herefs......28 C4
Clola Abers......103 K6
Clophill C Beds......32 F8
Clopton Nhants......32 F1
Clopton Suffk......35 K6
Clopton Corner Suffk......35 K6
Clos du Valle Guern......6 c1
Closeburn D & G......78 E9
Closeburnmill D & G......78 E9
Closworth Somset......7 N2
Clothall Herts......33 J9
Clotton Ches W......49 K3
Clough Foot Calder......58 B9
Clough Head Calder......58 E9
Cloughton N York......67 L8
Clousta Shet......111 k4
Clova Angus......94 F7
Clovelly Devon......14 F7
Clovenfords Border......79 P2
Clovulin Highld......90 D4
Clowne Derbys......51 L6
Clows Top Worcs......39 N7
Cluanie Inn Highld......97 Q7
Cluanie Lodge Highld......97 Q7
Clugston D & G......69 J7
Clun Shrops......38 F6
Clunas Highld......100 D6
Clunbury Shrops......38 G6
Clunderwen Carmth......25 K5
Clune Highld......99 L4
Clunes Highld......98 B10
Clungunford Shrops......38 H6
Clunie P & K......92 G6
Clunton Shrops......38 G6
Cluny Fife......86 F3
Clutton BaNES......17 N4
Clutton Ches W......49 J5
Clutton Hill BaNES......17 P4
Clydach Mons......27 P6
Clydach Swans......26 F8
Clydach Vale Rhondd......27 K9
Clydebank W Duns......84 H8
Clyffe Pypard Wilts......18 F5
Clynder Ag & B......84 D6
Clyne Neath......26 H8
Clynnog Fawr Gwynd......54 E10
Clyro Powys......38 E12
Clyst Honiton Devon......6 D4
Clyst Hydon Devon......6 D3
Clyst St George Devon......6 D5
Clyst St Lawrence Devon......6 D3
Clyst St Mary Devon......6 C5
Cnoc W Isls......111 d2
Cnwch Coch Cerdgn......37 L5
Coad's Green Cnwll......4 G5
Coalburn S Lans......78 D2
Coalburns Gatesd......73 K8
Coaley Gloucs......29 K8
Coalhill Essex......22 F4
Coalpit Heath S Glos......29 J11
Coal Pool Wsall......40 D7
Coalport Wrekin......39 M2
Coalsnaughton Clacks......85 Q4
Coaltown of Balgonie Fife......86 G3
Coaltown of Wemyss Fife......86 G3
Coalville Leics......41 K5
Coanwood Nthumb......72 C8
Coat Somset......17 L11
Coatbridge N Lans......85 M9
Coatdyke N Lans......85 M9
Coate Swindn......18 H4
Coate Wilts......18 F8

Coates Cambs......43 K9
Coates Gloucs......29 N8
Coates Lincs......52 C6
Coates W Susx......10 F6
Cobbaton Devon......15 K6
Coberley Gloucs......29 N5
Cobham Kent......22 D9
Cobham Surrey......20 H10
Cobham Services Surrey......20 H11
Cobnash Herefs......39 J9
Cobo Guern......6 b1
Cobridge C Stke......49 Q5
Coburby Abers......103 J3
Cockayne Hatley C Beds......33 J6
Cock Bridge Abers......101 K12
Cockburnspath Border......87 P7
Cock Clarks Essex......22 F3
Cockenzie and Port Seton
   E Loth......86 H7
Cockerham Lancs......63 J10
Cockermouth Cumb......71 J9
Cockernhoe Herts......32 G11
Cockett Swans......26 E9
Cockfield Dur......65 K3
Cockfield Suffk......34 E6
Cockfosters Gt Lon......21 L4
Cock Green Essex......34 B11
Cocking W Susx......10 E6
Cocking Causeway W Susx......10 E6
Cockington Torbay......6 B9
Cocklake Somset......17 L6
Cockley Cley Norfk......44 D8
Cock Marling E Susx......12 H6
Cockpole Green Wokham......20 C7
Cockshutt Shrops......48 H9
Cockthorpe Norfk......44 G2
Cockwood Devon......6 D6
Cockyard Derbys......50 D5
Coddenham Suffk......35 J6
Coddington Herefs......29 J1
Coddington Notts......52 B11
Codford St Mary Wilts......18 E11
Codford St Peter Wilts......18 E11
Codicote Herts......32 H11
Codmore Hill W Susx......10 G6
Codnor Derbys......51 K10
Codrington S Glos......29 K11
Codsall Staffs......39 Q2
Codsall Wood Staffs......39 Q2
Coedpoeth Wrexhm......48 F5
Coed Talon Flints......48 F4
Coed-y-paen Mons......28 D8
Coed-yr-ynys Powys......27 N5
Coffinswell Devon......6 B8
Cofton Devon......6 C6
Cofton Hackett Worcs......40 D11
Cogan V Glam......16 G2
Cogenhoe Nhants......32 B5
Cogges Oxon......31 J11
Coggeshall Essex......34 E11
Coignafearn Highld......99 K5
Coilacriech Abers......94 E13
Coilantogle Stirlg......85 K2
Coillore Highld......96 D3
Coity Brdgnd......27 K11
Col W Isls......111 d2
Colaboll Highld......107 J1
Colan Cnwll......3 K4
Colaton Raleigh Devon......6 E5
Colbost Highld......104 B11
Colburn N York......65 L7
Colby Cumb......64 C4
Colby IoM......56 b6
Colchester Essex......34 G10
Colchester Zoo Essex......34 F11
Cold Ash W Berk......19 N6
Cold Ashby Nhants......41 P11
Cold Ashton S Glos......17 Q2
Cold Aston Gloucs......30 F9
Coldbackie Highld......109 L4
Cold Brayfield M Keyn......32 D6
Coldean Br & H......11 M8
Coldeast Devon......5 Q5
Colden Calder......58 C8
Colden Common Hants......9 N3
Cold Hanworth Lincs......52 F6
Coldharbour Surrey......11 J2
Cold Higham Nhants......31 P4
Coldingham Border......81 J2
Cold Kirby N York......66 D10
Coldmeece Staffs......49 Q8
Cold Norton Essex......22 G4
Cold Overton Leics......42 B7
Coldred Kent......13 P1
Coldridge Devon......15 M10
Coldstream Border......80 H6
Coldwaltham W Susx......10 G6
Coldwells Abers......103 K7
Cole Somset......17 P9
Colebatch Shrops......38 G5
Colebrook Devon......6 D2
Colebrooke Devon......15 N11
Coleby Lincs......52 D10
Coleby N Linc......60 F9
Coleford Devon......15 N11
Coleford Gloucs......28 G6
Coleford Somset......17 P6
Colegate End Norfk......45 K11
Colehill Dorset......8 F7
Coleman's Hatch E Susx......11 N4
Colemere Shrops......48 H8
Colemore Hants......10 B4
Colenden P & K......92 G9
Colerne Wilts......18 B6
Colesbourne Gloucs......30 D10
Coleshill Bucks......20 F4
Coleshill Oxon......19 J3
Coleshill Warwks......40 G9
Coley BaNES......17 N5
Colgate W Susx......11 K4
Colinsburgh Fife......87 J2
Colinton C Edin......86 E8
Colintraive Ag & B......83 Q7
Colkirk Norfk......44 F5
Coll Ag & B......88 F5
Coll W Isls......111 d2
Collace P & K......93 J8
Collafirth Shet......111 k2
Coll Airport Ag & B......88 E5
Collaton Devon......5 P11
Collaton St Mary Torbay......6 B10
College of Roseisle Moray......100 H3
College Town Br For......20 D10
Collessie Fife......93 K11

Collier Row Gt Lon......21 P5
Collier's End Herts......33 L11
Collier Street Kent......12 E2
Colliston Abers......103 L9
Collin D & G......70 G1
Collingbourne Ducis Wilts......19 J9
Collingbourne Kingston Wilts......19 J9
Collingham Leeds......59 K5
Collingham Notts......52 B10
Collington Herefs......39 M9
Collingtree Nhants......31 Q3
Collins Green Warrtn......57 K9
Colliston Angus......93 Q6
Colliton Devon......6 E2
Collyweston Nhants......42 E9
Colmonell S Ayrs......68 F2
Colmworth Bed......32 F5
Colnabaichin Abers......101 K12
Colnbrook Slough......20 G7
Colne Cambs......33 L2
Colne Lancs......58 B6
Colne Engaine Essex......34 E10
Colney Norfk......45 K8
Colney Heath Herts......21 K3
Coln Rogers Gloucs......30 E11
Coln St Aldwyns Gloucs......30 F12
Coln St Dennis Gloucs......30 E11
Colonsay Ag & B......82 E4
Colonsay Airport Ag & B......82 E5
Colpy Abers......102 E8
Colquhar Border......79 M1
Colsterworth Lincs......42 D5
Colston Bassett Notts......41 P2
Coltfield Moray......100 H3
Coltishall Norfk......45 L6
Colton Cumb......62 G5
Colton Leeds......59 J7
Colton N York......59 M5
Colton Norfk......44 H7
Colton Staffs......40 D4
Colt's Hill Kent......12 D2
Colvend D & G......70 E5
Colwall Herefs......29 K1
Colwell Nthumb......72 G6
Colwich Staffs......40 D4
Colwinston V Glam......16 C2
Colworth W Susx......10 E9
Colwyn Bay Conwy......55 M6
Colyford Devon......6 H4
Colyton Devon......6 H4
Combe Oxon......31 K10
Combe W Berk......19 L8
Combe Down BaNES......18 B8
Combe Fishacre Devon......6 A9
Combe Florey Somset......16 F9
Combe Hay BaNES......17 Q4
Combeinteignhead Devon......6 B8
Combe Martin Devon......15 K3
Combe Raleigh Devon......6 F3
Comberbach Ches W......57 M12
Comberford Staffs......40 F6
Comberton Cambs......33 L5
Comberton Herefs......39 J8
Combe St Nicholas Somset......7 J1
Combrook Warwks......30 H4
Combs Derbys......50 D5
Combs Suffk......34 H5
Combs Ford Suffk......34 H5
Combwich Somset......16 H7
Comers Abers......95 L1
Cometrowe Somset......16 G10
Comhampton Worcs......39 Q8
Commins Coch Powys......47 N10
Commondale N York......66 F5
Common End Cumb......70 G10
Common Moor Cnwll......4 F6
Compstall Stockp......50 C3
Compstonend D & G......69 P8
Compton Devon......6 B9
Compton Hants......9 M3
Compton Staffs......39 P5
Compton Surrey......10 F1
Compton W Berk......19 N5
Compton W Susx......10 C7
Compton Wilts......18 G9
Compton Abbas Dorset......8 C4
Compton Abdale Gloucs......30 D10
Compton Bassett Wilts......18 F6
Compton Beauchamp Oxon......19 J4
Compton Bishop Somset......17 K5
Compton Chamberlayne
   Wilts......8 F2
Compton Dando BaNES......17 P4
Compton Dundon Somset......17 L9
Compton Durville Somset......17 K11
Compton Greenfield S Glos......28 G11
Compton Martin BaNES......17 M5
Compton Pauncefoot Somset......17 P10
Compton Valence Dorset......7 N4
Comrie Fife......86 B4
Comrie P & K......92 B10
Conaglen House Highld......90 E3
Conchra Highld......97 M4
Concraigie P & K......92 G6
Conderton Worcs......29 N2
Condicote Gloucs......30 F8
Condorrat N Lans......85 M8
Condover Shrops......39 J2
Coney Hill Gloucs......29 L5
Coneyhurst W Susx......10 H5
Coneysthorpe N York......66 G12
Coney Weston Suffk......34 F2
Congerstone Leics......41 J6
Congham Norfk......44 B5
Congleton Ches E......49 Q3
Congresbury N Som......17 L4
Conheath D & G......70 G2
Conicavel Moray......100 F5
Coningsby Lincs......52 H11
Conington Cambs......33 K4
Conington Cambs......42 H11
Conisbrough Donc......51 L2
Conisholme Lincs......53 L4
Coniston Cumb......62 F3
Coniston E R Yk......61 K7
Coniston Cold N York......58 B3
Conistone N York......58 C1
Connah's Quay Flints......48 F2
Connel Ag & B......90 C9
Connel Park E Ayrs......77 K8
Connor Downs Cnwll......2 E7
Conon Bridge Highld......107 J10
Cononley N York......58 C5
Consall Staffs......50 C10

Consett Dur......73 K10
Constable Burton N York......65 L8
Constable Lee Lancs......57 P4
Constantine Cnwll......2 H9
Constantine Bay Cnwll......3 K2
Contin Highld......106 G10
Conwy Conwy......55 L6
Conwy Castle Conwy......55 L6
Conyer's Green Suffk......34 E3
Cooden E Susx......12 E8
Cookbury Devon......14 G10
Cookham W & M......20 E6
Cookham Dean W & M......20 D6
Cookham Rise W & M......20 E6
Cookhill Worcs......30 D3
Cookley Suffk......35 M2
Cookley Worcs......39 Q6
Cookley Green Oxon......20 B5
Cookney Abers......95 P4
Cook's Green Essex......35 K11
Cooks Green Suffk......34 G6
Cooksmill Green Essex......22 D3
Coolham W Susx......10 H5
Cooling Medway......22 F8
Coombe Cnwll......3 L5
Coombe Devon......6 C9
Coombe Devon......6 E4
Coombe Gloucs......29 K9
Coombe Hants......9 Q4
Coombe Bissett Wilts......8 G3
Coombe Cellars Devon......6 B8
Coombe Hill Gloucs......29 M4
Coombe Keynes Dorset......8 C9
Coombe Pafford Torbay......6 C9
Coombes W Susx......11 J8
Coombes-Moor Herefs......38 G9
Coombeswood Dudley......40 C9
Coopersale Common Essex......21 P3
Copdock Suffk......35 J8
Copford Essex......34 F11
Copford Green Essex......34 F11
Copgrove N York......59 J2
Copister Shet......111 k3
Cople Bed......32 F7
Copley Dur......65 J3
Copmanthorpe C York......59 N5
Copmere End Staffs......49 P9
Copp Lancs......56 H2
Coppenhall Staffs......40 B4
Copperhouse Cnwll......2 E8
Coppingford Cambs......32 G2
Copplestone Devon......15 N10
Coppull Lancs......57 K6
Copsale W Susx......11 J5
Copster Green Lancs......57 M3
Copston Magna Warwks......41 L9
Cop Street Kent......23 P10
Copt Hewick N York......65 N12
Copthorne W Susx......11 L3
Copt Oak Leics......41 L5
Copythorne Hants......9 K5
Corbets Tey Gt Lon......22 C6
Corbière Jersey......7 a2
Corbridge Nthumb......72 H7
Corby Nhants......42 C11
Corby Glen Lincs......42 E5
Cordon N Ayrs......75 Q6
Coreley Shrops......39 L7
Corfe Somset......16 G11
Corfe Castle Dorset......8 E10
Corfe Mullen Dorset......8 E8
Corfton Shrops......39 J5
Corgarff Abers......94 E1
Corhampton Hants......9 Q4
Corlae D & G......77 L12
Corley Warwks......40 H9
Corley Services Warwks......40 H9
Cormuir Angus......94 E8
Cornard Tye Suffk......34 E8
Cornforth Dur......65 N1
Cornhill Abers......102 D4
Cornhill-on-Tweed Nthumb......81 J6
Cornholme Calder......58 B8
Cornoigmore Ag & B......88 C2
Cornsay Dur......73 K11
Cornsay Colliery Dur......73 L11
Corntown Highld......107 J10
Corntown V Glam......27 J12
Cornwall Airport Newquay
   Cnwll......3 K3
Cornwell Oxon......30 H8
Cornwood Devon......5 M8
Cornworthy Devon......6 Q8
Corpach Highld......90 F2
Corpusty Norfk......45 J4
Corrachree Abers......94 H2
Corran Highld......90 D4
Corran Highld......97 M7
Corrie D & G......79 K10
Corrie N Ayrs......75 Q4
Corriecravie N Ayrs......75 P7
Corriegills N Ayrs......75 Q5
Corriegour Lodge Hotel
   Highld......98 C9
Corriemoille Highld......106 F9
Corrimony Highld......98 E3
Corringham Lincs......52 C5
Corringham Thurr......22 E6
Corris Gwynd......47 M9
Corris Uchaf Gwynd......47 M9
Corrow Ag & B......84 D3
Corry Highld......96 H5
Corscombe Devon......15 L11
Corscombe Dorset......7 M2
Corse Gloucs......29 K3
Corse Lawn Gloucs......29 L3
Corsham Wilts......18 C6
Corsindae Abers......102 F12
Corsley Wilts......18 C10
Corsock D & G......78 C12
Corston BaNES......17 Q3
Corston Wilts......18 D4
Corstorphine C Edin......86 E7
Cortachy Angus......94 F9
Corton Suffk......45 Q10
Corton Wilts......18 D11
Corton Denham Somset......17 P10
Coruanan Highld......90 E3
Corwen Denbgs......48 C6
Coryton Devon......5 K4
Coryton Thurr......22 E6
Cosby Leics......41 M8
Coseley Dudley......40 C8

Cosgrove Nhants....32 B8
Cosham C Port....9 Q6
Cosheston Pembks....24 H7
Coshieville P & K....92 B6
Cossall Notts....51 L11
Cossington Leics....41 N5
Cossington Somset....17 J7
Costessey Norfk....45 K7
Costock Notts....41 M3
Coston Leics....42 B6
Coston Norfk....44 H8
Cote Oxon....19 L1
Cotebrook Ches W....49 L3
Cotehill Cumb....71 P5
Cotes Leics....41 M4
Cotesbach Leics....41 M10
Cotford St Luke Somset....16 G9
Cotgrave Notts....41 N1
Cothal Abers....102 H11
Cotham Notts....42 B1
Cotherstone Dur....64 H4
Cothill Oxon....19 M2
Cotleigh Devon....6 G3
Cotmanhay Derbys....51 L11
Coton Cambs....33 L5
Coton Nhants....41 P12
Coton Staffs....49 P10
Coton Clanford Staffs....49 Q10
Coton Hill Shrops....49 J11
Coton in the Elms Derbys....40 G4
Cotswold Airport Wilts....29 N9
Cotswolds....30 C11
Cotswold Wildlife Park & Gardens Oxon....30 G11
Cott Devon....5 Q7
Cottam Lancs....57 J3
Cottam Notts....52 B7
Cottenham Cambs....33 M4
Cottered Herts....33 K10
Cotteridge Birm....40 D10
Cotterstock Nhants....42 F11
Cottesbrooke Nhants....41 P11
Cottesmore Rutlnd....42 C7
Cottingham E R Yk....60 H7
Cottingham Nhants....42 B11
Cottingley C Brad....58 E6
Cottisford Oxon....31 N7
Cotton Suffk....34 H4
Cottown Abers....101 P9
Cottown Abers....102 G11
Cottown of Gight Abers....102 J7
Cotts Devon....5 J7
Coughton Warwks....30 E3
Coulaghailtro Ag & B....83 K9
Coulags Highld....97 N1
Coulby Newham Middsb....66 D5
Coull Abers....94 H2
Coulport Ag & B....84 D5
Coulsdon Gt Lon....21 L10
Coulston Wilts....18 D9
Coulter S Lans....78 G3
Coulton N York....66 E11
Coultra Fife....93 L10
Cound Shrops....39 K2
Coundon Dur....65 M2
Countersett N York....64 G9
Countess Wear Devon....6 C5
Countesswells C Aber....95 P2
Countesthorpe Leics....41 N8
Countisbury Devon....15 M3
Coupar Angus P & K....93 J7
Coupland Nthumb....81 K7
Cour Ag & B....75 M3
Courteachan Highld....97 J9
Courteenhall Nhants....31 Q4
Court Henry Carmth....26 D4
Courtsend Essex....23 K5
Courtway Somset....16 G8
Cousland Mdloth....86 H8
Cousley Wood E Susx....12 D4
Cove Ag & B....84 D6
Cove Border....87 P7
Cove Devon....16 C11
Cove Hants....20 D11
Cove Highld....105 M4
Cove Bay C Aber....95 Q2
Covehithe Suffk....35 Q1
Coven Staffs....40 B6
Coveney Cambs....33 M1
Covenham St Bartholomew Lincs....53 K5
Covenham St Mary Lincs....53 K5
Coventry Covtry....41 J10
Coverack Cnwll....2 H11
Coverack Bridges Cnwll....2 G9
Coverham N York....65 K9
Covington Cambs....32 F3
Covington S Lans....78 F2
Cowan Bridge Lancs....63 L7
Cowbeech E Susx....12 C7
Cowbit Lincs....43 J6
Cowbridge V Glam....16 D2
Cowden Kent....11 P3
Cowdenbeath Fife....86 D4
Cowers Lane Derbys....50 H10
Cowes IoW....9 N8
Cowesby N York....66 C9
Cowfold W Susx....11 K5
Cowhill S Glos....28 H9
Cowie Stirlg....85 P5
Cowley Devon....6 B4
Cowley Gloucs....29 N6
Cowley Gt Lon....20 G7
Cowley Oxon....31 M12
Cowling Lancs....57 L5
Cowling N York....58 C5
Cowling N York....65 M9
Cowlinge Suffk....34 B6
Cowpen Nthumb....73 N5
Cowplain Hants....10 B7
Cowshill Dur....72 F11
Cowslip Green N Som....17 L4
Cowthorpe N York....59 K4
Coxbank Ches E....49 M7
Coxbench Derbys....51 J11
Coxford Cnwll....14 C11
Coxford Norfk....44 E4
Coxheath Kent....22 E12
Coxhoe Dur....65 N1
Coxley Somset....17 M7
Coxley Wick Somset....17 M7
Coxtie Green Essex....22 C4
Coxwold N York....66 D11
Coychurch Brdgnd....27 K11

Coylton S Ayrs....76 G7
Coylumbridge Highld....99 N6
Coytrahen Brdgnd....27 J10
Crabbs Cross Worcs....30 D2
Crabtree W Susx....11 K5
Crackenthorpe Cumb....64 C3
Crackington Haven Cnwll....14 C11
Crackley Staffs....49 Q5
Crackleybank Shrops....49 N12
Cracoe N York....58 C3
Craddock Devon....6 E1
Cradley Dudley....40 C9
Cradley Herefs....39 N11
Cradley Heath Sandw....40 C9
Cradoc Powys....27 L3
Crafthole Cnwll....4 H9
Craggan Highld....100 F9
Cragganmore Moray....101 J7
Craghead Dur....73 L10
Cragside House & Garden Nthumb....73 J1
Crai Powys....27 J4
Craibstone Moray....101 P4
Craichie Angus....93 N6
Craig Angus....95 L10
Craig Highld....105 Q11
Craigbank E Ayrs....77 K8
Craigburn Border....86 F10
Craigcleuch D & G....79 M10
Craigdam Abers....102 H8
Craigdhu Ag & B....83 M2
Craigearn Abers....102 F11
Craigellachie Moray....101 K6
Craigend P & K....92 G10
Craigend Rens....84 H8
Craigendoran Ag & B....84 E6
Craigends Rens....84 G9
Craighlaw D & G....69 J6
Craighouse Ag & B....82 G9
Craigie P & K....92 G7
Craigie S Ayrs....76 G5
Craigiefold Abers....103 J3
Craigley D & G....70 C4
Craig Llangiwg Neath....26 G2
Craiglockhart C Edin....86 E7
Craigmillar C Edin....86 G7
Craigneston D & G....78 C10
Craigneuk N Lans....85 N10
Craigneuk N Lans....85 N9
Craignure Ag & B....89 P8
Craigo Angus....95 L8
Craigrothie Fife....93 L12
Craigruie Stirlg....91 M11
Craigton Angus....93 N7
Craigton C Aber....95 N2
Craigton E Rens....84 H11
Craigton of Airlie Angus....93 K5
Craik Border....79 M7
Crail Fife....87 L1
Crailing Border....80 F8
Craiselound N Linc....51 Q2
Crakehall N York....65 M9
Crambe N York....60 C2
Cramlington Nthumb....73 M5
Cramond C Edin....86 E7
Cramond Bridge C Edin....86 E7
Cranage Ches E....49 N2
Cranberry Staffs....49 P8
Cranborne Dorset....8 F5
Cranbourne Br For....20 E8
Cranbrook Devon....6 D4
Cranbrook Kent....12 F3
Cranfield C Beds....32 D8
Cranford Gt Lon....20 H7
Cranford St Andrew Nhants....32 D2
Cranford St John Nhants....32 D2
Cranham Gloucs....29 M6
Crank St Hel....57 J8
Cranleigh Surrey....10 G3
Cranmore Somset....17 P7
Cranoe Leics....41 Q8
Cransford Suffk....35 M4
Cranshaws Border....87 N9
Crantock Cnwll....2 H4
Cranwell Lincs....52 E12
Cranwich Norfk....44 C10
Cranworth Norfk....44 G8
Craobh Haven Ag & B....83 M2
Crarae Ag & B....83 Q4
Crask Inn Highld....109 J10
Crask of Aigas Highld....98 H1
Craster Nthumb....81 Q9
Cratfield Suffk....35 M2
Crathes Abers....95 M3
Crathie Abers....94 E3
Crathie Highld....98 H9
Crathorne N York....66 B6
Craven Arms Shrops....38 H5
Crawcrook Gatesd....73 K8
Crawford S Lans....78 F5
Crawfordjohn S Lans....78 E4
Crawley Hants....9 M1
Crawley Oxon....31 J10
Crawley W Susx....11 L3
Crawley Down W Susx....11 M3
Crawton Abers....95 P6
Cray N York....64 G10
Cray P & K....94 C8
Crayford Gt Lon....21 P8
Crayke N York....66 D12
Crays Hill Essex....22 E5
Creacombe Devon....15 P8
Creagan Inn Ag & B....90 D7
Creag Ghoraidh W Isls....111 b5
Creagorry W Isls....111 b5
Creaguaineach Lodge Highld....91 J3
Creaton Nhants....41 P12
Creca D & G....71 K2
Credenhill Herefs....39 J12
Crediton Devon....15 P11
Creebank D & G....69 J4
Creebridge D & G....69 K6
Creech Heathfield Somset....16 H10
Creech St Michael Somset....16 H10
Creed Cnwll....3 L6
Creekmouth Gt Lon....21 P7
Creeting St Mary Suffk....34 H5
Creeton Lincs....42 E6
Creetown D & G....69 L7
Cregneash IoM....56 a7
Creigiau Cardif....27 M11
Cremyll Cnwll....5 K9
Cressage Shrops....39 L2

Cressbrook Derbys....50 F6
Cresselly Pembks....25 J7
Cressex Bucks....20 D5
Cressing Essex....34 D11
Cresswell Nthumb....73 N3
Cresswell Pembks....25 J7
Cresswell Staffs....50 C11
Creswell Derbys....51 M6
Cretingham Suffk....35 K5
Cretshengan Ag & B....83 K9
Crewe Ches E....49 N4
Crewe-by-Farndon Ches W....48 H5
Crewe Green Ches E....49 N5
Crew Green Powys....48 G11
Crewkerne Somset....7 L2
Crewton C Derb....41 J2
Crianlarich Stirlg....91 K10
Cribyn Cerdgn....36 H9
Criccieth Gwynd....46 H4
Crich Derbys....51 J9
Crichton Mdloth....86 H9
Crick Nhants....41 N11
Crickadarn Powys....27 M1
Cricket St Thomas Somset....7 K2
Crickhowell Powys....27 P5
Cricklade Wilts....18 G3
Cricklewood Gt Lon....21 K6
Crieff P & K....92 C10
Criggion Powys....48 F11
Crigglestone Wakefd....58 H10
Crimond Abers....103 L4
Crimplesham Norfk....43 Q8
Crimscote Warwks....30 G5
Crinaglack Highld....98 F2
Crinan Ag & B....83 L4
Crindledyke N Lans....85 N10
Cringleford Norfk....45 K8
Crinow Pembks....25 K6
Croachy Highld....99 J4
Crockenhill Kent....21 P9
Crocker End Oxon....20 B6
Crockernwell Devon....5 P2
Crockerton Wilts....18 C11
Crocketford D & G....70 D2
Crockham Hill Kent....21 N12
Croes-goch Pembks....24 E3
Croes-lan Cerdgn....36 F10
Croesor Gwynd....47 K3
Croesyceiliog Carmth....25 P5
Croesyceiliog Torfn....28 C9
Croft Leics....41 L8
Croft Lincs....53 N10
Croft Warrtn....57 L9
Croftamie Stirlg....84 H6
Crofton Wakefd....59 J9
Croft-on-Tees N York....65 M5
Croftown Highld....106 C5
Crofts Moray....101 K5
Crofts Bank Traffd....57 N9
Crofts of Dipple Moray....101 L4
Crofts of Haddo Abers....102 H7
Crofts of Savoch Abers....103 L4
Crofty Swans....26 C9
Croggan Ag & B....89 P10
Croglin Cumb....71 R6
Croick Highld....106 H4
Cromarty Highld....107 N8
Crombie Fife....86 C5
Cromdale Highld....100 G9
Cromer Herts....33 J10
Cromer Norfk....45 K2
Cromford Derbys....50 H9
Cromhall S Glos....29 J10
Cromor W Isls....111 d2
Cromore W Isls....111 d2
Cromwell Notts....52 B10
Cronberry E Ayrs....77 K6
Crondall Hants....10 C1
Cronton Knows....57 J10
Crook Cumb....63 J3
Crook Dur....65 L1
Crookedholm E Ayrs....76 H4
Crookes Sheff....51 J4
Crookham Nthumb....81 J6
Crookham W Berk....19 P7
Crookham Village Hants....20 C11
Crook Inn Border....78 H4
Crooklands Cumb....63 K5
Crook of Devon P & K....86 C3
Cropredy Oxon....31 L5
Cropston Leics....41 M5
Cropthorne Worcs....30 D5
Cropton N York....66 G9
Cropwell Bishop Notts....41 P1
Cropwell Butler Notts....51 P12
Cros W Isls....111 e1
Crosbost W Isls....111 d2
Crosby Cumb....70 H7
Crosby IoM....56 c5
Crosby N Linc....60 F10
Crosby Sefton....56 G8
Crosby Garret Cumb....63 N1
Crosby Ravensworth Cumb....64 B5
Croscombe Somset....17 N7
Cross Somset....17 K5
Crossaig Ag & B....75 M3
Crossapol Ag & B....88 C7
Cross Ash Mons....28 E5
Cross-at-Hand Kent....12 F2
Crossbost W Isls....111 d2
Crosscanonby Cumb....70 H7
Crossdale Street Norfk....45 K3
Cross Flatts C Brad....58 E6
Crossford Fife....86 C5
Crossford S Lans....77 N3
Crossgatehall E Loth....86 H8
Crossgates E Ayrs....76 F3
Crossgates Fife....86 D5
Cross Gates Leeds....59 J7
Crossgates N York....67 M10
Crossgill Lancs....63 K9
Cross Green Leeds....59 J7
Cross Green Suffk....34 E5
Cross Green Suffk....34 G6
Cross Hands Carmth....26 D6
Crosshands E Ayrs....76 H5
Crosshill Fife....86 E3
Crosshill S Ayrs....76 F9
Crosshouse E Ayrs....76 G4
Cross Houses Shrops....39 K2
Cross in Hand E Susx....12 C5
Cross Inn Cerdgn....36 F8
Cross Inn Cerdgn....37 J7

Cross Keys Ag & B....84 F6
Crosskeys Caerph....27 P9
Crosskirk Highld....110 B2
Cross Lane IoW....9 N9
Cross Lane Head Shrops....39 N3
Crosslee Rens....84 G9
Crossmichael D & G....70 C3
Cross of Jackston Abers....102 G8
Cross o' th' hands Derbys....50 H10
Crossroads Abers....95 J1
Crossroads Abers....95 M3
Cross Street Suffk....35 K2
Crosston Angus....93 N5
Cross Town Ches E....57 N12
Crossway Green Worcs....39 Q8
Crossways Dorset....8 B9
Crosswell Pembks....25 K2
Crosthwaite Cumb....62 H4
Croston Lancs....57 J5
Crostwick Norfk....45 L7
Crouch End Gt Lon....21 L6
Croucheston Wilts....8 F3
Crouch Hill Dorset....7 Q1
Croughton Nhants....31 M7
Crovie Abers....102 G3
Crowan Cnwll....2 F8
Crowborough E Susx....11 P4
Crowborough Warren E Susx....11 P4
Crowcombe Somset....16 F8
Crowdecote Derbys....50 E7
Crowden Derbys....50 E2
Crow Edge Barns....58 F12
Crowell Oxon....20 C4
Crowfield Suffk....35 J5
Crowhill E Loth....87 N7
Crow Hill Herefs....28 H4
Crowhurst E Susx....12 F7
Crowhurst Surrey....11 M1
Crowland Lincs....43 J7
Crowland Suffk....34 G3
Crowlas Cnwll....2 D8
Crowle N Linc....60 D10
Crowle Worcs....30 B3
Crowle Green Worcs....30 B3
Crowmarsh Gifford Oxon....19 Q3
Crown Corner Suffk....35 L3
Crownhill C Plym....5 K8
Crownpits Surrey....10 F2
Crownthorpe Norfk....44 H9
Crowntown Cnwll....2 F9
Crows-an-Wra Cnwll....2 B9
Crowthorne Wokham....20 D9
Crowton Ches W....49 L1
Croxdale Dur....73 M12
Croxden Staffs....50 E11
Croxley Green Herts....20 H4
Croxteth Lpool....56 H9
Croxton Cambs....33 J5
Croxton N Linc....61 J10
Croxton Norfk....44 E11
Croxton Norfk....44 G4
Croxton Staffs....49 P8
Croxton Kerrial Leics....42 B4
Croy Highld....107 N11
Croy N Lans....85 M7
Croyde Devon....14 H4
Croydon Cambs....33 K6
Croydon Gt Lon....21 L9
Crubenmore Highld....99 K10
Cruckmeole Shrops....38 H1
Cruckton Shrops....48 H12
Cruden Bay Abers....103 M7
Crudgington Wrekin....49 L11
Crudie Abers....102 G4
Crudwell Wilts....29 N9
Crumlin Caerph....27 P8
Crumplehorn Cnwll....4 F9
Crumpsall Manch....57 Q8
Crundale Kent....13 K1
Crux Easton Hants....19 M9
Crwbin Carmth....26 C6
Cryers Hill Bucks....20 E4
Crymych Pembks....25 L2
Crynant Neath....26 H7
Crystal Palace Gt Lon....21 M8
Cuaig Highld....105 K10
Cuan Ag & B....89 P12
Cubert Cnwll....2 H4
Cublington Bucks....32 B11
Cublington Herefs....28 E2
Cuckfield W Susx....11 L5
Cucklington Somset....17 R10
Cuckney Notts....51 M6
Cuddesdon Oxon....31 N12
Cuddington Bucks....31 Q11
Cuddington Ches W....49 L2
Cuddington Heath Ches W....49 J6
Cudham Gt Lon....21 N10
Cudliptown Devon....5 L4
Cudnell BCP....8 F7
Cudworth Barns....59 K11
Cudworth Somset....7 K1
Cuffley Herts....21 L3
Cuil Highld....90 D5
Culbokie Highld....107 K9
Culburnie Highld....98 G1
Culcabock Highld....107 L12
Culcharry Highld....100 D5
Culcheth Warrtn....57 M9
Culdrain Abers....101 P8
Culduie Highld....97 K2
Culford Suffk....34 D3
Culgaith Cumb....64 B2
Culham Oxon....19 N2
Culkein Highld....108 B8
Culkein Drumbeg Highld....108 C8
Culkerton Gloucs....29 N7
Cullen Moray....101 N2
Cullercoats N Tyne....73 P6
Cullicudden Highld....107 K9
Cullingworth C Brad....58 E6
Cuillin Hills Highld....96 F5
Cullipool Ag & B....83 L1
Cullivoe Shet....111 k2
Culloden Highld....107 M12
Cullompton Devon....6 D2
Cullompton Services Devon....6 D2
Culm Davy Devon....16 F12
Culmington Shrops....39 J6
Culmstock Devon....16 E12
Culnacraig Highld....106 A2
Culnaightrie D & G....70 C5
Culnaknock Highld....104 G8

Culrain Highld....107 J4
Culross Fife....86 B5
Culroy S Ayrs....76 F8
Culsalmond Abers....102 E8
Culscadden D & G....69 L8
Culshabbin D & G....69 J8
Culswick Shet....111 j4
Cultercullen Abers....103 J9
Cults C Aber....95 P2
Culverstone Green Kent....22 D10
Culverthorpe Lincs....42 E3
Culworth Nhants....31 M5
Culzean Castle & Country Park S Ayrs....76 D8
Cumbernauld N Lans....85 M7
Cumbernauld Village N Lans....85 M7
Cumberworth Lincs....53 N8
Cuminestown Abers....102 G5
Cumledge Border....80 G3
Cummersdale Cumb....71 N5
Cummertrees D & G....71 J3
Cummingston Moray....100 H2
Cumnock E Ayrs....77 J7
Cumnor Oxon....31 L12
Cumrew Cumb....71 Q5
Cumrue D & G....78 H10
Cumwhinton Cumb....71 P5
Cumwhitton Cumb....71 Q5
Cundall N York....65 Q11
Cunninghamhead N Ayrs....76 F3
Cunningsburgh Shet....111 k4
Cupar Fife....93 L11
Cupar Muir Fife....93 L11
Curbar Derbys....50 G6
Curbridge Hants....9 N5
Curbridge Oxon....31 J11
Curdridge Hants....9 N5
Curdworth Warwks....40 F8
Curland Somset....16 H11
Curridge W Berk....19 N6
Currie C Edin....86 E8
Curry Mallet Somset....17 J10
Curry Rivel Somset....17 K10
Curtisden Green Kent....12 E3
Curtisknowle Devon....5 P9
Cury Cnwll....2 G10
Cushnie Abers....102 C11
Cusworth Donc....59 M12
Cutcloy D & G....69 L11
Cutcombe Somset....16 C8
Cuthill Highld....107 M5
Cutnall Green Worcs....39 Q8
Cutsdean Gloucs....30 E7
Cutthorpe Derbys....51 J6
Cuxham Oxon....19 Q2
Cuxton Medway....22 E9
Cuxwold Lincs....52 G4
Cwm Denbgs....56 C12
Cwmafan Neath....26 G9
Cwmaman Rhondd....27 L8
Cwmbach Carmth....25 M4
Cwmbâch Powys....27 N2
Cwmbach Rhondd....27 L8
Cwmbran Torfn....28 C9
Cwmcarn Caerph....27 P9
Cwmcarvan Mons....28 F7
Cwm-cou Cerdgn....36 E11
Cwmdare Rhondd....27 L7
Cwmdu Powys....27 P4
Cwmdu Swans....26 E9
Cwmduad Carmth....25 P3
Cwmfelin Brdgnd....27 J10
Cwmfelin Myr Td....27 M8
Cwmfelin Boeth Carmth....25 L5
Cwmfelinfach Caerph....27 P9
Cwmffrwd Carmth....25 P5
Cwmgiedd Powys....26 H6
Cwmgorse Carmth....26 F6
Cwmgwili Carmth....26 D6
Cwmhiraeth Carmth....25 N2
Cwm Llinau Powys....47 N9
Cwmllynfell Neath....26 G6
Cwmmawr Carmth....26 D6
Cwmparc Rhondd....27 K9
Cwmpengraig Carmth....25 N2
Cwmtillery Blae G....27 P7
Cwm-twrch Isaf Powys....26 G6
Cwm-twrch Uchaf Powys....26 G6
Cwm-y-glo Gwynd....54 H8
Cwmystwyth Cerdgn....37 N6
Cwrt-newydd Cerdgn....36 H10
Cyfarthfa Castle Museum Myr Td....27 L7
Cyffylliog Denbgs....48 C4
Cylibebyll Neath....26 G7
Cymer Neath....27 J9
Cymmer Rhondd....27 L10
Cyncoed Cardif....27 P11
Cynghordy Carmth....37 N11
Cynonville Neath....26 H9
Cynwyd Denbgs....48 C7
Cynwyl Elfed Carmth....25 P4

D

Daccombe Devon....6 B8
Dacre Cumb....71 P9
Dacre N York....58 F3
Dacre Banks N York....58 G2
Daddry Shield Dur....72 F12
Dadford Bucks....31 P6
Dadlington Leics....41 K7
Dafen Carmth....26 C8
Dagenham Gt Lon....21 P6
Daglingworth Gloucs....30 C12
Dagnall Bucks....32 E12
Dail bho Dheas W Isls....111 d1
Dailly S Ayrs....76 E10
Dairsie Fife....93 M11
Dalabrog W Isls....111 a6
Dalavich Ag & B....83 P1
Dalbeattie D & G....70 D4
Dalby IoM....56 b5
Dalby N York....66 F12
Dalcapon P & K....92 E5
Dalchalm Highld....107 Q2
Dalchreichart Highld....98 D6
Dalchrin P & K....91 Q11
Dalcrue P & K....92 F9
Dalditch Devon....6 E6
Dale Pembks....24 E7

Place	County	Page	Grid
Dale Abbey	Derbys	51	K12
Dalelia	Highld	89	P3
Dalgarven	N Ayrs	76	E3
Dalgety Bay	Fife	86	E5
Dalgig	E Ayrs	77	J8
Dalginross	P & K	92	B10
Dalguise	P & K	92	E6
Dalhalvaig	Highld	109	Q5
Dalham	Suffk	34	C4
Daliburgh	W Isls	111	a6
Dalkeith	Mdloth	86	G8
Dallas	Moray	100	H5
Dallinghoo	Suffk	35	L6
Dallington	E Susx	12	D6
Dallington	Nhants	31	Q2
Dalmally	Ag & B	90	G10
Dalmary	Stirlg	85	J4
Dalmellington	E Ayrs	76	H9
Dalmeny	C Edin	86	D6
Dalmore	Highld	107	L8
Dalmuir	W Duns	84	H8
Dalnabreck	Highld	89	P3
Dalnacardoch	P & K	91	Q3
Dalnahaitnach	Highld	99	M5
Dalnaspidal	P & K	91	P2
Dalnawillan Lodge	Highld	110	B7
Dalness	Highld	90	G6
Dalqueich	P & K	86	C2
Dalquhairn	S Ayrs	76	F11
Dalreavoch	Highld	107	M1
Dalry	N Ayrs	76	E2
Dalrymple	E Ayrs	76	F8
Dalserf	S Lans	77	N2
Dalsmeran	Ag & B	75	J9
Dalston	Cumb	71	M5
Dalston	Gt Lon	21	M6
Dalswinton	D & G	78	F10
Dalton	D & G	70	H2
Dalton	N York	65	K6
Dalton	N York	66	B11
Dalton	Nthumb	73	K6
Dalton-in-Furness	Cumb	62	E7
Dalton-le-Dale	Dur	73	P10
Dalton-on-Tees	N York	65	N6
Dalton Piercy	Hartpl	66	C2
Dalveich	Stirlg	91	P10
Dalwhinnie	Highld	99	J11
Dalwood	Devon	6	H3
Damerham	Hants	8	G4
Damgate	Norfk	45	N8
Damnaglaur	D & G	68	F11
Danbury	Essex	22	F3
Danby	N York	66	G6
Danby Wiske	N York	65	N7
Dandaleith	Moray	101	K6
Danderhall	Mdloth	86	G8
Danebridge	Ches E	50	C7
Dane End	Herts	33	K11
Danehill	E Susx	11	N5
Dane Hills	C Leic	41	M6
Dane Street	Kent	23	K11
Danshillock	Abers	102	F4
Danskine	E Loth	87	L8
Darenth	Kent	22	C8
Daresbury	Halton	57	L11
Darfield	Barns	59	K12
Dargate	Kent	23	L10
Dargavel	Rens	84	G8
Darite	Cnwll	4	C7
Darlaston	Wsall	40	C7
Darlaston Green	Wsall	40	C7
Darley	N York	58	G3
Darley Abbey	C Derb	51	J12
Darley Bridge	Derbys	50	H8
Darley Dale	Derbys	50	H7
Darley Green	Solhll	40	F11
Darleyhall	Herts	32	G11
Darley Head	N York	58	G3
Darlingscott	Warwks	30	G6
Darlington	Darltn	65	M5
Darlton	Notts	51	Q6
Darnick	Border	80	D7
Darowen	Powys	47	N10
Darra	Abers	102	F6
Darracott	Devon	14	E8
Darracott	Devon	14	H4
Darras Hall	Nthumb	73	K6
Darrington	Wakefd	59	L9
Darsham	Suffk	35	N3
Darshill	Somset	17	N7
Dartford	Kent	22	B8
Dartford Crossing	Kent	22	C8
Dartington	Devon	5	Q7
Dartmoor National Park	Devon	5	N4
Dartmouth	Devon	6	B11
Darton	Barns	58	H11
Darvel	E Ayrs	77	J4
Darwen	Bl w D	57	M4
Datchet	W & M	20	F7
Datchworth	Herts	33	J11
Daubhill	Bolton	57	M7
Daugh of Kinermony	Moray	101	K7
Dauntsey	Wilts	18	E4
Dava	Highld	100	F7
Davenham	Ches W	49	M2
Daventry	Nhants	31	M2
Davidson's Mains	C Edin	86	E7
Davidstow	Cnwll	4	E3
Davington	D & G	79	K8
Davington Hill	Kent	23	J10
Daviot	Abers	102	G9
Daviot	Highld	99	K2
Daviot House	Highld	99	K2
Davoch of Grange	Moray	101	N5
Davyhulme	Traffd	57	N9
Daw End	Wsall	40	D7
Dawesgreen	Surrey	11	K1
Dawley	Wrekin	39	M1
Dawlish	Devon	6	C7
Dawlish Warren	Devon	6	D7
Daybrook	Notts	51	M10
Daylesford	Gloucs	30	G8
Deal	Kent	23	Q11
Dean	Cumb	70	H9
Dean	Devon	5	P7
Dean	Devon	15	M3
Dean	Hants	9	P4
Dean	Oxon	31	J9
Dean	Somset	17	P7
Dean Bottom	Kent	22	C8
Deanburnhaugh	Border	79	N6
Deancombe	Devon	5	P7
Dean Court	Oxon	31	L11
Deane	Bolton	57	M7
Deane	Hants	19	P10
Deanhead	Kirk	58	D10
Deanland	Dorset	8	E4
Dean Prior	Devon	5	P7
Deanraw	Nthumb	72	E8
Deans	W Loth	86	B8
Deanscales	Cumb	70	H9
Deanshanger	Nhants	31	Q6
Deanshaugh	Moray	101	L5
Deanston	Stirlg	85	M3
Dearham	Cumb	70	H8
Debach	Suffk	35	L6
Debden	Essex	33	N4
Debden	Essex	33	N9
Debenham	Suffk	35	K4
Deblin's Green	Worcs	39	P11
Dechmont	W Loth	86	C7
Dechmont Road	W Loth	86	B8
Deddington	Oxon	31	L8
Dedham	Essex	34	H9
Dedworth	W & M	20	F8
Deene	Nhants	42	D10
Deenethorpe	Nhants	42	D10
Deepcar	Sheff	50	H2
Deeping Gate	C Pete	42	G8
Deeping St James	Lincs	42	G8
Deeping St Nicholas	Lincs	42	H7
Deerhurst	Gloucs	29	M3
Defford	Worcs	30	B5
Defynnog	Powys	27	K4
Deganwy	Conwy	55	L6
Degnish	Ag & B	83	L1
Deighton	C York	59	N5
Deighton	N York	65	P7
Deiniolen	Gwynd	54	H8
Delabole	Cnwll	4	D4
Delamere	Ches W	49	K2
Delfrigs	Abers	103	K10
Dellichurst	Highld	100	G8
Dell Quay	W Susx	10	D9
Delnabo	Moray	100	H11
Delny	Highld	107	M7
Delph	Oldham	58	C11
Delves	Dur	73	K10
Dembleby	Lincs	42	E3
Denaby	Donc	51	L2
Denbigh	Denbgs	48	C3
Denbrae	Fife	93	L11
Denbury	Devon	5	Q6
Denby	Derbys	51	K10
Denby Dale	Kirk	58	G11
Denchworth	Oxon	19	L3
Dendron	Cumb	62	E7
Denfield	P & K	92	E11
Denford	Nhants	32	E2
Dengie	Essex	23	J3
Denham	Bucks	20	G6
Denham	Suffk	34	C5
Denham	Suffk	35	K2
Denham Green	Bucks	20	G6
Denhead	Abers	103	K5
Denhead	Fife	93	N11
Denhead of Gray	C Dund	93	L8
Denholm	Border	80	D9
Denholme	C Brad	58	E7
Denmead	Hants	9	Q5
Denmore	C Aber	103	K11
Dennington	Suffk	35	L4
Denny	Falk	85	N6
Dennyloanhead	Falk	85	N7
Den of Lindores	Fife	93	J11
Denshaw	Oldham	58	C11
Denside of Durris	Abers	95	N3
Densole	Kent	13	N2
Denston	Suffk	34	C6
Denstone	Staffs	50	E11
Denstroude	Kent	23	L10
Dent	Cumb	63	N5
Denton	Cambs	42	G11
Denton	Darltn	65	L4
Denton	E Susx	11	P9
Denton	Kent	13	N1
Denton	Lincs	42	C4
Denton	N York	58	F4
Denton	Nhants	32	B5
Denton	Norfk	45	L11
Denton	Tamesd	50	B2
Denver	Norfk	43	P9
Denwick	Nthumb	81	P10
Deopham	Norfk	44	H9
Deopham Green	Norfk	44	H9
Depden	Suffk	34	C5
Deptford	Gt Lon	21	M7
Deptford	Wilts	18	E12
Derby	C Derb	41	J1
Derby	Devon	15	K5
Derbyhaven	IoM	56	b7
Derculich	P & K	92	D5
Dereham	Norfk	44	G7
Deri	Caerph	27	N8
Derringstone	Kent	23	M12
Derrington	Staffs	40	B3
Derry Hill	Wilts	18	E6
Derrythorpe	N Linc	52	B2
Dersingham	Norfk	44	B4
Dervaig	Ag & B	89	J6
Derwen	Denbgs	48	C5
Derwenlas	Powys	47	L10
Derwent Valley Mills	Derbys	50	H9
Derwent Water	Cumb	71	L10
Desborough	Nhants	42	B12
Desford	Leics	41	L6
Detling	Kent	22	F10
Devauden	Mons	27	F8
Devil's Bridge	Cerdgn	37	M5
Devizes	Wilts	18	E8
Devonport	C Plym	5	K8
Devonside	Clacks	85	Q4
Devoran	Cnwll	2	H7
Devoran & Perran	Cnwll	2	H7
Dewarton	Mdloth	86	H9
Dewlish	Dorset	8	B7
Dewsbury	Kirk	58	G9
Dewsbury Moor	Kirk	58	G9
Deytheur	Powys	48	E11
Dibden	Hants	9	L5
Dibden Purlieu	Hants	9	M6
Dickleburgh	Norfk	35	J1
Didbrook	Gloucs	30	D7
Didcot	Oxon	19	N3
Diddington	Cambs	32	H4
Diddlebury	Shrops	39	K5
Didling	W Susx	10	D6
Didmarton	Gloucs	29	B4
Didsbury	Manch	57	Q9
Digby	Lincs	52	F11
Digg	Highld	104	F8
Diggle	Oldham	58	D11
Digmoor	Lancs	57	J7
Dihewyd	Cerdgn	36	H9
Dilham	Norfk	45	M5
Dilhorne	Staffs	50	C11
Dillington	Cambs	32	G4
Dilston	Nthumb	72	H8
Dilton	Wilts	18	C10
Dilton Marsh	Wilts	18	C10
Dilwyn	Herefs	38	H10
Dinas	Gwynd	46	E4
Dinas Cross	Pembks	24	H2
Dinas-Mawddwy	Gwynd	47	P8
Dinas Powys	V Glam	16	F2
Dinder	Somset	17	N7
Dinedor	Herefs	28	G2
Dingestow	Mons	28	E6
Dingle	Lpool	56	G10
Dingley	Nhants	41	Q9
Dingwall	Highld	107	J9
Dinnet	Abers	94	H3
Dinnington	N u Ty	73	L6
Dinnington	Rothm	51	M4
Dinnington	Somset	17	K12
Dinorwig	Gwynd	54	H8
Dinorwig Slate Landscape	Gwynd	54	H8
Dinton	Bucks	31	Q11
Dinton	Wilts	8	E2
Dinwoodie	D & G	78	H10
Dinworthy	Devon	14	F8
Dipford	Somset	16	G10
Dippen	Ag & B	75	M5
Dippertown	Devon	5	J4
Dippin	N Ayrs	75	Q7
Dipple	Moray	101	L4
Dipple	S Ayrs	76	D10
Diptford	Devon	5	P8
Dipton	Dur	73	K9
Dirleton	E Loth	87	K5
Dirt Pot	Nthumb	72	F10
Diseworth	Leics	41	L3
Dishforth	N York	65	P11
Disley	Ches E	50	C4
Diss	Norfk	35	J1
Distington	Cumb	70	G10
Ditchampton	Wilts	8	G2
Ditcheat	Somset	17	P8
Ditchingham	Norfk	45	M11
Ditchling	E Susx	11	M7
Ditherington	Shrops	49	J11
Ditteridge	Wilts	18	B6
Dittisham	Devon	6	B10
Ditton	Kent	22	E10
Ditton Green	Cambs	33	Q5
Ditton Priors	Shrops	39	L4
Dixton	Mons	28	F6
Dobcross	Oldham	58	C11
Dobwalls	Cnwll	4	F7
Doccombe	Devon	5	Q3
Dochgarroch	Highld	99	J2
Docking	Norfk	44	C3
Docklow	Herefs	39	K10
Dockray	Cumb	71	N10
Doddinghurst	Essex	22	C4
Doddington	Cambs	43	L11
Doddington	Kent	23	H11
Doddington	Lincs	52	C9
Doddington	Nthumb	81	L7
Doddington	Shrops	39	L6
Doddiscombsleigh	Devon	6	B5
Dodd's Green	Ches E	49	L6
Dodford	Nhants	31	N3
Dodford	Worcs	40	C11
Dodington	S Glos	29	K11
Dodington	Somset	16	G7
Dodleston	Ches W	48	G4
Dodside	E Rens	84	H11
Dod's Leigh	Staffs	40	D1
Dodworth	Barns	58	H12
Doe Bank	Birm	40	E7
Dogdyke	Lincs	52	H11
Dogmersfield	Hants	20	C11
Dogsthorpe	C Pete	42	H9
Dolanog	Powys	48	C11
Dolbenmaen	Gwynd	46	H3
Dolfach	Powys	47	P10
Dolfor	Powys	38	C5
Dolgarrog	Conwy	55	L7
Dolgellau	Gwynd	47	M7
Doll	Highld	107	P2
Dollar	Clacks	85	Q4
Dollarfield	Clacks	85	Q4
Dolphin	Flints	48	E2
Dolphinholme	Lancs	63	K10
Dolphinton	S Lans	86	D11
Dolton	Devon	15	K9
Dolwen	Conwy	55	N6
Dolwyddelan	Conwy	55	K10
Domgay	Powys	48	F10
Doncaster	Donc	59	M12
Doncaster North Services	Donc	59	P11
Doncaster Sheffield Airport	Donc	51	P2
Donhead St Andrew	Wilts	8	D3
Donhead St Mary	Wilts	8	D3
Donibristle	Fife	86	E5
Doniford	Somset	16	E7
Donington	Lincs	42	H3
Donington on Bain	Lincs	52	H7
Donington Park Services	Leics	41	L3
Donisthorpe	Leics	40	H5
Donnington	Gloucs	30	F8
Donnington	Shrops	39	L1
Donnington	W Berk	19	M7
Donnington	W Susx	10	D9
Donnington	Wrekin	49	N11
Donnington Wood	Wrekin	49	N11
Donyatt	Somset	17	J12
Doonfoot	S Ayrs	76	F7
Dorback Lodge	Highld	100	G11
Dorchester	Dorset	7	Q5
Dorchester-on-Thames	Oxon	19	P2
Dordon	Warwks	40	H7
Dore	Sheff	50	H5
Dores	Highld	98	H3
Dorking	Surrey	21	J12
Dormansland	Surrey	11	N2
Dormington	Herefs	28	G2
Dormston	Worcs	30	C3
Dorney	Bucks	20	E7
Dornie	Highld	97	M5
Dornoch	Highld	107	N4
Dornock	D & G	71	K3
Dorrery	Highld	110	C5
Dorridge	Solhll	40	F11
Dorrington	Lincs	52	F11
Dorrington	Shrops	39	J2
Dorrington	Shrops	49	N7
Dorsington	Warwks	30	F4
Dorstone	Herefs	28	C1
Dorton	Bucks	31	P10
Douglas	IoM	56	d6
Douglas	S Lans	78	D3
Douglas and Angus	C Dund	93	M8
Douglas Pier	Ag & B	84	D3
Douglastown	Angus	93	M6
Douglas Water	S Lans	78	E2
Douglas West	S Lans	78	D3
Doulting	Somset	17	P7
Dounby	Ork	111	g2
Doune	Highld	106	G3
Doune	Stirlg	85	M3
Dounepark	S Ayrs	76	D11
Dounie	Highld	107	J4
Dousland	Devon	5	L6
Dove Dale	Derbys	50	F9
Dove Holes	Derbys	50	E5
Dovenby	Cumb	70	H8
Dover	Kent	13	P2
Dover Castle	Kent	13	P2
Dovercourt	Essex	35	L9
Doverdale	Worcs	39	Q8
Doveridge	Derbys	40	E1
Doversgreen	Surrey	11	K1
Dowally	P & K	92	E6
Dowdeswell	Gloucs	30	D9
Dowlais	Myr Td	27	M7
Dowland	Devon	15	K9
Dowlish Wake	Somset	17	K1
Down Ampney	Gloucs	18	G2
Downderry	Cnwll	4	G9
Downe	Gt Lon	21	N10
Downend	Gloucs	29	L8
Downend	S Glos	29	H12
Downfield	C Dund	93	L8
Downgate	Cnwll	4	H5
Downham	Essex	22	E4
Downham	Gt Lon	21	M8
Downham	Lancs	63	P12
Downham Market	Norfk	43	P9
Down Hatherley	Gloucs	29	M4
Downhead	Somset	17	N10
Downhead	Somset	17	Q7
Downhill	P & K	92	G9
Downholme	N York	65	K7
Downies	Abers	95	Q3
Downley	Bucks	20	D4
Down St Mary	Devon	15	M10
Downside	Surrey	20	H10
Down Thomas	Devon	5	K9
Downton	Wilts	8	H3
Dowsby	Lincs	42	G4
Doynton	S Glos	17	Q2
Draethen	Caerph	27	P10
Draffan	S Lans	77	N3
Drakeholes	Notts	51	P3
Drakemyre	N Ayrs	76	E2
Drakes Broughton	Worcs	30	B4
Draughton	N York	58	D4
Draughton	Nhants	41	Q11
Drax	N York	59	P8
Draycote	Warwks	41	K12
Draycott	Derbys	41	K2
Draycott	Gloucs	30	F7
Draycott	Somset	17	L6
Draycott in the Clay	Staffs	40	F2
Draycott in the Moors	Staffs	50	C11
Drayton	C Port	9	R6
Drayton	Leics	42	B10
Drayton	Norfk	45	K7
Drayton	Oxon	19	N2
Drayton	Oxon	31	K6
Drayton	Somset	17	K10
Drayton	Worcs	40	B11
Drayton Bassett	Staffs	40	G7
Drayton Beauchamp	Bucks	20	E2
Drayton Manor Park	Staffs	40	G7
Drayton Parslow	Bucks	32	B10
Drayton St Leonard	Oxon	19	P2
Dreen Hill	Pembks	24	G6
Drefach	Carmth	25	N2
Drefach	Carmth	26	D6
Drefach	Cerdgn	36	H10
Dreghorn	N Ayrs	76	F4
Drellingore	Kent	13	N2
Drem	E Loth	87	K6
Dresden	C Stke	50	B11
Drewsteignton	Devon	5	P3
Driffield	E R Yk	60	H3
Driffield	Gloucs	18	F2
Drift	Cnwll	2	C9
Drigg	Cumb	62	C3
Drighlington	Leeds	58	G8
Drimnin	Highld	89	L5
Drimpton	Dorset	7	K2
Drimsallie	Highld	90	C1
Dringhouses	C York	59	N4
Drinkstone	Suffk	34	F5
Drinkstone Green	Suffk	34	F5
Drointon	Staffs	40	D3
Droitwich Spa	Worcs	30	B2
Dron	P & K	92	H11
Dronfield	Derbys	51	J5
Drongan	E Ayrs	76	H7
Dronley	Angus	93	L8
Droop	Dorset	7	Q2
Droxford	Hants	9	Q4
Droylsden	Tamesd	50	B2
Druid	Denbgs	48	B6
Druidston	Pembks	24	F5
Druimarbin	Highld	90	E3
Druimavuic	Ag & B	90	D7
Druimdrishaig	Ag & B	83	L7
Druimindarroch	Highld	97	J11
Drum	Ag & B	83	P7
Drum	P & K	86	C3
Drumalbin	S Lans	78	E2
Drumbeg	Highld	108	C8
Drumblade	Abers	102	D7
Drumbreddon	D & G	68	E9
Drumbuie	Highld	97	K4
Drumburgh	Cumb	71	L4
Drumburn	D & G	70	E5
Drumburn	D & G	70	F3
Drumchapel	C Glas	85	J8
Drumclog	S Lans	77	L4
Drumeldrie	Fife	87	J2
Drumelzier	Border	79	J3
Drumfearn	Highld	97	J6
Drumfrennie	Abers	95	M3
Drumgley	Angus	93	M5
Drumguish	Highld	99	L8
Drumin	Moray	101	J8
Drumjohn	D & G	77	J10
Drumlamford	S Ayrs	68	H8
Drumlasie	Abers	95	K2
Drumleaning	Cumb	71	L5
Drumlemble	Ag & B	75	K8
Drumlithie	Abers	95	N6
Drummoddie	D & G	69	K9
Drummore	D & G	68	F10
Drummuir	Moray	101	M6
Drumnadrochit	Highld	98	G3
Drumnagorrach	Moray	102	C5
Drumoak	Abers	95	N3
Drumpark	D & G	78	E11
Drumrunie	Highld	106	C2
Drumshang	S Ayrs	76	E8
Drumuie	Highld	104	F11
Drumuillie	Highld	99	P5
Drumvaich	Stirlg	85	L3
Drunzie	P & K	86	D1
Drybeck	Cumb	64	C5
Drybridge	Moray	101	N3
Drybridge	N Ayrs	76	F4
Drybrook	Gloucs	28	H5
Dryburgh	Border	80	D7
Dry Doddington	Lincs	42	C2
Dry Drayton	Cambs	33	L4
Drymen	Stirlg	84	H5
Drymuir	Abers	103	J6
Drynoch	Highld	96	E4
Dubford	Abers	102	G3
Duchally	Highld	108	G11
Ducklington	Oxon	31	J11
Duddenhoe End	Essex	33	M9
Duddingston	C Edin	86	F7
Duddington	Nhants	42	E9
Duddlestone	Somset	16	H11
Duddo	Nthumb	81	K6
Duddon	Ches W	49	K3
Dudleston	Shrops	48	G7
Dudleston Heath	Shrops	48	G8
Dudley	Dudley	40	C9
Dudley	N Tyne	73	M6
Dudley Port	Sandw	40	C8
Dudsbury	Dorset	8	F7
Duffield	Derbys	51	J11
Duffryn	Neath	26	H9
Dufftown	Moray	101	L7
Duffus	Moray	101	J3
Dufton	Cumb	64	C3
Duggleby	N York	60	F2
Duirinish	Highld	97	L4
Duisdalemore	Highld	97	J7
Duisky	Highld	90	D2
Dukestown	Blae G	27	N6
Duke Street	Suffk	34	H8
Dukinfield	Tamesd	50	C2
Dulcote	Somset	17	N7
Dulford	Devon	6	E2
Dull	P & K	92	B6
Dullatur	N Lans	85	M7
Dullingham	Cambs	33	Q5
Dulnain Bridge	Highld	99	P4
Duloe	Bed	32	G5
Duloe	Cnwll	4	F8
Dulsie Bridge	Highld	100	E7
Dulverton	Somset	16	C9
Dulwich	Gt Lon	21	M8
Dumbarton	W Duns	84	G7
Dumbleton	Gloucs	30	D7
Dumfries	D & G	70	F1
Dumgoyne	Stirlg	85	J6
Dummer	Hants	19	P10
Dumpton	Kent	23	Q9
Dun	Angus	95	L9
Dunalastair	P & K	91	Q5
Dunan	Highld	96	G4
Dunan	P & K	91	L5
Dunaverty	Ag & B	75	K10
Dunball	Somset	17	J7
Dunbar	E Loth	87	M6
Dunbeath	Highld	110	D9
Dunbeg	Ag & B	90	B9
Dunblane	Stirlg	85	N3
Dunbog	Fife	93	K11
Duncanston	Highld	107	J10
Duncanstone	Abers	102	D9
Dunchideock	Devon	6	B5
Dunchurch	Warwks	41	L12
Duncow	D & G	78	F11
Duncrievie	P & K	86	D1
Duncton	W Susx	10	F6
Dundee	C Dund	93	M9
Dundee Airport	C Dund	93	L9
Dundon	Somset	17	L9
Dundonald	S Ayrs	76	F5
Dundonnell	Highld	106	B5
Dundraw	Cumb	71	K5
Dundreggan	Highld	98	D6
Dundrennan	D & G	70	C6
Dundry	N Som	17	N3
Dunecht	Abers	102	G12
Dunfermline	Fife	86	C5
Dunfield	Gloucs	18	G2
Dungavel	S Lans	77	L4
Dungeness	Kent	13	L6
Dunham Massey	Traffd	57	N10
Dunham-on-the-Hill	Ches W	49	J2
Dunham-on-Trent	Notts	52	B8
Dunhampton	Worcs	39	Q8
Dunham Town	Traffd	57	N10
Dunham Woodhouses	Traffd	57	N10
Dunholme	Lincs	52	E7
Dunino	Fife	93	P12
Dunipace	Falk	85	N6
Dunkeld	P & K	92	F7
Dunkerton	BaNES	17	Q4
Dunkeswell	Devon	6	F2
Dunkeswick	N York	58	H5
Dunkirk	Kent	23	L11

Place	County	Page	Grid
Dunkirk	S Glos	18	B4
Dunk's Green	Kent	22	C10
Dunlappie	Angus	95	K8
Dunley	Worcs	39	P8
Dunlop	E Ayrs	76	G2
Dunmaglass	Highld	98	H5
Dunmore	Falk	85	P5
Dunnet	Highld	110	E2
Dunnichen	Angus	93	N6
Dunning	P & K	92	F11
Dunnington	C York	59	P4
Dunnington	E R Yk	61	K4
Dunnington	Warwks	30	E4
Dunoon	Ag & B	84	C7
Dunphail	Moray	100	F5
Dunragit	D & G	68	F7
Duns	Border	80	G4
Dunsby	Lincs	42	F5
Dunscore	D & G	78	E11
Dunscroft	Donc	59	P11
Dunsdale	R & Cl	66	E4
Dunsden Green	Oxon	20	B7
Dunsdon	Devon	14	F9
Dunsfold	Surrey	10	G3
Dunsford	Devon	5	Q3
Dunshalt	Fife	86	F1
Dunshillock	Abers	103	K5
Dunsill	Notts	51	L8
Dunsley	N York	67	J5
Dunsley	Staffs	39	Q5
Dunsmore	Bucks	20	D3
Dunsop Bridge	Lancs	63	M11
Dunstable	C Beds	32	E11
Dunstall	Staffs	40	F4
Dunstan	Nthumb	81	Q9
Dunster	Somset	16	D7
Duns Tew	Oxon	31	L8
Dunston	Gatesd	73	M8
Dunston	Lincs	52	F10
Dunston	Norfk	45	K9
Dunston	Staffs	40	B4
Dunstone	Devon	5	M9
Dunstone	Devon	5	P5
Dunsville	Donc	59	N11
Dunswell	E R Yk	61	J7
Dunsyre	S Lans	86	C11
Dunterton	Devon	4	H4
Duntisbourne Abbots	Gloucs	29	N7
Duntisbourne Rouse	Gloucs	29	P7
Duntish	Dorset	7	Q2
Duntocher	W Duns	84	H8
Dunton	Bucks	32	B11
Dunton	C Beds	33	J7
Dunton	Norfk	44	E4
Dunton Bassett	Leics	41	M8
Dunton Green	Kent	21	P11
Duntulm	Highld	104	F7
Dunure	S Ayrs	76	E8
Dunvant	Swans	26	D9
Dunvegan	Highld	104	C11
Dunwich	Suffk	35	P3
Durgan	Cnwll	2	H9
Durgates	E Susx	12	D4
Durham	Dur	73	M11
Durham Cathedral	Dur	73	M11
Durham Services	Dur	73	N12
Durham Tees Valley Airport S on T		65	P5
Durisdeer	D & G	78	E8
Durisdeermill	D & G	78	E7
Durleigh	Somset	16	H8
Durley	Hants	9	N4
Durley	Wilts	19	J7
Durley Street	Hants	9	N4
Durlock	Kent	23	P10
Durlock	Kent	23	P9
Durness	Highld	108	G3
Durno	Abers	102	F9
Duror	Highld	90	D5
Durran	Ag & B	83	Q7
Durrington	W Susx	10	H8
Durrington	Wilts	18	H10
Dursley	Gloucs	29	K8
Dursley Cross	Gloucs	29	J5
Durston	Somset	16	H9
Durweston	Dorset	8	C6
Duston	Nhants	31	Q2
Duthil	Highld	99	P4
Dutton	Ches W	57	L11
Duxford	Cambs	33	M7
Duxford	Oxon	19	L2
Duxford IWM	Cambs	33	M7
Dwygyfylchi	Conwy	55	K6
Dwyran	IoA	54	F8
Dyce	C Aber	103	J11
Dyfatty	Carmth	26	B8
Dyffryn Ardudwy	Gwynd	47	J6
Dyffryn Cellwen	Neath	27	J6
Dyke	Lincs	42	F5
Dyke	Moray	100	F4
Dykehead	Angus	93	J5
Dykehead	Angus	94	F9
Dykehead	N Lans	85	P10
Dykehead	Stirlg	85	K4
Dykelands	Abers	95	L8
Dykends	Angus	93	J4
Dykeside	Abers	102	F6
Dykes of Gray	C Dund	93	L8
Dymchurch	Kent	13	L4
Dymock	Gloucs	29	J3
Dyrham	S Glos	17	Q2
Dysart	Fife	86	G4
Dyserth	Denbgs	56	C11

E

Place	County	Page	Grid
Eagland Hill	Lancs	62	H12
Eagle	Lincs	52	C9
Eaglesfield	Cumb	70	H9
Eaglesfield	D & G	71	K1
Eaglesham	E Rens	85	J11
Eagley	Bolton	57	N6
Eakring	Notts	51	P8
Ealand	N Linc	60	D10
Ealing	Gt Lon	21	J7
Eals	Nthumb	72	C9
Eamont Bridge	Cumb	71	Q9
Earby	Lancs	58	B5
Earcroft	Bl w D	57	M4
Eardington	Shrops	39	N4
Eardisland	Herefs	38	H9
Eardisley	Herefs	38	F11
Eardiston	Shrops	48	G9
Eardiston	Worcs	39	M8
Earith	Cambs	33	L2
Earlestown	St Hel	57	L9
Earley	Wokham	20	C8
Earlham	Norfk	45	K8
Earlish	Highld	104	E9
Earls Barton	Nhants	32	C4
Earls Colne	Essex	34	E10
Earls Common	Worcs	30	C3
Earl's Croome	Worcs	29	M1
Earlsdon	Covtry	40	H10
Earlsferry	Fife	87	J3
Earlsfield	Gt Lon	21	K8
Earlsford	Abers	102	H8
Earlsheaton	Kirk	58	H9
Earl Shilton	Leics	41	L7
Earl Soham	Suffk	35	L4
Earl Sterndale	Derbys	50	E7
Earlston	Border	80	D6
Earlston	E Ayrs	76	G4
Earlswood	Surrey	21	L12
Earlswood	Warwks	40	E11
Earnley	W Susx	10	D10
Earsdon	N Tyne	73	N6
Earsham	Norfk	45	M11
Eartham	W Susx	10	F8
Easby	N York	66	E6
Easdale	Ag & B	89	P11
Easebourne	W Susx	10	E5
Easenhall	Warwks	41	L10
Eashing	Surrey	10	F2
Easington	Bucks	31	P11
Easington	Dur	73	P11
Easington	E R Yk	61	P9
Easington	R & Cl	66	G4
Easington Colliery	Dur	73	Q11
Easington Lane	Sundld	73	P10
Easingwold	N York	59	M1
Eassie and Nevay	Angus	93	L6
East Aberthaw	V Glam	16	D3
East Allington	Devon	5	P10
East Anstey	Devon	15	P6
East Ardsley	Leeds	58	H8
East Ashey	IoW	9	P9
East Ashling	W Susx	10	D8
East Ayton	N York	67	L9
East Barkwith	Lincs	52	G7
East Barming	Kent	22	E11
East Barnby	N York	66	H5
East Barnet	Gt Lon	21	L4
East Barns	E Loth	87	N7
East Barsham	Norfk	44	F4
East Beckham	Norfk	45	J3
East Bedfont	Gt Lon	20	H8
East Bergholt	Suffk	34	H9
East Bilney	Norfk	44	F6
East Blatchington	E Susx	11	N8
East Boldon	S Tyne	73	P8
East Boldre	Hants	9	L7
Eastbourne	Darltn	65	N5
Eastbourne	E Susx	12	C9
East Bradenham	Norfk	44	F8
East Brent	Somset	17	J6
Eastbridge	Suffk	35	P4
East Bridgford	Notts	51	P11
East Buckland	Devon	15	L6
East Budleigh	Devon	6	E6
Eastburn	C Brad	58	D5
Eastbury	W Berk	19	K5
East Butterwick	N Linc	52	B3
Eastby	N York	58	D4
East Calder	W Loth	86	C8
East Carleton	Norfk	45	K9
East Carlton	Leeds	58	G5
East Carlton	Nhants	42	B11
East Chaldon	Dorset	8	B10
East Challow	Oxon	19	L3
East Charleton	Devon	5	P10
East Chelborough	Dorset	7	M2
East Chiltington	E Susx	11	M7
East Chinnock	Somset	17	L12
East Chisenbury	Wilts	18	G9
Eastchurch	Kent	23	J8
East Clandon	Surrey	20	G11
East Claydon	Bucks	31	Q8
East Coker	Somset	7	M1
Eastcombe	Gloucs	29	M7
East Compton	Somset	17	N7
East Cornworthy	Devon	6	B10
Eastcote	Gt Lon	20	H6
Eastcote	Nhants	31	P4
Eastcote	Solhll	40	G10
Eastcott	Wilts	18	F9
East Cottingwith	E R Yk	60	C6
Eastcourt	Wilts	19	J8
East Cowes	IoW	9	N8
East Cowick	E R Yk	59	P9
East Cowton	N York	65	N6
East Cranmore	Somset	17	P7
East Dean	E Susx	12	C9
East Dean	Gloucs	28	H5
East Dean	Hants	9	J3
East Dean	W Susx	10	E7
East Drayton	Notts	51	Q6
East Dulwich	Gt Lon	21	M8
East Dundry	N Som	17	N3
East Ella	C KuH	60	H8
Eastend	Essex	22	H5
East End	Hants	9	L7
East End	Hants	19	M8
East End	Kent	12	G3
East End	Oxon	31	K10
East End	Somset	17	P6
Easter Balmoral	Abers	94	E3
Easter Compton	S Glos	28	G11
Easter Dalziel	Highld	107	M10
Eastergate	W Susx	10	F8
Easterhouse	C Glas	85	L9
Easter Howgate	Mdloth	86	F9
Easter Kinkell	Highld	107	J10
Easter Moniack	Highld	98	H1
Eastern Green	Covtry	40	H10
Easter Ord	Abers	95	N2
Easter Pitkierie	Fife	87	K1
Easter Skeld	Shet	111	k4
Easter Softlaw	Border	80	G7
Easterton	Wilts	18	F9
East Everleigh	Wilts	18	H9
East Farleigh	Kent	22	E11
East Farndon	Nhants	41	Q9
East Ferry	Lincs	52	B4
Eastfield	N Lans	85	P9
Eastfield	N York	67	M10
East Fortune	E Loth	87	K6
East Garston	W Berk	19	L5
Eastgate	Dur	72	G12
Eastgate	Lincs	42	F6
Eastgate	Norfk	45	J5
East Goscote	Leics	41	N5
East Grafton	Wilts	19	J8
East Grimstead	Wilts	9	J2
East Grinstead	W Susx	11	N3
East Guldeford	E Susx	12	H6
East Haddon	Nhants	31	P1
East Hagbourne	Oxon	19	N3
East Halton	N Linc	61	K9
East Ham	Gt Lon	21	N6
Easthampton	Herefs	38	H9
East Hanney	Oxon	19	M3
East Hanningfield	Essex	22	F3
East Hardwick	Wakefd	59	L9
East Harling	Norfk	44	G11
East Harlsey	N York	65	Q7
East Harnham	Wilts	8	G2
East Harptree	BaNES	17	N5
East Harting	W Susx	10	C6
East Hatch	Wilts	8	D2
East Hatley	Cambs	33	J6
East Hauxwell	N York	65	L8
East Haven	Angus	93	N8
East Heckington	Lincs	42	H2
East Hedleyhope	Dur	73	K11
East Helmsdale	Highld	110	B11
East Hendred	Oxon	19	M3
East Heslerton	N York	67	K11
East Hoathly	E Susx	11	Q6
East Holme	Dorset	8	D9
East Horrington	Somset	17	N6
East Horsley	Surrey	20	H11
East Howe	BCP	8	F8
East Huntspill	Somset	17	J7
East Ilsley	W Berk	19	N5
Eastington	Devon	15	M9
Eastington	Gloucs	29	K7
Eastington	Gloucs	30	F10
East Keal	Lincs	53	L10
East Kennett	Wilts	18	G7
East Keswick	Leeds	59	J5
East Kilbride	S Lans	85	K11
East Kirkby	Lincs	53	K10
East Knighton	Dorset	8	B9
East Knoyle	Wilts	8	C2
East Lambrook	Somset	17	L11
Eastlands	D & G	70	D2
East Langdon	Kent	13	P2
East Langton	Leics	41	Q8
East Lavant	W Susx	10	D8
East Lavington	W Susx	10	F6
East Layton	N York	65	L5
Eastleach Martin	Gloucs	30	G12
Eastleach Turville	Gloucs	30	G11
East Leake	Notts	41	M3
Eastleigh	Devon	14	H6
Eastleigh	Hants	9	M4
East Lexham	Norfk	44	E6
Eastling	Kent	23	J11
East Linton	E Loth	87	L6
East Lockinge	Oxon	19	M4
East Lound	N Linc	52	B4
East Lulworth	Dorset	8	C10
East Lutton	N York	60	G1
East Lydford	Somset	17	N9
East Malling	Kent	22	E11
East Marden	W Susx	10	D7
East Markham	Notts	51	Q6
East Martin	Hants	8	F4
East Marton	N York	58	B4
East Meon	Hants	10	B5
East Mersea	Essex	23	K1
East Midlands Airport	Leics	41	K3
East Molesey	Surrey	21	J9
East Morden	Dorset	8	D8
East Morton	C Brad	58	E6
East Morton	N York	58	E8
East Ness	N York	66	F10
Eastney	C Port	9	Q7
Eastnor	Herefs	29	K2
East Norton	Leics	42	B9
Eastoft	N Linc	60	D10
East Ogwell	Devon	6	Q6
Easton	Cambs	32	G3
Easton	Devon	5	P3
Easton	Dorset	7	Q8
Easton	Hants	9	N2
Easton	Lincs	42	D5
Easton	Norfk	45	J7
Easton	Somset	17	M6
Easton	Suffk	35	L5
Easton	Wilts	18	D6
Easton Grey	Wilts	18	C4
Easton-in-Gordano	N Som	17	M2
Easton Maudit	Nhants	32	C5
Easton-on-the-Hill	Nhants	42	E8
Easton Royal	Wilts	18	H8
East Orchard	Dorset	8	C4
East Peckham	Kent	12	D1
East Pennard	Somset	17	N8
East Portlemouth	Devon	5	P11
East Prawle	Devon	5	Q11
East Preston	W Susx	10	H9
East Putford	Devon	14	G8
East Quantoxhead	Somset	16	F7
East Rainton	Sundld	73	N10
East Ravendale	NE Lin	52	H4
East Raynham	Norfk	44	E5
Eastrea	Cambs	43	J10
Eastriggs	D & G	71	L3
East Rigton	Leeds	59	J5
Eastrington	E R Yk	60	D8
Eastrop	Swindn	18	H3
East Rounton	N York	65	Q6
East Rudham	Norfk	44	D5
East Runton	Norfk	45	K2
East Ruston	Norfk	45	M5
Eastry	Kent	23	P11
East Saltoun	E Loth	87	J8
East Sheen	Gt Lon	21	K8
East Shefford	W Berk	19	L6
East Stockwith	Lincs	52	B5
East Stoke	Dorset	8	C9
East Stoke	Notts	51	Q10
East Stour	Dorset	8	B3
East Stourmouth	Kent	23	N10
East Stowford	Devon	15	L6
East Stratton	Hants	19	P11
East Studdal	Kent	23	P12
East Taphouse	Cnwll	4	E7
East-the-Water	Devon	14	H6
East Thirston	Nthumb	73	L2
East Tilbury	Thurr	22	D7
East Tisted	Hants	10	B4
East Torrington	Lincs	52	G6
East Tuddenham	Norfk	44	H7
East Tytherley	Hants	9	K2
East Tytherton	Wilts	18	E6
East Village	Devon	15	P10
Eastville	Bristl	17	N2
Eastville	Lincs	53	L11
East Walton	Norfk	44	C6
East Week	Devon	5	N2
Eastwell	Leics	41	Q2
East Wellow	Hants	9	K4
East Wemyss	Fife	86	G3
East Whitburn	W Loth	85	Q9
Eastwick	Herts	21	N1
East Wickham	Gt Lon	21	P7
East Williamston	Pembks	25	J7
East Winch	Norfk	44	B6
East Winterslow	Wilts	9	J1
East Wittering	W Susx	10	C9
East Witton	N York	65	K9
Eastwood	Notts	51	L10
Eastwood	Sthend	22	G6
East Woodburn	Nthumb	72	G4
East Woodhay	Hants	19	L8
East Worldham	Hants	10	C3
East Worthing	W Susx	11	J8
East Wretham	Norfk	44	F11
Eathorpe	Warwks	31	K1
Eaton	Ches E	49	Q3
Eaton	Ches W	49	L3
Eaton	Leics	42	B4
Eaton	Norfk	45	K8
Eaton	Notts	51	P5
Eaton	Oxon	31	K12
Eaton	Shrops	39	J4
Eaton Bray	C Beds	32	D11
Eaton Constantine	Shrops	39	L2
Eaton Green	C Beds	32	D11
Eaton Hastings	Oxon	19	J2
Eaton Mascott	Shrops	39	K2
Eaton Socon	Cambs	32	G5
Eaton upon Tern	Shrops	49	M10
Ebberston	N York	67	K10
Ebbesborne Wake	Wilts	8	E3
Ebbw Vale	Blae G	27	N6
Ebchester	Dur	73	K9
Ebford	Devon	6	D5
Ebley	Gloucs	29	L7
Ebnal	Ches W	49	J6
Ebrington	Gloucs	30	F6
Ecclaw	Border	87	P8
Ecclefechan	D & G	71	K1
Eccles	Border	80	G6
Eccles	Kent	22	E10
Eccles	Salfd	57	P8
Ecclesall	Sheff	50	H4
Ecclesfield	Sheff	51	J3
Eccleshall	Staffs	49	P9
Eccleshill	C Brad	58	F6
Ecclesmachan	W Loth	86	C7
Eccles Road	Norfk	44	G11
Eccleston	Ches W	49	H3
Eccleston	Lancs	57	K5
Eccleston	St Hel	57	J9
Echt	Abers	95	M2
Eckford	Border	80	F8
Eckington	Derbys	51	K5
Eckington	Worcs	29	N1
Ecton	Nhants	32	B4
Edale	Derbys	50	E4
Eday	Ork	111	h1
Eday Airport	Ork	111	h1
Edburton	W Susx	11	K7
Edderton	Highld	107	L5
Eddleston	Border	86	F11
Eddlewood	S Lans	85	M11
Edenbridge	Kent	11	N2
Edenfield	Lancs	57	P5
Edenhall	Cumb	71	Q8
Edenham	Lincs	42	F6
Eden Park	Gt Lon	21	M9
Eden Project	Cnwll	3	M5
Edensor	Derbys	50	G6
Edentaggart	Ag & B	84	F4
Edenthorpe	Donc	59	N11
Edern	Gwynd	46	E4
Edgbaston	Birm	40	D9
Edgcott	Bucks	31	P9
Edgcott	Somset	15	P4
Edge	Gloucs	29	L6
Edgefield	Norfk	44	H4
Edgefield Green	Norfk	44	H4
Edgerton	Kirk	58	F10
Edgeworth	Gloucs	29	N7
Edgmond	Wrekin	49	N10
Edgton	Shrops	38	H5
Edgware	Gt Lon	21	J5
Edgworth	Bl w D	57	N5
Edinbane	Highld	104	D11
Edinburgh	C Edin	86	F7
Edinburgh Airport	C Edin	86	D7
Edinburgh Castle	C Edin	86	F7
Edinburgh Old & New Town C Edin		86	F7
Edinburgh Royal Botanic Gardens	C Edin	86	F7
Edinburgh Zoo RZSS	C Edin	86	E7
Edingale	Staffs	40	G4
Edingham	D & G	70	D3
Edingley	Notts	51	P9
Edingthorpe	Norfk	45	M4
Edingthorpe Green	Norfk	45	M4
Edington	Border	81	J3
Edington	Nthumb	73	K4
Edington	Somset	17	K8
Edington	Wilts	18	D9
Edingworth	Somset	17	J5
Edithmead	Somset	17	J6
Edith Weston	Rutlnd	42	D8
Edlesborough	Bucks	32	D11
Edlingham	Nthumb	81	M11
Edlington	Lincs	52	H8
Edmondsham	Dorset	8	F5
Edmondsley	Dur	73	M10
Edmondthorpe	Leics	42	C6
Edmonton	Gt Lon	21	M5
Edmundbyers	Dur	72	H10
Ednam	Border	80	G6
Edradynate	P & K	92	D5
Edrom	Border	80	H3
Edstaston	Shrops	49	K8
Edstone	Warwks	30	F2
Edwalton	Notts	41	N1
Edwinstowe	Notts	51	N7
Edworth	C Beds	32	H8
Edwyn Ralph	Herefs	39	M9
Edzell	Angus	95	K8
Edzell Woods	Abers	95	K7
Efail-fach	Neath	26	G9
Efail Isaf	Rhondd	27	M11
Efailnewydd	Gwynd	46	F4
Efailwen	Carmth	25	K4
Efenechtyd	Denbgs	48	C4
Effgill	D & G	79	L9
Effingham	Surrey	20	H11
Egerton	Bolton	57	N6
Egerton	Kent	12	H1
Eggborough	N York	59	M9
Eggbuckland	C Plym	5	K8
Eggesford	Devon	15	M9
Eggington	C Beds	32	D10
Egginton	Derbys	40	H2
Eggleston	Dur	64	H3
Egham	Surrey	20	G8
Egleton	Rutlnd	42	C8
Eglingham	Nthumb	81	M9
Egloshayle	Cnwll	3	M2
Egloskerry	Cnwll	4	G3
Eglwysbach	Conwy	55	L7
Eglwys Cross	Wrexhm	49	J7
Eglwyswrw	Pembks	25	K2
Egmanton	Notts	51	Q7
Egremont	Cumb	70	G12
Egremont	Wirral	56	G9
Egton	N York	66	H6
Egton Bridge	N York	66	H6
Egypt	Bucks	20	F6
Eigg	Highld	96	F11
Eight Ash Green	Essex	34	F10
Eilanreach	Highld	97	L6
Eilean Donan Castle	Highld	97	M5
Eisgein	W Isls	111	d3
Eishken	W Isls	111	d3
Elan Valley	Powys	37	P7
Elan Village	Powys	37	Q7
Elberton	S Glos	28	H10
Elburton	C Plym	5	L9
Elcombe	Swindn	18	G5
Eldersfield	Worcs	29	L3
Elderslie	Rens	84	H9
Eldon	Dur	65	M2
Elerch	Cerdgn	37	L4
Elfhill	Abers	95	N5
Elford	Staffs	40	F5
Elgin	Moray	101	J3
Elgol	Highld	96	G6
Elham	Kent	13	M2
Elie	Fife	87	K3
Elim	IoA	54	E5
Eling	Hants	9	L5
Elkesley	Notts	51	P6
Elkstone	Gloucs	29	N6
Ella	Abers	102	E4
Ellacombe	Torbay	6	C9
Elland	Calder	58	E9
Ellary	Ag & B	83	L7
Ellastone	Staffs	50	E11
Ellel	Lancs	63	J10
Ellemford	Border	87	N9
Ellenabeich	Ag & B	89	P11
Ellenhall	Staffs	49	Q9
Ellen's Green	Surrey	10	H3
Ellerbeck	N York	66	B8
Ellerby	N York	66	H5
Ellerdine Heath	Wrekin	49	L10
Elleric	Ag & B	90	E6
Ellerker	E R Yk	60	F8
Ellerton	E R Yk	60	C6
Ellerton	N York	65	M7
Ellesborough	Bucks	20	D3
Ellesmere	Shrops	48	H8
Ellesmere Port	Ches W	56	H12
Ellingham	Norfk	45	N10
Ellingham	Nthumb	81	N8
Ellingstring	N York	65	L10
Ellington	Cambs	32	G3
Ellington	Nthumb	73	M3
Elliots Green	Somset	18	B10
Ellisfield	Hants	19	Q10
Ellishader	Highld	104	G8
Ellistown	Leics	41	K5
Ellon	Abers	103	K8
Ellonby	Cumb	71	N8
Elloughton	E R Yk	60	G8
Ellwood	Gloucs	28	G7
Elm	Cambs	43	M8
Elmbridge	Worcs	30	B1
Elmdon	Essex	33	M8
Elmdon	Solhll	40	F10
Elmer	W Susx	10	F9
Elmers End	Gt Lon	21	M9
Elmer's Green	Lancs	57	J7
Elmesthorpe	Leics	41	L8
Elmhurst	Staffs	40	E5
Elmley Castle	Worcs	30	N1
Elmley Lovett	Worcs	39	Q8
Elmore	Gloucs	29	K6
Elmore Back	Gloucs	29	K5
Elm Park	Gt Lon	21	Q6
Elmsett	Suffk	34	H7
Elmstead Market	Essex	34	H10
Elmsted	Kent	13	L2
Elmstone	Kent	23	N10
Elmstone Hardwicke	Gloucs	29	M4
Elmswell	E R Yk	60	G3
Elmswell	Suffk	34	G4
Elmton	Derbys	51	L6
Elphin	Highld	108	E12
Elphinstone	E Loth	86	H8
Elrick	Abers	95	N1
Elrig	D & G	69	J9
Elrington	Nthumb	72	F8
Elsdon	Nthumb	72	H2
Elsenham	Essex	33	N10
Elsfield	Oxon	31	M11
Elsham	N Linc	60	H10
Elsing	Norfk	44	H6
Elslack	N York	58	B4
Elson	Hants	9	P7
Elsrickle	S Lans	86	C12
Elstead	Surrey	10	E2

170 Elsted – Foleshill

Elsted W Susx 10 D6
Elsthorpe Lincs 42 F5
Elston Notts 51 Q10
Elstow Bed 32 F7
Elstree Herts 21 J4
Elstronwick E R Yk 61 L7
Elswick Lancs 56 H2
Elswick N u Ty 73 M7
Elsworth Cambs 33 K4
Elterwater Cumb 62 G2
Eltham Gt Lon 21 N8
Eltisley Cambs 33 J5
Elton Cambs 42 F10
Elton Ches W 49 J1
Elton Derbys 50 G8
Elton Herefs 39 J7
Elton S on T 65 P4
Elton-on-the-Hill Notts 51 Q11
Eltringham Nthumb 73 J8
Elvanfoot S Lans 78 F5
Elvaston Derbys 41 K2
Elveden Suffk 34 D2
Elvetham Heath Hants 20 C11
Elvingston E Loth 87 J7
Elvington C York 60 C5
Elvington Kent 23 P12
Elwick Hartpl 66 C2
Elworth Ches E 49 N3
Elworthy Somset 16 E8
Ely Cambs 33 N1
Ely Cardif 16 F2
Emberton M Keyn 32 C6
Embleton Cumb 71 J9
Embleton Nthumb 81 P9
Embo Highld 107 N4
Emborough Somset 17 N6
Embo Street Highld 107 N4
Embsay N York 58 D4
Emery Down Hants 9 K6
Emley Kirk 58 G10
Emmington Oxon 20 C3
Emneth Norfk 43 M8
Emneth Hungate Norfk 43 N8
Empingham Rutlnd 42 D8
Empshott Hants 10 C4
Emsworth Hants 10 C8
Enborne W Berk 19 M7
Enborne Row W Berk 19 M7
Enderby Leics 41 M7
Endmoor Cumb 63 K5
Endon Staffs 50 B9
Endon Bank Staffs 50 B9
Enfield Gt Lon 21 M4
Enfield Lock Gt Lon 21 M4
Enfield Wash Gt Lon 21 M4
Enford Wilts 18 G9
Engine Common S Glos 29 J11
Englefield W Berk 19 Q6
Englefield Green Surrey 20 F8
English Bicknor Gloucs 28 G5
Englishcombe BaNES 17 Q4
English Frankton Shrops 49 J9
Enham Alamein Hants 19 L10
Enmore Somset 16 H8
Enmore Green Dorset 8 C3
Ennerdale Bridge Cumb 70 H11
Enochdhu P & K 92 F3
Ensay Ag & B 88 H6
Ensbury BCP 8 F8
Ensdon Shrops 48 H11
Enstone Oxon 31 J8
Enterkinfoot D & G 78 E7
Enville Staffs 39 P5
Eochar W Isls 111 a5
Eòlaigearraidh W Isls 111 a6
Eoligarry W Isls 111 a6
Epney Gloucs 29 K6
Epperstone Notts 51 P10
Epping Essex 21 P3
Epping Green Essex 21 N3
Epping Upland Essex 21 N3
Eppleby N York 65 L5
Epsom Surrey 21 K10
Epwell Oxon 31 J6
Epworth N Linc 52 A3
Erbistock Wrexhm 48 G7
Erdington Birm 40 E8
Eridge Green E Susx 12 B3
Erines Ag & B 83 N7
Eriska Ag & B 90 C7
Eriskay W Isls 111 b6
Eriswell Suffk 34 C2
Erith Gt Lon 21 P7
Erlestoke Wilts 18 E9
Ermington Devon 5 M9
Erpingham Norfk 45 K4
Errogie Highld 98 H5
Errol P & K 93 J10
Erskine Rens 84 H8
Erskine Bridge Rens 84 H8
Ervie D & G 68 D5
Erwarton Suffk 35 K9
Erwood Powys 38 C12
Eryholme N York 65 N6
Eryrys Denbgs 48 E4
Escomb Dur 65 L2
Escrick N York 59 N5
Esgairgeiliog Powys 47 M9
Esh Dur 73 L11
Esher Surrey 21 J9
Eshott Nthumb 73 L2
Esh Winning Dur 73 L11
Eskadale Highld 98 F2
Eskbank Mdloth 86 G8
Eskdale Green Cumb 62 D3
Eskdalemuir D & G 79 L8
Esprick Lancs 56 H2
Essendine Rutlnd 42 F7
Essendon Herts 21 L2
Essich Highld 99 J2
Essington Staffs 40 C6
Esslemont Abers 103 J8
Eston R & Cl 66 D4
Etal Nthumb 81 K6
Etchilhampton Wilts 18 F8
Etchingham E Susx 12 E5
Etchinghill Kent 13 M3
Etchinghill Staffs 40 D4
Eton W & M 20 F7
Eton Wick W & M 20 F7
Etruria C Stke 49 Q6
Etteridge Highld 99 K9
Ettersgill Dur 64 F2
Ettiley Heath Ches E 49 N4
Ettingshall Wolves 40 B8
Ettington Warwks 30 H4
Etton C Pete 42 G8
Etton E R Yk 60 G5
Ettrick Border 79 L6
Ettrickbridge Border 79 N4
Ettrickhill Border 79 L6
Etwall Derbys 40 H2
Euston Suffk 34 E2
Euxton Lancs 57 K5
Evanton Highld 107 K8
Evedon Lincs 42 F1
Evelix Highld 107 M4
Evenjobb Powys 38 F9
Evenley Nhants 31 N7
Evenlode Gloucs 30 G8
Evenwood Dur 65 K3
Evercreech Somset 17 P8
Everingham E R Yk 60 D6
Everleigh Wilts 18 H9
Eversholt C Beds 32 E9
Evershot Dorset 7 N2
Eversley Hants 20 C10
Eversley Cross Hants 20 C10
Everthorpe E R Yk 60 F7
Everton C Beds 32 H6
Everton Hants 9 K8
Everton Lpool 56 G9
Everton Notts 51 P3
Evertown D & G 71 M1
Evesbatch Herefs 39 M11
Evesham Worcs 30 D5
Evington C Leic 41 N6
Ewden Village Sheff 50 H2
Ewell Surrey 21 K10
Ewell Minnis Kent 13 N2
Ewelme Oxon 19 Q3
Ewen Gloucs 18 E2
Ewenny V Glam 27 J12
Ewerby Lincs 42 G1
Ewhurst Surrey 10 H3
Ewhurst Green E Susx 12 F5
Ewhurst Green Surrey 10 H3
Ewloe Flints 48 F3
Ewood Bl w D 57 M4
Eworthy Devon 5 J2
Ewshot Hants 20 D12
Ewyas Harold Herefs 28 D3
Exbourne Devon 15 K10
Exbury Hants 9 M7
Exebridge Somset 16 C10
Exelby N York 65 N9
Exeter Devon 6 C4
Exeter Airport Devon 6 D4
Exeter Services Devon 6 C4
Exford Somset 15 P5
Exfordsgreen Shrops 39 J2
Exhall Warwks 30 E3
Exhall Warwks 41 J9
Exlade Street Oxon 19 Q4
Exminster Devon 6 C5
Exmoor National Park 15 P4
Exmouth Devon 6 D6
Exning Suffk 33 P4
Exton Devon 6 D5
Exton Hants 9 Q4
Exton Rutlnd 42 D7
Exton Somset 16 C9
Exwick Devon 6 B4
Eyam Derbys 50 G5
Eydon Nhants 31 M4
Eye C Pete 42 H9
Eye Herefs 39 J8
Eye Suffk 35 J3
Eyemouth Border 81 K2
Eyeworth C Beds 33 J7
Eyhorne Street Kent 22 G11
Eyke Suffk 35 M6
Eynesbury Cambs 32 H5
Eynsford Kent 22 B9
Eynsham Oxon 31 K11
Eype Dorset 7 L5
Eyre Highld 104 F10
Eythorne Kent 23 P12
Eyton Herefs 39 J9
Eyton Shrops 48 H10
Eyton on Severn Shrops 39 L2
Eyton upon the Weald Moors Wrekin 49 M11

F

Faccombe Hants 19 L8
Faceby N York 66 C7
Fachwen Powys 48 B11
Faddiley Ches E 49 L5
Fadmoor N York 66 F9
Faerdre Swans 26 F8
Faifley W Duns 84 H8
Failand N Som 17 M2
Failford S Ayrs 76 H6
Failsworth Oldham 50 B1
Fairbourne Gwynd 47 K8
Fairburn N York 59 L8
Fairfield Derbys 50 E6
Fairfield Worcs 40 C11
Fairford Gloucs 18 H1
Fairgirth D & G 70 E4
Fair Green Norfk 43 Q6
Fairhaven Lancs 56 G4
Fair Isle Shet 111 m5
Fair Isle Airport Shet 111 m5
Fairlands Surrey 20 F11
Fairlie N Ayrs 84 D11
Fairlight E Susx 12 G7
Fairmile Devon 6 E4
Fairmile Surrey 20 H10
Fairmilehead C Edin 86 F8
Fairnilee Border 79 P3
Fair Oak Hants 9 N4
Fairoak Staffs 49 N8
Fair Oak Green Hants 19 Q8
Fairseat Kent 22 D10
Fairstead Essex 34 C12
Fairstead Norfk 43 Q6
Fairwarp E Susx 11 P5
Fairwater Cardif 27 N12
Fairy Cross Devon 14 G7
Fakenham Norfk 44 F4
Fakenham Magna Suffk 34 E2
Fala Mdloth 87 J9
Fala Dam Mdloth 87 J9
Faldingworth Lincs 52 F6
Faldouët Jersey 7 c2
Falfield S Glos 29 J9
Falkenham Suffk 35 L8
Falkirk Falk 85 P7
Falkirk Wheel Falk 85 P7
Falkland Fife 86 F2
Fallburn S Lans 78 F2
Fallin Stirlg 85 N5
Fallodon Nthumb 81 P9
Fallowfield Manch 57 Q9
Fallowfield Nthumb 72 G7
Falmer E Susx 11 M8
Falmouth Cnwll 3 J8
Falnash Border 79 N7
Falsgrave N York 67 M9
Falstone Nthumb 72 D4
Fanagmore Highld 108 D6
Fancott C Beds 32 E10
Fanellan Highld 98 G1
Fangdale Beck N York 66 D8
Fangfoss E R Yk 60 D4
Fanmore Ag & B 89 J7
Fannich Lodge Highld 106 D8
Fans Border 80 E6
Far Bletchley M Keyn 32 C9
Farcet Cambs 42 H10
Far Cotton Nhants 31 Q3
Fareham Hants 9 P6
Farewell Staffs 40 E5
Faringdon Oxon 19 K2
Farington Lancs 57 K4
Farlam Cumb 71 Q4
Farleigh N Som 17 M3
Farleigh Surrey 21 M10
Farleigh Hungerford Somset 18 B8
Farleigh Wallop Hants 19 Q10
Farlesthorpe Lincs 53 M8
Farleton Cumb 63 K6
Farleton Lancs 63 L8
Farley Staffs 50 E11
Farley Wilts 9 J2
Farley Green Surrey 10 G2
Farley Hill Wokham 20 C9
Farleys End Gloucs 29 K6
Farlington C Port 10 B8
Farlington N York 59 N1
Farlow Shrops 39 L6
Farmborough BaNES 17 P4
Farmcote Gloucs 30 D8
Farmington Gloucs 30 F10
Farmoor Oxon 31 L11
Far Moor Wigan 57 K7
Farmtown Moray 101 P5
Farnborough Gt Lon 21 N9
Farnborough Hants 20 E11
Farnborough W Berk 19 M4
Farnborough Warwks 31 K4
Farnborough Park Hants 20 E11
Farncombe Surrey 10 F2
Farndish Bed 32 D4
Farndon Ches W 48 H5
Farndon Notts 51 Q9
Farne Islands Nthumb 81 P6
Farnell Angus 93 Q5
Farnham Dorset 8 E4
Farnham Essex 33 M10
Farnham N York 59 J3
Farnham Suffk 35 M5
Farnham Surrey 10 D1
Farnham Common Bucks 20 F6
Farnham Royal Bucks 20 F6
Farningham Kent 22 B9
Farnley Leeds 58 G7
Farnley N York 58 G5
Farnley Tyas Kirk 58 F10
Farnsfield Notts 51 P9
Farnworth Bolton 57 N7
Farnworth Halton 57 K10
Far Oakridge Gloucs 29 N7
Farr Highld 99 K3
Farr Highld 99 M8
Farr Highld 109 M3
Farraline Highld 98 H5
Farringdon Devon 6 D5
Farrington Gurney BaNES 17 P5
Far Sawrey Cumb 62 H3
Farsley Leeds 58 G7
Farthinghoe Nhants 31 M6
Farthingstone Nhants 31 N3
Fartown Kirk 58 F9
Fasnacloich Ag & B 90 D6
Fasnakyle Highld 98 D4
Fassfern Highld 90 D1
Fatfield Sundld 73 N9
Fauldhouse W Loth 85 Q10
Faulkbourne Essex 34 D12
Faulkland Somset 17 Q5
Fauls Shrops 49 L8
Faversham Kent 23 K10
Fawdington N York 66 B11
Fawdon N u Ty 73 M7
Fawkham Green Kent 22 C9
Fawler Oxon 31 J10
Fawley Bucks 20 C6
Fawley Hants 9 M6
Fawley W Berk 19 L5
Faxfleet E R Yk 60 E8
Faygate W Susx 11 K3
Fazakerley Lpool 56 G9
Fazeley Staffs 40 G7
Fearby N York 65 L10
Fearn Highld 107 N7
Fearnan P & K 91 Q7
Fearnbeg Highld 105 L9
Fearnmore Highld 105 K9
Fearnoch Ag & B 83 P7
Featherstone Staffs 40 C6
Featherstone Wakefd 59 K9
Feckenham Worcs 30 D2
Feering Essex 34 E11
Feetham N York 64 H7
Felbridge Surrey 11 M3
Felbrigg Norfk 45 K3
Felcourt Surrey 11 M2
Felindre Carmth 25 N2
Felindre Carmth 26 D5
Felindre Powys 38 D6
Felindre Swans 26 E8
Felindre Farchog Pembks 36 B11
Felinfoel Carmth 26 C8
Felingwmisaf Carmth 26 C4
Felingwmuchaf Carmth 26 C4
Felixkirk N York 66 C9
Felixstowe Suffk 35 L9
Felling Gatesd 73 M8
Felmersham Bed 32 E5
Felmingham Norfk 45 L4
Felpham W Susx 10 F9
Felsham Suffk 34 F5
Felsted Essex 34 B11
Feltham Gt Lon 20 H8
Felthamhill Surrey 20 H8
Felthorpe Norfk 45 J6
Felton Herefs 39 L11
Felton N Som 17 M3
Felton Nthumb 73 L2
Felton Butler Shrops 48 H11
Feltwell Norfk 44 B11
Fence Lancs 57 P2
Fence Rothm 51 K4
Fencott Oxon 31 M10
Fendike Corner Lincs 53 M10
Fen Ditton Cambs 33 M5
Fen Drayton Cambs 33 K4
Feniscliffe Bl w D 57 M4
Feniscowles Bl w D 57 M4
Feniton Devon 6 E3
Feniton Court Devon 6 F3
Fenn Green Shrops 39 P5
Fenn Street Medway 22 F8
Fenny Bentley Derbys 50 F10
Fenny Bridges Devon 6 F3
Fenny Compton Warwks 31 K4
Fenny Drayton Leics 41 J7
Fenstanton Cambs 33 K3
Fen Street Norfk 44 G10
Fenton Cambs 33 K2
Fenton Cumb 71 Q4
Fenton Lincs 52 B8
Fenton Lincs 52 C12
Fenton Notts 52 B6
Fenton Nthumb 81 K7
Fenton Barns E Loth 87 K6
Fenwick Donc 59 N10
Fenwick E Ayrs 76 H3
Fenwick Nthumb 73 J6
Fenwick Nthumb 81 M6
Feock Cnwll 3 J7
Feolin Ferry Ag & B 82 F8
Fergushill N Ayrs 76 F3
Feriniquarrie Highld 104 B11
Fern Angus 94 H9
Ferndale Rhondd 27 L9
Ferndown Dorset 8 F7
Ferness Highld 100 E6
Fernham Oxon 19 K3
Fernhill Heath Worcs 39 Q9
Fernhurst W Susx 10 E4
Fernie Fife 93 K11
Ferniegair S Lans 85 M11
Fernilea Highld 96 D3
Fernilee Derbys 50 D5
Fernwood Notts 52 B12
Ferrensby N York 59 J3
Ferrindonald Highld 97 J7
Ferring W Susx 10 H9
Ferrybridge Services Wakefd 59 L9
Ferryden Angus 95 M9
Ferryhill Dur 65 M2
Ferryhill Station Dur 65 N2
Ferry Point Highld 107 M5
Ferryside Carmth 25 N6
Fersfield Norfk 44 H12
Fersit Highld 91 K2
Feshiebridge Highld 99 M8
Fetcham Surrey 21 J11
Fetlar Shet 111 m2
Fetterangus Abers 103 K5
Fettercairn Abers 95 K7
Fewston N York 58 G4
Ffairfach Carmth 26 E5
Ffair Rhos Cerdgn 37 M7
Ffarmers Carmth 37 K10
Ffestiniog Railway Gwynd 47 K4
Fforest Carmth 26 D7
Ffostrasol Cerdgn 36 F10
Ffrith Flints 48 F4
Ffynnongroyw Flints 56 D11
Fickleshole Surrey 21 M10
Fiddington Somset 16 G7
Fiddleford Dorset 8 B5
Fiddlers Green Cnwll 3 J5
Field Staffs 40 D2
Field Dalling Norfk 44 G3
Field Head Leics 41 L5
Fifehead Magdalen Dorset 8 B3
Fifehead Neville Dorset 8 B5
Fifehead St Quintin Dorset 8 B5
Fife Keith Moray 101 M5
Fifield Oxon 30 G9
Fifield W & M 20 E7
Figheldean Wilts 18 H10
Filby Norfk 45 P7
Filey N York 67 N10
Filgrave M Keyn 32 C7
Filkins Oxon 30 G12
Filleigh Devon 15 L6
Fillingham Lincs 52 D6
Fillongley Warwks 40 H9
Filton S Glos 28 H11
Fimber E R Yk 60 F3
Finavon Angus 93 N4
Finberry Kent 13 K3
Fincham Norfk 44 B8
Finchampstead Wokham 20 C10
Fincharn Ag & B 83 N3
Finchdean Hants 10 B7
Finchingfield Essex 34 B9
Finchley Gt Lon 21 L5
Findern Derbys 40 H2
Findhorn Moray 100 G3
Findhorn Bridge Highld 99 M4
Findochty Moray 101 N2
Findo Gask P & K 92 E10
Findon Abers 95 Q3
Findon W Susx 10 H8
Findon Mains Highld 107 K9
Findon Valley W Susx 11 J8
Findrack House Abers 95 K2
Finedon Nhants 32 D3
Fingask P & K 92 H10
Fingest Bucks 20 C5
Finghall N York 65 L9
Fingland D & G 77 M7
Finglesham Kent 23 P11
Fingringhoe Essex 34 G11
Finlarig Stirlg 91 N9
Finmere Oxon 31 N7
Finnart P & K 91 M5
Finningham Suffk 34 H3
Finningley Donc 51 P2
Finsbay W Isls 111 c4
Finstall Worcs 40 C12
Finsthwaite Cumb 62 G5
Finstock Oxon 31 J10
Finstown Ork 111 h2
Fintry Abers 102 G4
Fintry Stirlg 85 K5
Finzean Abers 95 K4
Fionnphort Ag & B 88 G10
Fionnsbhagh W Isls 111 c4
Firbank Cumb 63 L4
Firbeck Rothm 51 M3
Firby N York 60 C2
Firby N York 65 M9
Firle E Susx 11 P8
Firsby Lincs 53 M10
Fir Tree Dur 65 K1
Fishbourne IoW 9 P8
Fishbourne W Susx 10 D8
Fishbourne Roman Palace W Susx 10 D8
Fishburn Dur 65 P2
Fishcross Clacks 85 P4
Fisherford Abers 102 E8
Fisherrow E Loth 86 G7
Fisher's Pond Hants 9 N4
Fisherton Highld 107 M11
Fisherton S Ayrs 76 E7
Fisherton de la Mere Wilts 18 E11
Fishery W & M 20 E7
Fishguard Pembks 24 G2
Fishlake Donc 59 P10
Fishnish Pier Ag & B 89 N7
Fishponds Bristl 17 P2
Fishtoft Lincs 43 K2
Fishtoft Drove Lincs 43 K1
Fishwick Lancs 57 K3
Fiskavaig Highld 96 D3
Fiskerton Lincs 52 F8
Fiskerton Notts 51 Q9
Fittleton Wilts 18 G10
Fittleworth W Susx 10 G6
Fitz Shrops 49 J11
Fitzhead Somset 16 F9
Fitzwilliam Wakefd 59 K10
Five Ash Down E Susx 11 P5
Five Ashes E Susx 12 B5
Fivehead Somset 17 J10
Fivelanes Cnwll 4 F4
Five Oak Green Kent 12 D2
Five Oaks Jersey 7 c2
Five Oaks W Susx 10 H4
Five Roads Carmth 26 C7
Flackwell Heath Bucks 20 E5
Fladbury Worcs 30 C5
Fladdabister Shet 111 k4
Flagg Derbys 50 F7
Flamborough E R Yk 67 Q12
Flamborough Head E R Yk 67 Q12
Flamingo Land Theme Park N York 66 H10
Flamstead Herts 20 H1
Flamstead End Herts 21 M3
Flansham W Susx 10 F9
Flanshaw Wakefd 58 H9
Flasby N York 58 C3
Flash Staffs 50 D7
Flashader Highld 104 D10
Flaunden Herts 20 G4
Flawborough Notts 42 B2
Flawith N York 59 L2
Flax Bourton N Som 17 M3
Flaxby N York 59 K3
Flaxley Gloucs 29 J6
Flaxpool Somset 16 F8
Flaxton N York 59 P2
Fleckney Leics 41 P8
Flecknoe Warwks 31 L2
Fledborough Notts 52 B8
Fleet Dorset 7 P6
Fleet Hants 20 D11
Fleet Lincs 43 L5
Fleet Hargate Lincs 43 L5
Fleet Services Hants 20 C11
Fleetwood Lancs 62 G11
Fleggburgh Norfk 45 P7
Flemingston V Glam 16 D3
Flemington S Lans 85 L10
Flempton Suffk 34 D3
Fletchertown Cumb 71 K7
Fletching E Susx 11 N5
Flexbury Cnwll 14 D10
Flexford Surrey 20 E12
Flimby Cumb 70 G8
Flimwell E Susx 12 E4
Flint Flints 48 E2
Flintham Notts 51 Q10
Flinton E R Yk 61 L7
Flitcham Norfk 44 C5
Flitch Green Essex 33 Q11
Flitton C Beds 32 F9
Flitwick C Beds 32 E9
Flixborough N Linc 60 E10
Flixborough Stather N Linc 60 E10
Flixton N York 67 M10
Flixton Suffk 45 M11
Flixton Traffd 57 N9
Flockton Kirk 58 G10
Flockton Green Kirk 58 G10
Flodigarry Highld 104 F7
Flookburgh Cumb 62 G7
Flordon Norfk 45 K10
Flore Nhants 31 N3
Flowton Suffk 34 H7
Flushing Cnwll 3 K8
Fluxton Devon 6 E4
Flyford Flavell Worcs 30 C3
Fobbing Thurr 22 E6
Fochabers Moray 101 L4
Fochriw Caerph 27 M7
Fockerby N Linc 60 E9
Foddington Somset 17 N9
Foel Powys 48 B12
Foggathorpe E R Yk 60 D6
Fogo Border 80 G4
Fogwatt Moray 101 K4
Foindle Highld 108 D6
Folda Angus 94 C8
Fole Staffs 50 D12
Foleshill Covtry 41 J10

Folke Dorset 17 P12
Folkestone Kent 13 N3
Folkestone Services Kent 13 L3
Folkingham Lincs 42 F4
Folkington E Susx 12 C8
Folksworth Cambs 42 G11
Folkton N York 67 M10
Folla Rule Abers 102 F8
Follifoot N York 59 J4
Folly Gate Devon 15 K11
Folly Hill Surrey 10 D11
Fonthill Bishop Wilts 8 D2
Fonthill Gifford Wilts 8 D2
Fontmell Magna Dorset 8 C4
Fontmell Parva Dorset 8 C5
Fontwell W Susx 10 F8
Foolow Derbys 50 F5
Forbestown Abers 101 M11
Forcett N York 65 L5
Ford Ag & B 83 N3
Ford Bucks 31 Q11
Ford Derbys 51 K5
Ford Devon 14 G7
Ford Gloucs 30 E8
Ford Nthumb 81 K6
Ford Somset 16 E9
Ford Staffs 50 E9
Ford W Susx 10 F8
Ford Wilts 18 C6
Fordcombe Kent 11 Q3
Fordell Fife 86 D5
Forden Powys 38 E2
Ford End Essex 34 B12
Forder Green Devon 5 Q6
Fordham Cambs 33 Q3
Fordham Essex 34 F10
Fordham Norfk 43 P9
Fordingbridge Hants 8 G5
Fordon E R Yk 67 M11
Fordoun Abers 95 M6
Fordstreet Essex 34 F10
Ford Street Somset 16 F11
Fordwich Kent 23 M10
Fordyce Abers 102 D3
Forebridge Staffs 40 B3
Forest Guern 6 b2
Forest Chapel Ches E 50 C6
Forest Gate Gt Lon 21 N6
Forest Green Surrey 10 H2
Forest Hall N Tyne 73 M6
Forest Hill Gt Lon 21 M8
Forest Hill Oxon 31 N11
Forest Lane Head N York 59 J3
Forest Mill Clacks 85 Q4
Forest of Bowland Lancs 63 L10
Forest of Dean Gloucs 28 H6
Forest Row E Susx 11 N3
Forestside W Susx 10 C7
Forest Town Notts 51 M8
Forfar Angus 93 M6
Forgandenny P & K 92 G11
Forge Hammer Torfn 28 C9
Forgie Moray 101 M4
Forgieside Moray 101 M5
Forgue Abers 102 D6
Formby Sefton 56 F7
Forncett End Norfk 45 J10
Forncett St Mary Norfk 45 J10
Forncett St Peter Norfk 45 J10
Fornham All Saints Suffk ...34 D4
Fornham St Martin Suffk 34 E4
Fornighty Highld 100 E5
Forres Moray 100 F4
Forsbrook Staffs 50 C11
Forse Highld 110 E8
Forsinard Highld 109 Q7
Forss Highld 110 B3
Fort Augustus Highld 98 E7
Forteviot P & K 92 F11
Forth S Lans 85 Q11
Forthampton Gloucs 29 M3
Forth Rail Bridge C Edin ...86 D6
Forth Road Bridge Fife 86 D6
Fortingall P & K 91 Q6
Forton Hants 19 M11
Forton Lancs 63 J11
Forton Shrops 48 H11
Forton Somset 7 J2
Forton Staffs 49 N10
Fortrie Abers 102 E6
Fortrose Highld 107 M10
Fortuneswell Dorset 7 P7
Fort William Highld 90 F2
Forty Hill Gt Lon 21 M4
Fosbury Wilts 19 K8
Foscot Oxon 30 G9
Fosdyke Lincs 43 K4
Foss P & K 92 B4
Fossebridge Gloucs 30 E11
Foster Street Essex 21 P2
Foston Derbys 40 F2
Foston Leics 41 N8
Foston Lincs 42 C2
Foston N York 59 P2
Foston on the Wolds E R Yk ..61 J3
Fotherby Lincs 53 K5
Fotheringhay Nhants 42 F10
Foula Shet 111 j5
Foula Airport Shet 111 j5
Foulden Border 81 K3
Foulden Norfk 44 C9
Foul End Warwks 40 G8
Foulness Island Essex 23 J5
Foulridge Lancs 58 B6
Foulsham Norfk 44 G5
Fountainhall Border 87 J11
Four Ashes Suffk 34 G3
Four Crosses Powys 48 F10
Four Elms Kent 11 P1
Four Forks Somset 16 G8
Four Gotes Cambs 43 M6
Four Lanes Cnwll 2 G7
Four Marks Hants 9 R1
Four Mile Bridge IoA 54 C6
Four Oaks Birm 40 E7
Four Oaks Solhll 40 G10
Fourpenny Highld 107 N4
Four Roads Carmth 25 Q7
Fourstones Nthumb 72 F7
Four Throws Kent 12 F4
Fovant Wilts 8 E2
Foveran Abers 103 K9
Fowey Cnwll 4 D9
Fowlhall Kent 12 E2

Fowlis Angus 93 K8
Fowlis Wester P & K 92 D10
Fowlmere Cambs 33 L7
Fownhope Herefs 28 G3
Foxbar Rens 84 H10
Foxcote Somset 17 Q5
Foxdale IoM 56 b5
Foxearth Essex 34 D7
Foxfield Cumb 62 E5
Foxhole Cnwll 3 L5
Foxholes N York 67 L11
Foxley Norfk 44 H6
Foxt Staffs 50 D10
Foxton Cambs 33 L7
Foxton Leics 41 P9
Foxton N York 65 Q8
Foxwood Shrops 39 L6
Foy Herefs 28 H3
Foyers Highld 98 G5
Foynesfield Highld 100 D5
Fraddon Cnwll 3 K4
Fradley Staffs 40 F5
Fradswell Staffs 40 C2
Fraisthorpe E R Yk 61 K2
Framfield E Susx 11 P6
Framingham Earl Norfk 45 L9
Framingham Pigot Norfk 45 L9
Framlingham Suffk 35 L4
Frampton Dorset 7 P4
Frampton Lincs 43 K3
Frampton Cotterell S Glos ..29 J11
Frampton Mansell Gloucs 29 N8
Frampton-on-Severn Gloucs ..29 K7
Framsden Suffk 35 K5
Framwellgate Moor Dur 73 M11
Franche Worcs 39 P6
Frankby Wirral 56 E10
Frankley Norfk 40 C10
Frankley Services Worcs 40 C10
Frankton Warwks 41 K12
Frant E Susx 12 C3
Fraserburgh Abers 103 K2
Frating Essex 34 H11
Frating Green Essex 34 H11
Fratton C Port 9 Q7
Freathy Cnwll 5 J9
Freckenham Suffk 33 Q3
Freckleton Lancs 56 H3
Freeby Leics 42 B6
Freefolk Hants 19 N10
Freeland Oxon 31 K10
Freethorpe Norfk 45 N8
Freethorpe Common Norfk 45 N8
Freiston Lincs 43 L2
Fremington Devon 15 J6
Fremington N York 65 J7
Frenchay S Glos 28 H12
Frenich P & K 92 C4
Frensham Surrey 10 D2
Freshfield Sefton 56 F7
Freshford Wilts 18 B8
Freshwater IoW 9 K9
Fressingfield Suffk 35 L2
Freston Suffk 35 J8
Freswick Highld 110 G3
Fretherne Gloucs 29 K6
Frettenham Norfk 45 L6
Freuchie Fife 86 F2
Freystrop Pembks 24 G6
Friar Park Sandw 40 D8
Friar's Bridge Cambs 43 M8
Friday Street Surrey 35 N5
Fridaythorpe E R Yk 60 E3
Friendly Calder 58 D8
Friern Barnet Gt Lon 21 L5
Friesthorpe Lincs 52 F6
Frieston Lincs 42 D1
Frieth Bucks 20 C5
Frilford Oxon 19 M2
Frilsham W Berk 19 P6
Frimley Surrey 20 E10
Frindsbury Medway 22 E9
Fring Norfk 44 C3
Fringford Oxon 31 N8
Frinsted Kent 22 H11
Frinton-on-Sea Essex 35 K11
Friockheim Angus 93 Q6
Frisby on the Wreake Leics .41 P4
Friskney Lincs 53 M11
Friston E Susx 12 B9
Friston Suffk 35 N5
Fritchley Derbys 51 J9
Fritham Hants 9 J5
Frithelstock Devon 14 H8
Frithelstock Stone Devon ...14 H8
Frithville Lincs 53 K12
Frittenden Kent 12 F2
Frittiscombe Devon 5 Q10
Fritton Norfk 45 K10
Fritton Norfk 45 N9
Fritwell Oxon 31 M8
Frizinghall C Brad 58 F7
Frizington Cumb 70 G11
Frocester Gloucs 29 K8
Frodesley Shrops 39 K2
Frodsham Ches W 57 K12
Frogden Border 80 G8
Frog End Cambs 33 L7
Froggatt Derbys 50 G5
Froghall Staffs 50 D10
Frogmore Devon 5 P10
Frognall Lincs 42 G7
Frog Pool Worcs 39 P8
Frogwell Cnwll 4 H6
Frolesworth Leics 41 L8
Frome Somset 18 B10
Frome St Quintin Dorset 7 N3
Fromes Hill Herefs 39 M11
Froncysyllte Wrexhm 48 F7
Fron-goch Gwynd 47 N4
Fron Isaf Wrexhm 48 F7
Froxfield Wilts 19 K7
Froxfield Green Hants 9 R3
Fryern Hill Hants 9 M4
Fryerning Essex 22 D4
Fryton N York 66 G12
Fuinary Highld 89 M7
Fulbeck Lincs 52 D12
Fulbourn Cambs 33 N5
Fulbrook Oxon 30 H10
Fulflood Hants 9 M2
Fulford C York 59 N4
Fulford Somset 16 G9
Fulford Staffs 50 C12

Fulham Gt Lon 21 K8
Fulking W Susx 11 K7
Fullarton N Ayrs 76 F4
Fuller Street Essex 34 C12
Fullerton Hants 19 L11
Fulletby Lincs 53 J8
Fullready Warwks 30 H5
Full Sutton E R Yk 60 D3
Fullwood E Ayrs 76 G2
Fulmer Bucks 20 F6
Fulmodeston Norfk 44 G4
Fulnetby Lincs 52 F7
Fulney Lincs 43 J5
Fulstow Lincs 53 K4
Fulwell Sundld 73 P8
Fulwood Lancs 57 K3
Fulwood Sheff 50 H4
Fundenhall Norfk 45 J10
Funtington W Susx 10 C8
Funtley Hants 9 Q6
Funtullich P & K 92 B9
Furley Devon 6 H2
Furnace Ag & B 83 Q3
Furnace Carmth 26 C8
Furness Vale Derbys 50 D4
Furneux Pelham Herts 33 L10
Furzley Hants 9 K4
Fyfield Essex 22 C3
Fyfield Hants 19 K10
Fyfield Oxon 19 M2
Fyfield Wilts 18 G7
Fyfield Wilts 18 H8
Fylingthorpe N York 67 K6
Fyning W Susx 10 D5
Fyvie Abers 102 G7

G

Gabroc Hill E Ayrs 76 H2
Gaddesby Leics 41 P5
Gaddesden Row Herts 20 G2
Gadgirth S Ayrs 76 G6
Gaerllwyd Mons 28 E9
Gaerwen IoA 54 F7
Gailes N Ayrs 76 F4
Gailey Staffs 40 B5
Gainford Dur 65 L4
Gainsborough Lincs 52 B5
Gainsborough Suffk 35 K8
Gainsford End Essex 34 C9
Gairloch Highld 105 M7
Gairlochy Highld 98 B11
Gairneybridge P & K 86 D3
Gaitsgill Cumb 71 N6
Galashiels Border 80 C7
Galgate Lancs 63 J10
Galhampton Somset 17 P9
Gallanachbeg Ag & B 90 B10
Gallanachmore Ag & B 89 R10
Gallatown Fife 86 G4
Galley Wood Essex 22 E3
Gallovie Highld 98 H10
Galloway Forest Park 69 L3
Gallowfauld Angus 93 M7
Gallowhill P & K 92 H8
Galltair Highld 97 L5
Galmisdale Highld 96 F11
Galmpton Devon 5 N11
Galmpton Torbay 6 B10
Galphay N York 65 M11
Galston E Ayrs 76 H4
Gamblesby Cumb 72 B11
Gamlingay Cambs 33 J6
Gamlingay Great Heath
  Cambs 32 H6
Gamrie Abers 102 G3
Gamston Notts 51 N12
Gamston Notts 51 P5
Ganavan Bay Ag & B 90 B9
Ganllwyd Gwynd 47 M6
Gannachy Angus 95 K7
Ganstead E R Yk 61 K7
Ganthorpe N York 66 F12
Ganton N York 67 L11
Garbity Moray 101 L5
Garboldisham Norfk 34 G1
Garbole Highld 99 L4
Garchory Abers 101 L12
Gardeners Green Wokham 20 D9
Gardenstown Abers 102 G3
Garden Village Sheff 50 H4
Garderhouse Shet 111 k4
Gare Hill Somset 18 B11
Garelochhead Ag & B 84 D5
Garford Oxon 19 M2
Garforth Leeds 59 K7
Gargrave N York 58 D4
Gargunnock Stirlg 85 M4
Garlic Street Norfk 45 K12
Garlieston D & G 69 L9
Garlinge Kent 23 P9
Garlinge Green Kent 23 L11
Garlogie Abers 95 M2
Garmond Abers 102 G5
Garmouth Moray 101 L3
Garmston Shrops 39 M2
Garndolbenmaen Gwynd 46 H3
Garnkirk N Lans 85 L8
Garnswllt Swans 26 E7
Garrabost W Isls 111 e2
Garrallan E Ayrs 77 J7
Garras Cnwll 2 G10
Garreg Gwynd 47 K3
Garrigill Cumb 72 D11
Garroch D & G 69 N3
Garrochtrie D & G 68 F10
Garrochty Ag & B 84 B11
Garros Highld 104 G9
Garsdale Head Cumb 64 E8
Garsdon Wilts 18 E4
Garshall Green Staffs 40 C1
Garsington Oxon 31 M12
Garstang Lancs 63 J12
Garston Herts 20 H4
Garston Lpool 56 H11
Gartachossan Ag & B 82 E10
Gartcosh N Lans 85 L9
Garth Powys 37 Q10
Garth Wrexhm 48 F7
Garth C Glas 85 L9
Garthamlock C Glas 85 L9
Garthmyl Powys 38 E3
Garthorpe Leics 42 B6
Garthorpe N Linc 60 E9
Garth Row Cumb 63 K3
Gartly Abers 102 C8

Gartmore Stirlg 85 J4
Gartness N Lans 85 N9
Gartness Stirlg 84 H5
Gartocharn W Duns 84 G6
Garton-on-the-Wolds E R Yk ..60 G3
Gartymore Highld 110 B11
Garva Bridge Highld 98 G9
Garvald Border 86 C11
Garvald E Loth 87 L7
Garvan Highld 90 D2
Garvard Ag & B 82 E5
Garvestone Norfk 44 G8
Garvock Inver 84 E8
Garway Herefs 28 E4
Garynahine W Isls 111 c2
Garyvard W Isls 111 d2
Gasper Wilts 8 B2
Gastard Wilts 18 C7
Gasthorpe Norfk 34 F1
Gaston Green Essex 33 N12
Gatcombe IoW 9 N9
Gateacre Lpool 56 H10
Gate Burton Lincs 52 B7
Gateforth N York 59 M8
Gatehead E Ayrs 76 G4
Gate Helmsley N York 59 P3
Gatehouse Nthumb 72 E3
Gatehouse of Fleet D & G ...69 N7
Gateley Norfk 44 F5
Gatenby N York 65 N9
Gateshaw Border 80 G9
Gateshead Gatesd 73 M8
Gateside Angus 93 M6
Gateside E Rens 84 H10
Gateside Fife 86 E1
Gateside N Ayrs 84 F11
Gateslack D & G 78 E8
Gatley Stockp 57 Q10
Gattonside Border 80 D7
Gatwick Airport W Susx 11 L2
Gaulby Leics 41 P7
Gauldry Fife 93 L10
Gauldswell P & K 93 J5
Gautby Lincs 52 H8
Gavinton Border 80 G4
Gawcott Bucks 31 P7
Gawsworth Ches E 50 B6
Gawthrop Cumb 63 M5
Gawthwaite Cumb 62 F5
Gaydon Warwks 31 J4
Gayhurst M Keyn 32 C7
Gayle N York 64 F9
Gayles N York 65 K6
Gayton Nhants 31 P4
Gayton Norfk 44 C6
Gayton Staffs 40 C2
Gayton le Marsh Lincs 53 L6
Gayton Thorpe Norfk 44 C6
Gaywood Norfk 43 Q6
Gazeley Suffk 34 C4
Gearraidh Bhaird W Isls ...111 d2
Gearraidh na h-Aibhne
  W Isls 111 c2
Geary Highld 104 C9
Gedding Suffk 34 F5
Geddington Nhants 42 C12
Gedling Notts 51 N11
Gedney Lincs 43 L5
Gedney Broadgate Lincs 43 L5
Gedney Drove End Lincs 43 M4
Gedney Dyke Lincs 43 L5
Gedney Hill Lincs 43 K7
Geeston Rutlnd 42 E8
Geirinis W Isls 111 b5
Geldeston Norfk 45 N10
Gellideg Myr Td 27 L7
Gellifor Denbgs 48 D3
Gelligaer Caerph 27 N9
Gellilydan Gwynd 47 L4
Gellinudd Neath 26 G7
Gellyburn P & K 92 G7
Gellywen Carmth 25 M4
Gelston D & G 70 C4
Gelston Lincs 42 C2
Gembling E R Yk 61 J3
Gentleshaw Staffs 40 D5
Georgefield D & G 79 L9
George Green Bucks 20 F7
Georgeham Devon 14 H4
Georgemas Junction Station
  Highld 110 D4
George Nympton Devon 15 M7
Georth Ork 111 h2
Gerinish W Isls 111 b5
Germansweek Devon 5 J2
Gerrans Cnwll 3 M6
Gerrards Cross Bucks 20 G6
Gerrick R & Cl 66 G5
Gestingthorpe Essex 34 D8
Geuffordd Powys 48 E11
Gidea Park Gt Lon 21 Q5
Giffnock E Rens 85 J10
Gifford E Loth 87 K8
Giffordtown Fife 93 K12
Giggleswick N York 63 P9
Gigha Ag & B 75 J3
Gilberdyke E R Yk 60 E8
Gilchriston E Loth 87 J8
Gilcrux Cumb 70 H7
Gildersome Leeds 58 G8
Gildingwells Rothm 51 M4
Gilesgate Moor Dur 73 N11
Gileston V Glam 16 D3
Gilfach Caerph 27 N8
Gilfach Goch Brdgnd 27 K10
Gilfachrheda Cerdgn 36 G8
Gilgarran Cumb 70 G10
Gillamoor N York 66 G8
Gillen Highld 104 C9
Gillesbie D & G 79 J9
Gilling East N York 66 E11
Gillingham Dorset 8 C3
Gillingham Medway 22 F9
Gillingham Norfk 45 N10
Gilling West N York 65 L6
Gillock Highld 110 E4
Gills Highld 110 G2
Gilmanscleuch Border 79 M5
Gilmerton C Edin 86 F8
Gilmerton P & K 92 D10
Gilmonby Dur 64 H5
Gilmorton Leics 41 M9

Gilsland Nthumb 72 B7
Gilston Border 87 J10
Gilston Herts 21 N2
Gilwern Mons 27 Q6
Gimingham Norfk 45 L3
Gipping Suffk 34 H4
Gipsey Bridge Lincs 53 J12
Girdle Toll N Ayrs 76 F3
Girlsta Shet 111 k4
Girsby N York 65 N6
Girthon D & G 69 N8
Girton Cambs 33 L4
Girton Notts 52 B9
Girvan S Ayrs 76 D10
Gisburn Lancs 63 P11
Gisleham Suffk 45 Q11
Gislingham Suffk 34 H3
Gissing Norfk 45 J11
Gittisham Devon 6 F3
Gladestry Powys 38 E10
Gladsmuir E Loth 87 J7
Glais Swans 26 F8
Glaisdale N York 66 H6
Glamis Angus 93 L6
Glanaman Carmth 26 F6
Glandford Norfk 44 H2
Glandwr Pembks 25 L3
Glandyfi Cerdgn 47 L11
Glanllynfi Brdgnd 27 J10
Glan-rhyd Powys 26 G7
Glanton Nthumb 81 M10
Glanvilles Wootton Dorset ...7 P2
Glan-y-don Flints 56 D11
Glapthorn Nhants 42 E11
Glapwell Derbys 51 L7
Glasbury Powys 27 P2
Glascote Staffs 40 G6
Glascwm Powys 38 D10
Glasfryn Conwy 55 N10
Glasgow C Glas 85 K9
Glasgow Airport Rens 84 H9
Glasgow Prestwick Airport
  S Ayrs 76 F6
Glasgow Science Centre
  C Glas 85 J9
Glasinfryn Gwynd 54 H7
Glasnacardoch Bay Highld ...97 J9
Glasnakille Highld 96 G7
Glasphein Highld 104 B11
Glassford S Lans 77 M2
Glasshouse Gloucs 29 J5
Glasshouses N York 58 F2
Glasslaw Abers 102 H4
Glasson Cumb 71 L4
Glasson Lancs 63 J10
Glassonby Cumb 72 B12
Glasson Dock Lancs 63 J10
Glasterlaw Angus 93 Q5
Glaston Rutlnd 42 C9
Glastonbury Somset 17 M8
Glatton Cambs 42 G11
Glazebrook Warrtn 57 M9
Glazebury Warrtn 57 M9
Glazeley Shrops 39 N5
Gleaston Cumb 62 F7
Glebe Highld 98 G5
Gledhow Leeds 58 H6
Gledpark D & G 69 P8
Gledrid Shrops 48 F7
Glemsford Suffk 34 D7
Glen Achulish Highld 90 E5
Glenallachie Moray 101 K7
Glenancross Highld 97 J10
Glenaros House Ag & B 89 L7
Glen Auldyn IoM 56 d3
Glenbarr Ag & B 75 K5
Glenbervie Abers 102 D4
Glenbeg Highld 89 M4
Glenbervie Abers 95 M6
Glenboig N Lans 85 M8
Glenborrodale Highld 89 M4
Glenbranter Ag & B 84 B4
Glenbreck Border 78 H5
Glenbrittle Highld 96 E5
Glenbuck E Ayrs 77 M5
Glencally Angus 94 F3
Glencaple D & G 70 G2
Glencarse P & K 92 H10
Glencoe Highld 90 F5
Glencothe Border 78 H3
Glencraig Fife 86 E4
Glencrosh D & G 78 C10
Glendale Highld 104 B11
Glenduruel Ag & B 83 Q6
Glendevon P & K 86 B2
Glendoe Lodge Highld 98 E7
Glendoick P & K 93 J10
Glenduckie Fife 93 K11
Glenegedale Ag & B 74 D3
Glenelg Highld 97 L6
Glenernie Moray 100 F6
Glenfarg P & K 92 G12
Glenfield Leics 41 M6
Glenfinnan Highld 90 C1
Glenfintaig Lodge Highld ...98 C10
Glenfoot P & K 92 H11
Glenfyne Lodge Ag & B 90 G12
Glengarnock N Ayrs 84 F11
Glengolly Highld 110 C3
Glengorm Castle Ag & B 89 K5
Glengrasco Highld 96 E1
Glenholm Border 78 H3
Glenhoul D & G 69 N2
Glenkin Ag & B 84 C7
Glenkindie Abers 101 N11
Glenlivet Moray 101 J9
Glenlochar D & G 70 C3
Glenlomond P & K 86 E2
Glenluce D & G 68 G7
Glenmassen Ag & B 84 B5
Glenmavis N Lans 85 M9
Glen Maye IoM 56 b5
Glenmore Highld 96 E2
Glenmore Lodge Highld 99 P7
Glen Nevis House Highld 90 F2
Glenochil Clacks 85 P4
Glen Parva Leics 41 M7
Glenquiech Angus 94 G3
Glenralloch Ag & B 83 M8
Glenridding Cumb 71 N11
Glenrothes Fife 86 F3
Glenshero Lodge Highld 98 H9
Glenstriven Ag & B 84 B7
Glentham Lincs 52 E5
Glentrool D & G 69 J4

172 Glen Trool Lodge – Hackbridge

Glen Trool Lodge D & G 69 K3
Glentruim Highld 99 K9
Glentworth Lincs 52 D6
Glenuig Highld 89 N2
Glenvarragill Highld 96 F2
Glen Vine IoM 56 c5
Glenwhilly D & G 68 G5
Glespin S Lans 78 D4
Glewstone Herefs 28 G4
Glinton C Pete 42 G8
Glooston Leics 41 Q8
Glossop Derbys 50 D3
Gloster Hill Nthumb 81 Q12
Gloucester Gloucs 29 L5
Gloucester Services Gloucs 29 L6
Gloucestershire Airport Gloucs 29 M5
Glusburn N York 58 D5
Glutt Lodge Highld 110 B8
Glympton Oxon 31 K9
Glynarthen Cerdgn 36 E10
Glyn Ceiriog Wrexhm 48 E7
Glyncoch Rhondd 27 M9
Glyncorrwg Neath 27 J8
Glynde E Susx 11 P8
Glyndyfrdwy Denbgs 48 D7
Glynneath Neath 27 J7
Glyntawe Powys 26 H5
Glynteg Carmth 25 N2
Gnosall Staffs 49 P10
Gnosall Heath Staffs 49 P10
Goadby Leics 41 Q7
Goadby Marwood Leics 41 R3
Goatacre Wilts 18 F5
Goathill Dorset 17 P11
Goathland N York 67 J7
Goathurst Somset 16 H8
Goat Lees Kent 13 J2
Gobowen Shrops 48 F8
Godalming Surrey 10 F2
Goddard's Green Kent 12 G3
Godmanchester Cambs 33 J3
Godmanstone Dorset 7 P4
Godmersham Kent 23 K12
Godney Somset 17 L7
Godolphin Cross Cnwll 2 F9
Godre'r-graig Neath 26 G7
Godshill IoW 9 N10
Godstone Surrey 21 M11
Goetre Mons 28 C7
Goff's Oak Herts 21 M3
Gogar C Edin 86 E7
Goginan Cerdgn 37 L4
Golan Gwynd 46 H3
Golant Cnwll 4 D8
Golberdon Cnwll 4 H6
Golborne Wigan 57 L8
Golcar Kirk 58 E10
Goldcliff Newpt 28 D11
Golden Green Kent 12 D1
Goldenhill C Stke 49 Q5
Golden Pot Hants 10 B2
Golders Green Gt Lon 21 K6
Goldhanger Essex 22 H2
Goldington Bed 32 F6
Goldsborough N York 59 J3
Goldsborough N York 67 J5
Golds Green Sandw 40 C8
Goldsithney Cnwll 2 E9
Goldthorpe Barns 59 L12
Goldworthy Devon 14 G7
Gollanfield Highld 107 N10
Golspie Highld 107 N3
Gomeldon Wilts 8 H1
Gomshall Surrey 10 H1
Gonalston Notts 51 P10
Gonerby Hill Foot Lincs 42 C3
Gonfirth Shet 111 k3
Good Easter Essex 22 D2
Gooderstone Norfk 44 C9
Goodleigh Devon 15 K5
Goodmanham E R Yk 60 F5
Goodmayes Gt Lon 21 P6
Goodnestone Kent 23 K10
Goodnestone Kent 23 N11
Goodrich Herefs 28 G5
Goodrington Torbay 6 B10
Goodshaw Lancs 57 P4
Goodwick Pembks 24 G2
Goodworth Clatford Hants 19 L11
Goole E R Yk 60 C9
Goom's Hill Worcs 30 D3
Goonbell Cnwll 2 G6
Goonhavern Cnwll 2 H5
Goonvrea Cnwll 2 G6
Goosecruives Abers 95 M5
Gooseford Devon 5 N2
Goose Green Essex 35 J10
Goose Green S Glos 17 P2
Goose Green Wigan 57 K8
Gooseham Cnwll 14 E8
Goosey Oxon 19 L3
Goosnargh Lancs 57 K2
Goostrey Ches E 49 P2
Gordano Services N Som 17 M2
Gordon Border 80 E5
Gordon Arms Hotel Border 79 L4
Gordonstown Abers 102 D4
Gordonstown Abers 102 F7
Gorebridge Mdloth 86 G9
Gorefield Cambs 43 L7
Gores Wilts 18 G8
Gorey Jersey 7 c2
Goring Oxon 19 P5
Goring-by-Sea W Susx 10 H9
Gorleston-on-Sea Norfk 45 Q8
Gorrachie Abers 102 F4
Gorran Churchtown Cnwll 3 M7
Gorran Haven Cnwll 3 M7
Gorsedd Flints 56 D12
Gorseddau Slate Landscape Gwynd 47 J3
Gorse Hill Swindn 18 H4
Gorseinon Swans 26 D8
Gorsgoch Cerdgn 36 H9
Gorslas Carmth 26 D6
Gorsley Gloucs 29 J4
Gorsley Common Herefs 29 J4
Gorstan Highld 106 F9
Gorsten Ag & B 89 P9
Gorsty Hill Staffs 40 E2
Gorthleck Highld 98 G5
Gorton Manch 50 B2
Gosbeck Suffk 35 J5
Gosberton Lincs 43 J4
Gosfield Essex 34 D10
Gosforth Cumb 62 C2
Gosforth N u Ty 73 M7
Gosport Hants 9 Q7
Gossington Gloucs 29 K8
Gotham Notts 41 M2
Gotherington Gloucs 29 N3
Gotton Somset 16 H9
Goudhurst Kent 12 E3
Goulceby Lincs 53 J7
Gourdas Abers 102 G7
Gourdie C Dund 93 L8
Gourdon Abers 95 N7
Gourock Inver 84 D7
Govan C Glas 85 J9
Goveton Devon 5 P10
Govilon Mons 28 B6
Gowdall E R Yk 59 N9
Gower Highld 106 H10
Gower Swans 26 C10
Gowerton Swans 26 D9
Gowkhall Fife 86 C5
Goxhill E R Yk 61 K5
Goxhill N Linc 61 J9
Grabhair W Isls 111 d3
Graffham W Susx 10 E6
Grafham Cambs 32 G3
Grafham Surrey 10 G2
Grafton N York 59 K2
Grafton Oxon 19 J1
Grafton Shrops 48 H10
Grafton Worcs 29 N2
Grafton Flyford Worcs 30 C3
Grafton Regis Nhants 31 Q5
Grafton Underwood Nhants 32 D2
Grafty Green Kent 12 G1
Graig Conwy 55 L7
Graigfechan Denbgs 48 D5
Grain Medway 22 H7
Grainsby Lincs 53 J4
Grainthorpe Lincs 53 L4
Grampound Cnwll 3 L6
Grampound Road Cnwll 3 K5
Gramsdal W Isls 111 b5
Gramsdale W Isls 111 b5
Granborough Bucks 31 Q8
Granby Notts 41 Q1
Grandborough Warwks 31 L2
Grand Chemins Jersey 7 c2
Grandes Rocques Guern 6 b1
Grandtully P & K 92 D5
Grange Cumb 71 L11
Grange Medway 22 F9
Grange P & K 93 K10
Grange Crossroads Moray 101 N4
Grange Hall Moray 100 G3
Grangehall S Lans 78 F1
Grange Hill Essex 21 N5
Grangemill Derbys 50 G8
Grange Moor Kirk 58 G10
Grangemouth Falk 85 Q6
Grange of Lindores Fife 93 J11
Grange-over-Sands Cumb 62 H6
Grangepans Falk 86 B6
Grange Park Nhants 31 Q3
Grangetown R & Cl 66 D4
Grangetown Sundld 73 P9
Grange Villa Dur 73 M9
Gransmoor E R Yk 61 J3
Granston Pembks 24 F2
Grantchester Cambs 33 M6
Grantham Lincs 42 D3
Granton C Edin 86 F6
Grantown-on-Spey Highld 100 F9
Grantshouse Border 87 P8
Grappenhall Warrtn 57 M10
Grasby Lincs 52 F3
Grasmere Cumb 62 G1
Grasscroft Oldham 58 C12
Grassendale Lpool 56 H10
Grassington N York 58 D2
Grassmoor Derbys 51 K7
Grassthorpe Notts 52 B9
Grateley Hants 19 J11
Graveley Cambs 33 J4
Graveley Herts 32 H10
Gravelly Hill Birm 40 E9
Graveney Kent 23 K10
Gravesend Kent 22 D8
Gravir W Isls 111 d3
Grayingham Lincs 52 D4
Grayrigg Cumb 63 L3
Grays Thurr 22 C7
Grayshott Hants 10 E3
Grayswood Surrey 10 E3
Greasbrough Rothm 51 K2
Greasby Wirral 56 F10
Great Abington Cambs 33 N7
Great Addington Nhants 32 D2
Great Alne Warwks 30 E3
Great Altcar Lancs 56 G7
Great Amwell Herts 21 M2
Great Asby Cumb 64 C5
Great Ashfield Suffk 34 G4
Great Ayton N York 66 D5
Great Baddow Essex 22 E3
Great Badminton S Glos 18 B4
Great Bardfield Essex 34 B10
Great Barford Bed 32 G6
Great Barr Sandw 40 D8
Great Barrington Gloucs 30 G10
Great Barrow Ches W 49 J2
Great Barton Suffk 34 E4
Great Barugh N York 66 G10
Great Bavington Nthumb 72 H5
Great Bealings Suffk 35 K7
Great Bedwyn Wilts 19 J7
Great Bentley Essex 35 J11
Great Billing Nhants 32 B4
Great Bircham Norfk 44 C4
Great Blakenham Suffk 35 J6
Great Blencow Cumb 71 P8
Great Bolas Wrekin 49 M10
Great Bookham Surrey 21 J11
Great Bourton Oxon 31 L5
Great Bowden Leics 41 Q9
Great Bradley Suffk 34 B6
Great Braxted Essex 22 G1
Great Bricett Suffk 34 G6
Great Brickhill Bucks 32 C10
Great Bridgeford Staffs 40 B3
Great Brington Nhants 31 P2
Great Bromley Essex 34 H10
Great Broughton Cumb 70 H8
Great Broughton N York 66 D6
Great Budworth Ches W 57 M12
Great Burdon Darltn 65 N4
Great Burstead Essex 22 D5
Great Busby N York 66 D6
Great Carlton Lincs 53 L6
Great Casterton Rutlnd 42 E8
Great Chalfield Wilts 18 C7
Great Chart Kent 13 J2
Great Chatwell Staffs 49 P11
Great Chell C Stke 49 Q5
Great Chesterford Essex 33 N8
Great Cheverell Wilts 18 E9
Great Chishill Cambs 33 L8
Great Clacton Essex 35 K12
Great Clifton Cumb 70 G9
Great Coates NE Lin 61 L11
Great Comberton Worcs 29 N1
Great Corby Cumb 71 P5
Great Cornard Suffk 34 E8
Great Cowden E R Yk 61 L6
Great Coxwell Oxon 19 J3
Great Cransley Nhants 32 B2
Great Cressingham Norfk 44 E9
Great Crosthwaite Cumb 71 L10
Great Cubley Derbys 50 F12
Great Cumbrae Island N Ayrs 84 C10
Great Dalby Leics 41 Q5
Great Denham Bed 32 E7
Great Doddington Nhants 32 C4
Great Dunham Norfk 44 E7
Great Dunmow Essex 33 Q11
Great Durnford Wilts 18 G12
Great Easton Essex 33 P10
Great Easton Leics 42 C10
Great Eccleston Lancs 56 H2
Great Ellingham Norfk 44 G10
Great Elm Somset 17 Q6
Great Everdon Nhants 31 N3
Great Eversden Cambs 33 K6
Great Fencote N York 65 M8
Great Finborough Suffk 34 G5
Greatford Lincs 42 F7
Great Fransham Norfk 44 E7
Great Gaddesden Herts 20 G2
Greatgate Staffs 50 D11
Great Gidding Cambs 42 G12
Great Givendale E R Yk 60 E4
Great Glemham Suffk 35 M4
Great Glen Leics 41 P7
Great Gonerby Lincs 42 C3
Great Gransden Cambs 33 J5
Great Green Cambs 33 J7
Great Green Suffk 34 F5
Great Habton N York 66 G11
Great Hale Lincs 42 G2
Great Hallingbury Essex 33 N11
Greatham Hants 10 C4
Greatham Hartpl 66 C3
Greatham W Susx 10 G6
Great Hampden Bucks 20 D3
Great Harrowden Nhants 32 C3
Great Harwood Lancs 57 N3
Great Haseley Oxon 19 Q1
Great Hatfield E R Yk 61 K5
Great Haywood Staffs 40 D3
Great Heck N York 59 N9
Great Henny Essex 34 E8
Great Hinton Wilts 18 D8
Great Hockham Norfk 44 F10
Great Holland Essex 35 K11
Great Hollands Br For 20 D9
Great Horkesley Essex 34 F9
Great Hormead Herts 33 L10
Great Horton C Brad 58 F7
Great Horwood Bucks 31 Q7
Great Houghton Barns 59 K11
Great Houghton Nhants 32 B5
Great Hucklow Derbys 50 F5
Great Kelk E R Yk 61 J3
Great Kimble Bucks 20 D3
Great Kingshill Bucks 20 E4
Great Langdale Cumb 62 F2
Great Langton N York 65 N8
Great Leighs Essex 34 C12
Great Limber Lincs 52 G2
Great Linford M Keyn 32 C8
Great Livermere Suffk 34 E3
Great Longstone Derbys 50 G6
Great Lumley Dur 73 N10
Great Malvern Worcs 39 P11
Great Maplestead Essex 34 D9
Great Marton Bpool 56 G2
Great Massingham Norfk 44 D5
Great Milton Oxon 19 Q1
Great Missenden Bucks 20 E3
Great Mitton Lancs 57 N2
Great Mongeham Kent 23 Q12
Great Moulton Norfk 45 J11
Great Musgrave Cumb 64 D5
Great Ness Shrops 48 H10
Great Notley Essex 34 C11
Great Oak Mons 28 D6
Great Oakley Essex 35 K10
Great Oakley Nhants 42 C11
Great Offley Herts 32 G10
Great Ormside Cumb 64 C4
Great Orton Cumb 71 M5
Great Ouseburn N York 59 K2
Great Oxendon Nhants 41 Q10
Great Park N u Ty 73 L6
Great Parndon Essex 21 N2
Great Paxton Cambs 32 H4
Great Plumpton Lancs 56 H3
Great Plumstead Norfk 45 L7
Great Ponton Lincs 42 D4
Great Preston Leeds 59 K8
Great Raveley Cambs 33 J1
Great Rissington Gloucs 30 G10
Great Rollright Oxon 31 J7
Great Ryburgh Norfk 44 F5
Great Ryton Shrops 39 J2
Great Saling Essex 34 B10
Great Salkeld Cumb 71 Q8
Great Sampford Essex 33 Q9
Great Saughall Ches W 48 G2
Great Shefford W Berk 19 L6
Great Shelford Cambs 33 M6
Great Smeaton N York 65 N6
Great Snoring Norfk 44 F4
Great Somerford Wilts 18 E4
Great Soudley Shrops 49 N9
Great Stainton Darltn 65 N3
Great Stambridge Essex 22 H5
Great Staughton Cambs 32 G4
Great Steeping Lincs 53 M9
Greatstone-on-Sea Kent 13 L5
Great Strickland Cumb 71 Q10
Great Stukeley Cambs 32 H2
Great Sturton Lincs 52 H7
Great Swinburne Nthumb 72 G6
Great Tew Oxon 31 K8
Great Tey Essex 34 E10
Great Thurlow Suffk 34 B6
Great Torrington Devon 15 J8
Great Tosson Nthumb 72 H2
Great Totham Essex 22 G2
Great Totham Essex 22 G2
Great Urswick Cumb 62 F7
Great Wakering Essex 22 H6
Great Waldingfield Suffk 34 E7
Great Walsingham Norfk 44 F3
Great Waltham Essex 22 E2
Great Warley Essex 22 C5
Great Washbourne Gloucs 29 N2
Great Weeke Devon 5 P3
Great Wenham Suffk 34 H8
Great Whittington Nthumb 72 H6
Great Wigborough Essex 23 J1
Great Wilbraham Cambs 33 N5
Great Wishford Wilts 8 F1
Great Witcombe Gloucs 29 M6
Great Witley Worcs 39 N8
Great Wolford Warwks 30 G7
Greatworth Nhants 31 M6
Great Wratting Suffk 34 B7
Great Wymondley Herts 32 H10
Great Wyrley Staffs 40 C6
Great Yarmouth Norfk 45 Q8
Great Yeldham Essex 34 C8
Greenburn W Loth 85 Q10
Green End Herts 33 K11
Green End Herts 33 K9
Greenfield Ag & B 84 D5
Greenfield C Beds 32 F9
Greenfield Flints 56 E12
Greenfield Highld 98 B8
Greenfield Oldham 58 C12
Greenford Gt Lon 21 J7
Greengairs N Lans 85 N8
Greengates C Brad 58 G6
Greenham Somset 16 E11
Green Hammerton N York 59 L3
Greenhaugh Nthumb 72 E4
Greenhead Nthumb 72 C7
Green Heath Staffs 40 C5
Greenhill D & G 78 H11
Greenhill Falk 85 N7
Greenhill Kent 23 M9
Greenhill Leics 41 K5
Greenhill S Lans 78 F3
Greenhills S Lans 85 K11
Greenhithe Kent 22 C8
Greenholm E Ayrs 77 J4
Greenhouse Border 80 D9
Greenhow Hill N York 58 E2
Greenland Highld 110 E3
Greenland Sheff 51 K3
Greenlaw Border 80 F5
Greenlea D & G 70 G1
Greenloaning P & K 85 N2
Greenmount Bury 57 P6
Greenock Inver 84 E7
Greenodd Cumb 62 G6
Green Ore Somset 17 N6
Green Park Readg 20 B9
Green Quarter Cumb 63 J2
Greenshields S Lans 86 B12
Greenside Gatesd 73 K8
Greenside Kirk 58 F10
Greens Norton Nhants 31 P4
Greenstead Green Essex 34 D10
Green Street Herts 21 J4
Green Street Herts 33 M11
Green Tye Herts 33 M11
Greenway Somset 17 J10
Greenwich Gt Lon 21 M7
Greenwich Maritime Gt Lon 21 M7
Greet Gloucs 30 D7
Greete Shrops 39 L7
Greetham Lincs 53 K8
Greetham Rutlnd 42 D7
Greetland Calder 58 E9
Greinton Somset 17 K8
Grenaby IoM 56 b6
Grendon Nhants 32 C5
Grendon Warwks 40 H7
Grendon Underwood Bucks 31 P9
Grenoside Sheff 51 J3
Greosabhagh W Isls 111 c3
Gresford Wrexhm 48 G5
Gresham Norfk 45 J3
Greshornish Highld 104 D10
Gressenhall Norfk 44 F7
Gressenhall Green Norfk 44 F6
Gressingham Lancs 63 K8
Greta Bridge Dur 65 J5
Gretna D & G 71 M3
Gretna Green D & G 71 M2
Gretna Services D & G 71 L2
Gretton Gloucs 30 D7
Gretton Nhants 42 C10
Gretton Shrops 39 K3
Grewelthorpe N York 65 M11
Greyrigg D & G 78 H10
Greys Green Oxon 20 B6
Greysouthen Cumb 70 H9
Greystoke Cumb 71 P8
Greystone Angus 93 P7
Greywell Hants 20 B12
Griff Warwks 41 J9
Griffithstown Torfn 28 C8
Grimeford Village Lancs 57 L6
Grimesthorpe Sheff 51 J3
Grimethorpe Barns 59 K11
Grimister Shet 111 k2
Grimley Worcs 39 Q9
Grimmet S Ayrs 76 F8
Grimoldby Lincs 53 L6
Grimpo Shrops 48 G9
Grimsargh Lancs 57 L3
Grimsby NE Lin 61 M11
Grimscote Nhants 31 P4
Grimscott Cnwll 14 E10
Grimshader W Isls 111 d2
Grimsthorpe Lincs 42 F5
Grimston Leics 41 P3
Grimston Norfk 44 C5
Grimstone Dorset 7 P4
Grimstone End Suffk 34 F3
Grindale E R Yk 67 N12
Grindleford Derbys 50 G5
Grindleton Lancs 63 N11
Grindley Brook Shrops 49 K7
Grindlow Derbys 50 F5
Grindon Staffs 50 E9
Gringley on the Hill Notts 51 Q3
Grinsdale Cumb 71 M4
Grinshill Shrops 49 K10
Grinton N York 65 J7
Griomsiadar W Isls 111 d2
Grishipoll Ag & B 88 F5
Gristhorpe N York 67 M10
Griston Norfk 44 F9
Gritley Ork 111 h2
Grittenham Wilts 18 F4
Grittleton Wilts 18 C5
Grizebeck Cumb 62 E5
Grizedale Cumb 62 G4
Groby Leics 41 M6
Groes Conwy 55 Q8
Groes-faen Rhondd 27 M11
Groeslon Gwynd 54 F9
Groes-Wen Caerph 27 N10
Grogarry W Isls 111 a5
Grogport Ag & B 75 M4
Groigearraidh W Isls 111 a5
Gronant Flints 56 C11
Groombridge E Susx 11 Q3
Grosebay W Isls 111 c3
Grosmont Mons 28 E4
Grosmont N York 67 J6
Groton Suffk 34 F8
Grouville Jersey 7 c2
Grove Notts 51 Q5
Grove Oxon 19 L3
Grove Green Kent 22 F11
Grove Park Gt Lon 21 N8
Grovesend Swans 26 D8
Gruinard Highld 105 P4
Gruinart Ag & B 82 D9
Grula Highld 96 D4
Gruline Ag & B 89 L8
Grundisburgh Suffk 35 K6
Gruting Shet 111 j4
Grutness Shet 111 k5
Gualachulain Highld 90 F7
Guardbridge Fife 93 M11
Guarlford Worcs 39 P11
Guay P & K 92 E6
Guernsey Guern 6 b2
Guernsey Airport Guern 6 b2
Guestling Green E Susx 12 G7
Guestling Thorn E Susx 12 G6
Guestwick Norfk 44 H5
Guide Bridge Tamesd 50 B2
Guilden Morden Cambs 33 J7
Guilden Sutton Ches W 49 J2
Guildford Surrey 20 F12
Guildtown P & K 92 G8
Guilsborough Nhants 41 P11
Guilsfield Powys 48 E12
Guiltreehill S Ayrs 76 F8
Guineaford Devon 15 J5
Guisborough R & Cl 66 E4
Guiseley Leeds 58 G6
Guist Norfk 44 G5
Guiting Power Gloucs 30 E8
Gullane E Loth 87 J5
Gulval Cnwll 2 D9
Gulworthy Devon 5 K5
Gumfreston Pembks 25 J8
Gumley Leics 41 P9
Gunby Lincs 42 D6
Gundleton Hants 9 Q2
Gun Hill E Susx 12 C7
Gunn Devon 15 L5
Gunnerside N York 64 G7
Gunnerton Nthumb 72 G6
Gunness N Linc 60 E11
Gunnislake Cnwll 5 J6
Gunnista Shet 111 k4
Gunthorpe C Pete 42 H9
Gunthorpe N Linc 52 B4
Gunthorpe Norfk 44 G3
Gunthorpe Notts 51 P11
Gunwalloe Cnwll 2 F10
Gurnard IoW 9 N8
Gurney Slade Somset 17 N6
Gurnos Powys 26 G7
Gussage All Saints Dorset 8 E5
Gussage St Andrew Dorset 8 E5
Gussage St Michael Dorset 8 E5
Guston Kent 13 P2
Gutcher Shet 111 k2
Guthrie Angus 93 P5
Guyhirn Cambs 43 L8
Guyzance Nthumb 81 P12
Gwaenysgor Flints 56 C11
Gwalchmai IoA 54 E6
Gwaun-Cae-Gurwen Carmth 26 F6
Gweek Cnwll 2 G9
Gwenddwr Powys 38 C12
Gwennap Cnwll 2 H7
Gwennap Mining District Cnwll 2 H7
Gwernaffield Flints 48 E3
Gwernesney Mons 28 E8
Gwernogle Carmth 26 D3
Gwernymynydd Flints 48 E3
Gwersyllt Wrexhm 48 G5
Gwespyr Flints 56 C11
Gwinear Cnwll 2 E8
Gwithian Cnwll 2 E7
Gwyddelwern Denbgs 48 C6
Gwyddgrug Carmth 26 C2
Gwytherin Conwy 55 N8

H

Habberley Shrops 38 H2
Habberley Worcs 39 P6
Habergham Lancs 57 P3
Habertoft Lincs 53 N9
Habrough NE Lin 61 K10
Hacconby Lincs 42 F5
Haceby Lincs 42 E3
Hacheston Suffk 35 M5
Hackbridge Gt Lon 21 L9

Hackenthorpe – Helstone 173

Hackenthorpe Sheff 51 K4
Hackford Norfk 44 H9
Hackforth N York 65 M8
Hackland Ork 111 h2
Hackleton Nhants 32 B6
Hacklinge Kent 23 Q11
Hackness N York 67 L9
Hackney Gt Lon 21 M6
Hackthorn Lincs 52 E7
Hackthorpe Cumb 71 Q10
Hadden Border 80 G7
Haddenham Bucks 20 B2
Haddenham Cambs 33 M2
Haddington E Loth 87 K7
Haddington Lincs 52 D10
Haddiscoe Norfk 45 P10
Haddon Cambs 42 G10
Hadfield Derbys 50 D2
Hadham Ford Herts 33 M11
Hadleigh Essex 22 F6
Hadleigh Suffk 34 G8
Hadley Worcs 39 Q8
Hadley Wrekin 49 M12
Hadley End Staffs 40 F4
Hadley Wood Gt Lon 21 L4
Hadlow Kent 22 D12
Hadlow Down E Susx 11 Q5
Hadnall Shrops 49 K10
Hadrian's Wall 72 G6
Hadstock Essex 33 N7
Hadzor Worcs 30 B2
Haggersta Shet 111 k4
Haggerston Nthumb 81 L5
Haggs Falk 85 N7
Hagley Herefs 28 G1
Hagley Worcs 40 B10
Hagworthingham Lincs 53 K9
Haile Cumb 62 B1
Hailey Oxon 31 J10
Hailsham E Susx 12 C8
Hail Weston Cambs 32 G4
Hainault Gt Lon 21 P5
Hainford Norfk 45 K6
Hainton Lincs 52 H6
Haisthorpe E R Yk 61 J2
Hakin Pembks 24 F7
Halam Notts 51 P9
Halbeath Fife 86 D5
Halberton Devon 6 D1
Halcro Highld 110 E4
Hale Cumb 63 J6
Hale Halton 57 J11
Hale Hants 8 H4
Hale Surrey 10 D1
Hale Traffd 57 P10
Hale Barns Traffd 57 P10
Hales Norfk 45 N10
Hales Staffs 49 N8
Halesowen Dudley 40 C10
Hales Place Kent 23 M10
Hale Street Kent 22 D12
Halesworth Suffk 35 N2
Halewood Knows 57 J10
Halford Devon 5 Q5
Halford Warwks 30 H5
Halfpenny Green Staffs 39 P4
Halfway House Shrops 48 G12
Halfway Houses Kent 22 H8
Halifax Calder 58 E8
Halket E Ayrs 84 G11
Halkirk Highld 110 D4
Halkyn Flints 48 E2
Hall E Rens 84 G11
Halland E Susx 11 P6
Hallaton Leics 42 B10
Hallatrow BaNES 17 P5
Hallbankgate Cumb 72 B8
Hall Dunnerdale Cumb 62 E3
Hallen S Glos 28 G11
Hallgarth Dur 73 N11
Hallglen Falk 85 P7
Hall Green Birm 40 E10
Hallin Highld 104 C9
Halling Medway 22 E10
Hallington Lincs 53 K6
Hallington Nthumb 72 H6
Halliwell Bolton 57 M6
Halloughton Notts 51 P9
Hallow Worcs 39 P9
Hall's Green Herts 33 J10
Hallyne Border 79 K2
Halmore Gloucs 29 J8
Halnaker W Susx 10 E8
Halsall Lancs 56 G6
Halse Nhants 31 M6
Halse Somset 16 F9
Halsetown Cnwll 2 D7
Halsham E R Yk 61 M8
Halstead Essex 34 D10
Halstead Kent 21 P10
Halstead Leics 41 Q6
Halstock Dorset 7 M2
Haltham Lincs 53 J10
Halton Bucks 20 E2
Halton Halton 57 K11
Halton Lancs 63 J8
Halton Leeds 59 J7
Halton Nthumb 72 H7
Halton Wrexhm 48 F7
Halton East N York 58 D4
Halton Gill N York 64 F11
Halton Holegate Lincs 53 L9
Halton Lea Gate Nthumb 72 C8
Halton Shields Nthumb 72 H7
Halton West N York 63 Q10
Haltwhistle Nthumb 72 D7
Halvergate Norfk 45 N8
Halwell Devon 5 Q9
Halwill Devon 14 H11
Halwill Junction Devon 14 H11
Ham Devon 6 H3
Ham Gloucs 29 J8
Ham Gt Lon 21 J8
Ham Kent 23 P11
Ham Somset 16 H10
Ham Wilts 19 K8
Hambleden Bucks 20 C6
Hambledon Hants 9 Q4
Hambledon Surrey 10 F3
Hamble-le-Rice Hants 9 N6
Hambleton Lancs 56 G1
Hambleton N York 59 M7
Hambridge Somset 17 K10
Hambrook W Susx 10 C8
Hameringham Lincs 53 K9
Hamerton Cambs 32 G2
Ham Green Worcs 30 D2
Hamilton S Lans 85 M11
Hamilton Services (northbound) S Lans 85 M10
Hamlet Dorset 7 N2
Hammersmith Gt Lon 21 K7
Hammerwich Staffs 40 E6
Hammoon Dorset 8 B5
Hamnavoe Shet 111 k4
Hampden Park E Susx 12 C9
Hampnett Gloucs 30 E10
Hampole Donc 59 L11
Hampreston Dorset 8 F7
Hampstead Gt Lon 21 L6
Hampstead Norreys W Berk 19 N5
Hampsthwaite N York 58 H3
Hampton C Pete 42 G10
Hampton Gt Lon 21 J9
Hampton Kent 23 M9
Hampton Shrops 39 N5
Hampton Swindn 18 H3
Hampton Worcs 30 D5
Hampton Bishop Herefs 28 G2
Hampton Court Palace Gt Lon 21 J9
Hampton Heath Ches W 49 J5
Hampton-in-Arden Solhll 40 G10
Hampton Lovett Worcs 30 B2
Hampton Lucy Warwks 30 G3
Hampton Magna Warwks 30 H2
Hampton Park Wilts 8 H2
Hampton Poyle Oxon 31 L10
Hampton Wick Gt Lon 21 J9
Hamptworth Wilts 9 J4
Hamsey E Susx 11 N7
Hamstall Ridware Staffs 40 E4
Hamstead Birm 40 D8
Hamstead Marshall W Berk 19 M7
Hamsterley Dur 65 K2
Hamsterley Dur 73 K9
Hamstreet Kent 13 J4
Ham Street Somset 17 M8
Hamworthy BCP 8 E8
Hanbury Staffs 40 F2
Hanbury Worcs 30 C2
Hanchurch Staffs 49 Q7
Handa Island Highld 108 C6
Hand and Pen Devon 6 E4
Handbridge Ches W 48 H3
Handcross W Susx 11 L4
Handforth Ches E 57 Q11
Handley Ches W 49 J4
Handley Derbys 51 J8
Handsworth Birm 40 D9
Handsworth Sheff 51 K4
Hanford C Stke 49 Q7
Hanging Heaton Kirk 58 G9
Hanging Houghton Nhants 41 Q11
Hanging Langford Wilts 18 F12
Hangleton Br & H 11 L8
Hanham S Glos 17 P2
Hankelow Ches E 49 M6
Hankerton Wilts 29 N9
Hanley C Stke 50 B10
Hanley Castle Worcs 39 Q12
Hanley Child Worcs 39 M8
Hanley Swan Worcs 39 P12
Hanley William Worcs 39 M8
Hanlith N York 58 B2
Hanmer Wrexhm 49 J7
Hannaford Devon 15 K6
Hannington Hants 19 N9
Hannington Nhants 32 B3
Hannington Swindn 18 H3
Hannington Wick Swindn 18 H2
Hanslope M Keyn 32 B7
Hanthorpe Lincs 42 F5
Hanwell Gt Lon 21 J7
Hanwell Oxon 31 K5
Hanwood Shrops 49 J12
Hanworth Gt Lon 20 H8
Hanworth Norfk 45 K3
Happendon S Lans 78 E3
Happendon Services S Lans 78 D3
Happisburgh Norfk 45 N4
Happisburgh Common Norfk 45 N4
Hapsford Ches W 49 J1
Hapton Lancs 57 P3
Hapton Norfk 45 K10
Harberton Devon 5 Q8
Harbertonford Devon 5 Q8
Harbledown Kent 23 L10
Harborne Birm 40 D10
Harborough Magna Warwks 41 L10
Harbottle Nthumb 81 K12
Harbourneford Devon 5 P7
Harburn W Loth 86 C9
Harbury Warwks 31 J3
Harby Leics 41 Q2
Harby Notts 52 C8
Harcombe Devon 6 B6
Harcombe Devon 6 F5
Harcombe Bottom Devon 7 J4
Harden C Brad 58 E6
Harden Wsall 40 D7
Hardenhuish Wilts 18 D6
Hardgate Abers 95 N2
Hardgate D & G 70 D3
Hardgate W Duns 84 H8
Hardham W Susx 10 G6
Hardingham Norfk 44 H8
Hardingstone Nhants 31 Q3
Hardington Somset 17 Q5
Hardington Mandeville Somset 7 M1
Hardington Marsh Somset 7 M2
Hardington Moor Somset 7 M1
Hardisworthy Devon 14 E7
Hardley Hants 9 M6
Hardley Street Norfk 45 N9
Hardraw N York 64 F8
Hardstoft Derbys 51 K8
Hardway Hants 9 Q7
Hardway Somset 17 Q8
Hardwick Bucks 32 B11
Hardwick Cambs 33 L5
Hardwick Nhants 32 C3
Hardwick Norfk 45 K11
Hardwick Oxon 31 J11
Hardwick Oxon 31 M7
Hardwick Wsall 40 E7
Hardwicke Gloucs 29 L6
Hardwicke Gloucs 29 M4
Hardwick Hall Derbys 51 L7
Hardy's Green Essex 34 F11
Hare Croft C Brad 58 E7
Harefield Gt Lon 20 G5
Hare Green Essex 34 H10
Hare Hatch Wokham 20 C7
Harehill Derbys 40 F1
Harehills Leeds 59 J7
Harelaw Border 80 C9
Harelaw D & G 79 N12
Harescombe Gloucs 29 L6
Haresfield Gloucs 29 L6
Harestock Hants 9 M2
Hare Street Essex 21 N2
Hare Street Herts 33 L10
Harewood Leeds 58 H5
Harewood End Herefs 28 F4
Harford Devon 5 M8
Hargrave Ches W 49 J3
Hargrave Nhants 32 E3
Hargrave Suffk 34 C5
Harkstead Suffk 35 K9
Harlaston Staffs 40 G5
Harlaxton Lincs 42 C4
Harlech Gwynd 47 J5
Harlech Castle Gwynd 47 J5
Harlescott Shrops 49 J11
Harlesden Gt Lon 21 K6
Harlesthorpe Derbys 51 L5
Harleston Devon 5 Q10
Harleston Norfk 45 L12
Harleston Suffk 34 G5
Harlestone Nhants 31 P2
Harle Syke Lancs 57 Q2
Harley Rothm 51 J2
Harley Shrops 39 L2
Harlington C Beds 32 E10
Harlington Donc 51 L1
Harlington Gt Lon 20 H7
Harlosh Highld 96 C2
Harlow Essex 21 N2
Harlow Carr RHS N York 58 H4
Harlow Hill Nthumb 73 J7
Harlthorpe E R Yk 60 C6
Harlton Cambs 33 L6
Harlyn Cnwll 3 K1
Harman's Cross Dorset 8 E10
Harmby N York 65 K9
Harmer Green Herts 33 J12
Harmer Hill Shrops 49 J10
Harmston Lincs 52 D10
Harnage Shrops 39 K2
Harnhill Gloucs 18 F1
Harold Hill Gt Lon 21 Q5
Haroldston West Pembks 24 F6
Haroldswick Shet 111 m2
Harold Wood Gt Lon 22 B5
Harome N York 66 F10
Harpenden Herts 21 J1
Harpford Devon 6 E5
Harpham E R Yk 61 J2
Harpley Norfk 44 D5
Harpley Worcs 39 M9
Harpole Nhants 31 P2
Harpsdale Highld 110 D5
Harpswell Lincs 52 D5
Harpurhey Manch 57 Q8
Harraby Cumb 71 N5
Harracott Devon 15 K6
Harrapool Highld 97 J5
Harras Cumb 70 F11
Harrietfield P & K 92 E9
Harrietsham Kent 22 G11
Harringay Gt Lon 21 L6
Harrington Cumb 70 G9
Harrington Lincs 53 L8
Harrington Nhants 41 Q10
Harringworth Nhants 42 D10
Harris W Isls 111 c3
Harrogate N York 58 H3
Harrold Bed 32 D5
Harrow Gt Lon 21 J6
Harrowbarrow Cnwll 5 J6
Harrowgate Village Darltn 65 N4
Harrow Green Suffk 34 E6
Harrow on the Hill Gt Lon 21 J6
Harrow Weald Gt Lon 21 J5
Harston Cambs 33 L6
Harston Leics 42 B4
Harswell E R Yk 60 E6
Hart Hartpl 66 C1
Hartburn Nthumb 73 J4
Hartburn S on T 65 Q4
Hartest Suffk 34 D6
Hartfield E Susx 11 P3
Hartford Cambs 33 J3
Hartford Ches W 49 L2
Hartfordbridge Hants 20 C10
Hartford End Essex 34 B12
Hartforth N York 65 L6
Hartgrove Dorset 8 C4
Harthill Ches W 49 J4
Harthill N Lans 85 Q9
Harthill Rothm 51 L5
Hartington Derbys 50 F8
Hartland Devon 14 E7
Hartland Quay Devon 14 D7
Hartlebury Worcs 39 Q7
Hartlepool Hartpl 66 C2
Hartley Cumb 64 E6
Hartley Kent 12 F3
Hartley Kent 22 C9
Hartley Wespall Hants 20 B10
Hartley Wintney Hants 20 C11
Hartlip Kent 22 G9
Harton N York 60 C2
Harton S Tyne 73 P7
Hartpury Gloucs 29 L4
Hartshead Kirk 58 F9
Hartshead Moor Services Calder 58 F8
Hartshill C Stke 49 Q6
Hartshill Warwks 41 J8
Hartshorne Derbys 41 J4
Hartwell Nhants 32 B6
Hartwith N York 58 G2
Hartwood N Lans 85 P10
Hartwoodmyres Border 79 N4
Harvel Kent 22 D10
Harvington Worcs 30 D4
Harvington Worcs 39 Q7
Harwell Notts 51 P3
Harwell Oxon 19 N3
Harwich Essex 35 L9
Harwood Dale N York 67 L8
Harworth Notts 51 N3
Hasbury Dudley 40 C10
Hascombe Surrey 10 G3
Haselbech Nhants 41 P11
Haselbury Plucknett Somset 7 L1
Haseley Warwks 30 G1
Haselor Warwks 30 E3
Hasfield Gloucs 29 L4
Haskayne Lancs 56 G7
Hasketon Suffk 35 L6
Haslemere Surrey 10 E4
Haslingden Lancs 57 P4
Haslingfield Cambs 33 L6
Haslington Ches E 49 N4
Hassingham Norfk 45 N8
Hassocks W Susx 11 L7
Hassop Derbys 50 G6
Haster Highld 110 G5
Hastingleigh Kent 13 L2
Hastings E Susx 12 G7
Hastingwood Essex 21 P2
Hastoe Herts 20 E2
Haswell Dur 73 P11
Haswell Plough Dur 73 P11
Hatch Beauchamp Somset 17 J11
Hatch End Gt Lon 21 J5
Hatchmere Ches W 49 K2
Hatch Warren Hants 19 Q10
Hatcliffe NE Lin 52 H4
Hatfield Donc 59 P11
Hatfield Herefs 39 L9
Hatfield Herts 21 K2
Hatfield Broad Oak Essex 33 N12
Hatfield Heath Essex 21 Q1
Hatfield Peverel Essex 22 F2
Hatfield Woodhouse Donc 59 P11
Hatford Oxon 19 K2
Hatherden Hants 19 K10
Hatherleigh Devon 15 J10
Hathern Leics 41 L3
Hatherop Gloucs 30 F11
Hathersage Derbys 50 G5
Hathersage Booths Derbys 50 G5
Hatherton Ches E 49 M6
Hatherton Staffs 40 C5
Hatley St George Cambs 33 J6
Hatt Cnwll 5 J7
Hattersley Tamesd 50 C2
Hatton Abers 103 L7
Hatton Angus 93 N7
Hatton Derbys 40 G2
Hatton Gt Lon 20 H8
Hatton Lincs 52 H7
Hatton Shrops 39 J4
Hatton Warrtn 57 L11
Hatton Warwks 30 G1
Hatton of Fintray Abers 102 H11
Hatton Park Warwks 30 G1
Haugh E Ayrs 76 H6
Haugham Lincs 53 K7
Haughhead E Duns 85 K7
Haughley Suffk 34 G4
Haughley Green Suffk 34 G4
Haugh of Glass Moray 101 M7
Haugh of Urr D & G 70 D3
Haughs of Kinnaird Angus 93 Q4
Haughton Ches E 49 L4
Haughton Shrops 48 H9
Haughton Staffs 49 Q10
Haughton le Skerne Darltn 65 N4
Haultwick Herts 33 K11
Haunton Staffs 40 G5
Hauxton Cambs 33 M6
Havant Hants 10 B8
Havenstreet IoW 9 P8
Havercroft Wakefd 59 K10
Haverfordwest Pembks 24 G6
Haverhill Suffk 33 Q7
Haverigg Cumb 62 D6
Havering-atte-Bower Gt Lon 21 P5
Haversham M Keyn 32 B8
Haverthwaite Cumb 62 G5
Havyatt N Som 17 L4
Hawarden Flints 48 G3
Hawbush Green Essex 34 D11
Hawen Cerdgn 36 F10
Hawes N York 64 F9
Hawe's Green Norfk 45 L9
Hawford Worcs 39 Q9
Hawick Border 80 C10
Hawkchurch Devon 7 J3
Hawkedon Suffk 34 D6
Hawkeridge Wilts 18 C9
Hawkesbury S Glos 18 B4
Hawkesbury Upton S Glos 18 B4
Hawkhead Rens 84 H9
Hawkhurst Kent 12 F4
Hawkinge Kent 13 N3
Hawkley Hants 10 C4
Hawkridge Somset 15 P6
Hawkshead Cumb 62 G3
Hawkshead Hill Cumb 62 G3
Hawksland S Lans 78 D2
Hawkstone Shrops 49 L9
Hawkswick N York 64 G12
Hawksworth Leeds 58 F6
Hawksworth Notts 51 Q11
Hawkwell Essex 22 G5
Hawley Hants 20 D10
Hawling Gloucs 30 E9
Hawnby N York 66 D9
Haworth C Brad 58 D6
Hawstead Suffk 34 E5
Hawthorn Dur 73 P10
Hawthorn Hill Lincs 52 H11
Hawton Notts 52 B12
Haxby C York 59 N3
Haxey N Linc 51 Q2
Haydock St Hel 57 K9
Haydon Bridge Nthumb 72 F7
Haydon Wick Swindn 18 G4
Hayes Gt Lon 20 H7
Hayes Gt Lon 21 N9
Hayes End Gt Lon 20 H7
Hayfield Ag & B 90 E10
Hayfield Derbys 50 D4
Hayhillock Angus 93 N7
Hayle Cnwll 2 E8
Hayle Port Cnwll 2 E8
Hayley Green Dudley 40 C10
Hayling Island Hants 10 B9
Hayne Devon 5 P3
Haynes C Beds 32 F8
Haynes Church End C Beds 32 F8
Haynes West End C Beds 32 F8
Hay-on-Wye Powys 27 P1
Hayscastle Pembks 24 F4
Hayscastle Cross Pembks 24 F4
Hay Street Herts 33 L10
Hayton Cumb 70 H7
Hayton Cumb 71 Q4
Hayton E R Yk 60 E5
Hayton Notts 51 Q4
Haytor Vale Devon 5 P5
Haytown Devon 14 G8
Haywards Heath W Susx 11 M5
Haywood Donc 59 N10
Hazelbank S Lans 77 P3
Hazelbury Bryan Dorset 7 Q2
Hazeleigh Essex 22 G3
Hazel Grove Stockp 50 B4
Hazelton Walls Fife 93 L10
Hazelwood Derbys 51 J10
Hazlemere Bucks 20 E4
Hazlerigg N u Ty 73 M6
Hazleton Gloucs 30 E9
Heacham Norfk 44 B3
Headbourne Worthy Hants 9 N2
Headcorn Kent 12 G2
Headingley Leeds 58 H7
Headington Oxon 31 M11
Headlam Dur 65 L4
Headlesscross N Lans 85 Q10
Headless Cross Worcs 30 D2
Headley Hants 10 D3
Headley Hants 19 N8
Headley Surrey 21 K11
Headley Down Hants 10 D3
Headon Notts 51 Q5
Heads Nook Cumb 71 P5
Heage Derbys 51 J10
Healaugh N York 59 L5
Healaugh N York 64 H7
Heald Green Stockp 57 Q10
Heale Somset 16 H11
Heale Somset 17 K10
Healey N York 65 L10
Healeyfield Dur 73 J10
Healing NE Lin 61 L11
Heamoor Cnwll 2 C9
Heanor Derbys 51 K10
Heanton Punchardon Devon 15 J5
Heapham Lincs 52 C6
Heart of Scotland Services N Lans 85 Q9
Heasley Mill Devon 15 M6
Heaste Highld 96 H6
Heath Derbys 51 K7
Heath Wakefd 59 J9
Heath and Reach C Beds 32 D10
Heathcote Derbys 50 F8
Heather Leics 41 K5
Heathfield E Susx 12 C6
Heathfield Somset 16 F10
Heath Green Worcs 40 E12
Heath Hall D & G 78 G11
Heath Hayes & Wimblebury Staffs 40 D5
Heath Hill Shrops 49 N11
Heathrow Airport Gt Lon 20 H8
Heathton Shrops 39 P4
Heath Town Wolves 40 B7
Heatley Warrtn 57 N10
Heaton C Brad 58 F7
Heaton N u Ty 73 M7
Heaton Staffs 50 C8
Heaton Chapel Stockp 57 Q9
Heaton Mersey Stockp 57 Q10
Heaton Norris Stockp 50 B3
Heaton's Bridge Lancs 56 H6
Heaverham Kent 22 C10
Heavitree Devon 6 C4
Hebburn S Tyne 73 N7
Hebden N York 58 D2
Hebden Bridge Calder 58 C8
Hebing End Herts 33 K11
Hebron Carmth 25 L4
Hebron Nthumb 73 L3
Heckfield Hants 20 B10
Heckfield Green Suffk 35 K2
Heckfordbridge Essex 34 F11
Heckington Lincs 42 G2
Heckmondwike Kirk 58 G9
Heddington Wilts 18 E7
Heddon-on-the-Wall Nthumb 73 K7
Hedenham Norfk 45 M10
Hedge End Hants 9 N5
Hedgerley Bucks 20 F6
Hedging Somset 17 J9
Hedley on the Hill Nthumb 73 J8
Hednesford Staffs 40 C5
Hedon E R Yk 61 K8
Hedsor Bucks 20 E6
Heeley Sheff 51 J4
Heglibister Shet 111 k4
Heighington Darltn 65 M3
Heighington Lincs 52 E9
Heightington Worcs 39 N7
Heiton Border 80 F7
Hele Devon 6 D3
Hele Devon 15 J4
Helensburgh Ag & B 84 E6
Helenton S Ayrs 76 G5
Helford Cnwll 2 H9
Helford Passage Cnwll 2 H9
Helhoughton Norfk 44 E5
Helions Bumpstead Essex 33 Q8
Helland Cnwll 3 N2
Hellescott Cnwll 4 G3
Hellesdon Norfk 45 K7
Hellidon Nhants 31 M3
Hellifield N York 63 Q10
Hellingly E Susx 12 C7
Helmdon Nhants 31 N5
Helme Kirk 58 E10
Helmingham Suffk 35 K5
Helmsdale Highld 110 B11
Helmshore Lancs 57 P5
Helmsley N York 66 E10
Helperby N York 59 K1
Helperthorpe N York 67 K12
Helpringham Lincs 42 G3
Helpston C Pete 42 G8
Helsby Ches W 49 J1
Helston Cnwll 2 F9
Helstone Cnwll 4 D4

Helton *Cumb* 71 Q10
Hemel Hempstead *Herts* 20 G2
Hemerdon *Devon* 5 L8
Hemingbrough *N York* 59 P7
Hemingby *Lincs* 53 J8
Hemingford Abbots *Cambs* 33 J3
Hemingford Grey *Cambs* 33 J3
Hemingstone *Suffk* 35 J6
Hemington *Leics* 41 L2
Hemington *Nhants* 42 F12
Hemington *Somset* 17 Q5
Hemley *Suffk* 35 L8
Hemlington *Middsb* 66 C5
Hempnall *Norfk* 45 L10
Hempnall Green *Norfk* 45 L10
Hempriggs *Moray* 100 H3
Hempstead *Essex* 33 Q8
Hempstead *Medway* 22 F9
Hempstead *Norfk* 44 H3
Hempstead *Norfk* 45 N5
Hempton *Norfk* 44 E4
Hempton *Oxon* 31 K7
Hemsby *Norfk* 45 P6
Hemswell *Lincs* 52 D5
Hemswell Cliff *Lincs* 52 D5
Hemsworth *Wakefd* 59 K10
Hemyock *Devon* 16 F12
Henbury *Bristl* 28 G11
Hendon *Gt Lon* 21 K5
Hendon *Sundld* 73 P9
Hendy *Carmth* 26 D7
Henfield *W Susx* 11 K6
Hengoed *Caerph* 27 N9
Hengoed *Powys* 38 E10
Hengrave *Suffk* 34 D3
Henham *Essex* 33 N10
Heniarth *Powys* 38 D1
Henlade *Somset* 16 H10
Henley *Dorset* 7 Q2
Henley *Somset* 17 L9
Henley *Suffk* 35 J6
Henley *W Susx* 10 E5
Henley Green *Covtry* 41 J10
Henley-in-Arden *Warwks* 30 F2
Henley-on-Thames *Oxon* 20 C6
Henley's Down *E Susx* 12 E7
Henllan *Cerdgn* 36 F11
Henllan *Denbgs* 55 Q7
Henllys *Torfn* 28 B9
Henlow *C Beds* 32 H8
Henlow Camp *C Beds* 32 G9
Hennock *Devon* 5 Q4
Henny Street *Essex* 34 E8
Henryd *Conwy* 55 L6
Henry's Moat (Castell Hendre) *Pembks* 24 H4
Hensall *N York* 59 N9
Henshaw *Nthumb* 72 D7
Hensingham *Cumb* 70 G11
Henstead *Suffk* 45 P11
Hensting *Hants* 9 N3
Henstridge *Somset* 17 Q11
Henstridge Ash *Somset* 17 Q11
Henton *Oxon* 20 C3
Henton *Somset* 17 L7
Henwick *Worcs* 39 Q10
Henwood *Cnwll* 4 G5
Heol-y-Cyw *Brdgnd* 27 K11
Hepple *Nthumb* 72 H1
Hepscott *Nthumb* 73 L4
Heptonstall *Calder* 58 C8
Hepworth *Kirk* 58 F11
Hepworth *Suffk* 34 G2
Herbrandston *Pembks* 24 F7
Hereford *Herefs* 28 F2
Hereson *Kent* 23 Q9
Heribusta *Highld* 104 E8
Heriot *Border* 86 H10
Hermiston *C Edin* 86 E8
Hermitage *Border* 79 P9
Hermitage *Dorset* 7 P2
Hermitage *W Berk* 19 N6
Hermon *Carmth* 25 N3
Hermon *Pembks* 25 L3
Herne *Kent* 23 M9
Herne Bay *Kent* 23 M9
Herne Hill *Gt Lon* 21 L8
Herne Pound *Kent* 22 D11
Hernhill *Kent* 23 K10
Herodsfoot *Cnwll* 4 F7
Heronsford *S Ayrs* 68 F3
Herriard *Hants* 19 Q10
Herringfleet *Suffk* 45 P9
Herringswell *Suffk* 34 C3
Herringthorpe *Rothm* 51 K3
Herrington *Sundld* 73 P9
Hersden *Kent* 23 M10
Hersham *Surrey* 20 H9
Herstmonceux *E Susx* 12 D7
Herston *Ork* 111 h3
Hertford *Herts* 21 M2
Hertford Heath *Herts* 21 M2
Hertingfordbury *Herts* 21 L2
Hesketh Bank *Lancs* 57 J4
Hesketh Lane *Lancs* 57 L1
Hesket Newmarket *Cumb* 71 M7
Hesleden *Dur* 73 Q12
Heslington *C York* 59 N4
Hessay *C York* 59 M4
Hessenford *Cnwll* 4 G8
Hessett *Suffk* 34 F4
Hessle *E R Yk* 60 H8
Hessle *Wakefd* 59 K9
Hest Bank *Lancs* 63 J8
Heston *Gt Lon* 20 H7
Heston Services *Gt Lon* 20 H7
Hestwall *Ork* 111 g2
Heswall *Wirral* 56 F11
Hethe *Oxon* 31 N8
Hethersett *Norfk* 45 J8
Hethersgill *Cumb* 71 P3
Hett *Dur* 73 M12
Hetton *N York* 58 C3
Hetton-le-Hole *Sundld* 73 N10
Heugh *Nthumb* 73 J6
Heughhead *Abers* 101 M11
Heugh Head *Border* 87 Q9
Heveningham *Suffk* 35 M3
Hever *Kent* 11 P2
Heversham *Cumb* 63 J5
Hevingham *Norfk* 45 K6
Hewas Water *Cnwll* 3 L6
Hewelsfield *Gloucs* 28 G8

Hewish *Somset* 7 K2
Hewood *Dorset* 7 J3
Hexham *Nthumb* 72 G7
Hextable *Kent* 21 P8
Hexthorpe *Donc* 51 M1
Hexton *Herts* 32 F10
Hexworthy *Cnwll* 4 H4
Hexworthy *Devon* 5 N6
Heybridge *Essex* 22 D4
Heybridge *Essex* 22 G2
Heybrook Bay *Devon* 5 K9
Heydon *Cambs* 33 M8
Heydon *Norfk* 45 J5
Heydour *Lincs* 42 E3
Heylipoll *Ag & B* 88 B7
Heylor *Shet* 111 j3
Heysham *Lancs* 62 H9
Heyshott *W Susx* 10 E6
Heytesbury *Wilts* 18 D11
Heythrop *Oxon* 31 J8
Heywood *Rochdl* 57 Q6
Heywood *Wilts* 18 C9
Hibaldstow *N Linc* 52 D3
Hickleton *Donc* 59 L12
Hickling *Norfk* 45 N5
Hickling *Notts* 41 P2
Hickling Green *Norfk* 45 N5
Hickstead *W Susx* 11 L6
Hidcote Bartrim *Gloucs* 30 F5
Hidcote Boyce *Gloucs* 30 F6
Higham *Barns* 58 H11
Higham *Derbys* 51 K8
Higham *Kent* 12 C1
Higham *Kent* 22 E8
Higham *Lancs* 57 P2
Higham *Suffk* 34 C4
Higham *Suffk* 34 G9
Higham Ferrers *Nhants* 32 D3
Higham Gobion *C Beds* 32 F9
Higham Hill *Gt Lon* 21 M5
Higham on the Hill *Leics* 41 J8
Highampton *Devon* 14 H10
Highams Park *Gt Lon* 21 M5
High Ardwell *D & G* 68 E10
High Auldgirth *D & G* 78 E10
High Bankhill *Cumb* 71 Q7
High Barnet *Gt Lon* 21 K4
High Beach *Essex* 21 N4
High Bentham *N York* 63 M8
High Bickington *Devon* 15 K7
High Biggins *Cumb* 63 L6
High Blantyre *S Lans* 85 L10
High Bonnybridge *Falk* 85 N7
High Bray *Devon* 15 M5
Highbridge *Somset* 17 J6
Highbrook *W Susx* 11 M4
High Brooms *Kent* 12 C2
Highburton *Kirk* 58 F10
Highbury *Gt Lon* 21 L6
Highbury *Somset* 17 Q6
High Catton *E R Yk* 60 C4
Highclere *Hants* 19 M8
Highcliffe *BCP* 8 H8
High Coniscliffe *Darltn* 65 M5
High Crosby *Cumb* 71 P4
High Cross *E Ayrs* 76 G3
High Cross *Hants* 10 B5
High Cross *Herts* 33 M11
High Cross *Warwks* 30 G1
High Drummore *D & G* 68 F11
High Easter *Essex* 22 C1
High Ellington *N York* 65 L10
Higher Ansty *Dorset* 8 B6
Higher Bartle *Lancs* 57 J3
Higher Bockhampton *Dorset* 7 Q4
Higher Brixham *Torbay* 6 C10
High Ercall *Wrekin* 49 L11
Higher Chillington *Somset* 7 K2
Higher Folds *Wigan* 57 M8
Higher Gabwell *Devon* 6 C8
Higher Heysham *Lancs* 62 H9
Higher Irlam *Salfd* 57 N9
Higher Kinnerton *Flints* 48 G4
Higher Muddiford *Devon* 15 K5
Higher Penwortham *Lancs* 57 K3
Higher Prestacott *Devon* 14 G11
Higher Town *Cnwll* 3 J6
Higher Town *Cnwll* 3 M4
Higher Town *IoS* 2 c1
Higher Walton *Lancs* 57 L4
Higher Walton *Warrtn* 57 L10
Higher Wambrook *Somset* 6 H2
Higher Waterston *Dorset* 7 Q4
Higher Wheelton *Lancs* 57 L4
Higher Whitley *Ches W* 57 L11
Higher Wincham *Ches W* 57 M12
Higher Wraxall *Dorset* 7 N3
Higher Wych *Ches W* 49 J6
High Etherley *Dur* 65 L2
Highfield *Gatesd* 73 K8
Highfield *N Ayrs* 76 E2
Highfields Caldecote *Cambs* 33 K5
High Garrett *Essex* 34 C10
Highgate *Gt Lon* 21 L6
Highgate *Kent* 12 F4
High Grantley *N York* 65 M12
High Green *Norfk* 45 J11
High Green *Norfk* 45 J8
High Green *Sheff* 51 J2
High Halden *Kent* 12 H3
High Halstow *Medway* 22 F8
High Ham *Somset* 17 M9
High Harrington *Cumb* 70 G9
High Harrogate *N York* 58 H3
High Hatton *Shrops* 49 L9
High Hauxley *Nthumb* 73 M1
High Hawsker *N York* 67 K6
High Hesket *Cumb* 71 P6
High Hoyland *Barns* 58 H11
High Hurstwood *E Susx* 11 P5
High Hutton *N York* 60 D1
High Ireby *Cumb* 71 K7
High Kilburn *N York* 66 D10
High Lands *Dur* 65 K3
Highlane *Derbys* 51 K4
High Lane *Stockp* 50 C4
High Lanes *Cnwll* 2 E8
Highleadon *Gloucs* 29 K4
High Legh *Ches E* 57 M11
Highleigh *W Susx* 10 D9
High Leven *S on T* 66 C5
Highley *Shrops* 39 N5
High Littleton *BaNES* 17 P5

High Lorton *Cumb* 71 J9
High Marnham *Notts* 52 B9
High Melton *Donc* 51 L1
High Mickley *Nthumb* 73 J8
Highmoor *Oxon* 20 B6
Highmoor Cross *Oxon* 20 B6
Highnam *Gloucs* 29 L5
High Newport *Sundld* 73 P9
High Newton *Cumb* 62 H5
High Newton-by-the-Sea *Nthumb* 81 P8
High Nibthwaite *Cumb* 62 F4
High Offley *Staffs* 49 P9
High Ongar *Essex* 22 C3
High Onn *Staffs* 49 P11
High Park Corner *Essex* 34 G11
High Pennyvenie *E Ayrs* 76 H9
High Pittington *Dur* 73 N11
High Roding *Essex* 33 P12
High Salvington *W Susx* 10 H8
High Spen *Gatesd* 73 K8
Highsted *Kent* 22 H10
High Street *Cnwll* 3 L5
Highstreet *Kent* 23 L10
Highstreet Green *Surrey* 10 F3
Hightae *D & G* 78 H11
Highter's Heath *Birm* 40 E10
Hightown *Sefton* 56 F7
Hightown Green *Suffk* 34 F5
High Toynton *Lincs* 53 J9
High Valleyfield *Fife* 86 B5
Highweek *Devon* 6 C8
Highwood *Essex* 22 D3
Highwood *W Susx* 11 J4
Highwood Hill *Gt Lon* 21 K5
Highworth *Swindn* 18 H3
High Wray *Cumb* 62 G3
High Wych *Herts* 33 P1
High Wycombe *Bucks* 20 D5
Hilborough *Norfk* 44 D9
Hilcott *Wilts* 18 G8
Hildenborough *Kent* 21 R12
Hilden Park *Kent* 12 C1
Hildersham *Cambs* 33 N7
Hilderstone *Staffs* 40 C1
Hilderthorpe *E R Yk* 61 K2
Hilgay *Norfk* 43 P9
Hill *S Glos* 28 H9
Hill *Warwks* 31 L2
Hillam *N York* 59 L8
Hill Brow *Hants* 10 C5
Hillbutts *Dorset* 8 E7
Hill Chorlton *Staffs* 49 P7
Hillclifflane *Derbys* 50 H10
Hill Common *Somset* 16 F10
Hilldyke *Lincs* 43 K1
Hill End *Fife* 86 C3
Hillend *Fife* 86 D5
Hill End *Gloucs* 29 M2
Hillend *Mdloth* 86 F8
Hillend *N Lans* 85 N9
Hillesden *Bucks* 31 P8
Hillesley *Gloucs* 29 K10
Hillfarrance *Somset* 16 F10
Hill Green *Kent* 22 G10
Hillhead *Abers* 102 D8
Hill Head *Hants* 9 P6
Hillhead *S Lans* 78 F2
Hillhead of Cocklaw *Abers* 103 M6
Hilliclay *Highld* 110 D3
Hillingdon *Gt Lon* 20 H6
Hillington *C Glas* 85 J9
Hillington *Norfk* 44 C5
Hillmorton *Warwks* 41 M11
Hill of Beath *Fife* 86 D4
Hill of Fearn *Highld* 107 N6
Hillowton *D & G* 70 C3
Hill Ridware *Staffs* 40 E4
Hillside *Abers* 95 Q3
Hillside *Angus* 95 L9
Hill Side *Kirk* 58 F10
Hills Town *Derbys* 51 L6
Hillstreet *Hants* 9 K4
Hillswick *Shet* 111 j3
Hill Top *Sandw* 40 C8
Hill Top *Wakefd* 59 J10
Hillwell *Shet* 111 k5
Hilmarton *Wilts* 18 E6
Hilperton *Wilts* 18 C8
Hilsea *C Port* 9 Q6
Hilston *E R Yk* 61 M7
Hilton *Border* 81 J4
Hilton *Cambs* 33 J4
Hilton *Cumb* 64 D4
Hilton *Derbys* 40 G2
Hilton *Dorset* 8 B6
Hilton *Dur* 65 L3
Hilton *S on T* 66 C5
Hilton *Shrops* 39 P3
Hilton of Cadboll *Highld* 107 P7
Hilton Park Services *Staffs* 40 C6
Himbleton *Worcs* 30 C3
Himley *Staffs* 39 Q4
Hincaster *Cumb* 63 K5
Hinchley Wood *Surrey* 21 J9
Hinckley *Leics* 41 K8
Hinderclay *Suffk* 34 G2
Hinderwell *N York* 66 H4
Hindhead *Surrey* 10 E3
Hindhead Tunnel *Surrey* 10 E3
Hindley *Wigan* 57 L7
Hindlip *Worcs* 39 Q9
Hindolveston *Norfk* 44 G4
Hindon *Wilts* 8 D2
Hindringham *Norfk* 44 G3
Hingham *Norfk* 44 G9
Hinstock *Shrops* 49 M9
Hintlesham *Suffk* 34 H7
Hinton *Herefs* 28 D2
Hinton *Nhants* 31 M4
Hinton *S Glos* 17 Q2
Hinton *Shrops* 38 H2
Hinton Ampner *Hants* 9 P2
Hinton Blewett *BaNES* 17 N5
Hinton Charterhouse *BaNES* 18 B8
Hinton-in-the-Hedges *Nhants* 31 M6
Hinton Martell *Dorset* 8 E6
Hinton on the Green *Worcs* 30 D6
Hinton Parva *Swindn* 19 J4
Hinton St George *Somset* 7 L2
Hinton St Mary *Dorset* 8 B4
Hinton Waldrist *Oxon* 19 L2
Hints *Staffs* 40 F6

Hinwick *Bed* 32 D5
Hinxhill *Kent* 13 K2
Hinxton *Cambs* 33 M7
Hinxworth *Herts* 32 H8
Hipperholme *Calder* 58 E8
Hipswell *N York* 65 L7
Hirn *Abers* 95 M2
Hirnant *Powys* 48 B10
Hirst *Nthumb* 73 M4
Hirst Courtney *N York* 59 N8
Hirwaun *Rhondd* 27 K7
Hiscott *Devon* 15 J7
Histon *Cambs* 33 M4
Hitcham *Suffk* 34 G6
Hitcham Causeway *Suffk* 34 G6
Hitcham Street *Suffk* 34 G6
Hitchin *Herts* 32 H10
Hither Green *Gt Lon* 21 M8
Hittisleigh *Devon* 5 P2
Hive *E R Yk* 60 E7
Hixon *Staffs* 40 D3
Hoaden *Kent* 23 N10
Hoar Cross *Staffs* 40 F3
Hoarwithy *Herefs* 28 G3
Hoath *Kent* 23 M9
Hobarris *Shrops* 38 F6
Hobkirk *Border* 80 D11
Hobson *Dur* 73 L9
Hoby *Leics* 41 P4
Hockering *Norfk* 44 H7
Hockerton *Notts* 51 Q9
Hockley *Essex* 22 G5
Hockley Heath *Solhll* 40 F11
Hockliffe *C Beds* 32 D10
Hockwold cum Wilton *Norfk* 44 C11
Hockworthy *Devon* 16 D11
Hoddesdon *Herts* 21 M2
Hoddlesden *Bl w D* 57 N4
Hoddom Cross *D & G* 71 J2
Hoddom Mains *D & G* 71 J2
Hodgeston *Pembks* 24 H8
Hodnet *Shrops* 49 L9
Hodsock *Notts* 51 N4
Hodsoll Street *Kent* 22 D10
Hodson *Swindn* 18 H5
Hodthorpe *Derbys* 51 M5
Hoe *Norfk* 44 G6
Hogben's Hill *Kent* 23 K11
Hoggeston *Bucks* 32 B10
Hoggrill's End *Warwks* 40 G8
Hoghton *Lancs* 57 L4
Hognaston *Derbys* 50 G10
Hogsthorpe *Lincs* 53 N8
Holbeach *Lincs* 43 K5
Holbeach Bank *Lincs* 43 K5
Holbeach Clough *Lincs* 43 K5
Holbeach Drove *Lincs* 43 K7
Holbeach Hurn *Lincs* 43 L5
Holbeach St Johns *Lincs* 43 K6
Holbeach St Mark's *Lincs* 43 L4
Holbeach St Matthew *Lincs* 43 L4
Holbeck *Notts* 51 M6
Holberrow Green *Worcs* 30 D3
Holbeton *Devon* 5 M9
Holborn *Gt Lon* 21 L7
Holbrook *Derbys* 51 J11
Holbrook *Suffk* 35 J9
Holbrooks *Covtry* 41 J10
Holbury *Hants* 9 M6
Holcombe *Devon* 6 C7
Holcombe *Somset* 17 P6
Holcombe Rogus *Devon* 16 E11
Holcot *Nhants* 32 B3
Holden *Lancs* 63 P11
Holdenby *Nhants* 31 P1
Holder's Green *Essex* 33 Q10
Holdgate *Shrops* 39 K4
Holdingham *Lincs* 42 F1
Holditch *Dorset* 7 J3
Holemoor *Devon* 14 H10
Holford *Somset* 16 F7
Holgate *C York* 59 N4
Holker *Cumb* 62 G6
Holkham *Norfk* 44 E2
Hollacombe *Devon* 14 G10
Holland Fen *Lincs* 52 H12
Holland-on-Sea *Essex* 35 K12
Hollandstoun *Ork* 111 i1
Hollee *D & G* 71 L2
Hollesley *Suffk* 35 M7
Hollicombe *Torbay* 6 B9
Hollingbourne *Kent* 22 G11
Hollingbury *Br & H* 11 L8
Hollingdon *Bucks* 32 C10
Hollington *Derbys* 50 G11
Hollington *Staffs* 50 D11
Hollingworth *Tamesd* 50 D2
Hollinsclough *Staffs* 50 E7
Hollins End *Sheff* 51 J4
Hollins Green *Warrtn* 57 M10
Hollinswood *Wrekin* 50 N1
Hollocombe *Devon* 15 L9
Holloway *Derbys* 51 J9
Holloway *Gt Lon* 21 L6
Hollowell *Nhants* 41 P11
Hollowmoor Heath *Ches W* 49 J2
Hollows *D & G* 79 N12
Hollybush *Caerph* 27 N7
Hollybush *E Ayrs* 76 G8
Hollybush *Herefs* 29 K2
Hollym *E R Yk* 61 N8
Holmbridge *Kirk* 58 E11
Holmbury St Mary *Surrey* 10 H2
Holmbush *Cnwll* 3 M5
Holmcroft *Staffs* 40 B3
Holme *Cambs* 42 H11
Holme *Cumb* 63 K6
Holme *Kirk* 58 E11
Holme *N York* 65 P10
Holme *Notts* 52 B10
Holme Chapel *Lancs* 57 Q3
Holme Hale *Norfk* 44 E8
Holme Lacy *Herefs* 28 G2
Holme Marsh *Herefs* 38 G10
Holme next the Sea *Norfk* 44 B2
Holme on the Wolds *E R Yk* 60 G5
Holme Pierrepont *Notts* 51 N11
Holmer *Herefs* 28 F1
Holmer Green *Bucks* 20 E4
Holme St Cuthbert *Cumb* 70 H4
Holmes Chapel *Ches E* 49 N3
Holmesfield *Derbys* 50 H5
Holmeswood *Lancs* 56 H5
Holmethorpe *Surrey* 21 L12

Holme upon Spalding Moor *E R Yk* 60 D6
Holmewood *Derbys* 51 K7
Holmfirth *Kirk* 58 F11
Holmhead *E Ayrs* 77 J7
Holmpton *E R Yk* 61 N9
Holmrook *Cumb* 62 C3
Holmside *Dur* 73 L10
Holne *Devon* 5 N6
Holnicote *Somset* 16 C6
Holsworthy *Devon* 14 F10
Holsworthy Beacon *Devon* 14 G9
Holt *Dorset* 8 F6
Holt *Norfk* 44 H3
Holt *Wilts* 18 C8
Holt *Worcs* 39 P9
Holt *Wrexhm* 48 H5
Holt End *Worcs* 40 E12
Holt Heath *Worcs* 39 P9
Holton *Oxon* 31 N11
Holton *Somset* 17 P10
Holton *Suffk* 35 N2
Holton cum Beckering *Lincs* 52 G7
Holton le Clay *Lincs* 53 J3
Holton le Moor *Lincs* 52 F4
Holton St Mary *Suffk* 34 H8
Holwell *Dorset* 7 Q1
Holwell *Herts* 32 G9
Holwell *Leics* 41 Q3
Holwell *Oxon* 30 G11
Holwick *Dur* 64 G3
Holybourne *Hants* 10 B2
Holyhead *IoA* 54 C5
Holy Island *IoA* 54 C5
Holy Island *Nthumb* 81 N5
Holy Island *Nthumb* 81 N6
Holymoorside *Derbys* 51 J7
Holyport *W & M* 20 E7
Holystone *Nthumb* 72 G1
Holytown *N Lans* 85 M10
Holywell *C Beds* 32 E12
Holywell *Cambs* 33 K3
Holywell *Cnwll* 2 H4
Holywell *Dorset* 7 N2
Holywell *Flints* 48 E1
Holywell Green *Calder* 58 E9
Holywell Lake *Somset* 16 F11
Holywell Row *Suffk* 34 B2
Holywood *D & G* 78 F11
Holywood Village *D & G* 78 F11
Homer *Shrops* 39 L2
Homersfield *Suffk* 45 L11
Homington *Wilts* 8 G3
Honeybourne *Worcs* 30 E5
Honeychurch *Devon* 15 L10
Honeystreet *Wilts* 18 G8
Honey Tye *Suffk* 34 F9
Honiley *Warwks* 40 G11
Honing *Norfk* 45 M5
Honingham *Norfk* 44 H7
Honington *Lincs* 42 D2
Honington *Suffk* 34 E2
Honington *Warwks* 30 H5
Honiton *Devon* 6 F3
Honley *Kirk* 58 F10
Hooe *Plym* 5 K9
Hooe *E Susx* 12 E7
Hoo Green *Ches E* 57 N11
Hoohill *Bpool* 56 G2
Hook *Gt Lon* 21 J9
Hook *E R Yk* 60 D8
Hook *Hants* 20 B11
Hook *Pembks* 24 G6
Hook *Wilts* 18 F4
Hooke *Dorset* 7 M3
Hook Green *Kent* 12 D3
Hook Norton *Oxon* 31 J7
Hookway *Devon* 15 P11
Hooley *Surrey* 21 L11
Hoo St Werburgh *Medway* 22 F8
Hooton Levitt *Rothm* 51 M3
Hooton Pagnell *Donc* 59 L11
Hooton Roberts *Rothm* 51 L2
Hope *Derbys* 50 F4
Hope *Devon* 5 N11
Hope *Flints* 48 F4
Hope *Staffs* 50 E9
Hope Bagot *Shrops* 39 L7
Hope Bowdler *Shrops* 39 J4
Hopehouse *Border* 79 L5
Hopeman *Moray* 100 H2
Hope Mansell *Herefs* 28 H5
Hopesay *Shrops* 38 H5
Hope under Dinmore *Herefs* 39 K10
Hopgrove *C York* 59 N3
Hopperton *N York* 59 K3
Hopstone *Shrops* 39 P4
Hopton *Derbys* 50 H9
Hopton *Staffs* 40 C3
Hopton *Suffk* 34 G2
Hopton Cangeford *Shrops* 39 K6
Hopton Castle *Shrops* 38 G6
Hoptonheath *Shrops* 38 H6
Hopton on Sea *Norfk* 45 Q9
Hopton Wafers *Shrops* 39 M6
Hopwas *Staffs* 40 F6
Hopwood *Worcs* 40 D11
Hopwood Park Services *Worcs* 40 D11
Horam *E Susx* 12 C6
Horbling *Lincs* 42 G3
Horbury *Wakefd* 58 H9
Horden *Dur* 73 Q11
Hordle *Hants* 9 J8
Hordley *Shrops* 48 H8
Horfield *Bristl* 17 N2
Horham *Suffk* 35 K3
Horkesley Heath *Essex* 34 G10
Horkstow *N Linc* 60 G9
Horley *Oxon* 31 K5
Horley *Surrey* 11 L2
Hornblotton Green *Somset* 17 N9
Hornby *Lancs* 63 L8
Hornby *N York* 65 L8
Hornby *N York* 65 P6
Horncastle *Lincs* 53 J9
Hornchurch *Gt Lon* 21 Q6
Horncliffe *Nthumb* 81 K4
Horndean *Border* 81 J4
Horndean *Hants* 10 B7
Horndon *Devon* 5 L4
Horndon on the Hill *Thurr* 22 D6
Horne *Surrey* 11 M2

Horner Somset...16 B7
Horning Norfk...45 M6
Horninghold Leics...42 B10
Horninglow Staffs...40 G3
Horningsea Cambs...33 M4
Horningsham Wilts...18 B11
Horningtoft Norfk...44 F5
Horns Cross Devon...14 G7
Hornsea E R Yk...61 K5
Hornsey Gt Lon...21 L5
Hornton Oxon...31 K6
Horrabridge Devon...5 K6
Horringer Suffk...34 D4
Horrocksford Lancs...63 N12
Horsebridge Devon...5 J5
Horsebridge E Susx...12 C7
Horsebridge Hants...9 L2
Horsehay Wrekin...39 M1
Horseheath Cambs...33 P7
Horsehouse N York...65 J10
Horsell Surrey...20 F10
Horseman's Green Wrexhm...49 J7
Horsey Norfk...45 P5
Horsey Somset...17 J8
Horsford Norfk...45 K6
Horsforth Leeds...58 G6
Horsham W Susx...11 J4
Horsham Worcs...39 N9
Horsham St Faith Norfk...45 K5
Horsington Lincs...52 H9
Horsington Somset...17 Q10
Horsley Derbys...51 J11
Horsley Gloucs...29 L8
Horsley Nthumb...72 F2
Horsley Nthumb...73 J7
Horsleycross Street Essex...35 J10
Horsleyhill Border...80 C9
Horsley Woodhouse Derbys...51 K11
Horsmonden Kent...12 E2
Horspath Oxon...31 M12
Horstead Norfk...45 L6
Horsted Keynes W Susx...11 M5
Horton Bucks...32 D11
Horton Dorset...8 F6
Horton Lancs...63 Q11
Horton Nhants...32 B6
Horton S Glos...18 A4
Horton Somset...17 J12
Horton Staffs...50 C8
Horton Swans...26 C10
Horton W & M...20 G8
Horton Wilts...18 F7
Horton Wrekin...49 M11
Horton-cum-Studley Oxon...31 N10
Horton Green Ches W...49 J5
Horton-in-Ribblesdale N York...64 E12
Horton Kirby Kent...22 C9
Horwich Bolton...57 M6
Horwood Devon...15 J6
Hoscote Border...79 N6
Hose Leics...41 Q2
Hosh P & K...92 C10
Hoswick Shet...111 k5
Hotham E R Yk...60 F7
Hothfield Kent...13 J2
Hoton Leics...41 M3
Hough Ches E...49 N5
Hougham Lincs...42 C2
Hough Green Halton...57 J10
Hough-on-the-Hill Lincs...42 D2
Houghton Cambs...33 J3
Houghton Hants...9 K2
Houghton Pembks...24 H7
Houghton W Susx...10 G7
Houghton Conquest C Beds...32 F8
Houghton Green E Susx...12 H5
Houghton-le-Spring Sundld...73 N10
Houghton on the Hill Leics...41 P6
Houghton Regis C Beds...32 E11
Houghton St Giles Norfk...44 F3
Hound Green Hants...20 B10
Houndslow Border...80 E5
Houndwood Border...87 Q9
Hounslow Gt Lon...21 J8
Househill Highld...100 D4
Houses Hill Kirk...58 G10
Housieside Abers...103 J9
Houston Rens...84 G9
Houstry Highld...110 D8
Houton Ork...111 g2
Hove Br & H...11 L8
Hoveringham Notts...51 P10
Hoveton Norfk...45 M6
Hovingham N York...66 F11
How Caple Herefs...28 H3
Howden E R Yk...60 D8
Howden-le-Wear Dur...65 L2
Howe Highld...110 F4
Howe N York...65 P10
Howe Norfk...45 L9
Howe Green Essex...22 E3
Howegreen Essex...22 G3
Howell Lincs...42 G2
Howe of Teuchar Abers...102 G6
Howes D & G...71 K3
Howe Street Essex...22 E1
Howe Street Essex...34 B9
Howey Powys...38 C9
Howgate Cumb...70 G10
Howgate Mdloth...86 F10
Howick Nthumb...81 Q10
Howlett End Essex...33 P9
Howley Somset...6 H2
How Mill Cumb...71 Q4
Howmore W Isls...111 a5
Hownam Border...80 G9
Howsham N Linc...52 E3
Howsham N York...60 C2
Howtel Nthumb...81 J7
How Wood Herts...21 J3
Howwood Rens...84 G10
Hoxa Ork...111 h3
Hoxne Suffk...35 K2
Hoy Ork...111 g3
Hoylake Wirral...56 E10
Hoyland Barns...51 J1
Hoylandswaine Barns...58 H12
Hubberston Pembks...24 F7
Huby N York...58 H5
Huby N York...59 M2
Hucclecote Gloucs...29 M5
Hucking Kent...22 G10
Hucknall Notts...51 M10
Huddersfield Kirk...58 F10

Huddington Worcs...30 C3
Hudswell N York...65 K7
Huggate E R Yk...60 F3
Hughenden Valley Bucks...20 D4
Hughley Shrops...39 K3
Hugh Town IoS...2 c2
Huish Devon...15 J9
Huish Wilts...18 G7
Huish Champflower Somset...16 E9
Huish Episcopi Somset...17 L10
Hùisinis W Isls...111 b3
Huisinish W Isls...111 b3
Hulcott Bucks...32 C12
Hulham Devon...6 D6
Hulland Derbys...50 G10
Hulland Ward Derbys...50 G10
Hullavington Wilts...18 D4
Hullbridge Essex...22 F4
Hull, Kingston upon C KuH...61 J8
Hulme Manch...57 Q9
Hulme Staffs...50 C10
Hulme Warrtn...57 L9
Hulme End Staffs...50 E8
Hulme Walfield Ches E...49 Q3
Hulton Lane Ends Bolton...57 M7
Hulverstone IoW...9 L9
Hulver Street Suffk...45 P11
Humber Bridge N Linc...60 H8
Humberside Airport N Linc...61 J11
Humberston NE Lin...53 K3
Humberstone C Leic...41 N6
Humbie E Loth...87 J9
Humbleton E R Yk...61 L7
Humby Lincs...42 E4
Hume Border...80 F6
Humshaugh Nthumb...72 G6
Huna Highld...110 G2
Huncote Leics...41 M7
Hundalee Border...80 E9
Hunderthwaite Dur...64 H4
Hundleby Lincs...53 L9
Hundle Houses Lincs...52 H11
Hundleton Pembks...24 G8
Hundon Suffk...34 C7
Hundred House Powys...38 C10
Hungarton Leics...41 P6
Hungerford Somset...16 E7
Hungerford W Berk...19 K7
Hungerford Newtown W Berk...19 L6
Hungerstone Herefs...28 E2
Hunmanby N York...67 N11
Hunningham Warwks...31 J1
Hunsbury Hill Nhants...31 Q3
Hunsdon Herts...21 N1
Hunsingore N York...59 K4
Hunslet Leeds...58 H7
Hunsonby Cumb...64 B1
Hunstanton Norfk...43 Q3
Hunstanworth Dur...72 G10
Hunsterson Ches E...49 M6
Hunston Suffk...34 F3
Hunston W Susx...10 D9
Hunstrete BaNES...17 P4
Hunsworth Kirk...58 F8
Hunter's Quay Ag & B...84 C7
Huntham Somset...17 J10
Hunthill Lodge Angus...94 H7
Huntingdon Cambs...33 J3
Huntingfield Suffk...35 M2
Huntington C York...59 N3
Huntington Ches W...48 H3
Huntington E Loth...87 J7
Huntington Herefs...38 F10
Huntington Staffs...40 C5
Huntingtowerfield P & K...92 G9
Huntley Gloucs...29 J5
Huntly Abers...102 C7
Hunton Kent...22 E12
Hunton N York...65 L8
Huntscott Somset...16 C7
Huntsham Devon...16 D11
Huntshaw Devon...15 J7
Huntspill Somset...17 J7
Huntstile Somset...16 H9
Huntworth Somset...17 J8
Hunwick Dur...65 L2
Hunworth Norfk...44 H3
Hurdcott Wilts...8 H1
Hurdsfield Ches E...50 B6
Hurley W & M...20 D6
Hurley Warwks...40 G8
Hurley Common Warwks...40 G7
Hurlford E Ayrs...76 H4
Hurn BCP...8 G7
Hursley Hants...9 M3
Hurst Wokham...20 C8
Hurstbourne Priors Hants...19 M10
Hurstbourne Tarrant Hants...19 L9
Hurst Green E Susx...12 E5
Hurst Green Essex...34 H12
Hurst Green Lancs...57 M2
Hurst Green Surrey...21 N12
Hurst Hill Dudley...40 B8
Hurstpierpoint W Susx...11 L6
Hurstwood Lancs...57 Q3
Hurtiso Ork...111 h2
Hurworth-on-Tees Darltn...65 N5
Hurworth Place Darltn...65 N5
Husbands Bosworth Leics...41 N10
Husborne Crawley C Beds...32 D9
Husthwaite N York...66 D11
Huthwaite Notts...51 L8
Huttoft Lincs...53 N8
Hutton BaNES...17 J4
Hutton Cumb...71 P7
Hutton E R Yk...60 H4
Hutton Essex...22 D4
Hutton Lancs...57 J4
Hutton N Som...17 J4
Hutton Buscel N York...67 L10
Hutton Conyers N York...65 N11
Hutton Cranswick E R Yk...60 H4
Hutton End Cumb...71 P7
Hutton Henry Dur...65 Q1
Hutton-le-Hole N York...66 G9
Hutton Lowcross R & Cl...66 E5
Hutton Magna Dur...65 K5
Hutton Roof Cumb...63 K6
Hutton Roof Cumb...71 M8
Hutton Rudby N York...66 C6
Hutton Sessay N York...66 C11
Hutton Wandesley N York...59 L4
Huxham Devon...6 C4
Huxley Ches W...49 K3
Huyton Knows...57 J9
Hycemoor Cumb...62 C4

Hyde Tamesd...50 C2
Hyde Heath Bucks...20 E4
Hyde Lea Staffs...40 B4
Hylands House & Park Essex...22 D3
Hyndford Bridge S Lans...78 E1
Hynish Ag & B...88 C8
Hyssington Powys...38 F4
Hythe Essex...34 G10
Hythe Hants...9 M6
Hythe Kent...13 M3
Hythe End W & M...20 G8

I

Ibberton Dorset...8 B6
Ible Derbys...50 G9
Ibsley Hants...8 H5
Ibstock Leics...41 K5
Ibstone Bucks...20 C5
Ibthorpe Hants...19 L9
Iburndale N York...67 J6
Ibworth Hants...19 P9
Ichrachan Ag & B...90 D9
Ickburgh Norfk...44 D10
Ickenham Gt Lon...20 H6
Ickford Bucks...31 N11
Ickham Kent...23 N10
Ickleford Herts...32 H9
Icklesham E Susx...12 G6
Ickleton Cambs...33 M7
Icklingham Suffk...34 C3
Ickornshaw N York...58 C5
Ickwell Green C Beds...32 G7
Icomb Gloucs...30 G9
Idbury Oxon...30 G9
Iddesleigh Devon...15 K9
Ide Devon...6 B5
Ideford Devon...6 B7
Ide Hill Kent...21 P11
Iden E Susx...12 H5
Iden Green Kent...12 E3
Iden Green Kent...12 F4
Idle C Brad...58 F6
Idless Cnwll...3 J6
Idlicote Warwks...30 H5
Idmiston Wilts...18 H12
Idole Carmth...25 P6
Idridgehay Derbys...50 H10
Idrigill Highld...104 E9
Idstone Oxon...19 J4
Iffley Oxon...31 M12
Ifield W Susx...11 K3
Ifold W Susx...10 G4
Iford BCP...8 G8
Iford E Susx...11 N8
Ifton Mons...28 F10
Ightfield Shrops...49 L7
Ightham Kent...22 C11
Iken Suffk...35 N6
Ilam Staffs...50 F10
Ilchester Somset...17 M10
Ilderton Nthumb...81 L9
Ilford Gt Lon...21 N6
Ilford Somset...17 K11
Ilfracombe Devon...15 J3
Ilkeston Derbys...51 L11
Ilketshall St Andrew Suffk...45 N11
Ilketshall St Margaret Suffk...45 M11
Ilkley C Brad...58 E5
Illand Cnwll...4 G5
Illey Dudley...40 C10
Illogan Cnwll...2 G7
Illston on the Hill Leics...41 P7
Ilmer Bucks...20 C3
Ilmington Warwks...30 G5
Ilminster Somset...17 J12
Ilsington Devon...5 Q5
Ilston Swans...26 D10
Ilton N York...65 L11
Ilton Somset...17 J11
Imachar N Ayrs...75 N4
Immingham NE Lin...61 K10
Immingham Dock NE Lin...61 K10
Impington Cambs...33 M4
Ince Ches W...57 J12
Ince Blundell Sefton...56 G8
Ince-in-Makerfield Wigan...57 L7
Inchbae Lodge Hotel Highld...106 G8
Inchbare Angus...95 K8
Inchberry Moray...101 L4
Incheril Highld...105 Q9
Inchinnan Rens...84 H8
Inchlaggan Highld...98 B8
Inchmichael P & K...93 J9
Inchmore Highld...107 J12
Inchnacardoch Highld...98 E4
Inchnadamph Highld...108 E10
Inchture P & K...93 K9
Inchyra P & K...92 H10
Indian Queens Cnwll...3 K4
Ingatestone Essex...22 D4
Ingbirchworth Barns...58 G11
Ingestre Staffs...40 C3
Ingham Lincs...52 D6
Ingham Norfk...45 N5
Ingham Suffk...34 E3
Ingham Corner Norfk...45 N5
Ingleby Derbys...41 J3
Ingleby Arncliffe N York...66 C7
Ingleby Barwick S on T...66 C5
Ingleby Greenhow N York...66 E6
Ingleigh Green Devon...15 K10
Inglesbatch BaNES...17 Q4
Inglesham Swindn...18 H2
Ingleston D & G...70 D2
Ingleton Dur...65 L4
Ingleton N York...63 M7
Inglewhite Lancs...57 K2
Ingoe Nthumb...73 J6
Ingol Lancs...57 K3
Ingoldisthorpe Norfk...44 B4
Ingoldmells Lincs...53 N9
Ingoldsby Lincs...42 E4
Ingram Nthumb...81 L10
Ingrave Essex...22 D5
Ingrow C Brad...58 D6
Ings Cumb...63 J3
Ingst S Glos...28 G10
Ingthorpe Rutlnd...42 E8
Ingworth Norfk...45 K4
Inkberrow Worcs...30 D3
Inkersall Green Derbys...51 K6
Inkhorn Abers...103 J7

Inkpen W Berk...19 L7
Inkstack Highld...110 F2
Innellan Ag & B...84 C8
Innerleithen Border...79 M2
Innerleven Fife...86 H3
Innermessan D & G...68 E6
Innerwick E Loth...87 N7
Innesmill Moray...101 K3
Insch Abers...102 E9
Insh Highld...99 M8
Inshes Highld...99 K1
Inskip Lancs...57 J2
Instow Devon...14 H6
Intake Sheff...51 K4
Inver Abers...94 D4
Inver Highld...107 P6
Inver P & K...92 F7
Inverailort Highld...97 K12
Inverallochy Abers...103 L3
Inveran Highld...107 J3
Inveraray Ag & B...84 B2
Inverarish Highld...96 G3
Inverarity Angus...93 M6
Inverarnan Stirlg...91 J11
Inverasdale Highld...105 M5
Inverbeg Ag & B...84 F4
Inverbervie Abers...95 N7
Inverboyndie Abers...102 F3
Invercreran Lodge Ag & B...90 D7
Inverdruie Highld...99 N6
Inveresk E Loth...86 G7
Inveresragan Ag & B...90 D8
Inverey Abers...94 B4
Inverfarigaig Highld...98 G4
Inverfolla Ag & B...90 C7
Invergarry Highld...98 D8
Invergeldie P & K...91 Q10
Inverglory Highld...98 C10
Invergordon Highld...107 L8
Invergowrie P & K...93 L9
Inverguseran Highld...97 K8
Inverhadden P & K...91 P5
Inverie Highld...97 K9
Inverinan Ag & B...90 D11
Inverinate Highld...97 N5
Inverkeilor Angus...93 R6
Inverkeithing Fife...86 D5
Inverkeithny Abers...102 E6
Inverkip Inver...84 D8
Inverkirkaig Highld...108 B10
Inverlael Highld...106 C5
Inverlair Highld...98 D11
Inverliever Lodge Ag & B...83 N2
Inverlochy Ag & B...90 G10
Invermark Angus...94 G6
Invermoriston Highld...98 F5
Invernaver Highld...109 M4
Inverneill Ag & B...83 M6
Inverness Highld...107 L12
Inverness Airport Highld...107 M11
Invernettie Abers...103 M6
Invernoaden Ag & B...84 C4
Inveroran Hotel Ag & B...90 H7
Inverquharity Angus...93 M4
Inverquhomery Abers...103 L6
Inverroy Highld...98 C11
Inversanda Highld...90 C4
Invershiel Highld...97 N6
Invershin Highld...107 J3
Invershore Highld...110 F8
Inversnaid Hotel Stirlg...84 F2
Inverugie Abers...103 M6
Inveruglas Ag & B...84 F2
Inveruglass Highld...99 M8
Inverurie Abers...102 G10
Inwardleigh Devon...15 K11
Inworth Essex...34 E12
Iochdar W Isls...111 a5
Iona Ag & B...88 G10
Iping W Susx...10 D5
iPort Logistics Park Donc...51 N2
Ipplepen Devon...5 Q7
Ipsden Oxon...19 Q4
Ipstones Staffs...50 D10
Ipswich Suffk...35 J7
Irby Wirral...56 F11
Irby in the Marsh Lincs...53 M10
Irby upon Humber NE Lin...52 H3
Irchester Nhants...32 D4
Ireby Cumb...71 K7
Ireby Lancs...63 M7
Ireleth Cumb...62 E6
Ireshopeburn Dur...72 F12
Irlam Salfd...57 N9
Irnham Lincs...42 E5
Iron Acton S Glos...29 J11
Ironbridge Wrekin...39 M2
Ironbridge Gorge Wrekin...39 M2
Ironmacannie D & G...69 P4
Ironville Derbys...51 L9
Irstead Norfk...45 M6
Irthington Cumb...71 P4
Irthlingborough Nhants...32 D3
Irton N York...67 L10
Irvine N Ayrs...76 F4
Isauld Highld...110 A3
Isbister Shet...111 k4
Isbister Shet...111 m3
Isfield E Susx...11 N6
Isham Nhants...32 C3
Isington Hants...10 C2
Islay Ag & B...82 E10
Islay Airport Ag & B...74 D3
Isle Abbotts Somset...17 J11
Isle Brewers Somset...17 K11
Isleham Cambs...33 Q2
Isle of Dogs Gt Lon...21 M7
Isle of Grain Medway...22 G7
Isle of Lewis W Isls...111 d2
Isle of Man IoM...56 c4
Isle of Man Ronaldsway Airport IoM...56 b7
Isle of Mull Ag & B...89 M8
Isle of Purbeck Dorset...8 E10
Isle of Sheppey Kent...23 J9
Isle of Skye Highld...96 E3
Isle of Thanet Kent...23 P9
Isle of Walney Cumb...62 E8
Isle of Whithorn D & G...69 L10
Isle of Wight IoW...9 N9
Isleornsay Highld...97 L2
Isles of Scilly IoS...2 c2

Isles of Scilly St Mary's Airport IoS...2 c2
Islesteps D & G...70 F2
Isleworth Gt Lon...21 J8
Isley Walton Leics...41 K3
Islibhig W Isls...111 b2
Islington Gt Lon...21 L6
Islip Nhants...32 E2
Islip Oxon...31 M10
Islivig W Isls...111 b2
Isombridge Wrekin...49 L11
Istead Rise Kent...22 D9
Itchen Abbas Hants...9 N2
Itchen Stoke Hants...9 P2
Itchingfield W Susx...11 J4
Itteringham Norfk...45 J4
Itton Mons...28 F9
Itton Common Mons...28 F9
Ivegill Cumb...71 N6
Iver Bucks...20 G7
Iver Heath Bucks...20 G6
Iveston Dur...73 K10
Ivinghoe Bucks...32 D12
Ivinghoe Aston Bucks...32 D12
Ivington Herefs...39 J10
Ivybridge Devon...5 M8
Ivychurch Kent...13 K5
Ivy Hatch Kent...22 C11
Iwade Kent...22 H9
Iwerne Courtney Dorset...8 C5
Iwerne Minster Dorset...8 C5
Ixworth Suffk...34 F3
Ixworth Thorpe Suffk...34 F3

J

Jack-in-the-Green Devon...6 D4
Jackton S Lans...85 K11
Jacobstow Cnwll...4 F2
Jacobstowe Devon...15 K10
Jameston Pembks...25 J8
Jamestown Highld...106 H10
Jamestown W Duns...84 G6
Janetstown Highld...110 E8
Janetstown Highld...110 G5
Jardine Hall D & G...78 H10
Jarrow S Tyne...73 N7
Jasper's Green Essex...34 C10
Jawcraig Falk...85 P7
Jaywick Essex...23 M1
Jedburgh Border...80 E9
Jeffreyston Pembks...25 J7
Jemimaville Highld...107 M8
Jerbourg Guern...6 c2
Jersey Jersey...7 b1
Jersey Airport Jersey...7 a2
Jesmond N u Ty...73 M7
Jevington E Susx...12 C9
Jockey End Herts...20 G1
Jodrell Bank Ches E...49 P2
Johnby Cumb...71 N8
John Lennon Airport Lpool...56 H11
John o' Groats Highld...110 H2
Johnshaven Abers...95 N8
Johnston Pembks...24 G6
Johnstone D & G...79 L8
Johnstone Rens...84 G9
Johnstonebridge D & G...78 H9
Johnstown Carmth...25 P5
Johnstown Wrexhm...48 F6
Joppa C Edin...86 G7
Joppa Cerdgn...37 J7
Joppa S Ayrs...76 G7
Jordanston Pembks...24 G3
Joyden's Wood Kent...21 P8
Juniper Nthumb...72 H9
Juniper Green C Edin...86 E8
Jura Ag & B...82 G6
Jurassic Coast Devon...7 J5
Jurby IoM...56 c2

K

Kaber Cumb...64 E5
Kaimend S Lans...86 B11
Kames Ag & B...83 P8
Kames E Ayrs...77 L6
Kea Cnwll...3 J7
Keadby N Linc...60 E10
Keal Cotes Lincs...53 K10
Kearsley Bolton...57 N7
Kearsney Kent...13 N2
Kearstwick Cumb...63 L6
Kedington Suffk...34 B7
Kedleston Derbys...50 H11
Keelby Lincs...61 K11
Keele Staffs...49 P6
Keele Services Staffs...49 P6
Keelham C Brad...58 E7
Keeston Pembks...24 F5
Keevil Wilts...18 D8
Kegworth Leics...41 L3
Kehelland Cnwll...2 F7
Keig Abers...102 D10
Keighley C Brad...58 D6
Keilarsbrae Clacks...85 P4
Keillour P & K...92 E9
Keiloch Abers...94 C4
Keils Ag & B...82 G8
Keinton Mandeville Somset...17 M9
Keir Mill D & G...78 F9
Keisley Cumb...64 D3
Keiss Highld...110 G4
Keith Moray...101 N5
Keithick P & K...93 J7
Keithock Angus...95 K8
Keithtown Highld...106 H10
Kelbrook Lancs...58 B5
Kelby Lincs...42 E2
Keld N York...64 F7
Kelfield N York...59 N6
Kelham Notts...51 Q9
Kelhead D & G...71 J2
Kellamergh Lancs...56 H3
Kellas Angus...93 M8
Kellas Moray...101 J5
Kellaton Devon...5 Q11
Kelling Norfk...44 H2
Kelloe Dur...73 N12

Kelloholm D & G ...77 M8
Kells Cumb ...70 F11
Kelly Devon ...5 J4
Kelmarsh Nhants ...41 Q10
Kelmscott Oxon ...19 J2
Kelsale Suffk ...35 N4
Kelsall Ches W ...49 K2
Kelshall Herts ...33 K9
Kelsick Cumb ...71 K5
Kelso Border ...80 G7
Kelstedge Derbys ...51 J7
Kelstern Lincs ...53 J5
Kelston BaNES ...17 Q3
Keltneyburn P & K ...92 B6
Kelton D & G ...70 G2
Kelty Fife ...86 D4
Kelvedon Essex ...34 E11
Kelvedon Hatch Essex ...22 C4
Kelynack Cnwll ...2 B9
Kemback Fife ...93 M11
Kemberton Shrops ...39 N2
Kemble Gloucs ...29 P8
Kemerton Worcs ...29 N2
Kemeys Commander Mons ...28 D7
Kemnay Abers ...102 F11
Kempley Gloucs ...29 J3
Kempley Green Gloucs ...29 J3
Kempsey Worcs ...39 Q11
Kempsford Gloucs ...18 H2
Kempshott Hants ...19 P10
Kempston Bed ...32 E7
Kempton Shrops ...38 G5
Kemp Town Br & H ...11 M8
Kemsing Kent ...22 B10
Kenardington Kent ...13 J4
Kenchester Herefs ...38 H12
Kencot Oxon ...30 G12
Kendal Cumb ...63 K4
Kenfig Brdgnd ...26 H11
Kenfig Hill Brdgnd ...26 H11
Kenilworth Warwks ...40 H12
Kenley Gt Lon ...21 L10
Kenley Shrops ...39 K3
Kenmore Highld ...105 L10
Kenmore P & K ...92 B6
Kenn Devon ...6 C6
Kenn N Som ...17 K3
Kennacraig Ag & B ...83 M9
Kennall Vale Cnwll ...2 H8
Kennerleigh Devon ...15 P10
Kennet Clacks ...85 Q5
Kennethmont Abers ...102 C9
Kennett Cambs ...34 B3
Kennford Devon ...6 C5
Kenninghall Norfk ...44 G11
Kennington Kent ...13 K2
Kennington Oxon ...19 N1
Kennington Lees Kent ...13 K2
Kennoway Fife ...86 G2
Kenny Somset ...17 J11
Kenny Hill Suffk ...33 Q2
Kennythorpe N York ...60 D2
Kenovay Ag & B ...88 C7
Kensaleyre Highld ...104 F11
Kensington Gt Lon ...21 K7
Kensington Palace Gt Lon ...21 K7
Kensworth Common C Beds ...32 E12
Kentallen Highld ...90 D5
Kentchurch Herefs ...28 E4
Kentford Suffk ...34 B4
Kentisbeare Devon ...6 E2
Kentisbury Devon ...15 L4
Kentish Town Gt Lon ...21 L6
Kentmere Cumb ...63 J2
Kenton Devon ...6 C6
Kenton Gt Lon ...21 J6
Kenton N u Ty ...73 L7
Kenton Suffk ...35 K4
Kenton Bankfoot N u Ty ...73 L7
Kentra Highld ...89 N3
Kentsboro Hants ...19 K11
Kent's Green Gloucs ...29 K4
Kent's Oak Hants ...9 K3
Kenwyn Cnwll ...3 J6
Keoldale Highld ...108 G3
Keppoch Highld ...97 M5
Kepwick N York ...66 C8
Keresley Covtry ...40 H10
Kerrera Ag & B ...89 Q10
Kerry Powys ...38 D4
Kerrycroy Ag & B ...84 B10
Kersall Notts ...51 Q8
Kersbrook Devon ...6 E6
Kersey Suffk ...34 G7
Kershader W Isls ...111 d2
Kerswell Devon ...6 E2
Kerswell Green Worcs ...39 Q11
Kesgrave Suffk ...35 K7
Kessingland Suffk ...45 Q11
Kestle Cnwll ...3 L6
Kestle Mill Cnwll ...3 J4
Keston Gt Lon ...21 N9
Keswick Cumb ...71 L10
Keswick Norfk ...45 K8
Kettering Nhants ...32 C2
Ketteringham Norfk ...45 J9
Kettins P & K ...93 J7
Kettlebaston Suffk ...34 F6
Kettlebridge Fife ...86 G2
Kettlebrook Staffs ...40 G6
Kettleburgh Suffk ...35 L5
Kettleholm D & G ...79 J12
Kettleshulme Ches E ...50 C5
Kettlesing N York ...58 G3
Kettlesing Bottom N York ...58 G3
Kettlestone Norfk ...44 F4
Kettlethorpe Lincs ...52 C8
Kettletoft Ork ...111 i1
Kettlewell N York ...64 H11
Ketton Rutlnd ...42 D8
Kew Gt Lon ...21 J7
Kew Royal Botanic Gardens Gt Lon ...21 J7
Kewstoke N Som ...17 J4
Kexby C York ...60 C4
Kexby Lincs ...52 C6
Key Green Ches E ...50 B7
Keyham Leics ...41 P6
Keyhaven Hants ...9 L7
Keyingham E R Yk ...61 L7
Keymer W Susx ...11 L7
Keynsham BaNES ...17 P3
Keysoe Bed ...32 F4
Keysoe Row Bed ...32 F5

Keyston Cambs ...32 F2
Keyworth Notts ...41 N2
Kibblesworth Gatesd ...73 M9
Kibworth Beauchamp Leics ...41 P8
Kibworth Harcourt Leics ...41 P8
Kidbrooke Gt Lon ...21 N7
Kidderminster Worcs ...39 Q6
Kidlington Oxon ...31 L10
Kidmore End Oxon ...20 B7
Kidsdale D & G ...69 L10
Kidsgrove Staffs ...49 Q5
Kidwelly Carmth ...25 P7
Kiel Crofts Ag & B ...90 C8
Kielder Nthumb ...72 B3
Kielder Forest ...72 B4
Kiells Ag & B ...82 F8
Kilbarchan Rens ...84 G9
Kilbeg Highld ...97 J8
Kilberry Ag & B ...83 K9
Kilbirnie N Ayrs ...84 E11
Kilbride Ag & B ...83 L7
Kilbride Ag & B ...83 Q9
Kilbuiack Moray ...100 G4
Kilburn Derbys ...51 J10
Kilburn Gt Lon ...21 K6
Kilburn N York ...66 D10
Kilby Leics ...41 N8
Kilchamaig Ag & B ...83 M10
Kilchattan Ag & B ...82 E4
Kilchattan Ag & B ...84 B11
Kilcheran Ag & B ...89 Q8
Kilchoan Highld ...89 K4
Kilchoman Ag & B ...82 C9
Kilchrenan Ag & B ...90 E10
Kilconquhar Fife ...87 J2
Kilcot Gloucs ...29 J4
Kilcoy Highld ...107 J11
Kilcreggan Ag & B ...84 D6
Kildale N York ...66 E5
Kildalloig Ag & B ...75 L8
Kildary Highld ...107 M7
Kildavaig Ag & B ...83 Q9
Kildavanan Ag & B ...83 Q9
Kildonan Highld ...109 Q10
Kildonan N Ayrs ...75 Q8
Kildonan Lodge Highld ...109 Q10
Kildonnan Highld ...96 F11
Kildrochet House D & G ...68 E7
Kildrummy Abers ...101 N10
Kildwick N York ...58 D5
Kilfinan Ag & B ...83 P7
Kilfinnan Highld ...98 C9
Kilgetty Pembks ...25 K7
Kilgrammie S Ayrs ...76 E10
Kilgwrrwg Common Mons ...28 F8
Kilham E R Yk ...60 H2
Kilkenneth Ag & B ...88 B7
Kilkenzie Ag & B ...75 K7
Kilkerran Ag & B ...75 L8
Kilkhampton Cnwll ...14 D9
Killamarsh Derbys ...51 L5
Killay Swans ...26 E9
Killean Ag & B ...75 J6
Killearn Stirlg ...85 J6
Killen Highld ...107 L10
Killerby Darltn ...65 L4
Killerton Devon ...6 D3
Killichonan P & K ...91 M5
Killiechonate Highld ...98 C11
Killiechronan Ag & B ...89 L7
Killiecrankie P & K ...92 D3
Killilan Highld ...97 N4
Killimster Highld ...110 G4
Killin Stirlg ...91 N9
Killinghall N York ...58 H3
Killington Cumb ...63 L5
Killington Lake Services Cumb ...63 L4
Killingworth N Tyne ...73 M6
Killochyett Border ...87 J12
Kilmacolm Inver ...84 F8
Kilmahog Stirlg ...85 K2
Kilmahumaig Ag & B ...83 L4
Kilmaluag Highld ...104 F7
Kilmany Fife ...93 L10
Kilmarnock E Ayrs ...76 G4
Kilmartin Ag & B ...83 M3
Kilmaurs E Ayrs ...76 G3
Kilmelford Ag & B ...83 M1
Kilmersdon Somset ...17 Q6
Kilmeston Hants ...9 P3
Kilmichael Ag & B ...75 K7
Kilmichael Glassary Ag & B ...83 N4
Kilmichael of Inverlussa Ag & B ...83 L6
Kilmington Devon ...6 H4
Kilmington Wilts ...18 B12
Kilmington Common Wilts ...8 B1
Kilmington Street Wilts ...8 B1
Kilmorack Highld ...106 H12
Kilmore Ag & B ...90 B10
Kilmore Highld ...97 J8
Kilmory Ag & B ...83 L3
Kilmory Highld ...89 L3
Kilmory N Ayrs ...75 P8
Kilmuir Highld ...104 C11
Kilmuir Highld ...104 E8
Kilmuir Highld ...107 L11
Kilmuir Highld ...107 M7
Kilmun Ag & B ...84 C6
Kilnave Ag & B ...82 D8
Kilncadzow S Lans ...77 P2
Kilndown Kent ...12 E3
Kilninver Ag & B ...89 Q11
Kilnsea E R Yk ...61 P10
Kilnsey N York ...58 C1
Kilnwick E R Yk ...60 G4
Kiloran Ag & B ...82 E4
Kilpatrick N Ayrs ...75 N7
Kilpeck Herefs ...28 E3
Kilpin E R Yk ...60 D8
Kilrenny Fife ...87 L2
Kilsby Nhants ...41 M12
Kilspindie P & K ...93 J9
Kilstay D & G ...68 F10
Kilsyth N Lans ...85 M7
Kiltarlity Highld ...98 G2
Kilton R & Cl ...66 F4
Kilton Thorpe R & Cl ...66 F4
Kilvaxter Highld ...104 E8
Kilve Somset ...16 F7
Kilvington Notts ...42 B2
Kilwinning N Ayrs ...76 E3
Kimberley Norfk ...44 H8
Kimberley Notts ...51 L11

Kimberworth Rothm ...51 K3
Kimblesworth Dur ...73 M10
Kimbolton Cambs ...32 F4
Kimbolton Herefs ...39 K9
Kimcote Leics ...41 N9
Kimmeridge Dorset ...8 D10
Kimpton Hants ...19 J10
Kimpton Herts ...32 H11
Kinbrace Highld ...109 Q8
Kinbuck Stirlg ...85 N3
Kincaple Fife ...93 N11
Kincardine Fife ...85 Q5
Kincardine Highld ...107 K5
Kincardine Bridge Fife ...85 Q5
Kincardine O'Neil Abers ...95 K3
Kinclaven P & K ...92 H7
Kincorth C Aber ...95 Q2
Kincorth House Moray ...100 F3
Kincraig Highld ...99 M7
Kincraigie P & K ...92 E6
Kindallachan P & K ...92 E6
Kinerarach Ag & B ...75 J2
Kineton Gloucs ...30 E8
Kineton Warwks ...31 J4
Kinfauns P & K ...92 H10
Kingarth Ag & B ...84 B10
Kingcausie Abers ...95 P3
Kingcoed Mons ...28 E7
Kingerby Lincs ...52 F5
Kingham Oxon ...30 H8
Kingholm Quay D & G ...70 F2
Kinghorn Fife ...86 F5
Kinglassie Fife ...86 E3
Kingoodie P & K ...93 L9
Kingsand Cnwll ...5 J9
Kingsbarns Fife ...93 Q12
Kingsbridge Devon ...5 P10
Kingsbridge Somset ...16 D8
King's Bromley Staffs ...40 E4
Kingsburgh Highld ...104 E10
Kingsbury Gt Lon ...21 J5
Kingsbury Warwks ...40 G8
Kingsbury Episcopi Somset ...17 L11
King's Caple Herefs ...28 G3
Kingsclere Hants ...19 N8
King's Cliffe Nhants ...42 E10
Kings Clipstone Notts ...51 N7
Kingscote Gloucs ...29 L9
Kingscott Devon ...15 J8
King's Coughton Warwks ...30 E3
Kingscross N Ayrs ...75 Q6
Kingsdon Somset ...17 M10
Kingsdown Kent ...13 Q1
Kingsdown Swindn ...18 H3
Kingsdown Wilts ...18 B7
Kingseat Abers ...103 J10
Kingseat Fife ...86 D4
Kingsey Bucks ...20 C3
Kingsfold W Susx ...11 J3
Kingsford C Aber ...95 P1
Kingsford E Ayrs ...76 H2
Kingsgate Kent ...23 Q8
Kingshall Street Suffk ...34 F4
King's Heath Birm ...40 E10
Kings Hill Kent ...22 D11
King's Hill Wsall ...40 C8
Kings House Hotel Highld ...90 H5
Kingshurst Solhll ...40 F9
Kingskerswell Devon ...6 B8
Kingskettle Fife ...86 G1
Kingsland Herefs ...39 J9
Kingsland IoA ...54 C5
Kings Langley Herts ...20 H3
King's Lynn Norfk ...43 P6
Kings Meaburn Cumb ...64 B4
King's Mills Guern ...6 b2
Kingsmuir Angus ...93 N6
Kings Muir Border ...79 L3
Kingsmuir Fife ...87 K1
Kingsnorth Kent ...13 J3
King's Norton Birm ...40 D10
King's Norton Leics ...41 P7
Kings Nympton Devon ...15 M8
King's Pyon Herefs ...38 H11
Kings Ripton Cambs ...33 J2
King's Somborne Hants ...9 L2
King's Stag Dorset ...7 Q1
King's Stanley Gloucs ...29 L7
King's Sutton Nhants ...31 L6
Kingstanding Birm ...40 D8
Kingsteignton Devon ...6 B8
Kingsthorne Herefs ...28 F3
Kingsthorpe Nhants ...31 Q2
Kingston Cambs ...33 K6
Kingston Cnwll ...4 H5
Kingston Devon ...5 M10
Kingston Dorset ...7 Q2
Kingston Dorset ...8 D10
Kingston E Loth ...87 K6
Kingston IoW ...9 N10
Kingston Kent ...23 M12
Kingston Bagpuize Oxon ...19 L2
Kingston Blount Oxon ...20 B4
Kingston by Sea W Susx ...11 K8
Kingston Deverill Wilts ...18 C12
Kingstone Herefs ...28 E2
Kingstone Somset ...17 K12
Kingstone Staffs ...40 D2
Kingston Lacy House & Gardens Dorset ...8 E7
Kingston Lisle Oxon ...19 K4
Kingston near Lewes E Susx ...11 N8
Kingston on Soar Notts ...41 L2
Kingston on Spey Moray ...101 L3
Kingston Russell Dorset ...7 N5
Kingston St Mary Somset ...16 H10
Kingston Seymour N Som ...17 K3
Kingston upon Hull C KuH ...61 J7
Kingston upon Thames Gt Lon ...21 J9
King's Walden Herts ...32 H11
Kingswear Devon ...6 B11
Kingswells C Aber ...95 P1
Kings Weston Bristl ...28 G12
Kingswinford Dudley ...40 B9
Kingswood Bucks ...31 P9
Kingswood C KuH ...61 J7
Kingswood Gloucs ...29 K9
Kingswood S Glos ...28 P2

Kingswood Somset ...16 F8
Kingswood Surrey ...21 K11
Kingswood Warwks ...40 F12
Kingswood Common Staffs ...39 Q2
Kings Worthy Hants ...9 N2
Kingthorpe Lincs ...52 G8
Kington Herefs ...38 F10
Kington S Glos ...28 H10
Kington Worcs ...30 C3
Kington Langley Wilts ...18 D5
Kington Magna Dorset ...8 B3
Kington St Michael Wilts ...18 D5
Kingussie Highld ...107 L8
Kingweston Somset ...17 M9
Kinharrachie Abers ...103 J8
Kinharvie D & G ...70 F3
Kinkell Bridge P & K ...92 D11
Kinknockie Abers ...103 L7
Kinleith C Edin ...86 E8
Kinlet Shrops ...39 N6
Kinloch Highld ...96 E9
Kinloch Highld ...108 G8
Kinloch Highld ...109 K5
Kinloch P & K ...92 H6
Kinlochard Stirlg ...84 H3
Kinlochbervie Highld ...108 E4
Kinlocheil Highld ...90 D1
Kinlochewe Highld ...105 Q9
Kinloch Hourn Highld ...97 N8
Kinlochlaggan Highld ...98 G10
Kinlochleven Highld ...90 G4
Kinlochmoidart Highld ...89 P2
Kinlochnanuagh Highld ...97 K11
Kinloch Rannoch P & K ...91 P5
Kinloss Moray ...100 G3
Kinmel Bay Conwy ...55 P5
Kinmuck Abers ...102 H10
Kinmundy Abers ...103 J10
Kinnabus Ag & B ...74 D4
Kinnadie Abers ...103 K6
Kinnaird P & K ...92 E4
Kinneff Abers ...95 N6
Kinnelhead D & G ...78 G8
Kinnell Angus ...93 Q5
Kinnerley Shrops ...48 G10
Kinnersley Herefs ...38 G11
Kinnersley Worcs ...39 Q12
Kinnerton Powys ...38 E9
Kinnesswood P & K ...86 E2
Kinnordy Angus ...93 L5
Kinoulton Notts ...41 P2
Kinross P & K ...86 D2
Kinrossie P & K ...92 H8
Kinross Services P & K ...86 D2
Kinsham Herefs ...38 G8
Kinsham Worcs ...29 N2
Kinsley Wakefd ...59 K10
Kinson BCP ...8 F7
Kintail Highld ...97 P6
Kintbury W Berk ...19 L7
Kintessack Moray ...100 F4
Kintillo P & K ...92 G11
Kinton Herefs ...38 H7
Kinton Shrops ...48 G10
Kintore Abers ...102 G11
Kintour Ag & B ...74 F4
Kintra Ag & B ...74 D3
Kintra Ag & B ...88 H10
Kintraw Ag & B ...83 M3
Kintyre Ag & B ...75 L5
Kinveachy Highld ...99 N5
Kinver Staffs ...39 Q5
Kippax Leeds ...59 L4
Kippen Stirlg ...85 L4
Kippford D & G ...70 D5
Kipping's Cross Kent ...12 D3
Kirbister Ork ...111 h2
Kirby Bedon Norfk ...45 L8
Kirby Bellars Leics ...41 Q4
Kirby Cane Norfk ...45 N10
Kirby Cross Essex ...35 K11
Kirby Grindalythe N York ...60 F1
Kirby Hill N York ...59 K1
Kirby Hill N York ...65 K6
Kirby Knowle N York ...66 C9
Kirby-le-Soken Essex ...35 K11
Kirby Misperton N York ...66 H10
Kirby Muxloe Leics ...41 M6
Kirby Underdale E R Yk ...60 D3
Kirby Wiske N York ...65 P9
Kirdford W Susx ...10 G5
Kirk Highld ...110 F4
Kirkabister Shet ...111 k4
Kirkandrews D & G ...69 N9
Kirkandrews upon Eden Cumb ...71 M4
Kirkbampton Cumb ...71 L4
Kirkbean D & G ...70 F4
Kirk Bramwith Donc ...59 N10
Kirkbride Cumb ...71 K4
Kirkbuddo Angus ...93 N7
Kirkburn Border ...79 L2
Kirkburn E R Yk ...60 G3
Kirkburton Kirk ...58 G10
Kirkby Knows ...56 H8
Kirkby Lincs ...52 F5
Kirkby N York ...66 D6
Kirkby Fleetham N York ...65 M8
Kirkby Green Lincs ...52 F11
Kirkby-in-Ashfield Notts ...51 L9
Kirkby-in-Furness Cumb ...62 E6
Kirkby la Thorpe Lincs ...42 F2
Kirkby Lonsdale Cumb ...63 L6
Kirkby Malham N York ...58 B3
Kirkby Mallory Leics ...41 M6
Kirkby Malzeard N York ...65 M11
Kirkbymoorside N York ...66 F9
Kirkby on Bain Lincs ...53 J10
Kirkby Overblow N York ...59 J4
Kirkby Stephen Cumb ...64 E6
Kirkby Thore Cumb ...64 B3
Kirkby Underwood Lincs ...42 F5
Kirkby Wharf N York ...59 L6
Kirkcaldy Fife ...86 F4
Kirkcambeck Cumb ...71 Q2
Kirkchrist D & G ...69 P8
Kirkcolm D & G ...68 D5
Kirkconnel D & G ...77 M8
Kirkconnell D & G ...70 F2
Kirkcowan D & G ...69 J7
Kirkcudbright D & G ...69 P8
Kirkdale Lpool ...56 G9
Kirk Deighton N York ...59 K4
Kirk Ella E R Yk ...60 H8

Kirkfieldbank S Lans ...77 P3
Kirkgunzeon D & G ...70 E3
Kirk Hallam Derbys ...51 L11
Kirkham Lancs ...56 H3
Kirkham N York ...60 C2
Kirkhamgate Wakefd ...58 H9
Kirk Hammerton N York ...59 L3
Kirkhaugh Nthumb ...72 C10
Kirkheaton Kirk ...58 F9
Kirkheaton Nthumb ...72 H5
Kirkhill Highld ...107 J12
Kirkhope S Lans ...78 F7
Kirkibost Highld ...96 G6
Kirkinch P & K ...93 K6
Kirkinner D & G ...69 K8
Kirkintilloch E Duns ...85 L8
Kirk Ireton Derbys ...50 H10
Kirkland Cumb ...70 H11
Kirkland D & G ...77 M8
Kirkland D & G ...78 D10
Kirkland D & G ...78 G10
Kirk Langley Derbys ...50 H11
Kirkleatham R & Cl ...66 E3
Kirklevington S on T ...66 B5
Kirkley Suffk ...45 Q10
Kirklington N York ...65 N10
Kirklington Notts ...51 P8
Kirklinton Cumb ...71 N3
Kirkliston C Edin ...86 D7
Kirkmabreck D & G ...69 L7
Kirkmaiden D & G ...68 F10
Kirk Merrington Dur ...65 M2
Kirk Michael IoM ...56 c4
Kirkmichael P & K ...94 B9
Kirkmichael S Ayrs ...76 F9
Kirkmuirhill S Lans ...77 N3
Kirknewton Nthumb ...81 J8
Kirknewton W Loth ...86 D8
Kirkney Abers ...101 P8
Kirk of Shotts N Lans ...85 P9
Kirkoswald Cumb ...71 Q7
Kirkoswald S Ayrs ...76 D9
Kirkpatrick D & G ...78 E10
Kirkpatrick Durham D & G ...70 C2
Kirkpatrick-Fleming D & G ...71 L2
Kirk Sandall Donc ...59 N11
Kirksanton Cumb ...62 D6
Kirk Smeaton N York ...59 M10
Kirkstall Leeds ...58 H7
Kirkstead Lincs ...52 H10
Kirkstile Abers ...102 C8
Kirkstile D & G ...79 M10
Kirkstyle Highld ...110 G2
Kirkthorpe Wakefd ...59 J9
Kirkton Abers ...102 E9
Kirkton D & G ...78 F11
Kirkton Fife ...93 L10
Kirkton Highld ...97 L4
Kirkton Highld ...97 N2
Kirkton P & K ...92 E11
Kirkton Manor Border ...79 K2
Kirkton of Airlie Angus ...93 K5
Kirkton of Auchterhouse Angus ...93 L7
Kirkton of Barevan Highld ...107 N11
Kirkton of Collace P & K ...92 H8
Kirkton of Durris Abers ...95 M3
Kirkton of Glenbuchat Abers ...101 M11
Kirkton of Glenisla Angus ...94 D9
Kirkton of Kingoldrum Angus ...93 L5
Kirkton of Lethendy P & K ...92 G7
Kirkton of Logie Buchan Abers ...103 L7
Kirkton of Maryculter Abers ...95 P3
Kirkton of Menmuir Angus ...95 J8
Kirkton of Monikie Angus ...93 N7
Kirkton of Rayne Abers ...102 F8
Kirkton of Skene Abers ...95 N1
Kirkton of Tealing Angus ...93 M7
Kirkton of Tough Abers ...102 D11
Kirktown Abers ...103 K3
Kirktown Abers ...103 M5
Kirktown of Alvah Abers ...102 E4
Kirktown of Bourtie Abers ...102 G9
Kirktown of Deskford Moray ...101 P3
Kirktown of Fetteresso Abers ...95 P5
Kirktown of Mortlach Moray ...101 L7
Kirktown of Slains Abers ...103 L9
Kirkurd Border ...86 D12
Kirkwall Ork ...111 h2
Kirkwall Airport Ork ...111 h2
Kirkwhelpington Nthumb ...72 H4
Kirk Yetholm Border ...80 H8
Kirmington N Linc ...61 J11
Kirmond le Mire Lincs ...52 H5
Kirn Ag & B ...84 C7
Kirriemuir Angus ...93 L5
Kirstead Green Norfk ...45 L10
Kirtlebridge D & G ...71 K2
Kirtling Cambs ...34 B5
Kirtling Green Cambs ...34 B5
Kirtlington Oxon ...31 L9
Kirtomy Highld ...109 N3
Kirton Lincs ...43 K3
Kirton Notts ...51 P7
Kirton Suffk ...35 L8
Kirtonhill W Duns ...84 G7
Kirton in Lindsey N Linc ...52 D4
Kirwaugh D & G ...69 K8
Kishorn Highld ...97 L2
Kislingbury Nhants ...31 P3
Kitt Green Wigan ...57 K7
Kittisford Somset ...16 E10
Kitt's Green Birm ...40 F9
Kittybrewster C Aber ...95 Q1
Kivernoll Herefs ...28 F3
Kiveton Park Rothm ...51 L4
Knaith Lincs ...52 B6
Knap Corner Dorset ...8 B3
Knaphill Surrey ...20 F10
Knapp Somset ...17 J10
Knapton C York ...59 M4
Knapton N York ...67 J11
Knapton Norfk ...45 M4
Knapwell Cambs ...33 K4
Knaresborough N York ...59 J3
Knarsdale Nthumb ...72 C9
Knaven Abers ...103 J6
Knayton N York ...66 B9
Knebworth Herts ...33 J11
Knedlington E R Yk ...60 C8
Kneesall Notts ...51 P7
Kneeton Notts ...51 P10
Knelston Swans ...26 C10

Knenhall Staffs....50 B12
Knightcote Warwks....31 K4
Knightley Staffs....49 P9
Knighton C Leic....41 N7
Knighton Dorset....7 N1
Knighton Powys....38 F7
Knighton Somset....16 G7
Knighton Staffs....49 N7
Knighton Staffs....49 N9
Knighton on Teme Worcs....39 L7
Knightwick Worcs....39 N10
Knill Herefs....38 F9
Knipoch Ag & B....90 B10
Knipton Leics....42 B4
Kniveton Derbys....50 G10
Knock Cumb....64 C3
Knock Highld....97 J7
Knock Moray....102 C5
Knock W Isls....111 d2
Knockally Highld....110 D9
Knockan Highld....106 D1
Knockando Moray....101 J7
Knockbain Highld....98 H1
Knockbain Highld....107 K10
Knock Castle N Ayrs....84 D9
Knockdee Highld....110 D4
Knockdow Ag & B....84 B8
Knockdown Wilts....18 C3
Knockeen S Ayrs....76 E11
Knockenkelly N Ayrs....75 Q7
Knockentiber E Ayrs....76 G4
Knockholt Kent....21 P10
Knockholt Pound Kent....21 P10
Knockin Shrops....48 G10
Knockinlaw E Ayrs....76 G4
Knocknain D & G....68 C6
Knockrome Ag & B....82 H8
Knocksharry IoM....56 b4
Knocksheen D & G....69 N3
Knockvennie Smithy D & G....70 C2
Knodishall Suffk....35 N4
Knodishall Common Suffk....35 P5
Knole Somset....17 L10
Knolls Green Ches E....57 P11
Knolton Wrexhm....48 H7
Knook Wilts....18 D11
Knossington Leics....42 B8
Knott End-on-Sea Lancs....62 G11
Knotting Bed....32 E4
Knotting Green Bed....32 E4
Knottingley Wakefd....59 L9
Knotty Ash Lpool....56 H9
Knowbury Shrops....39 L7
Knowe D & G....69 J5
Knowehead D & G....69 N2
Knoweside S Ayrs....76 E8
Knowes of Elrick Abers....102 D5
Knowle Bristl....17 N3
Knowle Devon....6 D2
Knowle Devon....6 E6
Knowle Devon....15 J5
Knowle Devon....15 N10
Knowle Shrops....39 L7
Knowle Solhll....40 F11
Knowle Somset....16 C7
Knowlefield Cumb....71 N4
Knowle Green Lancs....57 L2
Knowle St Giles Somset....7 J1
Knowl Hill W & M....20 D7
Knowsley Knows....56 H9
Knowsley Safari Park Knows....57 J9
Knowstone Devon....15 P7
Knox Bridge Kent....12 F2
Knoydart Highld....97 L8
Knucklas Powys....38 F7
Knuston Nhants....32 D4
Knutsford Ches E....57 N12
Knutsford Services Ches E....57 N12
Krumlin Calder....58 D9
Kuggar Cnwll....2 G11
Kyleakin Highld....97 K4
Kyle of Lochalsh Highld....97 K4
Kylerhea Highld....97 L5
Kylesku Highld....108 E8
Kylesmorar Highld....97 L10
Kyles Scalpay W Isls....111 c3
Kylestrome Highld....108 E8
Kynnersley Wrekin....49 M11
Kyrewood Worcs....39 L8

L

Lacasaigh W Isls....111 d2
Lacasdal W Isls....111 d2
Laceby NE Lin....52 H3
Lacey Green Bucks....20 D4
Lach Dennis Ches W....49 N2
Lackford Suffk....34 D3
Lackford Green Suffk....34 D3
Lacock Wilts....18 D7
Ladbroke Warwks....31 K3
Laddingford Kent....12 E1
Ladock Cnwll....3 K5
Lady Ork....111 i1
Ladybank Fife....93 K12
Ladygill S Lans....78 F4
Lady Hall Cumb....62 E5
Ladykirk Border....81 J5
Ladywood Birm....40 D9
Ladywood Worcs....39 Q9
La Fontenelle Guern....6 c1
Lag D & G....78 E10
Laga Highld....89 N4
Lagavulin Ag & B....74 F4
Lagg N Ayrs....75 P7
Laggan Highld....98 D9
Laggan Highld....99 J9
Lagganlia Highld....99 M8
La Grève de Lecq Jersey....7 a1
Laid Highld....108 H4
Laide Highld....105 N4
Laig Highld....96 F11
Laigh Clunch E Ayrs....76 H2
Laigh Fenwick E Ayrs....76 H1
Laigh Glenmuir E Ayrs....77 K7
Laighstonehall S Lans....85 M11
Laindon Essex....22 D5
Lairg Highld....107 J2
Laisterdyke C Brad....58 F7
Lake IoW....9 P10
Lake Wilts....18 G11
Lake District Cumb....71 K12

Lake District National Park Cumb....71 K12
Lakenham Norfk....45 K8
Lakenheath Suffk....44 B12
Lakes End Norfk....43 N10
Laleston Brdgnd....27 J11
Lamarsh Essex....34 E9
Lamas Norfk....45 L5
Lambden Border....80 G5
Lamberhurst Kent....12 D3
Lamberhurst Down Kent....12 D3
Lamberton Border....81 K3
Lambeth Gt Lon....21 L7
Lambfair Green Suffk....34 B6
Lambley Notts....51 N10
Lambley Nthumb....72 C8
Lambourn W Berk....19 K5
Lambourne End Essex....21 P5
Lambs Green W Susx....11 K3
Lamerton Devon....5 K5
Lamesley Gatesd....73 M8
Lamington S Lans....78 F3
Lamlash N Ayrs....75 Q6
Lamonby Cumb....71 N8
Lamorna Cnwll....2 C10
Lamorran Cnwll....3 K7
Lampeter Cerdgn....37 J10
Lampeter Velfrey Pembks....25 K6
Lamphey Pembks....24 H8
Lamplugh Cumb....70 H10
Lamport Nhants....41 Q11
Lamyatt Somset....17 P8
Lanark S Lans....77 P3
Lancaster Lancs....63 J9
Lancaster Services Lancs....63 J10
Lanchester Dur....73 L10
Lancing W Susx....11 J8
L'Ancresse Guern....6 c1
Landbeach Cambs....33 M4
Landcross Devon....14 H7
Landerberry Abers....95 M2
Landford Wilts....9 J4
Land-hallow Highld....110 E8
Landimore Swans....26 C9
Landkey Devon....15 K6
Landore Swans....26 F9
Landrake Cnwll....4 H7
Landulph Cnwll....5 J7
Laneast Cnwll....4 F4
Lane Cnwll....3 J4
Lane End Bucks....20 D5
Lane End Kent....22 C8
Lane End Wilts....18 B10
Lane Ends Derbys....40 G1
Laneham Notts....52 B8
Lane Head Dur....65 K5
Lanehead Dur....72 F11
Lane Head Wsall....40 C7
Lane Side Lancs....57 P4
Langal Highld....89 P3
Langaller Somset....16 H10
Langar Notts....41 Q1
Langbank Rens....84 G8
Langbar N York....58 E4
Langcliffe N York....63 P8
Langdale End N York....67 K8
Langdon Hills Essex....22 D6
Langdown Hants....9 M6
Langdyke Fife....86 G2
Langenhoe Essex....34 G11
Langford C Beds....32 H8
Langford Devon....6 D3
Langford Essex....22 G2
Langford Notts....52 B10
Langford Oxon....30 G12
Langford Budville Somset....16 F10
Langham Essex....34 G9
Langham Norfk....44 G2
Langham Rutlnd....42 B7
Langham Suffk....34 F3
Langho Lancs....57 N3
Langholm D & G....79 M11
Langland Swans....26 E10
Langlee Border....80 C7
Langley Hants....9 M7
Langley Herts....32 H11
Langley Kent....22 F11
Langley Nthumb....72 E8
Langley Slough....20 G7
Langley Somset....16 E9
Langley W Susx....10 D4
Langley Warwks....30 F2
Langley Burrell Wilts....18 D6
Langley Green Essex....34 E11
Langley Marsh Somset....16 E9
Langley Mill Derbys....51 K10
Langley Park Dur....73 L11
Langley Street Norfk....45 N9
Langley Upper Green Essex....33 M9
Langney E Susx....12 D9
Langold Notts....51 N4
Langore Cnwll....4 G3
Langport Somset....17 K10
Langrick Lincs....43 J1
Langridge BaNES....17 Q3
Langrigg Cumb....71 J6
Langrish Hants....10 B5
Langsett Barns....50 G2
Langside P & K....92 B11
Langstone Hants....10 B8
Langthorne N York....65 M8
Langthorpe N York....59 K1
Langthwaite N York....64 H7
Langtoft E R Yk....60 H2
Langtoft Lincs....42 G7
Langton Dur....65 L4
Langton Lincs....52 H9
Langton Lincs....53 L9
Langton N York....60 D2
Langton by Wragby Lincs....52 G7
Langton Green Kent....12 B3
Langton Herring Dorset....7 N6
Langton Matravers Dorset....8 E10
Langtree Devon....14 H8
Langwathby Cumb....71 R8
Langwell House Highld....110 C2
Langwith Derbys....51 M6
Langwith Junction Derbys....51 L7
Langworth Lincs....52 F8
Lanhydrock House & Gardens Cnwll....3 N3
Lanivet Cnwll....3 M3

Lanlivery Cnwll....3 N4
Lanner Cnwll....2 G7
Lanreath Cnwll....4 E8
Lansallos Cnwll....4 E9
Lanteglos Cnwll....4 D4
Lanteglos Highway Cnwll....4 E9
Lanton Border....80 E9
Lanton Nthumb....81 K7
Laphroaig Ag & B....74 E4
Lapley Staffs....49 Q11
Lapworth Warwks....40 F12
Larachbeg Highld....89 N6
Larbert Falk....85 P6
Largie Abers....102 D8
Largiemore Ag & B....83 P6
Largs N Ayrs....84 D10
Largybeg N Ayrs....75 Q7
Largymore N Ayrs....75 Q7
Larkfield Inver....84 D7
Larkfield Kent....22 E10
Larkhall S Lans....77 M2
Larkhill Wilts....18 G11
Larling Norfk....44 F11
La Rocque Jersey....7 c2
Lartington Dur....64 H4
Lasham Hants....19 Q11
Lasswade Mdloth....86 G8
Lastingham N York....66 G9
Latchford Warrtn....57 L10
Latchingdon Essex....22 G4
Latchley Cnwll....5 J5
Lathbury M Keyn....32 C7
Latheron Highld....110 E8
Latheronwheel Highld....110 E8
Lathones Fife....87 J1
Latimer Bucks....20 G4
Latteridge S Glos....29 J10
Lattiford Somset....17 Q10
Latton Wilts....18 G2
Lauder Border....80 C5
Laugharne Carmth....25 M6
Laughterton Lincs....52 B8
Laughton E Susx....11 P7
Laughton Leics....41 P9
Laughton Lincs....42 F4
Laughton Lincs....52 B4
Laughton Common Rothm....51 L4
Laughton-en-le-Morthen Rothm....51 M4
Launcells Cnwll....4 H4
Launton Oxon....31 N9
Laurencekirk Abers....95 L7
Laurieston D & G....70 P6
Laurieston Falk....85 Q7
Lavendon M Keyn....32 D6
Lavenham Suffk....34 F7
Lavernock V Glam....16 G3
Laversdale Cumb....71 P3
Laverstock Wilts....8 H2
Laverstoke Hants....19 N10
Laverton Gloucs....30 E7
Laverton N York....65 M11
Laverton Somset....18 B9
La Villette Guern....6 b2
Lavister Wrexhm....48 G4
Law S Lans....85 N11
Lawers P & K....91 Q8
Lawford Essex....34 H9
Lawford Somset....16 F8
Law Hill S Lans....85 N11
Lawhitton Cnwll....4 H4
Lawkland N York....63 P8
Lawley Wrekin....39 M1
Lawnhead Staffs....49 Q10
Lawrence Weston Bristl....28 G11
Lawrenny Pembks....24 H7
Lawshall Suffk....34 E6
Laxay W Isls....111 d2
Laxdale W Isls....111 d2
Laxey IoM....56 d4
Laxfield Suffk....35 L3
Laxford Bridge Highld....108 E6
Laxo Shet....111 k3
Laxton E R Yk....60 D8
Laxton Nhants....42 D10
Laxton Notts....51 Q7
Laycock C Brad....58 D6
Layer Breton Essex....34 F11
Layer-de-la-Haye Essex....34 F11
Layer Marney Essex....34 F12
Layham Suffk....34 G8
Laymore Dorset....7 K2
Laytham E R Yk....60 C6
Lazenby R & Cl....66 E4
Lazonby Cumb....71 Q7
Lea Derbys....51 J8
Lea Herefs....28 H4
Lea Lincs....52 B6
Lea Shrops....38 G4
Lea Wilts....18 E4
Leachkin Highld....107 K12
Leadburn Border....86 F10
Leadenham Lincs....52 D11
Leaden Roding Essex....22 C1
Leadgate Dur....73 K9
Leadhills S Lans....78 E6
Leafield Oxon....30 H10
Leagrave Luton....32 F11
Leake Common Side Lincs....53 L11
Lealholm N York....66 G6
Lealt Highld....104 G9
Lea Marston Warwks....40 G8
Leamington Hastings Warwks....31 L1
Leamington Spa Warwks....30 H2
Leap Cross E Susx....12 C7
Learney Abers....95 K2
Leasgill Cumb....63 J5
Leasingham Lincs....42 F1
Leasingthorne Dur....65 M2
Leatherhead Surrey....21 J11
Leathley N York....58 G5
Leaton Shrops....49 J10
Leaveland Kent....23 J11
Leavenheath Suffk....34 F8
Leavening N York....60 D2
Leaves Green Gt Lon....21 N10
Lebberston N York....67 M10
Le Bourg Jersey....7 c2
Lechlade on Thames Gloucs....18 H2
Lecht Gruinart Ag & B....82 D10
Leck Lancs....63 M6
Leckbuie P & K....91 Q8
Leckford Hants....19 L12
Leckhampstead Bucks....31 Q6

Leckhampstead W Berk....19 M5
Leckhampstead Thicket W Berk....19 M5
Leckhampton Gloucs....29 N5
Leckmelm Highld....106 C4
Leconfield E R Yk....60 H5
Ledaig Ag & B....90 C8
Ledburn Bucks....32 C11
Ledbury Herefs....29 J2
Ledgemoor Herefs....38 H11
Ledmore Highld....108 E12
Ledsham Leeds....59 L8
Ledston Leeds....59 K8
Ledwell Oxon....31 K8
Lee Devon....14 H3
Lee Gt Lon....21 M8
Leebotwood Shrops....39 J3
Lee Brockhurst Shrops....49 K9
Leece Cumb....62 E8
Lee Chapel Essex....22 E6
Lee Clump Bucks....20 E3
Leeds Kent....22 G11
Leeds Leeds....58 H7
Leeds Bradford Airport Leeds....58 G6
Leeds Castle Kent....22 G11
Leeds Skelton Lake Services Leeds....59 J7
Leedstown Cnwll....2 E8
Leek Staffs....50 C9
Leek Wootton Warwks....30 H1
Lee Mill Devon....5 M8
Leeming N York....65 N9
Leeming Bar N York....65 M9
Leeming Bar Rest Area N York....65 M9
Lee-on-the-Solent Hants....9 P7
Lees Derbys....50 H12
Lees Oldham....58 C12
Lees Green Derbys....50 H12
Leeswood Flints....48 F4
Leftwich Ches W....49 M2
Legbourne Lincs....53 L6
Legerwood Border....80 D5
Legoland W & M....20 F8
Legsby Lincs....52 G6
Leicester C Leic....41 N6
Leicester Forest East Services Leics....41 M7
Leigh Dorset....7 N2
Leigh Gloucs....29 M4
Leigh Kent....12 B2
Leigh Surrey....11 K1
Leigh Wigan....57 M8
Leigh Wilts....18 F3
Leigh Worcs....39 P10
Leigh Beck Essex....22 F6
Leigh Delamere Wilts....18 C5
Leigh Delamere Services Wilts....18 D5
Leigh Green Kent....12 H4
Leigh Knoweglass S Lans....77 K2
Leigh-on-Sea Sthend....22 G6
Leigh Park Dorset....8 F7
Leigh Park Hants....10 B8
Leigh Sinton Worcs....39 P11
Leighswood Wsall....40 D7
Leighton Gloucs....29 L9
Leighton Powys....38 E2
Leighton Shrops....39 L2
Leighton Bromswold Cambs....32 G2
Leighton Buzzard C Beds....32 D10
Leigh upon Mendip Somset....17 Q6
Leigh Woods N Som....17 N2
Leinthall Earls Herefs....39 J8
Leinthall Starkes Herefs....38 H8
Leintwardine Herefs....38 H7
Leire Leics....41 M9
Leiston Suffk....35 P4
Leith C Edin....86 F7
Leitholm Border....80 G5
Lelant Cnwll....2 E8
Lelley E R Yk....61 L7
Lempitlaw Border....80 G7
Lemreway W Isls....111 d3
Lemsford Herts....21 K2
Lenchwick Worcs....30 D5
Lendalfoot S Ayrs....68 E7
Lendrick Stirlg....85 J2
Lendrum Terrace Abers....103 M7
Lenham Kent....22 H11
Lenham Heath Kent....22 H12
Lenie Highld....98 G4
Lennel Border....80 H6
Lennox Plunton D & G....69 N8
Lennoxtown E Duns....85 K7
Lent Bucks....20 E7
Lenton C Nott....51 M11
Lenton Lincs....42 E4
Lenwade Norfk....44 H6
Lenzie E Duns....85 L8
Leochel-Cushnie Abers....102 C12
Leominster Herefs....39 J9
Leonard Stanley Gloucs....29 L7
Lepe Hants....104 B11
Leppington N York....60 D2
Lepton Kirk....58 G9
Lerags Ag & B....90 B10
L'Erée Guern....6 a2
Lerryn Cnwll....4 D8
Lerwick Shet....111 k4
Lesbury Nthumb....81 P10
Leslie Abers....102 D9
Leslie Fife....86 F2
Lesmahagow S Lans....78 D2
Lesnewth Cnwll....4 E3
Les Quartiers Guern....6 c1
Les Quennevais Jersey....7 a2
Lessingham Norfk....45 N5
Lessonhall Cumb....71 K5
Leswalt D & G....68 D6
L'Etacq Jersey....7 a1
Letchmore Heath Herts....21 J4
Letchworth Garden City Herts....32 H9
Letcombe Bassett Oxon....19 L4
Letcombe Regis Oxon....19 L4
Letham Angus....93 P6
Letham Border....80 F11
Letham Falk....85 P6
Letham Fife....93 K11
Letham Grange Angus....93 Q6
Lethenty Abers....102 D10

Lethenty Abers....102 H7
Letheringham Suffk....35 L5
Letheringsett Norfk....44 H3
Letterewe Highld....105 P7
Letterfearn Highld....97 M5
Letterfinlay Lodge Hotel Highld....98 C10
Letters Highld....106 C5
Lettershaw S Lans....78 E5
Letterston Pembks....24 G3
Lettoch Highld....99 Q5
Lettoch Highld....100 H8
Letton Herefs....38 G11
Letty Green Herts....21 L2
Letwell Rothm....51 M4
Leuchars Fife....93 M10
Leumrabhag W Isls....111 d3
Leurbost W Isls....111 d2
Levan Inver....84 D7
Levedale Staffs....40 B4
Leven E R Yk....61 J5
Leven Fife....86 H3
Levens Cumb....63 J5
Levens Green Herts....33 K11
Levenshulme Manch....57 Q9
Levenwick Shet....111 k5
Leverburgh W Isls....111 c4
Leverington Cambs....43 M7
Leverstock Green Herts....20 H3
Leverton Lincs....43 L1
Le Villocq Guern....6 b1
Levington Suffk....35 K8
Levisham N York....67 J8
Lew Oxon....31 J11
Lewannick Cnwll....4 G4
Lewdown Devon....5 K3
Lewes E Susx....11 N7
Leweston Pembks....24 G4
Lewisham Gt Lon....21 M8
Lewiston Highld....98 G4
Lewistown Brdgnd....27 K10
Lewknor Oxon....20 B4
Lewson Street Kent....23 J10
Lewtrenchard Devon....5 K3
Lexden Essex....34 F10
Lexworthy Somset....16 H8
Leybourne Kent....22 D10
Leyburn N York....65 K9
Leygreen Herts....32 G10
Ley Hill Bucks....20 F3
Leyland Lancs....57 K4
Leylodge Abers....102 G11
Leys Abers....103 K5
Leys P & K....93 J7
Leysdown-on-Sea Kent....23 K8
Leysmill Angus....93 Q6
Leys of Cossans Angus....93 L6
Leysters Herefs....39 K8
Leyton Gt Lon....21 M6
Leytonstone Gt Lon....21 N6
Lezant Cnwll....4 H4
Lhanbryde Moray....101 K3
Libanus Powys....27 L3
Libberton S Lans....78 G1
Liberton C Edin....86 F8
Lichfield Staffs....40 E5
Lickey Worcs....40 C11
Lickey End Worcs....40 C11
Lickfold W Susx....10 E5
Liddesdale Highld....89 Q4
Liddington Swindn....18 H5
Lidgate Suffk....34 C5
Lidlington C Beds....32 E8
Liff Angus....93 L8
Lifford Birm....40 D10
Lifton Devon....5 J3
Liftondown Devon....4 H3
Lighthorne Warwks....31 J3
Lighthorne Heath Warwks....31 J3
Lightwater Surrey....20 E10
Lightwater Valley Theme Park N York....65 M11
Lightwood C Stke....50 B11
Lilbourne Nhants....41 M11
Lilleshall Wrekin....49 N11
Lilley Herts....32 G10
Lilliesleaf Border....80 C8
Lillingstone Dayrell Bucks....31 P6
Lillingstone Lovell Bucks....31 P6
Lillington Dorset....7 P1
Lilliput BCP....8 F9
Lilstock Somset....16 F7
Limbury Luton....32 F11
Lime Street Worcs....29 L3
Limekilnburn S Lans....77 M2
Limekilns Fife....86 C5
Limerigg Falk....85 P8
Limerstone IoW....9 M10
Lime Street Worcs....29 L3
Limington Somset....17 M10
Limmerhaugh E Ayrs....77 K6
Limpenhoe Norfk....45 N8
Limpley Stoke Wilts....18 B8
Limpsfield Surrey....21 N11
Limpsfield Chart Surrey....21 N11
Linby Notts....51 M9
Linchmere W Susx....10 D4
Lincluden D & G....78 F12
Lincoln Lincs....52 D8
Lincomb Worcs....39 P8
Lindale Cumb....62 H6
Lindal in Furness Cumb....62 F7
Lindfield W Susx....11 M5
Lindford Hants....10 D3
Lindley Kirk....58 E9
Lindores Fife....93 K11
Lindridge Worcs....39 M8
Lindsell Essex....33 Q10
Lindsey Suffk....34 G7
Lindsey Tye Suffk....34 G7
Lingdale R & Cl....66 H5
Lingen Herefs....38 G8
Lingfield Surrey....11 M2
Lingfield Common Surrey....11 M2
Lingwood Norfk....45 M8
Liniclate W Isls....111 b5
Linicro Highld....104 E8
Linkend Worcs....29 L3
Linkenholt Hants....19 L9
Linkinhorne Cnwll....4 G5
Linktown Fife....86 F4
Linkwood Moray....101 K3
Linley Shrops....38 G4
Linley Green Herefs....39 M10
Linlithgow W Loth....86 B6

Linsidemore Highld 107 J3
Linslade C Beds 32 C10
Linstead Parva Suffk 35 M2
Linstock Cumb 71 N4
Linthurst Worcs 40 D11
Linthwaite Kirk 58 E10
Lintlaw Border 87 Q9
Lintmill Moray 101 P3
Linton Border 80 G8
Linton Cambs 33 P7
Linton Derbys 40 H4
Linton Herefs 28 H4
Linton Kent 22 F12
Linton Leeds 59 K5
Linton N York 58 C2
Linton Hill Herefs 29 J4
Linton-on-Ouse N York 59 L3
Linwood Lincs 52 G6
Linwood Rens 84 G9
Lionacleit W Isls 111 b5
Lional W Isls 111 e1
Liphook Hants 10 D4
Liscard Wirral 56 F9
Liscombe Somset 15 P5
Liskeard Cnwll 4 F7
Lismore Ag & B 90 B7
Liss Hants 10 C5
Lissett E R Yk 61 K3
Lissington Lincs 52 G6
Lisvane Cardif 27 P11
Liswerry Newpt 28 D10
Litcham Norfk 44 E6
Litchborough Nhants 31 N4
Litchfield Hants 19 M9
Litherland Sefton 56 G8
Litlington Cambs 33 K8
Litlington E Susx 11 Q9
Little Abington Cambs 33 N7
Little Addington Nhants 32 D3
Little Airies D & G 69 K9
Little Alne Warwks 30 F2
Little Altcar Sefton 56 F7
Little Amwell Herts 21 M2
Little Aston Staffs 40 E7
Little Ayton N York 66 D5
Little Baddow Essex 22 F2
Little Badminton S Glos 18 B4
Little Bampton Cumb 71 L5
Little Bardfield Essex 33 Q9
Little Barford Bed 32 H5
Little Barningham Norfk 45 J4
Little Barrington Gloucs 30 G10
Little Barrow Ches W 49 J2
Little Bavington Nthumb 72 H5
Little Bedwyn Wilts 19 K7
Little Bentley Essex 35 J10
Little Berkhamsted Herts 21 L2
Little Billing Nhants 32 B4
Little Billington C Beds 32 D11
Little Birch Herefs 28 F3
Little Blakenham Suffk 34 H7
Little Blencow Cumb 71 P8
Little Bloxwich Wsall 40 D6
Little Bognor W Susx 10 G6
Little Bollington Ches E 57 N10
Little Bookham Surrey 20 H11
Littleborough Notts 52 B7
Littleborough Rochdl 58 C10
Littlebourne Kent 23 N11
Little Bourton Oxon 31 L5
Little Braxted Essex 22 G1
Little Brechin Angus 95 J9
Littlebredy Dorset 7 N5
Little Brickhill M Keyn 32 C9
Little Brington Nhants 31 P2
Little Bromley Essex 34 H10
Little Budworth Ches W 49 L3
Littleburn Highld 107 K10
Little Burstead Essex 22 D5
Littlebury Essex 33 N8
Littlebury Green Essex 33 M8
Little Bytham Lincs 42 E6
Little Carlton Lincs 53 L6
Little Casterton Rutlnd 42 E8
Little Cawthorpe Lincs 53 K6
Little Chalfont Bucks 20 F4
Little Chart Kent 12 H2
Little Chesterford Essex 33 N8
Little Cheverell Wilts 18 E9
Little Chishill Cambs 33 L8
Little Clacton Essex 35 J11
Little Clifton Cumb 70 H9
Little Coates NE Lin 53 J2
Little Comberton Worcs 30 C5
Little Common E Susx 12 E8
Little Compton Warwks 30 H7
Little Cornard Suffk 34 E8
Little Cowarne Herefs 39 L11
Little Coxwell Oxon 19 K3
Little Crakehall N York 65 M9
Little Cressingham Norfk 44 E9
Little Crosby Sefton 56 G8
Little Cubley Derbys 50 F12
Little Dalby Leics 41 Q5
Littledean Gloucs 29 J6
Little Dewchurch Herefs 28 F3
Little Ditton Cambs 33 Q5
Little Downham Cambs 43 N12
Little Driffield E R Yk 60 H3
Little Dunham Norfk 44 E7
Little Dunkeld P & K 92 F7
Little Dunmow Essex 33 Q11
Little Durnford Wilts 8 G1
Little Easton Essex 33 P11
Little Eaton Derbys 51 J11
Little Ellingham Norfk 44 G9
Little Everdon Nhants 31 N3
Little Eversden Cambs 33 L6
Little Faringdon Oxon 19 J1
Little Fencote N York 65 M8
Little Fenton N York 59 M7
Littleferry Highld 107 N4
Little Fransham Norfk 44 E7
Little Gaddesden Herts 20 F2
Little Glemham Suffk 35 M5
Little Gorsley Herefs 29 J4
Little Gransden Cambs 33 J6
Little Green Somset 17 Q6
Little Hadham Herts 33 M11
Little Hale Lincs 42 H2
Little Hallam Derbys 51 L11
Little Hallingbury Essex 33 N12
Littleham Devon 6 D6
Littleham Devon 14 H7

Littlehampton W Susx 10 G9
Little Harrowden Nhants 32 C3
Little Haseley Oxon 19 Q1
Little Haven Pembks 24 F6
Littlehaven W Susx 11 J4
Little Hay Staffs 40 E7
Little Haywood Staffs 40 D3
Littlehempston Devon 5 Q7
Little Hereford Herefs 39 L4
Little Horkesley Essex 34 F9
Little Hormead Herts 33 L10
Little Horsted E Susx 11 P6
Little Horton C Brad 58 F7
Little Horwood Bucks 32 B10
Little Houghton Barns 59 K11
Little Houghton Nhants 32 B5
Little Hucklow Derbys 50 F5
Little Hutton N York 66 C11
Little Irchester Nhants 32 C4
Little Keyford Somset 18 B10
Little Kimble Bucks 20 D3
Little Kineton Warwks 31 J4
Little Kingshill Bucks 20 E4
Little Knox D & G 70 D4
Little Langdale Cumb 62 G2
Little Langford Wilts 18 F12
Little Leigh Ches W 49 L1
Little Leighs Essex 34 C12
Little Lever Bolton 57 N7
Little Linford M Keyn 32 B7
Little Load Somset 17 L10
Little London Cambs 43 L10
Little London E Susx 12 C6
Little London Hants 19 L10
Little London Hants 19 Q8
Little Longstone Derbys 50 F6
Little Maplestead Essex 34 D9
Little Marcle Herefs 29 J2
Little Marlow Bucks 20 E6
Little Massingham Norfk 44 D5
Little Melton Norfk 45 J8
Littlemill Abers 94 E3
Littlemill Highld 100 E5
Little Mill Mons 28 C8
Little Milton Oxon 19 Q1
Little Missenden Bucks 20 E4
Littlemore Oxon 31 M12
Little Musgrave Cumb 64 D5
Little Ness Shrops 48 H10
Little Newcastle Pembks 24 G3
Little Newsham Dur 65 K4
Little Norton Somset 17 L11
Little Oakley Essex 35 K10
Little Oakley Nhants 42 C11
Little Orton Cumb 71 M5
Littleover C Derb 41 J1
Little Packington Warwks 40 G9
Little Paxton Cambs 32 H4
Little Petherick Cnwll 3 K2
Little Plumstead Norfk 45 M7
Little Ponton Lincs 42 D4
Littleport Cambs 43 P11
Little Preston Nhants 31 N4
Littler Ches W 49 L3
Little Raveley Cambs 33 J2
Little Reedness E R Yk 60 D9
Little Ribston N York 59 J4
Little Rissington Gloucs 30 F9
Little Rollright Oxon 30 H7
Little Ryburgh Norfk 44 F5
Little Salkeld Cumb 71 Q8
Little Sampford Essex 33 Q9
Little Saughall Ches W 48 G2
Little Saxham Suffk 34 D4
Little Scatwell Highld 106 F10
Little Shelford Cambs 33 M6
Little Singleton Lancs 56 G2
Little Skipwith N York 59 P6
Little Smeaton N York 59 M10
Little Snoring Norfk 44 F4
Little Sodbury S Glos 18 A4
Little Somborne Hants 9 L2
Little Somerford Wilts 18 E4
Little Soudley Shrops 49 N9
Little Stainton Darltn 65 N4
Little Stanney Ches W 48 H1
Little Staughton Bed 32 F4
Little Steeping Lincs 53 M10
Little Stoke Staffs 40 B2
Littlestone-on-Sea Kent 13 L5
Little Stonham Suffk 35 J5
Little Stretton Leics 41 P7
Little Stretton Shrops 39 J4
Little Strickland Cumb 71 Q10
Little Stukeley Cambs 32 H2
Little Sugnall Staffs 49 P8
Little Swinburne Nthumb 72 G5
Little Sypland D & G 70 B5
Little Tew Oxon 31 J8
Little Tey Essex 34 E11
Little Thetford Cambs 33 N2
Little Thorpe Dur 73 Q11
Littlethorpe Leics 41 M7
Littlethorpe N York 59 J1
Little Thurlow Suffk 34 B6
Little Thurrock Thurr 22 D7
Littleton Ches W 48 H3
Littleton D & G 69 P7
Littleton Hants 9 M2
Littleton Somset 17 L9
Littleton Surrey 20 H9
Littleton Drew Wilts 18 C5
Littleton-on-Severn S Glos 28 H10
Littleton Panell Wilts 18 E9
Little Torrington Devon 15 J8
Little Town Lancs 57 M2
Little Urswick Cumb 62 F7
Little Wakering Essex 22 H6
Little Walden Essex 33 N8
Little Waldingfield Suffk 34 F7
Little Walsingham Norfk 44 F3
Little Waltham Essex 22 E2
Little Weighton E R Yk 60 G7
Little Wenlock Wrekin 39 M2
Little Weston Somset 17 N10
Little Whitefield IoW 9 P9
Littlewick Green W & M 20 D7
Little Wilbraham Cambs 33 N5
Little Witcombe Gloucs 29 M6
Little Witley Worcs 39 P8
Little Wittenham Oxon 19 P3
Little Wolford Warwks 30 H7

Little Woodcote Gt Lon 21 L10
Littleworth Oxon 19 K2
Littleworth Staffs 40 C3
Littleworth Worcs 30 B4
Little Wymington Bed 32 D4
Little Wymondley Herts 32 H10
Little Wyrley Staffs 40 D6
Little Yeldham Essex 34 C8
Littley Green Essex 34 B12
Litton Derbys 50 F6
Litton N York 64 G11
Litton Somset 17 N5
Litton Cheney Dorset 7 M5
Liurbost W Isls 111 d2
Liverpool Lpool 56 G10
Liversedge Kirk 58 G9
Liverton Devon 5 Q5
Liverton R & Cl 66 G4
Livingston W Loth 86 C8
Livingston Village W Loth 86 C8
Lixwm Flints 48 D2
Lizard Cnwll 2 G12
Llanaelhaearn Gwynd 46 F3
Llanafan Cerdgn 37 L6
Llanafan-Fawr Powys 37 Q9
Llanallgo IoA 54 G5
Llanarmon Dyffryn Ceiriog Wrexhm 48 D8
Llanarmon-yn-Ial Denbgs 48 E4
Llanarth Cerdgn 36 G8
Llanarth Mons 28 D6
Llanarthne Carmth 26 D5
Llanasa Flints 56 C11
Llanbadarn Fawr Cerdgn 37 K4
Llanbadarn Fynydd Powys 38 C6
Llanbadoc Mons 28 D8
Llanbeder Newpt 28 D10
Llanbedr Gwynd 47 J4
Llanbedr Powys 27 P5
Llanbedr-Dyffryn-Clwyd Denbgs 48 D4
Llanbedrgoch IoA 54 G5
Llanbedrog Gwynd 46 E5
Llanbedr-y-Cennin Conwy 55 J7
Llanberis Gwynd 54 H9
Llanbethêry V Glam 16 D3
Llanbister Powys 38 C7
Llanblethian V Glam 16 D2
Llanboidy Carmth 25 L4
Llanbradach Caerph 27 N10
Llanbrynmair Powys 47 P10
Llancadle V Glam 16 D3
Llancarfan V Glam 16 E2
Llancloudy Herefs 28 F5
Llandaff Cardif 27 N12
Llandanwg Gwynd 47 J5
Llanddaniel Fab IoA 54 F6
Llanddarog Carmth 26 C5
Llanddeiniol Cerdgn 37 J6
Llanddeiniolen Gwynd 54 G8
Llandderfel Gwynd 47 R4
Llanddeusant IoA 54 D5
Llanddew Powys 27 M3
Llanddewi Swans 26 B10
Llanddewi Brefi Cerdgn 37 L9
Llanddewi Rhydderch Mons 28 D6
Llanddewi Velfrey Pembks 25 K5
Llanddewi Ystradenni Powys 38 C8
Llanddoged Conwy 55 L8
Llanddona IoA 54 H5
Llanddowror Carmth 25 M6
Llanddulas Conwy 55 N6
Llanddwywe Gwynd 47 J2
Llanddyfnan IoA 54 G6
Llandefaelog-Tre'r-Graig Powys 27 N3
Llandefalle Powys 27 M3
Llandegfan IoA 54 H6
Llandegla Denbgs 48 E5
Llandegley Powys 38 D8
Llandegveth Mons 28 D9
Llandeilo Carmth 26 E4
Llandeilo Graban Powys 38 C12
Llandeloy Pembks 24 F4
Llandenny Mons 28 E7
Llandevaud Newpt 28 E10
Llandevenny Mons 28 E10
Llandinam Powys 38 B5
Llandissilio Pembks 25 K5
Llandogo Mons 28 F7
Llandough V Glam 16 D2
Llandough V Glam 16 F2
Llandovery Carmth 26 G2
Llandow V Glam 16 C2
Llandre Carmth 37 L4
Llandre Cerdgn 37 K4
Llandre Isaf Pembks 25 K3
Llandrillo Denbgs 48 B7
Llandrillo-yn-Rhôs Conwy 55 M5
Llandrindod Wells Powys 38 C9
Llandrinio Powys 48 F11
Llandudno Conwy 55 L5
Llandudno Junction Conwy 55 L6
Llandulas Powys 37 P11
Llandwrog Gwynd 54 F9
Llandybie Carmth 26 E6
Llandyfaelog Carmth 25 P6
Llandyfriog Cerdgn 36 F11
Llandygai Gwynd 54 H7
Llandygwydd Cerdgn 36 F10
Llandyrnog Denbgs 48 C3
Llandyssil Powys 38 E3
Llandysul Cerdgn 36 G11
Llanedeyrn Cardif 27 P11
Llanedi Carmth 25 P4
Llaneglwys Powys 27 M2
Llanegryn Gwynd 47 K9
Llanegwad Carmth 26 D4
Llaneilian IoA 54 F3
Llanelian-yn-Rhôs Conwy 55 M6
Llanelidan Denbgs 48 C5
Llanelieu Powys 27 N3
Llanellen Mons 28 C6
Llanelli Carmth 26 C8
Llanelltyd Gwynd 47 L7
Llanelwedd Powys 38 B10
Llanenddwyn Gwynd 47 J2
Llanengan Gwynd 46 E6
Llanerchymedd IoA 54 F5
Llanerfyl Powys 38 B1
Llanfachraeth IoA 54 D5
Llanfachreth Gwynd 47 M6
Llanfaelog IoA 54 D7
Llanfaelrhys Gwynd 46 D6
Llanfaethlu IoA 54 D4

Llanfair Gwynd 47 J5
Llanfair Caereinion Powys 38 C2
Llanfair Clydogau Cerdgn 37 K9
Llanfair Dyffryn Clwyd Denbgs 48 D4
Llanfairfechan Conwy 55 K6
Llanfairpwllgwyngyll IoA 54 G7
Llanfair Talhaiarn Conwy 55 N7
Llanfair Waterdine Shrops 38 F6
Llanfairynghornwy IoA 54 D4
Llanfair-yn-Neubwll IoA 54 D6
Llanfallteg Carmth 25 K5
Llanfallteg West Carmth 25 K5
Llanfarian Cerdgn 37 J5
Llanfechain Powys 48 E10
Llanfechell IoA 54 E4
Llanferres Denbgs 48 E4
Llan Ffestiniog Gwynd 47 L3
Llanfihangel-ar-arth Carmth 36 G11
Llanfihangel Glyn Myfyr Conwy 55 P10
Llanfihangel Nant Bran Powys 27 K2
Llanfihangel Rhydithon Powys 38 D8
Llanfihangel Rogiet Mons 28 E10
Llanfihangel-y-Creuddyn Cerdgn 37 L5
Llanfihangel-yn-Ngwynfa Powys 48 C11
Llanfihangel yn Nhowyn IoA 54 D6
Llanfilo Powys 27 N3
Llanfoist Mons 28 C6
Llanfor Gwynd 47 Q4
Llanfrechfa Torfn 28 C9
Llanfrynach Powys 27 M4
Llanfwrog Denbgs 48 D4
Llanfwrog IoA 54 D5
Llanfyllin Powys 48 D10
Llanfynydd Carmth 26 D4
Llanfynydd Flints 48 F4
Llanfyrnach Pembks 25 L3
Llangadfan Powys 38 B12
Llangadog Carmth 26 F3
Llangadwaladr IoA 54 E7
Llangaffo IoA 54 F7
Llangammarch Wells Powys 37 Q10
Llangan V Glam 27 K12
Llangarron Herefs 28 F5
Llangathen Carmth 26 D4
Llangattock Powys 27 P5
Llangattock Lingoed Mons 28 D5
Llangedwyn Powys 48 E10
Llangefni Gwynd 54 F6
Llangeinor Brdgnd 27 J10
Llangeitho Cerdgn 37 K8
Llangeler Carmth 36 F11
Llangelynin Gwynd 47 J9
Llangennech Carmth 26 D8
Llangennith Swans 25 P9
Llangernyw Conwy 55 N7
Llangian Gwynd 46 E5
Llangloffan Pembks 24 F3
Llanglydwen Carmth 25 L4
Llangoed IoA 54 H6
Llangollen Denbgs 48 E7
Llangolman Pembks 25 K4
Llangors Powys 27 N4
Llangower Gwynd 47 P5
Llangrannog Cerdgn 36 E9
Llangristiolus IoA 54 F6
Llangrove Herefs 28 F5
Llangunllo Powys 38 E7
Llangunnor Carmth 25 P5
Llangurig Powys 37 P5
Llangwm Conwy 47 Q3
Llangwm Mons 28 E8
Llangwm Pembks 24 H6
Llangwnnadl Gwynd 46 D5
Llangwyryfon Cerdgn 37 K6
Llangybi Cerdgn 37 K9
Llangybi Gwynd 46 G3
Llangybi Mons 28 D9
Llangyndeyrn Carmth 26 B6
Llangynhafal Denbgs 48 D3
Llangynidr Powys 27 N5
Llangynin Carmth 25 M5
Llangynog Carmth 25 N6
Llangynog Powys 48 B9
Llangynwyd Brdgnd 27 J10
Llanhamlach Powys 27 M4
Llanharan Rhondd 27 L11
Llanharry Rhondd 27 L11
Llanhennock Mons 28 D9
Llanhilleth Blae G 27 P8
Llanidloes Powys 37 Q4
Llaniestyn Gwynd 46 E5
Llanigon Powys 27 P2
Llanilar Cerdgn 37 M5
Llanilid Rhondd 27 K11
Llanina Cerdgn 36 G8
Llanishen Cardif 27 N11
Llanishen Mons 28 F7
Llanllechid Gwynd 55 J7
Llanllowell Mons 28 D8
Llanllugan Powys 38 C2
Llanllwch Carmth 25 P5
Llanllwchaiarn Powys 38 D4
Llanllwni Carmth 36 H11
Llanllyfni Gwynd 54 F10
Llanmadoc Swans 25 Q9
Llanmaes V Glam 16 D3
Llanmartin Newpt 28 D10
Llanmiloe Carmth 25 M7
Llannefydd Conwy 55 N6
Llannon Carmth 26 D7
Llannor Gwynd 46 F4
Llanon Cerdgn 36 H7
Llanover Mons 28 C7
Llanpumsaint Carmth 25 P3
Llanrhaeadr-ym-Mochnant Powys 48 D9
Llanrhian Pembks 24 E3
Llanrhidian Swans 26 C9
Llanrhychwyn Conwy 55 L8
Llanrhyddlad IoA 54 D4
Llanrhystud Cerdgn 36 J6
Llanrug Gwynd 54 G8
Llanrumney Cardif 27 P11
Llanrwst Conwy 55 L8
Llansadurnen Carmth 25 M6
Llansadwrn Carmth 26 E3
Llansadwrn IoA 54 H6
Llansaint Carmth 25 P7

Llansamlet Swans 26 F8
Llansanffraid Glan Conwy Conwy 55 L6
Llansannan Conwy 55 N8
Llansantffraed Powys 27 N4
Llansantffraed-Cwmdeuddwr Powys 37 Q7
Llansantffraed-in-Elvel Powys 38 C10
Llansantffraid Cerdgn 36 H7
Llansantffraid-ym-Mechain Powys 48 E10
Llansawel Carmth 26 E2
Llansilin Powys 48 E9
Llansoy Mons 28 E8
Llanspyddid Powys 27 L3
Llanstadwell Pembks 24 G7
Llansteffan Carmth 25 N6
Llantarnam Torfn 28 C9
Llanteg Pembks 25 L6
Llanthewy Skirrid Mons 28 D5
Llanthony Mons 28 C4
Llantilio-Crossenny Mons 28 D6
Llantilio Pertholey Mons 28 C5
Llantrisant Mons 28 D9
Llantrisant Rhondd 27 L11
Llantrithyd V Glam 16 E2
Llantwit Fardre Rhondd 27 M10
Llantwit Major V Glam 16 C3
Llanuwchllyn Gwynd 47 P5
Llanvaches Newpt 28 E9
Llanvair Discoed Mons 28 E9
Llanvapley Mons 28 D6
Llanvetherine Mons 28 D5
Llanvihangel Crucorney Mons 28 C5
Llanwddyn Powys 48 B10
Llanwenog Cerdgn 36 H10
Llanwern Newpt 28 D10
Llanwinio Carmth 25 M4
Llanwnda Gwynd 54 F9
Llanwnda Pembks 24 G2
Llanwnnen Cerdgn 37 J10
Llanwnog Powys 38 B4
Llanwrda Carmth 26 F3
Llanwrin Powys 47 M9
Llanwrthwl Powys 37 Q7
Llanwrtyd Wells Powys 37 P10
Llanwyddelan Powys 38 C2
Llanyblodwel Shrops 48 E10
Llanybri Carmth 25 N6
Llanybydder Carmth 36 H10
Llanycefn Pembks 25 J4
Llanychaer Pembks 24 H2
Llanymawddwy Gwynd 47 P7
Llanymynech Powys 48 F10
Llanynghenedl IoA 54 D5
Llanynys Denbgs 48 C3
Llanyre Powys 38 B9
Llanystumdwy Gwynd 46 H4
Llanywern Powys 27 N3
Llawhaden Pembks 25 J5
Llawryglyn Powys 37 Q3
Llay Wrexhm 48 G4
Llechrhyd Caerph 27 M7
Llechryd Cerdgn 36 D11
Lledrod Cerdgn 37 K6
Llithfaen Gwynd 46 F3
Lloc Flints 56 D12
Llowes Powys 27 P1
Llwydcoed Rhondd 27 L7
Llwydiarth Powys 48 B11
Llwyncelyn Cerdgn 36 G8
Llwyndafydd Cerdgn 36 F9
Llwyngwril Gwynd 47 J9
Llwynmawr Wrexhm 48 E7
Llwynypia Rhondd 27 L9
Llynclys Shrops 48 F10
Llynfaes IoA 54 E6
Llŷn Peninsula Gwynd 46 E4
Llysfaen Conwy 55 N6
Llyswen Powys 27 N2
Llysworney V Glam 16 C2
Llys-y-frân Pembks 24 H4
Llywel Powys 27 J3
Loan Falk 85 Q7
Loanhead Mdloth 86 F8
Loaningfoot D & G 70 F4
Loans S Ayrs 76 F5
Lobhillcross Devon 5 K3
Lochailort Highld 97 K12
Lochaline Highld 89 N7
Lochans D & G 68 E7
Locharbriggs D & G 78 G11
Lochavich Ag & B 90 C12
Lochawe Ag & B 90 F10
Loch Baghasdail W Isls 111 b6
Lochboisdale W Isls 111 b6
Lochbuie Ag & B 89 M10
Lochcarron Highld 97 M2
Lochdon Ag & B 89 P9
Lochdonhead Ag & B 89 P9
Lochead Ag & B 83 L7
Lochearnhead Stirlg 91 N10
Lochee C Dund 93 L8
Loch Eil Highld 90 E1
Locheilside Station Highld 90 D1
Lochend Highld 98 H2
Locheport W Isls 111 b4
Loch Euphoirt W Isls 111 b4
Lochfoot D & G 70 E2
Lochgair Ag & B 83 P5
Lochgelly Fife 86 E4
Lochgilphead Ag & B 83 N5
Lochgoilhead Ag & B 84 D3
Lochieheads Fife 93 J11
Lochill Moray 101 K3
Lochindorb Lodge Highld 100 E8
Lochinver Highld 108 C10
Loch Lomond and The Trossachs National Park 84 H1
Loch Loyal Lodge Highld 109 L6
Lochluichart Highld 106 F10
Lochmaben D & G 78 H11
Lochmaddy W Isls 111 b4
Loch nam Madadh W Isls 111 b4
Loch Ness Highld 98 G4
Lochore Fife 86 E3
Loch Portain W Isls 111 b4
Lochportain W Isls 111 b4
Lochranza N Ayrs 75 P3
Loch Sgioport W Isls 111 b5
Lochside Abers 95 M8
Lochside D & G 78 F12
Lochside Highld 107 N11

Place	County/Region	Page	Grid
Lochskipport	W Isls	111	b5
Lochslin	Highld	107	N6
Lochton	S Ayrs	68	H3
Lochty	Angus	95	J9
Lochty	Fife	87	K1
Lochuisge	Highld	89	Q5
Lochwinnoch	Rens	84	F10
Lochwood	D & G	78	H9
Lockengate	Cnwll	3	M4
Lockerbie	D & G	79	J11
Lockeridge	Wilts	18	G7
Lockerley	Hants	9	K3
Locking	N Som	17	J4
Locking Stumps	Warrtn	57	M9
Lockington	E R Yk	60	H5
Lockleywood	Shrops	49	M9
Locksbottom	Gt Lon	21	N9
Locks Heath	Hants	9	N6
Lockton	N York	67	J9
Loddington	Leics	42	B9
Loddington	Nhants	32	B2
Loddiswell	Devon	5	P9
Loddon	Norfk	45	M9
Lode	Cambs	33	N4
Lode Heath	Solhll	40	F10
Loders	Dorset	7	L4
Lodsworth	W Susx	10	E5
Lofthouse	Leeds	59	J8
Lofthouse	N York	65	K11
Lofthouse Gate	Wakefd	59	J8
Loftus	R & Cl	66	G4
Logan	E Ayrs	77	K7
Loganlea	W Loth	86	B9
Loggerheads	Staffs	49	N8
Logie	Angus	95	L8
Logie	Fife	93	M10
Logie	Moray	100	F5
Logie Coldstone	Abers	94	G2
Logie Newton	Abers	102	E7
Logie Pert	Angus	95	L8
Logierait	P & K	92	E5
Logierieve	Abers	103	J9
Login	Carmth	25	K4
Lolworth	Cambs	33	L4
Lonbain	Highld	105	K10
Londesborough	E R Yk	60	E5
London	Gt Lon	21	M7
London Apprentice	Cnwll	3	M6
London Ashford Airport	*Kent*	*13*	*K6*
London City Airport	*Gt Lon*	*21*	*N7*
London Colney	Herts	21	J3
Londonderry	N York	65	N9
London Gateway Services	*Gt Lon*	*21*	*K5*
London Gatwick Airport	*W Susx*	*11*	*L2*
London Heathrow Airport	*Gt Lon*	*20*	*H8*
London Luton Airport	*Luton*	*32*	*G11*
London Oxford Airport	*Oxon*	*31*	*L10*
London Southend Airport	*Essex*	*22*	*G2*
London Stansted Airport	*Essex*	*33*	*N11*
Londonthorpe	Lincs	42	D3
London Zoo ZSL	Gt Lon	21	L6
Londubh	Highld	105	M6
Lonemore	Highld	105	L6
Long Ashton	N Som	17	M3
Long Bank	Worcs	39	N7
Long Bennington	Lincs	42	B3
Longbenton	N Tyne	73	M7
Longborough	Gloucs	30	F8
Long Bredy	Dorset	7	N5
Longbridge	Birm	40	D11
Longbridge Deverill	Wilts	18	C11
Long Buckby	Nhants	31	N1
Longburton	Dorset	7	P1
Long Clawson	Leics	41	Q3
Longcliffe	Derbys	50	G9
Longcombe	Devon	5	Q8
Long Compton	Staffs	49	Q10
Long Compton	Warwks	30	H7
Longcot	Oxon	19	J3
Long Crendon	Bucks	20	B2
Long Crichel	Dorset	8	E5
Longden	Shrops	38	H2
Long Ditton	Surrey	21	J9
Longdon	Staffs	40	E5
Longdon	Worcs	29	L2
Longdon Green	Staffs	40	E5
Longdon upon Tern	Wrekin	49	L11
Longdown	Devon	6	B5
Longdowns	Cnwll	2	H8
Long Duckmanton	Derbys	51	K6
Long Eaton	Derbys	41	L2
Longfield	Kent	22	C9
Longford	Covtry	41	J10
Longford	Derbys	50	G12
Longford	Gloucs	29	L5
Longford	Shrops	49	M8
Longford	Wrekin	49	N10
Longforgan	P & K	93	K9
Longformacus	Border	87	N10
Longframlington	Nthumb	73	K1
Long Green	Ches W	49	J2
Longham	Dorset	8	F7
Longham	Norfk	44	F7
Long Hanborough	Oxon	31	K10
Longhaven	Abers	103	M7
Longhirst	Nthumb	73	L3
Longhope	Gloucs	29	J5
Longhope	Ork	111	g3
Longhorsley	Nthumb	73	K2
Longhoughton	Nthumb	81	P10
Long Itchington	Warwks	31	K2
Longlane	Derbys	50	G12
Long Lawford	Warwks	41	L11
Longleat Safari & Adventure Park	Wilts	18	B11
Longlevens	Gloucs	29	L5
Longleys	P & K	93	K7
Long Load	Somset	17	L10
Longmanhill	Abers	102	F3
Long Marston	Herts	20	E1
Long Marston	N York	59	L4
Long Marston	Warwks	30	F4
Long Marton	Cumb	64	C3
Long Melford	Suffk	34	E7
Longmoor Camp	Hants	10	C4
Longmorn	Moray	101	K4
Longmoss	Ches E	50	B6
Long Newnton	Gloucs	29	M9
Longnewton	Border	80	D8
Long Newton	E Loth	87	K8
Longnewton	S on T	65	P4
Longney	Gloucs	29	K6
Longniddry	E Loth	87	J7
Longnor	Shrops	39	J3
Longnor	Staffs	50	E7
Longparish	Hants	19	M10
Long Preston	N York	63	Q9
Longridge	Lancs	57	L2
Longridge	W Loth	85	Q9
Longriggend	N Lans	85	N8
Long Riston	E R Yk	61	J6
Longrock	Cnwll	2	D9
Longsdon	Staffs	50	C9
Longside	Abers	103	L6
Longstanton	Cambs	33	L4
Longstock	Hants	19	L12
Longstowe	Cambs	33	K6
Long Stratton	Norfk	45	K10
Long Street	M Keyn	32	B7
Longstreet	Wilts	18	G9
Long Sutton	Hants	10	B1
Long Sutton	Lincs	43	L5
Long Sutton	Somset	17	L10
Longthorpe	C Pete	42	G9
Long Thurlow	Suffk	34	G3
Longthwaite	Cumb	71	N10
Longton	Lancs	57	J4
Longtown	Cumb	71	N2
Longtown	Herefs	28	C3
Longueville	Jersey	7	c2
Longville in the Dale	Shrops	39	K4
Long Waste	Wrekin	49	L11
Long Whatton	Leics	41	L3
Longwick	Bucks	20	C3
Long Wittenham	Oxon	19	P3
Longwitton	Nthumb	73	J3
Longwood	D & G	70	B4
Longworth	Oxon	19	L2
Longyester	E Loth	87	K8
Lonmay	Abers	103	L4
Lonmore	Highld	104	C12
Looe	Cnwll	4	F9
Loose	Kent	22	F11
Loosley Row	Bucks	20	D4
Lootcherbrae	Abers	102	D5
Lopen	Somset	17	K12
Loppington	Shrops	49	J9
Lordshill	C Sotn	9	L4
Lords Wood	Medway	22	F10
Lornty	P & K	92	H6
Loscoe	Derbys	51	K10
Losgaintir	W Isls	111	c3
Lossiemouth	Moray	101	K2
Lostock Gralam	Ches W	49	M1
Lostock Green	Ches W	49	M2
Lostwithiel	Cnwll	4	D8
Lothbeg	Highld	107	Q1
Lothersdale	N York	58	C5
Lothmore	Highld	110	A12
Loudwater	Bucks	20	E5
Loudwater	Herts	20	G4
Loughborough	Leics	41	M4
Loughor	Swans	26	D8
Loughton	Essex	21	N4
Loughton	M Keyn	32	B8
Lound	Lincs	42	F6
Lound	Notts	51	P4
Lound	Suffk	45	Q9
Lount	Leics	41	K4
Louth	Lincs	53	K6
Lover	Wilts	8	H4
Loversall	Donc	51	M2
Loveston	Pembks	25	J7
Lovington	Somset	17	N9
Low Ackworth	Wakefd	59	K10
Low Barbeth	D & G	68	D6
Low Bentham	N York	63	M8
Low Biggins	Cumb	63	L6
Low Borrowbridge	Cumb	63	L3
Low Bradfield	Sheff	50	H3
Low Bradley	N York	58	D5
Low Burnham	N Linc	52	A3
Lowca	Cumb	70	F10
Low Catton	E R Yk	60	C4
Low Crosby	Cumb	71	P4
Lowdham	Notts	51	P10
Low Dinsdale	Darltn	65	N5
Lower Aisholt	Somset	16	G8
Lower Ansty	Dorset	8	B6
Lower Apperley	Gloucs	29	M4
Lower Arboll	Highld	107	P6
Lower Ashton	Devon	6	A6
Lower Assendon	Oxon	20	C6
Lower Badcall	Highld	108	D7
Lower Bartle	Lancs	57	J3
Lower Basildon	W Berk	19	Q5
Lower Beeding	W Susx	11	K5
Lower Benefield	Nhants	42	E11
Lower Bentley	Worcs	30	C2
Lower Boddington	Nhants	31	L4
Lower Bourne	Surrey	10	D2
Lower Brailes	Warwks	30	H6
Lower Breakish	Highld	97	J5
Lower Broadheath	Worcs	39	P10
Lower Broxwood	Herefs	38	G10
Lower Bullingham	Herefs	28	F2
Lower Burgate	Hants	8	H4
Lower Caldecote	C Beds	32	H7
Lower Chapel	Powys	27	L2
Lower Chicksgrove	Wilts	8	E2
Lower Chute	Wilts	19	K9
Lower Clapton	Gt Lon	21	M6
Lower Clent	Worcs	40	B10
Lower Cumberworth	Kirk	58	G11
Lower Darwen	Bl w D	57	M4
Lower Dean	Bed	32	F3
Lower Diabaig	Highld	105	L9
Lower Dicker	E Susx	12	B7
Lower Down	Shrops	38	G5
Lower Dunsforth	N York	59	K2
Lower Egleton	Herefs	39	L11
Lower End	M Keyn	32	D8
Lower Eythorne	Kent	23	P12
Lower Failand	N Som	17	M2
Lower Farringdon	Hants	10	B3
Lower Feltham	Gt Lon	20	H8
Lower Froyle	Hants	10	C2
Lower Gabwell	Devon	6	C8
Lower Gledfield	Highld	107	K4
Lower Godney	Somset	17	L7
Lower Gornal	Dudley	40	B8
Lower Gravenhurst	C Beds	32	G9
Lower Green	Kent	12	C3
Lower Green	Kent	12	D2
Lower Halstow	Kent	22	G9
Lower Hamworthy	BCP	8	E8
Lower Hardres	Kent	23	M11
Lower Hartwell	Bucks	20	C2
Lower Hergest	Herefs	38	F10
Lower Heyford	Oxon	31	L8
Lower Heysham	Lancs	62	H9
Lower Houses	Kirk	58	F10
Lower Irlam	Salfd	57	N9
Lower Killeyan	Ag & B	74	D4
Lower Langford	N Som	17	L4
Lower Largo	Fife	86	H2
Lower Leigh	Staffs	40	D1
Lower Loxhore	Devon	15	K5
Lower Lydbrook	Gloucs	28	G5
Lower Lye	Herefs	38	H8
Lower Machen	Newpt	27	P10
Lower Merridge	Somset	16	G8
Lower Middleton Cheney	Nhants	31	L6
Lower Moor	Worcs	30	C5
Lower Morton	S Glos	28	H9
Lower Nazeing	Essex	21	N3
Lower Oddington	Gloucs	30	G8
Lower Penarth	V Glam	16	G3
Lower Penn	Staffs	39	Q3
Lower Peover	Ches E	49	N1
Lower Place	Rochdl	58	B10
Lower Quinton	Warwks	30	F5
Lower Raydon	Suffk	34	G8
Lower Roadwater	Somset	16	D8
Lower Seagry	Wilts	18	E5
Lower Shelton	C Beds	32	E8
Lower Shiplake	Oxon	20	C7
Lower Shuckburgh	Warwks	31	L2
Lower Slaughter	Gloucs	30	F9
Lower Standen	Kent	13	N3
Lower Stanton St Quintin	Wilts	18	D5
Lower Stoke	Medway	22	G8
Lower Stondon	C Beds	32	G9
Lower Stone	Gloucs	29	J9
Lower Stow Bedon	Norfk	44	F10
Lower Street	Norfk	45	L3
Lower Street	Suffk	35	J6
Lower Swanwick	Hants	9	N5
Lower Swell	Gloucs	30	F8
Lower Tasburgh	Norfk	45	K10
Lower Tean	Staffs	50	D12
Lower Town	Devon	5	P5
Lower Town	Pembks	24	G2
Lower Upham	Hants	9	N4
Lower Weare	Somset	17	K5
Lower Welson	Herefs	38	F11
Lower Westmancote	Worcs	29	N2
Lower Whatley	Somset	17	Q6
Lower Whitley	Ches W	57	L11
Lower Wield	Hants	19	Q11
Lower Willingdon	E Susx	12	C9
Lower Withington	Ches E	49	P2
Lower Woodford	Wilts	8	G2
Lower Wraxall	Dorset	7	N3
Lowesby	Leics	41	Q6
Lowestoft	Suffk	45	Q10
Loweswater	Cumb	71	J10
Low Etherley	Dur	65	L2
Low Fell	Gatesd	73	M8
Lowfield Heath	W Susx	11	L1
Low Gartachorrans	Stirlg	84	H6
Low Grantley	N York	65	M12
Low Ham	Somset	17	L9
Low Harrogate	N York	58	H3
Low Hesket	Cumb	71	P6
Low Hutton	N York	60	D1
Lowick	Nhants	32	E1
Lowick	Nthumb	81	L6
Lowick Green	Cumb	62	F5
Low Lorton	Cumb	71	J9
Low Marnham	Notts	52	B9
Low Mill	N York	66	F8
Low Moorsley	Sundld	73	N10
Low Moresby	Cumb	70	G10
Low Newton	Cumb	62	H6
Low Row	Cumb	72	B8
Low Row	N York	64	H7
Low Salchrie	D & G	68	D6
Low Santon	N Linc	60	G10
Lowsonford	Warwks	30	F1
Low Tharston	Norfk	45	K10
Lowther	Cumb	71	Q10
Lowthorpe	E R Yk	61	J3
Lowton	Somset	16	G11
Lowton Common	Wigan	57	L8
Low Torry	Fife	86	B5
Low Worsall	N York	65	P5
Low Wray	Cumb	62	G2
Loxbeare	Devon	16	C11
Loxhill	Surrey	10	G3
Loxhore	Devon	15	K4
Loxley	Warwks	30	H4
Loxton	N Som	17	K5
Loxwood	W Susx	10	G4
Lubenham	Leics	41	P9
Luccombe	Somset	16	C7
Luccombe Village	IoW	9	P10
Lucker	Nthumb	81	N8
Luckett	Cnwll	5	J5
Lucking Street	Essex	34	D9
Luckington	Wilts	18	C4
Lucklawhill	Fife	93	M10
Luckwell Bridge	Somset	16	B8
Ludag	W Isls	111	b6
Ludborough	Lincs	53	J4
Ludbrook	Devon	5	N8
Ludchurch	Pembks	25	K6
Luddenden	Calder	58	D8
Luddenden Foot	Calder	58	D8
Luddesdown	Kent	22	D9
Luddington	N Linc	60	E10
Luddington	Warwks	30	F4
Luddington in the Brook	Nhants	42	F12
Ludford	Lincs	52	H5
Ludford	Shrops	39	K7
Ludgershall	Bucks	31	P10
Ludgershall	Wilts	19	J9
Ludgvan	Cnwll	2	D8
Ludham	Norfk	45	N6
Ludlow	Shrops	39	K7
Ludney	Somset	7	K1
Ludwell	Wilts	8	D3
Ludworth	Dur	73	P11
Luffness	E Loth	87	J6
Lugar	E Ayrs	77	K7
Luggate Burn	E Loth	87	L7
Luggiebank	N Lans	85	M8
Lugton	E Ayrs	84	G11
Lugwardine	Herefs	28	G1
Luib	Highld	96	G4
Luing	Ag & B	83	L2
Lulham	Herefs	28	E1
Lullington	Derbys	40	G5
Lullington	Somset	18	B9
Lulsgate Bottom	N Som	17	M3
Lulsley	Worcs	39	N10
Lumb	Calder	58	D9
Lumby	N York	59	L7
Lumphanan	Abers	95	J2
Lumphinnans	Fife	86	E4
Lumsden	Abers	101	N10
Lunan	Angus	95	L10
Lunanhead	Angus	93	N5
Luncarty	P & K	92	G9
Lund	E R Yk	60	G5
Lund	N York	59	P7
Lundie	Angus	93	K8
Lundin Links	Fife	86	H2
Lundin Mill	Fife	86	H2
Lundy	Devon	14	C3
Lunga	Ag & B	83	K2
Lunna	Shet	111	k3
Lunsford	Kent	22	E10
Lunsford's Cross	E Susx	12	E7
Lunt	Sefton	56	G8
Luppitt	Devon	6	F2
Lupset	Wakefd	58	H9
Lupton	Cumb	63	K6
Lurgashall	W Susx	10	F5
Lurley	Devon	16	C12
Luscombe	Devon	5	Q8
Luskentyre	W Isls	111	c3
Luss	Ag & B	84	F4
Lussagiven	Ag & B	83	J6
Lusta	Highld	104	C10
Lustleigh	Devon	5	Q4
Luston	Herefs	39	J9
Luthermuir	Abers	95	L8
Luthrie	Fife	93	K10
Luton	Devon	6	B7
Luton	Devon	6	E3
Luton	Luton	32	F11
Luton	Medway	22	F9
Luton Airport	*Luton*	*32*	*G11*
Lutterworth	Leics	41	M9
Lutton	Devon	5	M8
Lutton	Devon	5	N7
Lutton	Lincs	43	M5
Lutton	Nhants	42	G11
Luxborough	Somset	16	D8
Luxulyan	Cnwll	3	M4
Luxulyan Valley	*Cnwll*	*3*	*N4*
Lybster	Highld	110	F8
Lydbury North	Shrops	38	G5
Lydd	Kent	13	K6
Lydd Airport	*Kent*	*13*	*K6*
Lydden	Kent	13	N2
Lydden	Kent	23	Q9
Lyddington	Rutlnd	42	C10
Lydeard St Lawrence	Somset	16	F9
Lyde Green	S Glos	29	J12
Lydford	Devon	5	K3
Lydford on Fosse	Somset	17	N9
Lydgate	Calder	58	B8
Lydham	Shrops	38	G4
Lydiard Millicent	Wilts	18	G4
Lydiard Tregoze	Swindn	18	G4
Lydiate	Sefton	56	G7
Lydiate Ash	Worcs	40	C11
Lydlinch	Dorset	17	Q12
Lydney	Gloucs	28	H7
Lydstep	Pembks	25	J8
Lye	Dudley	40	B10
Lye Green	E Susx	11	P4
Lye Green	Warwks	30	G2
Lye's Green	Wilts	18	B10
Lyford	Oxon	19	L2
Lymbridge Green	Kent	13	L2
Lyme Regis	Dorset	7	J4
Lyminge	Kent	13	M2
Lymington	Hants	9	K8
Lyminster	W Susx	10	G8
Lymm	Wartn	57	M10
Lymm Services	*Wartn*	*57*	*M11*
Lympne	Kent	13	L3
Lympsham	Somset	17	J5
Lympstone	Devon	6	D6
Lynchat	Highld	99	L8
Lynch Green	Norfk	45	J8
Lyndhurst	Hants	9	K6
Lyndon	Rutlnd	42	C8
Lyndon Green	Birm	40	F9
Lyne	Border	79	K1
Lyne	Surrey	20	G9
Lyneal	Shrops	49	J8
Lyneham	Oxon	30	H9
Lyneham	Wilts	18	F5
Lynemouth	Nthumb	73	N3
Lyne of Skene	Abers	102	G12
Lyness	Ork	111	g3
Lyng	Norfk	44	H6
Lyng	Somset	17	J9
Lynmouth	Devon	15	M3
Lynsted	Kent	22	H10
Lynton	Devon	15	M3
Lyon's Gate	Dorset	7	P2
Lyonshall	Herefs	38	G10
Lytchett Matravers	Dorset	8	E7
Lytchett Minster	Dorset	8	E8
Lyth	Highld	110	F3
Lytham	Lancs	56	G4
Lytham St Annes	Lancs	56	G4
Lythe	N York	67	J5
Lythmore	Highld	110	C3

M

Place	County/Region	Page	Grid
Maaruig	W Isls	111	c3
Mabe Burnthouse	Cnwll	2	H8
Mablethorpe	Lincs	53	N6
Macclesfield	Ches E	50	B6
Macduff	Abers	102	F3
Macharioch	Ag & B	75	L9
Machen	Caerph	27	P10
Machrie	N Ayrs	75	N5
Machrihanish	Ag & B	75	J8
Machrins	Ag & B	82	E4
Machroes	Gwynd	46	E6
Machynlleth	Powys	47	M10
Machynys	Carmth	26	C8
Mackworth	Derbys	50	H12
Macmerry	E Loth	87	J7
Madderty	P & K	92	E10
Maddiston	Falk	85	Q7
Madeley	Staffs	49	P6
Madeley	Wrekin	39	M2
Madingley	Cambs	33	L5
Madley	Herefs	28	E2
Madresfield	Worcs	39	P11
Madron	Cnwll	2	C9
Maenclochog	Pembks	25	J4
Maendy	V Glam	16	D2
Maentwrog	Gwynd	47	L3
Maen-y-groes	Cerdgn	36	F8
Maer	Staffs	49	P7
Maerdy	Conwy	48	B6
Maerdy	Rhondd	27	K8
Maesbrook	Shrops	48	F10
Maesbury	Shrops	48	F9
Maesbury Marsh	Shrops	48	G9
Maesllyn	Cerdgn	36	F10
Maesteg	Brdgnd	27	J10
Maesybont	Carmth	26	D5
Maesycwmmer	Caerph	27	N9
Maggieknockater	Moray	101	L6
Magham Down	E Susx	12	C7
Maghull	Sefton	56	G8
Magna Park	Leics	41	L9
Magor	Mons	28	E10
Magor Services	*Mons*	*28*	*E10*
Maidenbower	W Susx	11	L3
Maiden Bradley	Wilts	18	B11
Maidencombe	Torbay	6	C8
Maidenhayne	Devon	6	H4
Maiden Head	N Som	17	N3
Maidenhead	W & M	20	E7
Maiden Newton	Dorset	7	N4
Maidens	S Ayrs	76	D9
Maiden's Green	Br For	20	E8
Maiden Wells	Pembks	24	G8
Maidford	Nhants	31	N4
Maids Moreton	Bucks	31	P7
Maidstone	Kent	22	F11
Maidstone Services	*Kent*	*22*	*G11*
Maidwell	Nhants	41	Q11
Mail	Shet	111	k4
Maindee	Newpt	28	C10
Mainland	Ork	111	h2
Mainland	Shet	111	k4
Mainsforth	Dur	65	N2
Mains of Balhall	Angus	94	H8
Mains of Balnakettle	Abers	95	K7
Mains of Dalvey	Highld	100	H8
Mains of Haulkerton	Abers	95	L7
Mains of Lesmoir	Abers	101	N9
Mains of Melgunds	Angus	93	P5
Mainsriddle	D & G	70	F4
Mainstone	Shrops	38	F5
Maisemore	Gloucs	29	L5
Major's Green	Worcs	40	E11
Malborough	Devon	5	P11
Maldon	Essex	22	G3
Malham	N York	58	B2
Maligar	Highld	104	G9
Mallaig	Highld	97	J9
Mallaigvaig	Highld	97	J9
Malleny Mills	C Edin	86	E8
Malltraeth	IoA	54	E7
Mallwyd	Gwynd	47	P8
Malmesbury	Wilts	18	D4
Malmsmead	Devon	15	N3
Malpas	Ches W	49	J6
Malpas	Cnwll	3	J7
Malpas	Newpt	28	C10
Maltby	Lincs	51	M3
Maltby	S on T	66	C5
Maltby le Marsh	Lincs	53	M7
Maltman's Hill	Kent	12	H2
Malton	N York	66	H12
Malvern	Worcs	39	P11
Malvern Hills		39	P12
Malvern Link	Worcs	39	P11
Malvern Wells	Worcs	29	K1
Mamble	Worcs	39	M7
Mamhilad	Mons	28	C7
Manaccan	Cnwll	2	H10
Manafon	Powys	38	C2
Mànais	W Isls	111	c3
Manaton	Devon	5	P4
Manby	Lincs	53	L6
Mancetter	Warwks	40	H7
Manchester	Manch	57	Q8
Manchester Airport	*Manch*	*57*	*P11*
Mancot	Flints	48	G3
Mandally	Highld	98	D8
Manea	Cambs	43	M11
Maney	Birm	40	E8
Manfield	N York	65	L5
Mangersta	W Isls	111	b2
Mangotsfield	S Glos	17	P2
Mangurstadh	W Isls	111	b2
Manish	W Isls	111	c3
Manley	Ches W	49	J2
Manmoel	Caerph	27	P7
Mannal	Ag & B	88	C8
Manningford Bohune	Wilts	18	G8
Manningford Bruce	Wilts	18	G8
Manningham	C Brad	58	F7
Mannings Heath	W Susx	11	K4
Mannington	Dorset	8	F6
Manningtree	Essex	34	H9
Mannofield	C Aber	95	Q2
Manor Park	Gt Lon	21	N6
Manorbier	Pembks	25	J8
Manorbier Newton	Pembks	24	H8
Manorhill	Border	80	F7
Manorowen	Pembks	24	G2
Mansell Gamage	Herefs	38	H12
Mansell Lacy	Herefs	38	H11
Mansfield	E Ayrs	77	K8
Mansfield	Notts	51	M8
Mansfield Woodhouse	Notts	51	M7
Manston	Dorset	8	B4
Manston	Kent	23	Q9
Manston	Leeds	59	J7
Manswood	Dorset	8	E6
Manthorpe	Lincs	42	F7
Manton	N Linc	52	D3
Manton	Rutlnd	42	C8

Manton Wilts 18 H7
Manuden Essex 33 M10
Maperton Somset 17 P10
Maplebeck Notts 51 P8
Mapledurham Oxon 19 R5
Mapledurwell Hants 20 B12
Maplehurst W Susx 11 J3
Maplescombe Kent 22 C9
Mapleton Derbys 50 F10
Mapperley Derbys 51 K11
Mapperley Park C Nott 51 M11
Mapperton Dorset 7 M3
Mappleborough Green Warwks 30 E2
Mappleton E R Yk 61 L5
Mapplewell Barns 59 J11
Mappowder Dorset 7 Q2
Màraig W Isls 111 c3
Marazion Cnwll 2 D9
Marbhig W Isls 111 d2
Marbury Ches E 49 K6
March Cambs 43 L10
March S Lans 78 G6
Marcham Oxon 19 M2
Marchamley Shrops 49 L9
Marchington Staffs 40 F2
Marchwiel Wrexhm 48 G6
Marchwood Hants 9 L5
Marcross V Glam 16 C3
Marden Herefs 39 K11
Marden Kent 12 E2
Marden Wilts 18 G8
Marden Thorn Kent 12 F2
Mardy Mons 28 C5
Mareham le Fen Lincs 53 J10
Mareham on the Hill Lincs 53 J9
Marehill W Susx 10 H5
Maresfield E Susx 11 P5
Marfleet C KuH 61 K8
Marford Wrexhm 48 G4
Margam Neath 26 G10
Margaret Marsh Dorset 8 B4
Margaretting Essex 22 D3
Margaretting Tye Essex 22 D3
Margate Kent 23 Q8
Margnaheglish N Ayrs 75 Q6
Margrie D & G 69 N8
Margrove Park R & Cl 66 F4
Marham Norfk 44 B7
Marhamchurch Cnwll 14 D10
Marham Park Suffk 34 D4
Marholm C Pete 42 G9
Mariansleigh Devon 15 M7
Marine Town Kent 22 H8
Marionburgh Abers 95 L1
Marishader Highld 104 G9
Maristow Devon 5 K7
Marjoriebanks D & G 78 H11
Mark Somset 17 K6
Markbeech Kent 11 P2
Markby Lincs 53 M7
Mark Cross E Susx 12 C4
Market Bosworth Leics 41 K6
Market Deeping Lincs 42 G7
Market Drayton Shrops 49 M8
Market Harborough Leics 41 Q9
Market Lavington Wilts 18 E9
Market Overton RutInd 42 C6
Market Rasen Lincs 52 G5
Market Stainton Lincs 52 H7
Market Warsop Notts 51 M7
Market Weighton E R Yk 60 F6
Market Weston Suffk 34 G2
Markfield Leics 41 L5
Markham Caerph 27 N8
Markham Moor Notts 51 Q6
Markinch Fife 86 G2
Markington N York 58 H2
Markle E Loth 87 L6
Marksbury BaNES 17 P4
Marks Tey Essex 34 E11
Markyate Herts 32 F12
Marlborough Wilts 18 H7
Marlcliff Warwks 30 E4
Marldon Devon 6 B9
Marlesford Suffk 35 M5
Marlingford Norfk 45 J8
Marloes Pembks 24 E7
Marlow Bucks 20 D6
Marlow Bottom Bucks 20 D6
Marlpit Hill Kent 11 N1
Marnhull Dorset 8 B4
Marple Stockp 50 C3
Marr Donc 59 L12
Marrick N York 65 J7
Marsden Kirk 58 D10
Marsden S Tyne 73 P7
Marshalswick Herts 21 J2
Marsham Norfk 45 K5
Marsh Baldon Oxon 19 P2
Marshborough Kent 23 P11
Marshbrook Shrops 38 H4
Marshchapel Lincs 53 K4
Marsh Farm Luton 32 F10
Marshfield Newpt 28 B11
Marshfield S Glos 18 B6
Marshgate Cnwll 4 E2
Marsh Gibbon Bucks 31 N9
Marsh Green Devon 6 E4
Marsh Green Kent 11 N2
Marshland St James Norfk 43 N8
Marsh Lane Derbys 51 K5
Marsh Street Somset 16 D7
Marshwood Dorset 7 K3
Marske N York 65 K7
Marske-by-the-Sea R & Cl 66 E3
Marston Ches E 38 G10
Marston Lincs 42 C2
Marston Oxon 31 M11
Marston Staffs 40 B3
Marston Wilts 18 E9
Marston Green Solhll 40 F9
Marston Magna Somset 17 N10
Marston Meysey Wilts 18 G2
Marston Montgomery Derbys 50 F12
Marston Moretaine C Beds 32 E8
Marston on Dove Derbys 40 G2
Marston St Lawrence Nhants 31 M5
Marston Trussell Nhants 41 P9
Marstow Herefs 28 G5
Marsworth Bucks 20 E1
Marten Wilts 19 K8
Martham Norfk 45 P6
Martin Hants 8 F4

Martin Kent 13 Q1
Martin Lincs 52 G10
Martinhoe Devon 15 L3
Martin Hussingtree Worcs 39 Q9
Martinstown Dorset 7 P5
Martlesham Suffk 35 L7
Martlesham Heath Suffk 35 L7
Martletwy Pembks 24 H6
Martley Worcs 39 N9
Martock Somset 17 L11
Marton Ches E 49 Q2
Marton E R Yk 61 K6
Marton Lincs 52 B7
Marton Middsb 66 D4
Marton N York 59 K2
Marton N York 66 G10
Marton Shrops 38 F2
Marton Warwks 31 K1
Marton-le-Moor N York 65 P12
Martyr Worthy Hants 9 N2
Marvig W Isls 111 d2
Marwell Wildlife Hants 9 N3
Marwood Devon 15 J5
Marybank Highld 106 H10
Maryburgh Highld 107 J10
Marygold Border 87 P9
Maryhill C Glas 85 J8
Marykirk Abers 95 L8
Marylebone Gt Lon 21 L7
Marylebone Wigan 57 L7
Marypark Moray 101 J7
Maryport Cumb 70 G8
Maryport D & G 68 F11
Marystow Devon 5 J4
Mary Tavy Devon 5 K4
Maryton Angus 95 L10
Marywell Abers 95 J3
Marywell Abers 95 Q3
Marywell Angus 93 Q6
Masham N York 65 L10
Masongill N York 63 M7
Mastin Moor Derbys 51 L5
Matching Green Essex 21 Q2
Matching Tye Essex 21 P2
Matfen Nthumb 73 J6
Matfield Kent 12 D2
Mathern Mons 28 F9
Mathon Herefs 39 N11
Mathry Pembks 24 F3
Matlask Norfk 45 J3
Matlock Derbys 50 H8
Matlock Bath Derbys 50 H8
Matson Gloucs 29 L5
Mattersey Notts 51 P3
Mattingley Hants 20 B10
Mattishall Norfk 44 H7
Mattishall Burgh Norfk 44 H7
Mauchline E Ayrs 76 H6
Maud Abers 103 J6
Maufant Jersey 7 c1
Maugersbury Gloucs 30 G8
Maughold IoM 56 e3
Mauld Highld 98 E2
Maulden C Beds 32 F8
Maulds Meaburn Cumb 64 B4
Maunby N York 65 N9
Maundown Somset 16 E9
Mautby Norfk 45 P7
Mavesyn Ridware Staffs 40 E4
Mavis Enderby Lincs 53 K9
Mawbray Cumb 70 H6
Mawdesley Lancs 57 J6
Mawdlam Brdgnd 26 H11
Mawgan Cnwll 2 G10
Mawgan Porth Cnwll 3 J3
Mawla Cnwll 2 G6
Mawnan Cnwll 2 H9
Mawnan Smith Cnwll 2 H9
Mawsley Nhants 32 B2
Maxey C Pete 42 G8
Maxstoke Warwks 40 G9
Maxton Border 80 E7
Maxton Kent 13 P2
Maxwelltown D & G 70 F1
Maxworthy Cnwll 4 G2
May Bank Staffs 49 Q6
Maybole S Ayrs 76 E8
Maybury Surrey 20 G10
Mayfield E Susx 12 C5
Mayfield Mdloth 86 G8
Mayfield Staffs 50 F10
Mayford Surrey 20 F11
May Hill Gloucs 29 J5
Mayland Essex 22 H3
Maylandsea Essex 22 H3
Maynard's Green E Susx 12 C6
Maypole Birm 40 E10
Maypole Green Norfk 45 N10
Maypole Green Suffk 34 F5
Meadgate BaNES 17 P5
Meadle Bucks 20 C3
Meadowfield Dur 73 M11
Meadwell Devon 5 J4
Mealabost W Isls 111 d2
Meanwood Leeds 58 H6
Meare Somset 17 L7
Meare Green Somset 16 H10
Meare Green Somset 17 J10
Mearns E Rens 85 J11
Mears Ashby Nhants 32 B4
Measham Leics 41 J5
Meath Green Surrey 11 L2
Meathop Cumb 62 H6
Meavaig W Isls 111 c2
Meavy Devon 5 L6
Medbourne Leics 42 B10
Meddon Devon 14 E8
Meden Vale Notts 51 M6
Medmenham Bucks 20 D6
Medomsley Dur 73 K9
Medstead Hants 19 Q12
Medway Services Medway 22 G10
Meerbrook Staffs 50 C8
Meesden Herts 33 L9
Meeth Devon 15 J9
Meeting House Hill Norfk 45 M5
Meidrim Carmth 25 M5
Meifod Powys 48 D11
Meigle P & K 93 K6
Meikle Carco D & G 77 N8
Meikle Earnock S Lans 85 M11
Meikle Ferry Highld 107 M5
Meikle Kilmory Ag & B 83 R10

Meikle Obney P & K 92 F8
Meikleour P & K 92 H7
Meikle Wartle Abers 102 F8
Meinciau Carmth 26 B6
Meir C Stke 50 C11
Melbost W Isls 111 d2
Melbourn Cambs 33 L7
Melbourne Derbys 41 J3
Melbourne E R Yk 60 D5
Melbury Abbas Dorset 8 C4
Melbury Bubb Dorset 7 N2
Melbury Osmond Dorset 7 N2
Melchbourne Bed 32 E4
Melcombe Bingham Dorset 8 B6
Meldon Devon 5 L2
Meldon Nthumb 73 K4
Meldreth Cambs 33 L7
Meldrum Stirlg 85 M3
Melfort Ag & B 90 B12
Meliden Denbgs 56 C11
Melin-y-wig Denbgs 48 B6
Melkinthorpe Cumb 71 Q9
Melkridge Nthumb 72 D7
Melksham Wilts 18 D7
Melling Lancs 63 L7
Melling Sefton 56 H8
Mellis Suffk 34 H2
Mellon Charles Highld 105 M4
Mellon Udrigle Highld 105 N3
Mellor Lancs 57 M3
Mellor Stockp 50 C3
Mellor Brook Lancs 57 M3
Mells Somset 17 Q6
Melmerby Cumb 72 B12
Melmerby N York 65 J9
Melmerby N York 65 N11
Melness Highld 109 K4
Melplash Dorset 7 L3
Melrose Border 80 D7
Melsetter Ork 111 g3
Melsonby N York 65 L6
Meltham Kirk 58 E11
Melton E R Yk 60 G8
Melton Suffk 35 L6
Melton Constable Norfk 44 H4
Melton Mowbray Leics 41 Q4
Melton Ross N Linc 60 H11
Melvaig Highld 105 L5
Melverley Shrops 48 G11
Melvich Highld 109 Q3
Membury Devon 6 H3
Membury Services W Berk 19 K5
Memsie Abers 103 K3
Memus Angus 93 M4
Menai Bridge IoA 54 H7
Mendham Suffk 45 L12
Mendip Hills 17 M5
Mendlesham Suffk 34 H4
Mendlesham Green Suffk 34 G4
Menheniot Cnwll 4 G7
Mennock D & G 77 N9
Menston C Brad 58 F5
Menstrie Clacks 85 P4
Mentmore Bucks 32 C11
Meoble Highld 97 L11
Meole Brace Shrops 49 J12
Meonstoke Hants 9 Q4
Meopham Kent 22 D9
Mepal Cambs 33 M1
Meppershall C Beds 32 G9
Mere Ches E 57 N11
Mere Wilts 8 B2
Mere Brow Lancs 56 H5
Mereclough Lancs 57 Q3
Mere Green Birm 40 E7
Mereworth Kent 22 D11
Meriden Solhll 40 G10
Merkadale Highld 96 D4
Merley BCP 8 F7
Merrion Pembks 24 G8
Merriott Somset 7 L1
Merrow Surrey 20 G12
Merry Hill Herts 21 J5
Merryhill Wolves 40 B7
Merrymeet Cnwll 4 G7
Mersea Island Essex 23 K1
Mersey Gateway Bridge Halton 57 K12
Mersham Kent 13 K3
Merstham Surrey 21 L11
Merston W Susx 10 E9
Merstone IoW 9 N9
Merthyr Cynog Powys 27 J1
Merthyr Mawr Brdgnd 27 J12
Merthyr Tydfil Myr Td 27 M7
Merthyr Vale Myr Td 27 M8
Merton Devon 15 J9
Merton Gt Lon 21 K9
Merton Norfk 44 G9
Merton Oxon 31 M9
Meshaw Devon 15 N8
Messing Essex 34 E11
Messingham N Linc 52 C3
Metfield Suffk 35 L1
Metherell Cnwll 5 J6
Metheringham Lincs 52 F10
Methil Fife 86 H3
Methilhill Fife 86 H3
Methley Leeds 59 J8
Methlick Abers 102 H7
Methven P & K 92 F9
Methwold Norfk 44 C10
Methwold Hythe Norfk 44 B10
Mettingham Suffk 45 M11
Metton Norfk 45 K3
Mevagissey Cnwll 3 M6
Mexborough Donc 51 L2
Mey Highld 110 F2
Meysey Hampton Gloucs 18 G1
Miabhaig W Isls 111 c2
Michaelchurch Herefs 28 F4
Michaelchurch Escley Herefs 28 C3
Michaelstone-y-Fedw Newpt 27 P11
Michaelston-le-Pit V Glam 16 F2
Michaelstow Cnwll 4 D4
Michaelwood Services Gloucs 29 J9
Micheldever Hants 9 N11
Micheldever Station Hants 19 N11
Michelmersh Hants 9 L3
Mickfield Suffk 35 J4
Micklebring Donc 51 L2
Mickleby N York 66 H5
Micklefield Leeds 59 K7
Mickleham Surrey 21 J11

Mickleover C Derb 40 H1
Mickleton Dur 64 H3
Mickleton Gloucs 30 F5
Mickle Trafford Ches W 49 J2
Mickley N York 65 M11
Mickley Square Nthumb 73 J8
Mid Ardlaw Abers 103 K3
Midbea Ork 111 h1
Mid Beltie Abers 95 K2
Mid Calder W Loth 86 C8
Mid Clyth Highld 110 F8
Mid Culbeuchly Abers 102 E3
Middle Aston Oxon 31 L8
Middle Barton Oxon 31 K8
Middlebie D & G 71 K1
Middlebridge P & K 92 D3
Middle Chinnock Somset 7 L1
Middle Claydon Bucks 31 Q8
Middlecroft Derbys 51 K6
Middleham N York 65 K9
Middle Handley Derbys 51 K5
Middlehill Wilts 18 B7
Middlehope Shrops 39 J4
Middle Kames Ag & B 83 N5
Middle Littleton Worcs 30 E5
Middlemarsh Dorset 7 P2
Middle Mayfield Staffs 50 F10
Middle Rasen Lincs 52 F5
Middle Rocombe Devon 6 B8
Middlesbrough Middsb 66 C4
Middleshaw Cumb 63 K5
Middlesmoor N York 65 J11
Middle Stoke Medway 22 G8
Middlestone Dur 65 M2
Middlestown Wakefd 58 H10
Middlethird Border 80 F5
Middleton Ag & B 88 B7
Middleton Derbys 50 G8
Middleton Derbys 50 H9
Middleton Essex 34 E8
Middleton Hants 19 M11
Middleton Herefs 39 K8
Middleton Leeds 58 H8
Middleton N York 58 E4
Middleton N York 66 H9
Middleton Nhants 42 B11
Middleton Norfk 43 Q6
Middleton Nthumb 73 J4
Middleton P & K 86 D2
Middleton Rochdl 57 Q7
Middleton Shrops 39 K6
Middleton Suffk 35 N3
Middleton Swans 26 P10
Middleton Warwks 40 F7
Middleton Cheney Nhants 31 L6
Middleton-in-Teesdale Dur 64 G3
Middleton Moor Suffk 35 N4
Middleton One Row Darltn 65 P5
Middleton-on-Sea W Susx 10 F9
Middleton on the Hill Herefs 39 K8
Middleton on the Wolds E R Yk 60 G4
Middleton Park C Aber 103 J11
Middleton Quernhow N York 65 N10
Middleton St George Darltn 65 N5
Middleton Scriven Shrops 39 M5
Middleton Stoney Oxon 31 M9
Middleton Tyas N York 65 M6
Middle Town IoS 2 b3
Middletown Powys 48 F11
Middle Tysoe Warwks 31 J5
Middle Wallop Hants 19 K12
Middlewich Ches E 49 N3
Middle Winterslow Wilts 9 J2
Middlewood Cnwll 4 G5
Middle Woodford Wilts 18 G12
Middlewood Green Suffk 34 H5
Middlezoy Somset 17 K9
Midford BaNES 18 B8
Midgham W Berk 19 P7
Midgley Calder 58 D8
Midgley Wakefd 58 H10
Midhopestones Sheff 50 G2
Midhurst W Susx 10 E6
Mid Lavant W Susx 10 D8
Midlem Border 80 C8
Mid Mains Highld 98 F2
Midpark Ag & B 83 Q10
Midsomer Norton BaNES 17 P5
Midtown Highld 109 K4
Mid Yell Shet 111 k2
Migdale Highld 107 K4
Migvie Abers 94 G1
Milborne Port Somset 17 P11
Milborne St Andrew Dorset 8 B7
Milborne Wick Somset 17 P11
Milbourne Nthumb 73 K6
Milbourne Wilts 18 D4
Milburn Cumb 64 C2
Milbury Heath S Glos 29 J10
Milby N York 59 K1
Milcombe Oxon 31 K7
Milden Suffk 34 F7
Mildenhall Suffk 34 B2
Mildenhall Wilts 18 H6
Mileham Norfk 44 F6
Mile Oak Br & H 11 K8
Milesmark Fife 86 C5
Miles Platting Manch 57 Q8
Mile Town Kent 22 H8
Milfield Nthumb 81 K7
Milford Derbys 51 J10
Milford Devon 14 E7
Milford Staffs 40 C4
Milford Surrey 10 F2
Milford Haven Pembks 24 F7
Milford on Sea Hants 9 K6
Milkwall Gloucs 28 G7
Milland W Susx 10 D4
Mill Bank Calder 58 D9
Millbreck Abers 103 K6
Millbridge Surrey 10 D2
Millbrook C Beds 32 E8
Millbrook C Sotn 9 L5
Millbrook Cnwll 5 J9
Millbrook Jersey 7 b2
Mill Brow Stockp 50 C3
Millbuie Abers 102 G12
Millbuie Highld 107 J11
Millcorner E Susx 12 G5
Millcraig Highld 107 L7
Milldale Staffs 50 F9
Mill End Bucks 20 C6
Mill End Herts 33 K9

Millerhill Mdloth 86 G8
Miller's Dale Derbys 50 F6
Millerston C Glas 85 L9
Mill Green Cambs 33 P7
Mill Green Essex 22 D3
Mill Green Lincs 42 H5
Mill Green Suffk 34 F8
Mill Green Suffk 34 G5
Mill Green Suffk 35 J5
Millhalf Herefs 38 F11
Millheugh S Lans 77 M2
Mill Hill Gt Lon 21 K5
Milhouse Ag & B 83 P8
Millhousebridge D & G 78 H10
Millhouse Green Barns 58 G12
Millhouses Sheff 51 J4
Milliken Park Rens 84 G9
Mill of Drumellan P & K 92 C11
Mill of Haldane W Duns 84 G6
Millom Cumb 62 D6
Millport N Ayrs 84 C11
Mill Street Suffk 34 H3
Millthrop Cumb 63 M4
Milltimber C Aber 95 P2
Milltown Abers 101 K12
Milltown Abers 101 N11
Milltown D & G 71 M1
Milltown Devon 15 K4
Milltown Derbys 97 J2
Milltown of Auchindoun Moray 101 L7
Milltown of Campfield Abers 95 L2
Milltown of Edinvillie Moray 101 K7
Milltown of Rothiemay Moray 102 C5
Milnathort P & K 86 D2
Milngavie E Duns 85 J7
Milnrow Rochdl 58 B10
Milnthorpe Cumb 63 J6
Milovaig Highld 104 B11
Milson Shrops 39 M7
Milstead Kent 22 H10
Milston Wilts 18 H10
Milthorpe Nhants 31 N5
Milton C Stke 50 B10
Milton Cambs 33 M4
Milton Cumb 71 Q4
Milton D & G 68 G8
Milton D & G 70 D2
Milton Derbys 40 H3
Milton Highld 98 G3
Milton Highld 107 J11
Milton Highld 110 G5
Milton Highld 107 M7
Milton Inver 84 F8
Milton Kent 22 D8
Milton Moray 101 J10
Milton Moray 101 P3
Milton N Som 16 J4
Milton Notts 51 P6
Milton Oxon 19 N3
Milton Oxon 31 J7
Milton P & K 92 B9
Milton Pembks 24 H8
Milton Somset 17 L10
Milton Stirlg 84 H3
Milton W Duns 84 G7
Milton Abbas Dorset 8 B7
Milton Abbot Devon 5 J4
Milton Bridge Mdloth 86 F9
Milton Bryan C Beds 32 D10
Milton Clevedon Somset 17 P8
Milton Combe Devon 5 K7
Milton Damerel Devon 14 G9
Milton Ernest Bed 32 E5
Milton Green Ches W 49 J4
Milton Hill Oxon 19 M3
Milton Keynes M Keyn 32 C8
Milton Lilbourne Wilts 18 H8
Milton Malsor Nhants 31 Q3
Milton Morenish P & K 91 P8
Milton of Auchinhove Abers 95 J2
Milton of Balgonie Fife 86 G3
Milton of Buchanan Stirlg 84 G5
Milton of Campsie E Duns 85 L7
Milton of Finavon Angus 93 N4
Milton of Leys Highld 99 K1
Milton of Murtle C Aber 95 P2
Milton on Stour Dorset 8 B2
Milton Regis Kent 22 H9
Milton-under-Wychwood Oxon 30 H9

Milverton Somset 16 F10
Milverton Warwks 30 H2
Milwich Staffs 40 C2
Minard Ag & B 83 P4
Minchinhampton Gloucs 29 M8
Minehead Somset 16 C6
Minera Wrexhm 48 F5
Minety Wilts 18 F3
Minffordd Gwynd 47 J4
Mingarrypark Highld 89 N3
Miningsby Lincs 53 K10
Minions Cnwll 4 G6
Minishant S Ayrs 76 F8
Minllyn Gwynd 47 P8
Minnigaff D & G 69 K6
Minnonie Abers 102 G4
Minskip N York 59 K2
Minstead Hants 9 K5
Minsted W Susx 10 D6
Minster Kent 23 P9
Minsterley Shrops 38 G2
Minster Lovell Oxon 30 H10
Minster-on-Sea Kent 23 J8
Minsterworth Gloucs 29 K5
Minterne Magna Dorset 7 P2
Minting Lincs 52 H8
Mintlaw Abers 103 K6
Minto Border 80 D9
Minton Shrops 38 H4
Mirehouse Cumb 70 F11
Mireland Highld 110 G4
Mirfield Kirk 58 G9
Miserden Gloucs 29 N7
Miskin Rhondd 27 L11
Misson Notts 51 P2
Misterton Notts 51 Q2
Misterton Somset 7 L2
Mistley Essex 35 J9
Mitcham Gt Lon 21 L9
Mitcheldean Gloucs 29 J5
Mitchell Cnwll 3 J5

Mitchellslacks – Newington 181

Mitchellslacks D & G 78 F9
Mitchel Troy Mons 28 F6
Mitford Nthumb 73 L4
Mithian Cnwll 2 H5
Mixbury Oxon 31 N7
Mobberley Ches E 57 P11
Mobberley Staffs 50 D11
Mochdre Powys 38 C4
Mochrum D & G 69 J9
Mockbeggar Kent 12 E1
Mockerkin Cumb 70 H10
Modbury Devon 5 N9
Moddershall Staffs 50 B12
Moelfre IoA 54 G4
Moelfre Powys 48 E9
Moffat D & G 78 H7
Moggerhanger C Beds 32 G6
Moira Leics 40 H4
Molash Kent 23 K11
Mol-chlach Highld 96 E7
Mold Flints 48 E3
Moldgreen Kirk 58 F10
Molehill Green Essex 33 P10
Molescroft E R Yk 60 H6
Molesworth Cambs 32 F2
Moll Highld 96 G4
Molland Devon 15 N6
Mollington Ches W 48 H2
Mollington Oxon 31 K5
Mollinsburn N Lans 85 M8
Mondynes Abers 95 M6
Monewden Suffk 35 L5
Moneydie P & K 92 F9
Moniaive D & G 78 C10
Monifieth Angus 93 N8
Monikie Angus 93 N7
Monimail Fife 93 K11
Monken Hadley Gt Lon 21 K4
Monk Fryston N York 59 L8
Monkhide Herefs 39 L12
Monkhill Cumb 71 M4
Monkhopton Shrops 39 L4
Monkland Herefs 39 J10
Monkleigh Devon 14 H7
Monknash V Glam 16 C3
Monkokehampton Devon 15 K10
Monkseaton N Tyne 73 N6
Monks Eleigh Suffk 34 F7
Monk's Gate W Susx 11 K5
Monks Heath Ches E 49 Q1
Monk Sherborne Hants 19 Q9
Monksilver Somset 16 E8
Monks Kirby Warwks 41 L10
Monk Soham Suffk 35 K4
Monks Risborough Bucks 20 D3
Monksthorpe Lincs 53 M9
Monk Street Essex 33 P10
Monkswood Mons 28 D8
Monkton Devon 6 G3
Monkton Kent 23 P9
Monkton S Ayrs 76 F6
Monkton S Tyne 73 N8
Monkton Combe BaNES 18 B8
Monkton Deverill Wilts 18 C12
Monkton Farleigh Wilts 18 B7
Monkton Heathfield Somset 16 H10
Monkton Wyld Dorset 7 J4
Monkwearmouth Sundld 73 P8
Monkwood Hants 9 Q2
Monmore Green Wolves 40 B7
Monmouth Mons 28 F6
Monnington on Wye Herefs 38 G12
Monreith D & G 69 J10
Montacute Somset 17 M11
Montford Shrops 48 H11
Montford Bridge Shrops 48 H11
Montgarrie Abers 102 D10
Montgomery Powys 38 E3
Montrose Angus 95 L9
Mont Saint Guern 6 b2
Monxton Hants 19 K11
Monyash Derbys 50 F7
Monymusk Abers 102 F11
Monzie P & K 92 C9
Moodiesburn N Lans 85 L8
Moonzie Fife 93 L11
Moor Allerton Leeds 58 H6
Moorby Lincs 53 J10
Moor Crichel Dorset 8 E6
Moordown BCP 8 G8
Moore Halton 57 L11
Moor End Calder 58 D8
Moorends Donc 59 P10
Moorhead C Brad 58 F6
Moorhouse Cumb 71 M4
Moorhouse Notts 51 Q7
Moorhouse Bank Surrey 21 N11
Moorlinch Somset 17 K8
Moor Monkton N York 59 L3
Moorsholm R & Cl 66 F5
Moorside Dorset 8 B4
Moorswater Cnwll 4 F7
Moorthorpe Wakefd 59 L11
Moortown Leeds 58 H6
Moortown Lincs 52 F4
Morangie Highld 107 M6
Morar Highld 97 J10
Morborne Cambs 42 G10
Morchard Bishop Devon 15 N10
Morcombelake Dorset 7 K4
Morcott Rutlnd 42 D9
Morda Shrops 48 F9
Morden Dorset 8 D8
Morden Gt Lon 21 K9
Mordiford Herefs 28 G2
Mordon Dur 65 N3
More Shrops 38 G4
Morebath Devon 16 C10
Morebattle Border 80 G8
Morecambe Lancs 62 H8
Moredon Swindn 18 G4
Morefield Highld 106 B4
Morehall Kent 13 N3
Moreleigh Devon 5 P9
Morenish P & K 91 N8
Morestead Hants 9 N3
Moreton Dorset 8 B9
Moreton Essex 21 Q3
Moreton Herefs 39 J8
Moreton Oxon 20 B3
Moreton Wirral 56 F10
Moreton Corbet Shrops 49 K10
Moreton Hall Suffk 34 E4
Moretonhampstead Devon 5 P3
Moreton-in-Marsh Gloucs 30 G7
Moreton Jeffries Herefs 39 L11
Moreton Morrell Warwks 30 H3
Moreton on Lugg Herefs 39 J11
Moreton Pinkney Nhants 31 M4
Moreton Say Shrops 49 L8
Moreton Valence Gloucs 29 K6
Morfa Nefyn Gwynd 46 E4
Morham E Loth 87 K7
Morland Cumb 64 B3
Morley Ches E 57 P11
Morley Derbys 51 K11
Morley Leeds 58 H8
Morley Green Ches E 57 P11
Morley St Botolph Norfk 44 H9
Morningside C Edin 86 F7
Morningside N Lans 85 N11
Morningthorpe Norfk 45 K10
Morpeth Nthumb 73 L4
Morphie Abers 95 L8
Morrey Staffs 40 E4
Morriston Swans 26 F8
Morston Norfk 44 G2
Mortehoe Devon 14 H3
Morthen Rothm 51 L3
Mortimer W Berk 19 Q7
Mortimer West End Hants 19 Q7
Mortlake Gt Lon 21 K8
Morton Cumb 71 N5
Morton Derbys 51 K8
Morton Lincs 42 F5
Morton Lincs 52 B5
Morton Notts 51 Q9
Morton Shrops 48 F9
Morton-on-Swale N York 65 N8
Morton on the Hill Norfk 45 J6
Morvah Cnwll 2 B8
Morvich Highld 97 N5
Morville Shrops 39 M4
Morwenstow Cnwll 14 D8
Mosborough Sheff 51 K5
Moscow E Ayrs 76 H4
Moseley Birm 40 E10
Moseley Wolves 40 C7
Moseley Worcs 39 P9
Moss Ag & B 88 B7
Moss Donc 59 N10
Mossat Abers 101 N10
Mossbank Shet 111 k3
Moss Bank St Hel 57 K8
Mossbay Cumb 70 G9
Mossblown S Ayrs 76 G6
Mossburnford Border 80 F10
Mossdale D & G 69 P5
Mossdale E Ayrs 76 H9
Moss Edge Lancs 62 H12
Mossend N Lans 85 M10
Mossley Tamesd 50 C1
Mosspaul Hotel Border 79 N8
Moss-side Highld 100 D4
Mosstodloch Moray 101 L4
Mossyard D & G 69 M8
Mossy Lea Lancs 57 K6
Mosterton Dorset 7 L2
Moston Manch 57 Q8
Mostyn Flints 56 D11
Motcombe Dorset 8 C3
Mothecombe Devon 5 M10
Motherby Cumb 71 N9
Motherwell N Lans 85 M10
Motspur Park Gt Lon 21 K9
Mottingham Gt Lon 21 N8
Mottisfont Hants 9 K3
Mottisfont Hants 9 K3
Mottistone IoW 9 L10
Mottram in Longdendale Tamesd 50 C2
Mottram St Andrew Ches E 57 Q12
Mouldsworth Ches W 49 J2
Moulin P & K 92 E4
Moulsecoomb Br & H 11 M8
Moulsford Oxon 19 P4
Moulsoe M Keyn 32 C8
Moultavie Highld 107 K7
Moulton Ches W 49 M2
Moulton Lincs 43 K5
Moulton N York 65 M6
Moulton Nhants 32 B4
Moulton Suffk 34 B4
Moulton V Glam 16 E3
Moulton Chapel Lincs 43 J6
Moulton St Mary Norfk 45 N8
Moulton Seas End Lincs 43 K5
Mount Cnwll 4 E6
Mountain C Brad 58 E7
Mountain Ash Rhondd 27 L8
Mountain Cross Border 86 D11
Mount Ambrose Cnwll 2 G7
Mount Bures Essex 34 E9
Mountfield E Susx 12 E6
Mountgerald Highld 107 J9
Mount Hawke Cnwll 2 G6
Mountjoy Cnwll 3 K4
Mount Lothian Mdloth 86 F10
Mountnessing Essex 22 D4
Mounton Mons 28 F9
Mount Pleasant Derbys 51 J10
Mount Pleasant Suffk 34 C7
Mountsorrel Leics 41 M5
Mount Tabor Calder 58 D8
Mousehole Cnwll 2 C9
Mouswald D & G 70 H2
Mow Cop Ches E 49 Q4
Mowhaugh Border 80 H9
Mowmacre Hill C Leic 41 N6
Mowsley Leics 41 N9
Moy Highld 98 F11
Moy Highld 99 L3
Moyle Highld 97 M6
Moylegrove Pembks 36 B10
Muasdale Ag & B 75 K4
Muchalls Abers 95 P4
Much Birch Herefs 28 F3
Much Cowarne Herefs 39 L11
Much Dewchurch Herefs 28 F3
Muchelney Somset 17 K10
Muchelney Ham Somset 17 L10
Much Hadham Herts 33 L11
Much Hoole Lancs 57 J4
Muchlarnick Cnwll 4 F8
Much Marcle Herefs 28 H3
Much Wenlock Shrops 39 L3
Muck Highld 89 J1
Muckleburgh Collection Norfk 44 H2
Mucklestone Staffs 49 N7
Muckton Lincs 53 L7
Muddiford Devon 15 K5
Muddles Green E Susx 12 B7
Mudeford BCP 8 H8
Mudford Somset 17 N11
Mudford Sock Somset 17 M11
Mugdock Stirlg 85 J7
Mugeary Highld 96 E2
Mugginton Derbys 50 H11
Muirden Abers 102 F5
Muirdrum Angus 93 P8
Muiresk Abers 102 F5
Muirhead Angus 93 L8
Muirhead Fife 86 F2
Muirhead N Lans 85 L8
Muirhouses Falk 86 B6
Muirkirk E Ayrs 77 L6
Muirmill Stirlg 85 M6
Muir of Fowlis Abers 102 D11
Muir of Miltonduff Moray 101 J4
Muir of Ord Highld 107 J11
Muirshearlich Highld 98 A11
Muirtack Abers 103 K7
Muirton P & K 85 Q1
Muirton Mains Highld 106 H10
Muirton of Ardblair P & K 92 H7
Muker N York 64 G7
Mulbarton Norfk 45 K9
Mulben Moray 101 L5
Mull Ag & B 89 M8
Mullardoch Highld 98 C3
Mullion Cnwll 2 G11
Mullion Cove Cnwll 2 F11
Mumby Lincs 53 N8
Munderfield Row Herefs 39 M10
Munderfield Stocks Herefs 39 M11
Mundesley Norfk 45 M3
Mundford Norfk 44 D10
Mundham Norfk 45 M9
Mundon Hill Essex 22 G3
Mungrisdale Cumb 71 M9
Munlochy Highld 107 K10
Munnoch N Ayrs 76 E2
Munsley Herefs 29 J1
Munslow Shrops 39 K5
Murchington Devon 5 N3
Murcott Oxon 31 N10
Murkle Highld 110 D3
Murlaggan Highld 97 P10
Murroes Angus 93 N8
Murrow Cambs 43 L8
Mursley Bucks 32 B10
Murston Kent 22 H9
Murthill Angus 93 N4
Murthly P & K 92 G7
Murton C York 59 P4
Murton Cumb 64 D3
Murton Dur 73 P10
Murton Nthumb 81 K5
Musbury Devon 6 H4
Musselburgh E Loth 86 G7
Muston Leics 42 B3
Muston N York 67 N10
Muswell Hill Gt Lon 21 L5
Mutehill D & G 69 P8
Mutford Suffk 45 P11
Muthill P & K 92 C11
Mybster Highld 110 D5
Myddfai Carmth 26 G3
Myddle Shrops 49 J10
Mydroilyn Cerdgn 36 G9
Myland Essex 34 G10
Mylor Cnwll 3 J8
Mylor Bridge Cnwll 3 J8
Mynachlog ddu Pembks 25 K3
Mynydd-bach Mons 28 F9
Mynydd-Bach Swans 26 E8
Mynyddgarreg Carmth 25 P7
Mynydd Isa Flints 48 F3
Myrebird Abers 95 M3
Myredykes Border 72 B2
Mytchett Surrey 20 E11
Mytholm Calder 58 C8
Mytholmroyd Calder 58 D8
Myton-on-Swale N York 59 K2

N

Naast Highld 105 M6
Na Buirgh W Isls 111 c3
Naburn C York 59 N5
Nackington Kent 23 M11
Nacton Suffk 35 K8
Nafferton E R Yk 60 H3
Nailsbourne Somset 16 G9
Nailsea N Som 17 L3
Nailstone Leics 41 K6
Nailsworth Gloucs 29 L8
Nairn Highld 100 D4
Nannerch Flints 48 D2
Nanpantan Leics 41 L4
Nanpean Cnwll 3 L5
Nanstallon Cnwll 3 M3
Nanternis Cerdgn 36 F8
Nantgaredig Carmth 26 C5
Nantglyn Denbgs 55 Q8
Nantlle Valley Slate Landscape Gwynd 54 G10
Nantmel Powys 38 B8
Nantmor Gwynd 47 K3
Nant Peris Gwynd 54 H9
Nantwich Ches E 49 M5
Nantyglo Blae G 27 P6
Nant-y-moel Brdgnd 27 K9
Naphill Bucks 20 D4
Napton on the Hill Warwks 31 L2
Narberth Pembks 25 J6
Narborough Leics 41 M7
Narborough Norfk 44 C7
Nasareth Gwynd 54 F10
Naseby Nhants 41 P10
Nash Bucks 32 B9
Nash Newpt 28 D11
Nash Shrops 39 L7
Nassington Nhants 42 F10
Nateby Cumb 64 E6
Nateby Lancs 63 J12
National Memorial Arboretum Staffs 40 F5
National Motor Museum (Beaulieu) Hants 9 L6
National Space Centre C Leic 41 N6
Natland Cumb 63 K4
Naughton Suffk 34 G7
Naunton Gloucs 30 E9
Naunton Worcs 29 M2
Naunton Beauchamp Worcs 30 C4
Navenby Lincs 52 E10
Navestock Essex 21 Q4
Navestock Side Essex 22 C4
Navidale Highld 110 B11
Navity Highld 107 N8
Nawton N York 66 F9
Nayland Suffk 34 F9
Nazeing Essex 21 N3
Neap Shet 111 k4
Near Cotton Staffs 50 E10
Near Sawrey Cumb 62 G3
Neasden Gt Lon 21 K6
Neasham Darltn 65 N5
Neath Neath 26 G8
Neatham Hants 10 C3
Neatishead Norfk 45 M6
Nebo Cerdgn 37 J7
Nebo Conwy 55 M9
Nebo Gwynd 54 F10
Nebo IoA 54 F4
Necton Norfk 44 E8
Nedd Highld 108 C8
Nedging Suffk 34 G7
Nedging Tye Suffk 34 G6
Needham Norfk 35 K1
Needham Market Suffk 34 H6
Needingworth Cambs 33 K3
Neen Savage Shrops 39 M6
Neen Sollars Shrops 39 M7
Neenton Shrops 39 M5
Nefyn Gwynd 46 E4
Neilston E Rens 84 H10
Nelson Caerph 27 M9
Nelson Lancs 57 Q2
Nemphlar S Lans 77 P3
Nempnett Thrubwell BaNES 17 M4
Nenthead Cumb 72 E11
Nenthorn Border 80 F6
Nerabus Ag & B 82 C11
Nercwys Flints 48 E4
Nerston S Lans 85 L10
Nesbit Nthumb 81 K7
Nesfield N York 58 E4
Nesscliffe Shrops 48 H10
Neston Ches W 56 F12
Neston Wilts 18 C7
Netchwood Shrops 39 L4
Nether Abington S Lans 78 F4
Nether Alderley Ches E 49 Q1
Netheravon Wilts 18 G10
Nether Blainslie Border 80 D5
Netherbrae Abers 102 G4
Nether Broughton Leics 41 P3
Netherburn S Lans 77 N2
Netherbury Dorset 7 L3
Netherby N York 59 J5
Nether Cerne Dorset 7 P3
Nethercleuch D & G 79 J10
Nether Compton Dorset 17 N11
Nether Crimond Abers 102 H10
Nether Dallachy Moray 101 M3
Netherend Gloucs 28 G8
Netherfield E Susx 12 E6
Netherfield Notts 51 N11
Nether Fingland S Lans 78 F6
Netherhampton Wilts 8 G2
Nether Handwick Angus 93 L7
Nether Haugh Rothm 51 K2
Netherhay Dorset 7 K2
Nether Headon Notts 51 Q5
Nether Heage Derbys 51 J10
Nether Heyford Nhants 31 P3
Nether Kellet Lancs 63 J8
Nether Kinmundy Abers 103 L6
Nether Langwith Notts 51 M6
Netherley Abers 95 P4
Netherley Lpool 56 H10
Nethermill D & G 78 G10
Nethermuir Abers 103 J6
Netherne-on-the-Hill Surrey 21 L11
Netheroyd Hill Kirk 58 F9
Nether Padley Derbys 50 G5
Nether Poppleton C York 59 M4
Netherseal Derbys 40 H5
Nether Silton N York 66 C8
Nether Stowey Somset 16 G8
Netherthird E Ayrs 77 K7
Netherthong Kirk 58 F11
Netherton Angus 93 P4
Netherton Devon 6 B8
Netherton Dudley 40 C9
Netherton Kirk 58 F10
Netherton N Lans 85 N11
Netherton Nthumb 81 K11
Netherton P & K 92 H5
Netherton Sefton 56 G8
Netherton Stirlg 85 J7
Netherton Wakefd 58 H10
Nethertown Cumb 62 B1
Nethertown Highld 110 G1
Nethertown Staffs 40 E4
Netherurd Border 86 D12
Nether Wallop Hants 19 K12
Nether Wasdale Cumb 62 D2
Nether Westcote Gloucs 30 G9
Nether Whitacre Warwks 40 G8
Nether Whitecleuch S Lans 78 D5
Nether Winchendon Bucks 31 Q10
Netherwitton Nthumb 73 K3
Nethy Bridge Highld 99 Q5
Netley Hants 9 M6
Netley Marsh Hants 9 K5
Nettlebed Oxon 20 B6
Nettlebridge Somset 17 P6
Nettlecombe Dorset 7 M4
Nettleden Herts 20 G2
Nettleham Lincs 52 E8
Nettlestead Kent 22 D11
Nettlestead Green Kent 22 D12
Nettlestone IoW 9 Q8
Nettlesworth Dur 73 M10
Nettleton Lincs 52 G4
Nettleton Wilts 18 B5
Netton Wilts 18 G12
Nevern Pembks 36 B11
Nevill Holt Leics 42 B10
New Abbey D & G 70 F3
New Aberdour Abers 103 J3
New Addington Gt Lon 21 M10
Newall Leeds 58 G5
New Alresford Hants 9 P2
New Alyth P & K 93 J6
Newark C Pete 42 H9
Newark Ork 111 i1
Newark-on-Trent Notts 52 B11
New Arley Warwks 40 H9
Newarthill N Lans 85 N10
New Ash Green Kent 22 C9
New Balderton Notts 52 B11
New Barn Kent 22 C9
New Barnet Gt Lon 21 L4
Newbattle Mdloth 86 G8
New Bewick Nthumb 81 M9
Newbie D & G 71 K3
Newbiggin Cumb 64 B2
Newbiggin Cumb 71 P9
Newbiggin Cumb 71 Q6
Newbiggin Dur 64 G3
Newbiggin N York 64 H9
Newbiggin-by-the-Sea Nthumb 73 N4
Newbigging Angus 93 K7
Newbigging Angus 93 M8
Newbigging Angus 93 N8
Newbigging S Lans 86 B11
Newbiggin-on-Lune Cumb 63 N2
New Bilton Warwks 41 L11
Newbold Derbys 51 J6
Newbold on Avon Warwks 41 L11
Newbold on Stour Warwks 30 G5
Newbold Pacey Warwks 30 H3
Newbold Verdon Leics 41 K6
New Bolingbroke Lincs 53 K11
Newborough C Pete 42 H8
Newborough IoA 54 F8
Newborough Staffs 40 F3
New Boultham Lincs 52 D8
Newbourne Suffk 35 L8
New Bradwell M Keyn 32 B8
New Brampton Derbys 51 J6
New Brancepeth Dur 73 M11
Newbridge C Edin 86 D7
Newbridge Caerph 27 P8
Newbridge Cnwll 2 C9
Newbridge D & G 78 F11
Newbridge Hants 9 K4
Newbridge IoW 9 M9
Newbridge Green Worcs 29 L2
Newbridge-on-Wye Powys 38 B9
New Brighton Wirral 56 F9
Newbrough Nthumb 72 F7
New Buckenham Norfk 44 H11
Newbuildings Devon 15 N10
Newburgh Abers 103 K4
Newburgh Abers 103 K9
Newburgh Fife 93 J11
Newburgh Lancs 57 J6
Newburn N u Ty 73 L7
Newbury Somset 17 Q6
Newbury W Berk 19 M7
Newbury Park Gt Lon 21 N6
Newby Cumb 64 B4
Newby Lancs 63 P11
Newby N York 63 N8
Newby N York 66 C5
Newby N York 67 L9
Newby Bridge Cumb 62 G5
Newby East Cumb 71 P4
New Byth Abers 102 H5
Newby West Cumb 71 M5
Newcastle Mons 28 E5
Newcastle Shrops 38 F5
Newcastle Airport Nthumb 73 L6
Newcastle Emlyn Carmth 36 E11
Newcastleton Border 79 P10
Newcastle-under-Lyme Staffs 49 Q6
Newcastle upon Tyne N u Ty 73 M7
Newchapel Pembks 36 D11
Newchapel Surrey 11 M2
Newchurch IoW 9 P9
Newchurch Kent 13 K4
Newchurch Mons 28 E8
Newchurch Powys 38 E11
Newchurch Staffs 40 F3
New Costessey Norfk 45 K7
Newcraighall C Edin 86 G7
New Crofton Wakefd 59 K10
New Cross Gt Lon 21 M7
New Cross Somset 17 K11
New Cumnock E Ayrs 77 K8
New Deer Abers 103 J6
New Denham Bucks 20 G6
Newdigate Surrey 11 K2
New Duston Nhants 31 Q2
New Earswick C York 59 N3
New Edlington Donc 51 M2
New Elgin Moray 101 J3
New Ellerby E R Yk 61 K6
Newell Green Br For 20 E8
New Eltham Gt Lon 21 N8
New End Worcs 30 D3
Newenden Kent 12 G5
New England C Pete 42 H9
Newent Gloucs 29 J4
New Ferry Wirral 56 G10
Newfield Dur 65 L2
Newfield Highld 107 N7
New Fletton C Pete 42 H9
New Forest National Park 9 K6
Newgale Pembks 24 E4
New Galloway D & G 69 P4
Newgate Street Herts 21 L3
New Gilston Fife 87 J1
New Grimsby IoS 2 b1
Newhall Ches E 49 L6
New Hartley Nthumb 73 N5
Newhaven C Edin 86 F7
Newhaven E Susx 11 N9
New Haw Surrey 20 G10
New Hedges Pembks 25 K8
New Holland N Linc 61 J9
Newholm N York 67 J5
New Houghton Derbys 51 L7
New Houghton Norfk 44 D5
Newhouse N Lans 85 N10
New Hutton Cumb 63 K4
Newick E Susx 11 N6
Newington Kent 13 M3
Newington Kent 22 G9

182 Newington – Old Bridge of Urr

Newington Oxon 19 Q2
New Inn Carmth 26 C2
New Inn Torfn 28 C8
New Invention Shrops 38 F6
New Lanark S Lans 78 E1
New Lanark Village S Lans 78 E1
Newland C KuH 61 J7
Newland Gloucs 28 G6
Newland N York 59 P8
Newland Somset 15 P5
Newland Worcs 39 P11
Newlandrig Mdloth 86 H9
Newlands Border 79 Q9
Newlands Nthumb 73 J9
Newlands of Dundurcas Moray 101 L5
New Langholm D & G 79 M11
New Leake Lincs 53 L11
New Leeds Abers 103 K4
New Lodge Barns 59 J11
New Longton Lancs 57 K4
New Luce D & G 68 G6
Newlyn Cnwll 2 C9
Newmachar Abers 103 J10
Newmains N Lans 85 N10
New Malden Gt Lon 21 K9
Newman's Green Suffk 34 E7
Newmarket Suffk 33 Q4
Newmarket W Isls 111 d2
New Marske R & Cl 66 E4
New Marston Oxon 31 M11
New Mill Abers 95 N5
Newmill Border 79 P6
New Mill Cnwll 2 C8
New Mill Kirk 58 F11
Newmill Moray 101 N5
Newmillerdam Wakefd 59 J10
Newmill of Inshewan Angus 94 G9
Newmills C Edin 86 E8
New Mills Derbys 50 D4
Newmills Fife 86 B5
Newmills Mons 28 F7
New Mills Powys 38 C2
Newmiln P & K 92 G9
Newmilns E Ayrs 77 J4
New Milton Hants 9 J8
New Mistley Essex 35 J9
New Moat Pembks 25 J4
Newney Green Essex 22 D3
Newnham Hants 20 B11
Newnham Herts 33 J8
Newnham Kent 23 J11
Newnham Nhants 31 M3
Newnham Bridge Worcs 39 M8
Newnham on Severn Gloucs 29 J6
New Ollerton Notts 51 P7
New Oscott Birm 40 E8
New Pitsligo Abers 103 J4
Newport Cnwll 4 H3
Newport E R Yk 60 E7
Newport Essex 33 N9
Newport Gloucs 29 J8
Newport Highld 110 D10
Newport IoW 9 N9
Newport Newpt 28 C10
Newport Pembks 25 J2
Newport Wrekin 49 N10
Newport-on-Tay Fife 93 M9
Newport Pagnell M Keyn 32 C7
Newport Pagnell Services M Keyn 32 C7
New Prestwick S Ayrs 76 F6
New Quay Cerdgn 36 F8
Newquay Cnwll 3 J4
Newquay Zoo Cnwll 3 J4
New Rackheath Norfk 45 L7
New Radnor Powys 38 E9
New Ridley Nthumb 73 J8
New Romney Kent 13 K5
New Rossington Donc 51 N2
New Sauchie Clacks 85 P4
Newseat Abers 102 F8
Newsham Lancs 57 K2
Newsham N York 65 K5
Newsham N York 65 P9
Newsham Nthumb 73 N5
New Sharlston Wakefd 59 J9
Newsholme E R Yk 60 C8
New Silksworth Sundld 73 P9
Newsome Kirk 58 F10
New Somerby Lincs 42 D3
Newstead Border 80 D7
Newstead Notts 51 L9
Newstead Nthumb 81 N8
New Stevenston N Lans 85 M10
New Swanage Dorset 8 F10
Newthorpe Notts 51 L10
New Thundersley Essex 22 F5
Newton Ag & B 83 Q4
Newton Border 80 E9
Newton Brdgnd 26 H12
Newton C Beds 32 H7
Newton Cambs 33 M6
Newton Cambs 43 M7
Newton Ches W 48 H2
Newton Ches W 49 J4
Newton Cumb 62 E7
Newton Derbys 51 K8
Newton Herefs 28 D3
Newton Herefs 39 K10
Newton Highld 107 J11
Newton Highld 107 M11
Newton Highld 107 M8
Newton Highld 110 G6
Newton Lincs 42 F3
Newton Mdloth 86 G8
Newton Moray 100 H3
Newton Moray 101 L3
Newton Nhants 42 C12
Newton Norfk 44 D7
Newton Notts 51 P11
Newton Nthumb 73 J7
Newton S Lans 78 F3
Newton S Lans 85 L10
Newton Sandw 40 D8
Newton Staffs 40 D3
Newton Suffk 34 F8
Newton W Loth 86 C6
Newton Warwks 41 M10
Newton Abbot Devon 6 B8
Newton Arlosh Cumb 71 K5
Newton Aycliffe Dur 65 M3
Newton Bewley Hartpl 66 C3
Newton Blossomville M Keyn 32 D6
Newton Bromswold Nhants 32 E4
Newton Burgoland Leics 41 J6
Newton by Toft Lincs 52 F6
Newton Ferrers Devon 5 L9
Newton Ferry W Isls 111 b4
Newton Flotman Norfk 45 K9
Newtongrange Mdloth 86 G8
Newton Green Mons 28 F9
Newton Harcourt Leics 41 N7
Newton Heath Manch 57 Q8
Newtonhill Abers 95 P4
Newton-in-Bowland Lancs 63 M11
Newton Kyme N York 59 L5
Newton-le-Willows N York 65 L9
Newton-le-Willows St Hel 57 L9
Newtonloan Mdloth 86 G9
Newton Longville Bucks 32 C9
Newton Mearns E Rens 85 J11
Newtonmill Angus 95 K8
Newtonmore Highld 99 K8
Newton Morrell N York 65 M5
Newton of Balcanquhal P & K 92 H12
Newton of Balcormo Fife 87 K2
Newton of Belltrees Rens 84 F10
Newton-on-Ayr S Ayrs 76 F6
Newton-on-Ouse N York 59 L3
Newton-on-Rawcliffe N York 66 H9
Newton-on-the-Moor Nthumb 81 N12
Newton on Trent Lincs 52 B8
Newton Poppleford Devon 6 E5
Newton Purcell Oxon 31 N7
Newton Regis Warwks 40 H6
Newton Reigny Cumb 71 P8
Newton St Cyres Devon 15 Q11
Newton St Faith Norfk 45 K6
Newton St Loe BaNES 17 Q3
Newton St Petrock Devon 14 G9
Newton Solney Derbys 40 H3
Newton Stacey Hants 19 M11
Newton Stewart D & G 69 K6
Newton Tony Wilts 19 J11
Newton Tracey Devon 15 J6
Newton under Roseberry R & Cl 66 D5
Newton upon Derwent E R Yk 60 C4
Newton Valence Hants 10 B4
Newton Wamphray D & G 78 H9
Newton with Scales Lancs 57 J3
Newtown BCP 8 F8
Newtown Cumb 70 H6
Newtown Cumb 71 P3
Newtown D & G 77 N8
Newtown Devon 6 E3
Newtown Devon 15 N7
New Town E Susx 11 P6
Newtown Gloucs 29 J8
Newtown Hants 9 Q5
Newtown Herefs 39 L12
Newtown Highld 98 E7
Newtown IoW 9 M8
Newtown Nthumb 81 L8
Newtown Powys 38 C4
Newtown Shrops 49 J8
Newtown Somset 6 H1
Newtown Staffs 50 B8
Newtown Wigan 57 K7
Newtown Worcs 39 Q10
Newtown Linford Leics 41 M5
Newtown St Boswells Border 80 D7
New Tredegar Caerph 27 N8
New Trows S Lans 77 N4
Newtyle Angus 93 K7
New Walsoken Cambs 43 M8
New Waltham NE Lin 53 J3
New Winton E Loth 87 J7
Newyork Ag & B 83 P2
New York Lincs 53 J11
New York N Tyne 73 N6
Neyland Pembks 24 G7
Nicholashayne Devon 16 E11
Nicholaston Swans 26 C10
Nidd N York 58 H3
Nigg C Aber 95 Q2
Nigg Highld 107 N7
Nigg Ferry Highld 107 N8
Ninebanks Nthumb 72 E9
Nine Elms Swindn 18 G4
Ninfield E Susx 12 E7
Ningwood IoW 9 L9
Nisbet Border 80 F8
Nisbet Hill Border 80 H4
Niton IoW 9 N11
Nitshill C Glas 85 J10
Nocton Lincs 52 F10
Noke Oxon 31 M10
Nolton Pembks 24 F5
Nolton Haven Pembks 24 F5
No Man's Heath Ches W 49 K6
No Man's Heath Warwks 40 H6
Nomansland Devon 15 P9
Nomansland Wilts 9 J4
Noneley Shrops 49 J9
Nonington Kent 23 N11
Nook Cumb 63 K6
Norbiton Gt Lon 21 K9
Norbury Ches E 49 K6
Norbury Derbys 50 F11
Norbury Gt Lon 21 L9
Norbury Shrops 38 G4
Norbury Staffs 49 P10
Norchard Worcs 39 Q8
Nordelph Norfk 43 N9
Nordley Shrops 39 M3
Norfolk Broads Norfk 45 P8
Norham Nthumb 81 J5
Norley Ches W 49 K2
Norleywood Hants 9 L7
Normanby Lincs 52 E6
Normanby N Linc 60 F10
Normanby N York 66 G10
Normanby R & Cl 66 D4
Normanby le Wold Lincs 52 G5
Normandy Surrey 20 E11
Norman's Green Devon 6 E3
Normanton C Derb 41 J2
Normanton Leics 42 B2
Normanton Notts 51 P9
Normanton Wakefd 59 J9
Normanton le Heath Leics 41 J5
Normanton on Cliffe Lincs 42 D2
Normanton on Soar Notts 41 L3
Normanton on the Wolds Notts 41 N2
Normanton on Trent Notts 52 B9
Norris Green Lpool 56 H9
Norris Hill Leics 41 J4
Norristhorpe Kirk 58 G9
Northall Bucks 32 D11
Northallerton N York 65 P8
Northam C Sotn 9 M5
Northam Devon 14 H6
Northampton Nhants 31 Q2
Northampton Worcs 39 Q8
Northampton Services Nhants 31 Q3
North Anston Rothm 51 M4
North Ascot Br For 20 E9
North Aston Oxon 31 L8
Northaw Herts 21 L3
Northay Somset 6 H1
North Baddesley Hants 9 L4
North Ballachulish Highld 90 E4
North Barrow Somset 17 N9
North Barsham Norfk 44 F3
Northbay W Isls 111 a7
North Benfleet Essex 22 F5
North Berwick E Loth 87 K5
North Boarhunt Hants 9 P5
Northborough C Pete 42 G8
Northbourne Kent 23 P11
North Bovey Devon 5 P4
North Bradley Wilts 18 C9
North Brentor Devon 5 K4
North Brewham Somset 17 Q8
Northbrook Hants 19 N11
North Buckland Devon 14 H4
North Burlingham Norfk 45 N7
North Cadbury Somset 17 P10
North Carlton Lincs 52 D7
North Carlton Notts 51 N4
North Cave E R Yk 60 F7
North Cerney Gloucs 30 D11
North Chailey E Susx 11 N6
Northchapel W Susx 10 F4
North Charford Hants 8 H4
North Charlton Nthumb 81 N9
North Cheam Gt Lon 21 K9
North Cheriton Somset 17 Q10
North Chideock Dorset 7 K4
Northchurch Herts 20 F2
North Cliffe E R Yk 60 E6
North Clifton Notts 52 B8
North Cockerington Lincs 53 L5
North Connel Ag & B 90 C9
North Cornelly Brdgnd 26 H11
North Cotes Lincs 53 K4
Northcott Devon 4 H2
Northcourt Oxon 19 N2
North Cove Suffk 45 P11
North Cowton N York 65 M6
North Crawley M Keyn 32 D7
North Creake Norfk 44 E3
North Curry Somset 17 J10
North Dalton E R Yk 60 F4
North Deighton N York 59 K4
Northdown Kent 23 Q8
North Downs 22 H11
North Duffield N York 59 P6
North Elmham Norfk 44 G6
North Elmsall Wakefd 59 L10
North End C Port 9 Q7
North End Essex 33 Q11
North End Hants 8 G4
North End Nhants 32 D3
North End W Susx 10 F8
Northend Warwks 31 K4
Northenden Manch 57 P10
North Erradale Highld 105 L6
North Evington C Leic 41 N6
North Fambridge Essex 22 G4
North Ferriby E R Yk 60 G8
Northfield Birm 40 D10
Northfield C Aber 95 P1
Northfield E R Yk 60 H8
Northfields Lincs 42 E8
Northfleet Kent 22 D8
North Frodingham E R Yk 61 J4
North Gorley Hants 8 H5
North Green Suffk 35 M4
North Greetwell Lincs 52 E8
North Grimston N York 60 E1
North Hayling Hants 10 B9
North Hill Cnwll 4 G5
North Hillingdon Gt Lon 20 H6
North Hinksey Village Oxon 31 L11
North Holmwood Surrey 11 J1
North Huish Devon 5 P8
North Hykeham Lincs 52 D9
Northiam E Susx 12 G5
Northill C Beds 32 G7
Northington Hants 19 P12
North Kelsey Lincs 52 F3
North Kessock Highld 107 L11
North Killingholme N Linc 61 K10
North Kilvington N York 65 Q9
North Kilworth Leics 41 N10
North Kyme Lincs 52 G11
North Landing E R Yk 67 Q12
Northlands Lincs 53 K11
Northleach Gloucs 30 E10
North Lee Bucks 20 D2
Northleigh Devon 6 G4
North Leigh Oxon 31 K10
North Leverton with Habblesthorpe Notts 52 B7
Northlew Devon 15 J11
North Littleton Worcs 30 E5
North Lopham Norfk 44 G12
North Luffenham Rutlnd 42 D9
North Marden W Susx 10 D6
North Marston Bucks 31 Q9
North Middleton Mdloth 86 G9
North Millbrex Abers 102 H6
North Milmain D & G 68 E8
North Molton Devon 15 M6
Northmoor Oxon 19 M1
North Moreton Oxon 19 P3
Northmuir Angus 93 L5
North Mundham W Susx 10 E9
North Muskham Notts 52 B10
North Newbald E R Yk 60 F6
North Newington Oxon 31 K6
North Newnton Wilts 18 G8
North Newton Somset 17 J9
Northney Hants 10 B8
North Nibley Gloucs 29 K9
Northolt Gt Lon 21 J6
Northolt Airport Gt Lon 20 H6
Northop Flints 48 E2
Northop Hall Flints 48 F2
North Ormesby Middsb 66 D4
North Ormsby Lincs 53 J5
Northorpe Kirk 58 G9
Northorpe Lincs 42 H3
Northorpe Lincs 52 C4
North Otterington N York 65 P9
North Owersby Lincs 52 F5
Northowram Calder 58 E8
North Perrott Somset 7 L2
North Petherton Somset 16 H9
North Petherwin Cnwll 4 G3
North Pickenham Norfk 44 E8
North Piddle Worcs 30 C3
North Poorton Dorset 7 M3
Northport Dorset 8 D9
North Queensferry Fife 86 D6
North Rauceby Lincs 42 E2
Northrepps Norfk 45 L3
North Reston Lincs 53 L6
North Rigton N York 58 H4
North Rode Ches E 50 B7
North Roe Shet 111 k3
North Ronaldsay Ork 111 i1
North Ronaldsay Airport Ork 111 i1
North Runcton Norfk 43 Q6
North Scarle Lincs 52 C9
North Shian Ag & B 90 C7
North Shields N Tyne 73 N7
North Shoebury Sthend 22 H6
North Shore Bpool 56 F2
North Side C Pete 43 J9
North Somercotes Lincs 53 L4
North Stainley N York 65 M11
North Stifford Thurr 22 C7
North Stoke BaNES 17 Q3
North Stoke Oxon 19 Q4
North Stoke W Susx 10 G7
Northstowe Cambs 33 L4
North Street Kent 23 K10
North Street W Berk 19 Q6
North Sunderland Nthumb 81 P7
North Tamerton Cnwll 14 F11
North Tawton Devon 15 L10
North Third Stirlg 85 M5
North Thoresby Lincs 53 J4
North Tolsta W Isls 111 e1
Northton W Isls 111 b3
North Town Devon 15 J9
North Town Somset 17 N7
North Town W & M 20 E7
North Tuddenham Norfk 44 G7
North Uist W Isls 111 a4
Northumberland National Park Nthumb 72 E5
North Walsham Norfk 45 L4
North Waltham Hants 19 P10
North Warnborough Hants 20 B12
North Weald Bassett Essex 21 P3
North Wheatley Notts 51 Q4
Northwich Ches W 49 M2
Northwick Worcs 39 Q9
North Widcombe BaNES 17 N5
North Willingham Lincs 52 G6
North Wingfield Derbys 51 K7
North Witham Lincs 42 D6
Northwold Norfk 44 C10
Northwood C Stke 50 B10
Northwood Gt Lon 20 H5
Northwood IoW 9 N8
Northwood Shrops 49 J8
Northwood Green Gloucs 29 J5
North Wootton Dorset 17 P12
North Wootton Norfk 43 Q5
North Wootton Somset 17 N7
North Wraxall Wilts 18 B6
North York Moors National Park 66 G7
Norton Donc 59 M10
Norton E Susx 11 P9
Norton Gloucs 29 M4
Norton Halton 57 K11
Norton Nhants 31 N2
Norton Notts 51 M6
Norton Powys 38 F8
Norton S on T 66 C3
Norton Sheff 51 J5
Norton Shrops 39 N3
Norton Suffk 34 F4
Norton Swans 26 E10
Norton W Susx 10 E8
Norton Wilts 18 C4
Norton Worcs 30 D5
Norton Worcs 39 Q10
Norton Bavant Wilts 18 D11
Norton Canes Staffs 40 D6
Norton Canes Services Staffs 40 D6
Norton Canon Herefs 38 H11
Norton Disney Lincs 52 C10
Norton Fitzwarren Somset 16 G10
Norton Green IoW 9 K9
Norton Hawkfield BaNES 17 N4
Norton Heath Essex 22 C3
Norton in Hales Shrops 49 N7
Norton-Juxta-Twycross Leics 41 J6
Norton-le-Clay N York 65 P12
Norton-le-Moors C Stke 50 B9
Norton Lindsey Warwks 30 G2
Norton Little Green Suffk 34 F4
Norton Malreward BaNES 17 N3
Norton-on-Derwent N York 66 H12
Norton St Philip Somset 18 B9
Norton Subcourse Norfk 45 N9
Norton sub Hamdon Somset 17 L11
Norwell Notts 51 Q8
Norwell Woodhouse Notts 51 Q8
Norwich Norfk 45 K8
Norwich Airport Norfk 45 K7
Norwick Shet 111 m2
Norwood Clacks 85 P4
Norwood Green Gt Lon 21 J7
Norwood Hill Surrey 11 K2
Norwoodside Cambs 43 L9
Noss Mayo Devon 5 L10
Nosterfield N York 65 M10
Nostie Highld 97 M4
Notgrove Gloucs 30 E9
Nottage Brdgnd 26 H12
Nottingham C Nott 51 M11
Notton Wakefd 59 J10
Notton Wilts 18 D6
Noutard's Green Worcs 39 P8
Nuffield Oxon 19 Q4
Nunburnholme E R Yk 60 E5
Nuneaton Warwks 41 J8
Nunhead Gt Lon 21 M8
Nun Monkton N York 59 L3
Nunney Somset 17 Q7
Nunnington N York 66 F10
Nunsthorpe NE Lin 53 J2
Nunthorpe C York 59 N4
Nunthorpe Middsb 66 D5
Nunthorpe Village Middsb 66 D5
Nunton Wilts 8 H3
Nunwick N York 65 N11
Nursling Hants 9 L4
Nutbourne W Susx 10 C8
Nutbourne W Susx 10 H6
Nutfield Surrey 21 L12
Nuthall Notts 51 M11
Nuthampstead Herts 33 L9
Nuthurst W Susx 11 J5
Nutley E Susx 11 N5
Nuttall Bury 57 P5
Nybster Highld 110 G3
Nyetimber W Susx 10 E9
Nyewood W Susx 10 C6
Nymans W Susx 11 L4
Nymet Rowland Devon 15 M9
Nymet Tracey Devon 15 M11
Nympsfield Gloucs 29 L8
Nynehead Somset 16 F10
Nyton W Susx 10 E8

O

Oadby Leics 41 N7
Oad Street Kent 22 G10
Oakamoor Staffs 50 D11
Oakbank W Loth 86 C8
Oak Cross Devon 15 J11
Oakdale Caerph 27 P8
Oake Somset 16 F10
Oaken Staffs 39 Q2
Oakenclough Lancs 63 K11
Oakengates Wrekin 49 M12
Oakenshaw Dur 73 L12
Oakenshaw Kirk 58 F8
Oakford Cerdgn 36 G8
Oakford Devon 16 C11
Oakham Rutlnd 42 C8
Oakhanger Hants 10 C3
Oakhill Somset 17 P6
Oakington Cambs 33 L4
Oaklands Herts 33 J12
Oakle Street Gloucs 29 K5
Oakley Bed 32 E6
Oakley Bucks 31 N10
Oakley Fife 86 B4
Oakley Hants 19 P9
Oakley Suffk 35 J2
Oakridge Lynch Gloucs 29 M7
Oaksey Wilts 29 P9
Oakthorpe Leics 40 H5
Oakwood C Derb 51 J12
Oakworth C Brad 58 D6
Oare Kent 23 J10
Oare Somset 15 N3
Oare Wilts 18 H7
Oasby Lincs 42 E3
Oath Somset 17 K10
Oathlaw Angus 93 N4
Oatlands Park Surrey 20 H9
Oban Ag & B 90 B9
Oban Airport Ag & B 90 C8
Obley Shrops 38 G6
Obney P & K 92 F8
Oborne Dorset 17 P11
Occold Suffk 35 J3
Occumster Highld 110 F8
Ochiltree E Ayrs 76 H7
Ockbrook Derbys 41 K1
Ocker Hill Sandw 40 C8
Ockham Surrey 20 H11
Ockle Highld 89 L3
Ockley Surrey 11 J3
Ocle Pychard Herefs 39 L11
Odcombe Somset 17 M11
Odd Down BaNES 17 Q4
Oddingley Worcs 30 B3
Oddington Oxon 31 M10
Odell Bed 32 D5
Odiham Hants 20 C12
Odsal C Brad 58 F8
Odsey Cambs 33 J8
Odstock Wilts 8 G3
Odstone Leics 41 K6
Offchurch Warwks 31 J2
Offenham Worcs 30 D5
Offerton Stockp 50 B3
Offham E Susx 11 N7
Offham Kent 22 D11
Offham W Susx 10 G8
Offord Cluny Cambs 32 H4
Offord D'Arcy Cambs 32 H4
Offton Suffk 34 H6
Offwell Devon 6 G3
Ogbourne Maizey Wilts 18 H6
Ogbourne St Andrew Wilts 18 H6
Ogbourne St George Wilts 18 H6
Ogle Nthumb 73 K5
Oglet Lpool 56 H11
Ogmore V Glam 16 B2
Ogmore-by-Sea V Glam 16 B2
Ogmore Vale Brdgnd 27 K10
Okeford Fitzpaine Dorset 8 B5
Okehampton Devon 5 M2
Oker Side Derbys 50 H8
Okewood Hill Surrey 11 J3
Old Nhants 32 B3
Old Aberdeen C Aber 95 Q1
Old Alresford Hants 9 P1
Oldany Highld 108 C8
Old Arley Warwks 40 H8
Old Auchenbrack D & G 77 M11
Old Basford C Nott 51 M11
Old Basing Hants 19 Q9
Old Beetley Norfk 44 F6
Oldberrow Warwks 30 E2
Old Bewick Nthumb 81 M9
Old Bolingbroke Lincs 53 K9
Old Boxted Essex 34 G9
Old Bramhope Leeds 58 G5
Old Brampton Derbys 51 J6
Old Bridge of Urr D & G 70 C3

Old Buckenham – Perry Barr 183

Old Buckenham Norfk 44 H10
Old Burghclere Hants 19 M8
Oldbury Sandw 40 C9
Oldbury Shrops 39 N4
Oldbury Warwks 40 H8
Oldbury-on-Severn S Glos 28 H9
Oldbury on the Hill Gloucs 18 B3
Old Byland N York 66 D9
Old Cantley Donc 51 N1
Oldcastle Mons 28 C4
Old Catton Norfk 45 K7
Old Clee NE Lin 53 J2
Old Cleeve Somset 16 E7
Old Colwyn Conwy 55 M6
Oldcotes Notts 51 N3
Old Coulsdon Gt Lon 21 L11
Old Dailly S Ayrs 76 D10
Old Dalby Leics 41 P3
Old Deer Abers 103 K6
Old Edlington Donc 51 M2
Old Ellerby E R Yk 61 K6
Old Felixstowe Suffk 35 M9
Oldfield Worcs 39 Q8
Old Fletton C Pete 42 H10
Oldford Somset 18 B10
Old Forge Herefs 28 G5
Old Grimsby IoS 2 b1
Old Hall Green Herts 33 L11
Oldham Oldham 58 B12
Oldhamstocks E Loth 87 N7
Old Harlow Essex 21 P2
Old Hunstanton Norfk 44 B2
Old Hurst Cambs 33 J2
Old Hutton Cumb 63 K5
Old Inns Services N Lans 85 N7
Old Kilpatrick W Duns 84 H8
Old Knebworth Herts 32 H11
Old Lakenham Norfk 45 K8
Oldland S Glos 17 P2
Old Langho Lancs 57 M2
Old Leake Lincs 53 L12
Old Malton N York 66 H11
Oldmeldrum Abers 102 H9
Oldmill Cnwll 4 H5
Old Milverton Warwks 30 H1
Oldmixon N Som 17 J5
Old Newton Suffk 34 H4
Old Portlethen Abers 95 Q3
Old Radford C Nott 51 M11
Old Radnor Powys 38 F9
Old Rayne Abers 102 E9
Old Romney Kent 13 K5
Old Shoreham W Susx 11 K8
Oldshoremore Highld 108 D4
Old Sodbury S Glos 29 K11
Old Somerby Lincs 42 D4
Oldstead N York 66 D10
Old Stratford Nhants 31 Q6
Old Struan P & K 92 C3
Old Swinford Dudley 40 B10
Old Thirsk N York 66 B10
Old Town Cumb 63 L5
Old Town E Susx 12 C9
Old Town IoS 2 c2
Old Trafford Traffd 57 P9
Oldwall Cumb 71 P4
Oldwalls Swans 26 C9
Old Warden C Beds 32 G7
Old Weston Cambs 32 F2
Old Wick Highld 110 G6
Old Windsor W & M 20 F8
Old Wives Lees Kent 23 K11
Old Woking Surrey 20 G11
Olgrinmore Highld 110 C5
Olive Green Staffs 40 E4
Oliver's Battery Hants 9 M2
Ollaberry Shet 111 k3
Ollach Highld 96 F3
Ollerton Ches E 57 P12
Ollerton Notts 51 P7
Ollerton Shrops 49 M9
Olney M Keyn 32 C6
Olrig House Highld 110 E3
Olton Solhll 40 F10
Olveston S Glos 28 H10
Ombersley Worcs 39 Q8
Ompton Notts 51 P7
Onchan IoM 56 d5
Onecote Staffs 50 D9
Onibury Shrops 39 J6
Onich Highld 90 E4
Onllwyn Neath 26 H6
Onneley Staffs 49 N6
Onslow Green Essex 33 Q12
Onslow Village Surrey 20 F12
Onston Ches W 49 L1
Opinan Highld 105 L7
Orbliston Moray 101 L4
Orbost Highld 96 B2
Orby Lincs 53 M9
Orchard Portman Somset 16 H10
Orcheston Wilts 18 F10
Orcop Herefs 28 F4
Orcop Hill Herefs 28 F4
Ord Abers 102 E4
Ordhead Abers 102 E11
Ordie Abers 94 G2
Ordiequish Moray 101 L4
Ordsall Notts 51 P5
Ore E Susx 12 G7
Orford Suffk 35 N6
Orford Warrtn 57 L10
Organford Dorset 8 D8
Orkney Islands Ork 111 h2
Orkney Neolithic Ork 111 g2
Orlestone Kent 13 J3
Orleton Herefs 39 J8
Orleton Worcs 39 M8
Orlingbury Nhants 32 C3
Ormesby R & Cl 66 D4
Ormesby St Margaret Norfk 45 P7
Ormesby St Michael Norfk 45 P7
Ormiscaig Highld 105 M4
Ormiston E Loth 86 H8
Ormsaigmore Highld 89 K4
Ormsary Ag & B 83 L8
Ormskirk Lancs 56 H7
Oronsay Ag & B 82 E5
Orphir Ork 111 h2
Orpington Gt Lon 21 P9
Orrell Sefton 56 G9
Orrell Wigan 57 K7
Orroland D & G 70 C6
Orsett Thurr 22 D7
Orslow Staffs 49 P11
Orston Notts 51 Q11
Orton Cumb 63 L1
Orton Nhants 32 B2
Orton Staffs 39 Q3
Orton Longueville C Pete 42 G10
Orton-on-the-Hill Leics 40 H6
Orton Waterville C Pete 42 G10
Orwell Cambs 33 K6
Osbaldeston Lancs 57 M3
Osbaldwick C York 59 N4
Osbaston Leics 41 K6
Osbaston Shrops 48 G10
Osborne House IoW 9 N8
Osbournby Lincs 42 F3
Oscroft Ches W 49 J3
Ose Highld 96 C2
Osgathorpe Leics 41 K4
Osgodby Lincs 52 F5
Osgodby N York 59 N7
Osgodby N York 67 M9
Oskaig Highld 96 G3
Oskamull Ag & B 89 K8
Osmaston Derbys 50 G11
Osmington Dorset 7 Q6
Osmington Mills Dorset 7 Q6
Osmondthorpe Leeds 59 J7
Osmotherley N York 66 C7
Osney Oxon 31 L11
Ospringe Kent 23 J10
Ossett Wakefd 58 H9
Ossington Notts 51 Q7
Osterley Gt Lon 21 J7
Oswaldkirk N York 66 E10
Oswaldtwistle Lancs 57 N4
Oswestry Shrops 48 F9
Otairnis W Isls 111 b4
Otford Kent 21 Q10
Otham Kent 22 F11
Othery Somset 17 K9
Otley Leeds 58 G5
Otley Suffk 35 K5
Otterbourne Hants 9 M3
Otterburn N York 63 Q9
Otterburn Nthumb 72 F3
Otter Ferry Ag & B 83 P6
Otterham Cnwll 4 E3
Otterhampton Somset 16 H7
Otternish W Isls 111 b4
Ottershaw Surrey 20 G9
Otterswick Shet 111 k3
Otterton Devon 6 E6
Ottery St Mary Devon 6 E4
Ottinge Kent 13 M2
Ottringham E R Yk 61 M8
Oughterside Cumb 71 J7
Oughtibridge Sheff 50 H3
Oughtrington Warrtn 57 M10
Oulston N York 66 D11
Oulton Cumb 71 K5
Oulton Norfk 45 J4
Oulton Staffs 40 B1
Oulton Suffk 45 Q10
Oulton Broad Suffk 45 Q10
Oulton Street Norfk 45 J5
Oundle Nhants 42 E11
Ounsdale Staffs 39 Q4
Our Dynamic Earth C Edin 86 F7
Ousby Cumb 64 B1
Ousden Suffk 34 C5
Ousefleet E R Yk 60 E9
Ouston Dur 73 M9
Outgate Cumb 62 G3
Outhgill Cumb 64 E7
Outhill Warwks 30 E2
Outlane Kirk 58 E9
Out Rawcliffe Lancs 56 H1
Out Skerries Shet 111 m3
Outwell Norfk 43 N8
Outwood Surrey 11 L2
Outwoods Staffs 49 P10
Ouzlewell Green Leeds 59 J8
Ovenden Calder 58 E8
Over Cambs 33 L3
Over Ches W 49 M3
Overbury Worcs 29 N2
Overcombe Dorset 7 Q6
Over Compton Dorset 17 N11
Over Haddon Derbys 50 G7
Over Hulton Bolton 57 M7
Over Kellet Lancs 63 K8
Over Kiddington Oxon 31 K9
Overleigh Somset 17 L8
Over Norton Oxon 30 H8
Over Peover Ches E 49 P1
Overpool Ches W 56 H12
Overscaig Highld 108 H10
Overseal Derbys 40 H4
Over Silton N York 66 C8
Oversland Kent 23 K11
Overstone Nhants 32 B4
Over Stowey Somset 16 G8
Overstrand Norfk 45 L3
Over Stratton Somset 17 L11
Overthorpe Nhants 31 L6
Overton C Aber 102 H11
Overton Hants 19 N10
Overton Lancs 62 H9
Overton N York 59 M3
Overton Shrops 39 J7
Overton Swans 26 B10
Overton Wakefd 58 H10
Overton Wrexhm 48 G7
Overtown N Lans 85 N11
Over Wallop Hants 19 K11
Over Whitacre Warwks 40 G8
Over Worton Oxon 31 K8
Oving Bucks 32 A11
Oving W Susx 10 E8
Ovingdean Br & H 11 M8
Ovingham Nthumb 73 J7
Ovington Dur 65 K5
Ovington Essex 34 C8
Ovington Hants 9 P2
Ovington Norfk 44 F9
Ovington Nthumb 73 J7
Ower Hants 9 K4
Owermoigne Dorset 8 B9
Owlerton Sheff 51 J3
Owlsmoor Br For 20 D10
Owlswick Bucks 20 C3
Owmby Lincs 52 E6
Owmby Lincs 52 F3
Owslebury Hants 9 N3
Owston Donc 59 M11
Owston Leics 41 Q6
Owston Ferry N Linc 52 B4
Owstwick E R Yk 61 M7
Owthorne E R Yk 61 N8
Owthorpe Notts 41 P2
Owton Manor Hartpl 66 C2
Oxborough Norfk 44 C9
Oxcombe Lincs 53 K7
Oxenholme Cumb 63 K4
Oxenhope C Brad 58 D7
Oxen Park Cumb 62 G5
Oxenpill Somset 17 L7
Oxenton Gloucs 29 N3
Oxenwood Wilts 19 K8
Oxford Oxon 31 L11
Oxford Airport Oxon 31 L10
Oxford Services Oxon 31 N12
Oxgangs C Edin 86 F8
Oxhey Herts 20 H4
Oxhill Dur 73 L9
Oxhill Warwks 30 H5
Oxley Wolves 40 B7
Oxley Green Essex 22 H1
Oxlode Cambs 43 M11
Oxnam Border 80 F9
Oxnead Norfk 45 K5
Oxshott Surrey 21 J10
Oxspring Barns 50 H1
Oxted Surrey 21 N11
Oxton Border 80 C4
Oxton N York 59 L5
Oxton Notts 51 N9
Oxton Wirral 56 F10
Oxwich Swans 26 C10
Oxwich Green Swans 26 C10
Oykel Bridge Highld 106 F3
Oyne Abers 102 E9
Oystermouth Swans 26 E10

P

Pabail W Isls 111 e2
Packington Leics 41 J5
Packmoor C Stke 49 Q5
Padanaram Angus 93 M5
Padbury Bucks 31 Q7
Paddington Gt Lon 21 L7
Paddlesworth Kent 13 M3
Paddlesworth Kent 22 D10
Paddock Wood Kent 12 D2
Padiham Lancs 57 P3
Padside N York 58 F3
Padstow Cnwll 3 K1
Padworth W Berk 19 Q7
Pagham W Susx 10 E9
Paglesham Essex 22 H5
Paignton Torbay 6 B10
Pailton Warwks 41 L10
Painscastle Powys 38 D11
Painshawfield Nthumb 73 J8
Painsthorpe E R Yk 60 E3
Painswick Gloucs 29 M6
Painter's Forstal Kent 23 J10
Paisley Rens 84 H9
Pakefield Suffk 45 Q11
Pakenham Suffk 34 F4
Paley Street W & M 20 E7
Palfrey Wsall 40 D7
Palgrave Suffk 35 J2
Pallington Dorset 8 B8
Palmarsh Kent 13 L4
Palmerston E Ayrs 76 H7
Palnackie D & G 70 D4
Palnure D & G 69 L6
Palterton Derbys 51 L7
Pamber End Hants 19 Q8
Pamber Green Hants 19 Q8
Pamber Heath Hants 19 Q8
Pamington Gloucs 29 N3
Pamphill Dorset 8 E7
Pampisford Cambs 33 N7
Panbride Angus 93 P8
Pancrasweek Devon 14 F10
Pandy Mons 28 D4
Pandy Wrexhm 48 G5
Pandy Tudur Conwy 55 M8
Panfield Essex 34 C10
Pangbourne W Berk 19 Q5
Pangdean W Susx 11 L7
Pannal N York 58 H4
Pannal Ash N York 58 H4
Pant Shrops 48 F10
Pantasaph Flints 48 D1
Pant-ffrwyth Brdgnd 27 K11
Pant Glas Gwynd 46 H2
Pantglas Powys 47 M10
Panton Lincs 52 H7
Pantside Caerph 27 P8
Pant-y-dwr Powys 37 R6
Pantymwyn Flints 48 E3
Panxworth Norfk 45 M7
Papa Stour Shet 111 j3
Papa Stour Airport Shet 111 j4
Papa Westray Ork 111 h1
Papa Westray Airport Ork 111 h1
Papcastle Cumb 70 H8
Papigoe Highld 110 H5
Papple E Loth 87 L7
Papplewick Notts 51 M9
Papworth Everard Cambs 33 J4
Papworth St Agnes Cambs 33 J4
Par Cnwll 3 N5
Parbold Lancs 57 J6
Parbrook Somset 17 N8
Parc Gwynd 47 P5
Parc Seymour Newpt 28 E9
Pardshaw Cumb 70 H9
Parham Suffk 35 M5
Park D & G 78 E10
Park Nthumb 72 C8
Park Corner Oxon 20 B6
Parkend Gloucs 28 H7
Parker's Green Kent 12 C1
Park Farm Kent 13 J3
Parkgate Ches W 56 F12
Parkgate D & G 78 G10
Park Gate Hants 9 N6
Park Gate Leeds 58 F6
Parkgate Surrey 11 K2
Parkhall W Duns 84 H8
Parkham Devon 14 G7
Parkmill Swans 26 D10
Park Royal Gt Lon 21 K7
Parkside Dur 73 Q10
Parkside N Lans 85 N10
Parkstone BCP 8 F8
Park Street Herts 21 J3
Parracombe Devon 15 L3
Parson Drove Cambs 43 L8
Parson's Heath Essex 34 G10
Partick C Glas 85 J9
Partington Traffd 57 N9
Partney Lincs 53 L9
Parton Cumb 70 F10
Partridge Green W Susx 11 J6
Parwich Derbys 50 F9
Passenham Nhants 32 A8
Paston C Pete 42 H9
Paston Norfk 45 M4
Patcham Br & H 11 L8
Patching W Susx 10 H8
Patchway S Glos 28 H11
Pateley Bridge N York 58 F2
Pathhead Fife 86 F4
Pathhead Mdloth 86 H9
Path of Condie P & K 92 G12
Patna E Ayrs 76 G8
Patney Wilts 18 F8
Patrick IoM 56 b5
Patrick Brompton N York 65 L8
Patricroft Salfd 57 N8
Patrington E R Yk 61 M9
Patrington Haven E R Yk 61 M9
Patrixbourne Kent 23 M11
Patterdale Cumb 71 N11
Pattingham Staffs 39 P3
Pattishall Nhants 31 P4
Pattiswick Green Essex 34 D11
Paul Cnwll 2 C9
Paulerspury Nhants 31 Q5
Paull E R Yk 61 K8
Paulton BaNES 17 P5
Paultons Park Hants 9 K4
Pauperhaugh Nthumb 73 K2
Pavenham Bed 32 E5
Pawlett Somset 16 H7
Paxford Gloucs 30 F6
Paxton Border 81 K4
Payhembury Devon 6 E3
Paythorne Lancs 63 P10
Peacehaven E Susx 11 N9
Peak District National Park 50 F3
Peak Forest Derbys 50 E5
Peakirk C Pete 42 G8
Peasedown St John BaNES 17 Q5
Peasemore W Berk 19 M5
Peasenhall Suffk 35 M3
Pease Pottage W Susx 11 L4
Pease Pottage Services W Susx 11 L4
Peaslake Surrey 10 H2
Peasley Cross St Hel 57 K9
Peasmarsh E Susx 12 H5
Peathill Abers 103 J3
Peat Inn Fife 87 J1
Peatling Magna Leics 41 N8
Peatling Parva Leics 41 N9
Pebmarsh Essex 34 E9
Pebsham E Susx 12 F8
Pebworth Worcs 30 F5
Pecket Well Calder 58 C8
Peckforton Ches E 49 K4
Peckham Gt Lon 21 M8
Peckleton Leics 41 L7
Pedlinge Kent 13 L3
Pedmore Dudley 40 B10
Pedwell Somset 17 K8
Peebles Border 79 L2
Peel IoM 56 b4
Peene Kent 13 M3
Pegsdon C Beds 32 G9
Pegswood Nthumb 73 M4
Pegwell Kent 23 Q9
Peinchorran Highld 96 G3
Peinlich Highld 104 F10
Peldon Essex 34 G12
Pelsall Wsall 40 D6
Pelton Dur 73 M9
Pelynt Cnwll 4 F8
Pemberton Carmth 26 D8
Pemberton Wigan 57 K7
Pembrey Carmth 25 P8
Pembridge Herefs 38 H9
Pembroke Pembks 24 H8
Pembroke Dock Pembks 24 G7
Pembrokeshire Coast National Park Pembks 24 E5
Pembury Kent 12 D2
Pen-allt Herefs 28 G3
Penallt Mons 28 F6
Penally Pembks 25 K8
Penarth V Glam 16 G2
Pen-bont Rhydybeddau Cerdgn 37 L4
Penbryn Cerdgn 36 E9
Pencader Carmth 25 Q2
Pencaitland E Loth 87 J8
Pencarnisiog IoA 54 D6
Pencarreg Carmth 37 J10
Pencelli Powys 27 M4
Penclawdd Swans 26 D9
Pencoed Brdgnd 27 K11
Pencombe Herefs 39 L10
Pencraig Herefs 28 G5
Pencraig Powys 48 B9
Pendeen Cnwll 2 B8
Penderyn Rhondd 27 K7
Pendine Carmth 25 L7
Pendlebury Salfd 57 P8
Pendleton Lancs 57 N2
Pendock Worcs 29 K3
Pendoggett Cnwll 4 C4
Pendomer Somset 7 M1
Pendoylan V Glam 16 E2
Penegoes Powys 47 M10
Pen-ffordd Pembks 25 J4
Pengam Caerph 27 N8
Pengam Cardif 27 P12
Penge Gt Lon 21 M8
Pengelly Cnwll 4 D4
Penhallow Cnwll 2 H5
Penhalvean Cnwll 2 G8
Penhill Swindn 18 H3
Penhow Newpt 28 E10
Penicuik Mdloth 86 F9
Penifiler Highld 96 F2
Peninver Ag & B 75 L7
Penistone Barns 50 G1
Penkill S Ayrs 76 D10
Penkridge Staffs 40 B5
Penley Wrexhm 48 H7
Penllyn V Glam 16 C2
Penmachno Conwy 55 L10
Penmaen Caerph 27 P8
Penmaen Swans 26 D10
Penmaenmawr Conwy 55 K6
Penmaenpool Gwynd 47 L7
Penmark V Glam 16 E3
Penmynydd IoA 54 G6
Pennal Gwynd 47 L10
Pennan Abers 102 H3
Pennant Powys 47 P10
Pennar Pembks 24 G8
Pennerley Shrops 38 G3
Pennines 58 C7
Pennington Cumb 62 F6
Pennorth Powys 27 M4
Penn Street Bucks 20 E4
Penny Bridge Cumb 62 F5
Pennycross Ag & B 89 L10
Pennyghael Ag & B 89 L10
Pennyglen S Ayrs 76 E8
Pennymoor Devon 15 P9
Pennywell Sundld 73 P9
Penparc Cerdgn 36 D10
Penperlleni Mons 28 C7
Penpoll Cnwll 4 E8
Penponds Cnwll 2 F7
Penpont D & G 78 D9
Pen-rhiw Pembks 36 D11
Penrhiwceiber Rhondd 27 M8
Pen Rhiwfawr Neath 26 G6
Penrhiwllan Cerdgn 36 F11
Penrhiwpal Cerdgn 36 F10
Penrhos Gwynd 46 F5
Penrhos Mons 28 E6
Penrhyn Bay Conwy 55 M5
Penrhyn-coch Cerdgn 37 K4
Penrhyndeudraeth Gwynd 47 K4
Penrhyn Slate Landscape Gwynd 55 J8
Penrice Swans 26 C10
Penrioch N Ayrs 75 N4
Penrith Cumb 71 Q9
Penrose Cnwll 3 K2
Penruddock Cumb 71 N9
Penryn Cnwll 2 H8
Pensarn Conwy 55 P6
Pensax Worcs 39 N8
Penselwood Somset 17 R9
Pensford BaNES 17 N4
Pensham Worcs 30 C5
Penshaw Sundld 73 N9
Penshurst Kent 11 Q2
Pensilva Cnwll 4 G6
Pensnett Dudley 40 B9
Pentewan Cnwll 3 M6
Pentir Gwynd 54 H8
Pentire Cnwll 2 H4
Pentlow Essex 34 D7
Pentney Norfk 44 C7
Pentonbridge Cumb 79 P12
Penton Mewsey Hants 19 K10
Pentraeth IoA 54 G6
Pentre Mons 28 E8
Pentre Rhondd 27 K9
Pentre Shrops 48 G11
Pentrebach Myr Td 27 M7
Pentre-bach Powys 27 J3
Pentre Berw IoA 54 F7
Pentrecelyn Denbgs 48 D5
Pentre-celyn Powys 47 P9
Pentre-chwyth Swans 26 F9
Pentre-cwrt Carmth 25 P2
Pentredwr Denbgs 48 E6
Pentrefelin Gwynd 47 J4
Pentrefoelas Conwy 55 M10
Pentregat Cerdgn 36 F9
Pentre-Gwenlais Carmth 26 E5
Pentre Hodrey Shrops 38 G6
Pentre Llanrhaeadr Denbgs 48 C3
Pentre Meyrick V Glam 16 C2
Pentre-tafarn-y-fedw Conwy 55 M8
Pentrich Derbys 51 J9
Pentridge Dorset 8 F4
Pentwyn Cardif 27 P11
Pen-twyn Mons 28 F7
Pentwynmaur Caerph 27 P9
Pentyrch Cardif 27 M11
Penwithick Cnwll 3 M5
Penybanc Carmth 26 E4
Penybont Powys 38 C8
Pen-y-bont Powys 48 E10
Penybontfawr Powys 48 C9
Pen-y-bryn Pembks 36 C11
Penycae Wrexhm 48 F6
Pen-y-clawdd Mons 28 E7
Pen-y-coedcae Rhondd 27 M10
Penycwn Pembks 24 E4
Pen-y-felin Flints 48 D2
Penyffordd Flints 48 F4
Pen-y-Garnedd Powys 48 C10
Pen-y-graig Gwynd 46 C5
Penygraig Rhondd 27 L10
Penygroes Carmth 26 D6
Penygroes Gwynd 54 F10
Pen-y-Mynydd Carmth 26 C7
Penymynydd Flints 48 F3
Penysarn IoA 54 F4
Pen-y-stryt Denbgs 48 E5
Penywaun Rhondd 27 K7
Penzance Cnwll 2 D9
Peopleton Worcs 30 C4
Peplow Shrops 49 L9
Perceton N Ayrs 76 F4
Percyhorner Abers 103 K3
Perham Down Wilts 19 J10
Periton Somset 16 C7
Perivale Gt Lon 21 J6
Perkins Village Devon 6 D5
Perlethorpe Notts 51 N6
Perranarworthal Cnwll 2 H7
Perranporth Cnwll 2 H5
Perranuthnoe Cnwll 2 D9
Perranwell Cnwll 2 H7
Perranzabuloe Cnwll 2 H5
Perry Birm 40 E8
Perry Cambs 32 G4
Perry Barr Birm 40 E8

Perry Green Wilts...18 E3
Pershall Staffs...49 P9
Pershore Worcs...30 C5
Pertenhall Bed...32 F4
Perth P & K...92 G10
Perthy Shrops...48 G8
Perton Herefs...28 H2
Perton Staffs...39 Q3
Peterborough C Pete...42 H9
Peterborough Services Cambs...42 G10
Peterchurch Herefs...28 D2
Peterculter C Aber...95 N2
Peterhead Abers...103 M6
Peterlee Dur...73 Q11
Petersfield Hants...10 C5
Peter's Green Herts...32 G11
Petersham Gt Lon...21 J8
Peters Marland Devon...14 H9
Peterstone Wentlooge Newpt...28 B11
Peterston-super-Ely V Glam...16 E2
Peterstow Herefs...28 G4
Peter Tavy Devon...5 K5
Petham Kent...23 L12
Petherwin Gate Cnwll...4 G3
Petrockstow Devon...15 J9
Pett E Susx...12 G7
Pettaugh Suffk...35 J5
Petterden Angus...93 M7
Pettinain S Lans...77 Q3
Pettistree Suffk...35 L6
Petton Devon...16 D10
Petts Wood Gt Lon...21 N9
Pettycur Fife...86 F5
Pettymuk Abers...103 J9
Petworth W Susx...10 F6
Pevensey E Susx...12 D8
Pevensey Bay E Susx...12 D8
Pewsey Wilts...18 H8
Pewsham Wilts...18 D6
Phepson Worcs...30 C3
Philham Devon...14 E7
Philiphaugh Border...79 N4
Phillack Cnwll...2 E7
Philleigh Cnwll...3 K7
Philpstoun W Loth...86 C6
Phoenix Green Hants...20 C11
Pibsbury Somset...17 L10
Pickburn Donc...59 L11
Pickering N York...66 H10
Pickford Covtry...40 H10
Pickhill N York...65 N10
Picklescott Shrops...38 H3
Pickmere Ches E...57 M12
Pickney Somset...16 G9
Pickwell Leics...42 B7
Pickworth Lincs...42 F4
Pickworth Rutlnd...42 F2
Picton Ches W...48 H2
Picton N York...65 P6
Piddinghoe E Susx...11 N9
Piddington Nhants...32 B6
Piddington Oxon...31 N10
Piddlehinton Dorset...7 Q4
Piddletrenthide Dorset...7 Q3
Pidley Cambs...33 K2
Piercebridge Darltn...65 L4
Pierowall Ork...111 h1
Pilgrims Hatch Essex...22 C4
Pilham Lincs...52 C5
Pillaton Cnwll...4 H7
Pillerton Hersey Warwks...30 H4
Pillerton Priors Warwks...30 H5
Pilley Barns...51 J1
Pilley Hants...9 K7
Pillgwenlly Newpt...28 C10
Pilling Lancs...62 H11
Pilning S Glos...28 G10
Pilsbury Derbys...50 E7
Pilsdon Dorset...7 K3
Pilsley Derbys...50 G6
Pilsley Derbys...51 K8
Pilson Green Norfk...45 N7
Piltdown E Susx...11 N5
Pilton Devon...15 K5
Pilton Nhants...42 E12
Pilton Rutlnd...42 D9
Pilton Somset...17 N7
Pimlico Gt Lon...21 H3
Pimperne Dorset...8 D5
Pinchbeck Lincs...43 J5
Pin Green Herts...33 J10
Pinhoe Devon...6 C4
Pinley Green Warwks...30 G2
Pinminnoch S Ayrs...76 D11
Pinmore S Ayrs...76 D11
Pinn Devon...6 E5
Pinner Gt Lon...20 H5
Pinner Green Gt Lon...20 H5
Pinvin Worcs...30 C4
Pinwherry S Ayrs...68 G2
Pinxton Derbys...51 L9
Pipe and Lyde Herefs...39 J12
Pipe Aston Herefs...39 J7
Pipe Gate Shrops...49 N7
Piperdam Angus...93 K8
Piperhill Highld...100 D5
Pipewell Nhants...42 B11
Pirbright Surrey...20 F11
Pirnie Border...80 E8
Pirnmill N Ayrs...75 N4
Pirton Herts...32 G9
Pishill Oxon...20 B5
Pistyll Gwynd...46 E3
Pitblae Abers...103 K3
Pitcairngreen P & K...92 F9
Pitcalnie Highld...107 N7
Pitcaple Abers...102 F7
Pitcarity Angus...94 F8
Pitchcombe Gloucs...29 L7
Pitchcott Bucks...31 Q9
Pitchford Shrops...39 K2
Pitch Green Bucks...20 C3
Pitchroy Moray...101 J7
Pitcombe Somset...17 P9
Pitcox E Loth...87 M7
Pitfichie Abers...102 E11
Pitglassie Abers...102 F6
Pitgrudy Highld...107 M3
Pitlessie Fife...86 G1
Pitlochry P & K...92 D4
Pitmachie Abers...102 E9
Pitmain Highld...99 J8
Pitmedden Abers...103 J9

Pitmedden Garden Abers...103 J9
Pitminster Somset...16 G11
Pitmuies Angus...93 P6
Pitmunie Abers...102 E11
Pitney Somset...17 L9
Pitroddie P & K...93 J10
Pitscottie Fife...93 M11
Pitsea Essex...22 E6
Pitsford Nhants...31 Q3
Pitstone Bucks...20 F1
Pittarrow Abers...95 M7
Pittenweem Fife...87 K2
Pitteuchar Fife...86 F3
Pittodrie House Hotel Abers...102 F9
Pitton Wilts...8 H2
Pittulie Abers...103 K2
Pity Me Dur...73 M10
Pixham Surrey...21 J12
Plains N Lans...85 N9
Plaish Shrops...39 K3
Plaistow Gt Lon...21 N6
Plaistow W Susx...10 H4
Plaitford Hants...9 J4
Plawsworth Dur...73 M10
Plaxtol Kent...22 C11
Playden E Susx...12 H6
Playford Suffk...35 K7
Play Hatch Oxon...20 B7
Playing Place Cnwll...3 J7
Playley Green Gloucs...29 K3
Plealey Shrops...38 H2
Plean Stirlg...85 P5
Pleasance Fife...93 J12
Pleasington Bl w D...57 M4
Pleasley Derbys...51 L7
Pleasurewood Hills Suffk...45 Q10
Plemstall Ches W...49 J2
Pleshey Essex...22 D1
Plockton Highld...97 L3
Plowden Shrops...38 H5
Pluckley Kent...12 H2
Pluckley Thorne Kent...12 H2
Plumbland Cumb...71 J7
Plumley Ches E...49 N1
Plumpton Cumb...71 P7
Plumpton E Susx...11 M7
Plumpton Nhants...31 N5
Plumpton Green E Susx...11 M6
Plumstead Gt Lon...21 N7
Plumstead Norfk...45 J3
Plumtree Notts...41 N2
Plungar Leics...41 Q1
Plurenden Kent...12 H3
Plush Dorset...7 Q3
Plwmp Cerdgn...36 F9
Plymouth C Plym...5 K8
Plympton C Plym...5 L8
Plymstock C Plym...5 L8
Plymtree Devon...6 E3
Pockley N York...66 F9
Pocklington E R Yk...60 D4
Podimore Somset...17 M10
Podington Bed...32 D4
Podmore Staffs...49 P8
Pointon Lincs...42 G4
Pokesdown BCP...8 G8
Polbain Highld...105 J1
Polbathic Cnwll...4 H8
Polbeth W Loth...86 B9
Poldark Mine Cnwll...2 G9
Polebrook Nhants...42 F11
Polegate E Susx...12 C8
Polesden Lacey Surrey...21 J11
Polesworth Warwks...40 H7
Polglass Highld...105 Q2
Polgooth Cnwll...3 M5
Polgown D & G...77 M9
Poling W Susx...10 G8
Poling Corner W Susx...10 G8
Polkerris Cnwll...4 D9
Pollington E R Yk...59 N9
Polloch Highld...89 Q3
Pollok C Glas...85 J9
Pollokshaws C Glas...85 J10
Pollokshields C Glas...85 J9
Polmassick Cnwll...3 L6
Polmont Falk...85 Q7
Polnish Highld...97 K12
Polperro Cnwll...4 F9
Polruan Cnwll...4 E9
Polstead Suffk...34 G8
Poltalloch Ag & B...83 M4
Poltimore Devon...6 C4
Polton Mdloth...86 F8
Polwarth Border...80 G4
Polyphant Cnwll...4 G4
Polzeath Cnwll...4 B4
Pomathorn Mdloth...86 F9
Pondersbridge Cambs...43 J10
Ponders End Gt Lon...21 M4
Ponsanooth Cnwll...2 H8
Ponsworthy Devon...5 N5
Pont Abraham Services Carmth...26 D7
Pontamman Carmth...25 Q6
Pontantwn Carmth...25 Q6
Pontardawe Neath...26 F7
Pontarddulais Swans...26 D7
Pont-ar-gothi Carmth...25 C5
Pontarsais Carmth...25 Q3
Pontblyddyn Flints...48 F4
Pontcysyllte Aqueduct Wrexhm...48 F7
Pontefract Wakefd...59 L9
Ponteland Nthumb...73 L6
Ponterwyd Cerdgn...37 M4
Pontesbury Shrops...38 H2
Pontesford Shrops...38 H2
Pontfadog Wrexhm...48 E7
Pontfaen Pembks...24 H3
Pont-faen Powys...27 J3
Pontgarreg Cerdgn...36 F9
Pont Henri Carmth...26 C5
Ponthir Torfn...28 C9
Ponthirwaun Cerdgn...36 D10
Pontllanfraith Caerph...27 P9
Pontlliw Swans...26 E8
Pontllyfni Gwynd...54 F10
Pontlottyn Caerph...27 N7
Pontnêddféchan Neath...27 J7
Pontnewydd Torfn...28 C9
Pontrhydfendigaid Cerdgn...37 M7
Pontrhydyfen Neath...26 H9
Pont-rhyd-y-groes Cerdgn...37 M6
Pontrilas Herefs...28 D3

Pont Robert Powys...48 C11
Pontsian Cerdgn...36 G10
Pontsticill Myr Td...27 M6
Pontwelly Carmth...36 G11
Pontyates Carmth...26 C7
Pontyberem Carmth...26 C6
Pontyclun Rhondd...27 L11
Pontycymer Brdgnd...27 J9
Pontymister Caerph...27 P10
Pont-y-pant Conwy...55 L10
Pontypool Torfn...28 C8
Pontypridd Rhondd...27 M10
Pontywaun Caerph...27 P9
Pool Cnwll...2 G7
Poole BCP...8 E8
Poole Keynes Gloucs...18 E2
Poolewe Highld...105 M6
Pooley Bridge Cumb...71 P10
Poolfold Staffs...50 B8
Poolhill Gloucs...29 K3
Pool in Wharfedale Leeds...58 G5
Pool of Muckhart Clacks...86 B3
Pool Street Essex...34 C8
Poplar Gt Lon...21 M7
Porchfield IoW...9 M8
Poringland Norfk...45 L9
Porkellis Cnwll...2 G8
Porlock Somset...15 Q3
Porlock Weir Somset...15 P3
Portachoillan Ag & B...83 L10
Port-an-Eorna Highld...97 K4
Port Appin Ag & B...90 C7
Port Askaig Ag & B...82 F8
Portavadie Ag & B...83 P8
Port Bannatyne Ag & B...84 B9
Portbury N Som...17 M2
Port Carlisle Cumb...71 K3
Port Charlotte Ag & B...82 C10
Portchester Hants...9 Q6
Port Driseach Ag & B...83 Q8
Port Ellen Ag & B...74 E4
Port Elphinstone Abers...102 G10
Portencalzie D & G...68 D5
Portencross N Ayrs...76 C2
Port Erin IoM...56 a6
Portesham Dorset...7 N5
Portessie Moray...101 N3
Port Eynon Swans...26 C10
Portfield Gate Pembks...24 G6
Portgate Devon...5 K4
Port Gaverne Cnwll...4 C4
Port Glasgow Inver...84 F7
Portgordon Moray...101 M3
Portgower Highld...110 B11
Porth Cnwll...3 J4
Porth Rhondd...27 L9
Porthallow Cnwll...2 H10
Porthallow Cnwll...4 F9
Porthcawl Brdgnd...26 H12
Porthcothan Cnwll...3 K2
Porthcurno Cnwll...2 B10
Port Henderson Highld...105 L7
Porthgain Pembks...24 E3
Porthgwarra Cnwll...2 B10
Porthill Staffs...49 Q6
Porthkerry V Glam...16 E3
Porthleven Cnwll...2 F9
Porthmadog Gwynd...47 J4
Porthmadog Gwynd...47 J4
Porth Navas Cnwll...2 H9
Porthoustock Cnwll...3 J10
Porthpean Cnwll...3 M5
Porthtowan Cnwll...2 G6
Porthyrhyd Carmth...26 C5
Portincaple Ag & B...84 D4
Portington E R Yk...60 D7
Portinnisherrich Ag & B...83 P2
Portinscale Cumb...71 L10
Port Isaac Cnwll...4 C4
Portishead N Som...17 L2
Portknockie Moray...101 N2
Portland Dorset...7 P8
Portlethen Abers...95 Q3
Portling D & G...70 E5
Portloe Cnwll...3 L7
Port Logan D & G...68 E10
Portmahomack Highld...107 Q5
Port Mary D & G...70 C6
Portmeirion Gwynd...47 J4
Portmellon Cnwll...3 M7
Port Mòr Highld...89 J1
Portnacroish Ag & B...90 C6
Portnaguran W Isls...111 e2
Portnahaven Ag & B...74 B2
Portnalong Highld...96 D3
Portnancon Highld...108 H4
Port nan Giùran W Isls...111 e2
Port nan Long W Isls...111 b4
Port Nis W Isls...111 e1
Portobello C Edin...86 G7
Portobello Wolves...40 C7
Port of Menteith Stirlg...85 K3
Port of Ness W Isls...111 e1
Porton Wilts...18 H12
Portpatrick D & G...68 D8
Port Quin Cnwll...4 B4
Port Ramsay Ag & B...90 B7
Portreath Cnwll...2 F6
Portreath Harbour Cnwll...2 F6
Portree Highld...96 F2
Port Righ Ag & B...75 M5
Port St Mary IoM...56 b7
Portscatho Cnwll...3 K8
Portsea C Port...9 Q7
Portskerra Highld...109 Q3
Portskewett Mons...28 F10
Portslade Br & H...11 K8
Portslade-by-Sea Br & H...11 L8
Portslogan D & G...68 D7
Portsmouth C Port...9 Q7
Portsmouth Calder...58 C8
Portsmouth Dockyard C Port...9 Q7
Port Soderick IoM...56 c6
Portsonachan Hotel Ag & B...83 E11
Portsoy Abers...102 D3
Portswood C Sotn...9 M5
Port Talbot Neath...26 G10
Port Tennant Swans...26 F9
Portuairk Highld...89 K3
Portway Sandw...40 C9
Portway Worcs...40 E11
Port Wemyss Ag & B...74 B3

Port William D & G...69 J9
Portwrinkle Cnwll...4 H9
Portyerrock D & G...69 L10
Poslingford Suffk...34 C7
Posso Border...79 K3
Postbridge Devon...5 N4
Postcombe Oxon...20 B4
Postling Kent...13 M3
Postwick Norfk...45 L8
Potarch Abers...95 K3
Potten End Herts...20 G2
Potter Brompton N York...67 L11
Potterhanworth Lincs...52 F9
Potterhanworth Booths Lincs...52 F9
Potter Heigham Norfk...45 N6
Potterne Wilts...18 E8
Potterne Wick Wilts...18 E8
Potters Bar Herts...21 K3
Potters Corner Kent...13 J2
Potters Crouch Herts...20 H3
Potters Marston Leics...41 L8
Potterspury Nhants...31 Q5
Potter Street Essex...21 P2
Potterton Abers...103 K11
Potto N York...66 C6
Potton C Beds...32 H6
Pott Shrigley Ches E...50 C5
Poughill Cnwll...14 D10
Poughill Devon...15 P9
Poulner Hants...8 H6
Poulshot Wilts...18 E8
Poulton Gloucs...18 G1
Poulton Wirral...56 G10
Poulton-le-Fylde Lancs...56 G2
Poundbury Dorset...7 P5
Poundffald Swans...26 D9
Pound Green E Susx...11 P5
Pound Green Suffk...34 C6
Pound Hill W Susx...11 L3
Poundon Bucks...31 N8
Poundsgate Devon...5 N6
Poundstock Cnwll...14 D11
Pouton D & G...69 L9
Povey Cross Surrey...11 L2
Powburn Nthumb...81 M10
Powderham Devon...6 C6
Powerstock Dorset...7 M4
Powfoot D & G...71 J3
Powick Worcs...39 Q10
Powmill P & K...86 B3
Poxwell Dorset...7 Q6
Poyle Slough...20 G7
Poynings W Susx...11 L7
Poyntington Dorset...17 P11
Poynton Ches E...50 B4
Poynton Green Wrekin...49 K10
Praa Sands Cnwll...2 E9
Praze-an-Beeble Cnwll...2 F8
Prees Shrops...49 K8
Preesall Lancs...62 G11
Prees Green Shrops...49 K8
Prees Heath Shrops...49 K7
Prees Higher Heath Shrops...49 K8
Pren-gwyn Cerdgn...36 G10
Prenteg Gwynd...47 J3
Prescot Knows...57 J9
Prescott Devon...16 E12
Presnerb Angus...94 C8
Prestatyn Denbgs...56 C11
Prestbury Ches E...50 B5
Prestbury Gloucs...29 N4
Presteigne Powys...38 G8
Prestleigh Somset...17 P7
Preston Border...87 P10
Preston Br & H...11 L8
Preston Devon...6 B7
Preston Dorset...7 Q6
Preston E R Yk...61 K7
Preston Gloucs...18 F1
Preston Herts...32 H10
Preston Kent...23 K10
Preston Kent...23 N10
Preston Lancs...57 K3
Preston Rutlnd...42 C9
Preston Somset...16 E8
Preston Torbay...6 B9
Preston Wilts...18 F5
Preston Bagot Warwks...30 F2
Preston Bissett Bucks...31 P8
Preston Bowyer Somset...16 F10
Preston Brockhurst Shrops...49 K9
Preston Brook Halton...57 K11
Preston Candover Hants...19 Q11
Preston Capes Nhants...31 M3
Preston Green Warwks...30 F2
Preston Gubbals Shrops...49 J10
Preston on Stour Warwks...30 G4
Preston on the Hill Halton...57 K11
Preston on Wye Herefs...28 D1
Prestonpans E Loth...86 H7
Preston Patrick Cumb...63 K5
Preston Plucknett Somset...17 M11
Preston St Mary Suffk...34 F6
Preston-under-Scar N York...65 J8
Preston upon the Weald Moors Wrekin...49 M11
Preston Wynne Herefs...39 K11
Prestwich Bury...57 P7
Prestwick S Ayrs...76 F6
Prestwick Airport S Ayrs...76 F6
Prestwood Bucks...20 E4
Prickwillow Cambs...33 P1
Priddy Somset...17 M6
Priest Hutton Lancs...63 K7
Priestland E Ayrs...77 J4
Priest Weston Shrops...38 F3
Primrosehill Border...87 P10
Primrose Hill Dudley...40 C9
Primsidemill Border...80 H8
Prince of Wales Bridge Mons...28 F10
Princes Risborough Bucks...20 D3
Princethorpe Warwks...41 K12
Princetown Devon...5 M5
Priors Hardwick Warwks...31 L3
Priorslee Wrekin...49 N12
Priors Marston Warwks...31 L3
Priors Norton Gloucs...29 M4
Priors Park Gloucs...29 M3
Priston BaNES...17 Q4
Prittlewell Sthend...22 G6
Privett Hants...10 B5
Prixford Devon...15 J5

Probus Cnwll...3 K6
Prora E Loth...87 K6
Prospect Cumb...71 J7
Prospidnick Cnwll...2 F9
Protstonhill Abers...102 H3
Prudhoe Nthumb...73 K8
Pubil P & K...91 L7
Publow BaNES...17 P4
Puckeridge Herts...33 L11
Puckington Somset...17 K11
Pucklechurch S Glos...17 Q2
Puddinglake Ches W...48 G2
Puddington Devon...15 P9
Puddletown Dorset...7 Q4
Pudsey Leeds...58 G7
Pulborough W Susx...10 G6
Pulford Ches W...48 G4
Pulham Dorset...7 Q2
Pulham Market Norfk...45 K11
Pulham St Mary Norfk...45 K11
Pulloxhill C Beds...32 F9
Pulverbatch Shrops...38 H2
Pumpherston W Loth...86 C8
Pumsaint Carmth...37 K11
Puncheston Pembks...24 H3
Puncknowle Dorset...7 M5
Punnett's Town E Susx...12 C6
Purbrook Hants...10 B8
Purfleet-on-Thames Thurr...22 B7
Puriton Somset...17 J7
Purleigh Essex...22 G3
Purley Gt Lon...21 L10
Purley on Thames W Berk...19 Q5
Purse Caundle Dorset...17 Q11
Purtington Somset...7 K2
Purton Gloucs...29 J7
Purton Gloucs...29 J7
Purton Wilts...18 G4
Purton Stoke Wilts...18 G3
Pury End Nhants...31 P5
Pusey Oxon...19 L2
Putley Herefs...28 H2
Putley Green Herefs...28 H2
Putney Gt Lon...21 K8
Puttenham Surrey...10 E1
Puxley Nhants...31 Q6
Puxton N Som...17 K4
Pwll Carmth...26 C8
Pwll-glâs Denbgs...48 C5
Pwllgloyw Powys...27 L3
Pwllheli Gwynd...46 F4
Pwllmeyric Mons...28 F9
Pwll-trap Carmth...25 M5
Pwll-y-glaw Neath...26 H9
Pye Bridge Derbys...51 K9
Pyecombe W Susx...11 L7
Pyle Brdgnd...26 H11
Pyleigh Somset...16 F9
Pylle Somset...17 N8
Pymoor Cambs...43 M11
Pymore Dorset...7 L4
Pyrford Surrey...20 G10
Pyrton Oxon...20 B3
Pytchley Nhants...32 C2
Pyworthy Devon...14 F10

Q

Quadring Lincs...42 H4
Quadring Eaudike Lincs...43 J4
Quainton Bucks...31 Q9
Quantock Hills Somset...16 G8
Quarff Shet...111 k4
Quarley Hants...19 J11
Quarndon Derbys...51 J11
Quarrier's Village Inver...84 F9
Quarrington Lincs...42 F2
Quarrington Hill Dur...73 N12
Quarry Bank Dudley...40 B9
Quarrywood Moray...101 J3
Quarter N Ayrs...84 D10
Quarter S Lans...85 M11
Quatford Shrops...39 N4
Quatt Shrops...39 N5
Quebec Dur...73 L11
Quedgeley Gloucs...29 L6
Queen Adelaide Cambs...33 P1
Queenborough Kent...22 H8
Queen Camel Somset...17 N10
Queen Charlton BaNES...17 P3
Queen Elizabeth Forest Park Stirlg...84 H3
Queen Elizabeth II Bridge Thurr...22 C8
Queenhill Worcs...29 M2
Queen Oak Dorset...8 B2
Queen's Bower IoW...9 P9
Queensbury C Brad...58 E7
Queensferry Flints...48 G2
Queensferry Crossing Fife...86 D6
Queenslie C Glas...85 L9
Queen's Park Bed...32 E6
Queen's Park Essex...22 D4
Queen's Park Nhants...31 Q2
Queenzieburn N Lans...85 L7
Quendon Essex...33 N10
Queniborough Leics...41 N5
Quenington Gloucs...30 F12
Queslett Birm...40 E8
Quethiock Cnwll...4 G7
Quidenham Norfk...44 G11
Quidhampton Wilts...8 G2
Quinton Nhants...31 R4
Quintrell Downs Cnwll...3 J4
Quixwood Border...87 P9
Quoig P & K...92 C10
Quorn Leics...41 M4
Quothquan S Lans...78 G2
Quoyburray Ork...111 h2
Quoyloo Ork...111 g2

R

Raasay Highld...96 G2
Rachan Mill Border...79 J3
Rachub Gwynd...55 J7
Rackenford Devon...15 P8
Rackham W Susx...10 G7
Rackheath Norfk...45 L7
Racks D & G...70 G1

Rackwick – Rudgwick 185

Rackwick Ork 111 g3
Radbourne Derbys 40 H1
Radcliffe Bury 57 P7
Radcliffe on Trent Notts 51 N11
Radclive Bucks 31 P7
Raddery Highld 107 L9
Radernie Fife 87 J1
Radford Covtry 41 J10
Radford Semele Warwks 31 J2
Radlett Herts 21 J4
Radley Oxon 19 N2
Radley Green Essex 22 D3
Radnage Bucks 20 C4
Radstock BaNES 17 P5
Radstone Nhants 31 N6
Radway Warwks 31 J5
Radwell Bed 32 E5
Radwell Herts 32 H9
Radwinter Essex 33 P8
Radyr Cardif 27 N11
Rafford Moray 100 G4
RAF Museum Cosford Shrops 39 P2
RAF Museum Hendon Gt Lon 21 K5
Ragdale Leics 41 P4
Raglan Mons 28 E7
Ragnall Notts 52 B8
Raigbeg Highld 99 M4
Rainbow Hill Worcs 39 Q10
Rainford St Hel 57 J8
Rainham Gt Lon 21 Q7
Rainham Medway 22 F9
Rainhill St Hel 57 J9
Rainhill Stoops St Hel 57 J10
Rainow Ches E 50 C6
Rainton N York 65 P11
Rainworth Notts 51 N8
Rait P & K 93 J9
Raithby Lincs 53 K6
Raithby Lincs 53 L9
Rake Hants 10 C5
Ralia Highld 99 K9
Ramasaig Highld 96 A2
Rame Cnwll 2 G8
Rame Cnwll 5 J9
Rampisham Dorset 7 N3
Rampside Cumb 62 E8
Rampton Cambs 33 L3
Rampton Notts 52 B7
Ramsbottom Bury 57 P5
Ramsbury Wilts 19 J6
Ramscraigs Highld 110 D9
Ramsdean Hants 10 B5
Ramsdell Hants 19 P8
Ramsden Oxon 31 J10
Ramsden Bellhouse Essex 22 E5
Ramsey Cambs 43 J11
Ramsey Essex 35 K10
Ramsey IoM 56 e3
Ramsey Forty Foot Cambs 43 K11
Ramsey Heights Cambs 43 J12
Ramsey Island Essex 23 J3
Ramsey Island Pembks 24 C4
Ramsey Mereside Cambs 43 J11
Ramsey St Mary's Cambs 43 J11
Ramsgate Kent 23 Q9
Ramsgill N York 65 K12
Ramshope Nthumb 80 G12
Ramshorn Staffs 50 E10
Ramsnest Common Surrey 10 F4
Ranby Lincs 52 H7
Ranby Notts 51 P5
Rand Lincs 52 F7
Randwick Gloucs 29 L7
Ranfurly Rens 84 G9
Rangemore Staffs 40 F3
Rangeworthy S Glos 29 J10
Rankinston E Ayrs 76 H8
Rannoch Station P & K 91 L5
Ranscombe Somset 16 C7
Ranskill Notts 51 P4
Ranton Staffs 49 Q10
Ranton Green Staffs 49 Q10
Ranworth Norfk 45 M7
Raploch Stirlg 85 N4
Rapness Ork 111 h1
Rascarrel D & G 70 D6
Rashfield Ag & B 84 C6
Rashwood Worcs 30 B2
Raskelf N York 66 C12
Rastrick Calder 58 F9
Ratagan Highld 97 N6
Ratby Leics 41 L6
Ratcliffe Culey Leics 41 J7
Ratcliffe on Soar Notts 41 L2
Ratcliffe on the Wreake Leics 41 N5
Rathen Abers 103 K3
Rathillet Fife 93 L10
Rathmell N York 63 P9
Ratho C Edin 86 D7
Ratho Station C Edin 86 D7
Rathven Moray 101 N3
Ratley Warwks 31 J5
Ratling Kent 23 N11
Ratlinghope Shrops 38 H3
Rattar Highld 110 F2
Rattery Devon 5 P7
Rattlesden Suffk 34 F5
Ratton Village E Susx 12 C9
Rattray P & K 92 H6
Raunds Nhants 32 E3
Ravenfield Rothm 51 L2
Ravenglass Cumb 62 C3
Raveningham Norfk 45 N10
Ravenscar N York 67 L7
Ravenscraig N Lans 85 N10
Ravensden Bed 32 F6
Ravenshead Notts 51 M9
Ravensthorpe Kirk 58 G9
Ravensthorpe Nhants 41 P12
Ravenstone Leics 41 K5
Ravenstone M Keyn 32 C6
Ravenstonedale Cumb 63 N2
Ravenstruther S Lans 77 Q3
Ravensworth N York 65 K6
Rawcliffe C York 59 M4
Rawcliffe E R Yk 59 P9
Rawdon Leeds 58 G6
Rawling Street Kent 22 H10
Rawmarsh Rothm 51 K2
Rawreth Essex 22 F5
Rawridge Devon 6 G2
Rawtenstall Lancs 57 P4
Raydon Suffk 34 H8
Rayleigh Essex 22 F5
Rayne Essex 34 C11
Raynes Park Gt Lon 21 K9
Reach Cambs 33 P4
Read Lancs 57 P2
Reading Readg 20 B8
Reading Services W Berk 20 A9
Reading Street Kent 12 H4
Reading Street Kent 23 Q9
Reagill Cumb 64 B4
Rearquhar Highld 107 M4
Rearsby Leics 41 P5
Reawla Cnwll 2 F8
Reay Highld 110 A3
Reculver Kent 23 N9
Red Ball Devon 16 E11
Redberth Pembks 25 J7
Redbourn Herts 20 H2
Redbourne N Linc 52 D4
Redbrook Gloucs 28 G6
Redbrook Wrexhm 49 K7
Redbrook Street Kent 12 H3
Redburn Highld 100 E6
Redcar R & Cl 66 E3
Redcastle D & G 70 D3
Redcastle Highld 107 J11
Redding Falk 85 Q7
Reddingmuirhead Falk 85 Q7
Reddish Stockp 50 B3
Redditch Worcs 30 D1
Rede Suffk 34 D5
Redenhall Norfk 45 L12
Redesmouth Nthumb 72 F5
Redford Abers 95 M7
Redford Angus 93 P6
Redford W Susx 10 D5
Redfordgreen Border 79 M6
Redgate Rhondd 27 L10
Redgorton P & K 92 G9
Redgrave Suffk 34 H2
Redhill Abers 95 M2
Red Hill BCP 8 G8
Redhill Herts 33 J9
Redhill N Som 17 M4
Redhill Surrey 21 L12
Redisham Suffk 45 N12
Redland Bristl 17 N2
Redland Ork 111 h2
Redlingfield Suffk 35 K3
Redlingfield Green Suffk 35 K3
Red Lodge Suffk 34 B3
Redlynch Somset 17 Q9
Redlynch Wilts 8 H3
Redmarley Worcs 39 N8
Redmarley D'Abitot Gloucs 29 K3
Redmarshall S on T 65 P4
Redmile Leics 42 B3
Redmire N York 65 J8
Redmyre Abers 95 M6
Rednal Shrops 48 G9
Redpath Border 80 D7
Red Point Highld 105 K8
Red Roses Carmth 25 L6
Red Row Nthumb 73 M2
Redruth Cnwll 2 G7
Redstone P & K 92 H8
Red Street Staffs 49 P5
Red Wharf Bay IoA 54 G5
Redwick Newpt 28 E11
Redwick S Glos 28 G10
Redworth Darltn 65 M3
Reed Herts 33 K9
Reedham Norfk 45 N9
Reedness E R Yk 60 D9
Reeds Holme Lancs 57 P4
Reepham Lincs 52 E8
Reepham Norfk 44 H5
Reeth N York 65 J7
Reeves Green Solhll 40 H11
Regil N Som 17 M4
Reiff Highld 108 A11
Reigate Surrey 21 K12
Reighton N York 67 N11
Reinigeadal W Isls 111 c3
Reisque Abers 103 J10
Reiss Highld 110 G5
Relubbus Cnwll 2 E8
Relugas Moray 100 F5
Remenham Wokham 20 C6
Remenham Hill Wokham 20 C6
Rempstone Notts 41 M3
Rendcomb Gloucs 30 D11
Rendham Suffk 35 M4
Rendlesham Suffk 35 M6
Renfrew Rens 84 H9
Renhold Bed 32 F6
Renishaw Derbys 51 K5
Rennington Nthumb 81 P9
Renton W Duns 84 G7
Renwick Cumb 72 B11
Repps Norfk 45 N6
Repton Derbys 40 H3
Reraig Highld 97 L4
Resaurie Highld 107 L12
Resipole Burn Highld 89 P4
Reskadinnick Cnwll 2 F7
Resolis Highld 107 L8
Resolven Neath 26 H8
Rest and be thankful Ag & B 84 D2
Reston Border 87 R9
Reswallie Angus 93 N5
Retford Notts 51 P5
Rettendon Common Essex 22 F4
Rettendon Village Essex 22 F4
Revesby Lincs 53 J10
Rewe Devon 6 C3
Rew Street IoW 9 M8
Reymerston Norfk 44 G8
Reynalton Pembks 25 J7
Reynoldston Swans 26 C10
Rezare Cnwll 4 H5
Rhandirmwyn Carmth 37 M11
Rhayader Powys 37 Q7
Rheindown Highld 106 H11
Rhenigidale W Isls 111 c3
Rhes-y-cae Flints 48 E2
Rhewl Denbgs 48 C4
Rhewl Denbgs 48 D6
Rhicarn Highld 108 C10
Rhiconich Highld 108 E5
Rhicullen Highld 107 L7
Rhigos Rhondd 27 K7
Rhives Highld 107 N3
Rhiwbina Cardif 27 N11
Rhiwderyn Newpt 28 B10
Rhiwlas Gwynd 54 H8
Rhoden Green Kent 12 D2
Rhodes Minnis Kent 13 M2
Rhodiad-y-brenin Pembks 24 D4
Rhonehouse D & G 70 C4
Rhoose V Glam 16 E3
Rhos Carmth 25 P2
Rhos Neath 26 G8
Rhoscolyn IoA 54 C6
Rhoscrowther Pembks 24 F8
Rhosesmor Flints 48 E2
Rhosgoch Powys 38 E11
Rhoshill Pembks 36 C11
Rhoshirwaun Gwynd 46 C5
Rhoslefain Gwynd 47 J9
Rhosllanerchrugog Wrexhm 48 F6
Rhosmeirch IoA 54 F6
Rhosneigr IoA 54 D7
Rhosnesni Wrexhm 48 G5
Rhôs-on-Sea Conwy 55 M5
Rhossili Swans 25 P10
Rhostryfan Gwynd 54 G9
Rhostyllen Wrexhm 48 F6
Rhosybol IoA 54 F4
Rhos-y-gwaliau Gwynd 47 Q4
Rhosymedre Wrexhm 48 F7
Rhu Ag & B 84 E6
Rhuallt Denbgs 48 C1
Rhubodach Ag & B 83 Q8
Rhuddlan Denbgs 55 Q6
Rhue Highld 106 B3
Rhunahaorine Ag & B 75 K3
Rhyd Gwynd 47 K3
Rhydargaeau Carmth 25 Q4
Rhydcymerau Carmth 26 D2
Rhyd-Ddu Gwynd 54 H10
Rhydlewis Cerdgn 36 F10
Rhydowen Cerdgn 36 G10
Rhyd-uchaf Gwynd 47 P4
Rhyd-y-clafdy Gwynd 46 E4
Rhyd-y-foel Conwy 55 N6
Rhydyfro Neath 26 F7
Rhyd-y-groes Gwynd 54 H8
Rhyd-y-pennau Cerdgn 37 K4
Rhyl Denbgs 55 Q5
Rhymney Caerph 27 N7
Rhynd P & K 92 H10
Rhynie Abers 101 P9
Rhynie Highld 107 P6
Ribbesford Worcs 39 P7
Ribbleton Lancs 57 K3
Ribchester Lancs 57 M2
Riby Lincs 52 H3
Riccall N York 59 N6
Riccarton Border 79 Q9
Riccarton E Ayrs 76 G4
Richards Castle Herefs 39 J8
Richmond Gt Lon 21 J8
Richmond N York 65 L7
Richmond Sheff 51 K4
Rickerscote Staffs 40 B4
Rickford N Som 17 L4
Rickham Devon 5 P11
Rickinghall Suffk 34 H2
Rickling Green Essex 33 N10
Rickmansworth Herts 20 G5
Riddell Border 80 C8
Riddlecombe Devon 15 K8
Riddlesden C Brad 58 E5
Ridge Dorset 8 D9
Ridge Herts 21 K4
Ridge Wilts 8 D2
Ridge Lane Warwks 40 H8
Ridgeway Derbys 51 K5
Ridgewell Essex 34 C8
Ridgewood E Susx 11 P6
Ridgmont C Beds 32 D9
Riding Mill Nthumb 72 H8
Ridlington Norfk 45 M4
Ridlington Rutlnd 42 C9
Ridsdale Nthumb 72 G4
Rievaulx N York 66 E9
Rigg D & G 71 L3
Riggend N Lans 85 M8
Righoul Highld 100 D5
Rigsby Lincs 53 L8
Rigside S Lans 78 E2
Riley Green Lancs 57 L4
Rilla Mill Cnwll 4 G5
Rillington N York 67 J11
Rimington Lancs 63 P11
Rimpton Somset 17 N10
Rimswell E R Yk 61 M8
Rinaston Pembks 24 H4
Rindleford Shrops 39 N3
Ringford D & G 69 Q7
Ringland Norfk 45 J7
Ringmer E Susx 11 N7
Ringmore Devon 5 N10
Ringmore Devon 6 C8
Ringorm Moray 101 K6
Ringsfield Suffk 45 N11
Ringsfield Corner Suffk 45 N11
Ringshall Herts 20 F1
Ringshall Suffk 34 G6
Ringshall Stocks Suffk 34 H6
Ringstead Nhants 32 E2
Ringstead Norfk 44 B3
Ringwood Hants 8 H6
Ringwould Kent 13 Q1
Rinmore Abers 101 M11
Ripe E Susx 11 P7
Ripley Derbys 51 K10
Ripley Hants 8 H7
Ripley N York 58 H3
Ripley Surrey 20 G11
Riplington Hants 9 Q3
Ripon N York 65 N12
Rippingale Lincs 42 F5
Ripple Kent 23 Q12
Ripple Worcs 29 M2
Ripponden Calder 58 D9
Risabus Ag & B 74 D4
Risbury Herefs 39 K10
Risby Suffk 34 D4
Risca Caerph 27 P9
Rise E R Yk 61 K6
Risegate Lincs 42 H4
Riseley Bed 32 F4
Riseley Wokham 20 B10
Rishangles Suffk 35 J3
Rishton Lancs 57 N3
Rishworth Calder 58 D9
Risley Derbys 41 L1
Risley Warrtn 57 M9
Risplith N York 58 G1
River Kent 13 P2
River W Susx 10 F5
Riverford Highld 107 J10
Riverhead Kent 21 P11
Rivington Lancs 57 L6
Rivington Services Lancs 57 L6
Roade Nhants 31 Q4
Roadmeetings S Lans 77 P2
Roadside E Ayrs 77 K7
Roadside Highld 110 D4
Roadwater Somset 16 D8
Roag Highld 96 C2
Roan of Craigoch S Ayrs 76 E9
Roath Cardif 27 P12
Roberton Border 79 N6
Roberton S Lans 78 F3
Robertsbridge E Susx 12 E5
Roberttown Kirk 58 G9
Robeston Wathen Pembks 25 J5
Robgill Tower D & G 71 L2
Robin Hood's Bay N York 67 K6
Roborough Devon 5 K7
Roborough Devon 15 K8
Robroyston C Glas 85 K8
Roby Knows 56 H10
Rocester Staffs 50 E11
Roch Pembks 24 F5
Rochdale Rochdl 58 B10
Roche Cnwll 3 L4
Rochester Medway 22 E9
Rochester Nthumb 72 E2
Rochford Essex 22 G5
Rochford Worcs 39 L8
Rock Cnwll 3 L1
Rock Nthumb 81 P9
Rock Worcs 39 N7
Rockbeare Devon 6 D4
Rockbourne Hants 8 G4
Rockcliffe Cumb 71 M4
Rockcliffe D & G 70 D5
Rockend Torbay 6 C9
Rock Ferry Wirral 56 G10
Rockfield Highld 107 Q6
Rockfield Mons 28 F6
Rockford Devon 15 N3
Rockhampton S Glos 28 H9
Rockhill Shrops 38 F6
Rockingham Nhants 42 C10
Rockland All Saints Norfk 44 G10
Rockland St Mary Norfk 45 M8
Rockland St Peter Norfk 44 G9
Rockley Notts 51 Q6
Rockliffe Lancs 57 Q4
Rockville Ag & B 84 D5
Rockwell End Bucks 20 C6
Rodborough Gloucs 29 L7
Rodbourne Swindn 18 G4
Rodbourne Wilts 18 D4
Rodden Dorset 7 N6
Rode Somset 18 B9
Rode Heath Ches E 49 P4
Rodel W Isls 111 c4
Roden Wrekin 49 L11
Rodhuish Somset 16 D8
Rodington Wrekin 49 L11
Rodington Heath Wrekin 49 L11
Rodley Gloucs 29 K6
Rodley Leeds 58 G6
Rodmarton Gloucs 29 N8
Rodmell E Susx 11 N8
Rodmersham Kent 22 H10
Rodmersham Green Kent 22 H10
Rodney Stoke Somset 17 L6
Rodsley Derbys 50 G11
Roecliffe N York 59 J2
Roe Green Herts 21 K2
Roe Green Herts 33 K9
Roehampton Gt Lon 21 K8
Roffey W Susx 11 K4
Rogart Highld 107 M2
Rogate W Susx 10 D5
Rogerstone Newpt 28 C10
Roghadal W Isls 111 c4
Rogiet Mons 28 E10
Roke Oxon 19 Q3
Roker Sundld 73 P8
Rollesby Norfk 45 P7
Rolleston Leics 41 Q7
Rolleston Notts 51 Q9
Rolleston on Dove Staffs 40 G3
Rolston E R Yk 61 L5
Rolvenden Kent 12 G4
Rolvenden Layne Kent 12 G4
Romaldkirk Dur 64 H3
Romanby N York 65 P8
Romanno Bridge Border 86 D11
Romansleigh Devon 15 M7
Romesdal Highld 104 E10
Romford Dorset 8 F5
Romford Gt Lon 21 P5
Romiley Stockp 50 C3
Romsey Cambs 33 M5
Romsey Hants 9 L3
Romsley Shrops 39 P5
Romsley Worcs 40 C10
Rona Highld 105 J10
Ronachan Ag & B 83 L11
Rookhope Dur 72 G11
Rookley IoW 9 N9
Rooks Bridge Somset 17 K5
Rooks Nest Somset 16 E9
Rookwith N York 65 L9
Roos E R Yk 61 M7
Roothams Green Bed 32 F5
Ropley Hants 9 Q2
Ropley Dean Hants 9 Q2
Ropsley Lincs 42 E4
Rora Abers 103 L5
Rorrington Shrops 38 F3
Rosarie Moray 101 M5
Rose Cnwll 2 H5
Rose Ash Devon 15 N7
Rosebank S Lans 77 N2
Rosebush Pembks 25 J3
Rosedale Abbey N York 66 G8
Rose Green Essex 34 E10
Rose Green Suffk 34 F7
Rose Green Suffk 34 F8
Rose Green W Susx 10 E9
Rosehall Highld 106 H2
Rosehearty Abers 103 J3
Rose Hill Lancs 57 P3
Roseisle Moray 100 H2
Roselands E Susx 12 C9
Rosemarket Pembks 24 G7
Rosemarkie Highld 107 M10
Rosemary Lane Devon 16 F12
Rosemount P & K 92 H7
Rosenannon Cnwll 3 L3
Rosewell Mdloth 86 F9
Roseworth S on T 65 Q3
Rosgill Cumb 71 Q11
Roskhill Highld 96 C1
Rosley Cumb 71 M6
Roslin Mdloth 86 F9
Rosliston Derbys 40 G4
Rosneath Ag & B 84 E6
Ross D & G 69 P9
Rossett Wrexhm 48 G4
Rossett Green N York 58 H4
Rossington Donc 51 N2
Ross-on-Wye Herefs 28 H4
Roster Highld 110 F7
Rostherne Ches E 57 N11
Rosthwaite Cumb 71 L11
Roston Derbys 50 F11
Rosyth Fife 86 D5
Rothbury Nthumb 73 J1
Rotherby Leics 41 P4
Rotherfield E Susx 12 B4
Rotherfield Greys Oxon 20 B7
Rotherfield Peppard Oxon 20 B7
Rotherham Rothm 51 K3
Rothersthorpe Nhants 31 Q3
Rotherwick Hants 20 B11
Rothes Moray 101 K5
Rothesay Ag & B 84 B9
Rothiebrisbane Abers 102 G7
Rothiemurchus Lodge Highld 99 P7
Rothienorman Abers 102 F7
Rothley Leics 41 N5
Rothmaise Abers 102 F8
Rothwell Leeds 59 J8
Rothwell Lincs 52 G4
Rothwell Nhants 32 B1
Rottal Lodge Angus 94 F7
Rottingdean Br & H 11 M9
Rottington Cumb 70 F11
Roucan D & G 78 G12
Rougham Norfk 44 D6
Rougham Suffk 34 E4
Rough Common Kent 23 L10
Roughpark Abers 101 L11
Roughton Lincs 53 J9
Roughton Norfk 45 K3
Roughton Shrops 39 N4
Roundbush Green Essex 22 C1
Round Green Luton 32 F11
Roundham Somset 7 K2
Roundhay Leeds 59 J6
Rounds Green Sandw 40 C9
Roundswell Devon 15 J6
Roundway Wilts 18 E7
Roundyhill Angus 93 L5
Rousay Ork 111 h1
Rousdon Devon 6 H5
Rousham Oxon 31 L8
Rous Lench Worcs 30 D4
Routenburn N Ayrs 84 D10
Routh E R Yk 61 J6
Row Cumb 63 J4
Rowanburn D & G 79 N12
Rowardennan Stirlg 84 F4
Rowarth Derbys 50 D3
Rowberrow Somset 17 L5
Rowde Wilts 18 E8
Rowen Conwy 55 L7
Rowfoot Nthumb 72 C8
Rowhedge Essex 34 G11
Rowington Warwks 30 G1
Rowland Derbys 50 G6
Rowland's Castle Hants 10 B7
Rowlands Gill Gatesd 73 L8
Rowledge Surrey 10 D2
Rowley Dur 73 J10
Rowley Regis Sandw 40 C9
Rowlstone Herefs 28 D4
Rowly Surrey 10 G2
Rowner Hants 9 P7
Rowney Green Worcs 40 D12
Rownhams Hants 9 L4
Rownhams Services Hants 9 L4
Rowrah Cumb 70 H10
Rowsham Bucks 32 C12
Rowsley Derbys 50 G7
Rowston Lincs 52 F11
Rowton Ches W 49 J3
Rowton Wrekin 49 L10
Roxburgh Border 80 F7
Roxby N Linc 60 F10
Roxton Bed 32 G6
Roxwell Essex 22 D2
Royal Leamington Spa Warwks 30 H2
Royal Sutton Coldfield Birm 40 E8
Royal Tunbridge Wells Kent 12 C3
Royal Wootton Bassett Wilts 18 F4
Royal Yacht Britannia C Edin 86 F6
Roy Bridge Highld 98 C11
Roydon Essex 21 N2
Roydon Norfk 34 H1
Roydon Norfk 44 B5
Roydon Hamlet Essex 21 N2
Royston Barns 59 J11
Royston Herts 33 K8
Royton Oldham 58 B11
Rozel Jersey 7 c1
Ruabon Wrexhm 48 F6
Ruaig Ag & B 88 D6
Ruan Lanihorne Cnwll 3 K7
Ruan Major Cnwll 2 G11
Ruan Minor Cnwll 2 G11
Ruardean Gloucs 28 H5
Ruardean Hill Gloucs 28 H5
Ruardean Woodside Gloucs 28 H5
Rubery Birm 40 C11
Rubha Ban W Isls 111 b6
Ruckhall Herefs 28 E2
Ruckinge Kent 13 K4
Ruckley Shrops 39 K3
Rudby N York 66 C6
Rudchester Nthumb 73 K7
Ruddington Notts 41 M2
Rudge Somset 18 C9
Rudgeway S Glos 28 H10
Rudgwick W Susx 10 H4

186 Rudheath – Seatown

Rudheath Ches W 49 M2
Rudley Green Essex 22 G3
Rudloe Wilts 18 C6
Rudry Caerph 27 P10
Rudston E R Yk 61 J1
Rudyard Staffs 50 C8
Ruecastle Border 80 E9
Rufford Lancs 57 J6
Rufford Abbey Notts 51 N7
Rufforth C York 59 M4
Rugby Warwks 41 L11
Rugby Services Warwks 41 L10
Rugeley Staffs 40 D4
Ruigh'riabhach Highld 105 Q4
Ruisgarry W Isls 111 b4
Ruishton Somset 16 H10
Ruisigearraidh W Isls 111 b4
Ruislip Gt Lon 20 H6
Rùm Highld 96 D9
Rumbach Moray 101 M5
Rumbling Bridge P & K 86 B3
Rumburgh Suffk 35 M1
Rumford Cnwll 3 K2
Rumford Falk 85 Q7
Rumney Cardif 27 P11
Runcorn Halton 57 K11
Runcton W Susx 10 E9
Runcton Holme Norfk 43 P8
Runfold Surrey 10 D1
Runhall Norfk 44 H8
Runham Norfk 45 P7
Runnington Somset 16 F10
Runswick N York 66 H4
Runtaleave Angus 94 E8
Runwell Essex 22 F5
Ruscombe Wokham 20 C8
Rushall Herefs 28 H2
Rushall Norfk 45 K12
Rushall Wilts 18 G9
Rushall Wsall 40 D7
Rushbrooke Suffk 34 E5
Rushbury Shrops 39 K4
Rushden Herts 33 K9
Rushden Nhants 32 D4
Rushenden Kent 22 H8
Rushford Norfk 34 F1
Rush Green Essex 23 M1
Rush Green Gt Lon 21 P6
Rush Green Warrtn 57 M10
Rushlake Green E Susx 12 D6
Rushmere Suffk 45 P11
Rushmoor Surrey 10 E3
Rushock Worcs 40 B12
Rusholme Manch 57 Q9
Rushton Nhants 42 B12
Rushton Spencer Staffs 50 C8
Rushwick Worcs 39 P10
Rushyford Dur 65 M2
Ruskie Stirlg 85 K3
Ruskington Lincs 52 F12
Rusland Cross Cumb 62 G5
Rusper W Susx 11 K3
Ruspidge Gloucs 29 J6
Russell's Water Oxon 20 B5
Russ Hill Surrey 11 K3
Rusthall Kent 12 C3
Rustington W Susx 10 G9
Ruston N York 67 K10
Ruston Parva E R Yk 60 H2
Ruswarp N York 67 J5
Rutherford Border 80 E7
Rutherglen S Lans 85 K10
Ruthernbridge Cnwll 3 M3
Ruthin Denbgs 48 D4
Ruthrieston C Aber 95 Q2
Ruthven Abers 101 P6
Ruthven Angus 93 K6
Ruthven Highld 99 L8
Ruthven Highld 99 M3
Ruthvoes Cnwll 3 K4
Ruthwell D & G 70 H3
Ruyton-XI-Towns Shrops 48 H10
Ryal Nthumb 72 H6
Ryall Dorset 7 K4
Ryall Worcs 29 M1
Ryarsh Kent 22 D10
Rydal Cumb 62 G2
Ryde IoW 9 P8
Rye E Susx 12 H6
Rye Foreign E Susx 12 H5
Rye Street Worcs 29 K2
Ryhall Rutlnd 42 E7
Ryhill Wakefd 59 J10
Ryhope Sundld 73 P9
Ryland Lincs 52 E7
Rylands Notts 41 M1
Rylstone N York 58 C3
Ryme Intrinseca Dorset 7 N1
Ryther N York 59 M6
Ryton Gatesd 73 K7
Ryton Shrops 39 N2
Ryton-on-Dunsmore Warwks 41 J11
RZSS Edinburgh Zoo C Edin 86 E7

S

Sabden Lancs 57 P2
Sacombe Herts 33 K11
Sacriston Dur 73 M10
Sadberge Darltn 65 N4
Saddell Ag & B 75 L6
Saddington Leics 41 P8
Saddlebow Norfk 43 P7
Saddlescombe W Susx 11 L7
Saffron Walden Essex 33 N8
Sageston Pembks 25 J7
Saham Hills Norfk 44 E9
Saham Toney Norfk 44 E9
Saighton Ches W 49 J3
St Abbs Border 81 J1
St Agnes Border 87 M9
St Agnes Cnwll 2 G5
St Agnes IoS 2 b3
St Agnes Mining District Cnwll 2 G6
St Albans Herts 21 J2
St Allen Cnwll 3 J5
St Andrew Guern 6 b2
St Andrews Fife 93 N11
St Andrews Botanic Garden Fife 93 N11
St Andrews Major V Glam 16 F2
St Andrews Well Dorset 7 L4
St Anne's Lancs 56 G3
St Ann's D & G 78 H9
St Ann's Chapel Cnwll 5 J6
St Ann's Chapel Devon 5 N10
St Anthony-in-Meneage Cnwll 2 H10
St Anthony's Hill E Susx 12 D9
St Arvans Mons 28 F9
St Asaph Denbgs 48 B1
St Athan V Glam 16 D3
St Aubin Jersey 7 b2
St Austell Cnwll 3 M5
St Bees Cumb 70 F12
St Blazey Cnwll 3 N5
St Boswells Border 80 D7
St Brelade Jersey 7 a2
St Brelade's Bay Jersey 7 a2
St Breock Cnwll 3 L2
St Breward Cnwll 4 D5
St Briavels Gloucs 28 G7
St Brides Major V Glam 16 B2
St Brides-super-Ely V Glam 27 M12
St Brides Wentlooge Newpt 28 C11
St Budeaux C Plym 5 K8
Saintbury Gloucs 30 E6
St Buryan Cnwll 2 C9
St Catherines Ag & B 84 C2
St Chloe Gloucs 29 L8
St Clears Carmth 25 M5
St Cleer Cnwll 4 F6
St Clement Cnwll 3 J7
St Clement Jersey 7 c2
St Clether Cnwll 4 F4
St Colmac Ag & B 83 Q9
St Columb Major Cnwll 3 K3
St Columb Minor Cnwll 3 J4
St Columb Road Cnwll 3 K4
St Combs Abers 103 L3
St Cross South Elmham Suffk 45 L12
St Cyrus Abers 95 M8
St David's P & K 92 E10
St Davids Pembks 24 D4
St Davids Cathedral Pembks 24 D4
St Day Cnwll 2 G7
St Dennis Cnwll 3 L4
St Dogmaels Pembks 36 C10
St Dominick Cnwll 5 J6
St Donats V Glam 16 C3
St Endellion Cnwll 4 C5
St Enoder Cnwll 3 K4
St Erme Cnwll 3 J6
St Erney Cnwll 4 H8
St Erth Cnwll 2 E8
St Erth Praze Cnwll 2 E8
St Ervan Cnwll 3 K2
St Eval Cnwll 3 K3
St Ewe Cnwll 3 L6
St Fagans Cardif 27 N12
St Fagans: National History Museum Cardif 27 N12
St Fergus Abers 103 M5
St Fillans P & K 91 Q10
St Florence Pembks 25 J8
St Gennys Cnwll 4 C11
St George Conwy 55 P6
St Georges N Som 17 K4
St George's V Glam 16 E2
St Germans Cnwll 4 H8
St Giles in the Wood Devon 15 J8
St Giles-on-the-Heath Devon 4 H3
St Harmon Powys 38 B7
St Helen Auckland Dur 65 L3
St Helen's E Susx 12 G7
St Helens IoW 9 Q9
St Helens St Hel 57 K9
St Helier Gt Lon 21 L9
St Helier Jersey 7 b2
St Hilary Cnwll 2 E9
St Hilary V Glam 16 D2
St Ippolyts Herts 32 H10
St Ishmael's Pembks 24 E7
St Issey Cnwll 3 L2
St Ive Cnwll 4 G6
St Ives Cambs 33 K3
St Ives Cnwll 2 D7
St James's End Nhants 31 Q3
St James South Elmham Suffk 35 M1
St Jidgey Cnwll 3 L2
St John Cnwll 5 J9
St John Jersey 7 b1
St John's E Susx 11 P4
St John's IoM 56 b5
St John's Kent 21 Q11
St Johns Surrey 20 F10
St Johns Worcs 39 Q10
St John's Chapel Devon 15 J6
St John's Chapel Dur 72 F12
St John's Fen End Norfk 43 N7
St John's Kirk S Lans 78 F2
St John's Town of Dalry D & G 69 N3
St John's Wood Gt Lon 21 L6
St Judes IoM 56 d3
St Just Cnwll 2 B9
St Just-in-Roseland Cnwll 3 J8
St Just Mining District Cnwll 2 B8
St Katherines Abers 102 G8
St Keverne Cnwll 2 H10
St Kew Cnwll 3 M1
St Kew Highway Cnwll 3 M1
St Keyne Cnwll 4 F7
St Lawrence Essex 23 J3
St Lawrence IoW 9 N11
St Lawrence Jersey 7 b1
St Lawrence Kent 23 Q9
St Leonards Bucks 20 E3
St Leonards Dorset 8 G6
St Leonards E Susx 12 F8
St Levan Cnwll 2 B10
St Lythans V Glam 16 F2
St Mabyn Cnwll 3 M2
St Madoes P & K 92 H10
St Margarets Herefs 28 D3
St Margarets Herts 21 M2
St Margaret's at Cliffe Kent 13 Q2
St Margaret's Hope Ork 111 h3
St Margaret South Elmham Suffk 45 M12
St Marks IoM 56 c6
St Martin Cnwll 2 H10
St Martin Cnwll 4 G8
St Martin Guern 6 b2
St Martin Jersey 7 c1
St Martin's IoS 2 c1
St Martin's P & K 92 H9
St Martin's Shrops 48 G8
St Mary Jersey 7 a1
St Mary Bourne Hants 19 M10
St Marychurch Torbay 6 C9
St Mary Church V Glam 16 D2
St Mary Cray Gt Lon 21 P9
St Mary in the Marsh Kent 13 K5
St Mary's IoS 2 c2
St Mary's Ork 111 h2
St Mary's Bay Kent 13 L5
St Mary's Hoo Medway 22 F7
St Mary's Platt Kent 22 D11
St Maughans Green Mons 28 F5
St Mawes Cnwll 3 J8
St Mawgan Cnwll 3 K3
St Mellion Cnwll 5 J7
St Mellons Cardif 27 P11
St Merryn Cnwll 3 K2
St Michael Caerhays Cnwll 3 L7
St Michael Church Somset 17 J9
St Michael Penkevil Cnwll 3 J7
St Michaels Kent 12 H3
St Michaels Worcs 39 L8
St Michael's Mount Cnwll 2 D9
St Michael's on Wyre Lancs 57 J1
St Minver Cnwll 3 L1
St Monans Fife 87 K2
St Neot Cnwll 4 E6
St Neots Cambs 32 H5
St Newlyn East Cnwll 3 J5
St Nicholas Pembks 24 F2
St Nicholas V Glam 16 E2
St Nicholas-at-Wade Kent 23 N9
St Ninians Stirlg 85 N5
St Olaves Norfk 45 P9
St Osyth Essex 23 L1
St Ouen Jersey 7 a1
St Owen's Cross Herefs 28 G4
St Paul's Cray Gt Lon 21 P9
St Paul's Walden Herts 32 H11
St Peter Jersey 7 a1
St Peter Port Guern 6 c2
St Peter's Guern 6 b2
St Peter's Kent 23 Q9
St Peter's Hill Cambs 33 J3
St Pinnock Cnwll 4 F7
St Quivox S Ayrs 76 F6
St Sampson Guern 6 c1
St Saviour Guern 6 b2
St Saviour Jersey 7 b2
St Stephen Cnwll 3 L5
St Stephens Cnwll 4 H3
St Stephens Cnwll 5 J8
St Teath Cnwll 4 D4
St Thomas Devon 6 B5
St Tudy Cnwll 3 N1
St Twynnells Pembks 24 G8
St Veep Cnwll 4 E8
St Vigeans Angus 93 Q7
St Wenn Cnwll 3 L3
St Weonards Herefs 28 F4
Salcombe Devon 5 P11
Salcombe Regis Devon 6 F5
Salcott-cum-Virley Essex 23 J1
Sale Traffd 57 P9
Saleby Lincs 53 M7
Sale Green Worcs 30 B3
Salehurst E Susx 12 E5
Salem Cerdgn 37 L4
Salen Ag & B 89 M7
Salen Highld 89 N4
Salford C Beds 32 D8
Salford Oxon 30 H8
Salford Salfd 57 P8
Salford Priors Warwks 30 E4
Salfords Surrey 11 L2
Salhouse Norfk 45 M7
Saline Fife 86 B4
Salisbury Wilts 8 G2
Salisbury Plain Wilts 18 F10
Salkeld Dykes Cumb 71 Q7
Sallachy Highld 107 J1
Salle Norfk 45 J5
Salmonby Lincs 53 K8
Salperton Gloucs 30 E9
Salsburgh N Lans 85 N9
Salt Staffs 40 C2
Saltaire C Brad 58 F6
Saltaire C Brad 58 F6
Saltash Cnwll 5 J8
Saltburn Highld 107 M8
Saltburn-by-the-Sea R & Cl 66 F4
Saltby Leics 42 C5
Saltcoats N Ayrs 76 D3
Saltcotes Lancs 56 G4
Saltdean Br & H 11 M9
Salterbeck Cumb 70 G9
Salterforth Lancs 58 B5
Salterswall Ches W 49 L3
Salterton Wilts 18 G12
Saltfleet Lincs 53 M5
Saltfleetby All Saints Lincs 53 M5
Saltfleetby St Clement Lincs 53 M5
Saltfleetby St Peter Lincs 53 M5
Saltford BaNES 17 P3
Salthouse Norfk 44 H2
Saltley Birm 40 E9
Saltmarshe E R Yk 60 D8
Saltney Flints 48 H3
Salton N York 66 G10
Saltrens Devon 14 H7
Saltwood Kent 13 M3
Salvington W Susx 10 H8
Salwarpe Worcs 39 Q9
Salway Ash Dorset 7 L4
Sambourne Warwks 30 D2
Sambrook Wrekin 49 N9
Sampford Arundel Somset 16 F11
Sampford Brett Somset 16 E7
Sampford Courtenay Devon 15 L11
Sampford Moor Somset 16 F11
Sampford Peverell Devon 16 D12
Sampford Spiney Devon 5 L6
Samsonlane Ork 111 i2
Samuelston E Loth 87 J7
Sanaigmore Ag & B 82 C8
Sancreed Cnwll 2 C9
Sancton E R Yk 60 F6
Sandaig Highld 97 K8
Sandal Magna Wakefd 59 J9
Sanday Ork 111 i1
Sanday Airport Ork 111 i1
Sandbach Ches E 49 N4
Sandbach Services Ches E 49 P4
Sandbank Ag & B 84 C6
Sandbanks BCP 8 F9
Sandend Abers 102 D3
Sanderstead Gt Lon 21 M10
Sandford Cumb 64 D4
Sandford Devon 15 P10
Sandford Dorset 8 D9
Sandford Hants 8 H7
Sandford IoW 9 N10
Sandford N Som 17 K4
Sandford S Lans 77 M3
Sandford-on-Thames Oxon 19 N1
Sandford Orcas Dorset 17 P11
Sandford St Martin Oxon 31 K8
Sandgate Kent 13 M3
Sandhaven Abers 103 K2
Sandhead D & G 68 E8
Sand Hills Leeds 59 J6
Sandhills Oxon 31 M11
Sandhills Surrey 10 F3
Sandhoe Nthumb 72 H7
Sandhole Ag & B 83 Q4
Sand Hole E R Yk 60 D6
Sandholme E R Yk 60 E7
Sandhurst Br For 20 D10
Sandhurst Gloucs 29 L4
Sandhurst Kent 12 F4
Sand Hutton N York 59 P3
Sandhutton N York 65 P10
Sandiacre Derbys 51 L12
Sandilands Lincs 53 N7
Sandleheath Hants 8 G4
Sandleigh Oxon 19 M1
Sandley Dorset 8 B3
Sandness Shet 111 j4
Sandon Essex 22 E3
Sandon Herts 33 K9
Sandon Staffs 40 C2
Sandon Bank Staffs 40 C2
Sandown IoW 9 P9
Sandplace Cnwll 4 F8
Sandridge Herts 21 J2
Sandringham Norfk 44 B4
Sandsend N York 67 J5
Sandtoft N Linc 60 D11
Sandway Kent 22 H12
Sandwich Kent 23 P10
Sandwick Shet 111 k5
Sandwick W Isls 111 d2
Sandwith Cumb 70 F11
Sandy C Beds 32 G7
Sandyford D & G 79 K9
Sandygate Devon 6 B7
Sandygate IoM 56 d3
Sandyhills D & G 70 E5
Sandylands Lancs 62 H9
Sandy Lane Wilts 18 E7
Sandy Park Devon 5 P3
Sangobeg Highld 108 H3
Sangomore Highld 108 H3
Sankyn's Green Worcs 39 P8
Sanna Highld 89 K3
Sanndabhaig W Isls 111 d2
Sannox N Ayrs 75 Q4
Sanquhar D & G 77 N8
Santon Bridge Cumb 62 C2
Santon Downham Suffk 44 D11
Sapcote Leics 41 L8
Sapey Common Herefs 39 M8
Sapiston Suffk 34 F2
Sapley Cambs 33 J2
Sapperton Gloucs 29 N7
Sapperton Lincs 42 E4
Saracen's Head Lincs 43 K5
Sarclet Highld 110 G7
Sarisbury Hants 9 N5
Sarn Powys 38 E4
Sarnau Cerdgn 36 E9
Sarnau Powys 48 E11
Sarn Mellteyrn Gwynd 46 D5
Sarn Park Services Brdgnd 27 J11
Saron Carmth 26 E6
Saron Gwynd 54 G8
Sarratt Herts 20 G4
Sarre Kent 23 N9
Sarsden Oxon 30 H9
Satley Dur 73 K11
Satterleigh Devon 15 L7
Satterthwaite Cumb 62 G4
Sauchen Abers 102 F11
Saucher P & K 92 H8
Sauchieburn Abers 95 L7
Saul Gloucs 29 K7
Saundby Notts 52 B6
Saundersfoot Pembks 25 K7
Saunderton Bucks 20 C3
Saunton Devon 14 H5
Sausthorpe Lincs 53 L9
Savile Town Kirk 58 G9
Sawbridge Warwks 31 L2
Sawbridgeworth Herts 21 P1
Sawdon N York 67 K9
Sawley Derbys 41 L2
Sawley Lancs 63 P11
Sawley N York 58 G1
Sawston Cambs 33 M7
Sawtry Cambs 42 G12
Saxby Leics 42 B6
Saxby Lincs 52 E6
Saxby All Saints N Linc 60 G10
Saxelbye Leics 41 P4
Saxham Street Suffk 34 H5
Saxilby Lincs 52 C8
Saxlingham Norfk 44 G3
Saxlingham Green Norfk 45 L10
Saxlingham Nethergate Norfk 45 K10
Saxlingham Thorpe Norfk 45 K9
Saxmundham Suffk 35 N4
Saxondale Notts 51 P11
Saxon Street Cambs 34 B5
Saxtead Suffk 35 L4
Saxtead Green Suffk 35 L4
Saxtead Little Green Suffk 35 L4
Saxthorpe Norfk 45 J4
Saxton N York 59 L6
Sayers Common W Susx 11 L6
Scackleton N York 66 F11
Scadabay W Isls 111 c3
Scadabhagh W Isls 111 c3
Scafell Pike Cumb 62 E2
Scaftworth Notts 51 P3
Scagglethorpe N York 67 J11
Scalasaig Ag & B 82 E4
Scalby E R Yk 60 E8
Scalby N York 67 L9
Scaldwell Nhants 41 Q11
Scaleby Cumb 71 P3
Scalebyhill Cumb 71 P3
Scales Cumb 62 F7
Scales Cumb 71 M9
Scalford Leics 41 Q3
Scaling N York 66 G5
Scalloway Shet 111 k4
Scalpay Highld 96 H4
Scalpay W Isls 111 c3
Scamblesby Lincs 53 J7
Scamodale Highld 90 B2
Scampston N York 67 J11
Scampton Lincs 52 D7
Scaniport Highld 99 J2
Scapegoat Hill Kirk 58 E10
Scarba Ag & B 83 K3
Scarborough N York 67 M9
Scarcewater Cnwll 3 K5
Scarcliffe Derbys 51 L7
Scarcroft Leeds 59 J6
Scarfskerry Highld 110 F2
Scarinish Ag & B 88 C7
Scarisbrick Lancs 56 H6
Scarning Norfk 44 F7
Scarrington Notts 51 Q11
Scartho NE Lin 53 J3
Scatsta Airport Shet 111 k3
Scaur D & G 70 D5
Scawby N Linc 52 D3
Scawsby Donc 59 M12
Scawthorpe Donc 59 M11
Scawton N York 66 D10
Scayne's Hill W Susx 11 M5
Scethrog Powys 27 M4
Scholar Green Ches E 49 Q4
Scholes Kirk 58 F11
Scholes Leeds 59 J6
Scholes Rothm 51 K2
Scholes Wigan 57 L7
Scissett Kirk 58 G11
Scleddau Pembks 24 G2
Scofton Notts 51 N5
Scole Norfk 35 J2
Scone P & K 92 H9
Sconser Highld 96 F4
Scoonie Fife 86 H2
Scopwick Lincs 52 F11
Scoraig Highld 105 Q3
Scorborough E R Yk 60 H5
Scorrier Cnwll 2 G7
Scorton Lancs 63 J11
Scorton N York 65 M7
Scotby Cumb 71 P5
Scotch Corner N York 65 L6
Scotch Corner Rest Area N York 65 L6
Scotforth Lancs 63 J9
Scothern Lincs 52 E7
Scotlandwell P & K 86 E2
Scotscalder Station Highld 110 C5
Scot's Gap Nthumb 73 J4
Scotsmill Abers 102 D10
Scotstoun C Glas 85 J9
Scotswood N u Ty 73 L7
Scotter Lincs 52 C4
Scotterthorpe Lincs 52 C3
Scottish Seabird Centre E Loth 87 K5
Scotton Lincs 52 C4
Scotton N York 59 J3
Scotton N York 65 L8
Scoulton Norfk 44 G9
Scourie Highld 108 D6
Scourie More Highld 108 D7
Scousburgh Shet 111 k5
Scrabster Highld 110 C2
Scraesburgh Border 80 F9
Scrane End Lincs 43 L2
Scraptoft Leics 41 P6
Scratby Norfk 45 Q7
Scrayingham N York 60 C3
Scredington Lincs 42 F3
Scremby Lincs 53 M9
Scremerston Nthumb 81 L4
Screveton Notts 51 Q11
Scriven N York 59 J3
Scrooby Notts 51 P3
Scropton Derbys 40 G2
Scrub Hill Lincs 52 H11
Scruton N York 65 N8
Scullomie Highld 109 L4
Sculthorpe Norfk 44 E4
Scunthorpe N Linc 60 F11
Seaborough Dorset 7 K2
Seabridge Staffs 49 Q6
Seabrook Kent 13 M3
Seaburn Sundld 73 P8
Seacombe Wirral 56 G10
Seacroft Leeds 59 J7
Seafield W Loth 86 B8
Seaford E Susx 11 P9
Seaforth Sefton 56 G9
Seagrave Leics 41 N4
Seaham Dur 73 P10
Seahouses Nthumb 81 P7
Seal Kent 22 B11
Sealand Flints 48 G2
Seale Surrey 10 E1
Seamer N York 66 C5
Seamer N York 67 L10
Seamill N Ayrs 76 D2
Sea Palling Norfk 45 N5
Searby Lincs 52 F3
Seasalter Kent 23 L9
Seascale Cumb 62 B3
Seathwaite Cumb 62 E3
Seatoller Cumb 71 L11
Seaton Cnwll 4 G8
Seaton Cumb 70 G8
Seaton Devon 6 H5
Seaton E R Yk 61 K5
Seaton Kent 23 N10
Seaton Nthumb 73 N5
Seaton Rutlnd 42 C9
Seaton Carew Hartpl 66 D2
Seaton Delaval Nthumb 73 N6
Seaton Ross E R Yk 60 D6
Seaton Sluice Nthumb 73 N5
Seatown Dorset 7 K4
Seatown Moray 101 K2

Seave Green N York 66 D7
Seaview IoW 9 Q8
Seaville Cumb 71 J5
Seavington St Mary Somset 17 K12
Seavington St Michael
  Somset 17 K12
Sebastopol Torfn 28 C8
Sebergham Cumb 71 M7
Seckington Warwks 40 H6
Second Severn Crossing
  Mons 28 F10
Sedbergh Cumb 63 M4
Sedbury Gloucs 28 Q9
Sedbusk N York 64 F8
Sedgeberrow Worcs 30 D6
Sedgebrook Lincs 42 C3
Sedgefield Dur 65 P2
Sedgeford Norfk 44 B3
Sedgehill Wilts 8 C2
Sedgemoor Services Somset ...17 J5
Sedgley Dudley 40 B8
Sedgley Park Bury 57 P8
Sedgwick Cumb 63 K5
Sedlescombe E Susx 12 F6
Sedrup Bucks 20 C2
Seend Wilts 18 D8
Seend Cleeve Wilts 18 D8
Seer Green Bucks 20 F5
Seething Norfk 45 M9
Sefton Sefton 56 G8
Seighford Staffs 49 Q9
Seion Gwynd 54 H8
Seisdon Staffs 39 Q3
Selattyn Shrops 48 F8
Selborne Hants 10 C4
Selby N York 59 N7
Selham W Susx 10 E6
Selhurst Gt Lon 21 M9
Selkirk Border 79 P3
Sellack Herefs 28 G4
Sellafield Station Cumb 62 B2
Sellafirth Shet 111 k2
Sellindge Kent 13 L3
Selling Kent 23 K11
Sells Green Wilts 18 D8
Selly Oak Birm 40 D10
Selmeston E Susx 11 P8
Selsdon Gt Lon 21 M10
Selsey W Susx 10 D10
Selside N York 64 E11
Selsley Gloucs 29 L7
Selsted Kent 13 N2
Selston Notts 51 L9
Selworthy Somset 16 C6
Semer Suffk 34 G7
Semington Wilts 18 D8
Semley Wilts 8 D3
Send Surrey 20 G11
Senghenydd Caerph 27 N10
Sennen Cnwll 2 B10
Sennen Cove Cnwll 2 B9
Sennybridge Powys 27 K3
Sessay N York 66 C11
Setchey Norfk 43 Q7
Seton Mains E Loth 87 J7
Settle N York 63 P9
Settrington N York 67 J12
Sevenhampton Gloucs 30 D9
Sevenhampton Swindn 18 H3
Seven Kings Gt Lon 21 P6
Sevenoaks Kent 21 Q11
Sevenoaks Weald Kent 21 Q12
Seven Sisters Neath 26 H7
Severn Beach S Glos 28 G10
Severn Bridge S Glos 28 G10
Severn Stoke Worcs 39 Q12
Severn View Services S Glos ...28 G10
Sevington Kent 13 K2
Sewards End Essex 33 P8
Sewell C Beds 32 E11
Sewerby E R Yk 61 L1
Seworgan Cnwll 2 G9
Sewstern Leics 42 C6
Sgalpaigh W Isls 111 c3
Sgiogarstaigh W Isls 111 e1
Shabbington Bucks 31 P11
Shackerstone Leics 41 J6
Shackleford Surrey 10 E2
Shader W Isls 111 d1
Shadforth Dur 73 N11
Shadingfield Suffk 45 P12
Shadoxhurst Kent 13 J3
Shadwell Leeds 59 J6
Shadwell Norfk 44 F12
Shaftenhoe End Herts 33 L8
Shaftesbury Dorset 8 C3
Shafton Barns 59 K11
Shakerley Wigan 57 M8
Shalbourne Wilts 19 K7
Shalden Hants 10 B2
Shaldon Devon 6 C8
Shalfleet IoW 9 M9
Shalford Essex 34 C10
Shalford Surrey 10 G1
Shalford Green Essex 34 B10
Shalmsford Street Kent 23 L11
Shalstone Bucks 31 N6
Shamley Green Surrey 10 G2
Shandford Angus 94 H9
Shandon Ag & B 84 E6
Shandwick Highld 107 P7
Shangton Leics 41 Q8
Shanklin IoW 9 P10
Shantron Ag & B 84 F5
Shap Cumb 71 Q11
Shapinsay Ork 111 h2
Shapwick Dorset 8 D7
Shapwick Somset 17 K8
Shard End Birm 40 F9
Shardlow Derbys 41 K2
Shareshill Staffs 40 C6
Sharlston Wakefd 59 K9
Sharmans Cross Solihll 40 F10
Sharnbrook Bed 32 E5
Sharnford Leics 41 L8
Sharoe Green Lancs 57 K3
Sharow N York 65 N12
Sharpenhoe C Beds 32 F10
Sharperton Nthumb 81 K12
Sharpness Gloucs 29 J8
Sharrington Norfk 44 G3
Shatterford Worcs 39 P6
Shaugh Prior Devon 5 L7
Shavington Ches E 49 M5

Shaw Oldham 58 C11
Shaw Swindn 18 G4
Shaw W Berk 19 N7
Shaw Wilts 18 D7
Shawbirch Wrekin 49 M11
Shawbost W Isls 111 d1
Shawbury Shrops 49 K10
Shawell Leics 41 M10
Shawford Hants 9 M3
Shawhead D & G 70 E1
Shaw Mills N York 58 G2
Shearington D & G 70 G3
Shearsby Leics 41 N8
Shearston Somset 16 H9
Shebbear Devon 14 H9
Shebdon Staffs 49 N9
Shebster Highld 110 D3
Shedfield Hants 9 P5
Sheen Staffs 50 E8
Sheepridge Kirk 58 F9
Sheepscar Leeds 58 H7
Sheepscombe Gloucs 29 M6
Sheepstor Devon 5 L6
Sheepwash Devon 14 H10
Sheepy Magna Leics 41 J7
Sheepy Parva Leics 41 J7
Sheering Essex 21 P1
Sheerness Kent 22 H8
Sheerwater Surrey 20 G10
Sheet Hants 10 C5
Sheffield Sheff 51 J4
Sheffield Park E Susx 11 N5
Shefford C Beds 32 G8
Sheigra Highld 108 D4
Sheinton Shrops 39 L2
Shelderton Shrops 38 H6
Sheldon Birm 40 F9
Sheldon Derbys 50 F7
Sheldon Devon 6 F2
Sheldwich Kent 23 K11
Shelfanger Norfk 45 J12
Shelford Notts 51 P11
Shelley Kirk 58 G11
Shelley Suffk 34 G8
Shellingford Oxon 19 K3
Shellow Bowells Essex 22 C2
Shelsley Beauchamp Worcs ...39 N9
Shelsley Walsh Worcs 39 N9
Shelton Bed 32 E3
Shelton Norfk 45 K11
Shelton Notts 42 B2
Shelton Lock C Derb 41 J2
Shelton Under Harley Staffs ..49 P7
Shelve Shrops 38 G3
Shelwick Herefs 28 F1
Shenfield Essex 22 C4
Shenington Oxon 31 J5
Shenley Herts 21 J4
Shenley Brook End M Keyn 32 B9
Shenley Church End M Keyn ...32 B9
Shenmore Herefs 28 D2
Shennanton D & G 69 J6
Shenstone Staffs 40 E6
Shenstone Worcs 39 Q7
Shenton Leics 41 J7
Shenval Moray 101 J8
Shephall Herts 33 J11
Shepherd's Bush Gt Lon 21 K7
Shepherdswell Kent 13 N1
Shepley Kirk 58 G11
Shepperton Surrey 20 H9
Shepreth Cambs 33 L7
Shepshed Leics 41 L4
Shepton Beauchamp Somset ...17 K11
Shepton Mallet Somset 17 N7
Shepton Montague Somset 17 P9
Shepway Kent 22 F11
Sheraton Dur 66 C1
Sherborne Dorset 17 P11
Sherborne Gloucs 30 F10
Sherborne Somset 17 N5
Sherborne St John Hants 19 Q9
Sherbourne Warwks 30 H2
Sherburn Dur 73 N11
Sherburn N York 67 K11
Sherburn Hill Dur 73 N11
Sherburn in Elmet N York 59 L7
Shere Surrey 10 H1
Shereford Norfk 44 E4
Sherfield English Hants 9 K3
Sherfield on Loddon Hants 20 B10
Sherford Devon 5 Q10
Sheriffhales Shrops 49 N11
Sheriff Hutton N York 59 P2
Sheringham Norfk 45 J2
Sherington M Keyn 32 C7
Shernborne Norfk 44 B4
Sherrington Wilts 18 E11
Sherston Wilts 18 C4
Sherwood C Nott 51 M11
Sherwood Forest Notts 51 N8
Shetland Islands Shet 111 k4
Shettleston C Glas 85 L9
Shevington Wigan 57 K7
Shevington Vale Wigan 57 K7
Sheviock Cnwll 4 H8
Shibden Head C Brad 58 E8
Shide IoW 9 N9
Shidlaw Nthumb 80 H6
Shiel Bridge Highld 97 N6
Shieldaig Highld 105 M10
Shieldhill D & G 78 G11
Shieldhill Falk 85 P7
Shieldhill House Hotel S Lans ...78 G2
Shields N Lans 85 N11
Shielfoot Highld 89 N3
Shielhill Angus 93 M4
Shielhill Inver 84 D8
Shifnal Shrops 39 N1
Shilbottle Nthumb 81 P11
Shildon Dur 65 M3
Shillford E Rens 84 H10
Shillingford Devon 16 D10
Shillingford Oxon 19 P3
Shillingford Abbot Devon 6 B5
Shillingford St George Devon ...6 B5
Shillingstone Dorset 8 C5
Shillington C Beds 32 G9
Shilton Oxon 30 H11
Shilton Warwks 41 K9
Shimpling Norfk 45 J12
Shimpling Suffk 34 E6
Shimpling Street Suffk 34 E6

Shincliffe Dur 73 N11
Shiney Row Sundld 73 N9
Shinfield Wokham 20 B9
Shinness Highld 109 J11
Shipbourne Kent 22 C11
Shipdham Norfk 44 F8
Shipham Somset 17 L5
Shiphay Torbay 6 B9
Shiplake Oxon 20 C7
Shipley C Brad 58 F6
Shipley W Susx 11 J6
Shipley Bridge Surrey 11 L3
Shipmeadow Suffk 45 N11
Shippon Oxon 19 N2
Shipston-on-Stour Warwks 30 G6
Shipton Gloucs 30 D9
Shipton N York 59 M3
Shipton Shrops 39 K4
Shipton Bellinger Hants 19 J10
Shipton Gorge Dorset 7 M5
Shipton Green W Susx 10 C9
Shipton Moyne Gloucs 29 M10
Shipton-on-Cherwell Oxon 31 L10
Shiptonthorpe E R Yk 60 E9
Shipton-under-Wychwood
  Oxon 30 H9
Shirburn Oxon 20 B4
Shirdley Hill Lancs 56 G6
Shirebrook Derbys 51 M7
Shiregreen Sheff 51 J3
Shirehampton Bristl 28 G12
Shiremoor N Tyne 73 N6
Shirenewton Mons 28 F9
Shireoaks Notts 51 M5
Shirland Derbys 51 K8
Shirley C Sotn 9 L5
Shirley Derbys 50 G11
Shirley Gt Lon 21 M9
Shirley Solihll 40 E10
Shirrell Heath Hants 9 P5
Shirwell Devon 15 K5
Shiskine N Ayrs 75 N6
Shobdon Herefs 38 H9
Shobrooke Devon 15 P11
Sholden Kent 23 Q11
Sholing C Sotn 9 M5
Shoby Leics 41 P4
Shocklach Ches W 48 H5
Shoeburyness Sthend 22 H6
Sholden Kent 23 Q11
Shop Cnwll 4 E8
Shoreditch Gt Lon 21 M6
Shoreditch Somset 16 H10
Shoreham Kent 21 P10
Shoreham-by-Sea W Susx 11 K8
Shorley Hants 9 P3
Shorne Kent 22 E8
Shortgate E Susx 11 P7
Short Heath Birm 40 E8
Short Heath Wsall 40 C7
Shortlanesend Cnwll 3 J6
Shortlees E Ayrs 76 G4
Shorwell IoW 9 M10
Shoscombe BaNES 17 Q5
Shotesham Norfk 45 L9
Shotgate Essex 22 F5
Shotley Suffk 35 K9
Shotley Bridge Dur 73 J9
Shotley Gate Suffk 35 L9
Shottenden Kent 23 K11
Shottery Warwks 30 F3
Shotteswell Warwks 31 K5
Shottisham Suffk 35 M7
Shottlegate Derbys 50 H10
Shotton Dur 73 P11
Shotton Flints 48 F2
Shotton Colliery Dur 73 P11
Shotts N Lans 85 P10
Shotwick Ches W 48 G2
Shougle Moray 101 J4
Shouldham Norfk 44 B8
Shouldham Thorpe Norfk 43 Q8
Shoulton Worcs 39 P9
Shrawardine Shrops 48 H11
Shrawley Worcs 39 P8
Shrewley Warwks 30 G1
Shrewsbury Shrops 49 J11
Shrewton Wilts 18 F11
Shripney W Susx 10 F9
Shrivenham Oxon 19 J3
Shropham Norfk 44 G10
Shroton Dorset 8 C5
Shrub End Essex 34 F11
Shucknall Herefs 28 G1
Shudy Camps Cambs 33 P7
Shuna Ag & B 83 L2
Shurdington Gloucs 29 N5
Shurlock Row W & M 20 D8
Shurrery Highld 110 B4
Shurrery Lodge Highld 110 B4
Shurton Somset 16 G7
Shustoke Warwks 40 G8
Shute Devon 6 H4
Shute Devon 15 Q11
Shutford Oxon 31 J6
Shut Heath Staffs 49 Q10
Shuthonger Gloucs 29 M2
Shutlanger Nhants 31 Q4
Shuttington Warwks 40 G6
Shuttlewood Derbys 51 L6
Shuttleworth Bury 57 P5
Siabost W Isls 111 d1
Siadar W Isls 111 d1
Sibbertoft Nhants 41 P10
Sibford Ferris Oxon 31 J5
Sibford Gower Oxon 31 J6
Sible Hedingham Essex 34 C9
Sibley's Green Essex 33 P10
Sibsey Lincs 53 K12
Sibson Cambs 42 F10
Sibson Leics 41 J7
Sibster Highld 110 G5
Sibthorpe Notts 51 Q6
Sibton Suffk 35 M3
Sicklesmere Suffk 34 E5
Sicklinghall N York 59 J5
Sidbury Devon 6 F4
Sidbury Shrops 39 M5
Sidcot N Som 17 K5
Sidcup Gt Lon 21 P8
Siddington Ches E 49 Q2
Siddington Gloucs 18 F2
Sidestrand Norfk 45 L3
Sidford Devon 6 F5

Sidlesham W Susx 10 D9
Sidley E Susx 12 E8
Sidmouth Devon 6 F5
Sigglesthorne E R Yk 61 K5
Sigingstone V Glam 16 C2
Silchester Hants 19 Q8
Sileby Leics 41 N5
Silecroft Cumb 62 D6
Silfield Norfk 45 J9
Silkstone Barns 58 H11
Silkstone Common Barns 58 H12
Silk Willoughby Lincs 42 F2
Silloth Cumb 70 H5
Silpho N York 67 L8
Silsden C Brad 58 D5
Silsoe C Beds 32 F9
Silton Dorset 8 B2
Silverburn Mdloth 86 E9
Silverdale Lancs 63 J7
Silverdale Staffs 49 P6
Silver End Essex 34 D11
Silverford Abers 102 G3
Silver Jubilee Bridge Halton ..57 K11
Silverstone Nhants 31 P5
Silverton Devon 6 C3
Silvington Shrops 39 L6
Simonburn Nthumb 72 F6
Simonsbath Somset 15 N4
Simonstone Lancs 57 P3
Simprim Border 80 H5
Simpson Bucks 32 C9
Simpson Cross Pembks 24 F5
Sinclair's Hill Border 80 H4
Sinclairston E Ayrs 76 H7
Sinderby N York 65 N10
Sinderland Green Traffd 57 N10
Sindlesham Wokham 20 C9
Sinfin C Derb 41 J2
Singleton Kent 13 J2
Singleton Lancs 56 H2
Singleton W Susx 10 E7
Singlewell Kent 22 D8
Sinnahard Abers 101 N11
Sinnington N York 66 G9
Sinton Worcs 39 P9
Sinton Worcs 39 Q9
Sinton Green Worcs 39 P9
Sissinghurst Kent 12 F3
Siston S Glos 17 P2
Sithney Cnwll 2 F9
Sittingbourne Kent 22 H10
Six Ashes Shrops 39 P4
Six Hundred Cambs 33 P5
Sixmile Bottom Cambs 33 P5
Sixpenny Handley Dorset 8 E4
Skaill Ork 111 h2
Skara Brae Ork 111 g2
Skares E Ayrs 77 J7
Skateraw Abers 95 P4
Skateraw E Loth 87 N7
Skeabost Highld 104 F11
Skeeby N York 65 L7
Skeffington Leics 41 Q7
Skeffling E R Yk 61 N9
Skegby Notts 51 L8
Skegby Notts 51 B9
Skegness Lincs 53 P10
Skelbo Highld 107 N4
Skelbo Street Highld 107 N4
Skelbrooke Donc 59 L10
Skeldyke Lincs 43 K3
Skellingthorpe Lincs 52 D8
Skellow Donc 59 M11
Skelmanthorpe Kirk 58 G11
Skelmersdale Lancs 57 J7
Skelmorlie N Ayrs 84 D9
Skelpick Highld 109 M5
Skelston D & G 78 D10
Skelton C York 59 M3
Skelton Cumb 71 N8
Skelton E R Yk 60 D8
Skelton R & Cl 66 F4
Skelton on Ure N York 59 J1
Skelwith Bridge Cumb 62 G2
Skendleby Lincs 53 M9
Skene House Abers 102 G12
Skenfrith Mons 28 E5
Skerne E R Yk 60 H3
Skerray Highld 109 L3
Skerricha Highld 108 F4
Skerton Lancs 63 J9
Sketchley Leics 41 K8
Sketty Swans 26 E9
Skewsby N York 66 E12
Skiall Highld 110 B3
Skidby E R Yk 60 H7
Skigersta W Isls 111 e1
Skilgate Somset 16 D10
Skillington Lincs 42 C5
Skinburness Cumb 71 J4
Skinflats Falk 85 Q6
Skinidin Highld 104 C11
Skipness Ag & B 83 N10
Skipper's Bridge D & G 79 M11
Skipsea E R Yk 61 K3
Skipton N York 58 C4
Skipton-on-Swale N York 65 P10
Skipwith N York 59 P6
Skirbeck Lincs 43 K2
Skirlaugh E R Yk 61 K6
Skirling Border 78 H2
Skirmett Bucks 20 C5
Skirpenbeck E R Yk 60 D3
Skirwith Cumb 64 B2
Skirza Highld 110 H3
Skokholm Island Pembks 24 D7
Skomer Island Pembks 24 C7
Skulamus Highld 97 J5
Skye Green Essex 34 E11
Skye of Curr Highld 99 P4
Slack Calder 58 C8
Slackbuie Highld 99 K1
Slacks of Cairnbanno Abers ...102 H6
Slad Gloucs 29 M7
Slade Devon 15 J3
Slade Green Gt Lon 21 Q7
Slade Hooton Rothm 51 M3
Slaggyford Nthumb 72 C9
Slaidburn Lancs 63 N10
Slaithwaite Kirk 58 E10
Slaley Nthumb 72 H8
Slamannan Falk 85 P9
Slapton Bucks 32 D11
Slapton Devon 5 Q10

Slapton Nhants 31 N5
Slaugham W Susx 11 K5
Slaughterford Wilts 18 C6
Slawston Leics 41 R8
Sleaford Hants 10 C3
Sleaford Lincs 42 F2
Sleagill Cumb 64 B4
Sleap Shrops 49 L11
Sleasdairidh Highld 107 K3
Sledmere E R Yk 60 F2
Sleetbeck Cumb 79 P12
Sleights N York 67 J6
Slickly Highld 110 F3
Sliddery N Ayrs 75 P7
Sligachan Highld 96 F4
Sligrachan Ag & B 84 C5
Slimbridge Gloucs 29 K7
Slindon Staffs 49 P8
Slindon W Susx 10 F8
Slinfold W Susx 10 H4
Slingsby N York 66 F11
Slip End C Beds 32 F11
Slip End Herts 33 J8
Slipton Nhants 32 D2
Slitting Mill Staffs 40 D4
Slockavullin Ag & B 83 M4
Sloncombe Devon 5 P3
Sloothby Lincs 53 M8
Slough Slough 20 F7
Slough Green Somset 16 H11
Slumbay Highld 97 M2
Slyfield Surrey 20 F11
Slyne Lancs 63 J8
Smailholm Border 80 E7
Smallburgh Norfk 45 M5
Smallburn E Ayrs 77 L6
Small Dole W Susx 11 K7
Smalley Derbys 51 K11
Smallfield Surrey 11 L2
Small Heath Birm 40 E9
Small Hythe Kent 12 H4
Smallridge Devon 7 J3
Smallthorne C Stke 50 B10
Smallworth Norfk 34 G1
Smannell Hants 19 L10
Smarden Kent 12 G2
Smarden Bell Kent 12 G2
Smart's Hill Kent 11 Q2
Smeatharpe Devon 6 G1
Smeeth Kent 13 K3
Smeeton Westerby Leics 41 P8
Smerral Highld 110 D8
Smestow Staffs 39 Q4
Smethwick Sandw 40 D9
Smirisary Highld 89 N2
Smisby Derbys 41 J4
Smithfield Cumb 71 P3
Smith's Green Essex 33 Q8
Smithstown Highld 105 L6
Smithton Highld 107 L12
Smoo Highld 108 H3
Smythe's Green Essex 34 F11
Snade D & G 78 D10
Snailbeach Shrops 38 G2
Snailwell Cambs 33 Q4
Snainton N York 67 K10
Snaith E R Yk 59 N9
Snape N York 65 M10
Snape Suffk 35 N5
Snape Street Suffk 35 N5
Snaresbrook Gt Lon 21 N5
Snarestone Leics 41 J5
Snarford Lincs 52 F7
Snargate Kent 13 J4
Snave Kent 13 K4
Sneaton N York 67 J6
Snelland Lincs 52 F7
Snelston Derbys 50 F11
Snetterton Norfk 44 G11
Snettisham Norfk 44 B4
Snitter Nthumb 81 L12
Snitterby Lincs 52 E5
Snitterfield Warwks 30 G3
Snitton Shrops 39 K7
Snodland Kent 22 E10
Snowdon Gwynd 54 H10
Snowdonia National Park 47 N5
Snow End Herts 33 L9
Snowshill Gloucs 30 E7
Soake Hants 9 Q5
Soay Highld 96 E7
Soberton Hants 9 Q4
Soberton Heath Hants 9 P5
Sockburn Darltn 65 N6
Soham Cambs 33 P3
Solas W Isls 111 b4
Soldridge Hants 9 Q1
Sole Street Kent 22 D9
Sole Street Kent 23 L12
Solihull Solihll 40 F10
Sollas W Isls 111 b4
Sollers Dilwyn Herefs 38 H10
Sollers Hope Herefs 28 H3
Solva Pembks 24 E4
Solwaybank D & G 79 L12
Somerby Leics 41 R5
Somerby Lincs 52 F3
Somercotes Derbys 51 K9
Somerford BCP 8 H8
Somerford Keynes Gloucs 18 E2
Somerley W Susx 10 D9
Somerleyton Suffk 45 P10
Somersal Herbert Derbys 40 F1
Somersby Lincs 53 K8
Somersham Cambs 33 K2
Somersham Suffk 34 H7
Somerton Oxon 31 L8
Somerton Somset 17 L9
Somerton Suffk 34 D6
Sompting W Susx 11 J8
Sonning Wokham 20 C8
Sonning Common Oxon 20 B7
Sopley Hants 8 H7
Sopwell Herts 21 J3
Sopworth Wilts 18 C4
Sorbie D & G 69 L9
Sordale Highld 110 D4
Sorisdale Ag & B 88 G4
Sorn E Ayrs 77 J5
Sornhill E Ayrs 77 J4
Sortat Highld 110 F3
Sotby Lincs 52 H7
Sotterley Suffk 45 P12
Soughton Flints 48 E3

Place	County	Page	Grid
Soulbury	Bucks	32	C10
Soulby	Cumb	64	D5
Souldern	Oxon	31	M7
Souldrop	Bed	32	E4
Sound	Ches E	49	L6
Sound Muir	Moray	101	M5
Soundwell	S Glos	17	P2
Sourton	Devon	5	L3
Soutergate	Cumb	62	E6
South Acre	Norfk	44	D7
South Alkham	Kent	13	N2
Southall	Gt Lon	20	H7
South Allington	Devon	5	Q11
South Alloa	Falk	85	P5
Southam	Gloucs	29	N4
Southam	Warwks	31	K2
South Ambersham	W Susx	10	E6
Southampton	C Soton	9	M5
Southampton Airport	*Hants*	*9*	*M4*
South Anston	Rothm	51	L4
South Ashford	Kent	13	J2
South Baddesley	Hants	9	L7
South Bank	C York	59	N4
South Barrow	Somset	17	N9
South Beddington	Gt Lon	21	L10
South Benfleet	Essex	22	F6
Southborough	Gt Lon	21	N9
Southborough	Kent	12	C2
Southbourne	BCP	8	G8
Southbourne	W Susx	10	C8
South Bramwith	Donc	59	N11
South Brent	Devon	5	N8
South Brewham	Somset	17	Q8
South Broomhill	Nthumb	73	M2
Southburgh	Norfk	44	G8
South Burlingham	Norfk	45	N8
Southburn	E R Yk	60	G4
South Cadbury	Somset	17	P10
South Carlton	Lincs	52	D8
South Carlton	Notts	51	N4
South Cave	E R Yk	60	F7
South Cerney	Gloucs	18	F2
South Chailey	E Susx	11	N6
South Charlton	Nthumb	81	N9
South Cheriton	Somset	17	Q10
South Church	Dur	65	L2
Southchurch	Sthend	22	H6
South Cliff	N York	67	M9
South Cliffe	E R Yk	60	F7
South Clifton	Notts	52	B9
South Cockerington	Lincs	53	L6
South Cornelly	Brdgnd	26	H11
Southcott	Cnwll	4	F2
Southcott	Devon	5	P4
Southcourt	Bucks	20	D2
South Cove	Suffk	35	P1
South Creake	Norfk	44	E3
South Croxton	Leics	41	P5
South Dalton	E R Yk	60	G5
South Darenth	Kent	22	C9
South Dell	W Isls	111	d1
South Downs National Park		*11*	*M8*
South Duffield	N York	59	P7
South Earlswood	Surrey	11	L1
Southease	E Susx	11	N8
South Elkington	Lincs	53	J6
South Elmsall	Wakefd	59	L11
Southend	Ag & B	75	K10
Southend Airport	*Essex*	*22*	*G5*
Southend-on-Sea	Sthend	22	H6
Southerndown	V Glam	16	B2
Southerness	D & G	70	F5
South Erradale	Highld	105	L7
Southerton	Devon	6	E5
Southery	Norfk	43	P10
South Fambridge	Essex	22	G5
South Ferriby	N Linc	60	G9
South Field	E R Yk	60	H8
Southfield	Falk	85	P8
Southfleet	Kent	22	C8
Southgate	Gt Lon	21	L5
Southgate	Swans	26	D10
South Gorley	Hants	8	H5
South Gosforth	N u Ty	73	M7
South Green	Essex	22	D5
South Green	Kent	22	G10
South Green	Norfk	44	H7
South Gyle	C Edin	86	E7
South Hanningfield	Essex	22	E4
South Harting	W Susx	10	C6
South Hayling	Hants	10	B9
South Heath	Bucks	20	E3
South Heighton	E Susx	11	N9
South Hetton	Dur	73	P10
South Hiendley	Wakefd	59	K10
South Hill	Cnwll	4	H5
South Hinksey	Oxon	31	L12
South Holmwood	Surrey	11	J2
South Hornchurch	Gt Lon	21	P6
South Huish	Devon	5	N11
South Hykeham	Lincs	52	D9
South Hylton	Sundld	73	P9
Southill	C Beds	32	G8
Southington	Hants	19	N10
South Kelsey	Lincs	52	E4
South Kessock	Highld	107	L11
South Killingholme	N Linc	61	K10
South Kilvington	N York	65	N10
South Kilworth	Leics	41	N10
South Kirkby	Wakefd	59	K11
South Kyme	Lincs	52	G12
Southleigh	Devon	6	G4
South Leigh	Oxon	31	K11
South Leverton	Notts	52	A7
South Littleton	Worcs	30	E5
South Lopham	Norfk	34	G1
South Luffenham	Rutlnd	42	D9
South Lynn	Norfk	43	P6
South Malling	E Susx	11	N7
South Marston	Swindn	18	H3
South Merstham	Surrey	21	L11
South Milford	N York	59	L7
South Milton	Devon	5	N10
South Mimms	Herts	21	K4
South Mimms Services	*Herts*	*21*	*K4*
Southminster	Essex	23	J4
South Molton	Devon	15	M7
South Moor	Dur	73	L9
Southmoor	Oxon	19	L2
South Moreton	Oxon	19	P3
Southmuir	Angus	93	L5
South Mundham	W Susx	10	E9
South Newbald	E R Yk	60	F7
South Newington	Oxon	31	K7
South Newton	Wilts	8	G1
South Nitshill	C Glas	85	J10
South Normanton	Derbys	51	K9
South Norwood	Gt Lon	21	M9
South Ockendon	Thurr	22	C6
Southoe	Cambs	32	H4
Southolt	Suffk	35	K3
South Ormsby	Lincs	53	L8
Southorpe	C Pete	42	F9
South Otterington	N York	65	P9
Southover	Dorset	7	N4
South Owersby	Lincs	52	F5
South Park	Surrey	11	K1
South Perrott	Dorset	7	L2
South Petherton	Somset	17	L11
South Petherwin	Cnwll	4	G4
South Pickenham	Norfk	44	E8
South Pill	Cnwll	5	J8
South Pool	Devon	5	Q11
South Poorton	Dorset	7	M4
Southport	Sefton	56	G5
South Queensferry	C Edin	86	D6
South Rauceby	Lincs	42	F2
South Raynham	Norfk	44	E5
South Reddish	Stockp	50	B3
Southrepps	Norfk	45	L3
South Reston	Lincs	53	L6
Southrey	Lincs	52	G9
South Ronaldsay	Ork	111	h3
Southrop	Gloucs	30	G12
Southrope	Hants	19	Q10
South Runcton	Norfk	43	Q8
South Scarle	Notts	52	B10
Southsea	C Port	9	Q7
South Shian	Ag & B	90	C7
South Shields	S Tyne	73	P7
South Shore	Bpool	56	F3
Southside	Dur	65	K3
South Stainley	N York	58	H2
South Stifford	Thurr	22	C7
South Stoke	BaNES	17	Q4
South Stoke	Oxon	19	P4
South Stoke	W Susx	10	G7
South Street	Kent	23	K10
South Street	Kent	23	L9
South Tarbrax	S Lans	86	B10
South Tawton	Devon	5	N2
South Tehidy	Cnwll	2	H7
South Thoresby	Lincs	53	L7
Southtown	Norfk	45	Q8
South Uist	W Isls	111	b6
Southwaite	Cumb	71	P6
Southwaite Services	*Cumb*	*71*	*P6*
South Walsham	Norfk	45	N7
Southwark	Gt Lon	21	L7
South Warnborough	Hants	10	B1
Southwater	W Susx	11	J5
Southway	C Plym	5	K7
South Weald	Essex	22	C5
Southwell	Notts	51	P9
South Weston	Oxon	20	B4
South Wheatley	Notts	51	Q4
Southwick	Hants	9	Q6
Southwick	Nhants	42	E10
Southwick	Sundld	73	P8
Southwick	W Susx	11	K8
Southwick	Wilts	18	C9
South Widcombe	BaNES	17	N5
South Wigston	Leics	41	N7
South Willingham	Lincs	52	H6
South Wingfield	Derbys	51	J9
South Witham	Lincs	42	D6
Southwold	Suffk	35	Q2
South Woodham Ferrers	Essex	22	F4
South Wootton	Norfk	43	Q5
South Wraxall	Wilts	18	C7
South Zeal	Devon	5	N2
Sovereign Harbour	E Susx	12	D9
Sowerby	Calder	58	D9
Sowerby	N York	66	B10
Sowerby Bridge	Calder	58	D9
Sowood	Calder	58	E9
Sowton	Devon	5	K7
Sowton	Devon	6	D4
Soyland Town	Calder	58	D9
Spain's End	Essex	33	Q8
Spalding	Lincs	43	J5
Spaldington	E R Yk	60	D7
Spaldwick	Cambs	32	G3
Spalford	Notts	52	B9
Spanby	Lincs	42	F3
Sparham	Norfk	44	H6
Spark Bridge	Cumb	62	F5
Sparkford	Somset	17	N10
Sparkhill	Birm	40	E10
Sparkwell	Devon	5	M8
Sparrowpit	Derbys	50	E5
Sparrows Green	E Susx	12	D4
Sparsholt	Hants	9	M2
Sparsholt	Oxon	19	L4
Spaunton	N York	66	G9
Spaxton	Somset	16	G8
Spean Bridge	Highld	98	C11
Spearywell	Hants	9	K2
Speen	Bucks	20	D4
Speen	W Berk	19	M7
Speeton	N York	67	N11
Speke	Lpool	56	H11
Speldhurst	Kent	12	B2
Spellbrook	Herts	33	M12
Spencers Wood	Wokham	20	B9
Spen Green	Ches E	49	P4
Spennithorne	N York	65	K9
Spennymoor	Dur	65	M2
Spetchley	Worcs	30	B4
Spetisbury	Dorset	8	D7
Spexhall	Suffk	35	N2
Spey Bay	Moray	101	L3
Speybridge	Highld	100	G9
Speyview	Moray	101	K6
Spilsby	Lincs	53	L9
Spinkhill	Derbys	51	L5
Spinningdale	Highld	107	L4
Spital	Wirral	56	G11
Spital Hill	Donc	51	N3
Spittal	E Loth	87	J6
Spittal	Highld	110	D5
Spittal	Nthumb	81	L4
Spittal	Pembks	24	G4
Spittalfield	P & K	92	G7
Spittal of Glenmuick	Abers	94	D4
Spittal of Glenshee	P & K	94	B7
Spittal-on-Rule	Border	80	D9
Spixworth	Norfk	45	L7
Splatt	Devon	15	K10
Splayne's Green	E Susx	11	N5
Splott	Cardif	16	G2
Spofforth	N York	59	J4
Spondon	C Derb	41	K1
Spooner Row	Norfk	44	H10
Sporle	Norfk	44	E7
Spott	E Loth	87	M7
Spottiswoode	Border	80	E4
Spratton	Nhants	41	Q12
Spreakley	Surrey	10	D2
Spreyton	Devon	15	M11
Spriddlestone	Devon	5	L9
Spridlington	Lincs	52	E6
Springburn	C Glas	85	K8
Springfield	D & G	71	M2
Springfield	Essex	22	E2
Springfield	Fife	93	L12
Springholm	D & G	70	D2
Springside	N Ayrs	76	F4
Springthorpe	Lincs	52	C5
Springwell	Sundld	73	M8
Sproatley	E R Yk	61	K7
Sproston Green	Ches W	49	N3
Sprotbrough	Donc	51	M11
Sproughton	Suffk	35	J7
Sprouston	Border	80	G7
Sprowston	Norfk	45	L7
Sproxton	Leics	42	C5
Sproxton	N York	66	E10
Spurstow	Ches E	49	K4
Spyway	Dorset	7	M4
Stableford	Shrops	39	N3
Stacey Bank	Sheff	50	H3
Stackhouse	N York	63	P8
Stackpole	Pembks	24	H9
Stackpole Elidor	Pembks	24	H8
Staddiscombe	C Plym	5	K9
Stadhampton	Oxon	19	Q2
Stadhlaigearraidh	W Isls	111	a5
Staffield	Cumb	71	Q7
Staffin	Highld	104	G8
Stafford	Staffs	40	B3
Stafford Services (northbound)	*Staffs*	*40*	*B2*
Stafford Services (southbound)	*Staffs*	*40*	*B2*
Stagsden	Bed	32	E7
Stainburn	Cumb	70	G9
Stainby	Lincs	42	C5
Staincross	Barns	59	J11
Staindrop	Dur	65	K4
Staines-upon-Thames	Surrey	20	G8
Stainforth	Donc	59	N10
Stainforth	N York	63	P8
Staining	Lancs	56	G2
Stainland	Calder	58	E9
Stainsacre	N York	67	K6
Stainton	Cumb	63	K5
Stainton	Cumb	71	P9
Stainton	Donc	51	M3
Stainton	Dur	65	J4
Stainton	Middsb	66	C5
Stainton by Langworth	Lincs	52	F7
Staintondale	N York	67	L7
Stainton le Vale	Lincs	52	H5
Stainton with Adgarley	Cumb	62	F7
Stair	E Ayrs	76	G6
Stairhaven	D & G	68	G8
Staithes	N York	66	H4
Stakes	Hants	10	B8
Stalbridge	Dorset	17	Q11
Stalbridge Weston	Dorset	17	Q11
Stalham	Norfk	45	N5
Stalisfield Green	Kent	23	J11
Stallen	Dorset	17	N11
Stallingborough	NE Lin	61	K11
Stalmine	Lancs	62	G12
Stalybridge	Tamesd	50	C2
Stambourne	Essex	34	C8
Stambourne Green	Essex	34	B8
Stamford	Lincs	42	E8
Stamford Bridge	Ches W	49	J3
Stamford Bridge	E R Yk	60	C3
Stamfordham	Nthumb	73	J6
Stamford Hill	Gt Lon	21	M6
Stanbridge	C Beds	32	D11
Stanbury	C Brad	58	D6
Stand	N Lans	85	M8
Standburn	Falk	85	Q7
Standeford	Staffs	40	B6
Standen	Kent	12	G3
Standerwick	Somset	18	B10
Standford	Hants	10	D3
Standingstone	Cumb	70	H8
Standish	Wigan	57	K6
Standlake	Oxon	31	K12
Standon	Hants	9	M3
Standon	Herts	33	L11
Standon	Staffs	49	P8
Stane	N Lans	85	P10
Stanfield	Norfk	44	F6
Stanford	C Beds	32	G8
Stanford	Kent	13	L3
Stanford Bishop	Herefs	39	M10
Stanford Bridge	Worcs	39	N8
Stanford Dingley	W Berk	19	P6
Stanford in the Vale	Oxon	19	K3
Stanford le Hope	Thurr	22	D7
Stanford on Avon	Nhants	41	N10
Stanford on Soar	Notts	41	M3
Stanford on Teme	Worcs	39	N8
Stanfree	Derbys	51	L6
Stanghow	R & Cl	66	F4
Stanground	C Pete	42	H10
Stanhoe	Norfk	44	D3
Stanhope	Border	79	J3
Stanhope	Dur	72	H11
Stanhope	Kent	13	J2
Stanion	Nhants	42	D11
Stanley	Derbys	51	K11
Stanley	Dur	73	L9
Stanley	P & K	92	G8
Stanley	Staffs	50	B9
Stanley Crook	Dur	73	L12
Stanley Pontlarge	Gloucs	30	D7
Stanmer	Br & H	11	M7
Stanmore	Gt Lon	21	J5
Stanmore	Hants	9	M2
Stannersburn	Nthumb	72	D4
Stanningfield	Suffk	34	E5
Stannington	Nthumb	73	L5
Stannington	Sheff	50	H4
Stannington Station	Nthumb	73	L5
Stansbatch	Herefs	38	G9
Stansfield	Suffk	34	C6
Stanstead	Suffk	34	D7
Stanstead Abbotts	Herts	21	M2
Stansted	Kent	22	C10
Stansted Airport	*Essex*	*33*	*N11*
Stansted Mountfitchet	Essex	33	N10
Stanton	Gloucs	30	E7
Stanton	Nthumb	73	K3
Stanton	Staffs	50	E10
Stanton	Suffk	34	F3
Stanton by Bridge	Derbys	41	J3
Stanton by Dale	Derbys	51	L12
Stanton Drew	BaNES	17	N4
Stanton Fitzwarren	Swindn	18	H3
Stanton Harcourt	Oxon	31	K11
Stanton in Peak	Derbys	50	G7
Stanton Lacy	Shrops	39	J6
Stanton Lees	Derbys	50	G8
Stanton Long	Shrops	39	L4
Stanton-on-the-Wolds	Notts	41	N2
Stanton Prior	BaNES	17	P4
Stanton St Bernard	Wilts	18	G8
Stanton St John	Oxon	31	M11
Stanton St Quintin	Wilts	18	D5
Stanton Street	Suffk	34	F4
Stanton under Bardon	Leics	41	L5
Stanton upon Hine Heath	Shrops	49	K10
Stanton Wick	BaNES	17	N4
Stanway	Essex	34	F11
Stanway	Gloucs	30	D7
Stanwell	Surrey	20	G8
Stanwick	Nhants	32	E3
Stanwix	Cumb	71	N4
Staoinebrig	W Isls	111	a5
Stape	N York	66	H8
Stapeley	Ches E	49	M5
Stapenhill	Staffs	40	G3
Staple	Kent	23	P11
Staple Cross	Devon	16	D11
Staplecross	E Susx	12	F5
Staplefield	W Susx	11	L5
Staple Fitzpaine	Somset	16	H11
Stapleford	Cambs	33	M6
Stapleford	Herts	33	K12
Stapleford	Leics	42	B6
Stapleford	Lincs	52	C11
Stapleford	Notts	51	L12
Stapleford	Wilts	18	F12
Stapleford Abbotts	Essex	21	P5
Staplegrove	Somset	16	G10
Staplehay	Somset	16	G10
Staplehurst	Kent	12	F2
Staplestreet	Kent	23	K10
Stapleton	Herefs	38	G8
Stapleton	Leics	41	K7
Stapleton	N York	65	M5
Stapleton	Shrops	39	J2
Stapleton	Somset	17	L11
Stapley	Somset	16	G12
Staploe	Bed	32	G5
Staplow	Herefs	29	J1
Star	Fife	86	G2
Star	Pembks	25	M2
Star	Somset	17	L5
Starbeck	N York	59	J3
Starbotton	N York	64	G11
Starcross	Devon	6	C6
Stareton	Warwks	41	J12
Starlings Green	Essex	33	M9
Starston	Norfk	45	K12
Startforth	Dur	65	J4
Startley	Wilts	18	D4
Statenborough	Kent	23	P11
Statham	Warrtn	57	M10
Stathe	Somset	17	K9
Stathern	Leics	41	Q2
Staunton	Gloucs	28	G6
Staunton	Gloucs	29	K3
Staunton on Arrow	Herefs	38	G9
Staunton on Wye	Herefs	38	G12
Staveley	Cumb	63	J3
Staveley	Derbys	51	K6
Staveley	N York	59	J3
Staveley-in-Cartmel	Cumb	62	H5
Staverton	Devon	5	Q7
Staverton	Gloucs	29	M4
Staverton	Nhants	31	M2
Staverton	Wilts	18	C8
Stawell	Somset	17	K8
Stawley	Somset	16	E10
Staxigoe	Highld	110	H5
Staxton	N York	67	L10
Staynall	Lancs	62	G12
Stean	N York	65	J11
Stearsby	N York	66	E12
Steart	Somset	16	H7
Stebbing	Essex	33	Q11
Stechford	Birm	40	F9
Stedham	W Susx	10	D5
Steel Road	Border	79	Q9
Steen's Bridge	Herefs	39	K10
Steep	Hants	10	C5
Steep Lane	Calder	58	D9
Steeple	Dorset	8	D10
Steeple	Essex	22	H3
Steeple Ashton	Wilts	18	D9
Steeple Aston	Oxon	31	L8
Steeple Bumpstead	Essex	34	B8
Steeple Claydon	Bucks	31	P8
Steeple Gidding	Cambs	32	G1
Steeple Langford	Wilts	18	F12
Steeple Morden	Cambs	33	J8
Steeton	C Brad	58	D5
Stein	Highld	104	C10
Stelling Minnis	Kent	13	M1
Stembridge	Somset	17	M4
Stenalees	Cnwll	3	M4
Stenhouse	D & G	77	N11
Stenhousemuir	Falk	85	P6
Stenness	Ork	111	g2
Stenscholl	Highld	104	F8
Stenson Fields	Derbys	41	J2
Stenton	E Loth	87	M7
Steornabhagh	W Isls	111	d2
Stepaside	Pembks	25	K7
Stepford	D & G	78	E11
Stepney	Gt Lon	21	M7
Steppingley	C Beds	32	E9
Stepps	N Lans	85	L8
Sternfield	Suffk	35	N5
Stert	Wilts	18	F8
Stetchworth	Cambs	33	Q5
Stevenage	Herts	32	H10
Stevenston	N Ayrs	76	E3
Steventon	Hants	19	P10
Steventon	Oxon	19	M3
Steventon End	Essex	33	P8
Stevington	Bed	32	E6
Stewartby	Bed	32	E8
Stewartfield	S Lans	85	K11
Stewarton	Ag & B	75	K8
Stewarton	E Ayrs	76	G3
Stewkley	Bucks	32	C10
Stewley	Somset	17	J11
Steyning	W Susx	11	J7
Steynton	Pembks	24	G7
Stibb	Cnwll	14	D9
Stibbard	Norfk	44	G4
Stibb Cross	Devon	14	H8
Stibb Green	Wilts	19	J8
Stibbington	Cambs	42	F9
Stichill	Border	80	F6
Sticker	Cnwll	3	L6
Stickford	Lincs	53	K10
Sticklepath	Devon	5	N2
Stickney	Lincs	53	K11
Stiffkey	Norfk	44	F2
Stifford Clays	Thurr	22	C7
Stilligarry	W Isls	111	a5
Stillingfleet	N York	59	N6
Stillington	N York	59	N1
Stillington	S on T	65	P3
Stilton	Cambs	42	G11
Stinchcombe	Gloucs	29	K8
Stinsford	Dorset	7	Q5
Stiperstones	Shrops	38	G3
Stirchley	Wrekin	39	M1
Stirling	Abers	103	M6
Stirling	Stirlg	85	N4
Stirling Castle	*Stirlg*	*85*	*N4*
Stirling Services	*Stirlg*	*85*	*N5*
Stirtloe	Cambs	32	H4
Stirton	N York	58	C4
Stisted	Essex	34	D10
Stithians	Cnwll	2	H8
Stivichall	Covtry	41	J11
Stixwould	Lincs	52	H9
St Michaels	Fife	93	M10
Stoak	Ches W	48	H2
Stobo	Border	79	K2
Stoborough	Dorset	8	D9
Stobs Castle	Border	80	C11
Stobswood	Nthumb	73	L2
Stock	Essex	22	E4
Stock	N Som	17	L4
Stockbridge	Hants	9	L1
Stockbridge	W Susx	10	D8
Stockbriggs	S Lans	77	N4
Stockbury	Kent	22	G10
Stockcross	W Berk	19	M7
Stockerston	Leics	42	B9
Stock Green	Worcs	30	C3
Stocking	Herefs	28	H3
Stockingford	Warwks	41	J8
Stocking Pelham	Herts	33	M10
Stockland	Devon	6	H2
Stockland Bristol	Somset	16	H7
Stockleigh English	Devon	15	P10
Stockleigh Pomeroy	Devon	15	P10
Stockley	Wilts	18	E7
Stocklinch	Somset	17	K11
Stockport	Stockp	50	B3
Stocksbridge	Sheff	50	H2
Stocksfield	Nthumb	73	J8
Stockton	Herefs	39	K9
Stockton	Norfk	45	N10
Stockton	Shrops	39	N3
Stockton	Warwks	31	K2
Stockton	Wilts	18	E12
Stockton	Wrekin	49	P11
Stockton Brook	Staffs	50	B9
Stockton Heath	Warrtn	57	L10
Stockton-on-Tees	S on T	66	C4
Stockton on Teme	Worcs	39	N8
Stockton on the Forest	C York	59	P3
Stockwell End	Wolves	40	B7
Stockwood	Bristl	17	P3
Stockwood	Dorset	7	N2
Stock Wood	Worcs	30	D3
Stodmarsh	Kent	23	N10
Stody	Norfk	44	H3
Stoer	Highld	108	B9
Stoford	Somset	17	N12
Stoford	Wilts	8	F1
Stogumber	Somset	16	E8
Stogursey	Somset	16	G7
Stoke	Covtry	41	J10
Stoke	Devon	14	E7
Stoke	Hants	10	B9
Stoke	Hants	19	L9
Stoke	Medway	22	G8
Stoke Abbott	Dorset	7	L3
Stoke Albany	Nhants	42	B11
Stoke Ash	Suffk	35	J3
Stoke Bardolph	Notts	51	N11
Stoke Bliss	Worcs	39	M9
Stoke Bruerne	Nhants	31	Q4
Stoke-by-Clare	Suffk	34	C7
Stoke-by-Nayland	Suffk	34	G9
Stoke Canon	Devon	6	C3
Stoke Charity	Hants	19	N1
Stoke Climsland	Cnwll	4	H5
Stoke Cross	Herefs	39	L11
Stoke D'Abernon	Surrey	20	H10
Stoke Doyle	Nhants	42	E11
Stoke Dry	Rutlnd	42	C10
Stoke Edith	Herefs	28	H1
Stoke Farthing	Wilts	8	F3
Stoke Ferry	Norfk	44	B9
Stoke Fleming	Devon	6	B11
Stokeford	Dorset	8	C9
Stoke Gabriel	Devon	6	B10
Stoke Gifford	S Glos	28	H11
Stoke Golding	Leics	41	K7
Stoke Goldington	M Keyn	32	B7
Stokeham	Notts	52	A7
Stoke Hammond	Bucks	32	C10
Stoke Holy Cross	Norfk	45	K9
Stokeinteignhead	Devon	6	C8
Stoke Lacy	Herefs	39	L11
Stoke Lyne	Oxon	31	M8
Stoke Mandeville	Bucks	20	D2

Stokenchurch Bucks 20 C4
Stoke Newington Gt Lon 21 M6
Stokenham Devon 5 Q10
Stoke Orchard Gloucs 29 M3
Stoke-on-Trent C Stke 50 B10
Stoke Poges Bucks 20 F6
Stoke Prior Herefs 39 K10
Stoke Prior Worcs 30 C1
Stoke Rivers Devon 15 L5
Stoke Rochford Lincs 42 D5
Stoke Row Oxon 20 B6
Stoke St Gregory Somset 17 J10
Stoke St Mary Somset 16 H10
Stoke St Michael Somset 17 P6
Stoke St Milborough Shrops 39 K5
Stokesby Norfk 45 N7
Stokesley N York 66 D6
Stoke sub Hamdon Somset 17 L11
Stoke Talmage Oxon 20 B4
Stoke Trister Somset 17 Q9
Stoke upon Tern Shrops 49 M9
Stolford Somset 16 G7
Stondon Massey Essex 22 C4
Stone Bucks 20 C2
Stone Gloucs 29 J9
Stone Rothm 51 M3
Stone Staffs 40 B1
Stone Worcs 39 Q7
Stone Allerton Somset 17 K6
Ston Easton Somset 17 N5
Stonebridge N Som 17 K4
Stonebridge Warwks 40 G10
Stonebroom Derbys 51 K8
Stone Cross Kent 23 P11
Stonecrouch Kent 12 E4
Stoneferry C KuH 61 J7
Stonefield Castle Hotel Ag & B 83 N8
Stonegate E Susx 12 D4
Stonegrave N York 66 F11
Stonehaven Abers 95 P5
Stonehenge Wilts 18 G11
Stonehouse C Plym 5 K9
Stonehouse Gloucs 29 L7
Stonehouse S Lans 77 M3
Stone in Oxney Kent 12 H5
Stoneleigh Warwks 41 J11
Stonesby Leics 42 B5
Stonesfield Oxon 31 K10
Stones Green Essex 35 J10
Stone Street Kent 22 C11
Stone Street Suffk 35 N1
Stonewells Moray 101 K3
Stoneybridge W Isls 111 a5
Stoneyburn W Loth 86 B9
Stoneygate C Leic 41 N7
Stoneykirk D & G 68 E8
Stoney Middleton Derbys 50 G6
Stoney Stanton Leics 41 L8
Stoney Stoke Somset 17 Q9
Stoney Stratton Somset 17 P8
Stoneywood C Aber 103 J11
Stoneywood Falk 85 N6
Stonham Aspal Suffk 35 J5
Stonnall Staffs 40 E6
Stonor Oxon 20 B6
Stonton Wyville Leics 41 Q8
Stonybreck Shet 111 m5
Stony Houghton Derbys 51 L7
Stony Stratford M Keyn 32 B8
Stoodleigh Devon 15 L6
Stoodleigh Devon 16 C11
Stopham W Susx 10 G6
Stopsley Luton 32 F11
Stornoway W Isls 111 d2
Stornoway Airport W Isls 111 d2
Storridge Herefs 39 N11
Storrington W Susx 10 H7
Storth Cumb 63 J6
Storwood E R Yk 60 C5
Stotfield Moray 101 J2
Stotfold C Beds 32 H9
Stottesdon Shrops 39 M5
Stoughton Leics 41 N7
Stoughton Surrey 20 F12
Stoughton W Susx 10 C7
Stoulton Worcs 30 B4
Stourbridge Dudley 40 B10
Stourhead Wilts 8 B1
Stourpaine Dorset 8 C5
Stourport-on-Severn Worcs 39 P7
Stour Provost Dorset 8 B3
Stour Row Dorset 8 B3
Stourton Staffs 39 Q5
Stourton Warwks 30 H6
Stourton Wilts 8 B1
Stourton Caundle Dorset 17 Q12
Stove Shet 111 k5
Stoven Suffk 35 P1
Stow Border 87 J12
Stow Lincs 52 C7
Stow Bardolph Norfk 43 P8
Stow Bedon Norfk 44 F10
Stowbridge Norfk 43 P8
Stow-cum-Quy Cambs 33 N5
Stowe Shrops 38 F7
Stowe-by-Chartley Staffs 40 D3
Stowell Somset 17 P10
Stowey BaNES 17 N4
Stowford Devon 5 J3
Stowford Devon 6 F5
Stowlangtoft Suffk 34 F3
Stow Longa Cambs 32 G3
Stow Maries Essex 22 G4
Stowmarket Suffk 34 H5
Stow-on-the-Wold Gloucs 30 H8
Stowting Kent 13 L2
Stowupland Suffk 34 H5
Straad IoM 83 Q9
Straanruie Highld 99 P6
Strachan Abers 95 L4
Strachur Ag & B 84 B3
Stradbroke Suffk 35 K3
Stradishall Suffk 34 C6
Stradsett Norfk 43 Q8
Stragglethorpe Lincs 52 C11
Straiton Mdloth 86 F8
Straiton S Ayrs 76 G9
Straloch Abers 102 H10
Straloch P & K 92 F3
Stramshall Staffs 40 E1
Strang IoM 56 c5
Strangeways Salfd 57 P8
Strangford Herefs 28 G4
Stranraer D & G 68 E7

Stratfield Mortimer W Berk 19 Q7
Stratfield Saye Hants 20 B10
Stratfield Turgis Hants 20 B10
Stratford Gt Lon 21 M6
Stratford St Andrew Suffk 35 M5
Stratford St Mary Suffk 34 H9
Stratford sub Castle Wilts 8 G2
Stratford Tony Wilts 8 G3
Stratford-upon-Avon Warwks 30 G3
Strath Highld 105 L6
Strathan Highld 108 C10
Strathan Highld 109 K3
Strathaven S Lans 77 L3
Strathblane Stirlg 85 J7
Strathcanaird Highld 106 C3
Strathcarron Highld 97 N2
Strathcoil Ag & B 89 N9
Strathdon Abers 101 L11
Strathkinness Fife 93 M11
Strathloanhead W Loth 85 Q8
Strathmashie House Highld 98 H10
Strathmiglo Fife 86 E1
Strathpeffer Highld 106 H10
Strathtay P & K 92 D5
Strathwhillan N Ayrs 75 Q5
Strathy Highld 109 P3
Strathy Inn Highld 109 P3
Strathyre Stirlg 91 N11
Stratton Cnwll 14 E10
Stratton Dorset 7 P4
Stratton Gloucs 30 D12
Stratton Audley Oxon 31 N8
Stratton-on-the-Fosse Somset 17 P6
Stratton St Margaret Swindn 18 H4
Stratton St Michael Norfk 45 K10
Stratton Strawless Norfk 45 K6
Streat E Susx 11 M7
Streatham Gt Lon 21 L8
Streatley C Beds 32 F10
Streatley W Berk 19 P5
Street Devon 6 G5
Street Somset 17 L8
Street Ashton Warwks 41 L10
Street Dinas Shrops 48 G7
Street End Kent 23 M11
Street End W Susx 10 D9
Streethay Staffs 40 F5
Streetlam N York 65 N7
Streetly End Cambs 33 P7
Street on the Fosse Somset 17 N8
Strelitz P & K 92 H8
Strelley Notts 51 L11
Strensall C York 59 N3
Strensham Services (northbound) Worcs 29 M1
Strensham Services (southbound) Worcs 29 M2
Stretcholt Somset 16 H7
Strete Devon 5 R10
Stretford Traffd 57 P9
Strethall Essex 33 M8
Stretham Cambs 33 N2
Strettington W Susx 10 E8
Stretton Ches W 49 K8
Stretton Derbys 51 K8
Stretton Rutlnd 42 D7
Stretton Staffs 40 B5
Stretton Staffs 40 G3
Stretton Warrtn 57 L11
Stretton Grandison Herefs 39 L12
Stretton-on-Dunsmore Warwks 41 K11
Stretton on Fosse Warwks 30 G6
Stretton Sugwas Herefs 28 E1
Stretton under Fosse Warwks 41 L10
Stretton Westwood Shrops 39 L3
Strichen Abers 103 K4
Stringston Somset 16 G7
Strixton Nhants 32 C4
Stroat Gloucs 28 G8
Strollamus Highld 96 H4
Stroma Highld 110 G1
Stromeferry Highld 97 M3
Stromness Ork 111 g2
Stronaba Highld 98 B11
Stronachlachar Stirlg 84 G2
Stronafian Ag & B 83 Q6
Stronchrubie Highld 108 E11
Strone Ag & B 84 D6
Strone Highld 98 A11
Strone Highld 98 G4
Stronmilchan Ag & B 90 F10
Stronsay Ork 111 i2
Stronsay Airport Ork 111 i2
Strontian Highld 89 Q4
Strood Medway 22 E9
Strood Gloucs 29 L7
Strood Hants 10 B5
Strood Green Gloucs 29 L7
Stroxton Lincs 42 C4
Struan Highld 96 D3
Struan P & K 92 B3
Strumpshaw Norfk 45 M8
Strutherhill S Lans 77 M2
Struthers Fife 86 H1
Struy Highld 98 E2
Stuartfield Abers 103 K6
Stubbington Hants 9 P6
Stubbins Lancs 57 P5
Stubton Lincs 42 C1
Stuckton Hants 8 H5
Studham C Beds 32 E12
Studland Dorset 8 F10
Studlands Park Suffk 33 Q4
Studley Warwks 30 E2
Studley Wilts 18 E6
Studley Common Warwks 30 E2
Studley Roger N York 65 N12
Studley Royal N York 65 M12
Studley Royal Park & Fountains Abbey N York 58 H1
Stuntney Cambs 33 N3
Sturmer Essex 34 B7
Sturminster Common Dorset 8 B5
Sturminster Marshall Dorset 8 D7
Sturminster Newton Dorset 8 B5
Sturry Kent 23 M10
Sturton N Linc 52 D3
Sturton by Stow Lincs 52 C7
Sturton le Steeple Notts 52 B6
Stuston Suffk 35 J2
Stutton N York 59 L6
Stutton Suffk 35 J9
Styal Ches E 57 Q11

Stynie Moray 101 L3
Styrrup Notts 51 N3
Succoth Ag & B 84 E2
Suckley Worcs 39 N10
Sudborough Nhants 32 D1
Sudbourne Suffk 35 N6
Sudbrook Lincs 42 D2
Sudbrook Mons 28 F10
Sudbrooke Lincs 52 E8
Sudbury Derbys 40 F2
Sudbury Gt Lon 21 J6
Sudbury Suffk 34 E8
Suffield N York 67 L8
Suffield Norfk 45 K4
Sugnall Staffs 49 P8
Sugwas Pool Herefs 28 E1
Suisnish Highld 96 H6
Sulby IoM 56 d3
Sulgrave Nhants 31 M5
Sulham W Berk 19 Q6
Sulhamstead W Berk 19 Q7
Sullom Shet 111 k3
Sullom Voe Shet 111 k3
Sully V Glam 16 F3
Sumburgh Airport Shet 111 k5
Summerbridge N York 58 G2
Summercourt Cnwll 3 K5
Summerfield Norfk 44 C3
Summerhill Pembks 25 K7
Summerhouse Darltn 65 L4
Summersdale W Susx 10 D8
Summerseat Bury 57 P6
Summertown Oxon 31 L11
Sunbury-on-Thames Surrey 20 H9
Sundaywell D & G 78 D11
Sunderland Ag & B 82 C9
Sunderland Cumb 71 J8
Sunderland Lancs 62 H10
Sunderland Sundld 73 P9
Sunderland Bridge Dur 73 M12
Sundhope Border 79 M4
Sundon Park Luton 32 F10
Sundridge Kent 21 P11
Sunningdale W & M 20 F9
Sunninghill W & M 20 F9
Sunningwell Oxon 19 N1
Sunniside Dur 73 K12
Sunniside Gatesd 73 L8
Sunnyhill C Derb 41 J2
Sunnyhurst Bl w D 57 M4
Sunnylaw Stirlg 85 N4
Sunnymead Oxon 31 L11
Surbiton Gt Lon 21 J9
Surfleet Lincs 43 J5
Surlingham Norfk 45 M8
Surrex Essex 34 E11
Sustead Norfk 45 K3
Susworth Lincs 52 B3
Sutcombe Devon 14 F9
Sutcombemill Devon 14 F9
Sutterby Lincs 53 L8
Sutterton Lincs 43 J3
Sutton C Beds 32 H7
Sutton C Pete 42 F9
Sutton Cambs 33 M2
Sutton Devon 5 N10
Sutton E Susx 11 P9
Sutton Gt Lon 21 K9
Sutton Kent 23 P12
Sutton N York 59 L8
Sutton Norfk 45 N5
Sutton Notts 51 Q12
Sutton Oxon 31 K11
Sutton Shrops 39 N5
Sutton Shrops 49 J12
Sutton Shrops 49 N10
Sutton Suffk 35 M7
Sutton W Susx 10 F7
Sutton-at-Hone Kent 22 B9
Sutton Bassett Nhants 41 Q9
Sutton Benger Wilts 18 D5
Sutton Bonington Notts 41 L3
Sutton Bridge Lincs 43 M6
Sutton Cheney Leics 41 K7
Sutton Coldfield Birm 40 E8
Sutton Courtenay Oxon 19 N2
Sutton cum Lound Notts 51 P4
Sutton Green Surrey 20 G11
Sutton Heath Suffk 35 M7
Sutton Howgrave N York 65 N10
Sutton-in-Ashfield Notts 51 L8
Sutton-in-Craven N York 58 D5
Sutton Maddock Shrops 39 N2
Sutton Mallet Somset 17 K8
Sutton Mandeville Wilts 8 E2
Sutton Montis Somset 17 P10
Sutton-on-Hull C KuH 61 J7
Sutton on Sea Lincs 53 N7
Sutton-on-the-Forest N York 59 M2
Sutton on the Hill Derbys 40 G2
Sutton on Trent Notts 52 B9
Sutton St Edmund Lincs 43 L7
Sutton St James Lincs 43 L6
Sutton St Nicholas Herefs 39 K11
Sutton Scotney Hants 19 M11
Sutton-under-Brailes Warwks 30 H6
Sutton-under-Whitestonecliffe N York 66 C10
Sutton upon Derwent E R Yk 60 C5
Sutton Valence Kent 12 F1
Sutton Veny Wilts 18 D11
Sutton Waldron Dorset 8 C4
Sutton Weaver Ches W 57 K11
Sutton Wick BaNES 17 N4
Sutton Wick Oxon 19 N2
Swaby Lincs 53 L8
Swadlincote Derbys 40 H4
Swaffham Norfk 44 D8
Swaffham Bulbeck Cambs 33 N4
Swaffham Prior Cambs 33 P4
Swafield Norfk 45 L4
Swainby N York 66 C7
Swainsthorpe Norfk 45 K9
Swainswick BaNES 18 B7
Swalcliffe Oxon 31 J6
Swalecliffe Kent 23 L9
Swallow Lincs 52 H3
Swallow Beck Lincs 52 D9
Swallowcliffe Wilts 8 E2
Swallowfield Wokham 20 B9
Swanage Dorset 8 F10
Swanbourne Bucks 32 B10
Swan Green Ches W 49 N1

Swanland E R Yk 60 G8
Swanley Kent 21 P9
Swanley Village Kent 21 Q9
Swanmore Hants 9 P4
Swannington Leics 41 K4
Swannington Norfk 45 J6
Swanpool Lincs 52 D9
Swanscombe Kent 22 C8
Swansea Swans 26 E9
Swansea Airport Swans 26 D9
Swansea West Services Swans 26 E8
Swanton Abbot Norfk 45 L5
Swanton Morley Norfk 44 G6
Swanton Novers Norfk 44 G4
Swan Village Sandw 40 C8
Swanwick Derbys 51 K9
Swanwick Hants 9 N5
Swarby Lincs 42 F3
Swardeston Norfk 45 K9
Swarkestone Derbys 41 J2
Swarland Nthumb 81 N12
Swarraton Hants 19 P12
Swarthmoor Cumb 62 F6
Swaton Lincs 42 G3
Swavesey Cambs 33 K3
Sway Hants 9 J7
Swayfield Lincs 42 E5
Swaythling C Sotn 9 M4
Sweetham Devon 15 Q11
Sweethaws E Susx 11 P4
Sweets Cnwll 4 E2
Sweetshouse Cnwll 3 N4
Swefling Suffk 35 M4
Swepstone Leics 41 J5
Swerford Oxon 31 J7
Swettenham Ches E 49 P3
Swilland Suffk 35 K6
Swillington Leeds 59 J7
Swimbridge Devon 15 L6
Swimbridge Newland Devon 15 K6
Swinbrook Oxon 30 H10
Swincliffe N York 58 G3
Swinderby Lincs 52 C10
Swindon Gloucs 29 N4
Swindon Staffs 39 Q4
Swindon Swindn 18 G4
Swine E R Yk 61 K7
Swinefleet E R Yk 60 D9
Swineshead Bed 32 F4
Swineshead Lincs 43 J3
Swiney Highld 110 E8
Swinford Leics 41 M10
Swingfield Minnis Kent 13 N2
Swingfield Street Kent 13 N2
Swingleton Green Suffk 34 F7
Swinhoe Nthumb 81 P8
Swinithwaite N York 65 J9
Swinside Cumb 71 K10
Swinstead Lincs 42 E5
Swinton Border 80 H5
Swinton N York 65 L10
Swinton N York 66 G11
Swinton Rothm 51 K2
Swinton Salfd 57 P8
Swiss Valley Carmth 26 C8
Swithland Leics 41 M5
Swordale Highld 107 J8
Swordland Highld 97 L10
Swordly Highld 109 N3
Swynnerton Staffs 49 Q8
Swyre Dorset 7 M5
Sychtyn Powys 38 B1
Syde Gloucs 29 N6
Sydenham Gt Lon 21 M8
Sydenham Oxon 20 B3
Sydenham Damerel Devon 5 J5
Syderstone Norfk 44 D4
Sydling St Nicholas Dorset 7 P3
Sydmonton Hants 19 M8
Syerston Notts 51 Q10
Sykehouse Donc 59 N10
Symbister Shet 111 k3
Symington S Ayrs 76 G5
Symington S Lans 78 E2
Symondsbury Dorset 7 L4
Symonds Yat (West) Herefs 28 G5
Syre Highld 109 M7
Syreford Gloucs 30 D9
Syresham Nhants 31 N5
Syston Leics 41 N5
Syston Lincs 42 D2
Sytchampton Worcs 39 Q8
Sywell Nhants 32 B4

T

Tackley Oxon 31 L9
Tacolneston Norfk 45 J10
Tadcaster N York 59 L5
Taddington Derbys 50 F6
Tadley Hants 19 P8
Tadlow Cambs 33 J7
Tadmarton Oxon 31 K6
Tadpole Swindn 18 G3
Tadworth Surrey 21 K11
Taff's Well Rhondd 27 N11
Taibach Neath 26 G10
Tain Highld 107 M6
Tain Highld 110 E3
Takeley Essex 33 P11
Takeley Street Essex 33 N11
Talaton Devon 6 E4
Talbenny Pembks 24 E6
Talbot Village BCP 8 F8
Taleford Devon 6 E4
Talerddig Powys 47 Q10
Talgarreg Cerdgn 36 G9
Talgarth Powys 27 N3
Talisker Highld 96 D4
Talke Staffs 49 Q5
Talke Pits Staffs 49 Q5
Talkin Cumb 71 Q4
Talla Linnfoots Border 79 J5
Tallaminnock S Ayrs 76 G10
Tallarn Green Wrexhm 49 J6
Tallentire Cumb 70 H8
Talley Carmth 26 E3
Tallington Lincs 42 F8
Talmine Highld 109 K3
Talog Carmth 25 N4

Talsarn Cerdgn 37 J9
Talsarnau Gwynd 47 K4
Talskiddy Cnwll 3 K3
Talwrn IoA 54 G6
Tal-y-bont Cerdgn 37 K3
Tal-y-Bont Conwy 55 L7
Talybont Gwynd 47 J2
Tal-y-bont Gwynd 54 H7
Talybont-on-Usk Powys 27 N4
Tal-y-Cafn Conwy 55 L7
Tal-y-coed Mons 28 E6
Talysarn Gwynd 54 G10
Tamar Valley Mining District Devon 5 J7
Tamerton Foliot C Plym 5 K7
Tamworth Staffs 40 G6
Tamworth Services Warwks 40 G7
Tandridge Surrey 21 M12
Tanfield Dur 73 L9
Tanfield Lea Dur 73 L9
Tangasdale W Isls 111 a7
Tangley Hants 19 K9
Tangmere W Susx 10 E8
Tankerness Ork 111 h2
Tankersley Barns 51 J2
Tankerton Kent 23 L9
Tannach Highld 110 G6
Tannachie Abers 95 N5
Tannadice Angus 93 N4
Tanner's Green Worcs 40 E11
Tannington Suffk 35 L4
Tannochside N Lans 85 L10
Tansley Derbys 51 J8
Tansor Nhants 42 F11
Tantobie Dur 73 L9
Tanworth in Arden Warwks 40 E12
Tan-y-groes Cerdgn 36 E10
Taobh Tuath W Isls 111 b3
Taplow Bucks 20 E7
Tarbert Ag & B 75 J3
Tarbert Ag & B 83 N8
Tarbert W Isls 111 c3
Tarbet Ag & B 84 F3
Tarbet Highld 97 L10
Tarbet Highld 108 D7
Tarbolton S Ayrs 76 G6
Tarbrax S Lans 86 B10
Tardebigge Worcs 30 D1
Tarfside Angus 94 H1
Tarland Abers 94 H2
Tarleton Lancs 57 J5
Tarlton Gloucs 29 N8
Tarnock Somset 17 K5
Tarporley Ches W 49 K3
Tarrant Crawford Dorset 8 D6
Tarrant Gunville Dorset 8 D5
Tarrant Hinton Dorset 8 D5
Tarrant Keyneston Dorset 8 D6
Tarrant Launceston Dorset 8 D5
Tarrant Monkton Dorset 8 D5
Tarrant Rawston Dorset 8 D6
Tarrant Rushton Dorset 8 D6
Tarring Neville E Susx 11 N8
Tarrington Herefs 28 H1
Tarskavaig Highld 96 H6
Tarves Abers 102 H8
Tarvin Ches W 49 J3
Tasburgh Norfk 45 K10
Tasley Shrops 39 N3
Tatenhill Staffs 40 G3
Tathwell Lincs 53 K6
Tatsfield Surrey 21 N11
Tattenhall Ches W 49 J4
Tatterford Norfk 44 E5
Tattersett Norfk 44 D4
Tattershall Lincs 52 H11
Tattershall Thorpe Lincs 52 H10
Tattingstone Suffk 35 J8
Tattingstone White Horse Suffk 35 J8
Tatton Park Ches E 57 N11
Tatworth Somset 7 J2
Tauchers Moray 101 M5
Taunton Somset 16 G10
Taunton Deane Services Somset 16 G11
Taverham Norfk 45 J7
Tavernspite Pembks 25 L6
Tavistock Devon 5 K5
Tavistock Devon 5 K5
Taw Green Devon 15 L11
Tawstock Devon 15 K6
Taxal Derbys 50 D5
Tay Bridge C Dund 93 M9
Tay Forest Park P & K 92 B4
Tayinloan Ag & B 75 K4
Taynton Gloucs 29 J4
Taynton Oxon 30 G10
Taynuilt Ag & B 90 D9
Tayport Fife 93 M9
Tayvallich Ag & B 83 L5
Tealby Lincs 52 G5
Tealing Angus 93 M7
Team Valley Gatesd 73 M8
Teangue Highld 97 J7
Teanord Highld 107 K9
Tebay Cumb 63 L2
Tebay Services Cumb 63 L2
Tebworth C Beds 32 E10
Tedburn St Mary Devon 5 Q2
Teddington Gloucs 29 N3
Teddington Gt Lon 21 J8
Tedstone Delamere Herefs 39 M9
Tedstone Wafer Herefs 39 M9
Teeton Nhants 41 P12
Teffont Evias Wilts 8 E2
Teffont Magna Wilts 8 E2
Tegryn Pembks 25 L3
Teigh Rutlnd 42 C7
Teigngrace Devon 6 B7
Teignmouth Devon 6 C8
Teindside Border 79 P7
Telford Wrekin 39 M1
Telford Services Shrops 39 N1
Tellisford Somset 18 B9
Telscombe E Susx 11 N8
Tempar P & K 91 Q5
Templand D & G 78 H10
Temple Cnwll 4 D5
Temple Mdloth 86 G9
Temple Bar Cerdgn 37 J9
Temple Cloud BaNES 17 P4
Templecombe Somset 17 Q10
Temple Grafton Warwks 30 E3

Temple Guiting Gloucs...30 E8
Temple Hirst N York...59 N8
Temple Normanton Derbys...51 K7
Temple of Fiddes Abers...95 N5
Temple Sowerby Cumb...64 B3
Templeton Devon...15 Q9
Templeton Pembks...25 K6
Templetown Dur...73 K10
Tempsford C Beds...32 G6
Tenbury Wells Worcs...39 L8
Tenby Pembks...25 K8
Tendring Essex...35 J11
Tendring Green Essex...35 J10
Tendring Heath Essex...35 J10
Ten Mile Bank Norfk...43 P10
Tenterden Kent...12 H4
Terling Essex...22 F1
Ternhill Shrops...49 L8
Terregles D & G...78 F12
Terrington N York...66 F12
Terrington St Clement Norfk...43 N6
Terrington St John Norfk...43 N6
Teston Kent...22 E11
Testwood Hants...9 L5
Tetbury Gloucs...29 M9
Tetchill Shrops...48 H8
Tetcott Devon...14 F11
Tetford Lincs...53 K8
Tetney Lincs...53 K4
Tetsworth Oxon...20 B3
Tettenhall Wolves...40 B7
Tettenhall Wood Wolves...39 Q3
Teversal Notts...51 L8
Teversham Cambs...33 M5
Teviothead Border...79 N7
Tewin Herts...21 L1
Tewkesbury Gloucs...29 M3
Teynham Kent...23 J10
Thackley C Brad...58 F6
Thainstone Abers...102 G10
Thakeham W Susx...10 H6
Thame Oxon...20 B3
Thames Ditton Surrey...21 J9
Thamesmead Gt Lon...21 P7
Thamesport Medway...22 G8
Thanington Kent...23 L11
Thankerton S Lans...78 F2
Tharston Norfk...45 K10
Thatcham W Berk...19 N7
Thaxted Essex...33 P9
Theakston N York...65 N9
Thealby N Linc...60 F9
Theale Somset...17 L7
Theale W Berk...19 Q6
Thearne E R Yk...61 J6
The Beeches Gloucs...18 F1
Theberton Suffk...35 P4
The Braes Highld...96 G3
The Bridge Kent...22 B8
The Brunt E Loth...87 M7
The Bungalow IoM...56 d4
The Burf Worcs...39 P8
The City Bucks...20 C4
The Common Wilts...9 J2
Theddingworth Leics...41 P9
Theddlethorpe All Saints Lincs...53 M6
Theddlethorpe St Helen Lincs...53 M6
The Deep C KuH...61 J8
The Den N Ayrs...76 F2
The Forstal Kent...13 K3
The Green Cumb...62 D5
The Green Essex...34 C11
The Green N York...66 H6
The Green Wilts...8 C2
The Hill Cumb...62 D5
The Lee Bucks...20 E3
The Lhen IoM...56 d2
Thelnetham Suffk...34 G2
The Lochs Moray...101 L3
Thelveton Norfk...35 J1
Thelwall Warrtn...57 M10
Themelthorpe Norfk...44 H6
The Middles Dur...73 L9
The Moor Kent...12 F4
The Mumbles Swans...26 E10
The Murray S Lans...85 K11
The Neuk Abers...95 M3
Thenford Nhants...31 M6
The Reddings Gloucs...29 M5
Therfield Herts...33 K8
The Ross P & K...92 B10
The Spring Warwks...40 H11
The Stocks Kent...12 H5
The Strand Wilts...18 D8
Thetford Norfk...44 E12
Thetford Forest Park...44 D11
Theydon Bois Essex...21 N4
Thickwood Wilts...18 C6
Thimbleby Lincs...53 J9
Thimbleby N York...66 C8
Thingwall Wirral...56 F11
Thirkleby N York...66 C10
Thirlby N York...66 C10
Thirlestane Border...80 D5
Thirn N York...65 L9
Thirsk N York...65 Q10
Thistleton Lancs...56 H2
Thistleton Rutlnd...42 D6
Thistley Green Suffk...33 Q2
Thixendale N York...60 E3
Thockrington Nthumb...72 G5
Tholomas Drove Cambs...43 L8
Tholthorpe N York...59 L2
Thomastown Abers...102 D7
Thompson Norfk...44 F10
Thomshill Moray...101 L4
Thongsbridge Kirk...58 F11
Thoralby N York...64 H9
Thoresway Lincs...52 G4
Thorganby Lincs...52 H4
Thorganby N York...59 P6
Thorgill N York...66 G9
Thorington Suffk...35 N2
Thorington Street Suffk...34 G9
Thorlby N York...58 C4
Thorley Herts...33 M11
Thorley Street IoW...9 L9
Thormanby N York...66 C11
Thornaby-on-Tees S on T...66 C4
Thornage Norfk...44 H3
Thornborough Bucks...31 Q7
Thornborough N York...65 N10

Thornbury C Brad...58 G7
Thornbury Devon...14 G9
Thornbury Herefs...39 L9
Thornbury S Glos...28 H10
Thornby Nhants...41 P11
Thorncliff Staffs...50 D8
Thorncombe Dorset...7 K3
Thorndon Suffk...35 J3
Thorndon Cross Devon...5 L2
Thorne Donc...59 P10
Thorner Leeds...59 J6
Thorne St Margaret Somset...16 E11
Thorney C Pete...43 J8
Thorney Notts...52 C8
Thorney Somset...17 K10
Thorney Hill Hants...9 H7
Thorney Island W Susx...10 C9
Thornfalcon Somset...16 H10
Thornford Dorset...17 N12
Thorngrafton Nthumb...72 E7
Thorngumbald E R Yk...61 L8
Thornham Norfk...44 C2
Thornham Magna Suffk...34 H3
Thornham Parva Suffk...35 J3
Thornhaugh C Pete...42 F9
Thornhill C Sotn...9 M5
Thornhill Cumb...62 B11
Thornhill D & G...78 E9
Thornhill Derbys...50 E4
Thornhill Kirk...58 G9
Thornhill Stirlg...85 L3
Thornholme E R Yk...61 J2
Thornicombe Dorset...8 C6
Thornington Nthumb...81 J7
Thornley Dur...73 K12
Thornley Dur...73 P11
Thornliebank E Rens...85 J10
Thorns Suffk...34 C6
Thornsett Derbys...50 D4
Thornthwaite Cumb...71 K9
Thornthwaite N York...58 F3
Thornton Angus...93 M6
Thornton Bucks...31 Q7
Thornton C Brad...58 E7
Thornton E R Yk...60 D3
Thornton Fife...86 F3
Thornton Lancs...56 G1
Thornton Leics...41 L6
Thornton Middsb...66 C5
Thornton Nthumb...81 K5
Thornton Curtis N Linc...61 J9
Thorntonhall S Lans...85 K11
Thornton Heath Gt Lon...21 L9
Thornton Hough Wirral...56 F11
Thornton-in-Craven N York...58 B5
Thornton in Lonsdale N York...63 M7
Thornton-le-Beans N York...65 P9
Thornton-le-Clay N York...59 N2
Thornton-le-Dale N York...67 J10
Thornton le Moor Lincs...52 F4
Thornton-le-Moor N York...65 P9
Thornton-le-Moors Ches W...48 H1
Thornton-le-Street N York...65 P9
Thorntonloch E Loth...87 N7
Thornton Rust N York...64 G9
Thornton Steward N York...65 L9
Thornton Watlass N York...65 M9
Thornydykes Border...80 E5
Thornythwaite Cumb...71 N10
Thoroton Notts...51 Q11
Thorp Arch Leeds...59 K5
Thorpe Derbys...50 F10
Thorpe E R Yk...60 G5
Thorpe N York...58 D2
Thorpe Notts...51 Q10
Thorpe Surrey...20 G9
Thorpe Abbotts Norfk...35 K2
Thorpe Arnold Leics...41 Q4
Thorpe Audlin Wakefd...59 L10
Thorpe Bassett N York...67 J11
Thorpe Bay Sthend...22 H6
Thorpe by Water Rutlnd...42 C10
Thorpe Constantine Staffs...40 H6
Thorpe End Norfk...45 L7
Thorpe Green Essex...35 J11
Thorpe Green Suffk...34 F6
Thorpe Hesley Rothm...51 J2
Thorpe in Balne Donc...59 N11
Thorpe Langton Leics...41 Q8
Thorpe Lea Surrey...20 G8
Thorpe-le-Soken Essex...35 K11
Thorpe le Street E R Yk...60 E5
Thorpe Malsor Nhants...32 B2
Thorpe Mandeville Nhants...31 M5
Thorpe Market Norfk...45 L3
Thorpe Marriot Norfk...45 K7
Thorpe Morieux Suffk...34 F6
Thorpeness Suffk...35 P5
Thorpe on the Hill Lincs...52 C9
Thorpe Park Surrey...20 G9
Thorpe St Andrew Norfk...45 L8
Thorpe St Peter Lincs...53 M10
Thorpe Salvin Rothm...51 M5
Thorpe Satchville Leics...41 Q5
Thorpe Thewles S on T...65 P3
Thorpe Tilney Lincs...52 G11
Thorpe Underwood N York...59 L3
Thorpe Waterville Nhants...32 E1
Thorpe Willoughby N York...59 M7
Thorrington Essex...34 H11
Thorverton Devon...6 C3
Thrandeston Suffk...35 J2
Thrapston Nhants...32 E2
Threapwood Ches W...48 H6
Threapwood Staffs...50 D11
Threave S Ayrs...76 F9
Three Bridges W Susx...11 L3
Three Chimneys Kent...12 G3
Three Cocks Powys...27 N2
Three Crosses Swans...26 D9
Three Cups Corner E Susx...12 D6
Threekingham Lincs...42 F3
Three Leg Cross E Susx...12 D4
Three Legged Cross Dorset...8 F6
Three Mile Cross Wokham...20 B9
Threemilestone Cnwll...2 H6
Threemiletown W Loth...86 C7
Threlkeld Cumb...71 M9
Threshers Bush Essex...21 P2
Threshfield N York...58 C2
Thrigby Norfk...45 P7
Thrintoft N York...65 N8
Thriplow Cambs...33 M7

Throcking Herts...33 K10
Throckley N u Ty...73 K7
Throckmorton Worcs...30 C4
Throop BCP...8 G8
Thropton Nthumb...72 H1
Throsk Stirlg...85 P5
Throughgate D & G...78 E11
Throwleigh Devon...5 N3
Throwley Forstal Kent...23 J11
Thrumpton Notts...41 L2
Thrumster Highld...110 G6
Thrunscoe NE Lin...53 K2
Thrupp Gloucs...29 M7
Thrussington Leics...41 P4
Thruxton Hants...19 K10
Thruxton Herefs...28 E2
Thrybergh Rothm...51 L2
Thulston Derbys...41 K2
Thundersley Essex...22 F6
Thurcaston Leics...41 M5
Thurcroft Rothm...51 L3
Thurgarton Norfk...45 K3
Thurgarton Notts...51 P10
Thurgoland Barns...50 H2
Thurlaston Leics...41 L7
Thurlaston Warwks...41 L12
Thurlbear Somset...16 H11
Thurlby Lincs...42 F6
Thurlby Lincs...52 C10
Thurlby Lincs...53 M8
Thurleigh Bed...32 F5
Thurlestone Devon...5 N10
Thurloxton Somset...16 H9
Thurlstone Barns...58 G12
Thurlton Norfk...45 N9
Thurmaston Leics...41 N5
Thurnby Leics...41 N6
Thurne Norfk...45 N7
Thurnham Kent...22 F11
Thurning Nhants...42 F12
Thurning Norfk...44 H4
Thurnscoe Barns...59 L11
Thursby Cumb...71 M5
Thursford Norfk...44 G4
Thursley Surrey...10 E3
Thurso Highld...110 D3
Thurstaston Wirral...56 F11
Thurston Suffk...34 F4
Thurstonfield Cumb...71 M4
Thurstonland Kirk...58 F11
Thurton Norfk...45 M9
Thurvaston Derbys...50 G12
Thuxton Norfk...44 G8
Thwaite N York...64 F7
Thwaite Suffk...35 J3
Thwaite Head Cumb...62 G4
Thwaite St Mary Norfk...45 M10
Thwing E R Yk...67 M12
Tibbermore P & K...92 F10
Tibbers D & G...78 E9
Tibberton Gloucs...29 K4
Tibberton Worcs...30 B3
Tibberton Wrekin...49 M10
Tibenham Norfk...45 J11
Tibshelf Derbys...51 K8
Tibthorpe E R Yk...60 G3
Ticehurst E Susx...12 E4
Tichborne Hants...9 P2
Tickencote Rutlnd...42 E8
Tickenham N Som...17 L2
Tickhill Donc...51 N3
Ticklerton Shrops...39 J4
Ticknall Derbys...41 J3
Tickton E R Yk...60 H6
Tidcombe Wilts...19 K8
Tiddington Oxon...31 P12
Tiddington Warwks...30 G3
Tidebrook E Susx...12 C4
Tideford Cnwll...4 H8
Tidenham Gloucs...28 G9
Tideswell Derbys...50 F6
Tidmarsh W Berk...19 Q6
Tidmington Warwks...30 H6
Tidworth Wilts...19 J10
Tiers Cross Pembks...24 F6
Tiffield Nhants...31 P4
Tigerton Angus...95 J8
Tigh a' Ghearraidh W Isls...111 a4
Tigharry W Isls...111 a4
Tighnabruaich Ag & B...83 P8
Tigley Devon...5 P7
Tilbrook Cambs...32 F3
Tilbury Thurr...22 D8
Tile Cross Birm...40 F9
Tile Hill Covtry...40 H11
Tilehurst Readg...19 Q6
Tilford Surrey...10 E2
Tilgate W Susx...11 L3
Tilham Street Somset...17 M8
Tillicoultry Clacks...85 Q4
Tillietudlem S Lans...77 N3
Tillingham Essex...23 J3
Tillington Herefs...39 J12
Tillington W Susx...10 F5
Tillington Common Herefs...39 J11
Tillybirloch Abers...95 L1
Tillyfourie Abers...102 E11
Tillygreig Abers...103 J10
Tillyrie P & K...86 D2
Tilmanstone Kent...23 P12
Tilney All Saints Norfk...43 P6
Tilney High End Norfk...43 N6
Tilney St Lawrence Norfk...43 N7
Tilshead Wilts...18 F10
Tilstock Shrops...49 K7
Tilston Ches W...49 J5
Tilstone Fearnall Ches W...49 K4
Tilsworth C Beds...32 E11
Tilton on the Hill Leics...41 Q6
Tiltups End Gloucs...29 L8
Timberland Lincs...52 G10
Timbersbrook Ches E...50 B8
Timberscombe Somset...16 C7
Timble N York...58 F4
Timpanheck D & G...71 M1
Timperley Traffd...57 P10
Timsbury BaNES...17 P4
Timsbury Hants...9 L3
Timsgearraidh W Isls...111 c2
Timworth Suffk...34 E3
Timworth Green Suffk...34 E3

Tincleton Dorset...8 B8
Tindale Cumb...72 B8
Tingewick Bucks...31 P7
Tingrith C Beds...32 E9
Tingwall Airport Shet...111 k4
Tingwell Ork...111 h2
Tinhay Devon...5 J3
Tinsley Sheff...51 K3
Tinsley Green W Susx...11 L3
Tintagel Cnwll...4 C3
Tintern Mons...28 F8
Tintinhull Somset...17 M11
Tintwistle Derbys...50 D2
Tinwald D & G...78 G11
Tinwell Rutlnd...42 E8
Tipton Sandw...40 C8
Tipton Green Sandw...40 C8
Tipton St John Devon...6 E5
Tiptree Essex...34 E12
Tiptree Heath Essex...34 G1
Tirabad Powys...37 P11
Tiree Ag & B...88 C7
Tiree Airport Ag & B...88 C7
Tiretigan Ag & B...83 K9
Tirley Gloucs...29 L3
Tiroran Ag & B...89 K10
Tirphil Caerph...27 N7
Tirril Cumb...71 P9
Tisbury Wilts...8 D2
Tissington Derbys...50 F9
Titchberry Devon...14 E6
Titchfield Hants...9 P6
Titchmarsh Nhants...32 E2
Titchwell Norfk...44 C2
Tithby Notts...51 P12
Titley Herefs...38 G9
Titsey Surrey...21 N11
Titson Cnwll...14 E10
Tittensor Staffs...49 Q7
Tittleshall Norfk...44 E6
Titton Worcs...39 P7
Tiverton Ches W...49 K4
Tiverton Devon...6 C1
Tivetshall St Margaret Norfk...45 K11
Tivetshall St Mary Norfk...45 J11
Tixall Staffs...40 C3
Tixover Rutlnd...42 D9
Toab Shet...111 k5
Tobermory Ag & B...89 L5
Toberonochy Ag & B...83 L2
Tobha Mòr W Isls...111 a5
Tocher Abers...102 F8
Tochieneal Moray...101 P3
Tockenham Wilts...18 F5
Tockholes Bl w D...57 M4
Tockington S Glos...28 H10
Tockwith N York...59 L4
Todber Dorset...8 B4
Toddington C Beds...32 E10
Toddington Gloucs...30 D7
Toddington Services C Beds...32 E10
Todenham Gloucs...30 G7
Todhills Angus...93 M7
Todhills Rest Area Cumb...71 N3
Todmorden Calder...58 C8
Todwick Rothm...51 L4
Toft Cambs...33 K5
Toft Lincs...42 F6
Toft Shet...111 k3
Toft Hill Dur...65 K2
Toft Monks Norfk...45 N10
Toft next Newton Lincs...52 E6
Toftrees Norfk...44 E5
Togston Nthumb...73 M1
Tokavaig Highld...96 H7
Tokers Green Oxon...20 B7
Tolastadh bho Thuath W Isls...111 e1
Tolland Somset...16 E9
Tollard Royal Wilts...8 D4
Toll Bar Donc...59 M11
Toller Fratrum Dorset...7 N4
Toller Porcorum Dorset...7 N3
Tollerton N York...59 L2
Tollerton Notts...41 N1
Tollesbury Essex...23 J2
Tolleshunt D'Arcy Essex...22 H2
Tolleshunt Knights Essex...22 H1
Tolleshunt Major Essex...22 H2
Toll of Birness Abers...103 K8
Tolpuddle Dorset...8 B8
Tolworth Gt Lon...21 J9
Tomatin Highld...99 M4
Tomchrasky Highld...98 C6
Tomdoun Highld...98 B8
Tomich Highld...98 D4
Tomich Highld...107 J11
Tomich Highld...107 K2
Tomich Highld...107 L8
Tomintoul Moray...101 J10
Tomnacross Highld...98 G2
Tomnavoulin Moray...101 J9
Tonbridge Kent...12 C2
Tondu Brdgnd...27 J11
Tonedale Somset...16 F11
Tong C Brad...58 G7
Tong Kent...23 J11
Tong Shrops...39 P1
Tong W Isls...111 d2
Tonge Leics...41 K3
Tongham Surrey...10 E1
Tongland D & G...69 Q8
Tong Norton Shrops...39 P1
Tongue Highld...109 K4
Tongwynlais Cardif...27 N11
Tonmawr Neath...26 H9
Tonna Neath...26 G8
Tonwell Herts...33 K12
Tonypandy Rhondd...27 L9
Tonyrefail Rhondd...27 L10
Toot Baldon Oxon...19 P1
Toot Hill Essex...21 P3
Toothill Swindn...18 G4
Tooting Gt Lon...21 L8
Tooting Bec Gt Lon...21 L8
Topcliffe N York...65 P11
Topcroft Norfk...45 L10
Topcroft Street Norfk...45 L10
Toppesfield Essex...34 C8
Toprow Norfk...45 K9
Topsham Devon...6 C5
Torbeg N Ayrs...75 N6
Torboll Highld...107 M3
Torbreck Highld...99 J2

Torbryan Devon...5 Q6
Torcastle Highld...90 F1
Torcross Devon...5 Q10
Tore Highld...107 K10
Torinturk Ag & B...83 M9
Torksey Lincs...52 B7
Torlundy Highld...90 F2
Tormarton S Glos...18 B5
Tormore N Ayrs...75 N6
Tornagrain Highld...107 M11
Tornaveen Abers...95 K2
Torness Highld...98 H4
Toronto Dur...65 L2
Torpenhow Cumb...71 K7
Torphichen W Loth...86 A7
Torphins Abers...95 K2
Torpoint Cnwll...5 J8
Torquay Torbay...6 C9
Torquhan Border...87 J11
Torran Highld...104 H11
Torrance E Duns...85 K8
Torranyard N Ayrs...76 F3
Torridon Highld...105 N10
Torridon House Highld...105 M10
Torrin Highld...96 G5
Torrisdale Ag & B...75 M5
Torrisdale Highld...109 M4
Torrish Highld...110 A11
Torrisholme Lancs...63 J9
Torrobull Highld...107 K2
Torry C Aber...95 Q2
Torryburn Fife...86 B5
Torteval Guern...6 a2
Torthorwald D & G...78 G12
Tortington W Susx...10 G8
Torton Worcs...39 Q7
Tortworth S Glos...29 J9
Torvaig Highld...96 F2
Torver Cumb...62 F4
Torwood Falk...85 P6
Torwoodlee Border...79 P2
Torworth Notts...51 P4
Toscaig Highld...97 J3
Toseland Cambs...33 J4
Tosside Lancs...63 P10
Tostock Suffk...34 F4
Totaig Highld...104 B11
Tote Highld...104 F11
Tote Highld...104 G9
Totland IoW...9 K9
Totley Sheff...50 H5
Totnes Devon...5 Q7
Toton Notts...41 L1
Totronald Ag & B...88 E5
Totscore Highld...104 E8
Tottenham Gt Lon...21 M5
Tottenhill Norfk...43 Q7
Totteridge Gt Lon...21 K5
Totternhoe C Beds...32 E11
Tottington Bury...57 P6
Totton Hants...9 L5
Toulston N York...59 K6
Toulvaddie Highld...107 P6
Tovil Kent...22 F11
Toward Ag & B...84 C8
Toward Quay Ag & B...84 B9
Towcester Nhants...31 P4
Towednack Cnwll...2 D7
Tower of London Gt Lon...21 M7
Towersey Oxon...20 B3
Towie Abers...101 N11
Tow Law Dur...73 K11
Town End Cambs...43 L10
Townend W Duns...84 G7
Townhead Barns...50 H2
Townhead D & G...78 G10
Townhead of Greenlaw D & G...70 C3
Townhill Fife...86 D4
Town Littleworth E Susx...11 N6
Townshend Cnwll...2 E8
Town Street Suffk...44 C11
Town Yetholm Border...80 H8
Towthorpe C York...59 N3
Towton N York...59 L6
Towyn Conwy...55 P6
Toxteth Lpool...56 G10
Toynton All Saints Lincs...53 L10
Toy's Hill Kent...21 P12
Trabboch E Ayrs...76 H5
Trabbochburn E Ayrs...76 H7
Tradespark Highld...100 D4
Trafford Park Traffd...57 P9
Trallong Powys...27 K3
Tranent E Loth...86 H7
Tranmere Wirral...56 G10
Trantelbeg Highld...109 Q5
Trantlemore Highld...109 Q5
Trap Carmth...26 E5
Traprain E Loth...87 L7
Traquair Border...79 M3
Trawden Lancs...58 B6
Trawsfynydd Gwynd...47 L4
Trealaw Rhondd...27 L9
Treales Lancs...56 H3
Trearddur Bay IoA...54 B5
Trebetherick Cnwll...4 B5
Treborough Somset...16 D8
Trebullett Cnwll...4 H5
Treburley Cnwll...4 H5
Trecastle Powys...27 J3
Trecwn Pembks...24 G3
Trecynon Rhondd...27 L7
Tredegar Blae G...27 N7
Tredington Gloucs...29 M3
Tredington Warwks...30 H5
Tredunnock Mons...28 D9
Treen Cnwll...2 B10
Treeton Rothm...51 K4
Trefasser Pembks...24 F2
Trefecca Powys...27 N3
Trefechan Myr Td...27 L7
Trefeglwys Powys...37 Q3
Treffgarne Pembks...24 G4
Treffgarne Owen Pembks...24 F4
Trefilan Cerdgn...37 J3
Trefin Pembks...24 E3
Trefnant Denbgs...48 B3
Trefonen Shrops...48 F9
Trefor Gwynd...46 E3
Treforest Rhondd...27 M10
Trefriw Conwy...55 L8
Tregadillett Cnwll...4 G4
Tregare Mons...28 E6

Tregaron Cerdgn 37 L8
Tregarth Gwynd 54 H7
Tregeare Cnwll 4 F3
Tregeiriog Wrexhm 48 D8
Tregele IoA 54 E3
Treglemais Pembks 24 E3
Tregonetha Cnwll 3 L3
Tregonning & Gwinear
Mining District Cnwll 2 E9
Tregony Cnwll 3 K6
Tregorrick Cnwll 3 M5
Tregoyd Powys 27 P2
Tre-groes Cerdgn 36 G10
Tre-gynwr Carmth 25 P5
Trehafod Rhondd 27 L10
Trehan Cnwll 5 J8
Treharris Myr Td 27 M9
Treherbert Rhondd 27 K8
Trekenner Cnwll 4 H5
Treknow Cnwll 4 C3
Trelawnyd Flints 56 C11
Trelech Carmth 25 M3
Treleddyd-fawr Pembks 24 D3
Trelewis Myr Td 27 M9
Trelights Cnwll 4 B4
Trelill Cnwll 4 C5
Trellech Mons 28 F7
Trelogan Flints 56 D11
Tremadog Gwynd 47 J4
Tremail Cnwll 4 E3
Tremain Cerdgn 36 D10
Tremaine Cnwll 4 F3
Tremar Cnwll 4 G6
Trematon Cnwll 5 J8
Tremeirchion Denbgs 48 C2
Trenance Cnwll 3 J3
Trenance Cnwll 3 L2
Trench Wrekin 49 M11
Trenear Cnwll 2 G9
Treneglos Cnwll 4 F3
Trent Dorset 17 N11
Trentham C Stke 49 Q7
Trentishoe Devon 15 L3
Trent Vale C Stke 49 Q6
Treoes V Glam 27 K12
Treorchy Rhondd 27 K8
Trequite Cnwll 3 M1
Trerhyngyll V Glam 27 L12
Trerulefoot Cnwll 4 H8
Tresaith Cerdgn 36 E9
Tresco IoS 2 b2
Trescowe Cnwll 2 E9
Tresean Cnwll 2 H4
Tresham Gloucs 29 L9
Treshnish Isles Ag & B 88 G7
Tresillian Cnwll 3 K6
Treskinnick Cross Cnwll 14 D11
Tresmeer Cnwll 4 F3
Tresparrett Cnwll 4 E2
Tressait P & K 92 C4
Tresta Shet 111 k4
Tresta Shet 111 m2
Treswell Notts 52 A7
Tre Taliesin Cerdgn 37 L3
Trethevey Cnwll 4 D3
Trethewey Cnwll 2 B10
Trethurgy Cnwll 3 M5
Tretire Herefs 28 F4
Tretower Powys 27 P5
Treuddyn Flints 48 F4
Trevalga Cnwll 4 D3
Trevalyn Wrexhm 48 H4
Trevarrian Cnwll 3 J3
Treveal Cnwll 2 H4
Treveighan Cnwll 4 D4
Trevellas Downs Cnwll 2 H5
Trevelmond Cnwll 4 F7
Treverva Cnwll 2 H9
Trevescan Cnwll 2 B10
Treviscoe Cnwll 3 L5
Trevone Cnwll 3 K1
Trevor Wrexhm 48 F7
Trewalder Cnwll 4 D4
Trewarmett Cnwll 4 D3
Trewavas Mining District
Cnwll 2 E9
Trewen Cnwll 4 F4
Trewint Cnwll 4 F4
Trewithian Cnwll 3 K8
Trewoon Cnwll 3 L5
Treyford W Susx 10 D6
Trimdon Dur 65 P1
Trimdon Colliery Dur 65 P1
Trimdon Grange Dur 65 P1
Trimingham Norfk 45 L3
Trimley St Martin Suffk 35 L8
Trimley St Mary Suffk 35 L9
Trimsaran Carmth 26 B7
Trimstone Devon 15 J4
Trinafour P & K 91 Q4
Tring Herts 20 E2
Trinity Angus 95 K9
Trinity Jersey 7 b1
Trinity Gask P & K 92 E11
Triscombe Somset 16 F8
Trislaig Highld 90 E2
Trispen Cnwll 3 J6
Tritlington Nthumb 73 L3
Trochry P & K 92 E7
Troedyraur Cerdgn 36 E10
Troedyrhiw Myr Td 27 M8
Troon Cnwll 2 F8
Troon S Ayrs 76 F5
Tropical World Roundhay
Park Leeds 59 J6
Trossachs Stirlg 84 H2
Trossachs Pier Stirlg 84 H2
Troston Suffk 34 E3
Trotshill Worcs 30 B3
Trottiscliffe Kent 22 D10
Trotton W Susx 10 D5
Troutbeck Cumb 62 H2
Troutbeck Bridge Cumb 62 H3
Troway Derbys 51 K5
Trowbridge Wilts 18 C8
Trowell Notts 51 L11
Trowell Services Notts 51 L11
Trowle Common Wilts 18 C8
Trowse Newton Norfk 45 L8
Trudoxhill Somset 17 Q7
Trull Somset 16 G10
Trumpan Highld 104 C9
Trumpet Herefs 28 H2
Trumpington Cambs 33 M6
Trunch Norfk 45 L3
Truro Cnwll 3 J6
Trusham Devon 6
Trusley Derbys 40 G1
Trusthorpe Lincs 53 N6
Trysull Staffs 39 Q4
Tubney Oxon 19 M2
Tuckenhay Devon 5 Q8
Tuckhill Shrops 39 P5
Tuckingmill Cnwll 2 F7
Tuckingmill Wilts 8 D2
Tuckton BCP 8 G8
Tuddenham Suffk 34 C3
Tuddenham Suffk 35 K7
Tudeley Kent 12 C2
Tudhoe Dur 65 M1
Tudweiliog Gwynd 46 D4
Tuffley Gloucs 29 L6
Tufton Hants 19 M10
Tufton Pembks 24 H3
Tugby Leics 41 Q7
Tugford Shrops 39 K5
Tughall Nthumb 81 P8
Tullibody Clacks 85 P4
Tullich Abers 94 F3
Tullich Highld 99 J4
Tullich Highld 107 P7
Tulliemet P & K 92 E5
Tulloch Abers 102 G8
Tullochgorm Ag & B 83 P4
Tulloch Station Highld 98 E11
Tullymurdoch P & K 92 H5
Tullynessle Abers 102 D10
Tulse Hill Gt Lon 21 L8
Tumble Carmth 26 D6
Tumby Lincs 53 J10
Tumby Woodside Lincs 53 J11
Tummel Bridge P & K 92 B4
Tunbridge Wells Kent 12 C3
Tundergarth D & G 79 J11
Tunga W Isls 111 d2
Tunley BaNES 17 Q4
Tunstall E R Yk 61 M7
Tunstall Kent 22 H10
Tunstall Lancs 63 L7
Tunstall N York 65 L8
Tunstall Norfk 45 N8
Tunstall Staffs 49 P9
Tunstall Suffk 35 M6
Tunstall Sundld 73 P9
Tunstead Derbys 50 E6
Tunstead Norfk 45 L6
Tunstead Milton Derbys 50 D5
Tupsley Herefs 28 G2
Turgis Green Hants 8 B10
Turkdean Gloucs 30 E9
Tur Langton Leics 41 Q8
Turleigh Wilts 18 B8
Turnastone Herefs 28 D2
Turnberry S Ayrs 76 D9
Turnditch Derbys 50 H10
Turners Hill W Susx 11 M3
Turnhouse C Edin 86 D7
Turnworth Dorset 8 B6
Turriff Abers 102 F5
Turton Bottoms Bl w D 57 N6
Turves Cambs 43 K10
Turvey Bed 32 D6
Turville Bucks 20 C5
Turweston Bucks 31 N6
Tutbury Staffs 40 G2
Tutnall Worcs 30 C9
Tuttington Norfk 45 K5
Tuxford Notts 51 Q6
Twatt Ork 111 g2
Twatt Shet 111 k4
Twechar E Duns 85 L7
Tweedbank Border 80 C7
Tweedmouth Nthumb 81 L4
Tweedsmuir Border 78 H4
Twelveheads Cnwll 2 H7
Twemlow Green Ches E 49 P2
Twenty Lincs 42 G6
Twerton BaNES 17 Q4
Twickenham Gt Lon 21 J8
Twigworth Gloucs 29 L4
Twineham W Susx 11 K6
Twinstead Essex 34 E9
Twitchen Devon 15 N6
Two Dales Derbys 50 H8
Two Gates Staffs 40 G7
Two Waters Herts 20 G3
Twycross Leics 41 J6
Twycross Zoo Leics 40 H6
Twyford Bucks 31 P8
Twyford Hants 9 N3
Twyford Leics 41 Q5
Twyford Norfk 45 G5
Twyford Wokham 20 C8
Twynholm D & G 69 P8
Twyning Gloucs 29 M2
Twynllanan Carmth 26 G4
Twywell Nhants 32 D2
Tyberton Herefs 28 D2
Tyburn Birm 40 F8
Tycroes Carmth 26 E6
Tycrwyn Powys 48 C10
Tydd Gote Lincs 43 M6
Tydd St Giles Cambs 43 L6
Tydd St Mary Lincs 43 M6
Tye Green Essex 33 P9
Tyldesley Wigan 57 M8
Tyler Hill Kent 23 L10
Tylorstown Rhondd 27 L9
Tyn-nant Conwy 48 B6
Ty'n-dwr Denbgs 48 E7
Tyndrum Stirlg 91 J9
Tynemouth N Tyne 73 P7
Tyne Tunnel S Tyne 73 N7
Tyningham E Loth 87 L6
Tynron D & G 77 N11
Tyn-y-Groes Conwy 55 L7
Tyrie Abers 103 J3
Tyringham M Keyn 32 C7
Tyseley Birm 40 E9
Tythegston Brdgnd 27 J11
Tytherington Ches E 50 B6
Tytherington S Glos 29 J10
Tytherington Wilts 18 D11
Tytherleigh Devon 7 J3
Tytherton Lucas Wilts 18 D6
Tywardreath Cnwll 3 N5
Tywyn Gwynd 47 J10

U

Ubbeston Green Suffk 35 M3
Ubley BaNES 17 M5
Uckfield E Susx 11 P6
Uckinghall Worcs 29 M2
Uckington Gloucs 29 M4
Uddingston S Lans 85 L10
Uddington S Lans 78 E3
Udimore E Susx 12 G6
Udny Green Abers 103 J9
Udny Station Abers 103 J9
Uffculme Devon 16 E12
Uffington Lincs 42 F8
Uffington Oxon 19 K3
Uffington Shrops 49 K11
Ufford C Pete 42 F8
Ufford Suffk 35 L6
Ufton Warwks 31 J2
Ufton Nervet W Berk 19 Q7
Ugadale Ag & B 75 L6
Ugborough Devon 5 N8
Uggeshall Suffk 35 P2
Ugglebarnby N York 67 J6
Ughill Sheff 50 G3
Ugley Essex 33 N10
Ugley Green Essex 33 N10
Ugthorpe N York 66 H5
Uibhist A Deas W Isls 111 b6
Uibhist A Tuath W Isls 111 a4
Uig Ag & B 88 E5
Uig Highld 104 B10
Uig Highld 104 E9
Uig W Isls 111 c2
Uigshader Highld 104 F12
Uisken Ag & B 89 J11
Ulbster Highld 110 G5
Ulceby Lincs 53 L8
Ulceby Lincs 61 J10
Ulceby Skitter N Linc 61 J10
Ulcombe Kent 12 G1
Uldale Cumb 71 L7
Uley Gloucs 29 K8
Ulgham Nthumb 73 M3
Ullapool Highld 106 B4
Ullenhall Warwks 30 E1
Ulleskelf N York 59 M6
Ullesthorpe Leics 41 L9
Ulley Rothm 51 L4
Ullingswick Herefs 39 L11
Ullock Cumb 70 H10
Ullswater Cumb 71 N10
Ullswater Steamers Cumb 71 N11
Ulpha Cumb 62 E4
Ulrome E R Yk 61 K3
Ulsta Shet 111 k3
Ulva Ag & B 89 J8
Ulverley Green Solhll 40 F10
Ulverston Cumb 62 F6
Ulwell Dorset 8 F10
Ulzieside D & G 77 N9
Umberleigh Devon 15 K7
Unapool Highld 108 E8
Underbarrow Cumb 63 J4
Under Burnmouth Border 79 P11
Undercliffe C Brad 58 F7
Underdale Shrops 49 J11
Underriver Kent 22 B11
Underwood Notts 51 L10
Undy Mons 28 E10
Union Mills IoM 56 c5
Unst Shet 111 m2
Unstone Derbys 51 J5
Upavon Wilts 18 G9
Upchurch Kent 22 G9
Upcott Devon 15 N6
Up Exe Devon 6 C3
Upgate Norfk 45 J6
Uphall Dorset 7 M3
Uphall W Loth 86 C7
Upham Devon 15 Q9
Upham Hants 9 N4
Uphampton Herefs 38 H9
Uphampton Worcs 39 Q8
Uphill N Som 17 J5
Up Holland Lancs 57 K7
Uplawmoor E Rens 84 G11
Upleadon Gloucs 29 K4
Upleatham R & Cl 66 E4
Uploders Dorset 7 M4
Uplowman Devon 16 D11
Uplyme Devon 7 J4
Up Marden W Susx 10 C7
Upminster Gt Lon 22 C6
Up Mudford Somset 17 N11
Up Nately Hants 20 B11
Upottery Devon 6 G2
Upper Affcot Shrops 39 J5
Upper Arley Worcs 39 N6
Upper Badcall Highld 108 D7
Upper Basildon W Berk 19 P5
Upper Beeding W Susx 11 K7
Upper Benefield Nhants 42 E11
Upper Bentley Worcs 30 C2
Upper Broadheath Worcs 39 P10
Upper Broughton Notts 41 P3
Upper Bucklebury W Berk 19 P7
Upper Burgate Hants 8 H4
Upperby Cumb 71 N5
Upper Caldecote C Beds 32 G7
Upper Chapel Powys 27 L1
Upper Chicksgrove Wilts 8 E2
Upper Chute Wilts 19 K9
Upper Clapton Gt Lon 21 M6
Upper Clatford Hants 19 L11
Upper Cound Shrops 39 K2
Upper Cumberworth Kirk 58 G11
Upper Dallachy Moray 101 M3
Upper Deal Kent 23 Q11
Upper Dean Bed 32 F4
Upper Denby Kirk 58 G11
Upper Dicker E Susx 12 B7
Upper Dovercourt Essex 35 M9
Upper Drumbane Stirlg 85 L2
Upper Dunsforth N York 59 K2
Upper Eashing Surrey 10 F2
Upper Eathie Highld 107 M9
Upper Egleton Herefs 39 M12
Upper Elkstone Staffs 50 D8
Upper Ellastone Staffs 50 E11
Upper Farringdon Hants 10 B3
Upper Framilode Gloucs 29 K6
Upper Froyle Hants 10 C2
Upperglen Highld 104 D11
Upper Godney Somset 17 L7
Upper Gravenhurst C Beds 32 G9
Upper Green W Berk 19 L7
Upper Grove Common Herefs 28 G4
Upper Hale Surrey 10 D1
Upper Halliford Surrey 20 H9
Upper Hambleton Rutlnd 42 D8
Upper Harbledown Kent 23 L10
Upper Hartfield E Susx 11 P3
Upper Hatherley Gloucs 29 M5
Upper Heaton Kirk 58 F9
Upper Helmsley N York 59 P3
Upper Hergest Herefs 38 F10
Upper Heyford Nhants 31 P3
Upper Heyford Oxon 31 L8
Upper Hill Herefs 39 J10
Upper Hopton Kirk 58 G9
Upper Hulme Staffs 50 D8
Upper Inglesham Swindn 18 H2
Upper Killay Swans 26 D9
Upper Kinchrackine Ag & B 90 G10
Upper Knockando Moray 101 J6
Upper Lambourn W Berk 19 K5
Upper Landywood Staffs 40 C6
Upper Langford N Som 17 L4
Upper Langwith Derbys 51 L6
Upper Largo Fife 87 J2
Upper Leigh Staffs 50 D12
Upper Lochton Abers 95 L3
Upper Longdon Staffs 40 D5
Upper Lybster Highld 110 F8
Upper Lydbrook Gloucs 28 H6
Upper Lye Herefs 38 H8
Uppermill Oldham 58 C11
Upper Milton Worcs 39 P7
Upper Minety Wilts 18 E3
Upper Mulben Moray 101 L5
Upper Netchwood Shrops 39 L4
Upper Nobut Staffs 40 D1
Upper Norwood W Susx 10 F6
Upper Oddington Gloucs 30 G8
Upper Poppleton C York 59 M4
Upper Ratley Hants 9 K3
Upper Rissington Gloucs 30 G9
Upper Rochford Worcs 39 L8
Upper Ruscoe D & G 69 N6
Upper Sapey Herefs 39 M8
Upper Seagry Wilts 18 D5
Upper Shelton C Beds 32 E7
Upper Sheringham Norfk 45 J2
Upper Skelmorlie N Ayrs 84 D9
Upper Slaughter Gloucs 30 F9
Upper Soudley Gloucs 29 H6
Upper Standen Kent 13 N3
Upper Stoke Norfk 45 L9
Upper Stondon C Beds 32 G9
Upper Stowe Nhants 31 N3
Upper Street Hants 8 H4
Upper Street Norfk 45 M6
Upper Street Norfk 45 M6
Upper Street Suffk 34 C6
Upper Street Suffk 35 L7
Upper Sundon C Beds 32 F10
Upper Swell Gloucs 30 F8
Upper Tean Staffs 50 D11
Upperthong Kirk 58 F11
Upperton W Susx 10 F5
Upper Town Herefs 39 L11
Uppertown Highld 110 G1
Upper Town N Som 17 M3
Upper Town Suffk 34 F4
Upper Tumble Carmth 26 D6
Upper Tysoe Warwks 31 J5
Upper Victoria Angus 93 P8
Upper Wardington Oxon 31 L5
Upper Welland Worcs 29 K1
Upper Wellingham E Susx 11 N7
Upper Weybread Suffk 35 K2
Upper Wield Hants 19 Q11
Upper Winchendon Bucks 31 Q10
Upper Woodford Wilts 18 G12
Upper Wraxall Wilts 18 B6
Uppingham Rutlnd 42 C9
Uppington Shrops 39 L1
Upsall N York 66 C9
Upsettlington Border 81 J5
Upshire Essex 21 N4
Up Somborne Hants 9 L2
Upstreet Kent 23 N10
Upton Bucks 31 Q10
Upton C Pete 42 G9
Upton Cambs 32 H2
Upton Ches W 48 H2
Upton Cnwll 4 G6
Upton Devon 6 E3
Upton Devon 5 P10
Upton Dorset 7 Q6
Upton Dorset 8 E8
Upton Halton 57 J10
Upton Hants 9 L4
Upton Hants 19 L9
Upton Leics 41 J7
Upton Lincs 52 C6
Upton Norfk 45 N7
Upton Notts 51 N9
Upton Notts 51 Q9
Upton Oxon 19 N4
Upton Slough 20
Upton Somset 16 D9
Upton Somset 17 L10
Upton Wakefd 59 L10
Upton Wirral 56 F10
Upton Bishop Herefs 28 H4
Upton Cheyney S Glos 17 Q3
Upton Cressett Shrops 39 M4
Upton Grey Hants 10 B1
Upton Hellions Devon 15 N11
Upton Lovell Wilts 18 D11
Upton Magna Shrops 49 K11
Upton Noble Somset 17 Q8
Upton Pyne Devon 6 C3
Upton St Leonards Gloucs 29 M6
Upton Scudamore Wilts 18 C10
Upton Snodsbury Worcs 30 C4
Upton-upon-Severn Worcs 29 L1
Upton Warren Worcs 30 B1
Upwaltham W Susx 10 F7
Upwell Norfk 43 N9
Upwood Cambs 43 J12
Urchfont Wilts 18 F8
Urmston Traffd 57 P9
Urquhart Moray 101 K3
Urquhart Castle Highld 98 G4
Urra N York 66 D7
Urray Highld 106 H10
Ury Abers 95 P4
Uryside Abers 102 G10
Usan Angus 95 M10
Ushaw Moor Dur 73 M11
Usk Mons 28 D8
Usselby Lincs 52 F5
Usworth Sundld 73 N8
Utkinton Ches W 49 K3
Utley C Brad 58 D5
Uton Devon 15 P11
Utterby Lincs 53 K5
Uttoxeter Staffs 40 E2
Uxbridge Gt Lon 20 G6
Uyeasound Shet 111 m2
Uzmaston Pembks 24 G6

V

Vale Guern 6 c1
Valley IoA 54 D6
Valtos Highld 104 G9
Valtos W Isls 111 c2
Vange Essex 22 E6
Vatsetter Shet 111 k2
Vatten Highld 96 C2
Vaynor Myr Td 27 L6
Veensgarth Shet 111 k4
Velindre Powys 27 P2
Venngreen Devon 14 G9
Venn Ottery Devon 6 E5
Verwood Dorset 8 G5
Veryan Cnwll 3 K7
Vickerstown Cumb 62 E8
Victoria Cnwll 3 L4
Viewfield Moray 101 K3
Viewpark N Lans 85 M10
Vigo Kent 22 D10
Village de Putron Guern 6 c2
Vines Cross E Susx 12 C6
Virginia Water Surrey 20 G9
Virginstow Devon 4 H2
Vobster Somset 17 Q6
Voe Shet 111 k3
Vowchurch Herefs 28 D2

W

Waberthwaite Cumb 62 C4
Wackerfield Dur 65 K3
Wacton Norfk 45 K10
Wadborough Worcs 30 B5
Waddesdon Bucks 31 Q10
Waddesdon Manor Bucks 31 Q10
Waddeton Devon 6 B10
Waddingham Lincs 52 E4
Waddington Lancs 63 N12
Waddington Lincs 52 D9
Waddon Gt Lon 21 L9
Wadebridge Cnwll 3 L2
Wadeford Somset 7 J1
Wadenhoe Nhants 42 E12
Wadesmill Herts 33 K12
Wadhurst E Susx 12 D4
Wadshelf Derbys 50 H6
Wadworth Donc 51 M2
Wainfleet All Saints Lincs 53 N10
Wainfleet St Mary Lincs 53 M10
Wainhouse Corner Cnwll 4 E8
Wainscott Medway 22 E8
Wainstalls Calder 58 D8
Waitby Cumb 64 D9
Waithe Lincs 53 J4
Wakefield Wakefd 59 J9
Wake Green Birm 40 E10
Wakehurst Place W Susx 11 M4
Wakerley Nhants 42 D9
Wakes Colne Essex 34 E10
Walberswick Suffk 35 P2
Walberton W Susx 10 F8
Walbutt D & G 70 C2
Walcombe Somset 17 M6
Walcot Lincs 42 F3
Walcot Shrops 49 L11
Walcot Swindn 18 H4
Walcot Telford 49 M10
Walcot Green Norfk 35 J1
Walcott Lincs 52 G1
Walcott Norfk 45 M4
Walden Stubbs N York 59 M10
Walderslade Medway 22 F10
Walderton W Susx 10 C7
Walditch Dorset 7 L4
Waldridge Dur 73 M10
Waldringfield Suffk 35 L7
Waldron E Susx 12 B6
Wales Rothm 51 L4
Wales Somset 17 N10
Walesby Lincs 52 G5
Walesby Notts 51 P6
Walford Herefs 28 G5
Walford Herefs 38 H7
Walford Heath Shrops 49 J10
Walgherton Ches E 49 M6
Walgrave Nhants 32 B3
Walkden Salfd 57 N8
Walker N u Ty 73 M7
Walkerburn Border 79 M2
Walkeringham Notts 51 Q3
Walkerith Lincs 52 B5
Walkern Herts 33 J10
Walker's Heath Birm 40 D10
Walkerton Fife 86 F3
Walkford BCP 8 H8
Walkhampton Devon 5 L6
Walkington E R Yk 60 G6

192 Walkley – Westonzoyland

Walkley Sheff 51 J3
Walk Mill Lancs 57 Q3
Walkwood Worcs 30 D2
Wall Nthumb 72 G7
Wall Staffs 40 E6
Wallacetown S Ayrs 76 E10
Wallacetown S Ayrs 76 F6
Wallands Park E Susx 11 N7
Wallasey Wirral 56 F9
Wallasey (Kingsway) Tunnel Wirral 56 G9
Wall Heath Dudley 40 B9
Wallingford Oxon 19 P3
Wallington Gt Lon 21 L9
Wallington Hants 9 P6
Wallington Herts 33 J9
Wallington Heath Wsall 40 C6
Wallisdown BCP 8 F8
Walliswood Surrey 10 H3
Walls Shet 111 j4
Wallsend N Tyne 73 N7
Wallyford E Loth 86 H7
Walmer Kent 23 Q12
Walmer Bridge Lancs 57 J4
Walmley Birm 40 F8
Walmley Ash Birm 40 F8
Walpole Suffk 35 M2
Walpole Cross Keys Norfk 43 N6
Walpole Highway Norfk 43 N7
Walpole St Andrew Norfk 43 N6
Walpole St Peter Norfk 43 N6
Walsall Wsall 40 D7
Walsden Calder 58 C9
Walsgrave on Sowe Covtry 41 J10
Walsham le Willows Suffk 34 G3
Walshford N York 59 K4
Walsoken Norfk 43 M7
Walston S Lans 86 C12
Walsworth Herts 32 H10
Walter's Ash Bucks 20 D4
Waltham Kent 13 L1
Waltham NE Lin 53 J3
Waltham Abbey Essex 21 M4
Waltham Chase Hants 9 P4
Waltham Cross Herts 21 M4
Waltham on the Wolds Leics 42 B5
Waltham St Lawrence W & M 20 D7
Walthamstow Gt Lon 21 M5
Walton C Pete 42 H9
Walton Cumb 71 Q3
Walton Derbys 51 J7
Walton Leeds 59 K5
Walton Leics 41 N9
Walton M Keyn 32 C9
Walton Powys 38 F9
Walton Somset 17 L8
Walton Suffk 35 L9
Walton W Susx 10 D8
Walton Wakefd 59 J10
Walton Wrekin 49 L10
Walton Cardiff Gloucs 29 M3
Walton East Pembks 24 H4
Walton Highway Norfk 43 M7
Walton-in-Gordano N Som 17 K2
Walton-le-Dale Lancs 57 K4
Walton-on-Thames Surrey 20 H9
Walton-on-the-Hill Staffs 40 C4
Walton-on-the-Hill Surrey 21 K11
Walton-on-the-Naze Essex 35 L11
Walton on the Wolds Leics 41 N4
Walton-on-Trent Derbys 40 G4
Walton Park N Som 17 K2
Walton West Pembks 24 F6
Walworth Darltn 65 M4
Walworth Gt Lon 21 M7
Walwyn's Castle Pembks 24 F6
Wambrook Somset 6 H2
Wanborough Surrey 10 E1
Wanborough Swindn 18 H4
Wandsworth Gt Lon 21 K8
Wangford Suffk 35 P2
Wanlip Leics 41 N5
Wanlockhead D & G 78 E6
Wannock E Susx 12 C8
Wansford C Pete 42 F9
Wansford E R Yk 60 H3
Wanshurst Green Kent 12 F2
Wanstead Gt Lon 21 N6
Wanstrow Somset 17 Q7
Wanswell Gloucs 29 J8
Wantage Oxon 19 L3
Wappenbury Warwks 41 J12
Wappenham Nhants 31 N5
Warbleton E Susx 12 C6
Warborough Oxon 19 P3
Warboys Cambs 33 K2
Warbreck Bpool 56 G2
Warbstow Cnwll 4 F3
Warburton Traffd 57 M10
Warcop Cumb 64 D5
Warden Nthumb 72 G7
Ward End Birm 40 E9
Wardington Oxon 31 L5
Wardle Ches E 49 L4
Wardle Rochdl 58 B10
Wardley Gatesd 73 N8
Wardley Rutlnd 42 B9
Wardlow Derbys 50 F6
Wardy Hill Cambs 33 M1
Ware Herts 21 M1
Wareham Dorset 8 D9
Warehorne Kent 13 J4
Warenford Nthumb 81 N8
Wareside Herts 21 N1
Waresley Cambs 33 J6
Warfield Br For 20 E8
Warfleet Devon 6 B11
Wargrave Wokham 20 C7
Warham Norfk 44 F2
Wark Nthumb 72 F5
Wark Nthumb 80 H6
Warkleigh Devon 15 L7
Warkton Nhants 32 C2
Warkworth Nhants 31 L6
Warkworth Nthumb 81 P11
Warlaby N York 65 N8
Warleggan Cnwll 4 E6
Warley Town Calder 58 D8
Warlingham Surrey 21 M10
Warmfield Wakefd 59 J9
Warmingham Ches E 49 N4
Warmington Nhants 42 F11
Warmington Warwks 31 K5
Warminster Wilts 18 C10
Warmley S Glos 17 P2
Warmsworth Donc 51 M1
Warmwell Dorset 7 Q5
Warner Bros. Studio Tour Herts 20 H4
Warnford Hants 9 Q3
Warnham W Susx 11 J4
Warningcamp W Susx 10 G8
Warninglid W Susx 11 K5
Warren Ches E 50 B6
Warren Pembks 24 G8
Warrenhill S Lans 78 F2
Warren Row W & M 20 D7
Warren Street Kent 22 H11
Warrington M Keyn 32 C6
Warrington Warrtn 57 L10
Warriston C Edin 86 F7
Warsash Hants 9 N6
Warslow Staffs 50 E8
Warter E R Yk 60 E4
Warthermaske N York 65 L10
Warthill N York 59 P3
Wartling E Susx 12 D8
Wartnaby Leics 41 P3
Warton Lancs 56 H3
Warton Lancs 63 J7
Warton Warwks 40 H6
Warwick Warwks 30 H2
Warwick Bridge Cumb 71 P4
Warwick Castle Warwks 30 H2
Warwick Services Warwks 31 J3
Wasbister Ork 111 h1
Wasdale Head Cumb 62 E1
Washaway Cnwll 3 M2
Washbourne Devon 5 Q8
Washbrook Suffk 35 J8
Washfield Devon 16 C11
Washford Somset 16 E7
Washford Pyne Devon 15 N9
Washingborough Lincs 52 E8
Washington Sundld 73 N9
Washington W Susx 10 H7
Washington Services Gatesd 73 M9
Washwood Heath Birm 40 E9
Wasperton Warwks 30 H3
Wass N York 66 D10
Wast Water Cumb 62 D2
Watchet Somset 16 E7
Watchfield Oxon 19 J3
Watchgate Cumb 63 K3
Water Devon 5 P4
Waterbeach Cambs 33 M4
Waterbeach W Susx 10 E8
Waterbeck D & G 79 L12
Water End E R Yk 60 D6
Waterfall Staffs 50 E9
Waterfoot Ag & B 75 M5
Waterfoot E Rens 85 J11
Waterfoot Lancs 57 Q5
Waterford Herts 21 L1
Waterheads Border 86 F11
Waterhouses Staffs 50 E10
Wateringbury Kent 22 E11
Waterloo Highld 97 J5
Waterloo N Lans 85 N11
Waterloo P & K 92 F8
Waterloo Pembks 24 G7
Waterloo Sefton 56 G8
Waterlooville Hants 10 B7
Watermead Bucks 20 D1
Watermillock Cumb 71 P10
Water Newton Cambs 42 G10
Water Orton Warwks 40 F8
Waterperry Oxon 31 N11
Waterrow Somset 16 E10
Watersfield W Susx 10 G6
Waterside Bl w D 57 N4
Waterside E Ayrs 76 G9
Waterside E Ayrs 76 H3
Waterside E Duns 85 L8
Waterstein Highld 104 A11
Waterstock Oxon 31 N11
Waterston Pembks 24 G7
Water Stratford Bucks 31 P7
Waters Upton Wrekin 49 L10
Watford Herts 20 H4
Watford Nhants 31 N1
Watford Gap Services Nhants 31 N1
Wath N York 58 F1
Wath N York 65 N11
Wath upon Dearne Rothm 51 K1
Watlington Norfk 43 P7
Watlington Oxon 20 B5
Watten Highld 110 F5
Wattisfield Suffk 34 G2
Wattisham Suffk 34 G6
Watton Dorset 7 L4
Watton E R Yk 60 H4
Watton Norfk 44 F9
Watton-at-Stone Herts 33 K11
Wattston N Lans 85 N8
Wattsville Caerph 27 P9
Waulkmill Abers 95 K4
Waunarlwydd Swans 26 E9
Waunfawr Cerdgn 37 K4
Waunfawr Gwynd 54 G9
Wavendon M Keyn 32 C8
Waverbridge Cumb 71 K6
Waverley Rothm 51 K4
Waverton Ches W 49 J3
Waverton Cumb 71 K6
Wawne E R Yk 61 J6
Waxham Norfk 45 P5
Wayford Somset 7 K2
Waytown Dorset 7 L4
Way Village Devon 15 Q9
Weacombe Somset 16 F7
Weald Oxon 19 K1
Wealdstone Gt Lon 21 J5
Weardley Leeds 58 H5
Weare Somset 17 K5
Weare Giffard Devon 14 H7
Wearhead Dur 72 F11
Wearne Somset 17 K9
Weasenham All Saints Norfk 44 E6
Weasenham St Peter Norfk 44 E5
Weaste Salfd 57 P8
Weaverham Ches W 49 L1
Weaverthorpe N York 67 L12
Webheath Worcs 30 D2
Wedderlairs Abers 102 H8
Weddington Warwks 41 J8
Wedhampton Wilts 18 F8
Wedmore Somset 17 L6
Wednesbury Sandw 40 C8
Wednesfield Wolves 40 C7
Weedon Bucks 32 B12
Weedon Bec Nhants 31 N3
Weedon Lois Nhants 31 N5
Weeford Staffs 40 F6
Weeke Hants 9 M2
Weekley Nhants 32 C1
Week St Mary Cnwll 14 E11
Weel E R Yk 60 H6
Weeley Essex 35 J11
Weeley Heath Essex 35 J11
Weem P & K 92 C6
Weethley Warwks 30 D3
Weeting Norfk 44 C11
Weeton E R Yk 61 N9
Weeton Lancs 56 H2
Weeton N York 58 H5
Weetwood Leeds 58 H6
Weir Lancs 57 Q4
Weir Quay Devon 5 J7
Weisdale Shet 111 k4
Welborne Norfk 44 H7
Welbourn Lincs 52 D11
Welburn N York 60 C1
Welbury N York 65 P7
Welby Lincs 42 D3
Welcombe Devon 14 E8
Weldon Nhants 42 D11
Welford Nhants 41 N10
Welford W Berk 19 L6
Welford-on-Avon Warwks 30 F4
Welham Leics 41 Q8
Welham Notts 51 Q5
Welham Green Herts 21 K3
Well Hants 10 C2
Well Lincs 53 M8
Well N York 65 M10
Welland Worcs 29 L2
Wellbank Angus 93 N8
Wellesbourne Warwks 30 H3
Well Head Herts 32 H10
Welling Gt Lon 21 P8
Wellingborough Nhants 32 C3
Wellingham Norfk 44 E6
Wellingore Lincs 52 E11
Wellington Cumb 62 C2
Wellington Herefs 39 J11
Wellington Somset 16 F11
Wellington Wrekin 49 M12
Wellington Heath Herefs 29 J1
Wellow BaNES 17 Q5
Wellow IoW 9 L9
Wellow Notts 51 P7
Wells Somset 17 M7
Wells-next-the-Sea Norfk 44 F2
Wellstye Green Essex 33 Q11
Welltree P & K 92 E10
Wellwood Fife 86 C5
Welney Norfk 43 N10
Welshampton Shrops 48 H8
Welsh Frankton Shrops 48 G8
Welsh Newton Herefs 28 F5
Welshpool Powys 38 E1
Welsh St Donats V Glam 16 D2
Welton Cumb 71 M6
Welton E R Yk 60 G8
Welton Lincs 52 E7
Welton Nhants 31 N2
Welton le Marsh Lincs 53 M9
Welton le Wold Lincs 53 J6
Welwick E R Yk 61 N9
Welwyn Herts 32 H12
Welwyn Garden City Herts 21 K2
Wem Shrops 49 K9
Wembdon Somset 16 H8
Wembley Gt Lon 21 J6
Wembury Devon 5 L9
Wembworthy Devon 15 L9
Wemyss Bay Inver 84 D8
Wendens Ambo Essex 33 N9
Wendlebury Oxon 31 M9
Wendling Norfk 44 F7
Wendover Bucks 20 D3
Wendron Cnwll 2 G9
Wendron Mining District Cnwll 2 G8
Wendy Cambs 33 K7
Wenhaston Suffk 35 N2
Wennington Cambs 33 J2
Wennington Gt Lon 22 B7
Wennington Lancs 63 L8
Wensley Derbys 50 H8
Wensley N York 65 J9
Wentbridge Wakefd 59 L10
Wentnor Shrops 38 H4
Wentworth Cambs 33 M2
Wentworth Rothm 51 J2
Wenvoe V Glam 16 F2
Weobley Herefs 38 H10
Wepham W Susx 10 G8
Wereham Norfk 44 B9
Werrington C Pete 42 G9
Werrington Cnwll 4 H3
Wervin Ches W 48 H2
Wesham Lancs 56 H3
Wessington Derbys 51 J8
West Acre Norfk 44 C7
West Alvington Devon 5 P10
West Anstey Devon 15 P6
West Ashby Lincs 53 J8
West Ashling W Susx 10 D8
West Ashton Wilts 18 C9
West Auckland Dur 65 L3
West Ayton N York 67 L9
West Bagborough Somset 16 G9
West Bank Halton 57 K11
West Barkwith Lincs 52 G7
West Barnby N York 66 H5
West Barns E Loth 87 M6
West Barsham Norfk 44 E4
West Bay Dorset 7 L5
West Beckham Norfk 45 J3
West Bedfont Surrey 20 H8
Westbere Kent 23 M10
West Bergholt Essex 34 F10
West Bexington Dorset 7 M5
West Bilney Norfk 44 B7
West Blatchington Br & H 11 L8
West Boldon S Tyne 73 P8
Westborough Lincs 42 C2
Westbourne BCP 8 F8
Westbourne W Susx 10 C8
West Bowling C Brad 58 F7
West Bradenham Norfk 44 F8
West Bradford Lancs 63 N12
West Bradley Somset 17 M8
West Bretton Wakefd 58 H10
West Bridgford Notts 51 N12
West Bromwich Sandw 40 D8
Westbrook Kent 23 Q8
Westbrook W Berk 19 M6
West Buckland Devon 15 L6
West Buckland Somset 16 G11
West Burrafirth Shet 111 j4
West Burton N York 64 H9
Westbury Bucks 31 N7
Westbury Shrops 38 G1
Westbury Wilts 18 C9
Westbury Leigh Wilts 18 C10
Westbury-on-Severn Gloucs 29 J6
Westbury-on-Trym Bristl 28 G12
Westbury-sub-Mendip Somset 17 M6
West Butterwick N Linc 52 B3
Westby Lancs 56 H3
West Byfleet Surrey 20 G10
West Cairngaan D & G 68 F11
West Caister Norfk 45 Q7
West Calder W Loth 86 B9
West Camel Somset 17 N10
West Chaldon Dorset 8 B10
West Challow Oxon 19 L3
West Charleton Devon 5 P10
West Chiltington W Susx 10 H6
West Chinnock Somset 17 L12
West Clandon Surrey 20 G11
West Cliffe Kent 13 Q2
Westcliff-on-Sea Sthend 22 G6
West Coker Somset 17 M12
Westcombe Somset 17 P8
West Compton Somset 17 N7
West Compton Abbas Dorset 7 N4
Westcote Gloucs 30 G9
Westcote Barton Oxon 31 K8
Westcott Bucks 31 Q10
Westcott Devon 6 D2
Westcott Surrey 11 J1
West Cottingwith N York 59 P6
Westcourt Wilts 19 J8
West Cowick E R Yk 59 P9
West Cross Swans 26 E10
West Curthwaite Cumb 71 M6
Westdean E Susx 11 Q9
West Dean W Susx 10 D7
West Dean Wilts 9 J3
West Deeping Lincs 42 G8
West Derby Lpool 56 H9
West Dereham Norfk 43 Q9
West Down Devon 15 J4
Westdowns Cnwll 4 C4
West Drayton Gt Lon 20 G7
West Drayton Notts 51 P6
West Dunnet Highld 110 E2
West Ella E R Yk 60 H8
West End Bed 32 E6
West End Hants 9 M5
West End N Som 17 L3
West End Norfk 45 Q7
West End Surrey 20 F10
West End Surrey 20 H10
West End Wilts 8 E3
West End Green Hants 19 Q8
Wester Aberchalder Highld 98 H5
Wester Balblair Highld 106 H12
Westerdale Highld 110 D5
Westerdale N York 66 F6
Westerfield Suffk 35 K7
Westergate W Susx 10 F8
Westerham Kent 21 N11
Westerhope N u Ty 73 L7
Westerland Devon 6 B9
Westerleigh S Glos 29 J11
Western Isles W Isls 111 c3
Wester Ochiltree W Loth 86 B7
Wester Pitkierie Fife 87 K2
Wester Ross Highld 105 P6
Westerton of Rossie Angus 93 R5
Westerwick Shet 111 j4
West Farleigh Kent 22 E11
West Farndon Nhants 31 M4
West Felton Shrops 48 G9
Westfield BaNES 17 P5
Westfield Cumb 70 G9
Westfield E Susx 12 F7
Westfield Highld 110 C3
Westfield N Lans 85 M8
Westfield Norfk 44 G8
Westfield Surrey 20 G11
Westfield W Loth 85 Q8
Westfields Herefs 28 F1
Westfields of Rattray P & K 92 H6
Westgate Dur 72 G12
Westgate N Linc 60 D11
Westgate-on-Sea Kent 23 P8
West Grafton Wilts 19 J8
West Green Hants 20 C11
West Grimstead Wilts 8 H3
West Grinstead W Susx 11 J5
West Haddlesey N York 59 M8
West Haddon Nhants 41 N12
West Hagbourne Oxon 19 N3
West Hagley Worcs 40 B10
Westhall Suffk 35 N1
West Hallam Derbys 51 K11
West Halton N Linc 60 F9
Westham Dorset 7 P7
Westham E Susx 12 D8
West Ham Gt Lon 21 N6
Westham Somset 17 K6
Westhampnett W Susx 10 E8
West Handley Derbys 51 K5
West Hanney Oxon 19 L3
West Hanningfield Essex 22 E4
West Harnham Wilts 8 G2
West Harptree BaNES 17 M5
West Harting W Susx 10 C6
West Hatch Somset 16 H11
West Hatch Wilts 8 D2
West Haven Angus 93 P8
Westhay Somset 17 L7
West Heath Birm 40 D11
West Helmsdale Highld 110 B11
West Hendred Oxon 19 M3
West Heslerton N York 67 K11
West Hewish N Som 17 K4
Westhide Herefs 39 L12
Westhill Abers 95 N1
West Hill Devon 6 E4
Westhill Highld 107 L12
West Hoathly W Susx 11 M4
West Holme Dorset 8 C9
Westhope Herefs 39 J11
Westhope Shrops 39 J5
West Horndon Essex 22 D6
Westhorpe Lincs 42 H4
Westhorpe Suffk 34 H3
West Horrington Somset 17 N6
West Horsley Surrey 20 H11
West Hougham Kent 13 N3
Westhoughton Bolton 57 M7
Westhouse N York 63 M7
Westhouses Derbys 51 K8
West Howe BCP 8 F8
Westhumble Surrey 21 J11
West Huntingtower P & K 92 G10
West Huntspill Somset 17 J7
West Hythe Kent 13 L3
West Ilsley W Berk 19 M4
West Itchenor W Susx 10 C9
West Kennett Wilts 18 G7
West Kilbride N Ayrs 76 D2
West Kingsdown Kent 22 C10
West Kington Wilts 18 B5
West Kirby Wirral 56 E10
West Knapton N York 67 J11
West Knighton Dorset 7 Q5
West Knoyle Wilts 8 C2
Westlake Devon 5 M9
West Lambrook Somset 17 K11
West Langdon Kent 13 P1
West Lavington W Susx 10 E6
West Lavington Wilts 18 E9
West Layton N York 65 K5
West Leake Notts 41 M3
Westleigh Devon 14 H6
Westleigh Devon 16 E11
West Leigh Somset 16 F9
Westleton Suffk 35 P3
West Lexham Norfk 44 D6
Westley Suffk 34 D4
Westley Waterless Cambs 33 P5
West Lilling N York 59 P2
Westlington Bucks 31 Q11
West Linton Border 86 D10
Westlinton Cumb 71 N3
West Littleton S Glos 18 B5
West Lockinge Oxon 19 M4
West Lulworth Dorset 8 B10
West Lutton N York 60 F1
West Lydford Somset 17 N9
West Lyng Somset 17 J9
West Lynn Norfk 43 P6
West Malling Kent 22 D10
West Malvern Worcs 39 N11
West Marden W Susx 10 C7
West Markham Notts 51 Q6
Westmarsh Kent 23 P10
West Marsh NE Lin 61 L11
West Marton N York 58 B4
West Melbury Dorset 8 C4
West Meon Hants 9 Q3
West Mersea Essex 23 J2
Westmeston E Susx 11 M7
West Midland Safari Park Worcs 39 P7
Westmill Herts 33 K10
West Milton Dorset 7 M4
Westminster Gt Lon 21 L7
Westminster Abbey & Palace Gt Lon 21 L7
West Molesey Surrey 21 J9
West Monkton Somset 16 H9
West Moors Dorset 8 F6
West Morden Dorset 8 D8
West Morriston Border 80 E6
West Mudford Somset 17 N11
Westmuir Angus 93 L5
West Ness N York 66 F10
Westnewton Cumb 71 J6
West Newton E R Yk 61 L6
West Newton Norfk 44 B5
West Newton Somset 16 H9
West Norwood Gt Lon 21 L8
Westoe S Tyne 73 P7
West Ogwell Devon 5 Q6
Weston BaNES 17 Q3
Weston Ches E 49 N5
Weston Devon 6 F3
Weston Devon 6 F5
Weston Hants 10 B6
Weston Herts 33 J10
Weston Lincs 43 J5
Weston N York 58 F5
Weston Nhants 31 N5
Weston Notts 51 Q7
Weston Shrops 39 L4
Weston Shrops 48 F9
Weston Staffs 40 C3
Weston W Berk 19 L6
Weston Beggard Herefs 28 G1
Westonbirt Gloucs 18 C3
Weston by Welland Nhants 41 Q8
Weston Colville Cambs 33 P6
Weston Corbett Hants 10 B1
Weston Coyney C Stke 50 C11
Weston Favell Nhants 32 B4
Weston Green Cambs 33 P6
Weston Heath Shrops 49 P11
Westoning C Beds 32 E9
Weston-in-Gordano N Som 17 L2
Weston Jones Staffs 49 N10
Weston Longville Norfk 45 J7
Weston Lullingfields Shrops 48 H9
Weston-on-the-Green Oxon 31 M9
Weston Park Staffs 49 P12
Weston Patrick Hants 10 B1
Weston Rhyn Shrops 48 F8
Weston-sub-Edge Gloucs 30 E6
Weston-super-Mare N Som 17 J4
Weston Turville Bucks 20 D2
Weston-under-Lizard Staffs 49 P12
Weston under Penyard Herefs 28 H4
Weston-under-Redcastle Shrops 49 K9
Weston under Wetherley Warwks 41 J12
Weston Underwood Derbys 50 H11
Weston Underwood M Keyn 32 C6
Weston-upon-Trent Derbys 41 K2
Westonzoyland Somset 17 J8

West Orchard Dorset......8 B4
West Overton Wilts......18 G7
Westow N York......60 D2
West Park Abers......95 N3
West Parley Dorset......8 G7
West Peckham Kent......22 D11
West Pelton Dur......73 M9
West Pennard Somset......17 M8
West Pentire Cnwll......2 H4
West Porlock Somset......15 P3
Westport Somset......17 K11
West Putford Devon......14 G8
West Quantoxhead Somset......16 F7
Westquarter Falk......85 Q7
West Rainton Dur......73 N10
West Rasen Lincs......52 F5
Westray Ork......111 h1
Westray Airport Ork......111 h1
West Raynham Norfk......44 E5
Westrigg W Loth......85 Q9
Westrop Swindn......18 H3
West Rounton N York......65 P6
West Row Suffk......34 B2
West Rudham Norfk......44 D5
West Runton Norfk......45 K2
Westruther Border......80 E4
Westry Cambs......43 L9
West Saltoun E Loth......87 J8
West Sandford Devon......15 N10
West Sandwick Shet......111 k3
West Scrafton N York......65 J10
West Stafford Dorset......7 Q5
West Stockwith Notts......52 B5
West Stoke W Susx......10 D8
West Stour Dorset......8 B3
West Stourmouth Kent......23 N10
West Stow Suffk......34 D3
West Stowell Wilts......18 G8
West Street Suffk......34 G3
West Tanfield N York......65 M10
West Taphouse Cnwll......4 E7
West Tarbert Ag & B......83 M9
West Tarring W Susx......10 H8
West Thirston Nthumb......73 L2
West Thorney W Susx......10 C9
West Thorpe Notts......41 N3
West Thurrock Thurr......22 C7
West Tilbury Thurr......22 D7
West Tisted Hants......9 Q2
West Torrington Lincs......52 G7
West Town Hants......10 B9
West Town N Som......17 L3
West Tytherley Hants......9 J2
West Walton Norfk......43 M7
Westward Cumb......71 L6
Westward Ho! Devon......14 H6
Westwell Kent......13 J1
Westwell Oxon......30 G11
Westwell Leacon Kent......13 J1
West Wellow Hants......9 K4
West Wembury Devon......5 L9
West Wemyss Fife......86 G4
Westwick Cambs......33 L4
West Wickham Cambs......33 P6
West Wickham Gt Lon......21 M9
West Williamston Pembks......24 H7
West Winch Norfk......43 Q6
West Winterslow Wilts......9 J2
West Wittering W Susx......10 C9
West Witton N York......65 J9
Westwood Devon......6 D3
Westwood Kent......23 Q9
Westwood Wilts......18 B8
West Woodburn Nthumb......72 F4
West Woodhay W Berk......19 L8
Westwoodside N Linc......51 Q2
West Worldham Hants......10 C3
West Worthing W Susx......11 J9
West Wratting Cambs......33 P6
West Wylam Nthumb......73 K8
Wetheral Cumb......71 P5
Wetherby Leeds......59 K5
Wetherby Services N York......59 K4
Wetherden Suffk......34 G4
Wetheringsett Suffk......35 J4
Wethersfield Essex......34 B9
Wetherup Street Suffk......35 J4
Wetley Rocks Staffs......50 C10
Wettenhall Ches E......49 L4
Wetton Staffs......50 E9
Wetwang E R Yk......60 F3
Wetwood Staffs......49 P8
Wexcombe Wilts......19 J8
Weybourne Norfk......45 J2
Weybourne Surrey......10 D1
Weybread Suffk......35 L1
Weybread Street Suffk......35 L2
Weybridge Surrey......20 H9
Weycroft Devon......7 J3
Weydale Highld......110 D3
Weyhill Hants......19 K10
Weymouth Dorset......7 P7
Whaddon Bucks......32 B9
Whaddon Cambs......33 K7
Whaddon Gloucs......29 L6
Whaddon Wilts......8 H3
Whaddon Wilts......18 C8
Whaley Derbys......51 L6
Whaley Bridge Derbys......50 D5
Whaley Thorns Derbys......51 M6
Whaligoe Highld......110 G7
Whalley Lancs......57 N2
Whalsay Shet......111 m3
Whalton Nthumb......73 K5
Whaplode Lincs......43 K5
Whaplode Drove Lincs......43 K7
Wharf Warwks......31 K4
Wharfe N York......63 P8
Wharles Lancs......57 J2
Wharley End C Beds......32 D7
Wharncliffe Side Sheff......50 H2
Wharram-le-Street N York......60 E2
Wharton Ches W......49 M3
Wharton Herefs......39 J10
Whashton N York......65 K6
Whasset Cumb......63 K6
Whatcote Warwks......30 H5
Whateley Warwks......40 G7
Whatfield Suffk......34 G7
Whatley Somset......7 J2
Whatley Somset......17 Q6
Whatley's End S Gloucs......28 H11
Whatlington E Susx......12 F6
Whatton-in-the-Vale Notts......51 Q11

Whauphill D & G......69 K8
Wheal Peevor Cnwll......2 G6
Wheatacre Norfk......45 P10
Wheathampstead Herts......21 J1
Wheatley Hants......10 C3
Wheatley Oxon......31 N11
Wheatley Hill Dur......73 P11
Wheatley Hills Donc......59 N12
Wheaton Aston Staffs......49 Q11
Wheddon Cross Somset......16 C8
Wheeler's Green Wokham......20 C8
Wheelock Ches E......49 N4
Wheelton Lancs......57 L5
Wheldrake C York......59 P5
Whelford Gloucs......18 H2
Whelpley Hill Bucks......20 F3
Whempstead Herts......33 K11
Whenby N York......66 L12
Whepstead Suffk......34 D5
Wherstead Suffk......35 J8
Wherwell Hants......19 L11
Wheston Derbys......50 F5
Whetsted Kent......12 D2
Whetstone Gt Lon......21 L5
Whetstone Leics......41 M7
Whicham Cumb......62 D6
Whichford Warwks......30 H4
Whickham Gatesd......73 L8
Whiddon Down Devon......5 N10
Whigstreet Angus......93 N6
Whilton Nhants......31 N2
Whimple Devon......6 E4
Whimpwell Green Norfk......45 N4
Whinburgh Norfk......44 G8
Whinnieliggate D & G......70 B5
Whinnyfold Abers......103 M8
Whippingham IoW......9 N8
Whipsnade C Beds......32 E12
Whipsnade Zoo ZSL C Beds......32 E12
Whipton Devon......6 C4
Whisby Lincs......52 C9
Whissendine Rutlnd......42 B7
Whissonsett Norfk......44 F5
Whistlefield Ag & B......84 D4
Whistlefield Inn Ag & B......84 C5
Whistley Green Wokham......20 C8
Whiston Knows......57 J9
Whiston Nhants......32 C5
Whiston Rothm......51 K3
Whiston Staffs......40 B5
Whiston Staffs......50 D10
Whitbeck Cumb......62 D5
Whitbourne Herefs......39 N10
Whitburn S Tyne......73 P8
Whitburn W Loth......85 Q9
Whitby Ches W......48 H2
Whitby N York......67 J5
Whitchester Border......87 N9
Whitchurch BaNES......17 N3
Whitchurch Bucks......32 B11
Whitchurch Cardif......27 N11
Whitchurch Devon......5 K5
Whitchurch Hants......19 M10
Whitchurch Herefs......28 G5
Whitchurch Oxon......19 Q5
Whitchurch Pembks......24 E4
Whitchurch Shrops......49 K7
Whitchurch Canonicorum
    Dorset......7 K4
Whitchurch Hill Oxon......19 Q5
Whitcombe Dorset......7 Q5
Whitcot Shrops......38 H4
Whitcott Keysett Shrops......38 F5
Whiteacre Heath Warwks......40 G8
White Ball Somset......16 E11
Whitebridge Highld......98 G6
Whitebrook Mons......28 G7
Whitebushes Surrey......11 L1
Whitecairns Abers......103 J10
Whitechapel Gt Lon......21 M7
White Chapel Lancs......57 K2
White Colne Essex......34 E10
Whitecraig E Loth......86 G8
Whitecrook D & G......68 F7
White Cross Cnwll......2 G10
Whitecross Falk......85 R7
Whiteface Highld......107 L5
Whitefarland N Ayrs......75 N4
Whitefaulds S Ayrs......76 E8
Whitefield Bury......57 P7
Whitefield Somset......16 E9
Whiteford Abers......102 F9
Whitegate Ches W......49 L2
Whitehall Ork......111 i2
Whitehaven Cumb......70 F11
Whitehill Hants......10 C4
Whitehills Abers......102 E3
Whitehouse Abers......102 E11
Whitehouse Ag & B......83 M10
Whitehouse Common Birm......40 F7
Whitekirk E Loth......87 L6
White Lackington Dorset......7 Q3
Whitelackington Somset......17 K11
White Ladies Aston Worcs......30 B4
Whiteleaf Bucks......20 D3
Whiteley Hants......9 N5
Whiteley Bank IoW......9 P10
Whitemire Moray......100 F5
Whitemoor C Nott......51 M11
Whitemoor Cnwll......3 L4
Whiteness Shet......111 k4
White Notley Essex......34 D11
Whiteparish Wilts......9 J3
White Pit Lincs......53 L7
Whiterashes Abers......102 H9
White Roding Essex......22 C1
Whiterow Highld......110 G6
Whiterow Moray......100 F4
Whiteshill Gloucs......29 L7
Whitesmith E Susx......11 Q7
Whitestaunton Somset......6 H1
Whitestone Warwks......41 J9
Whitestone Cross Devon......6 B4
White Waltham W & M......20 D7
Whitewell Lancs......63 M11
Whitfield C Dund......93 M8
Whitfield Kent......13 P2
Whitfield Nhants......31 N6
Whitfield Nthumb......72 E8
Whitfield S Glos......29 J9
Whitford Devon......6 H4
Whitford Flints......56 D12
Whitgift E R Yk......60 E9
Whitgreave Staffs......40 B2
Whithorn D & G......69 L10

Whiting Bay N Ayrs......75 Q7
Whitkirk Leeds......59 J7
Whitland Carmth......25 L5
Whitlaw Border......80 C10
Whitletts S Ayrs......76 F6
Whitley N York......59 M9
Whitley Readg......20 B8
Whitley Sheff......51 J2
Whitley Wilts......18 C7
Whitley Bay N Tyne......73 N6
Whitley Chapel Nthumb......72 G8
Whitley Lower Kirk......58 G10
Whitminster Gloucs......29 K7
Whitmore Staffs......49 P7
Whitnage Devon......16 D11
Whitnash Warwks......31 J2
Whitney-on-Wye Herefs......38 F11
Whitsbury Hants......8 H4
Whitsome Border......81 J4
Whitson Newpt......28 D11
Whitstable Kent......23 L9
Whitstone Cnwll......14 E11
Whittingham Nthumb......81 M10
Whittingslow Shrops......38 H4
Whittington Derbys......51 J6
Whittington Gloucs......30 D9
Whittington Lancs......63 L7
Whittington Norfk......44 B9
Whittington Shrops......48 G8
Whittington Staffs......39 Q5
Whittington Staffs......40 F6
Whittington Warwks......40 H7
Whittington Worcs......39 Q10
Whittlebury Nhants......31 P5
Whittle-le-Woods Lancs......57 L5
Whittlesey Cambs......43 J10
Whittlesford Cambs......33 M7
Whitton N Linc......60 F8
Whitton Nthumb......73 J1
Whitton Powys......38 F8
Whitton S on T......65 P3
Whitton Shrops......39 L7
Whittonstall Nthumb......73 J9
Whitway Hants......19 M8
Whitwell Derbys......51 M5
Whitwell Herts......32 H11
Whitwell IoW......9 N11
Whitwell N York......65 M7
Whitwell Rutlnd......42 D8
Whitwell-on-the-Hill N York......60 C2
Whitwell Street Norfk......44 H6
Whitwick Leics......41 K4
Whitworth Lancs......58 B9
Whixall Shrops......49 K8
Whixley N York......59 K3
Whorlton Dur......65 K5
Whyle Herefs......39 K9
Whyteleafe Surrey......21 M10
Wibsey C Brad......58 F7
Wibtoft Warwks......41 L9
Wichelstowe Swindn......18 G4
Wichenford Worcs......39 P9
Wichling Kent......22 H11
Wick BCP......8 H8
Wick Highld......110 G5
Wick S Glos......17 Q2
Wick V Glam......16 C2
Wick W Susx......10 G8
Wick Worcs......30 C5
Wicken Cambs......33 P3
Wicken Nhants......31 Q6
Wicken Bonhunt Essex......33 N9
Wickenby Lincs......52 F7
Wicken Green Village Norfk......44 D4
Wickersley Rothm......51 L3
Wicker Street Green Suffk......34 F8
Wickford Essex......22 E5
Wickham Hants......9 P5
Wickham W Berk......19 L6
Wickham Bishops Essex......22 G2
Wickhambreaux Kent......23 N10
Wickhambrook Suffk......34 C6
Wickhamford Worcs......30 E6
Wickham Green Suffk......34 H3
Wickham Market Suffk......35 M5
Wickhampton Norfk......45 N8
Wickham St Paul Essex......34 D9
Wickham Skeith Suffk......34 H3
Wickham Street Suffk......34 H3
Wick John o' Groats Airport
    Highld......110 G5
Wicklewood Norfk......44 H9
Wickmere Norfk......45 J4
Wick St Lawrence N Som......17 K3
Wicksteed Park Nhants......32 C2
Wickwar S Glos......29 J10
Widdington Essex......33 N9
Widdington Nthumb......73 M2
Widdrington Station Nthumb......73 M3
Widecombe in the Moor
    Devon......5 P5
Widegates Cnwll......4 G8
Widemouth Bay Cnwll......14 D10
Wide Open N Tyne......73 M6
Widford Essex......22 E3
Widford Herts......33 L12
Widmer End Bucks......20 E4
Widmerpool Notts......41 N2
Widmore Gt Lon......21 N9
Widnes Halton......57 K10
Widworthy Devon......6 G3
Wigan Wigan......57 L7
Wigborough Somset......17 L12
Wiggaton Devon......6 E4
Wiggenhall St Germans Norfk......43 P7
Wiggenhall St Mary
    Magdalen Norfk......43 P7
Wiggenhall St Mary the
    Virgin Norfk......43 P7
Wigginton C York......59 N3
Wigginton Herts......32 F2
Wigginton Oxon......31 K7
Wigginton Staffs......40 G6
Wigglesworth N York......63 P10
Wiggonby Cumb......71 L5
Wighill N York......59 L5
Wighton Norfk......44 F3
Wightwick Wolves......39 Q3
Wigley Hants......9 K4
Wigmore Herefs......38 H8
Wigmore Medway......22 F9
Wigsley Notts......52 C9
Wigsthorpe Nhants......42 F12
Wigston Leics......41 N7

Wigston Fields Leics......41 N7
Wigston Parva Leics......41 L9
Wigthorpe Notts......51 N4
Wigtoft Lincs......43 J3
Wigton Cumb......71 L6
Wigtown D & G......69 L7
Wike Leeds......59 J5
Wilbarston Nhants......42 B11
Wilberfoss E R Yk......60 C4
Wilburton Cambs......33 M2
Wilby Nhants......32 C4
Wilby Norfk......44 G11
Wilby Suffk......35 L3
Wilcot Wilts......18 G8
Wilcott Shrops......48 H10
Wildboarclough Ches E......50 C7
Wilden Bed......32 F6
Wilden Worcs......39 P7
Wildhern Hants......19 L9
Wildmanbridge S Lans......85 N11
Wildmill Brdgnd......27 J11
Wildmoor Worcs......40 C11
Wildsworth Lincs......52 B4
Wilford C Nott......51 M12
Wilkesley Ches E......49 L7
Wilkhaven Highld......107 Q5
Wilkieston W Loth......86 D8
Willand Devon......6 D1
Willaston Ches E......49 M5
Willaston Ches W......56 G12
Willen M Keyn......32 C8
Willenhall Covtry......41 J11
Willenhall Wsall......40 C7
Willerby E R Yk......60 H7
Willerby N York......67 L10
Willersey Gloucs......30 E6
Willesleigh Herefs......38 G11
Willesborough Kent......13 K2
Willesborough Lees Kent......13 K2
Willesden Gt Lon......21 K6
Willesley Wilts......18 C3
Willett Somset......16 F9
Willey Shrops......39 M3
Willey Warwks......41 L9
Willey Green Surrey......20 F12
Williamscot Oxon......31 L5
Willian Herts......32 H9
Willingale Essex......22 C2
Willingdon E Susx......12 C9
Willingham Cambs......33 L3
Willingham by Stow Lincs......52 C6
Willingham St Mary Suffk......45 P12
Willington Bed......32 G6
Willington Derbys......40 H2
Willington Dur......65 L1
Willington Kent......22 F11
Willington N Tyne......73 N7
Willington Warwks......30 H6
Willitoft E R Yk......60 C7
Williton Somset......16 E7
Willoughby Lincs......53 M8
Willoughby Warwks......31 M1
Willoughby-on-the-Wolds
    Notts......41 N3
Willoughby Waterleys Leics......41 M8
Willoughton Lincs......52 D5
Willows Green Essex......34 C11
Willtown Somset......17 K10
Wilmcote Warwks......30 F3
Wilmington BCP......8 G3
Wilmington E Susx......12 B8
Wilmington Kent......21 Q8
Wilmslow Ches E......57 Q11
Wilpshire Lancs......57 M3
Wilsden C Brad......58 E6
Wilsford Lincs......42 E2
Wilsford Wilts......18 G11
Wilsford Wilts......18 G8
Wilshaw Kirk......58 E11
Wilsill N York......58 F2
Wilson Leics......41 K3
Wilsontown S Lans......85 Q11
Wilstead Bed......32 F7
Wilsthorpe Lincs......42 F7
Wilstone Herts......20 E1
Wilton Herefs......28 G4
Wilton N York......67 J10
Wilton R & Cl......66 E4
Wilton Wilts......8 G2
Wilton Wilts......19 J8
Wilton Dean Border......80 C10
Wimbish Green Essex......33 P9
Wimbledon Gt Lon......21 K8
Wimblington Cambs......43 L10
Wimboldsley Ches W......49 M3
Wimborne Minster Dorset......8 E7
Wimborne St Giles Dorset......8 F5
Wimbotsham Norfk......43 P8
Wimpole Cambs......33 K6
Wimpstone Warwks......30 G4
Wincanton Somset......17 Q10
Winchburgh W Loth......86 C7
Winchcombe Gloucs......30 D8
Winchelsea E Susx......12 H6
Winchester Hants......9 N2
Winchester Services Hants......9 N1
Winchet Hill Kent......12 E2
Winchfield Hants......20 C11
Winchmore Hill Bucks......20 E4
Winchmore Hill Gt Lon......21 L5
Wincle Ches E......50 C7
Wincobank Sheff......51 J3
Windermere Cumb......62 H3
Windermere Jetty Cumb......62 H3
Winderton Warwks......31 J6
Windhill Highld......107 J11
Windlesham Surrey......20 E9
Windmill Cnwll......3 K2
Windmill Hill E Susx......12 D7
Windmill Hill Somset......17 J11
Windrush Gloucs......30 F10
Windsole Abers......102 D4
Windsor W & M......20 F7
Windsor Castle W & M......20 F7
Windsoredge Gloucs......29 L8
Windsor Green Suffk......34 E6
Windygates Fife......86 G3
Wineham W Susx......11 K6
Wineham E R Yk......61 M8
Winfarthing Norfk......45 J11
Winford IoW......9 P9
Winford N Som......17 M3
Winforton Herefs......38 F11
Winfrith Newburgh Dorset......8 B9
Wing Bucks......32 C11

Wing Rutlnd......42 C9
Wingate Dur......73 P12
Wingerworth Derbys......51 J7
Wingfield C Beds......32 E10
Wingfield Suffk......35 K2
Wingfield Wilts......18 B9
Wingham Kent......23 N11
Wingrave Bucks......32 C11
Winkburn Notts......51 P8
Winkfield Br For......20 E8
Winkfield Row Br For......20 E8
Winkhill Staffs......50 D9
Winkleigh Devon......15 L9
Winksley N York......65 M12
Winlaton Gatesd......73 L8
Winless Highld......110 G5
Winmarleigh Lancs......63 J11
Winnall Hants......9 N2
Winnersh Wokham......20 C8
Winnington Ches W......49 M1
Winscombe N Som......17 K5
Winsford Ches W......49 M3
Winsford Somset......16 B8
Winsham Somset......7 K2
Winshill Staffs......40 H3
Winshwen Swans......26 F9
Winskill Cumb......64 B1
Winsley Wilts......18 B8
Winslow Bucks......31 Q8
Winson Gloucs......30 E11
Winsor Hants......9 K5
Winster Cumb......62 H4
Winster Derbys......50 G8
Winston Dur......65 K4
Winston Suffk......35 K5
Winstone Gloucs......29 N6
Winswell Devon......15 J9
Winterborne Came Dorset......7 Q5
Winterborne Clenston Dorset......8 C6
Winterborne Houghton
    Dorset......8 B6
Winterborne Kingston Dorset......8 C7
Winterborne Monkton Dorset......7 P5
Winterborne Stickland Dorset......8 C6
Winterborne Whitechurch
    Dorset......8 C7
Winterborne Zelston Dorset......8 D7
Winterbourne S Glos......28 H11
Winterbourne W Berk......19 M6
Winterbourne Abbas Dorset......7 N5
Winterbourne Bassett Wilts......18 G6
Winterbourne Dauntsey Wilts......8 H1
Winterbourne Earls Wilts......8 H1
Winterbourne Gunner Wilts......8 H1
Winterbourne Monkton Wilts......18 G6
Winterbourne Steepleton
    Dorset......7 P5
Winterbourne Stoke Wilts......18 F11
Winterburn N York......58 C3
Wintringham N Linc......60 F9
Winterley Ches E......49 N4
Wintersiow Wilts......9 J2
Winterton N Linc......60 F9
Winterton-on-Sea Norfk......45 P6
Winthorpe Notts......52 B11
Winton BCP......8 G8
Winton Cumb......64 E5
Wintringham Cambs......32 H5
Wintringham N York......67 J11
Winwick Cambs......32 F1
Winwick Nhants......41 N11
Winwick Warrtn......57 L9
Wirksworth Derbys......50 H9
Wirral......56 F10
Wirswall Ches E......49 K6
Wisbech Cambs......43 M8
Wisbech St Mary Cambs......43 L8
Wisborough Green W Susx......10 G5
Wiseman's Bridge Pembks......25 K7
Wiseton Notts......51 Q3
Wishaw N Lans......85 N11
Wishaw Warwks......40 F8
Wisley Garden RHS Surrey......20 G10
Wispington Lincs......52 H8
Wissett Suffk......35 M2
Wissington Suffk......34 F9
Wistanstow Shrops......38 H5
Wistanswick Shrops......49 M9
Wistaston Ches E......49 M5
Wistaston Green Ches E......49 M5
Wiston Pembks......24 H5
Wiston S Lans......78 F3
Wiston W Susx......11 J7
Wistow Cambs......33 J1
Wistow N York......59 N7
Wiswell Lancs......57 N2
Witcham Cambs......33 M2
Witchampton Dorset......8 E6
Witchford Cambs......33 N2
Witcombe Somset......17 L10
Witham Essex......22 G1
Witham Friary Somset......17 Q7
Witham on the Hill Lincs......42 F6
Witham St Hughs Lincs......52 C10
Withcall Lincs......53 J6
Withdean Br & H......11 L8
Witherenden Hill E Susx......12 D5
Witheridge Devon......15 N8
Witherley Leics......41 J7
Withern Lincs......53 L7
Withernsea E R Yk......61 N8
Withernwick E R Yk......61 K6
Withersdale Street Suffk......35 L1
Withersfield Suffk......33 Q7
Witherslack Cumb......62 H5
Withiel Cnwll......3 M3
Withiel Florey Somset......16 D9
Withington Gloucs......30 D10
Withington Herefs......39 K12
Withington Manch......57 Q9
Withington Shrops......49 L11
Withington Staffs......40 D1
Withleigh Devon......6 B1
Withnell Lancs......57 L4
Withybed Green Worcs......40 D11
Withybrook Warwks......41 K10
Withycombe Somset......16 D7
Withyham E Susx......11 P3
Withypool Somset......15 P5
Withywood Bristl......17 N3
Witley Surrey......10 F3
Witnesham Suffk......35 K6
Witney Oxon......31 J11
Wittering C Pete......42 F9

Wittersham Kent 12 H5
Witton Birm 40 E8
Witton Norfk 45 M4
Witton Norfk 45 M8
Witton Gilbert Dur 73 M10
Witton le Wear Dur 65 K2
Witton Park Dur 65 L2
Wiveliscombe Somset 16 E9
Wivelrod Hants 19 R12
Wivelsfield E Susx 11 M6
Wivelsfield Green E Susx 11 M6
Wivenhoe Essex 34 G11
Wiveton Norfk 44 G2
Wix Essex 35 J10
Wixams Bed 32 F7
Wixford Warwks 30 E3
Wixoe Suffk 34 C8
Woburn C Beds 32 D9
Woburn Safari Park C Beds 32 D9
Woburn Sands M Keyn 32 D9
Woking Surrey 20 G10
Wokingham Wokham 20 D9
Woldingham Surrey 21 M11
Wold Newton E R Yk 67 M11
Wold Newton NE Lin 53 J4
Wolfclyde S Lans 78 G2
Wolferton Norfk 43 Q4
Wolfhill P & K 92 H8
Wolf's Castle Pembks 24 G4
Wolfsdale Pembks 24 G5
Wollaston Dudley 40 B9
Wollaston Nhants 32 C4
Wollaston Shrops 48 G11
Wollaton C Nott 51 M11
Wollaton Hall & Park C Nott 51 M11
Wollerton Shrops 49 L9
Wollescote Dudley 40 B10
Wolseley Bridge Staffs 40 D4
Wolsingham Dur 73 J12
Wolstanton Staffs 49 Q6
Wolston Warwks 41 K11
Wolvercote Oxon 31 L11
Wolverhampton Wolves 40 B7
Wolverhampton Halfpenny Green Airport Staffs 39 P4
Wolverley Worcs 39 P6
Wolverton Hants 19 P8
Wolverton M Keyn 32 B8
Wolverton Warwks 30 G2
Wolverton Wilts 8 B2
Wolvesnewton Mons 28 E8
Wolvey Warwks 41 K9
Wolvey Heath Warwks 41 K9
Wolviston S on T 66 C3
Wombleton N York 66 F10
Wombourne Staffs 39 Q4
Wombwell Barns 51 K1
Womenswold Kent 23 N12
Womersley N York 59 M9
Wonersh Surrey 10 G2
Wonford Devon 6 C4
Wonston Dorset 7 Q2
Wonston Hants 19 M11
Wooburn Bucks 20 E6
Wooburn Green Bucks 20 E6
Woodacott Devon 14 G9
Woodall Rothm 51 L5
Woodall Services Rothm 51 L5
Woodbastwick Norfk 45 M7
Wood Bevington Warwks 30 D4
Woodborough Notts 51 N10
Woodborough Wilts 18 G8
Woodbridge Suffk 35 L7
Woodbury Devon 6 D5
Woodbury Salterton Devon 6 D5
Woodchester Gloucs 29 L8
Woodchurch Kent 12 H3
Woodcombe Somset 16 C6
Woodcote Gt Lon 21 L10
Woodcote Oxon 19 Q4
Woodcote Wrekin 49 P11
Woodcroft Gloucs 28 G9
Wood Dalling Norfk 44 H5
Woodditton Cambs 33 Q5
Woodeaton Oxon 31 M10
Wood End Gt Lon 20 H7
Wood End Herts 33 K10
Woodend Highld 89 Q4
Woodend Nhants 31 N4
Woodend W Loth 85 Q8
Woodend W Susx 10 D8
Wood End Warwks 40 E11
Wood End Wolves 40 C7
Wood Enderby Lincs 53 J10
Woodfalls Wilts 8 H4
Woodford Cnwll 14 D9
Woodford Gloucs 29 J9
Woodford Gt Lon 21 N5
Woodford Nhants 32 D2
Woodford Stockp 50 B4
Woodford Bridge Gt Lon 21 N5
Woodford Green Gt Lon 21 N5
Woodford Halse Nhants 31 M4
Woodford Wells Gt Lon 21 N5
Woodgate Birm 40 D10
Woodgate Devon 16 E12
Woodgate W Susx 10 F8
Woodgate Worcs 30 C2
Wood Green Gt Lon 21 L5
Woodgreen Hants 8 H4
Woodhall N York 64 H9
Woodhall Spa Lincs 52 H10
Woodham Bucks 31 P9
Woodham Surrey 20 G10
Woodham Ferrers Essex 22 F4
Woodham Mortimer Essex 22 F3
Woodham Walter Essex 22 F3
Wood Hayes Wolves 40 C7
Woodhead Abers 102 G7
Woodhill Shrops 39 N5
Woodhill Somset 17 J10
Woodhorn Nthumb 73 N3
Woodhouse Leeds 58 H7
Woodhouse Leeds 41 M5
Woodhouse Sheff 51 K4
Woodhouse Wakefd 59 J9
Woodhouse Eaves Leics 41 M5
Woodhouselee Mdloth 86 F8
Woodhouselees D & G 71 N1
Woodhouses Oldham 50 B1
Woodhouses Staffs 40 F4
Woodhurst Cambs 33 K2
Woodingdean Br & H 11 M8
Woodkirk Leeds 58 H8

Woodland Abers 103 J9
Woodland Devon 5 M8
Woodland Devon 5 Q6
Woodland Dur 65 J3
Woodland S Ayrs 76 C11
Woodlands Donc 59 M11
Woodlands Dorset 8 F5
Woodlands Hants 9 K5
Woodlands Kent 59 J3
Woodlands Park W & M 20 D7
Woodland View Sheff 50 H3
Woodleigh Devon 5 P9
Woodley Wokham 20 C8
Woodmancote Gloucs 29 K8
Woodmancote Gloucs 29 N4
Woodmancote Gloucs 30 D11
Woodmancote W Susx 10 C8
Woodmancote W Susx 11 K7
Woodmancott Hants 19 P11
Woodmansey E R Yk 60 H6
Woodmansgreen W Susx 10 D5
Woodmansterne Surrey 21 L10
Woodnesborough Kent 23 P11
Woodnewton Nhants 42 E10
Wood Norton Norfk 44 G5
Woodplumpton Lancs 57 J2
Woodrising Norfk 44 G9
Wood's Corner E Susx 12 D6
Woodseaves Staffs 49 P9
Woodsetts Rothm 51 M4
Woodsford Dorset 8 A8
Wood's Green E Susx 12 D4
Woodside Br For 20 E8
Woodside Fife 86 H1
Woodside Gt Lon 21 M9
Woodside P & K 93 J7
Woodstock Oxon 31 K10
Woodston C Pete 42 H10
Wood Street Norfk 45 N6
Wood Street Village Surrey 20 F12
Woodton Norfk 45 L10
Woodtown Devon 14 G7
Woodville Derbys 40 H4
Wood Walton Cambs 32 H1
Woofferton Shrops 39 K8
Wookey Somset 17 M7
Wookey Hole Somset 17 M6
Wool Dorset 8 C9
Woolacombe Devon 14 H4
Woolage Green Kent 23 N12
Woolaston Gloucs 28 G8
Woolaston Common Gloucs 28 G8
Woolavington Somset 17 J7
Woolbeding W Susx 10 E5
Woolbrook Devon 6 F5
Wooler Nthumb 81 L9
Woolfardisworthy Devon 14 F7
Woolfardisworthy Devon 15 P9
Woolfords S Lans 86 B10
Woolhampton W Berk 19 P7
Woolhope Herefs 28 H2
Woolland Dorset 8 B6
Woolley BaNES 17 Q3
Woolley Cambs 32 G2
Woolley Wakefd 58 H10
Woolley Edge Services Wakefd 58 H10
Woolmere Green Worcs 30 C2
Woolmer Green Herts 33 J11
Woolminstone Somset 7 K2
Woolpit Suffk 34 F4
Woolstaston Shrops 39 J3
Woolsthorpe by Belvoir Lincs 42 B4
Woolsthorpe-by-Colsterworth Lincs 42 D5
Woolston C Sotn 9 M5
Woolston Shrops 48 G9
Woolston Somset 16 E6
Woolston Somset 17 P9
Woolston Warrtn 57 M10
Woolstone Gloucs 29 N3
Woolstone M Keyn 32 C8
Woolstone Oxon 19 K4
Woolston Green Devon 5 Q7
Woolton Lpool 56 H10
Woolton Hill Hants 19 M8
Woolverstone Suffk 35 K8
Woolverton Somset 18 B9
Woolwich Gt Lon 21 N7
Woonton Herefs 38 G10
Woore Shrops 49 N7
Wootten Green Suffk 35 K3
Wootton Bed 32 E7
Wootton Kent 13 N2
Wootton N Linc 61 J10
Wootton Nhants 31 Q3
Wootton Oxon 19 N1
Wootton Oxon 31 K9
Wootton Staffs 50 E10
Wootton Bassett Wilts 18 F4
Wootton Bridge IoW 9 P8
Wootton Courtenay Somset 16 C4
Wootton Fitzpaine Dorset 7 K4
Wootton Rivers Wilts 18 H8
Wootton St Lawrence Hants 19 P9
Wootton Wawen Warwks 30 F2
Worcester Worcs 39 Q10
Worcester Park Gt Lon 21 K9
Wordsley Dudley 40 B9
Worfield Shrops 39 N3
Workington Cumb 70 G9
Worksop Notts 51 N5
Worlaby N Linc 60 H10
Worlds End Hants 9 Q5
Worlds End W Susx 11 L6
Worle N Som 17 J4
Worleston Ches E 49 M4
Worlingham Suffk 45 P11
Worlington Devon 15 N9
Worlington Suffk 34 B3
Worlingworth Suffk 35 K3
Wormbridge Herefs 28 E3
Wormegay Norfk 43 Q7
Wormelow Tump Herefs 28 F3
Wormhill Derbys 50 E6
Wormingford Essex 34 F9
Worminghall Bucks 31 N11
Wormington Gloucs 30 D6
Wormit Fife 93 M9
Wormleighton Warwks 31 K4
Wormley Herts 21 M3
Wormley Surrey 10 F3

Wormshill Kent 22 G11
Wormsley Herefs 38 H11
Worplesdon Surrey 20 F11
Worrall Sheff 50 H3
Worsbrough Barns 51 J1
Worsbrough Bridge Barns 59 J12
Worsbrough Dale Barns 59 J12
Worsley Salfd 57 N8
Worstead Norfk 45 M5
Worsthorne Lancs 57 Q3
Worston Devon 5 M9
Worston Lancs 57 P1
Worth Kent 23 P11
Wortham Suffk 34 H2
Worthen Shrops 38 G2
Worthenbury Wrexhm 48 H6
Worthing Norfk 44 G6
Worthing W Susx 11 J9
Worthington Leics 41 K4
Worth Matravers Dorset 8 E11
Wortley Barns 50 H2
Wortley Leeds 58 H7
Worton N York 64 G9
Worton Wilts 18 E8
Wortwell Norfk 45 L12
Wotton-under-Edge Gloucs 29 K9
Wotton Underwood Bucks 31 P10
Woughton on the Green M Keyn 32 C8
Wouldham Kent 22 E9
Wrabness Essex 35 K9
Wrafton Devon 15 J5
Wragby Lincs 52 G7
Wragby Wakefd 59 K10
Wrangaton Devon 5 N8
Wrangle Lincs 53 L12
Wrangway Somset 16 F11
Wrantage Somset 17 J10
Wrawby N Linc 52 E2
Wraxall N Som 17 L2
Wraxall Somset 17 N8
Wray Lancs 63 L8
Wraysbury W & M 20 G8
Wrayton Lancs 63 L7
Wrea Green Lancs 56 H3
Wreay Cumb 71 N6
Wrecclesham Surrey 10 D2
Wrekenton Gatesd 73 M8
Wrelton N York 66 G9
Wrenbury Ches E 49 L6
Wreningham Norfk 45 J9
Wrentham Suffk 45 Q12
Wrentnall Shrops 38 H2
Wressle E R Yk 60 C7
Wressle N Linc 52 D2
Wrestlingworth C Beds 33 J7
Wretton Norfk 44 B9
Wrexham Wrexhm 48 G5
Wrexham Industrial Estate Wrexhm 48 H5
Wribbenhall Worcs 39 P7
Wrinehill Staffs 49 N6
Wrington N Som 17 L4
Writhlington BaNES 17 Q5
Writtle Essex 22 D3
Wrockwardine Wrekin 49 L11
Wroot N Linc 60 C12
Wrose C Brad 58 F6
Wrotham Kent 22 C10
Wroughton Swindn 18 G5
Wroxall IoW 9 P10
Wroxall Warwks 40 G12
Wroxeter Shrops 39 K1
Wroxham Norfk 45 L6
Wroxton Oxon 31 K6
Wyaston Derbys 50 F11
Wyberton Lincs 43 K2
Wyboston Bed 32 G5
Wybunbury Ches E 49 M5
Wychbold Worcs 30 B2
Wychnor Staffs 40 F4
Wyck Rissington Gloucs 30 D9
Wycliffe Dur 65 K5
Wycoller Lancs 58 C6
Wycomb Leics 41 Q3
Wycombe Marsh Bucks 20 E5
Wyddial Herts 33 L9
Wye Kent 13 K1
Wyke C Brad 58 F8
Wyke Dorset 8 B3
Wyke Champflower Somset 17 P8
Wykeham N York 67 L10
Wyken Covtry 41 J10
Wyken Shrops 39 N3
Wyke Regis Dorset 7 P7
Wykey Shrops 48 H9
Wylam Nthumb 73 K7
Wylde Green Birm 40 E8
Wylye Wilts 18 E12
Wymeswold Leics 41 N3
Wymington Bed 32 D4
Wymondham Leics 42 C6
Wymondham Norfk 45 J9
Wynford Eagle Dorset 7 N4
Wyre Piddle Worcs 30 C5
Wysall Notts 41 N3
Wythall Worcs 40 E11
Wytham Oxon 31 L11
Wythenshawe Manch 57 P10
Wyton Cambs 33 J3
Wyton E R Yk 61 K7
Wyverstone Suffk 34 G3
Wyverstone Street Suffk 34 G4

Y

Yaddlethorpe N Linc 52 C3
Yafforth N York 65 N8
Yalberton Torbay 6 B10
Yalding Kent 22 E12
Yanwath Cumb 71 Q9
Yanworth Gloucs 30 E10
Yapham E R Yk 60 D4
Yapton W Susx 10 F9
Yarborough N Som 17 K5
Yarburgh Lincs 53 K5
Yarcombe Devon 6 H3
Yard Devon 15 N7
Yardley Birm 40 E9
Yardley Gobion Nhants 31 Q5
Yardley Hastings Nhants 32 C5
Yardley Wood Birm 40 E10

Yarkhill Herefs 39 L12
Yarley Somset 17 M7
Yarlington Somset 17 P9
Yarm S on T 65 P5
Yarmouth IoW 9 L9
Yarnbrook Wilts 18 C9
Yarnfield Staffs 49 Q8
Yarnscombe Devon 15 K7
Yarnton Oxon 31 L10
Yarpole Herefs 39 J8
Yarrow Border 79 M4
Yarrow Feus Border 79 M4
Yarrowford Border 79 N3
Yarwell Nhants 42 F9
Yate S Glos 29 J11
Yateley Hants 20 D10
Yatesbury Wilts 18 F6
Yattendon W Berk 19 P6
Yatton Herefs 38 H8
Yatton N Som 17 L3
Yatton Keynell Wilts 18 C5
Yaverland IoW 9 Q9
Yaxham Norfk 44 G7
Yaxley Cambs 42 H10
Yaxley Suffk 35 J2
Yazor Herefs 38 H11
Yeading Gt Lon 20 H7
Yeadon Leeds 58 G6
Yealand Conyers Lancs 63 J7
Yealand Redmayne Lancs 63 J7
Yealmpton Devon 5 M9
Yearsley N York 66 E11
Yeaton Shrops 48 H10
Yeaveley Derbys 50 F11
Yeavering Nthumb 81 K7
Yedingham N York 67 J10
Yelford Oxon 31 J12
Yell Shet 111 k3
Yelling Cambs 33 J4
Yelvertoft Nhants 41 N11
Yelverton Devon 5 L6
Yelverton Norfk 45 L9
Yenston Somset 17 Q11
Yeoford Devon 15 N11
Yeolmbridge Cnwll 4 G3
Yeovil Somset 17 M11
Yeovil Marsh Somset 17 M11
Yeovilton Somset 17 M10
Yesnaby Ork 111 g2
Yetminster Dorset 7 N1
Yettington Devon 6 E5
Yetts o'Muckhart Clacks 86 B2
Yew Tree Sandw 40 D8
Y Felinheli Gwynd 54 G7
Y Ferwig Cerdgn 36 C10
Y Ffôr Gwynd 46 G4
Yielden Bed 32 E4
Yieldshields S Lans 77 P2
Yiewsley Gt Lon 20 G7
Ynys Gwynd 47 K4
Ynysboeth Rhondd 27 M9
Ynysddu Caerph 27 P9
Ynyshir Rhondd 27 L9
Ynystawe Swans 26 F8
Ynysybwl Rhondd 27 M9
Yockleton Shrops 48 H12
Yokefleet E R Yk 60 E8
Yoker C Glas 84 H8
York C York 59 N4
Yorkletts Kent 23 L10
Yorkley Gloucs 28 H7
Yorkshire Dales National Park 64 F11
York Town Surrey 20 D10
Youlgreave Derbys 50 G7
Youlthorpe E R Yk 60 D3
Youlton N York 59 L2
Yoxall Staffs 40 F4
Yoxford Suffk 35 N3
Y Rhiw Gwynd 46 D6
Ysbyty Ifan Conwy 55 M10
Ysbyty Ystwyth Cerdgn 37 M6
Ysceifiog Flints 48 D2
Ystalyfera Neath 26 G7
Ystrad Rhondd 27 L9
Ystrad Aeron Cerdgn 36 H9
Ystradfellte Powys 27 K6
Ystradgynlais Powys 26 H6
Ystrad Meurig Cerdgn 37 L7
Ystrad Mynach Caerph 27 N9
Ystradowen V Glam 27 L12
Ythanbank Abers 103 J8
Ythanwells Abers 102 E7
Ythsie Abers 103 J8

Z

Zeal Monachorum Devon 15 M10
Zeals Wilts 8 B2
Zelah Cnwll 3 J5
Zennor Cnwll 2 C7
Zouch Notts 41 L3
ZSL London Zoo Gt Lon 21 L6
ZSL Whipsnade Zoo C Beds 32 E12